Lecture Notes in Computer Science 10919

Commenced Publication in 1973
Founding and Former Series Editors:
Gerhard Goos, Juris Hartmanis, and Jan van Leeuwen

Editorial Board

More information about this series at http://www.springer.com/series/7409

Aaron Marcus · Wentao Wang (Eds.)

Design, User Experience, and Usability

Designing Interactions

7th International Conference, DUXU 2018
Held as Part of HCI International 2018
Las Vegas, NV, USA, July 15–20, 2018
Proceedings, Part II

 Springer

Editors
Aaron Marcus
Aaron Marcus and Associates
Berkeley, CA
USA

Wentao Wang
Baidu Inc.
Beijing
China

ISSN 0302-9743   ISSN 1611-3349 (electronic)
Lecture Notes in Computer Science
ISBN 978-3-319-91802-0   ISBN 978-3-319-91803-7 (eBook)
https://doi.org/10.1007/978-3-319-91803-7

Library of Congress Control Number: 2018944301

LNCS Sublibrary: SL3 – Information Systems and Applications, incl. Internet/Web, and HCI

Printed on acid-free paper

This Springer imprint is published by the registered company Springer International Publishing AG
part of Springer Nature.
The registered company address is: Gewerbestrasse 11, 6330 Cham, Switzerland

Foreword

The 20th International Conference on Human-Computer Interaction, HCI International 2018, was held in Las Vegas, NV, USA, during July 15–20, 2018. The event incorporated the 14 conferences/thematic areas listed on the following page.

A total of 4,373 individuals from academia, research institutes, industry, and governmental agencies from 76 countries submitted contributions, and 1,170 papers and 195 posters have been included in the proceedings. These contributions address the latest research and development efforts and highlight the human aspects of design and use of computing systems. The contributions thoroughly cover the entire field of human-computer interaction, addressing major advances in knowledge and effective use of computers in a variety of application areas. The volumes constituting the full set of the conference proceedings are listed in the following pages.

I would like to thank the program board chairs and the members of the program boards of all thematic areas and affiliated conferences for their contribution to the highest scientific quality and the overall success of the HCI International 2018 conference.

This conference would not have been possible without the continuous and unwavering support and advice of the founder, Conference General Chair Emeritus and Conference Scientific Advisor Prof. Gavriel Salvendy. For his outstanding efforts, I would like to express my appreciation to the communications chair and editor of *HCI International News*, Dr. Abbas Moallem.

July 2018   Constantine Stephanidis

HCI International 2018 Thematic Areas
and Affiliated Conferences

Thematic areas:

- Human-Computer Interaction (HCI 2018)
- Human Interface and the Management of Information (HIMI 2018)

Affiliated conferences:

- 15th International Conference on Engineering Psychology and Cognitive Ergonomics (EPCE 2018)
- 12th International Conference on Universal Access in Human-Computer Interaction (UAHCI 2018)
- 10th International Conference on Virtual, Augmented, and Mixed Reality (VAMR 2018)
- 10th International Conference on Cross-Cultural Design (CCD 2018)
- 10th International Conference on Social Computing and Social Media (SCSM 2018)
- 12th International Conference on Augmented Cognition (AC 2018)
- 9th International Conference on Digital Human Modeling and Applications in Health, Safety, Ergonomics, and Risk Management (DHM 2018)
- 7th International Conference on Design, User Experience, and Usability (DUXU 2018)
- 6th International Conference on Distributed, Ambient, and Pervasive Interactions (DAPI 2018)
- 5th International Conference on HCI in Business, Government, and Organizations (HCIBGO)
- 5th International Conference on Learning and Collaboration Technologies (LCT 2018)
- 4th International Conference on Human Aspects of IT for the Aged Population (ITAP 2018)

Conference Proceedings Volumes Full List

1. LNCS 10901, Human-Computer Interaction: Theories, Methods, and Human Issues (Part I), edited by Masaaki Kurosu
2. LNCS 10902, Human-Computer Interaction: Interaction in Context (Part II), edited by Masaaki Kurosu
3. LNCS 10903, Human-Computer Interaction: Interaction Technologies (Part III), edited by Masaaki Kurosu
4. LNCS 10904, Human Interface and the Management of Information: Interaction, Visualization, and Analytics (Part I), edited by Sakae Yamamoto and Hirohiko Mori
5. LNCS 10905, Human Interface and the Management of Information: Information in Applications and Services (Part II), edited by Sakae Yamamoto and Hirohiko Mori
6. LNAI 10906, Engineering Psychology and Cognitive Ergonomics, edited by Don Harris
7. LNCS 10907, Universal Access in Human-Computer Interaction: Methods, Technologies, and Users (Part I), edited by Margherita Antona and Constantine Stephanidis
8. LNCS 10908, Universal Access in Human-Computer Interaction: Virtual, Augmented, and Intelligent Environments (Part II), edited by Margherita Antona and Constantine Stephanidis
9. LNCS 10909, Virtual, Augmented and Mixed Reality: Interaction, Navigation, Visualization, Embodiment, and Simulation (Part I), edited by Jessie Y. C. Chen and Gino Fragomeni
10. LNCS 10910, Virtual, Augmented and Mixed Reality: Applications in Health, Cultural Heritage, and Industry (Part II), edited by Jessie Y. C. Chen and Gino Fragomeni
11. LNCS 10911, Cross-Cultural Design: Methods, Tools, and Users (Part I), edited by Pei-Luen Patrick Rau
12. LNCS 10912, Cross-Cultural Design: Applications in Cultural Heritage, Creativity, and Social Development (Part II), edited by Pei-Luen Patrick Rau
13. LNCS 10913, Social Computing and Social Media: User Experience and Behavior (Part I), edited by Gabriele Meiselwitz
14. LNCS 10914, Social Computing and Social Media: Technologies and Analytics (Part II), edited by Gabriele Meiselwitz
15. LNAI 10915, Augmented Cognition: Intelligent Technologies (Part I), edited by Dylan D. Schmorrow and Cali M. Fidopiastis
16. LNAI 10916, Augmented Cognition: Users and Contexts (Part II), edited by Dylan D. Schmorrow and Cali M. Fidopiastis
17. LNCS 10917, Digital Human Modeling and Applications in Health, Safety, Ergonomics, and Risk Management, edited by Vincent G. Duffy
18. LNCS 10918, Design, User Experience, and Usability: Theory and Practice (Part I), edited by Aaron Marcus and Wentao Wang

http://2018.hci.international/proceedings

7th International Conference on Design, User Experience, and Usability

Program Board Chair(s): **Aaron Marcus, USA** and **Wentao Wang,** *P.R. China*

- Sisira Adikari, Australia
- Claire Ancient, UK
- Jan Brejcha, Czech Republic
- Silvia De los Rios Perez, Spain
- Marc Fabri, UK
- Chao Liu, P.R. China
- Judith A. Moldenhauer, USA
- Jingyan Qin, P.R. China
- Francisco Rebelo, Portugal
- Christine Riedmann-Streitz, Germany
- Kerem Rizvanoglu, Turkey
- Elizabeth Rosenzweig, USA
- Patricia Search, USA
- Marcelo Márcio Soares, Brazil
- Carla G. Spinillo, Brazil
- Manfred Thüring, Germany
- Xuemei Yuan, P.R. China
- Paul Michael Zender, USA

The full list with the Program Board Chairs and the members of the Program Boards of all thematic areas and affiliated conferences is available online at:

http://www.hci.international/board-members-2018.php

HCI International 2019

The 21st International Conference on Human-Computer Interaction, HCI International 2019, will be held jointly with the affiliated conferences in Orlando, FL, USA, at Walt Disney World Swan and Dolphin Resort, July 26–31, 2019. It will cover a broad spectrum of themes related to Human-Computer Interaction, including theoretical issues, methods, tools, processes, and case studies in HCI design, as well as novel interaction techniques, interfaces, and applications. The proceedings will be published by Springer. More information will be available on the conference website: http://2019.hci.international/.

General Chair
Prof. Constantine Stephanidis
University of Crete and ICS-FORTH
Heraklion, Crete, Greece
E-mail: general_chair@hcii2019.org

http://2019.hci.international/

Contents – Part II

Design, Education and Creativity

GUI, Visualization and Image Design

Multimodal DUXU

Mobile DUXU

Design, Education and Creativity

Expanding Design Thinking with Methods from Futures Studies. Reflections on a Workshop with Chinese User Experience Students

Ellen De Vos[1]([⊠]), Xin Xin[2], and Marina Emmanouil[1]

[1] Ghent University, Marksesteenweg 58, Kortrijk, Belgium
ehidvos.devos@ugent.be
[2] Beijing Normal University, No. 19 XinJieKouWai Street, Haidian District,
Beijing, China

Abstract. Design thinking can be seen as a fundamental premise to approach solving a problem in an innovative way [1]. It is especially valuable at situations in which challenges are complex and ambiguous. Design thinking includes two distinct approaches: diverging and converging. It requires both a flexible way of understanding, to come with various ideas, and know-how to make informed decisions. These opposing activities are poured into an explanatory model. However, a rigorous design thinking process might be considered as a limitation on creative thinking. Also, the promise of a straightforward all-in-one solution for complex problems seems rather unrealistic [1]. Futures studies exceed design thinking on the aspect of the acceptance of plausible options by freeing the apparent certainties [2]. This is primarily useful at the early phase of a design thinking practice when the problem should be explored. Whether a focus on the future context of a designed product could be recognized as added value, must still be inquired. This is a reflective paper on a two-day workshop developed for User Experience students in China that applied techniques from futures studies combined with design thinking and narrative techniques. In particular, the participants were design thinking newbies used to operate in an educational context with focus on traditional lecture-based pedagogy [3].

Keywords: Design thinking · Practice · Novices · Creativity

1 Introduction

In 2016 a new master program titled 'User Experience' (UX) was founded at Beijing Normal University (BNU). A rising number of students (119 in 2016 and 225 in 2017) with different undergraduate degrees apply for the entrance exam of the exclusive program each year. However, no more than seventy students are admitted. This first UX training in China has - for Chinese education tradition - an innovative approach: interactive, practice-oriented and project-based learning [4]. In contrast to other Chinese educational institutions, BNU claims to recognize the role of design pedagogy, the increasing importance of an internationalized perspective and the teaching of critical and creative thinking [3]. In this framework, the first author of this paper, who would be named 'workshop leader' thereinafter, was invited to facilitate a workshop that took place in the first weeks of the students' induction to the program during fall semester in 2017. The existing cooperation between the universities, the reputation of Gent University (UGent), and the workshop leader's experience in both academic and industrial contexts formed the ground for this invitation.

The workshop is based on a design process framework, and by doing so, on design thinking. Literature posits that the open-endedness makes design suited to the inculcation of creativity in newcomers [5]. Besides designing material objects, design thinking can contribute to achieving an organic flow of experience in concrete situations, making experiences more intelligent, meaningful, and satisfying [6]. The workshop was supposed to open the mind of UX students, to bring them out of the comfort zone of their current knowledge domain and situations they are facing today. The future was defined as the main topic and students were free to imagine how that future would look like, and encouraged to work on a subject they are genuinely interested in. This was done in order to augment students' motivations, a requirement for any type of a creative act [7].

Three qualitative futures studies methods were carefully selected to enrich the design workshop. The use of trends and the extrapolation of historical and present events could inspire action towards a certain direction in the unknown future. Thirdly, extreme scenarios of an utopian and a dystopian future image could stipulate a detailed story. Undoubtedly, storytelling lies at the heart of scenarios' building, but also for creativity and design practices, narrative is central [8, 9]. Indeed, the creative insights of students who currently lack the experience or knowledge necessary to fully express their ideas may be undermined in favor of the few students who can more effectively communicate their ideas [7]. Another argument for the use of narratives is that it makes the workshop accessible for non-design students, because historically all people are seen as natural storytellers, who constantly create and maintain their identity by constructing and telling the stories of their lives [10].

The main question of this work-in-progress research is: how do methods from futures studies help non-design students in a design thinking process? This paper serves as a reflection tool to learn what worked well in this specific context and what can be improved in the future.

2 Background

2.1 Design Thinking

Design thinking has been defined as a fundamental premise to approach solving a problem in an innovative way [1]. The methodology behind design thinking is also highly needed in non-design disciplines such as, human resources management and business strategy, contexts in which problems are complex and ambiguous [6, 11, 12]. The traditional way of analytical thinking has not been sufficient [13]. Many models have been proposed to explain the process that often is seen as a magical intervention [1]. The Double Diamond Model of Design Thinking proposed by the British Design

Council makes a distinction between four complementary, yet necessary, sequential phases: Discover, Define, Develop and Deliver, known as the 4-D approach [14]. Design thinking offers multiple tools that allow people to reframe the way in which they understand a problem and to develop ideas from a variety of perspectives (Discover) [15, 16]. A similar flexible way of thinking, divergent thinking, is vital in the Develop-phase where a variety of concepts, that have addressed the initial problem, are generated. Equally valuable in the design process, are the moments where all gathered information is filtered (Define) and where the concepts are launched and prepared to receive feedback (Deliver). The willingness to take intellectual risks is among others a characteristic cognition during these decision-making steps; the umbrella term is convergent thinking [16]. Designers are thus concerned with invention as well as judgment [6].

The workshop aimed at using creativity techniques to come to a product concept. During the workshop the students went through different activities that characterize the front end of innovation: opportunity identification, idea generation, idea selection and concept development. However, the 4-D approach runs the risk of overly simplifying the complex practice that lies underneath [16]. Such a scheme makes the innovation process transparent both for designers and their stakeholders who follow the progress. It also gives a clear view on the characteristics of each step of what should be done. But there is no such a thing as a success formula of how to reach superior innovation.

Novelty, originality, imagination and usefulness fall under the most important features of creativity. People believe that creativity should be attributed to the individual human mind [17]. In our opinion, creativity can be both: all people are creative by nature, and also can improve their creativity through training [16]. Moreover, different cultural contexts may have an impact on the understanding of creativity. The Eastern perception differentiate on the fact that moral goodness, i.e. not only satisfying his own needs but also devote himself to other people and the interests of society as a whole, is a necessary feature of creativity [17].

2.2 Futures Studies

Predicting the future lies in the heart of any product development [18]. Since the mid-twentieth century, the acceleration at which the changes have occurred at the social, cultural, economic and technological areas has become more apparent [19]. These evolutions influence the context that is the frame of reference on which all design decisions are based and thus exploring this context should be the first step in a design process [20]. Just like design thinking, the discipline of futures studies focuses on solving the increasingly complex problems we face [2]. While design thinking is closely related to user-centered design [1], futures studies focus on the context of the user. While consumers relate back to what they know and are a valuable source for incremental user-centered design, radical innovation of meaning is not pulled by the market but results from a vision about a possible future [14]. Futures studies exceed design thinking on the aspect of the acceptance of plausible options, by freeing the apparent certainties [2]. Over the last decade many new practices of design were formed which included scenario-based design. Its speculative aspect, often combined with narrative representation strategies, has found ways of probing alternative futures and their impact on society [21]. Design pedagogy can benefit from methods of futures studies, as a tool for helping students as they engage in creative discovery. No scenario is exhaustive, so it can be fleshed out creatively with some details [22].

2.3   Narrative

Storytelling bridges analysis with synthesis [23] and is applicable to train both divergent and convergent thinking. Stories can be useful tools in several activities of the design process, including the actual development, the design communication or documentation and in evaluation [23]. Over the last three decades there has been a growing focus on narrative in psychology and in the social sciences [10]. Just as futures studies, narrative has only been linked to design practice recently.

Storytelling is a well-known method in futures studies. Futures are stories we tell ourselves, in which we constantly blend aspects from of our current life [24]. Considering that the created stories should not be random, different foresight methods are used to argument their directions: literature review, expert panels, interviews and scenarios are the four most widely used [19].

2.4   Educational Contexts

Project-based learning and learning-by-doing are considered in the Western part of the world as a standard in many design curricula [25]. These kinds of learning environments are highly collaborative and less formal, which might help students feel more comfortable with sharing their ideas [26]. While this practice is commonplace in UGent design studies, in China, active, student-based discovery and involved pedagogy is not often conducted. Instead, content knowledge is more included as a primary focus in the Chinese curriculum, in which students are used to traditional lecture-based pedagogy in large groups [27].

3   The Workshop

The outcome of the workshop was to create artifacts for the future. These artifacts definitely provide concrete materializations of devised ideas and are highly suited as a means for design communication [28]. However, students started with a look into the future context and afterwards they delved into the interactions and objects that could be encountered in that prospected world. This sequence could just as reasonably be regarded as a descent from chaotic environments to the unity provided by an object [6]. Hekkert also performs this approach in his book ViP-Vision in Design [20]. In this paper we use the terms 'method', 'technique' and 'tool' interchangeably to describe specific instruments we gave the participants of the workshop. Also, the focus of the workshop was on the design thinking mindset and less on the realization of a design piece. The initiators of the workshop, the teaching staff of BNU, were convinced that the students had to be instructed a methodology which could broaden their mind and inspire them to tackle problems differently instead of having a narrow and rigid view on problem solving. As the participants of the workshops were non-experienced, the outcome of each technique should be achievable for the intended audience. Exploration through visualization [15], for example, was implemented in different ways: drawing a storyboard, telling a story through given images, prototyping or filming and editing a video. As a consequence of working in groups, the students were able to divide the effort among them. Indeed, there is a thin line between challenging students and creating a culture of intimidation and insecurity.

The level of uncertainty that surrounds the students must be counterbalanced with assistance in building a belief in themselves and their work [29]. We therefore mold the workshop in a step-by-step-assignment, but even so, most introduced methods leave space for individual interpretations for further use of them after the workshop.

The framework of the workshop (see Fig. 1) builds on the 4-D approach of the Double Diamond Diagram of Design Thinking. Although we were only operating in the front end of innovation, it is important to go through the different steps of which design thinking consists. Some help to diverge, others to make decisions or communicate through the process. Importantly, students should first have a clear understanding of the future context, and therefore the emphasis lays on the first D, the Discover-phase. The students get the chance to unfold their capacity for empathy and enrich their perspective on situations, so they would see opportunities instead of limitations and challenges instead of problems. Essential in the Discover-phase are idea generation and exploration for opportunities [30].

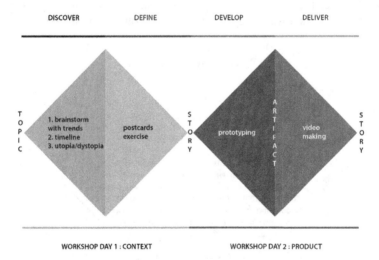

Fig. 1. Overview of the workshop. Model adapted from the 4-D approach of the double diamond diagram of design thinking [14].

Fifty-four students participated in the two-day workshop between nineteen and thirty-one-years old. Thirty-three participants were female and twenty-one male. Only four participants had a background in design. The students were divided in groups of four to six students. All groups had multidisciplinary teams (i.e., with different undergraduate degrees, such as psychology, biology and finance), and two groups had a homogeneous gender composition.

3.1 Discovering: Curiosity About the Future and First Story

Right at the start of the workshop and before students were split in groups, they were asked to use their imagination and formulate an answer on the question: what they think about the future. This question addressed their intuition, which is similar to the Wishful Thinking Technique. Wishful Thinking Technique challenges analytical thinkers to give alternative solutions in terms of a wish or fantasy before these wishful statements are converted into more practical ones [5]. The teams were formed around the topics that they brought forward. By doing so, we tried to augment the engagement of the participants, a condition for successful brainstorming afterwards [31]. Also, perception of competence is a prerequisite for sense making, which leads to sustained interest and the desire to explore [32].

After dividing the students in teams, they presented to each other favorite objects that they were supposed to bring to the workshop. Clearly, objects manifest how we experience the world around us, how we think, and which values we hold dear [33]. By explaining why the object is important to them, the students already created their first story, which reveals information to the listener. The objects had no relation to the topic, which was not yet known at the moment of the call to bring an object. This small episode can be seen as a way of getting to know the other team members.

Fig. 2. Taxonomy of futures research methodologies [34].

Once the topic was known, we guided the students through the Discover-phase. Almost the entire first day of the workshop was assigned to the exploration of the chosen topic. Before the students ended the day with a story, the result of all impressions passed through a filter, three different futures studies techniques were applied. A trend injected brainstorm, an experiential extrapolation, and a scenario exercise were selected because they are either interactive or because they challenge the creative skills of the participants [34] (See Fig. 2). The aim at this part of the workshop is to develop as many, and as diverse ideas as possible. The students had to make some decisions about which direction their imagination would take. Although the three techniques could have been implemented independently, the order in which they used them was the workshop leaders deliberate choice. At first the concept of a trend was launched. Trends identify today the seeds of what might affect future products, human behavior and organizations, and are therefore a useful tool [1]. Each team was appointed to brainstorm on three different trends. In the next assignment, students had to formulate the seeds, or predictive signs, they noticed themselves and relate them to fictional facts. Their subsequent job was creating entire fictional scenarios.

3.2 Brainstorming: Matching Subject with Trends

As a team creativity tool, brainstorming is perhaps the most popular and commonly used. Brainstorming is an approach to consciously leave team members unfettered, to identify opportunities and challenges, to choose a variety of issues, as well as, it is a way to generate ideas. This approach advocates producing derivative ideas and inconsistent thoughts [35]. The different perspectives (undergraduate degrees) of the team members to look at problems would offer more space and potential for creative ideas. The limitations the students were confronted with were their own knowledge, the topic they decided to work on and the available time. Brainstorming does not ensure that all facets of the problem have been addressed [5]. Therefore, after a first exploration on their own, some trends, selected from a trend map composed by Richard Watson [36+ see Fig. 3], were introduced to the teams. The students were asked to reflect on the combination of this trend, which was either a broad societal evolution (e.g., a shift from 'me' to 'we') or a technical innovation (e.g., surveillance drones) and their topic. Although it was our intention to enrich the groups' ideation process with the trends, some were mostly confused. As seen in Table 1, the trends were not chosen by reason of their evident link to the topic. Rather they had to challenge the students to think out-of-the-box and let uncommon associations trigger their mind. McFadzean [24] explains that it is advised to not confront newbies with the complexity of introducing new elements into a brainstorm session. The limited time spent by the workshop leader at explaining what trends are, how you can spot them, and why these particular trends are chosen for their topic could be another argument for the students misunderstanding of this exercise (Fig. 4).

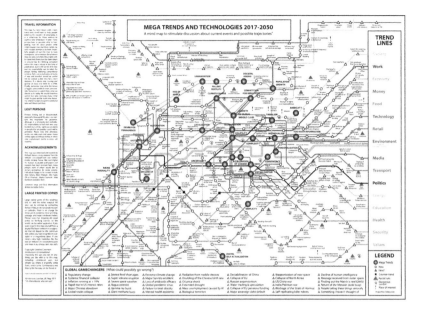

Fig. 3. Trend map [36].

Fig. 4. Example of a completed brainstorm template (topic: housing).

Table 1. Overview of trends assigned to the different teams.

Topic	Trend 1	Trend 2	Trend 3
Education	Permanent temporary staff	Shift from 'me' to 'we'	Mobile phones banned in schools
Housing	Growth in familiarity	Surveillance drones	Hacking
Communication	Speed	Growth of megacities	Open vs. closed
Healthcare	Increasing risk aversion	People living and working alone	Normalization of obesity
Beauty	1 in 2 people suffering from mental health problems	Desire for nostalgic romance	Male and female versions of common drugs
Time	Desire for nostalgic romance	Possibility of choice	Convenience
Social robot	Search for meaning (weekends only)	Equality of opportunity	Sending of 'feelings' as email attachments
Music	Peer-to-peer lending	Convenient access	Fear of missing out
Family	Population growth	Recognition of cognition diversity	Food security
Environment	Consumer choice	Growth of gated communities	Service replaces product
Social change	Doubling of dementia	Peer-to-peer lending	De-materialization
Robot at work	Volunteering	1 in 2 people suffering from mental health problems	Desire for nostalgic romance

3.3 Timeline with Facts and Fiction: Extrapolation

The contemporary context of the society we live in, describes a set of considerations that underlie existing products. The process of de-construction helps uncover them. The future context is the one the designer builds as the foundation for a new design. They can partly overlap, but it is optional [20]. Therefore, in the next assignment, the students were asked to write down past and present factual events that might influence the forthcoming position of their topic. Just like the trends, recalling important past issues or actions happening nowadays could inspire the students. In order to do this, students completed a timeline, which became a starting point to see where the world might move. One third of the timeline is reserved for fictional events, examples of this future setting.

We observed only few difficulties with this assignment that was quite straightforward. One group defined 'past' as 'their' past, and noted events they could remember themselves and not a more general memory. However, other teams referred to the common past of China, i.e., to different dynasties, or described an evolution from ancient times until eternity. As time was the only indication, the transformations vary in feasibility but remained without substantive direction (Fig. 5).

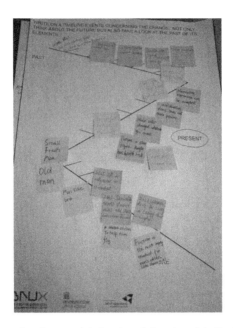

Fig. 5. Example of a completed extrapolation template (topic: beauty).

3.4   Quadrant Matrix: Utopian vs. Dystopian Scenarios

In order to take into account, the various directions our society could go from now on, a quadrant matrix diagram was given to the students. Their objective was to examine the interaction of two progressions of their choice, which was a crucial step in the scenario building [8]. The students developed scenarios for each of the quadrants and imagined four different future contexts [37]. They have been asked to regard these evolutions in either a highly positive or a very negative way. Hence the students created a best-case scenario (utopia) and a worst-case scenario (dystopia) for their future situation. The word utopia, meaning 'no place' in Greek, seems to be a good term for forecasts that neither want to tell truths nor point out causes [38]. Authors of utopias/dystopias often want to offer critiques about the society they live in, and sometimes indicate mechanisms behind a social development that they want to give warnings about [38].

We realized that the job's deadline was too tight, one team did not even finish the matrix, and that the groups faced difficulties in naming the axes of the matrix. Furthermore, a variation can be done without the focus on 'good' and 'bad'. That would leave more room for participants to form their own value judgments [37] (Fig. 6, Table 2).

The scenario assignment closed the Discover-phase. The students now were ready to build an image of a future context in which their topic has evolved. Their curiosity and empathy have been activated and many rough ideas were collected. The techniques applied in the three remaining phases, Define, Develop and Deliver, will be discussed less extended because they are not specific futures studies methods.

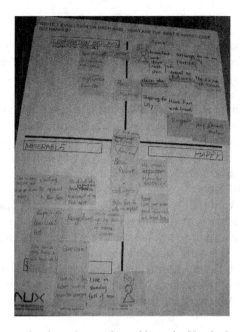

Fig. 6. Example of a completed matrix template with on the X-axis the range from 'miserable' to 'happy' on the Y-axis the zone from 'the cooperation between human' and robot rules' (topic: robot at work).

Table 2. Overview of characteristics of the utopian/dystopian scenarios of the different teams.

Topic	Dystopian scenario	Utopian scenario
Education	Inefficient & traditional	Efficient & digital
Housing	Low familiarity & not safe	High familiarity & safe
Communication	Closed & standard	Open & divers
Healthcare	Not important & dissatisfaction	Important & satisfaction
Beauty	Unhealthy & aesthetic uniformity	Healthy & aesthetic variety
Time	Inconvenient & not likeable	Convenient & likeable
Social robot	/	/
Music	Passive & inconvenient	Active & convenient
Family	Individualistic & unethical	Collectivistic & ethical
Environment	Not taking responsibility & no respect for nature and each other	Taking responsibility & respect for nature and each other
Social change	Unordered & property concentrated	Ordered & property average
Robot at work	Feeling miserable & robot rules	Feeling happy & cooperation between human and robot

3.5 Define a Vision of the Future: Building a Story on Postcards

At the end of the first day of the workshop, the first insights were reviewed, selected and discarded [30]. The participants had to select three images out of more than 150 postcards. Through this experiential encounter they had to tell a compelling and detailed story [22]. Stories are both a form of design communication that allows us to judge and an exercise of imagination that contributes to the process of composition [23].

The students had to mutually agree, which postcards mostly represented the scenario they had been working on. You could either adapt a story to the cards you found and that inspired you, or, with a clear story in mind, have looked for matching illustrations. Both an intuitive and a rational approach were possible [5]. The postcards belong to the personal archive of the workshop leader and show either photos or drawings. Curry and Ward [39] wrote an article about postcards as 'doorways'. They say that constructing a story around images feels safe, because it provides neutrality and a means for difficult truths to be conveyed, or personal offerings to be risked with reduced vulnerability. They also state that the multiple possibilities from combining and recombining stretch the imagination of the participants [39]. The postcards helped to narrow the thoughts of the students. It is important to have convergent techniques in the workshop process, which tell the participants when the search for new ideas is over [20] (Fig. 7).

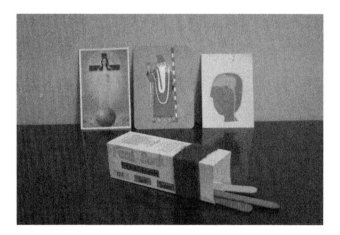

Fig. 7. Example of both the postcards and the prototyped artifact (topic: healthcare).

3.6 Prototyping an Artifact for a Prospected Society

As the second day of the workshop started, we entered the Develop-phase with a 'quick-and-dirty' prototyping session. The students were challenged to create the best possible object with a limited amount of material. In this Develop-phase, the students learned how to think with their hands, which is called tinkering. The creation of an artifact can build bridges of imaginations between abstract thoughts and concrete experience [22]. The designers' intentions concerning the interaction of the design and its surroundings, including its cultural and societal contexts, are all present in the artifact [21, 40]. The artifact does not only represent a certain function, but it is a tool that transfers a meaning.

3.7   Deliver a Video: Making User Experience Visible

As last assignment the students were asked to make a short video to present their artifacts. They were given a storyboard template (see Fig. 8) and asked to consider the protagonists as well as the environment of shooting.

The format of the video, a teleshopping video, is derived from a procedure by The Extrapolation Factory, a design-based research studio for participatory futures studies [37]. The final episode of the workshop required different skills of the students: writing a film scenario, acting, filming and editing image and sound, which of course could be divided among the team members. The advantage of this approach is that it gives space for reflection between the various stages of the creative process [41].

Although sales video is a specific kind of story, the teams were supposed to give a lot of information about the product, its use and context. If this contextualization has no linkage to the essentials of known activities, the resulting concepts may be too disruptive to potential users [18]. This can be done through introducing the problem or challenge at the beginning of the video. By showing stories of humans who interact with an object, you can help to make user experience more tangible [23]. Video has lately been used to create design fictions, while suggest, mediate and provoke discourse on future technologies and their implications rather than demonstrate fully developed solutions [42].

Fig. 8. Example of a completed storyboard template (topic: housing).

4   Conclusions

This paper does not rely on any quantitative evidence or rigorous modeling but on empirical experience. The workshop was based on a combination of reflecting on the changing circumstances, with the use of our imagination when designing for anticipation on these evolutions. Overall, the learning outcomes of the session are met, but there is still an opportunity to improve the outcomes and the flow of the workshop. The language related issues, e.g., added to the complexity of the project. Although this generation Chinese students learn English since primary school, we observed that they are not used to operate in an English-speaking environment. Especially listening and speaking seemed to be rather underdeveloped skills. To overcome this language-based obstacle, a Chinese-speaking assistant and translated templates and presentation slides would have helped in the communication process. Also, the use of (moving) images could have been explored more. For example, the postcards could have been used on the extrapolation timeline to illuminate and bring to life historic moments [39].

By reflecting on a workshop approach that is grounded on techniques from design thinking, futures studies and narratives, we contributed practical insights about a workshop that had as its final output an artifact for a possible future context.

This paper was limited to the reflection of futures studies techniques during the Discover-phase of design thinking. In further research we want to explore whether they can also have an added value in the following phases of the design thinking model.

References

1. Brown, T.: Change by Design: How Design Thinking Transforms Organizations and Inspires Innovation. HarperCollins Publishers, New York (2009)
2. Visser, W.: Designing as construction of representations: a dynamic viewpoint in cognitive design research. Hum. Comput. Interact. **21**(1), 103–152 (2006)
3. Hilton, C.: Cross-disciplinary pedagogy: from Chinese fan dance to designing a bandstand. In: Proceedings of the 18th International Conference on Engineering and Product Design Education (E&PDE16), pp. 539–544. Aalborg, Denmark (2016)
4. Beijing Normal University. School of Psychology Holds Ceremony for UX Lab and User Experience and Human-Computer Interaction & Professional Postgraduate UX Enrollment Conference (2017). http://english.bnu.edu.cn/universitynews/79105.htm. Accessed 10 Dec 2017
5. Couger, J.D., Higgins, L.F., McIntyre, S.C.: (Un)Structured creativity in information systems organizations. MIS Q. **17**(4), 375–397 (1993)
6. Buchanan, R.: Wicked problems in design thinking. Des. Issues **8**(2), 5–21 (1992)
7. Kaufman, J.C., Beghetto, R.A.: Beyond big and little: the four C model of creativity. Rev. Gen. Psychol. **13**(1), 1 (2009)
8. Raven, P.G., Elahi, S.: The new narrative: applying narratology to the shaping of futures outputs. Futures **74**, 49–61 (2015)
9. Selin, C., Kimbell, L., Ramirez, R., Bhatti, Y.: Scenarios and design: scoping the dialogue space. Futures **74**, 4–17 (2015)
10. Svanaes D., Seland G.: Putting the users center stage: role playing and low-fi prototyping enable end users to design mobile systems. In: Proceedings of the SIGCHI Conference on Human Factors in Computing Systems, ACM 2004, pp. 479–486 (2004)
11. Badke-Schaub, P., Roozenburg, N., Cardoso, C.: Design thinking: a paradigm on its way from dilution to meaninglessness. In: Proceedings of the 8th Design Thinking Research Symposium, pp. 19–20 (2010)

12. Norman D.: Design thinking. a useful myth? (2017). http://www.core77.com/blog/columns/design_thinking_a_useful_myth_16790.asp. Accessed 10 Dec 2017
13. Johansson-Söldberg, U., Woodilla, J., Çetinkaya, M.: Design thinking: past, present and possible futures. Creativity Innov. Manag. **22**(2), 121–146 (2013)
14. Design Council: The double diamond design process model (2017). https://www.designcouncil.org.uk. Accessed 10 Dec 2017
15. Gill, C., Graell, M.: Teaching design thinking: evolution of a teaching collaboration across disciplinary, academic and cultural boundaries. In: Proceedings of the 18th International Conference on Engineering and Product Design Education (E&PDE16), pp. 34–39. Aalborg, Denmark (2016)
16. Lewis, T.: Creativity: a framework for the design/problem solving discourse in technology education. J. Technol. Educ. **17**(1), 36 (2006)
17. Niu, W., Sternberg, R.J.: The philosophical roots of Western and Eastern conceptions of creativity. J. Theoret. Philos. Psychol. **26**(1–2), 18 (2006)
18. Salovaara, A., Mannonen, P.: Use of future-oriented information in user-centered product concept ideation. In: Costabile, M.F., Paternò, F. (eds.) INTERACT 2005. LNCS, vol. 3585, pp. 727–740. Springer, Heidelberg (2005). https://doi.org/10.1007/11555261_58
19. Guemes-Castorena, D.: Megatrend methodology to identify development opportunities. In: Management of Engineering & Technology PICMET 2009 Proceedings. Portland International Conference, pp. 2391–2396 (2009)
20. Hekkert, P., Van Dijk, M.: ViP-Vision in Design: A Guidebook for Innovators. BIS Publishers, Amsterdam (2011)
21. Gatto G., Mccardle J.: The designer and the scientist: the road to inspire transdisciplinary synergies. In: Proceedings of the 18th International Conference on Engineering and Product Design Education (E&PDE16), pp. 468–473. Aalborg, Denmark (2016)
22. Candy S.: Time machine/reverse archaeology, vol. 11, no. 11, p. 2014 (2013)
23. Parrish, P.: Design as storytelling. TechTrends **50**(4), 72–82 (2006)
24. McFadzean, E.: The creativity continuum: towards a classification of creative problem solving techniques. Creativity Innov. Manag. **7**(3), 131–139 (1998)
25. Bell, S.: Project-based learning for the 21st century: skills for the future. Clearing House **83**(2), 39–43 (2010)
26. Morgan, D., Skaggs, P.: Collaboration in the zone of proximal development. In: Proceedings of the 18th International Conference on Engineering and Product Design Education (E&PDE16), pp. 664–669. Aalborg, Denmark (2016)
27. Jin, L., Cortazzi, M.: Changing practices in Chinese cultures of learning. Lang. Cult. Curriculum **19**(1), 5–20 (2006)
28. Zimmerman, J., Forlizzi, J., Evenson, S.: Research through design as a method for interaction design research in HCI. In: Proceedings of the SIGCHI Conference on Human Factors in Computing Systems, ACM 2007, pp. 493–502 (2007)
29. Andriopoulos, C.: Six paradoxes in managing creativity: an embracing act. Long Range Plan. **36**, 375–388 (2003)
30. Tschimmel, K.: Design thinking as an effective toolkit for innovation. In: ISPIM Conference Proceedings. The International Society for Professional Innovation Management (ISPIM) (2012)
31. Kelley, T., Kelley, D.: Reclaim your creative confidence. Harvard Bus. Rev. **90**(12), 115–118 (2012)
32. Arnone, M.P., Small, R.V., Chauncey, S.A., McKenna, H.P.: Curiosity, interest and engagement in technology-pervasive learning environments: a new research agenda. Educ. Technol. Res. Dev. **59**(2), 181–198 (2011)

33. Nazli, C., Giaccardi, E., Tynan-OMahony, F., Speed, C., Caldwell, M.: Thing-centered narratives: a study of object personas. Seminar **3**, 22–23 (2015)
34. Gosselin, D., Tindemans, B.: Thinking Futures: Strategy at the Edge of Complexity and Uncertainty. Lannoo Meulenhoff, Belgium (2016)
35. Zhao, Z., Hou, J.: The study on influencing factors of team brainstorming effectiveness. Int. J. Bus. Manag. **5**(1), 181 (2009)
36. Watson, R.: Mega trends and technologies 2017–2050 (2017). https://nowandnext.com/PDF/Mega%20Trends%20and%20Technologies%202017-2050%20(Print).jpg. Accessed 10 Dec 2017
37. Montgomery, E.P., Woebken, C.: Extrapolation Factory - Operator's Manual, Publication version 1.0 (2016)
38. Bergman, A., Karlsson, J.C., Axelsson, J.: Truth claims and explanatory claims—an ontological typology of futures studies. Futures **42**(8), 857–865 (2010)
39. Curry, A., Ward, V.: Postcards as doorways. J. Futures Stud. **18**(3), 101–114 (2014)
40. Folkmann, M.N.: Enabling creativity. Imagination in design processes. In: Proceedings of the 1st International Conference on Design Creativity, ICDC 2010, pp. 66–72 (2010)
41. Firth, R., Stoltenberg, E.: Using moving image to facilitate storytelling as an ideation methodology and a platform to enhance the integration of international student cohorts within product design education. In: Proceedings of the 18th International Conference on Engineering and Product Design Education (E&PDE16), pp. 539–544. Aalborg, Denmark (2016)
42. Arnall, T., Martinussen, E.S.: Depth of field: discursive design research through film. Form Akademisk-forskningstidsskrift for design og designdidaktikk **3**(1), 100–122 (2010)

Exploring the Referral and Usage of Science Fiction in HCI Literature

Philipp Jordan[1]($\boxtimes$), Omar Mubin[2]($\boxtimes$), Mohammad Obaid[3]($\boxtimes$), and Paula Alexandra Silva[4]($\boxtimes$)

[1] University of Hawaii at Manoa, Honolulu, USA
philippj@hawaii.edu
[2] SCEM, Western Sydney University, Sydney, Australia
o.mubin@westernsydney.edu.au
[3] Uppsala University, Uppsala, Sweden
mohammad.obaid@it.uu.se
[4] DigiMedia Research Center, University of Aveiro, Aveiro, Portugal
palexa@gmail.com

Abstract. Research on science fiction (sci-fi) in scientific publications has indicated the usage of sci-fi stories, movies or shows to inspire novel Human-Computer Interaction (HCI) research. Yet no studies have analysed sci-fi in a top-ranked computer science conference at present. For that reason, we examine the CHI main track for the presence and nature of sci-fi referrals in relationship to HCI research. We search for six sci-fi terms in a dataset of 5812 CHI main proceedings and code the context of 175 sci-fi referrals in 83 papers indexed in the CHI main track. In our results, we categorize these papers into five contemporary HCI research themes wherein sci-fi and HCI interconnect: (1) Theoretical Design Research; (2) New Interactions; (3) Human-Body Modification or Extension; (4) Human-Robot Interaction and Artificial Intelligence; and (5) Visions of Computing and HCI. In conclusion, we discuss results and implications located in the promising arena of sci-fi and HCI research.

Keywords: Design fiction · Future visions · HCI inspiraton
Popular culture in science · Science fiction

1 Introduction

Sci-fi has inspired many technological innovations. Its influence is present in the invention, conceptualization, design and application of interfaces and technology. As an avenue of creativity and expression both, sci-fi literature and media have fueled advancements in interactive technology and proven to be a key source of inspiration for researchers in the field of computing technology [2].

There are numerous examples of interactive products, devices and systems in the real world whose origin can be traced back to sci-fi [22,41]. From the wristwatch used by fictional detective Dick Tracy to the communicators of *Star Trek* which predated nowadays mobile phones. From the video conferencing and

© Springer International Publishing AG, part of Springer Nature 2018
A. Marcus and W. Wang (Eds.): DUXU 2018, LNCS 10919, pp. 19–38, 2018.
https://doi.org/10.1007/978-3-319-91803-7_2

disobedient Artificial Intelligence (AI) as depicted in *2001: A Space Odyssey*, to the video-phones and robots of Fritz Lang's 1927 *Metropolis*, both considered influential and seminal sci-fi dystopian movies to this day. Upon closer investigation, we observe that this relationship is bi-directional to such an extent that sci-fi creators regularly consult with researchers and scientists [25], for instance Marvin Minsky's [45] contribution to *2001: A Space Odyssey*. The areas of HCI and sci-fi therefore seem to have the potential to grow in unison [35].

But how does the anecdotal, discursive symbiosis of HCI and sci-fi translate into scientific research and peer-reviewed publications? Our research question examines how sci-fi is used in a leading HCI venue, in this study, the ACM Conference on Human Factors in Computing Systems (CHI). Specifically, we explore what particular kinds of sci-fi HCI researchers mention in their papers and how these sci-fi referrals relate to the research itself. At this stage, we limit our investigation to the scientific publications produced in the main proceedings of CHI. Given the high ranking of this particular conference [11,15], and impact of the main proceedings (e.g. 10 of 10 of the highest cited papers of the CHI conference are indexed in the main CHI proceedings [1]), we exclude the CHI extended abstracts in this preliminary study.

In the remaining sections of the paper, we first present a summary of related work on the topic followed by an account of our process of sci-fi keyword analysis through a contextual analysis of HCI research. We then present our coding scheme, overviews, and details of our results and speculate on their meaning. In our future work, we outline the next steps of this research.

2   Background

Contemporary HCI research is gradually beginning to disseminate the past, present, and future value and impact of sci-fi visualizations on HCI research and vice-versa [22,23,36,41]. Among others, various case studies on the intersections of HCI and sci-fi movies [28,46], on novel sci-fi movie-based interaction techniques [14], sci-fi inspired future user interfaces and design heuristics [47,50] have been published. In a broader context, sci-fi prototyping [26] and the lately in vogue emergence of design fiction as a method in design research (e.g. [32]) substantiate a mutual relationship of HCI and sci-fi.

While it is acknowledged that HCI and interaction design can learn from sci-fi [37,38], the HCI community is realising that there is more to sci-fi's relationship with interactive technology than presenting an utopian vision; which is unfortunately what most overview papers get drawn into. Most HCI/sci-fi reviews [46] simply list sci-fi technologies that have been realized in the real world; the HCI community might find it difficult to utilize such insights to advance their research. Supplementing such overviews through sci-fi related search-and-retrieval queries in computer science conferences can facilitate a better description of the intersection and utilization of HCI and sci-fi; and therefore explain how HCI researchers actually use sci-fi in their research publications.

To create a better and more nuanced understanding of the sci-fi and HCI relationship in the case of scientific publications, this paper presents a preliminary study, where we collect and qualitatively analyse the presence of sci-fi in the CHI main proceedings, one of the most prestigious, contemporary HCI collections. By doing this analysis, we expect to gain a better understanding of the evolutionary, historic, and chronological pattern in the presence of sci-fi related referrals in HCI research. As prior research [33] has shown that CHI proceedings are prone to general topic shifts over extended periods of time, we do expect to uncover a similar shift towards sci-fi related referrals in the most recent CHI publications due to the variation in the popularity and propagation of particular sci-fi content.

An important parameter to judge the influence of any discipline on a field of research is the analysis of the research articles emerging from that area. Scientometrics, keyword- and citation-analyses [40] are defined as the area of research focusing on measuring and analyzing the impact of various factors on science and technology. The technique is now widely utilized in understanding publication trends and emerging fields in HCI. For example, we identify a variety of scientometric studies on HCI literature [20], and specifically the CHI conference [4,17,33]. Nevertheless, aside of one example [30], scientometric or topical studies that analyze the presence of sci-fi related terms and keywords in HCI or CHI literature seem to lack.

Hence, we believe that an analysis of the presence and referrals of sci-fi related keywords in the CHI main track is an important first step to determine a premature, but much more informed and data-based insight into the relationship of the two disciplines of HCI and sci-fi. The earlier introduced exception is Levin's [30] study on the presence of 20 sci-fi movies in the ISI web of science database. While this study is methodologically the closest related state-of-the-art to our study, it differs in two significant aspects:

Firstly, Levin [30] assessed the overall presence of these sci-fi movies across a broad range of research disciplines, for instance aerospace engineering, economics, political sciences and biology thereby extending beyond our current scope and research aim. Consequently, as Levin's study extended into such a wide variety of research topics, computing technology was under-represented.

Secondly, Levin's study [30] as well as our own research [22] on the usage of *Star Trek* in the ACM Digital Library, do both focus on very specific and selected sci-fi movies and franchises, e.g. *Blade Runner*, *Matrix* in the former and *Star Trek* in the latter study. We therefore assess in this study the general presence and usage of unspecific "sci-fi" in HCI publications through a more generic, inclusive search-query.

In the remaining part of the paper, we do summarize in Sect. 3 our method and data collection process, describe in Sect. 4 the results of our study, summarize the findings and conclusions in Sect. 5 and outline the future work in Sect. 6.

3 Method

Using the ACM Digital Library search interface, we query the full-text of the entire CHI proceedings in early 2018 for each of the six search terms: *"sci-fi"* *"sciencefiction"* *"science fiction"* *"scifi"* *"sci fi" or "science-fiction"*, see also Fig. 1.

Search Query

```
Search Run Date: 2018-01-05 at 7:40:44 PM EST
Search Result Count: 137
Query Syntax:
"query": { content.ftsec:("sci-fi" "sciencefiction"
"science fiction" "scifi" "sci fi" "science-fiction") }
"filter": {owners.owner=HOSTED},
{series.seriesAbbr.CHI}
```

ACM Digital Library

Search Run Date: [save as csv]
2018-01-05 at 7:40:44 PM EST

Search Result Count: 137

Query Syntax:

"query": { content.ftsec:("sci-fi"
"sciencefiction" "science fiction"
"scifi" "sci fi" "science-fiction") }

"filter":
{owners.owner=HOSTED},
{series.seriesAbbr=CHI}

ACM DIGITAL LIBRARY

Searched for content.ftsec:("sci-fi" "sciencefiction" "science fiction" "scifi" "sci fi" "science-fiction")

Searched The ACM Full-Text Collection: 489,636 records [Expand your search to The ACM Guide

Refinements [remove all] click each refinement below to remove
Proceeding Series: CHI

137 results found

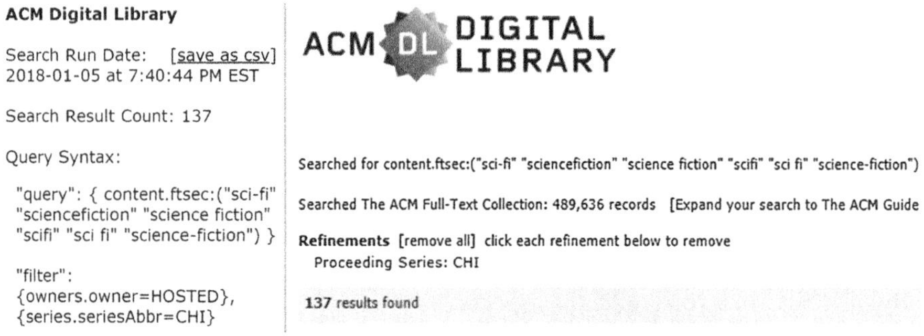

Fig. 1. ACM Digital Library search query and results

This query searches all records in the CHI conference in the ACM Digital Library and returns 137 records in January 2018. These 137 retrieved records can be categorized into 83 records indexed in the main CHI proceedings (CHI PRO) and 54 indexed in other CHI series (CHI OTH), see also Table 1. Among those papers in the CHI OTH series, we find the CHI extended abstracts, work-in-progress papers or panel-, interactivity- or student-sessions. In this preliminary study, we qualitatively analyze the 83 records retrieved in the main CHI proceedings.

First, we conducted an open coding process of the 83 records in the CHI main proceedings amid the authors. This open coding is based on the specifity of the sci-fi referral and the sci-fi referral relationship to the primary technologies, respectively the main research theme of the individual publication. To both, establish initial coding categories and ensure a basic reliability of these categories, each author first independently reviewed 15 papers of the 83 papers. Second, a group review of these 15 papers and codes advanced the coding scheme outlined below. Third, all authors then proceeded to code the remaining 68 papers using the coding scheme and, fourth, through a final group review did resolve any remaining inconsistencies. In detail, our coding scheme consists of three main items:

1. **Unspecific sci-fi referral** - describes the unspecific sci-fi refereed in the retrieved publication, such as a general referrals to sci-fi movies, television shows, sci-fi short stories, books or literature in the full-text, for example *"science-fiction stories"* or *"sci-fi movies"*.
2. **Specific sci-fi referral** - if applicable, describes the details of the sci-fi media type referred in the retrieved publication, such as the specific title of a sci-fi movie, show, book or an explicitly mentioned name of a sci-fi movie or book author, for example *"2001: A Space Odyssey"* or *"Bruce Sterling"*.
3. **Sci-fi/HCI relationship** - if applicable, describes the primary technologies or concepts from a sci-fi movie, show, or story in relationship to the research theme and focus of the individual, retrieved publication. Examples are herein *"shape-changing interfaces"*, *"autonomous cars"* but also theoretical papers on *"futurism"* and *"design research"*.

4   Results

Our query, as defined in Fig. 1, retrieves 137 records distributed into 83 records in the CHI main proceedings and 54 records in the other CHI proceedings. Figure 2 shows these records in relationship to the CHI year they appear in.

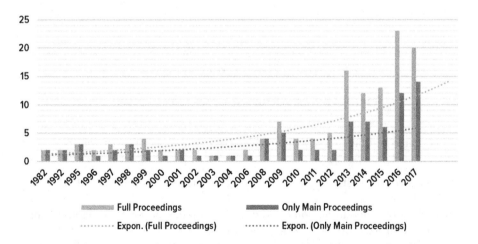

Fig. 2. Publications matching our sci-fi query over the full CHI proceedings (green bars, n = 137), and the main CHI proceedings (blue bars, n = 83). (Color figure online)

Exponential trends seem to indicate a proliferation of records matching our search-terms in both, the full and main proceedings from 2013 onward. The most recent three iterations of the CHI conference from 2015–2017 account with 33 retrieved records (Fig. 2, blue bars) for more than a one-third of the 83 publications in the main proceedings. Similarly, the other CHI papers from 2013–2017 cover with 38 records more than half of the 54 papers we retrieved with our search-query.

In the following analysis in this preliminary study, we will present the results of the analysis of the 83 CHI main proceedings we have retrieved and therefore not consider the 54 CHI extended abstracts at this time.

4.1   Frequency Analysis of the Sci-Fi Referrals

Of the 175 sci-fi referrals we retrieve in the 83 papers in the main CHI proceedings (Fig. 3), we find that 51 publications mention sci-fi as defined per our search query once (1*) within the full-text, a result consistent with related work, e.g. [30].

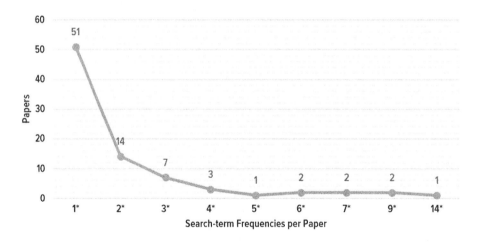

Fig. 3. 175 sci-fi referrals of our query in 83 papers

The three publications with the highest frequencies of sci-fi referrals on a sentence-level analysis are:

- Blythe's [7] 2014 CHI paper on imaginary abstracts with fourteen (14*) sci-fi referrals.
- A 1992 CHI panel discussion by Marcus, Norman, Rucker, Sterling and Vinge [37] on sci-fi with nine (9*) sci-fi referrals.
- Tannenbaum's [49] 2012 CHI paper on steampunk with nine (9*) sci-fi referrals.

The earliest mention of sci-fi is found in Devaris' [12] 1982 paper on information technologies and innovative workspaces, wherein he briefly compares (page 3):

*"[...] newly designed corporate office installations in Sweden, Switzerland, West Germany and Japan to the settings we would expect to see in a **science fiction** or space movie."*

4.2 Coding Results of the Sci-Fi in the 83 CHI Main Papers

In summary, out of the 83 retrieved publications, 31 refer to sci-fi in trivial ways with regards to our research question. For example, we retrieve papers which refer to sci-fi, but do in fact report on a usability evaluation of a video game set in a sci-fi universe. Other publications we consider as false-positives mention a movie recommendation system, wherein sci-fi is a genre among others in addition to publications which mention sci-fi in the publication references, but do not discuss them in a meaningful way in the remainder of the paper.

From the remaining 52 publications, 21 papers mention specific sci-fi in the context of the referral, such as movies (e.g. *Terminator*, *Star Wars*, *Doctor Who*, authors (e.g. Isaac Asimov, H.G. Wells, Bruce Sterling), or sci-fi writings and novels (e.g. *Dune*, *Schismatrix*, *Shaping Things*) and 31 papers refer unspecific sci-fi. Table 1 presents the overview of the 83 CHI main papers we have coded as false-positives or which refer either, unspecific or specific sci-fi.

Table 1. Retrieved papers, publication years and coding

CHI series	Range	Records	False-positives	Unspecific sci-fi	Specific sci-fi
CHI PRO	1982–2017	83	31	31	21
CHI OTH	1996–2017	54	Not analyzed	Not analyzed	Not analyzed
Total	1982–2017	137	Not analyzed	Not analyzed	Not analyzed

In cases of multiple types of mentions, a specific sci-fi referral (movie, show or story/writing) was given priority over an unspecific sci-fi referral in our coding. For example, if a paper mentions a science fiction movie and then proceeds to introduce the movie *Minority Report* in the text, we have coded that paper as referring specific sci-fi.

In order to exemplify our coding, we introduce in the following sections selected examples of our coding. As we have retrieved 175 sci-fi referrals of our search-terms across all 83 CHI main papers (see Fig. 3), we do provide overviews of the full coding in Tables 2 and 3 in the latter part of the paper. In addition to the overviews, we introduce below selected, representative examples for each code accordingly.

False-Positives: We find 31 instances of CHI papers which we evaluate as false-positives with regards to overall importance of the sci-fi referral in relationship to the paper focus and our research question. For instance Kim, McNally, Norooz and Druin's [24] study on adult internet searching habits refers our search-terms in quotes from study participants, for instance (page 4953 and page 4955):

*"I know several websites I would go to find **science fiction** books for kids;"*

*"Like P17, several adult search users had domain knowledge related to their hobbies or leisure activities (e.g., travel, pop music, **science fiction** book)."*

In other examples of false-positives, sci-fi is referred in the context of emotions and digital games, for instance in Bopp, Mekler and Opwis's [8] article describing the preferences of study participants (page 2998):

*"The three most popular genres were RPGs and action RPGs (n = 109), followed by adventure and action adventure games (n = 95), as well as strategy and real time strategy games (n = 71). Popular genres for other media were, for example, **science fiction**, comedy, drama, fantasy, and thrillers."*

Although sci-fi is mentioned within the full-text of the paper in these examples, we did assess these referrals as false-positives with respect to the research focus of the paper under review and the context of our content analysis.

Unspecific Sci-Fi: Krekhov, Emmerich, Babinski and Krüger [27] refer unspecifc sci-fi and prior studies as means to derive gestural interactions. Quoted below is an example of a sci-fi referral which did have a stronger connection to the research theme of the paper under scrutiny in our coding (page 5285):

*"Another interesting approach to generate comprehensible gestures is to rely on popular **science fiction** movies. Filmmakers have to create futuristic interactions that the audience should be able to understand intuitively."*

Yet serving as another example of an unspecific sci-fi referral, Bardzell, Bardzell and Stolterman [3] refer to sci-fi theory in their inquiry into critical design (page 1958):

*"Following **science fiction** theorists in distinguishing between 'cognitive speculation' and 'mere fantasy,' in which the former is speculation grounded in a rigorous understanding of the past and present and used to project possible futures, and the latter is mere escapism, this radio seems to be more on the order of fantasy than serious speculation, and therefore the design qua critical design is unsuccessful."*

Specific Sci-Fi: A paper by Reeves [44] on the future of ubicomp is one example of a case where we identified specific sci-fi in our qualitative review (page 1577):

*"Underkoffler would go on to produce a 'Minority Report' gestural interface, which he demoed at Technology, Entertainment, Design (TED) 2010 conference. It is important to see this within the context of a wider historical trend, i.e., that of substantial feedback between the **science fiction** imagination and technological development."*

In this example, Reeves [44] mentions specific sci-fi by naming the well-known sci-fi movie *Minority Report* and links it to future technological advances.

4.3   Research Themes Where Sci-Fi and HCI Research Intersect

The 52 publications which we consider relevant were further analyzed and - based on the research theme and focus of the individual paper - placed into five, mutually exclusive thematic categories. In order to exemplify the thematic coding of the sci-fi in our analysis, we will introduce yet again selected examples of the coding for each thematic area. Then, we will provide summaries and details of the coding and analysis of the usage of sci-fi in the CHI main proceedings.

Coding Examples of Theoretical Design Research: For instance, Bauer and Kientz [5] refer sci-fi in their CHI'13 paper on ideation through scenario-based design (page 1958):

> *"Other, less traditional ideation methods include bodystorming, futures and alternative news, and* **science fiction** *prototyping. [...]* **Science fiction** *prototyping aims to use science fiction writing as a way of inspiring futuristic ideas. These methods often require the designers to generate the ideas and present them to users for feedback, and thus DesignLibs makes a unique contribution by enabling potential end users to easily generate and contribute design ideas."*

Among others, Blythe [7] extensively writes about design fiction and refers specific sci-fi in the context of theoretical design research, for example (page 706):

> *"Literary techniques such as pastiche have been used to place concept designs in different fictional worlds, some from* **science fiction** *e.g. 1984 or A Clockwork Orange, but also other cultural contexts like Agatha Christies Miss Marple stories or the Simpsons."*

Coding Examples of Human-Robot Interaction and AI: To begin with, Pereira, Prada and Paiva's [43] 2014 case study on social presence in human-agent interactions leads with the observation that sci-fi robots are becoming reality (page 1449):

> *"**Science-fiction** films or books have long included characters such as intelligent computers, robots and androids that evoke the same type of social responses from the audience or the reader. With the evolution of technology, these* **science-fiction** *visions are now becoming a reality, and new interactive techniques and devices are designed to evoke social responses from users."*

Bucci, Cang, Valair, Marino, Tseng, Jung, Rantala, Schneider and MacLean [10] similarly write that (page 3683):

*"Companion robots that once existed only in **science fiction** are quickly becoming part of our present reality."*

Takayama, Groom and Nass [48] utilize a piece of dialogue from the seminal sci-fi movie *2001: A Space Odyssey* as title in their 2009 CHI paper on human agents: *"I'm Sorry, Dave: I'm Afraid I Won't Do That: Social Aspects of Human-Agent Conflict"*. The authors refer first to unspecific sci-fi, and then to the sci-fi movie *2001: A Space Odyssey* as well as sci-fi author Issac Asimov (page 2099):

*"On the other hand, Asimov's Second Law of Robotics places obedience to humans above everything (including the robot's self-preservation) other than harm to humans. This notion is echoed in **science fiction** : The disobedience of HAL, the computer from 2001, led to the death of his crew mates."*

Coding Examples of New Interactions: As the first example of the theme of New Interactions, we identify Marcus et al. CHI '92 panel [37], quoted below, which had the clear aim to identify synergies between sci-fi authors and HCI researchers (page 435):

*"This plenary panel will explore ideas about future user interfaces, their technology support, and their social context as proposed in the work of leading authors of **science fiction** characterized as the Cyberpunk movement."*

Elmqvist, Henry, Riche and Fekete [13] do acknowledge in 2008 that the source of inspiration for their paper on a novel interaction technique - space deformation - is a specific, 50-year old sci-fi story by sci-fi author Frank Herbert (page 1341):

*"The inspiration for the technique in this paper comes from Frank Herbert's classic **science-fiction** novel Dune from 1965, where interstellar space travel is performed through a process known as 'folding space'."*

As one last example, Grandhi, Joue and Mittelberg's [16] study on touchless gestural interfaces introduces the topic of novel interactions by means of a popular, specific sci-fi movie (page 821):

*"However, unlike touch gestures, touchless gestures remain largely a notion developed in science fiction (as depicted in the popular **sci-fi** movie Minority Report) and have only been implemented to a limited degree in a few proof-of concept research applications [...]."*

Coding Examples of Visions of Computing and HCI: In this thematic area, we code papers which refer sci-fi in conjunction with technology, agency, power and utopian and dystopian visions of the future. For example, autonomous cars are subject to Lee, Joo and Nass's [29] study, which refers to the US sci-fi show *Knight Rider* (page 3631):

*"Driverless car KITT in a famous American TV series is no longer **science fiction**."*

Mankoff, Rode and Faste's [34] paper on forecasting, HCI and futurism refers to a variety of sci-fi, for example (page 1629):

*"These authors ask us to dive into a world where **science fiction** bleeds into reality and the future suddenly seems surprisingly near and uncertain."*

Later on, the authors [34] proceed to state a clear synergy of sci-fi, HCI and the technological future (pages 1632–1633):

*"A critical examination of forecasts that arise from monitoring can inform HCI. An example is the analysis of **science fiction** to gain new insights into how ubiquitous computing technologies should engage with bureaucratic structures [...] by examining the cultural biases present in visions of the future (such as the powerful male who must escape from feminine control in movies such as The Truman Show), we create an opportunity to choose whether or not to reinforce them."*

As a last example in this category, we present a 2017 case study [42] of 22 participants who attended a men-versus-machine Go match. Interviews with the attendants suggest a future view of society, technology and AI, which seems mainly shaped by a variety of famous sci-fi movies (page 2526):

*"When asked about their thoughts and impressions of the term AI, most of the participants described experiences of watching **science fiction** movies. They mentioned the specific examples, such as Skynet from Terminator (1984), Ultron from The Avengers (2015), Hal from 2001: A Space Odyssey (1968), sentient machines from The Matrix (1999), and the robotic boy from A.I. Artificial Intelligence (2001)."*

Examples of Human-Body Modification or Extension: In the nascent research area of Human-Body Modification or Extension, we find referrals to sci-fi, for instance by Massimi, Odom, Banks and Kirk [39] (page 993):

*"The idea of using technology to prevent death entirely, or to 'speak from beyond the grave' has been a motif in **science fiction** for decades, but has begun to actually occur in current systems."*

Jamison-Powell, Briggs, Lawson, Linehan, Windle and Gross [21] observe a proliferation of posthumous messaging applications and mention unspecific sci-fi in their paper (page 2926):

*"Terming the second over-arching concept 'Transcendence' may initially sound rather futuristic and, even, reminiscent of **science-fiction** when applied to the subject of death and technology. However, our analysis shows that these posthumous services do, indeed, transcend."*

Permanent modification of the human body is subject to Heffernan, Vetere and Chang's [18] CHI '16 paper, who outline through specific sci-fi movies and shows the visual depictions of such interfaces in the past (all quotes, page 1799):

> *"This section describes the use of insertables as seen in popculture and the recent leap from **science fiction** into reality."*

> *"Insertable devices have accented **science fiction** for decades, from the Cyber Men of Doctor Who (1966) to The Terminator (1984). The 1970s TV series The Six Million Dollar Man and The Bionic Woman saw humans rebuilt; in their universes we had the technology."*

> *"While the above is not yet technically possible, the concept of insertables is no longer contained to the boundaries of **science fiction.**"*

Britton and Semaan [9] draw similar analogies of sci-fi and the human-machine symbiosis (page 2499):

> *"From The Terminator to Fit Bit, the fascination with merging body and technology has played a persistent role in science and **science fiction.**"*

In summary, we code the 52 CHI main papers into the five research themes as summarized below:

1. **Theoretical Design Research (n = 16):** Out of the 52 relevant publications, 16 papers which refer sci-fi in publications on critical design research, ideation and design fiction or sci-fi prototyping as the examples presented in [7].
2. **Human-Robot Interaction and AI (n = 10):** Out of the 52 relevant publications, 10 refer sci-fi in papers on human-robot or human-agent interaction and agency, artificial intelligence, natural language interfaces and ethics, for example [43].
3. **New Interactions (n = 9):** Out of the 52 relevant publications, 9 refer sci-fi in papers on novel interfaces and interaction modes (gestural, haptical, shape-changing, multi-modal) as the example presented in [16].
4. **Visions of Computing and HCI (n = 9):** Out of the 52 relevant publications, 9 refer sci-fi in publications on technology in conjunction with society, agency and power, for instance autonomous cars and systems or dystopian visions of ubiquitous computing in the conflict zone of privacy and security, e.g. [34].
5. **Human-body Modification or Extension (n = 8):** Out of the 52 relevant publications, 8 refer sci-fi in papers on DIY cyborgs or on-body fabrication of artifacts, implants, insertables and technologies for the digital afterlife, for example [18].

Table 2 summarizes the distribution of the 83 papers across our coding categories, while Table 3 shows the coding of each individual paper.

Excluding the 31 false-positives for illustration purposes, Fig. 4 shows the 52 main CHI proceedings we coded in one of the final five research themes. In order to indicate trends, the 52 papers have been further grouped into the decade the papers were published in.

Table 2. Coding overview of the 83 main CHI papers

Code	Coding	Range of papers	Coding
FP	False-Positives	1995–2017	31
TD	Theoretical Design Research	2000–2017	16
HRI	Human-Robot Interaction and AI	1996–2017	10
NI	New Interactions	1992–2017	9
VIS	Visions of Computing and HCI	1982–2017	9
HBM	Human-Body Modification	1999–2017	8
	Total	**1982–2017**	**83**

Table 3. Coding details of the 83 main CHI papers

	FP	TD	HRI	NI	VIS	HBM	Total
1982					2		2
1992			1	1			2
1995	3						3
1996	2						2
1997					2		2
1999	1					1	2
2000		1					1
2001	1			1			2
2002	1						1
2003	1						1
2004	1						1
2006	1						1
2008	1		2	1			4
2009	2		2	1			5
2010	1				1		2
2011				1		1	2
2012		2					2
2013	3	2			1	1	7
2014	2	2	2	1	1		8
2015	3	1		2			6
2016	4	2	3			4	13
2017	4	6	1	1	1	1	14
Total	**31**	**16**	**10**	**9**	**9**	**8**	**83**

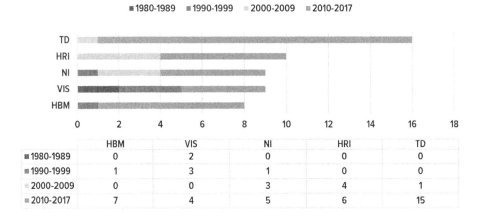

Fig. 4. Research themes per decade (n = 52) where sci-fi and HCI intersect in a meaningful way in the CHI main proceedings.

5   Findings and Conclusions

In order to address the lack of a study into the usage of sci-fi referrals in HCI research, our research question examined if, and how, general and specific sci-fi is used the ACM Conference on Human Factors in Computing Systems. In this preliminary study, we identified 137 records in the CHI proceedings which refer sci-fi - as defined with our six-term search and retrieval query. We also qualitatively analysed the 83 records indexed in the main CHI proceedings which fitted out inclusion criteria.

In our qualitative review, we further identified 52 publications which discuss sci-fi in a meaningful way with regards to our research question and in addition, five broader research themes which intersect with sci-fi in papers from 1982–2017. Specifically, we explored the usage of sci-fi, the specific type of sci-fi referral, the search-term frequency distribution of sci-fi referrals, and the associated technologies of sci-fi in scientific publications.

In general, it appears that sci-fi becomes more acknowledged in the CHI conference in recent years. The majority of relevant publications (37 out of 52) in our analysis are published in the 2010s onwards indicating an upsurge of sci-fi papers in recent years.

Our research also provided a better understanding of the evolutionary uses of sci-fi in HCI research in the case of the CHI main track. With regards to the research themes in focus on the papers we analysed, we observed that *Visions of Computing and HCI* of the future in conjunction with sci-fi are referred from the 1980s onwards. In contrast, *Human-Robot Interaction and AI* publications have been referring sci-fi in the 2000s forward through for instance, movies and fictional robots to explore robot ethics or the public perception of AI.

Since the 2010s, there are emerging research areas in computing research, predominantly the thematic area of *Theoretical Design Research*, but as well the areas of *New Interactions* or *Human-Body Modification*. In these thematic areas, sci-fi movies, shows or stories do provide an inspiration for the foremost and upcoming HCI challenges of our time, for example through the discussion of shape-changing interfaces, implantables or digital afterlife ethics.

This research was of an exploratory nature. By taking the CHI proceedings as a pilot dataset for analysis, we afforded ourselves the possibility to apply our tentative methodology. In the process, we learned its strengths and limitations. All in all, our methodology proved useful as we were able to identify specific sci-fi through a contextual review of the retrieved papers. We aim to use it to conduct further more fully fledged studies where we will investigate how sci-fi is used in HCI.

6   Discussion and Future Work

We acknowledge that our open, qualitative coding of the uses of sci-fi within the respective publications might be subjective as it might lack external validity and overall reliability. Although we discussed both, our coding scheme and the five general research themes thorough, in some cases the mutual exclusive coding of the sci-fi in the paper under review was challenging.

For instance, [42] shares aspects of both, the theme of Human-Robot Interaction and AI and Visions of Computing and HCI. In another, similar example, we find a paper [29] which refers specific sci-fi, namely KITT from *Knight Rider*. KITT is arguably an AI of some sorts embedded in a vehicle, hence the paper presents results of a study on human driver's loss of agency in the emergence of 'partially intelligent' cars in the near future.

To establish a basic reliability of our method, we did first find common ground through open coding 25% of the sample independently. Then we consolidated and, after one author finished the review of the remaining papers, conducted a final discussion of the coding between the raters. Still, we did not calculate a Krippendorff's alpha, respectively Fleiss' kappa, in this study, a limitation we aim to address in future studies in order to validate our coding scheme.

Moreover, the full-text query of the dataset we used did lead us to specific sci-fi authors, movie titles, and short stories in the context of the retrieved paper. Although, that is a reasonable expectation, we might have missed relevant publications not matching our initial six-term search query. Direct full-text searches for movie titles [30], such as *"Terminator"* or *"Avatar"*, can generate hundreds of false-positives which complicate the qualitative coding process.

This trade-off between recall and precision, or full-text versus metadata search and retrieval, is a classic dilemma in information retrieval [6,19,31]. In this study, we decided to search full-text for 'sci-fi' and its synonyms and therefore might not have caught all potential referrals of the concept. While this is a trade-off we will reconsider in a future instance of this ongoing research, we believe our results are interesting and shed light on remarkable trends in HCI research.

Our analysis shows that starting in the 2010s, there is an upsurge of retrieved publications, specifically from 2013 in the CHI extended abstracts, and from 2016 onwards in the main CHI proceedings. On the other hand, these initial results can only be of provisional nature and should be normalized against the distribution of all papers per year in the main CHI proceedings. Such a comparison might allow for a better insight into an above-average occurrence of sci-fi related papers. This is then an aspect of this preliminary study that warrants further investigation.

As of yet, our analysis does not include the other 54 CHI records, among those the records from the CHI extended abstracts (e.g. other work-in-progress papers, alt.chi contributions, plenary sessions, workshops, etc.). We aim to qualitatively review these 54 other records in the future, and plan to explore in more detail the specifics of the sci-fi referred in HCI research.

Beyond the extension of this study, future analysis will apply similar and more specific searches in a wider range of literature, conferences and venues. Exploring sci-fi referrals in conferences other than CHI, for example HCII, UIST, INTER-ACT, SIGGRAPH or even the IEEE *Xplore* Digital Library might allow for comparative assessments of both, research themes and cultural bias across conferences and periodicals in order to corroborate or refute the results of this study.

In the future, we aim to collect a larger, yet filtered, sample that is generated from cross-cultural and preferably, univocal, sci-fi titles and keywords in order to replicate and validate this pilot study. We also aim to investigate in more details the uses of specific types of sci-fi, for instance particular sci-fi movies, novels or characters and aim to investigate as well the uniformity - or diversity - of the sci-fi material consulted, refereed and discussed in HCI research.

Based on our analysis and findings, a last important future goal of this research effort will be to extrapolate any lessons that allow researchers and practitioners to understand why sci-fi is used and how the sci-fi supports the arguments of the papers where it is cited, to ultimately provide guidance on future research in this area.

We speculate that the explicit referral of sci-fi in HCI research represents a fraction of the actual inspiration and impact it has had on HCI research. Our future studies will therefore aim to conduct qualitative interviews with HCI researchers in order to investigate that claim and assess the reasons and reservations of authors in computer science, who refer, or rather decide consciously to not refer to sci-fi in their research output.

References

1. ACM Digital Library - Conference on Human Factors in Computing Systems (2018). https://dl.acm.org/event.cfm?id=RE151
2. Asimov, I.: How Easy to See the Future! Asimov on Science Fiction. Avon Books, New York (1975)
3. Bardzell, J., Bardzell, S., Stolterman, E.: Reading critical designs: supporting reasoned interpretations of critical design. In: Proceedings of the SIGCHI Conference on Human Factors in Computing Systems, CHI 2014, pp. 1951–1960. ACM, New York (2014). https://doi.org/10.1145/2556288.2557137

4. Bartneck, C., Hu, J.: Scientometric analysis of the CHI proceedings. In: Proceedings of the SIGCHI Conference on Human Factors in Computing Systems, CHI 2009, pp. 699–708. ACM, New York (2009). https://doi.org/10.1145/1518701.1518810

5. Bauer, J.S., Kientz, J.A.: Designlibs: a scenario-based design method for ideation. In: Proceedings of the SIGCHI Conference on Human Factors in Computing Systems, CHI 2013, pp. 1955–1958. ACM, New York (2013). https://doi.org/10.1145/2470654.2466258

6. Beall, J.: The weaknesses of full-text searching. J. Acad. Librarianship **34**(5), 438–444 (2008). https://doi.org/10.1016/j.acalib.2008.06.007

7. Blythe, M.: Research through design fiction: narrative in real and imaginary abstracts. In: Proceedings of the SIGCHI Conference on Human Factors in Computing Systems, CHI 2014, pp. 703–712. ACM, New York (2014). https://doi.org/10.1145/2556288.2557098

8. Bopp, J.A., Mekler, E.D., Opwis, K.: Negative emotion, positive experience? Emotionally moving moments in digital games. In: Proceedings of the 2016 CHI Conference on Human Factors in Computing Systems, CHI 2016, pp. 2996–3006. ACM, New York (2016). https://doi.org/10.1145/2858036.2858227

9. Britton, L.M.: Manifesting the Cyborg via techno body modification: from human computer interaction to integration. In: Companion of the 2017 ACM Conference on Computer Supported Cooperative Work and Social Computing, CSCW 2017 Companion, pp. 53–56. ACM, New York (2017). https://doi.org/10.1145/3022198.3024939

10. Bucci, P., Cang, X.L., Valair, A., Marino, D., Tseng, L., Jung, M., Rantala, J., Schneider, O.S., MacLean, K.E.: Sketching cuddlebits: coupled prototyping of body and behaviour for an affective robot pet. In: Proceedings of the 2017 CHI Conference on Human Factors in Computing Systems, CHI 2017, pp. 3681–3692. ACM, New York (2017). https://doi.org/10.1145/3025453.3025774

11. Core Conference Ranks (2018). http://portal.core.edu.au/conf-ranks/1053/

12. DeVaris, P.E.: The impact of electronics on humans and their work environment. In: Proceedings of the 1982 Conference on Human Factors in Computing Systems, CHI 1982, pp. 281–286. ACM, New York (1982). https://doi.org/10.1145/800049.801795

13. Elmqvist, N., Henry, N., Riche, Y., Fekete, J.D.: Melange: space folding for multifocus interaction. In: Proceedings of the SIGCHI Conference on Human Factors in Computing Systems, CHI 2008, pp. 1333–1342. ACM, New York (2008). https://doi.org/10.1145/1357054.1357263

14. Figueiredo, L.S., Pinheiro, M.G.G.M., Neto, E.X.V.,, Teichrieb, V.: An open catalog of hand gestures from Sci-Fi movies. In: Proceedings of the 33rd Annual ACM Conference Extended Abstracts on Human Factors in Computing Systems, CHI EA 2015, pp. 1319–1324. ACM, New York (2015). https://doi.org/10.1145/2702613.2732888

15. Google Scholar HCI Top Publications (2018). https://goo.gl/Xikppr

16. Grandhi, S.A., Joue, G., Mittelberg, I.: Understanding naturalness and intuitiveness in gesture production: insights for touchless gestural interfaces. In: Proceedings of the SIGCHI Conference on Human Factors in Computing Systems, CHI 2011, pp. 821–824. ACM, New York (2011). https://doi.org/10.1145/1978942.1979061

17. Guha, S., Steinhardt, S., Ahmed, S.I., Lagoze, C.: Following bibliometric footprints: the ACM digital library and the evolution of computer science. In: Proceedings of the 13th ACM/IEEE-CS Joint Conference on Digital Libraries, JCDL 2013, pp. 139–142. ACM, New York (2013). https://doi.org/10.1145/2467696.2467732

18. Heffernan, K.J., Vetere, F., Chang, S.: You put what, where?: Hobbyist use of insertable devices. In: Proceedings of the 2016 CHI Conference on Human Factors in Computing Systems, CHI 2016, pp. 1798–1809. ACM, New York (2016). https://doi.org/10.1145/2858036.2858392

19. Hemminger, B.M., Saelim, B., Sullivan, P.F., Vision, T.J.: Comparison of full-text searching to metadata searching for genes in two biomedical literature cohorts. J. Am. Soc. Inf. Sci. Technol. **58**(14), 2341–2352 (2007). https://doi.org/10.1002/asi.20708

20. Henry, N., Goodell, H., Elmqvist, N., Fekete, J.D.: 20 years of four HCI conferences: a visual exploration. Int. J. Hum. Comput. Interact. **23**(3), 239–285 (2007)

21. Jamison-Powell, S., Briggs, P., Lawson, S., Linehan, C., Windle, K., Gross, H.: "PS. I love you": understanding the impact of posthumous digital messages. In: Proceedings of the 2016 CHI Conference on Human Factors in Computing Systems, CHI 2016, pp. 2920–2932. ACM, New York (2016). https://doi.org/10.1145/2858036.2858504

22. Jordan, P., Auernheimer, B.: The fiction in computer science: a qualitative data analysis of the ACM digital library for traces of star trek. In: Ahram, T., Falcão, C. (eds.) AHFE 2017. AISC, vol. 607, pp. 508–520. Springer, Cham (2018). https://doi.org/10.1007/978-3-319-60492-3_48

23. Jordan, P., Mubin, O., Silva, P.A.: A conceptual research agenda and quantification framework for the relationship between science-fiction media and human-computer interaction. In: Stephanidis, C. (ed.) HCI 2016. CCIS, vol. 617, pp. 52–57. Springer, Cham (2016). https://doi.org/10.1007/978-3-319-40548-3_9

24. Kim, J., McNally, B., Norooz, L., Druin, A.: Internet search roles of adults in their homes. In: Proceedings of the 2017 CHI Conference on Human Factors in Computing Systems, CHI 2017, pp. 4948–4959. ACM, New York (2017). https://doi.org/10.1145/3025453.3025572

25. Kirby, D.: The future is now: diegetic prototypes and the role of popular films in generating real-world technological development. Soc. Stud. Sci. **40**(1), 41–70 (2010). https://doi.org/10.1177/0306312709338325

26. Kohno, T., Johnson, B.D.: Science fiction prototyping and security education: cultivating contextual and societal thinking in computer security education and beyond. In: Proceedings of the 42nd ACM Technical Symposium on Computer Science Education, SIGCSE 2011, pp. 9–14. ACM, New York (2011). https://doi.org/10.1145/1953163.1953173

27. Krekhov, A., Emmerich, K., Babinski, M., Krüger, J.: Gestures from the point of view of an audience: towards anticipatable interaction of presenters with 3d content. In: Proceedings of the 2017 CHI Conference on Human Factors in Computing Systems, CHI 2017, pp. 5284–5294. ACM, New York (2017). https://doi.org/10.1145/3025453.3025641

28. Larson, J.: Limited imagination: depictions of computers in science fiction film. Futures **40**(3), 293–299 (2008). https://doi.org/10.1016/j.futures.2007.08.015

29. Lee, K.J., Joo, Y.K., Nass, C.: Partially intelligent automobiles and driving experience at the moment of system transition. In: Proceedings of the SIGCHI Conference on Human Factors in Computing Systems, CHI 2014, pp. 3631–3634. ACM, New York (2014). https://doi.org/10.1145/2556288.2557370

30. Levin, L.G., De Filippo, D.: Films and science: quantification and analysis of the use of science fiction films in scientific papers. JCOM-J. Sci. Commun. 13(03) (2014). https://jcom.sissa.it/archive/13/03/JCOM_1303_2014_A07

31. Lin, J.: Is searching full text more effective than searching abstracts? BMC Bioinf. **10**(1), 46 (2009). https://doi.org/10.1186/1471-2105-10-46

32. Lindley, J., Coulton, P.: Back to the future: 10 years of design fiction. In: Proceedings of the 2015 British HCI Conference, British HCI 2015, pp. 210–211. ACM, New York (2015). https://doi.org/10.1145/2783446.2783592

33. Liu, Y., Goncalves, J., Ferreira, D., Xiao, B., Hosio, S., Kostakos, V.: Chi 1994–2013: mapping two decades of intellectual progress through co-word analysis. In: Proceedings of the 32nd Annual ACM Conference on Human Factors in Computing Systems, CHI 2014, pp. 3553–3562. ACM, New York (2014). https://doi.org/10.1145/2556288.2556969

34. Mankoff, J., Rode, J.A., Faste, H.: Looking past yesterday's tomorrow: using futures studies methods to extend the research horizon. In: Proceedings of the SIGCHI Conference on Human Factors in Computing Systems, CHI 2013, pp. 1629–1638. ACM, New York (2013). https://doi.org/10.1145/2470654.2466216

35. Marcus, A.: ACM Interactions Blog, February 2013. http://goo.gl/bvLdLV

36. Marcus, A.: The past 100 years of the future: HCI and user-experience design in science-fiction movies and television. In: SIGGRAPH Asia 2015 Courses, SA 2015, pp. 15:1–15:26. ACM, New York (2015). https://doi.org/10.1145/2818143.2818151

37. Marcus, A., Norman, D.A., Rucker, R., Sterling, B., Vinge, V.: Sci-Fi at CHI: cyberpunk novelists predict future user interfaces. In: Proceedings of the SIGCHI Conference on Human Factors in Computing Systems, CHI 1992, pp. 435–437. ACM, New York (1992). https://doi.org/10.1145/142750.142892

38. Marcus, A., Soloway, E., Sterling, B., Swanwick, M., Vinge, V.: Opening pleanary: Sci-fi @ CHI-99: science-fiction authors predict future user interfaces. In: CHI 1999 Extended Abstracts on Human Factors in Computing Systems, CHI EA 1999, pp. 95–96. ACM, New York (1999). https://doi.org/10.1145/632716.632775

39. Massimi, M., Odom, W., Banks, R., Kirk, D.: Matters of life and death: locating the end of life in lifespan-oriented HCI research. In: Proceedings of the SIGCHI Conference on Human Factors in Computing Systems, CHI 2011, pp. 987–996. ACM, New York (2011). https://doi.org/10.1145/1978942.1979090

40. Mingers, J., Leydesdorff, L.: A review of theory and practice in scientometrics. Eur. J. Oper. Res. **246**(1), 1–19 (2015). http://www.sciencedirect.com/science/article/pii/S037722171500274X

41. Mubin, O., Obaid, M., Jordan, P., Alves-Oliveria, P., Eriksson, T., Barendregt, W., Sjolle, D., Fjeld, M., Simoff, S., Billinghurst, M.: Towards an agenda for Sci-Fi inspired HCI research. In: Proceedings of the 13th International Conference on Advances in Computer Entertainment Technology, ACE 2016, pp. 10:1–10:6. ACM, New York (2016). https://doi.org/10.1145/3001773.3001786

42. Oh, C., Lee, T., Kim, Y., Park, S., Kwon, S.B., Suh, B.: Us vs. Them: understanding artificial intelligence technophobia over the Google deepmind challenge match. In: Proceedings of the 2017 CHI Conference on Human Factors in Computing Systems, CHI 2017, pp. 2523–2534. ACM, New York (2017). https://doi.org/10.1145/3025453.3025539

43. Pereira, A., Prada, R., Paiva, A.: Improving social presence in human-agent interaction. In: Proceedings of the SIGCHI Conference on Human Factors in Computing Systems, CHI 2014, pp. 1449–1458. ACM, New York (2014). https://doi.org/10.1145/2556288.2557180

44. Reeves, S.: Envisioning ubiquitous computing. In: Proceedings of the SIGCHI Conference on Human Factors in Computing Systems, CHI 2012, pp. 1573–1582. ACM, New York (2012). https://doi.org/10.1145/2207676.2208278

45. Rifkin, G.: Marvin Minsky, Pioneer in Artificial Intelligence, Dies at 88. The New York Times, January 2016. http://goo.gl/hL6AzW

46. Schmitz, M., Endres, C., Butz, A.: A survey of human-computer interaction design in science fiction movies. In: Proceedings of the 2nd International Conference on INtelligent TEchnologies for Interactive enterTAINment, INTETAIN 2008, pp. 7:1–7:10, ICST (Institute for Computer Sciences, Social-Informatics and Telecommunications Engineering), ICST, Brussels, Belgium, Belgium (2007). http://dl.acm.org/citation.cfm?id=1363200.1363210

47. Shedroff, N., Noessel, C.: Make it so: Learning from Sci-Fi interfaces. In: Proceedings of the International Working Conference on Advanced Visual Interfaces, AVI 2012, pp. 7–8. ACM, New York (2012). https://doi.org/10.1145/2254556.2254561

48. Takayama, L., Groom, V., Nass, C.: I'm sorry, Dave: I'm afraid I won't do that: social aspects of human-agent conflict. In: Proceedings of the SIGCHI Conference on Human Factors in Computing Systems, CHI 2009, pp. 2099–2108. ACM, New York (2009). https://doi.org/10.1145/1518701.1519021

49. Tanenbaum, J., Tanenbaum, K., Wakkary, R.: Steampunk as design fiction. In: Proceedings of the SIGCHI Conference on Human Factors in Computing Systems, CHI 2012, pp. 1583–1592. ACM, New York (2012). https://doi.org/10.1145/2207676.2208279

50. Troiano, G.M., Tiab, J., Lim, Y.K.: Sci-Fi: shape-changing interfaces, future interactions. In: Proceedings of the 9th Nordic Conference on Human-Computer Interaction, NordiCHI 2016, pp. 45:1–45:10. ACM, New York (2016). https://doi.org/10.1145/2971485.2971489

Pedagogy of Programming Education for Higher Education Using Block Based Programming Environment

Daehoon Kim, Jaewoong Choi, In-Ho Jung, and Changbeom Choi$^{(\boxtimes)}$

Handong Global University, Pohang-si, Kyunbuk 37554, Republic of Korea
{21200082, 21631005, 21631004, cbchoi}@handong.edu

Abstract. As the modern society utilizes various devices based on the Information, Communication Technology (ICT), the importance of the computer program has been increased. As the needs of the education of engineering increases, many researchers studied the pedagogy of the engineering education and the learning contents development. In general, the education of the programming language accompanies with the syntax learning and logic developments. The block-based programming language helps to build the logic of the students. Therefore, Block-based programming languages are used in the entry course to the engineering departments. However, the block-based learning languages are limited to develop conventional applications. The application of the block-based programming language requires the particular middleware to execute, and usually, the application cannot utilize the functionalities of the hardware. Therefore, students should learn the high-level programming language regardless of the block-based programming language to develop the ICT services. Unlike other pedagogy, this paper introduces the education contents and programming environment with high-level programming. Notably, this paper proposes the hybrid approaches to help students to build their programming logic and programming syntax.

Keywords: Human-computer-interactive learning · Web-based programming
Programming education environment

1 Introduction

1.1 The Importance of Programming Education

As the era of the 4th industrial revolution emerged, the importance of the programming education increased. Many policymakers for K-12 curriculum have decided to adopt programming education into their curriculum. As the importance of the programming education increases, many educators considered making effective pedagogy to teach their students. There are several issues in teaching programming skills, and among them increasing motivation and understanding are essential. For those who are new to programming course, the visualized languages may give more motivation and interest rather than the grammar-based languages. Therefore, the educators have utilized to use visual programming environment to their classroom. The visualized programming

© Springer International Publishing AG, part of Springer Nature 2018
A. Marcus and W. Wang (Eds.): DUXU 2018, LNCS 10919, pp. 39–50, 2018.
https://doi.org/10.1007/978-3-319-91803-7_3

environment, in general, utilize block image. By placing proper blocks and connecting them, a student may exercise to raise the computational thinking. Also, the educator may utilize visual programming environment to create various education contents by applying the environment to various domains, such as robotics, animation, application development.

Unfortunately, when the students are accustomed to the visual programming environment, and if they want to make complicated computer system, they must learn a grammar-based programming language, such as C++, Java, Python, and Scala. Therefore, an educator may teach visual programming environment to raise the computational thinking first, and after teaching visual programming environment, they have to teach grammar-based programming environment without taking advantage of the visual programming environment.

This research introduces a pedagogy for programming education using HIPE, the High-level Interactive Programming Environment to help students learn how to make a program using grammar-based programming language by taking advantage of the visual programming environment.

In this study, we introduce HIPE which provides ideal programming environment through interaction between human and computer and suggest how to interact with programming education. The rest of the paper is organized as follows. Section 2 introduces the background of the research. It introduces the characteristics of the visual programming environment and grammar-based programming environment. Also, HIPE will be introduced in this section. Section 3 shows programming education pedagogy using HIPE. Section 4 introduces the case study for HIPE, and finally, Sect. 5 concludes this paper.

2   Related Work

2.1   Text-Based Programming Environment

A well-known and popular programming environment is an environment in which a user can directly describe a program's code and complete a program. Such a programming environment can be defined as a text-based programming environment. Specifically, the text-based programming environment is an environment in which the programmer can directly insert and edit the program code in a place selected by the programmer using a keyboard and a mouse, and can convert the program code into a working program. A text-based programming environment consists of two tools. The first tool is a programming editing tool that allows the user to edit the program code using the tool. Another tool is an environment that provides a compile function and linking functions as a programming environment in which a program code described by a user is received as an executable program. A text-based programming environment can be divided into a console-based programming environment and an integrated development environment, depending on the editing tools and programming support tools. The console-based programming environment is a programming environment that utilizes the command line interface rather than the graphical user interface such as vi and gcc which are well-known tools for embedded programming environment or a

Linux programming environment. On the other hand, environments that can be edited and executed by using a graphical user interface without using a command line interface include a graphical code editing tool and a command line interface based programming support environment, or an integrated programming environment in which these tools are integrated have. Such a text-based programming environment can be utilized for learning programming while describing a user's intention as text and converting it into a form that can be executed, regardless of the graphical elements of the support tool.

In general, teachers and students use the text-based programming environment to gain programming knowledge in their classroom. The primary objectives of the teachers in programming course are two folds. First, the teachers should raise the computational thinking of the students. To help students to raise the computational thinking, the teachers prepare problem or contents, so that the students may build the logic of the program to solve the problem. On the other hand, the teachers teach the students to express their logic using programming language. Therefore, the teachers teach the syntax of the programming language to the students. As the primary objectives of the programming course are to build the computational thinking and improve the familiarity of the syntax usage of a programming language, the teachers use various tools and materials to help students. However, the text-based programming environments are not helpful to the teachers nor students. Since the text-based programming environment focuses on making a program rather than teaching students, the teachers and the students cannot take any advantages to improve the progress.

This research provides a visual educational environment for programming. The educational environment helps students to formulate logic and learn how to make a program by utilizing visual elements and generating an error-free code based on the visual elements.

2.2 Visual Programming Environment

In the programming education, a visual programming language is popular programming environment that lets users create a program by manipulating visual elements that represent the logic of the program. By visualizing logic of the program, the teachers and the students may utilize the programming environment to focus on the logic building. Also, the programming environment has an extension to control the animations, videos, music or robot to motivate students to improve the computational thinking. For instance, the Scratch, MIT App Inventor, and LEGO NXT are popular visual programming environment to teach programming beginners such as K-12 students in the STEM (Science, Technology, Engineering, and Mathematics) education.

There are several characteristics of the visual programming environment. First, it can be easily programmed and shared via the Internet. For example, everyone can do programming and build a simple application that works on a smartphone in 30 min using the App Inventor. Therefore, the results of programming can be verified through a mobile device. Another feature is that the visual programming environment gives feedback to a user through a graphical user interface. For example, the user may combine logic blocks to complete the program. During the combining phase, the programming environment prohibits the incorrect combination of the logic blocks.

Accordingly, the user may build a program without knowing a complex programming language and other tools. Also, the user may drag and drop the logic or function blocks to complete program easily.

However, the visual programming environment is not suitable to develop a commercial application. In general, a commercial application has complex features and business logic, so that a developer may use hundreds and thousands of blocks to build the application. Also, the developer may not reuse the pre-developed library to implement an application. Moreover, the application of the visual programming environment may not utilize the full performance of a device. To use the full performance and the features of a device, the developer should understand the capabilities of a programming language and the target device. This research focuses on the fact. After a student develops the computational thinking using visual programming languages, the student should learn high-level programming languages to build a computer program based on the text-based programming environment. Since the students are familiar with the visual programming language, the teachers may need times and efforts to help students adopt the text-based programming environment.

2.3   High-Level Interactive Programming Environment

As the demand for programming language education grows, many services are proposed to help teach programming using visualization elements, the blocks. The services take advantage of the visualization features to express one's logic in real-time.

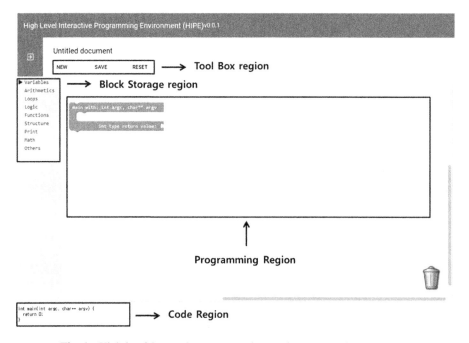

Fig. 1. High-level interactive programming environment web page screen

The feature may help a student who wants to improve the computational thinking; however, it may not help a student who wants to build a realistic program using high-level programming language. This research bridges the gap between two types of the students. The HIPE, High-level Interactive Programming Environment, is a web-based visualization programming editor that allows students to learn the structural and programming logic of the C/C++ language, intuitively.

The Fig. 1 shows the execution screen of the HIPE. The Toolbox region provides features to start building a new program or save the current status of the program. The Block storage region provides various blocks to a user based on the high-level programming language. The blocks are designed to reflect the functionalities of the high-level programming language. For example, the "print" block is designed to print out the contents to the standard output stream in C++ programming language. The Programming region is a region that the user may construct a program using block. Since the blocks are designed to prevent the syntax error, the user may not consider the syntax error of the code. Therefore, if a user tries to assemble the wrong combination of the block, the HIPE will give feedback to the user that the given block combination generates the syntax error.

Finally, the Code region shows the code generation results concerning the assembled blocks in real-time.

3 Visual Programming Pedagogy Based on HIPE

Most programming education environments are a text-oriented environment. The tutor provides theoretical contents to the students and provides programming tasks to check the progress of a student. Such type of education can be a high entry barrier for beginners. On the other hand, a visual programming environment has low entry barrier to the beginners. The students may check their logic in real-time using feedback from the visual programming environment. Therefore, the visual programming environments are used to help beginners to form correct programming logic and design capability. However, almost all commercial applications are developed using a text-based programming language and environment. Consequently, when a student wants to build such application, the student should learn how to use the text-based programming language and the environment. The HIPE is a useful tool to fill in the gap between the visual programming language and the text-based programming language. The HIPE may be utilized to tutors who want to help students to improve the programming logic and high-level programming skills at the same time. The tutors and the students may use HIPE to interact each other. Following subsections show the educational phases and interactions among the tutors, the students, and the HIPE during the educational phases.

3.1 Phase 1: Interactive Learning

In Phase I, a tutor and a student interact with each other using HIPE. Since the HIPE shows the logic of the program, the tutor may use the tool to show the code generation results when the tutor puts a block to the HIPE. For example, when the tutor puts a block to the programming region of the HIPE, the HIPE generates the codes based on the assembled blocks. Since the HIPE prohibits the syntax error in real-time, students may practice forming correct logic. Also, the tutor may use the tools to make a simple pop-up quiz by using the code generation features. Figure 2 shows the logic block and the code generation results. As shown in the figure, a user may put blocks to the programming region of the HIPE. Then, the HIPE analyzes the assembled blocks and generates the corresponding C++ code.

```
#include <iostream>

int main(int argc, char** argv) {
    int input = 0;
    return 0;
}
```

Fig. 2. Blocks and codes for variables

Figure 3 shows the sequence diagram of interaction among the tutor, the student, and the HIPE. When a tutor teaches a student, the tutor may place the block incrementally. Then, a student may watch how the program completes. Also, during the teaching session, the tutor may use HIPE to answer the students' questions.

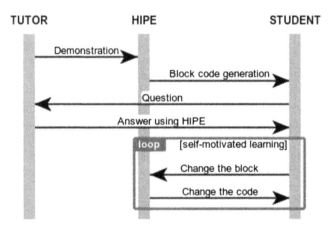

Fig. 3. Sequence diagram

Figure 4 and 5 shows an example of the Phase I. Figure 4 shows the code generation results when a user adds print block and input block. When the user adds print block to the HIPE, the HIPE translate the block to code which uses the standard output stream. Similarly, when the user adds input block, the HIPE translate the blocks to code.

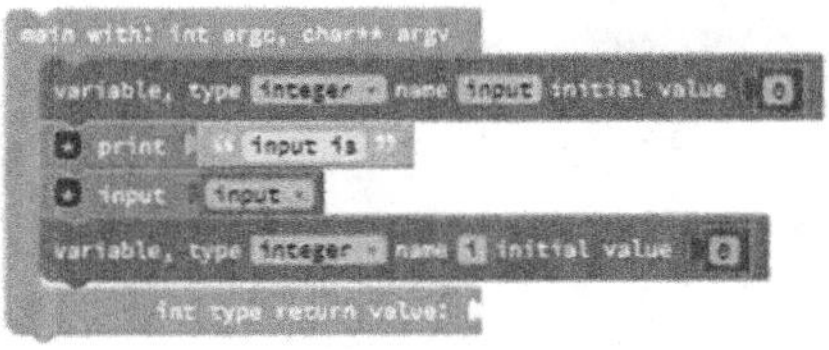

Fig. 4. Blocks and codes for input/output

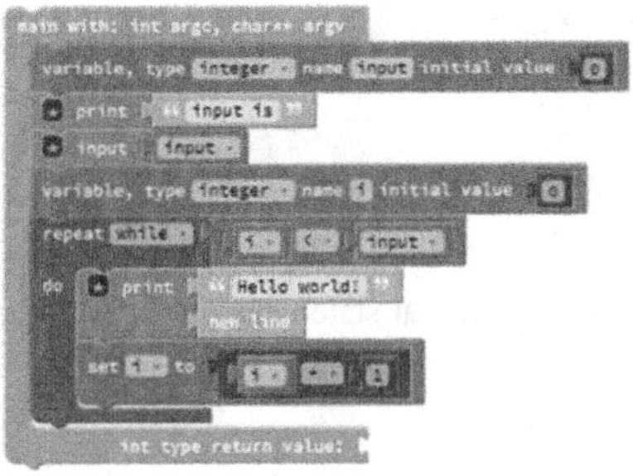

Fig. 5. Block and codes for while loop

Figure 5 shows the complex combination of the blocks. When the user adds the repeat blocks to the HIPE, the HIPE will generate the block into while block. During the session, a tutor may ask a question such as "Tell me what code is generated when you insert this block."

3.2 Phase II: Learning from Difference

The next step of the pedagogy using HIPE is the "Learning from difference" phase. In Phase II, students are encouraged to study by themselves. First, a tutor gives a problem to the students. Notably, the problem is a diagram of code blocks which denotes the logic of the student a problem with the block created using HIPE and write the code for the problem. It is the process of actually mastering Programming Syntax learned through Phase 1. The student can identify and train the wrong part of himself by comparing his written code with the results of the HIPE.

Figure 6 shows the example of Phase II. Figure 6 is a block diagram which shows a program that receives a score from a user and outputs a grade corresponding to the score using the multiple conditional statements with HIPE. During the practice session, the tutor provides the diagram to the students and encourage them to develop the program using text-based programming language. Then, the students may solve the problem or may not solve the problem using text-based programming language. If the students are not yet familiar with the programming syntax, the students may go back to the Phase I, and use the HIPE to enhance their skills.

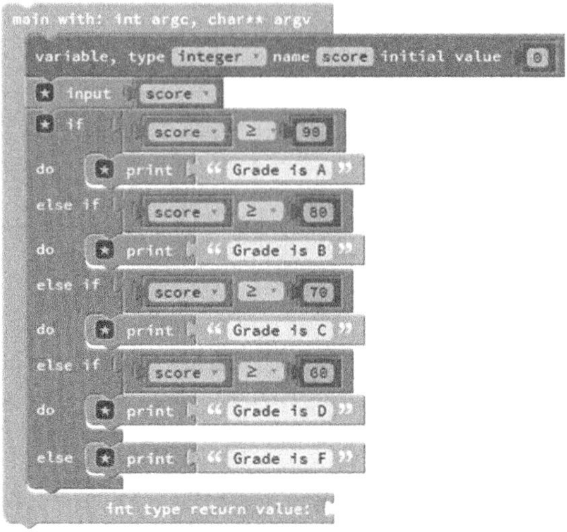

Fig. 6. Complete code block and codes for conditional statements

3.3   Phase 3: Traditional Learning

Phase III is the final phase. In this phase, the students are familiar with the given programming syntax. Therefore, a tutor may use the traditional education method to teach students. During the phase, the tutor may present the programming problem to the student without using HIPE. If the students have a syntax error in their code, or if the students do not fully understand the syntax, they may solve the problems in the text-based programming environment.

4   Case Study: Short-Term Programming Course

This section introduces the case study to show the effectiveness of the pedagogy at Handong Global University. Notably, the School of Global Entrepreneurship at Handong Global University opens short-term programming course twice a year for extracurricular activities. About 37 students have participated the programming course in 2017, and the course was specifically designed to apply the proposed pedagogy using HIPE. Approximately 70% of the participants have experienced the visual programming languages, and about 57% of the students have prior knowledge of C/C++ languages. After every session, a survey was taken to check the effectiveness of the pedagogy using HIPE.

4.1   Camp Operation

During the short-term programming course, the tutor explained the theoretical part of the C++ programming language, such as the basic syntax of C++ programming language, dynamic memory allocation, and other high-level features of the object-oriented programming language. After the lesson, there was a practice session to check the progress. The course had three parts as the proposed pedagogy. At the beginning of the course, HIPE was used for to help students to understand the difference between a visual programming language and a text-based programming language. After the programming lessons, the students were encouraged to use text-based programming environment during the practice session. Finally, at the end of the course, all students used the text-based programming language environment.

Figure 7 shows the problem used in the short-term programming course. The objective of the problem was to learn the syntax for input and output of the program. During the practice session, simple problems were provided to the students. Each problem has description part to introduce the objective of the program. Also, the problem has input/output boxes to provide a test case to check the correctness.

- **Problem**

Enter your age and print it out. Declare an integer variable, input the age, output it according to the output format, and output the following result.

(Assemble the given code block using HIPE and run the code.)

Input   23

Output   My age is 23
          Thank you

Fig. 7. Problem of the practice session during Phase I

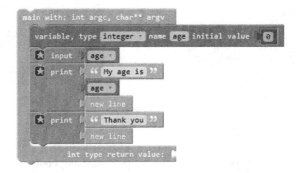

Fig. 8. Code blocks of the practice session during Phase I

During the practice session, students assembled a given block and checked the code generations. Figures 8 and 9 illustrate the code blocks and corresponding code of the practice session.

```
#include <iostream>

int main(int argc, char **argv){
    int age = 0;
    std::cin >> age;
    std::cout << "My age is" << age << std::endl;
    std::cout << "Thank you" << std::endl;
    retrn 0;
}
```

Fig. 9. Code of the practice session during Phase I

4.2   Questionnaire Results

Figure 10 shows the survey result. Almost 70% of the students are familiar with the visual programming language. Also, 56.8% of the students have prior knowledge of the C/C++ programming language. Based on the preliminary survey results, more than 40% of students begin with the visual programming languages to study programming.

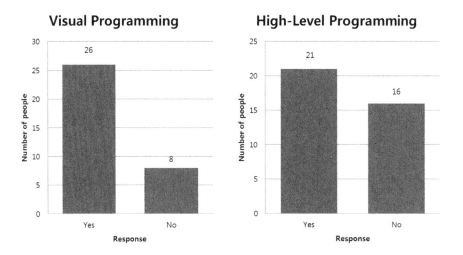

Fig. 10. Questionnaire result before short-term course

Figure 11 shows the survey results after the programming course. As a result, 81% of the students answered that the HIPE was helpful to understand the logic and the syntax of the programming language. This survey shows that the HIPE may be useful to the students who are familiar with the visual programming language, and the HIPE was useful to the students who have prior knowledge of the C/C++ programming language. Also, students have testified that the HIPE was useful to see the logic diagram and its code at the same time and it was helpful when the HIPE gives the feedback based on the combination of the blocks.

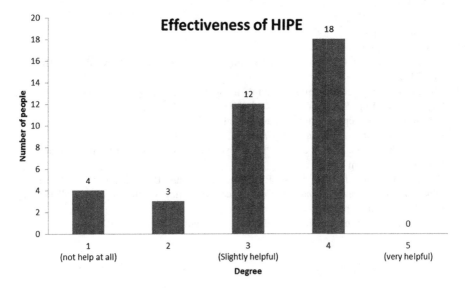

Fig. 11. Questionnaire result after short-term course

5 Conclusion

In the era of the fourth industrial revolution movement, the programming education is one of the hot issues in the education. To help beginners to form the computation thinking, many educators have utilized various teaching methods and tools. One of the programming education environment is block-based programming environment. The block-based programming environment is a visual programming environment using blocks to represent the logic of the program. Since the block-based programming language allows the correct block combination, a student may get feedbacks from the programming environment. After the students are familiar with the computational thinking, the students may want to build a complex application. Unfortunately, the students may not develop the complex or commercial application with the visual programming language, due to the limitation of the language. Therefore, the students should study text-based programming language. Since the students are familiar with the visual programming language, this research proposed a pedagogy using visual programming environment for a text-based programming language.

The programming environment, HIPE, fills the gap between building computational thinking and learning the syntax of the programming language. As proposed in the paper, a tutor may utilize the HIPE in various ways during the programming course.

For the future research, extending the programming pedagogy and programming environment to support specific topics, such as the Internet of Things and artificial intelligence.

References

1. https://www.vim.org/
2. https://gcc.gnu.org/
3. Malan, D.J., Leitner, H.H.: Scratch for budding computer scientists. ACM SIGCSE Bull. **39** (1), 223 (2007)
4. Wing, J.M.: Computational thinking and thinking about computing. Philos. Trans. Roy. Soc. A Math. Phys. Eng. Sci. **366**(1881), 3717 (2008)
5. Scratch official homepage. https://scratch.mit.edu/
6. App Inventor official homepage. http://appinventor.mit.edu/explore/
7. Lego NXT official homepage. http://www.lego.com/enus/mindstorms/?domainredir=mindstorms.lego.com
8. Maloney, J., Burd, L., Kafai, Y., Rusk, N., Silverman, B.: Scratch: a sneak preview [education]. In: Second International Conference on Creating, Connecting, and Collaborating through Computing, pp. 104–109 (2004)
9. Shu, N.C.: Visual Programming. Van Nostrand Reinhold, New York (1988)

A Design Provocation for Humble Designers and Empowered Users

Joon Suk Lee[1]([✉]), Margaret Dickey-Kurdziolek[2],
and Stacy Branham[3]

[1] Virginia State University, 1 Hayden Street, Petersburg, VA 23806, USA
joonsukl@acm.org
[2] Margaret Kurdziolek LLC, Pittsburgh, PA, USA
[3] UMBC, 1000 Hilltop Circle, Baltimore, MD 21250, USA

Abstract. Designs are ultimately imbued with the values and judgments of the designers who made them. This means that there is an inherent power imbalance between designers and users. Some design philosophies embrace the position of designer as empowered architect (*libertarian paternalism*), while others try to shift power to users by integrating them into the design process (*participatory design*). In this paper we present a third approach called *"use-time nudge,"* which maintains the authority of designer at *design-time*, yet grants the users more power at *use-time*. Use-time nudge challenges designers to question the values they imbue into their work at design-time and respond by deliberately deferring those judgments to the user to be made at use-time.

Keywords: Use-time nudge · Design provocation · Libertarian paternalism
Participatory design

1 Introduction

1.1 Re-imagining Designer-User Relationship

In his 1980 article, "Do Artifacts Have Politics?" Langdon Winner pointed out that no design is free from embedding designers' beliefs—designs inevitably represent designers' cultural, political, philosophical, religious, ethical, or aesthetic values [18]. No design is value neutral, and the act of designing is a form of articulating the designers' constant efforts to configure user activities (and users). As such, designers are destined to shape users' experiences in some way.

In this paper, we explore two established philosophies for navigating designer-user relationships: *participatory design*, which seeks to ameliorate the designer-user power imbalance, and *libertarian paternalism* [16], which embraces the position of designer as empowered experience architect. We then use these philosophies to introduce the idea of *use-time nudge* as a design provocation. We see use-time nudge as a way (1) for designers to reflect on the values they bring to their work, and (2) for users to design their experience with an artifact *after* the design of the artifact has been completed.

© Springer International Publishing AG, part of Springer Nature 2018
A. Marcus and W. Wang (Eds.): DUXU 2018, LNCS 10919, pp. 51–61, 2018.
https://doi.org/10.1007/978-3-319-91803-7_4

1.2   Philosophies on Designer-User Relationship

Different design professionals and researchers have tried to either embrace the imbalance of power in designer-user relationships or ameliorate it through different design practices.

For example, stemming from a Marxist commitment to democratize workplaces and empower workers, participatory design engages users in the design process [12]. Participatory design aims to democratize the design process and offset the unequally distributed power between designers and users by endowing users with opportunities to affect design decisions [3, 12].

On the other hand, we find approaches like that advocated by "Nudge: Improving Decisions About Health, Wealth, and Happiness" [16]. Drawing from social science findings, Thaler and Sunstein argue that people oftentimes make bad decisions—"decisions they would not have made if they had paid full attention and possessed complete information, unlimited cognitive abilities, and complete self-control [16, p. 5]." Based on this premise, they advocate the idea of designer as choice architect, whose responsibility it is to create designs that nudge people into making better decisions. To distance their idea of nudge from coercion, the authors introduce the term *Libertarian Paternalism* as a subtle and nonintrusive way of guiding users' behaviors [16]. This philosophy both acknowledges that designers have power over users and encourages designers to embrace that power as a *paternalistic figure*, strengthening (in a supposedly positive way) the inequality between designers and users.

While these two opposing approaches differ in how they view the roles of users and designers, they both inherently differentiate design practices from use practices. Such separation between "the setting of design (design-time) and the setting of use (use-time)" is often thought of as a by-product of the industrialization of design [10]. Design-time is seen as belonging to the design professionals whose job is to create completed design artifacts, while use-time is associated with unpredictable situations in which the artifacts are deployed into the ever-changing user context [10]. *Participatory Design* aims to reform the relationship between the designer and the user by shifting user involvement from use-time into design-time, whereas *Libertarian Paternalism* focuses on the designers' responsibilities and authority in design-time.

As opposed to the design praxis and theories that differentiate design-time and use-time, it has also been argued that design does not end when designers produce designed artifacts, but encompasses the entirety of use practices in which the designed artifacts are taken, appropriated, redefined and reconfigured by the users. Users and designed artifacts co-define and constantly reconfigure each other in situ [13, 17]. Design in this sense is an on-going process in which users are always a legitimate part. However, this account of design does not indicate how designers can actively aid users' design involvement in use-time.

2 Design Provocation

We propose *use-time nudge* as a design provocation and alternative way of design-thinking on the designer-user relationship. Our approach draws from the ideas of *participatory design* and *libertarian paternalism*, taking a situated perspective in understanding design praxis. Like participatory design, we advocate designer-user equality. Like libertarian paternalism, we accept that designers influence users. What makes our approach unique is a commitment to designing systems such that users can create and design their own interactions at *use-time*.

2.1 A Thought Experiment: Three Different Approaches to a Design Problem

In this section, we present an example of a design problem the authors have encountered first-hand. We then examine how our approach to this design problem changes if we take a participatory design, libertarian paternalism, or use-time nudge approach.

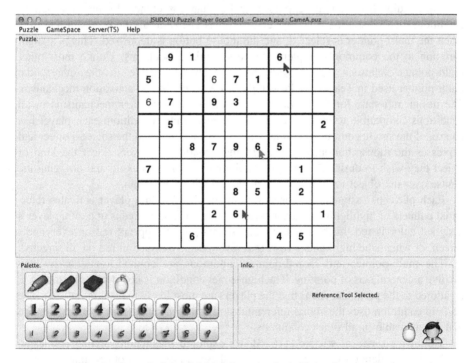

Fig. 1. Team Sudoku (Multi-pointer version) (Color figure online)

Design Task: Team Sudoku

Team Sudoku is a multi-user, parallel-distributed form of the Sudoku game. Sudoku presents the player with a 9 × 9 board with digits between 1 and 9 in some cells.

The goal of Sudoku is to fill the board so that each of the nine columns, nine rows and nine distinct 3×3 blocks contain exactly one instance of each digit from 1 to 9. Games are differentiated from one another by the number and location of starting digits. In the computerized form, each distinct game initially contains digits that cannot be written over or changed except by starting a new game, and that are a different color (black) from those that are in play (green).

Team Sudoku provides users three distinct features for manipulating the board. A pen tool enables users to insert entries on the board, and a pencil tool allows users to tentatively mark possibilities (note-entries). Users can delete any entries on the game board with an eraser tool. Team Sudoku is a multi-user collaborative variation of Sudoku in which players have their own computers with their own copies of the shared game board. When one player fills in a number, erases a number, or uses an indicating tool, the results are promptly shared on all players' screens.

Four different versions of Team Sudoku that vary in the support they provide for indicating were developed in-house. The four versions are a multi-pointer (shown in Fig. 1), a shared-pointer, a highlighter, and a no-pointer (no-help). In all cases, individual players use their private mouse indicators privately on their own screens. In the no-help condition, there is no explicit help for shared reference. In the multi-pointer condition, each person has a pointer that becomes visible to all the others in real time when the multi-pointer is selected, and the mouse button is depressed. This is a slight variation to the commonly implemented multi-pointer solutions. Unlike most other multi-pointer solutions that provide pointers always visible to the others, the multi-pointer used in Team Sudoku is only made visible by the activation mechanism. The design rationale for this variation is to make the activation mechanisms in all conditions compatible to each other. In the shared-pointer condition, each player has control of the single communal pointer when he/she has selected the shared-pointer and depresses the mouse button. In the highlighter condition, players select the kind of object they wish to designate (cell, row, column, block) by clicking and dragging the mouse over the object to show the other players what they mean.

Each player is assigned a color at system start up. When a player activates referential pointers or highlighters, his/her color appears on all the screens (e.g., if a player's assigned color is red, his/her multi-pointer/shared-pointer appears red on everyone's screen, or when s/he highlights a row, that row appears outlined in red on all screens).

The multi-pointer and shared-pointer conditions are context-free, that is, they involve a general sort of pointing. The highlighter condition is board-specific, that is, it is tailored to the particular items that the players are most likely to want to indicate. The no-help condition uses the verbal referential skills that we know from ordinary life and that are available in all other conditions.

Through a series of studies [4–6, 8], we explored interactions among collocated players in a collaborative Sudoku game. In these studies, we noticed that, in some groups, if a player made a critical mistake, the mistake would seemingly go unnoticed. However, subsequent data analysis revealed that many of the mistakes were noticed by the players, they simply decided not to discuss it. Some groups even decided not to exchange a single word during the entire gameplay [8].

As designers, we reflected on why some teams would hesitate to initiate social interaction even when it seemed critical in order to complete the game. This eventually led us to search and consider possible design interventions to remedy those situations and foster meaningful user interactions.

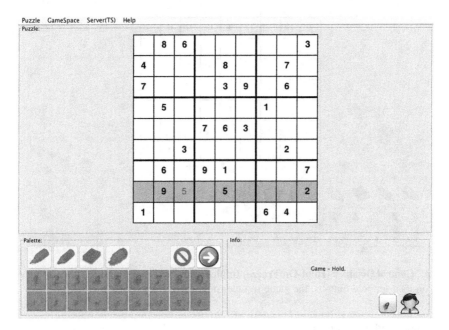

Fig. 2. Control Disabler (Hold-On/Freeze) Implemented in Team Sudoku: A player can click on the pause button to instantly put a hold on every player's game control buttons except the un-hold button.

Participatory Design Approach

First, a participatory design approach would lead us to actively involve users in designing the next phase of Team Sudoku. This could take the form of collaborative workshops, in which users discuss, sketch, and ultimately design solutions that account for their own values and desired experiences while playing the Team Sudoku game.

Libertarian Paternalism Approach

Alibertarian paternalism approach would lead us to design a solution that encourages users to behaviors we deem optimal. For instance, if we, designers, believe that mistakes need to be corrected quickly for optimal game play, we could make the Team Sudoku software monitor user entered numbers and alert the users when they make a mistake on the game board.

Similarly, if we believe that establishing "verbal equity" [1, 19] amongst group members is pivotal for an ideal group experience, we can design the software to monitor individual group member's contributions to the conversation, and to display each player's contributions to the group discussion (the amount of talk) on screen. In this way, we as designers *paternalistically* nudge users into making *better* behavioral decisions.

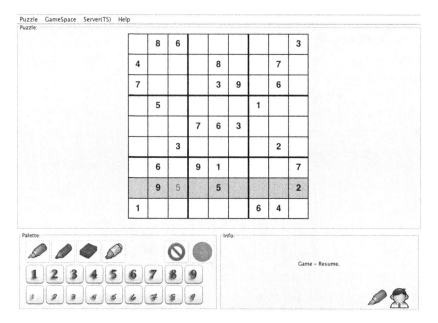

Fig. 3. Control Disabler (Hold-On/Freeze) Implemented in Team Sudoku: When all players click on their un-hold buttons, the game resumes on everyone's screen.

Use-Time Nudge Approach

Instead of taking an approach that tries to shape user-to-user interactions in design-time, we could try to enable users to find a solution to the problem during use-time. This section illustrates two sample examples of use-time nudge. By activating these interaction disruptors, users can create seamful moments in their interactions, and try to appropriate the moments to initiate desired social interactions. These designs are not intended to enforce certain kinds of user behaviors (e.g., talking), but only provide users opportunities to create seams in interaction. Users can use these disruptors to shape their interactions and influence other people's behaviors.

The first example (Figs. 2 and 3) is a "hold-on" button. The hold-on button would allow any of the participants to "hold" or "freeze" the game board until everyone in the group pushed the "un-hold" button.

Clicking the "hold-on" button would trigger a substantial, disruptive event during game play, encouraging user-to-user discussion. However, the decision to use the "hold-on" button is made completely by the users themselves during use-time. It grants them the ability to significantly shape their experience of the game.

The second example of interaction disruptors is a reverse-highlighter (Fig. 4). When activated, a reverse highlighter dims all the un-highlighted parts in the software on everyone's screen, creating visual distractions for other players. The group then can decide whether to ignore or appropriate the interactional opportunity initiated by one player.

These examples illustrate how designers in design-time can create features that nudge users, yet, by taking a use-time nudge approach, defer some value judgments to users at use-time. Users can thoughtfully leverage these affordances to shape their own experience as well as the experience of collocated collaborators.

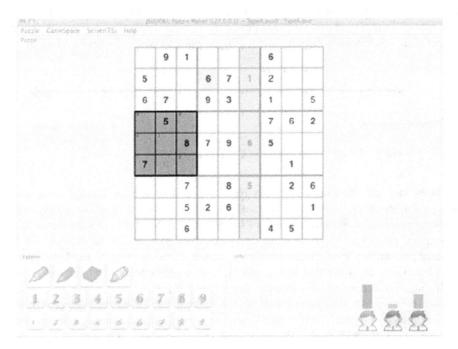

Fig. 4. Reverse highlighter implemented in Team Sudoku

3   Discussions

Processless design [7, 9] proposed and extended by the first author argues that intentional omission of embedding processes into digital artifacts delegates design responsibilities and powers to users, allowing users to construct more spontaneous, opportunistic and meaningful experiences and interactions in situ.

Like processless design, the idea of use-time nudge also enables and helps users to create and design their own situated experiences. Indeed, these two design concepts can collectively be used as conceptual guides for designing collaborative systems.

Yet, these two design ideas are mutually contradictory; by creating use-time nudge, designers inevitably embed processes into the system; by removing processes (that is, practicing processlessness), designers are forgoing opportunities to provide use-time nudge.

However, these two design ideas should not be understood as design axioms that must be practiced unconditionally. Nor should they be seen as constituent parts of possible design solutions in an ontological morphological design box (see [2]). Choosing to practice processlessness does not necessarily mean not designing use-time nudge, and designing use-time nudge should not be seen as refraining from processlessness. Instead, processlessness and use-time nudge should be understood as incommensurate dichotomous design concepts that constitute a *design tension* [14] between the two. In other words, the tension between the two competing ideas of processlessness and use-time nudge "conceptualize design not as problem solving but as goal balancing" [14, p. 415]. The acts of designing in this sense are designers' continual efforts and praxes to find a proper equilibrium within the continuum of two opposing design forces (see Fig. 5).

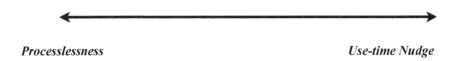

Processlessness   ***Use-time Nudge***

Fig. 5. Design tension between *Processlessness* and Use-Time Nudge

How then can designers go about balancing two contending design goals and design collaborative systems? The design tension between processlessness and use-time nudge does not provide bullet-listed design implications, but only works as a conceptual guide for design. It offers designers space to consider the different interactional possibilities their designs enable (or disable) in the moment of use. In addition, the idea of tension is not tied to any specific design methodology and can indeed be easily incorporated into many existing design methods. For instance, the conceptual tension between processlessness and use-time nudge can be handled effectively by scenario-based design which has been known to provide "simultaneously concrete and flexible" ways of handling the "complex [and] uncertain nature of design" [11, p. 26]. *Claims* [11] that augment the scenario-based design process by providing critical parameters for design choices can also provide an effective way to put the design tension idea into practice. Claims can also help designers capture their design practice of using the tensions into a reusable knowledge base (see [11] for in depth descriptions of *claims* and *critical parameters*). By requiring designers to generate design tradeoffs (*upsides* and *downsides*), claims help designers to recognize the different interactional possibilities their design—what they put in or what they leave out—can create or hinder. Table 1 shows an example of a typical claim for a control disabler (Hold-On/Freeze) feature.

Table 1. Claim for control disabler

Hold-On/Freeze
+ users can initiate disabling process to forcefully capture other people's attention
+ users can appropriate the seamful moment created by the control disabler to design desired social interaction
– control disable can be an annoyance
– control disable can be a distractor

Both *processless design* and *use-time nudge* embrace and augment *Zensign*, the idea that what we leave out of a design is as important as what we put in it [15]. These design provocations can be seen as radical ideas, yet they are still important alternatives to existing design thinking. These two ideas constitute a design tension which in turn can help to create designs that are open to multiple interactional possibilities. Yet, designers also have to acknowledge that even with such designs, they cannot anticipate the innumerable ways that users and designed artifacts can interact. Users and designed artifacts reform, reformulate and redefine each other. This in turn mandates research on how users behave around the newly designed artifacts. This is a dialectic relationship in which studies in qualitative research and studies in design research affect each other and trigger reformation on both sides iteratively.

Fig. 6. Who Designs and When? We propose use-time nudge (U-TN, highlighted in green) as a new design philosophy. Participatory Design (PD) emphasizes design-time collaboration between designer and user. Nudge emphasizes design-time activities of the designer. However, use-time nudge emphasizes the design-time activities of the designer as well as the use-time activities of the user.

4 Conclusion

Artifacts have politics. That is, the values of designers are infused into their designs and ultimately affect users. In this paper we proposed that designers can acknowledge and embrace this power without resorting to paternalistic design framing (as in libertarian paternalism), and can share the design process with users without design-time user engagement (as in participatory design). The alternative we offer is the use-time nudge, a design philosophy that draws both user and designer as empowered, situated actors. Figure 6 summarizes these three different design philosophies.

Use-time nudge distributes power between designer and user roles. In design-time, the designer has ultimate authority over the process, but is reflective and humble. The designer deliberately leaves pieces of the interaction design unfinished, and defers some values, judgments and system behaviors to be determined at use-time. At use-time, the user is mindful, active, and empowered. The user is afforded opportunities to reflect on and actively shape the interactions they and other users have with the artifact.

We see use-time nudge as a means of adding deliberate reflection into the design process. It challenges designers to identify and question the values imbued in their work, and scale their designs back to make space for the user.

References

1. Borge, M., Carroll, J.M.: Verbal equity, cognitive specialization, and performance. In: Proceedings of the 18th International Conference on Supporting Group Work (GROUP 2014), pp. 215–225. ACM, New York (2014). https://doi.org/10.1145/2660398.2660418
2. Card, S.K., Mackinlay, J.D., Robertson, G.G.: A morphological analysis of the design space of input devices. ACM Trans. Inf. Syst. **9**(2), 99–122 (1991). https://doi.org/10.1145/123078.128726
3. Kensing, F., Blomberg, J.: Participatory design: issues and concerns. Comput. Support. Coop. Work (CSCW) **7**(3), 167–185 (1998)
4. Lee, J.S., Tatar, D.: Impact of mediating technologies on talk and emotion: questioning "commonsense". In: 9th IEEE International Conference on Collaborative Computing: Networking, Applications and Worksharing, Austin, TX, pp. 380–389 (2013)
5. Lee, J.S., Tatar, D.: Form factor matters. In: Proceedings of the 2013 Conference on Computer Supported Cooperative Work (CSCW 2013), pp. 1481–1486. ACM, New York (2013). https://doi.org/10.1145/2441776.2441944
6. Lee, J.S., Tatar, D.: Sounds of silence: exploring contributions to conversations, non-responses and the impact of mediating technologies in triple space. In: Proceedings of the 17th ACM Conference on Computer Supported Cooperative Work and Social Computing (CSCW 2014), 1561–1572. ACM, New York (2014). https://doi.org/10.1145/2531602.2531655
7. Lee, J.S., Branham, S., Tatar, D., Harrison, S.: Processlessness: staying open to interactional possibilities. In: Proceedings of the Designing Interactive Systems Conference (DIS 2012), pp. 78–81. ACM, New York (2012). https://doi.org/10.1145/2317956.2317969
8. Lee, J.S., Tatar, D., Harrison, S.: Micro-coordination: because we did not already learn everything we need to know about working with others in kindergarten. In: Proceedings of the ACM 2012 Conference on Computer Supported Cooperative Work (CSCW 2012), pp. 1135–1144. ACM, New York (2012). https://doi.org/10.1145/2145204.2145372
9. Lee, J.-S.: Processless design extended. In: Marcus, A., Wang, W. (eds.) DUXU 2017. LNCS, vol. 10288, pp. 89–99. Springer, Cham (2017). https://doi.org/10.1007/978-3-319-58634-2_7
10. Maceli, M.G.: Bridging the design time – use time divide: towards a future of designing in use. In: Proceedings of the 8th ACM Conference on Creativity and Cognition (C&C 2011), pp. 461–462. ACM, New York (2011). https://doi.org/10.1145/2069618.2069751
11. Scott McCrickard, D.: Making claims: knowledge design, capture, and sharing in HCI. Synth. Lect. Hum. Centered Inf. **5**(3), 1–125 (2012)
12. Spinuzzi, C.: The methodology of participatory design. Techn. Commun. **52**(2), 163–174 (2005)
13. Suchman, L.: Human-Machine Reconfigurations: Plans and Situated Actions. Cambridge University Press, Cambridge (2007)
14. Tatar, D.: The design tensions framework. Hum. Comput. Interact. **22**(4), 413–451 (2007)

15. Tatar, D., Lee, J.S., Alaloula, N.: Playground games: a design strategy for supporting and understanding coordinated activity. In: Proceedings of the 7th ACM Conference on Designing Interactive Systems (DIS 2008), pp. 68–77. ACM, New York (2008). https://doi.org/10.1145/1394445.1394453
16. Thaler, R.H., Sunstein, C.R.: Nudge: Improving Decisions About Health, Wealth, and Happiness. Yale University Press, New Haven (2008)
17. Wertsch, J.V.: Mind as Action. Oxford University Press, New York (1998)
18. Winner, L.: Do artifacts have politics? Daedalus 109(1)
19. Woolley, A.W., Chabris, C.F., Pentland, A., Hashmi, N., Malone, T.W.: Evidence for a collective intelligence factor in the performance of human groups. Science 330(6004), 686–688 (2010). https://doi.org/10.1126/science.1193147

Internet AI Technology and Its Impact on China's High Education

Chao Liu[1(✉)], Chao Zhao[2], and Wentao Wang[3]

[1] Baidu User Experience Department, Baidu, Beijing 100085, China
Liuchao05@baidu.com
[2] Industrial Design Department, Academy of Art and Design,
Tsinghua University, Haidian, Beijing, China
zhaochao@tsinghua.edu.cn
[3] Baidu Education Department, Baidu, Beijing 100085, China
wangwentao@baidu.com

Abstract. This paper discussed the probable influence and changes of China's high education under the background of era of Internet artificial intelligence (AI). There are two trends of the future high education development influenced by the internet AI technology: firstly, the new internet based education products and services based on the AI technology will strongly affect the learning process and interaction between students and teachers. Secondly, AI technology will change the future talent cultivation methods and further replace some traditional job opportunities through creating the new working positions for the future graduates. The authors identified the opportunities and challenges faced by China's universities, and explored the new teaching methodologies within the context of AI era.

Keywords: Internet AI technology · High education · Chinese context
Baidu · Tsinghua University · Learning process

1 Introduction

The internet AI technology as specified in this paper is realizable on the basis of the verified internet product. All-purpose AI technology, such as, speech recognition, image recognition, natural semantic recognition, augmented reality, deep learning, education mapping knowledge domain (millions of education knowledge), education user portrait (learning interest and learning progress), education data intelligence (big data behavior analysis) (Fig. 1) will strongly impact on the future changes and development of China's education. The scope of this research mainly focus on the China's high education institutions, except for kindergarten, primary school, junior high school and senior high school education. This paper presented the pilot study for the design institutions which focus on cultivating the design graduates to meet the talents recruitment requirement of the new technological enterprises.

© Springer International Publishing AG, part of Springer Nature 2018
A. Marcus and W. Wang (Eds.): DUXU 2018, LNCS 10919, pp. 62–72, 2018.
https://doi.org/10.1007/978-3-319-91803-7_5

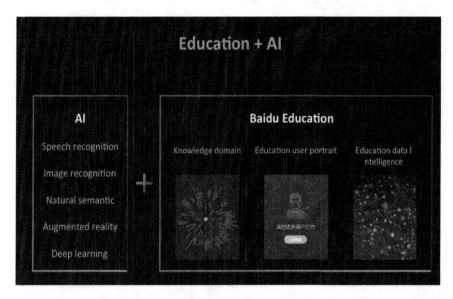

Fig. 1. All-purpose AI technology

2   Research Background and Problem

Based on the analyzing the big data released by 700 universities in China, the research team have identified 7 universities randomly to conduct survey (including 1 top university, 2 key universities, 2 regular high education universities and 2 higher vocational colleges). The survey shows that Chinese universities have invested more than USD 3 million in the teaching materials and hardware equipment. The investment amount of the key universities is over USD 10 million every year. However, the findings of survey indicate that the utilization rate of teaching materials and hardware equipment is not higher than the expectation. Moreover, it was difficult for the university students to find out the desirable materials from the huge number of teaching materials. This is because students don't know the teaching materials and hardware equipment purchased by universities, nor the correlation to their research topics. Therefore, the actual utilization rate of teaching resources is seriously affected and need to explore the solutions in this research.

3   Research Methodology and Coding System

In order to solve the knowledge screening problem of different students in different learning phases, the research team composed by co-operation between Baidu Company and Tsinghua University conducted the qualitative and quantitative research about the high education administration and academic affairs in the different universities. This research matched the knowledge points with the curriculum of each university to form a personalized educational AI knowledge map based on the different students in different disciplines. Firstly, the research team developed knowledge system to link the related knowledge documents within the Baidu internet system to the different disciplines. And then, this research build a coding system based on the analyzing amount of the reading and downloaded of knowledge data base. There are two categories in this coding system: document relevance, and document quality. Figure 2 shows the coding system to map the relationship among the different domain knowledge to build the body of knowledge for particular disciplinary. The Wisdom College PC System (Fig. 3) has been developed based on above understanding. It is worth noting that students retention rate of product utilization increased by 16% when AI mapping knowledge domain is launched on the line [1].

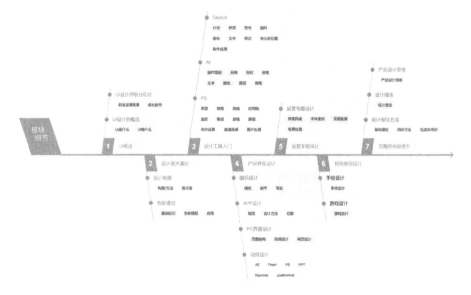

Fig. 2. Mapping of the domain knowledge

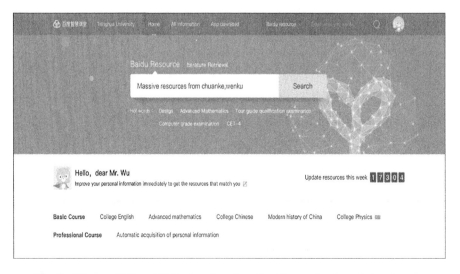

Fig. 3. Wisdom College PC System based on the AI mapping knowledge domain

4 AI Wisdom Class Schedule

AI mapping knowledge domain is established on the basis of the vast amount of knowledge documents' optimization of Baidu. However, this research found that the time sequence of knowledge points doesn't necessarily correspond with the learning time of students. So it is necessary to develop a product to increase the utilization frequency of knowledge document by students. The AI wisdom class schedule has been developed by this research through linking the AI mapping knowledge domain with the universities' curriculum. This product supports the teaching process with the multi-functions such as class time reminder, classroom location, campus map navigation, and the course tips (course complexity, roll call frequency, the course assignment and so on). Students can read their class schedule on the mobile phone at anytime and anywhere (Fig. 4).

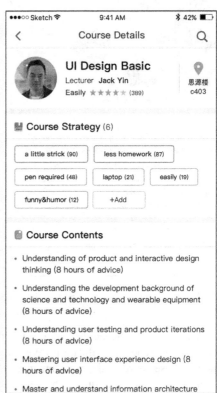

Fig. 4. AI wisdom class schedule

The value of the AI wisdom class schedule is not only enhancing the utilization frequency of students, but also provide new method of individual teaching knowledge data base. For example,

There are 15 million knowledge points and 0.2 billion knowledge documents in Baidu Baike linked with the universities' curriculum (Fig. 5).

Fig. 5. Huge amount of knowledge points and documents linked with universities curriculum

When the class schedule is docked with knowledge point, research team find out that the class schedule utilization frequency of students is increased for 200% and the students raise more utilization demands. Based on the functions such as the examination prompt and score query, this research analyze the learning state of every student at present to help the students planning next-step learning path through AI technology. In such case, the individual learning plan of students will be matched to AI mapping knowledge domain again (Fig. 6).

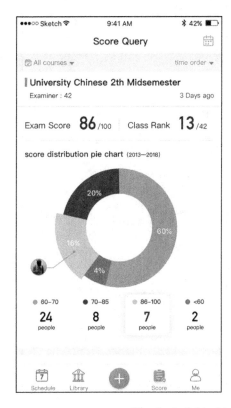
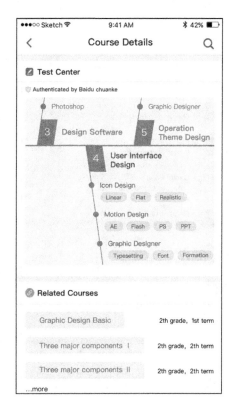

Fig. 6. Individual learning plan of students

5   AI Image Recognition Technology's Application in the University Education

It is well know that the basic application of AI technology includes image and speech recognition. How to use these technologies in the university education? The research team have developed following products to explore the solutions to answer this question:

One solution developed by research team is data extraction based on face recognition and student attention. Every educator knows that not all students have the strong self-control ability and not every teacher can attract the students during class. The traditional method is roll call, however, this time-consuming work is likely to provoke opposition between students and teachers. It is important to note that AI technology can solve this problem easily. AI face recognition technology can recognize the faces of all students within the short time and line out the possibly absent students under the supporting of camera installed in the university classroom. The professor can carry out roll call for small group of students who are suspected to be absent screened by AI technology (Fig. 7).

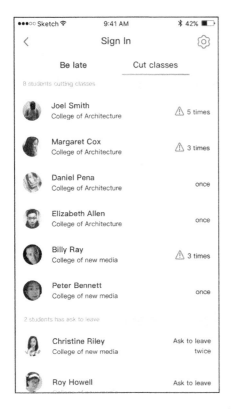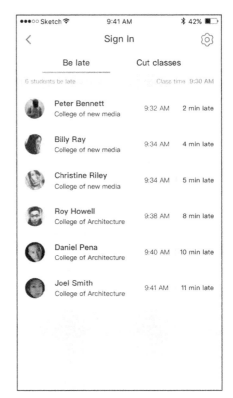

Fig. 7. Data extraction based on face recognition and student attention

Besides the reason of self-control ability of students, the quality of curriculum might be another factor to cause the students absenteeism. Therefore, AI face recognition technology might monitor the excitement and attention of each student in the class to evaluate the teaching quality. If most students are absent-minded and sleeping in the class, it means that the course has quality problem. Therefore, this system developed multiple dimensions to assess the curriculum quality.

Another solution is the AI based image recognition to support the copyright protection during the teaching process. Sometimes, it is difficult for professors to solve the copyright issue in the class. However, the AI image recognition technology might utilize the big data to protect copyright during the teaching process. With the image rechecking function, the product developed by this research can scan and check the students' homework, and then calculate the percentage of copying. In case of original homework, the professor can recommend the students to apply to the National Patent Office for design patent (Fig. 8).

AI speech and image recognition technology's application is valuable in the massive online teaching process. Now days, although the universities pay more attention to record the video courses to develop the massive online course, not all teachers have the capability to record the online course and edit the video. therefore,

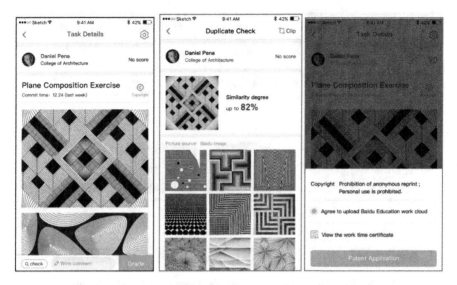

Fig. 8. AI based image recognition to support the copyright protection

many universities have employed the third-party companies to support professors recording the video course. Considering that most online courses might last for dozens of hours, the reviewing and editing process will cost a lot of money. The AI based speech and image recognition can help the judges and college leaders to check the problems of video, such as, whether there is long-playing empty image, and whether the course contents correspond with the online catalog.

6   Cloud-Based Education Data

The artificial intelligence is based on the huge amount of big data to provide service for the users' demands. **As an important** education **resource**, students' work and assignment are **always** ignored and **wasted in the traditional** offline **teaching proces**s. **However, as the learning records of individuals, these data** are very valuable to support every student learning process and provide learning demonstration for the future students. For this purpose, the research team have developed Baidu Homework Cloud Platform, zp.baidu.com (Fig. 9), within one year [2]. The university students can upload their daily homework and assignment to Baidu Homework Cloud Platform which is able to save homework for students forever. Meanwhile, the homework can be seen and praised by other students. To recruit talents from universities, many companies are willing to provide scholarship based on this homework cloud platform. If students do their homework well, they will win the scholarship and internship opportunity sponsored by the industries. Based to the analysis of huge amount data of homework, AI technology can link the students' homework to Baidu wisdom class schedule, which might help the next students who take the course with the reference materials.

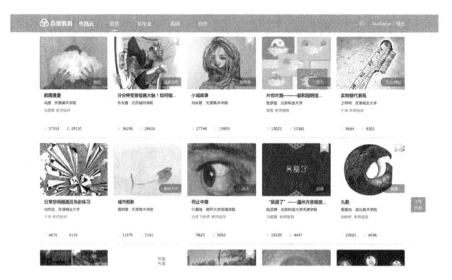

Fig. 9. Cloud-based education data and Homework Cloud Platform

The educational AI of Baidu big data shows its advantages to support universities and professors constantly optimizing curriculum. The only thing that professors need to do is entering the subject of the course and teaching directory into big data system (such as Baidu Wenku, Baidu Read, and Baidu Baike), so they can get massive research documents and papers from the data base. Moreover, the individual information of professors, including quantity of publications and number of prizes are also included by Baidu Scholar (Fig. 10).

Fig. 10. The educational AI of Baidu big data for professors

7   AI Technology's Influence on the Talent Cultivation Approach

As a service provider, AI technology will be widely used in various field within the next twenty years. The job opportunity competition is inevitable between human and AI service. This research explored the new approach and methodology for the future talent cultivation in AI era. It is important to note that some existing services will be replaced by AI technology because these services just provide simple and similar solutions for the public service with expensive cost. For example, web banner designers usually repeated similar job such as input text, Align text, Adjust Font, Adust text size, select color, and insert pictures for the different projects. These works are repeated constantly and might be completed by template. As the largest E-commerce platform of China, Alibaba company employed AI technology to develop a banner design program, Luban, to do the E-commerce advertisement web design job auto-matically [3] in 2016. Since then, the banner design costs are reduced to 1/10 of labor cost. This trend will challenge some job positions like graphic designers in the e-commerce industries (Fig. 11).

Fig. 11. AI based banner design program, Luban.

To face the challenge of AI technology in the high education areas, it is necessary to analyze the working mode of AI technology. It is a kind of in-depth learning process based on the big data, and it can master the certain rules and provide the specific solution automatically. There are three key points emerged during the AI working mode: 1. Vast amount of repeated big data. 2. Single field and domain. 3 Relatively high-quality solution based on the big data solution. On the basis of the above three points, this research suggests three principles for the talent cultivation within the high education context:

1. To do the innovative work rather than making the repeated work. For example, people should pay more attention to learn how to create the new coffee flavor rather than to learn how to keep the flavor consistency of Caffe Latte, because human being is not as good as machine for repeated work.
2. To create new areas based on the multidisciplinary collaboration. For example, there is a strong risk of English teaching replacement (based on the teaching materials) by AI; however, it is difficult for AI to replace the students who have linked the two disciplines, rugby and English, as rugby English. The reason is that the big data are absent in the trans-boundary field and AI is unable to find out the rules in small data.
3. Do the best product/service design innovation, instead of the common simple service. AI technology is able to provide the service with high cost performance, and human being cannot compete with AI technology to finish the simple task with the cost performance.

In conclusion, there are two trends of the future high education development influenced by the internet AI technology: firstly, the new internet based education products and services based on the AI technology will strongly affect the learning process and interaction between students and teachers. Secondly, AI technology will change the future talent cultivation methods and further replace some traditional job opportunities through creating the new working positions for the future graduates. The future high education should develop new curriculum based on the AI technology to cultivate the future talents with the high-quality innovation capability.

References

1. Website of Baidu wisdom university PC. eduai.baidu.com
2. Website of Baidu homework cloud. zp.baidu.com
3. Luban as an intelligent E-commerce AI design platform of Alibaba

Virtual Reality as a Tool
for Teaching Architecture

Guilherme Valle Loures Brandão[⊠],
Wilian Daniel Henriques do Amaral,
Caio Augusto Rabite de Almeida, and Jose Alberto Barroso Castañon

Universidade Federal de Juiz de Fora, Juiz de Fora, Brazil
{guilherme.loures, wilian.amaral}@engenharia.ufjf.br,
caioaugusto.arq@gmail.com, jose.castanon@ufjf.edu.br

Abstract. Every year many technologies are developed and implemented in such a way that fundamentally alters how we create, develop and interact with the environment. Virtual Reality has been broadly spread on architecture by allowing users to immerse on a digital universe or in an unbuilt project simulation. On engineering and architecture, project solutions and proposal visualization are essential for the diverse steps understanding and new project solutions development. Such tools help on speeding up processes, iterate and explore digital models faster and create the best solutions. The insertion of contents that support the student formation related to new technologies is an important step towards the qualification of future architects to new design tendencies. This paper aims to evaluate the further training methods on graphic representation and architectural design aid tools at the Juiz de Fora Federal University (UFJF). For this purpose, the use and evaluation of a VR experience used to show several architectural projects designed by the architecture students from the Federal University of Juiz de Fora presentations. The work starts from the premise that the technology applied to mobile devices such as cellphones or virtual reality goggles are reasonably cheap to acquire and become familiar to the student if presented on the first stages of learning, achieving a deep and complex status as the alumni progresses towards graduation. To conclude, it is perceived that after an initial adaptation period there was a perceivable acceptation and architectonic design comprehension by students.

Keywords: Architecture · Design process · Teaching · Virtual reality
Technology

1 Introduction

Broadly, virtual reality (VR) is a digital tool that transports the user to an environment in which one is not physically present but receives sensorial stimuli that lead to the sense of real presence in those spaces. Through computational modeling and simulation, it allows the user to interact with a three-dimensional (3D) artificial space, through visual perception and/or other sensory stimuli.

The VR application immerses the user in an artificially generated environment that simulates reality using devices that allow interactivity such as headsets, goggles, gloves

© Springer International Publishing AG, part of Springer Nature 2018
A. Marcus and W. Wang (Eds.): DUXU 2018, LNCS 10919, pp. 73–82, 2018.
https://doi.org/10.1007/978-3-319-91803-7_6

and clothing that exchange information with a computer. In its typical format, the user has coupled to the head a set of goggles or a helmet with stereoscopic screens that allow visualizing animations and simulations of an environment (Virtual Reality 2010).

Computer graphics, computer visualization and user interfaces enable new challenges upon shapes and concepts under the creation processes. Although the computer use as a project tool is widespread among the architectural offices, there are still unexplored and emerging forms of representation and visualization such as VR and augmented reality (AR), which can help and modify the built environment's production mode.

In the engineering and architecture fields, the design solutions and proposal visualizations are essential for understanding the various stages and new design solutions development. The VR allows the user visualization of elements, generating significant evolutions that affect all production stages, from the conception to building and interior materialization plus city elaboration and development.

Rebelo et al. (2011) affirm that VR has been applied in architecture to allow interaction between internal and external virtual environments, with different levels of realism. In these environments users can move freely and, in some cases, make modifications such as color changes, lighting and furniture placement in many different scales. In the field of applied ergonomics, VR has been developed for increasing environmental quality and training for the task executor, in addition to the general gain on product, environment and productive systems overall quality (Grave et al. 2001; Rebelo et al. 2011).

Digital modeling and analysis tools allow for greater control over creation and visualization on complex models, in which the drawing by hand has greater difficulty and time spent in representing. The time spent developing a work in the virtual environment is reduced in addition to allowing a greater amount of potentially relevant information and its visual and performance comparison, especially in cases of architectural projects and its spatial and ergonomic relations (Borgart and Kocaturk 2007).

Borsboom-Van Beurden et al. (2006) affirm that the use of virtual models, compared to the use of technical drawings, can contribute to greater efficiency in project communication. According to the authors, virtual models have a greater connection with the way that a human being perceives real objects, facilitating the identification and understanding of the object conceived. For Cross (2007, p. 33), designers need means which "allow ideas in the conception process to be expressed and reviewed, developed and corrected according to the design process" in an integrated way within the expected temporality.

According to Tversky (2005) when constructing external or internal representations, designers are involved in a spatial cognitive process in which the representation of the medium serves as cognitive auxiliaries for memory and information processing.

Schon (1992) states that with the execution of action and reflection, each level of representation makes the designers evolve in their own interpretations and ideas for design solutions. In this approach, the bias taken are the reflections caused using unconventional visualizations plus the stimuli and difficulties provided to users during the project development and reasoning, favoring the multifactorial approach and spatial experience during the preliminary phases of conception and materialization.

2 Justification

Tools that use computer aided design (CAD) and, more recently, building information modeling (BIM) help creating virtual models that increasingly resemble the final built object, with great implementation potential both in the craft as in teaching the disciplines that involve planning of the built environment (da Fonseca 2013).

In this context, Silvestri (2010) points out that virtual data and computer-generated drawings and information have quickly replaced physical and analog learning media such as hand-held drawings and mockups. Besides, these digital tools are at the center of a new way to approach the design process itself.

To Oxman (2006), expressions such as "digital design" or "digital architecture" are often used to describe contemporary architectural practices that are already assisted by these new platforms, as the latter depend on fundamentally on the first ones to conceive the project, its production and construction. The need to integrate new technologies such as VR into the product design process is generally recognized, especially in the design phase and, as such, provides new advances in CAD areas (Ye 2005).

These emerging technologies create new paradigms to overcome conventional interfaces drawbacks, such as product visualization for designer and consumer, both in conception and in understanding the object's tridimensionality and scale. Regarding the VR applied to architecture and ergonomics, researches indicates that the introduction of these tools in different fields of education is viable, including the various design and coordination stages, integrating the various disciplines approaching design (Fonseca et al. 2013).

Specifically, in the field of architecture and urbanism, VR can be used to predict the undertaking impact on the landscape and building rehabilitation, such as changing colors, materials and textures. It also allows for project overlap compatibility, such as structures, installations, enveloping, geographical location and solar study, thus enabling interference verification between systems in real time (Sánchez et al. 2013).

This being stated, this work justifies itself due to VR presenting itself as an important and useful tool for teaching architecture and contemporary urbanism integrating design, design, analysis, spatial perception, building fabrication and assembly around digital technologies. From this integration, the professionals involved have an opportunity to fundamentally redefine the relationships between technical projects from the most diverse disciplines and the effective production, with consequent quality improvement in the final product.

3 Objective

This article seeks to verify the future architectural professionals' perception in the use of virtual reality on teaching and developing the students holistic concept and spatial understanding skills on the Federal University of Juiz de Fora's undergraduate course in Architecture and Urbanism.

4   Methodology

For this study's elaboration, it was studied the use and evaluation of a virtual reality experience in visualization of 3D models (Fig. 1) and in the presentation of students' architectural projects in the Federal University of Juiz de Fora's Faculty of Architecture. The work starts on the premise that the technology used in conjunction with mobile devices is familiar to the undergraduate student and, if implemented in the initial stages of training, can achieve a greater depth of interest and involvement with the content proposed in classroom.

Fig. 1. Image rendered in stereoscopic format

The evaluation relies in the feasibility of using VR through the alumni mobile devices in educational environments, investigating the relationship between tool use and student participation, through interviews and monitoring the Digital Representation discipline, besides the contribution of understanding spatiality and instrumentation after technology use.

The strategies implemented were applied during Digital Representation I and Initiation to the Process of Computer Aided Modeling classes. Two types of visualization were used: through virtual reality goggles with coupled smartphones and augmented reality through mobile devices.

First, a brief explanation was made about the concept, applications and how to use the instruments and, at first, a demonstration of models already rendered in vision 360°. Subsequently, each student would use the Kubity® software introducing a model that was carried out previously in class which, in turn, would generate a QR Code to be introduced in the smartphone application to be visualized by students in virtual reality goggles. Finally, the students answered a questionnaire about the tool's application and importance in the process of learning and visualization of the projected spatiality, as well as their interest on the subject (Fig. 2).

Modelling   Save on app format   Generate QR code   Cellphone capture   VR glasses   Survey

Fig. 2. Sequence used to apply the methodology

The application was performed using virtual reality goggles, coupled with smartphones with the Kubity® software installed allowing the transformation of models developed in the class by students with the Trimble SKETCHUP® 3D modeling software, on which they performed the immersion in their own models. The VR Box virtual reality goggles (Fig. 3), which allow mobile devices to couple, have several models of easy access and acquisition. Cardboard box models (Fig. 4) can also be used, with its design easily found on the internet and run by the students themselves.

Fig. 3. VR Box goggles with smartphone coupled, model used. (source: VR Box)

Fig. 4. *Cardboard Box* goggles: Design and assembly with coupled smartphone (source: Google VR Cardboard)

This comparison was carried out through a workshop to collect people's perceptions on the experiment. The methodology application took place in the Digital representation I classes at the UFJF's Faculty of Architecture and Urbanism during the 2017 first school semester. For the study application were taken, to the place of the class, mobile devices with the Application Kubity® installed, virtual reality goggles, and models of the German Pavilion project from the 1929 World Fair, with architect Mies van der Rohe authorship, built in the city of Barcelona, Spain rendered in stereoscopic Vision 360° (Fig. 5).

Subsequently to the tools presentation to undergraduate students, 48 electronic questionnaires were applied to them, according to Table 1, to generate a critical analysis of the benefits and perceived limitations of the tools used.

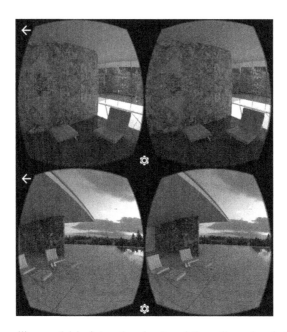

Fig. 5. German pavilion model in internal and external three-dimensional views (source: VR ArchViz Pavilion)

Table 1. Questionnaire applied to students

Question	Possible answers
Which semester are you in?	First; Second
Have you had previous contact with virtual reality?	Yes; No
Do you think that virtual reality allows you to understand a space's scale, shape, materials, distances and accesses?	Yes; No
Do you consider it relevant to use virtual reality on teaching architecture?	Yes; No
Would you use virtual reality in presentations for architectural design disciplines or other disciplines?	Yes; No

5   Results and Discussion

The compilation of the answers obtained came to the summary table presented below (Table 2).

From the respondent students, 44 are enrolled in the course's first semester and 04 are enrolled in the second semester, which was already expected since the discipline "Digital Representation I" integrates the first period in the Architecture and Urbanism course syllabus at FAU/UFJF.

When questioned about some previous VR contact, 44 students claim to have no prior contact with the technology presentation in classroom during the realization of

Table 2. Obtained answers summary table

Question	Answer	
	First	Second
Which semester are you in?	44	4
Question	Answer	
	Yes	No
Have you had previous contact with virtual reality?	4	44
Do you think that virtual reality allows you to understand the space's scale, shape, materials, distances and accesses?	48	—
Do you consider it relevant to use virtual reality in architectural teaching?	48	—
Would you use virtual reality in architectural design disciplines work presentations or other disciplines?	41	7

this work, while 04 students had previous contact. It was observed that most of the interviewed students made the first contact with the virtual reality through the performed practice, most of which had never used or knew the possibility of using the technology for digital representation in Architecture.

Asked later if the use of VR allowed the understanding of spatiality, texture and tectonic space presented, the total of the 48 students stated "Yes" and demonstrated surprise in the experimentation acuity on the object's scale. All students also recognize as important the use of digital media such as VR in the teaching of architecture and project disciplines that interfere in the built environment. Last asked about the possibility of using virtual reality in other disciplines as a form of designing and presenting projects, 41 students responded affirmatively while 7 said they would not use.

The students' responses and interest bring an indication that the introduction and application of new tools and technologies such as VR may trigger new dynamics between the parties involved in the process of design and learning, from conception to representation and presentation of the same, encompassing the manufacture of components and objects to the construction site and the building execution.

As results, the need for familiarization and use of technologies aided by mobile devices, interactive methods and VR for the visualization of architectural spatialization besides a development in perception of space and its components can be highlighted. It is understood that VR was welcomed by the students, who appreciated the use of the applied methodology, and the exercises performed enabled to improve their performance and spatial cognition capacity in a more dynamic way in the development of digital models. Students' interest in emerging technologies makes them able to be used as a didactic contribution to the development of spatial and design skills in those alumni.

However, the initial difficulty to produce adequate content for the proposed dynamics is emphasized, as well as the model optimization that allow for a more reliable and detailed view, in addition to the detailing process and the difficulty on adequacy of performed models. All the students interviewed evaluated, however, that the interaction with the content in virtual reality allows to maximize the learning process, not only in the disciplines regarding graphic representation, but also in architecture's techniques, theory and history.

This study recognizes the limitation of working with a restricted number of students available in the applied discipline and stresses the suggestion for future work in which there is a comparison of similar experiences between related courses and between the student enrolment and the semester in which they gain contact within the disciplines, as well as the proper orientation to produce more complex and detailed models.

6 Conclusion

The study presented demonstrated an experiment to verify the perception of students in the initial cycle of a course of undergraduate architecture and urbanism on the use of VR as a didactic contribution, incorporated in the visualization of design alternatives of the environment Built. It was found that the use of the strategy of visualization of spaces in VR contributes to an improvement in the understanding of proposals and solutions design, with interaction between the participants and the projected environment, assisting in the decision making.

The work pointed out the way technologies that use virtual reality can offer a faster and more intuitive interaction between the designer and the CAD program, with a simple approach to the creation and evaluation of proposed concepts and tectonics. However, formal CAD systems are not fully oriented to support the project design process due in its vast majority to the traditional interaction between human and computer, usually using its peripherals (mouse, keyboard) and a two-dimensional screen for interaction with these softwares. This may lead to loss of information and visualization through the conversion of 2D into 3D elements necessary for the decision interpretation and evaluation (Ye et al. 2006).

Unlike 2D technologies, which seek to display depth and perspective on flat screens in two dimensions, stereoscopic visualization provides the user with an immersive 3D visual perception of spatiality. Stereoscopic display is also a 3D visual channel output device. This then allows stereoscopic viewing to be much easier to interpret than 2D images typically displayed on computer monitors.

VR has already been applied in the field and studied in various related disciplines such as real estate, interior design and urban planning, enabling new possibilities to exploratory studies and use of the tool aiming to complement several new forms of architecture creation and production that emerge with the digital age.

VR's potential is to allow for a natural interaction with virtual models and to increase computer support and real-time changes throughout the project process. On the other hand, the use of virtual models impacts positively on the mental formation of three-dimensional images, increasing the perception of spatial compositions and reducing mental workload, since the three-dimensional representation facilitates the understanding and needs less effort for the user to interpret.

When VR technology is applied on built environment disciplines of the when used in vocational training or in the project process, offers a new look to understand different stages of a constructive process, allowing the verification and comparison between different scenarios and proposals before the final definition. To fulfil this premise, it is important to check the ability to visualize several models to demonstrate different layers (structure, installations, furniture, etc.), textures and geographical positions.

Although VR presents many advantages in the development of consumer goods, those who often applies the technology should be aware of some disadvantages. These are not strictly associated with modeling or situation analysis, but intrinsically linked to expectations associated with the human-computer interaction inherent in VR-based projects.

One of the main problems encountered in the experiences was the 3D model display and their manipulation on mobile devices so that different interactions occur freely using open source platforms. In the case of the Kubity® application the model view in free mode is restricted to 10 min per loaded model. It is verified that a greater adherence to VR as a didactic tool as a possibility depends mainly on the technology accessibility and the programs' and applications' ease of use and interface, which go against the greater perception and usability by the students.

In this sense, the use of VR as a tool for teaching and developing analytical skills and design also presents some limitations. One of the considerations to be made when deciding to use the tool is the immersion level offered by the chosen virtual reality system, being important to select a system that allows an appropriate level of immersion to the didactic and expected task (Rebelo et al. 2011).

The results are based on the hypothesis that representation tools have a convergence in the cognition process of and space perception and, consequently, are important tools during the design and space representation phases, both in the process as in the result necessary in the context of contemporary design.

In addition to empirical activities and bibliographic study, it is concluded that emerging technologies such as VR, even with some still existing gaps, can facilitate the development of senses beyond the visual aspects of a new generation of CAD tools that introduce collaboration and cognition concepts more integrated to the space production processes.

Acknowledgements. The authors thank CAPES and the PROAC - Built Environment Graduate Programme from Federal University of Juiz de Fora for the support received during this work execution.

References

Borgart, A., Kocaturk, T.: Free-form design as the digital "Zeitgeist". J. IASS **48**(4), 3–9 (2007). http://www.iass-structures.org/index.cfm/journal.article?aID=80

Borsboom-Van Beurden, J.A.M., Van Lammeren, R.J.A., Hoogerwerf, T., Bouwman, A.A.: Linking land use modeling and 3D visualization. In: Van Leeuwen, J.P., Timmermans, H.J. P. (eds.) Innovations in Design and Decision Support Systems in Architecture and Urban Planning, pp. 85–101. Springer, Dordrecht (2006). https://doi.org/10.1007/978-1-4020-5060-2_6

Cross, N.: From a design science to a design discipline: Understanding designerly ways of knowing and thinking. In: Design Research Now, pp. 41–54 (2007)

Cross, N., Dorst, K.: Co-evolution of problem and solution space in creative design. In: Gero, J. S., Maher, M.L. (eds.) Computational Models of Creative Design Computing, pp. 243–262. University of Sydney, Sydney (1999)

da Fonseca, A.G.M.F.: Aprendizagem, mobilidade e convergência: mobile learning com celulares e smartphones. Revista_Mídia_e_Cotidiano **2**(2), 265–283 (2013)

Fonseca, D., Villagrasa, S., Martí, N., Redondo, E., Sánchez, A.: Visualization methods in architecture education using 3D virtual models and augmented reality in mobile and social networks. In: Procedia - Social and Behavioral Sciences, vol. 93, pp. 1337–1343. (2013). https://doi.org/10.1016/j.sbspro.2013.10.040. ISSN 1877-0428

Fonseca, D., Martí, N., Redondo, E., Navarro, I., Sánchez, A.: Relationship between student profile, tool use, participation, and academic performance: with the use of Augmented Reality technology for visualized architecture models. Comput. Hum. Behav. **31**, 434–445 (2014). https://doi.org/10.1016/j.chb.2013.03.006

Grave, L., Escaleira, C., Silva, A.F., Marcos, A.: A Realidade Virtual como Ferramenta de Treino para Montagem de Cablagens Eléctricas. In: Proceddings of 10° Encontro Português de Computação Grafca, pp. 147–63 (2001)

Kubity® App. https://www.kubity.com/. Accessed 15 Aug 2017

Oxman, R.: Theory and design in the first digital age. Des. Stud. **27**(3), 229–265 (2006). https://doi.org/10.1016/j.destud.2005.11.002

Rebelo, F., Duarte, E., Noriega, P., Soares, M.M.: Virtual Reality in consumer product design: methods and applications. In: Karwowski, W., Soares, M.M., Stanton, N.A. (eds.) Human Factors and Ergonomics in Consumer Product Design: Methods and Techniques. pp. 381–402. CRC Press, Boca Raton (2011). https://doi.org/10.1201/b10950-28

Sánchez, A., Redondo, E., Fonseca, D., Navarro, I.: Construction processes using mobile augmented reality: a study case in Building Engineering degree. In: Rocha, A., Correia, A.M., Wilson, T., Stroetmann, K.A. (eds.) Advances in Information Systems and Technologies, pp. 1053–1062. Springer, Berlin (2013). https://doi.org/10.1007/978-3-642-36981-0_100

Schon, D.: Designing as reflective conversation with the materials of a design situation. Res. Eng. Des. **3**(3), 131–147 (1992). https://doi.org/10.1007/BF01580516

Silvestri, C., Motro, R., Maurin, B., Dresp-Langley, B.: Visual spatial learning of complex object morphologies through the interaction with virtual and real-world data. Des. Stud. **31**(4), 363–381 (2010). https://doi.org/10.1016/j.destud.2010.03.001

Tversky, B.: Functional significance of visuospatial representations. In: Shah, P., Miyake, A. (eds.) Handbook of Higher-Level Visuospatial Thinking, pp. 1–34. Cambridge University Press, Cambridge (2005). https://doi.org/10.1017/cbo9780511610448.002

Virtual Reality. In: Encyclopædia Britannica (2010). http://www.britannica.com/EBchecked/topic/630181/virtual-reality. Accessed 11 Aug 2017

Ye, J.: Integration of virtual reality techniques into computer aided product design. Thesis (Design Ph.D.) - Department of Design and Technology, Loughborough University, UK (2005)

Ye, J., Campbell, R.I., Page, T., Badni, K.S.: An investigation into the implementation of virtual reality technologies in support of conceptual design. Des. Stud. **27**(1), 77–97 (2006). https://doi.org/10.1016/j.destud.2005.06.002

The Research on the Practice of Traditional Handicraft Entering into College Quality Education Class

Qianhe Man[✉]

School of Design and Art, Beijing Institute of Technology,
5 South Zhongguancun Street, Haidian District, Beijing, China
manqianhe@hotmail.com

Abstract. This thesis summarizes a suitable practice teaching mode of tradi-tional handicraft course for colleges and universities. It is based on the practical class of college quality education. It conforms to the relationship between tra-ditional handicraft and college quality education, as well as the goals, practice content and features of college quality education. Traditional handicraft practice course can fully mobilize students' eyes, ears, hands and brains to make students get fully practiced in visual sense, auditory sense, tactile sense, and perception. Then, students can form a study method of learning widely, thinking smartly, acting flexibly, and comprehending ingeniously. This is a sublimation process that people learn something from the physiological visual sense to a new stage of mental perception, in line with the general rule that human beings know the world. Through the practice teaching of traditional handicraft, the students can achieve the harmony between hand and heart, the harmony of skill and art, and the harmony between man and thing. This whole teaching process shows the features of teaching through lively activities, learning to appreciate in lively activities, learning the virtue in the lively activities, and learning to be wise in the lively activities. Traditional handicraft enters into college in a brand new form and brings vitality and energy for quality education.

Keywords: Traditional handicraft · College quality education
Practice

1 Introduction

On writing this thesis, the author has done about 12 years teaching practice on taking the traditional handicraft into the college quality teaching class. During the whole process, the author has found that the quality education plays an important role in expanding the students' horizon and extending the students' knowledge structure.

Foundation item: humanity and social science research youth fund project of Ministry of education. The practice research of the folk traditional handicraft in college quality education (15YJC760072). The great traditional design wisdom published in gold standard of Chinese design. Einstein works, wrote by Einstein, in the third volume, commercial press,1st edition of 1979, p. 144.

© Springer International Publishing AG, part of Springer Nature 2018
A. Marcus and W. Wang (Eds.): DUXU 2018, LNCS 10919, pp. 83–95, 2018.
https://doi.org/10.1007/978-3-319-91803-7_7

However, for the students who are not in this major, the appreciation and actual practice of the traditional handicraft is a brand new area, which needs art education and practice ability. It needs to discuss about starting a traditional handicraft course of moderate difficulty. At the same time, there are a large number of students in this class, covering all undergraduate majors in the universities. It's another remaining issue of choosing a multi-operator traditional handicraft and how to practice it. Based on such preconditions, the author wants to analyze and summarize the relations, objectives, contents and teaching methods of the traditional handicraft practice and the quality education, with the expectation of promoting college quality education.

2   The Background of Traditional Handicraft Entering College Quality Education Class

With the reformation of university education mechanism and the adjustment of cultivation direction, it is a good time when the traditional handicraft enters into the university quality education. At present, the higher education in our country emphasizes the professional education should be based on quality education. The talent cultivation objective of the college has gradually transformed from the merely professional talent cultivation to comprehensive ability quality education and featured on cultivating professional ability. The study objective of the students has transformed from getting all credits to benefiting their all-aspect development. These changes set a new demand and new opportunity for college quality education.

Traditional handicraft carries on the past ethnic culture, and also embraces the appreciation contents of the folk, what's more, it has the character of the operation of the handicraft course. This course just satisfies the need of the college students, who want to be exposed to the culture, enjoy physical and mental pleasure and develop in all-round way. Jean Jacques Rousseau, who is a famous enlightenment thinker in France, in the book Emile, once said, "Handicraft has the best utility, which can do self-activity from the whole effect of visual sense, tactile sense, auditory sense and language. In this way, people can grow in a natural way, get the perceptual intuition of things and make sure the basis of knowledge and cultivate moral sentiment". In the eye of Rousseau, the handicraft makes the perfect combination of human behavior and the inner heart experience. This practice way is the oldest and the most upright teaching and learning way. Handicraft makes the harmony of body and mind, and can also help the students grow healthily. After many years teaching, the handicraft has accumulated a lot of experience and entered into the class of college quality education. Now this course is very popular among the students.

On the background of the cultivation orientation change of quality education, it is the appropriate time for traditional handicraft entering college quality education practice class, which offers complete realization way for quality education and teaching practice.

3 The Practice Objectives of Traditional Handicraft in College Education

(1) **Promoting Students All-Round Development**

Quality education is regarded as the "holistic education", which aims at cultivating human personal autonomy, people oriented spirits, and the understanding of the culture of different ethnic groups. It also develops people's full character and the ability of cooperation. Therefore, the students can gain humanity and culture, the basic social literacy, and the final goal is to cultivate the students into the kind of people who have a great view and with comprehensive ability. We call this kind of people "holistic person". The traditional handicraft method is a practical way to realize the "holistic education".

(2) **Cultivating Intelligent Students**

In China, one the problems of today's education is exam-oriented education, which causes the students do not have many chances to practice by themselves. The traditional handicraft can not only cultivate students' intelligent, but also cultivate students to do things with their imagination. In recent years, in most famous international universities, there is a general requirement on the credit of the courses that the students must take a proportion of the credit courses taken with labs. This requirement has fully stand for the practical teaching playing an important goal for us to cultivate the students.

(3) **Improving the Recognition of Multi-ethnic Cultural Identity**

Most of the folk traditional handicrafts are from minority area, so they are based on the culture and social formation of the minority areas. The process to learn and master the folk traditional handicrafts is also the process to understand and identify with the ethnic minority culture, which not only be good for the ethnic fusion, but also good for the contemporary university students to absorb and learn the cultures in different culture types. Therefore, the contemporary university students can form more opening and forgiving personality and a sense of national pride.

4 The Practice Contents of Traditional Handicraft in College Quality Education [1]

(1) **Learning the Traditional Culture Widely and Bearing the Culture**

The traditional handicraft entering into the university courses is a new teaching mode that people have found in the process of practice. The teaching contents of the traditional handicraft can be use one word to describe, the word is "wide". First of all, the wide range of the content. The content of the course mainly covers the process of the traditional handicraft, the cultural background, the features of the areas, the people and customs and also other related content. What's more, the wide range of teaching tools. The students can learn not only with the help of the pictures and the videos, as the way to know the media. The most important thing is that the students have many material object, in these material subjects, of which include the works of the graduated students and the excellent folk traditional handicrafts. With those things, the students can learn knowledge visually, actually, aurally. And last but not the least, the wide range of discussion. Small class teaching mode is a good way in handicraft learning, because in this way the students can fully communicate and discuss with other students and share their opinions so that they can learn the different ideas from different people and in different aspects. Therefore, this small class teaching mode can help the students to share their ideas and discuss the good plans. During the process of teaching, the plans of the students can be improved as the students learn more and know more about the traditional handicraft. And finally, after many discussions, the students will render the best design plan. This kind of teaching idea and teaching mode is very flexible, which can activate the students thinking. As a result, the students can not only master the way of making traditional handicraft, but also carrying on the good traditional culture. This is a good way in that it helps the students to make progress and even yield twice the result with half the effort (Fig. 1).

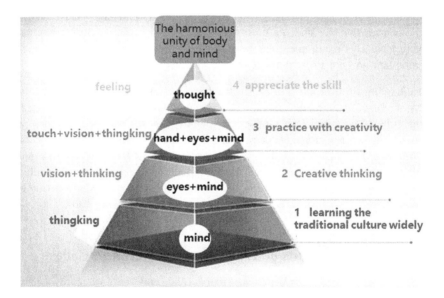

Fig. 1. The logic diagram of the practice contents of traditional handicraft in college quality education

Taking the filaments silver for example, at the beginning of this curse, the students can get filaments handicraft ornaments of different nationalities, including: the Miao nationality, the Dai nationality, the Bai nationality. And then during the class, the students will describe the ornaments in their hands. They will introduce the features of the ornaments in different areas and different nationalities, their pattern design, their aesthetic design and their regional culture. For example, in the Miao nationality, the butterfly is regarded as the mother, therefore in the Miao nationality, the ornaments with the butterfly pattern design is very common to see no matter on the clothes or on the silver sheet. In the Miao nationality, people always hold the opinion that the more, the more beautiful; the bigger, the better. That's why we often see that the girls in the Miao nationality always wear the silver ornaments from the head to the foot, and the skill of the ornaments is very excellent. Sisters Festival, the biggest festival in the Miao nationality, on that day, people wear beautiful traditional cloth and silver ornaments, the site is very grand, and many people will be attracted. After understanding the cultural background and the handicraft process, the students will closely see the ornaments in their hand and they will more easily understand what happened behind the ornaments. This is a way to recognize the handicraft in a new view of complete to part, and finally come back to complete, as a result, the students can accumulate the experience to do things in their future practical practice [2] (Fig. 2).

Fig. 2. The clothes and ornaments of Miao nationality, on the most famous Sisters Festival of the Miao nationality. Photo by Qianhe Man.

(2) **Designing Plan with Creativity**

On the basis of learning the tradition widely and carrying on the culture, the students can design the first draft plan according to their interests and beauty appreciation. In the design process, students can develop creative thinking, and what's more, it can also help students' "eye" and "brain" develop balanced. The students of quality education come from different colleges, they are in different majors, compared with the students who are major in design, and most of the students do not have the design experience. If the students want to make a design, they must think hard. In most cases, those students would like to draw simple sketch to show their ideas, or they would like to download the picture from the internet and then make some improvements, or they would like to take the previous students' works to talk about their ideas. In this teaching stage, the students and the teachers should discuss thoroughly and exchange the ideas of each other, they should make some improvements of the design plan, and they should also decide the making process.

Taking tie-dyeing crafts as an example, traditional tie-dyeing patterns emphasizes rendering effects and requires complex craft procedure, including three to five times of dip-dyeing. After being introduced to quality education class of college students, tie-dyeing has been given a brand new conception by college students and appears a new look. By designing skillfully, trying modern geometry pattern element, even handling very succinct color lumps, students have given modern sense to the traditional handicrafts. At the same time, combining kinds of using functions, students have developed new products, including practical products such as book-packing cloth, mobile phone bag and pot-holder etc. Because of the brevity of modern design pattern, the traditional handicraft procedure, relating to students' work, is greatly simplified and more suitable to the features of college quality education course [3] (Fig. 3).

Fig. 3. According to the traditional handicraft, the student Xiaoqing Song created the works about the old topic of butterfly loves flowers. Photo by Qianhe Man.

(3) **Practice with Creativity**

Practice with creativity is an important part of hands-on practice of traditional handicraft, which includes the process whether the students take part in practical practice, whether the students have finished the task with the hand, eye, brain balanced, and whether the students have finished the task with the tactile sense, visual sense, auditory sense, and sense of smell balanced, the result directly influences the quality of their works. During the process, the students actually take part in the process, they work hard to try many times, and finally they will find it is very interesting that they can overcome the difficulties, improve themselves, and feel happy in the hands-on practice.

Student's design plan varies from each other, because of this reason, the individual traditional handicraft in the process of practice may also be different. Therefore, every student should work hard with creativity to finish his own creative design. This practice process should manage the most adequate stages, and also use the most adequate tools and equipment, in the most adequate time to gain the most successful result. Not afraid of hardship and not afraid of tired is not the ideal way for practicing traditional handicraft, on the contrary, it is the creative thinking and skillful work that can be called the best way. At the end of the class, the practical practice work design and the condition of complete can be the standard of judgement instead of the general thesis and report, and this special method shows the teaching feature of the practical curse.

Enamel craft is a complicated traditional handicraft, of whom the predecessor is the well-known cloisonné. It is dated from Jintao period of Ming Dynasty, being a fine royal craft in the beginning, with a history of 500 years. In the nation's early period, cloisonné was an important export product. Eight years ago, cloisonné was introduced as a course into the campus of Beijing Institute of Technology. This course emphasizes craft practice and requires students to operate skillfully instead of acting rashly. All cloisonné craft procedure, including making copper mold, soldering, glazing, welding copper wire, filling colors, burning, grinding, polishing and burning again, have to be finished in order. When there are many same figures in the pattern, students can design their own special tools to finish. When they succeed using their own way to solve a craft issue, they will achieve both craft works and confidence. Therefore, in the process of operating and practicing crafts, students can train their patience, strengthen their problem-solving ability and develop their logical thinking [4] (Fig. 4).

(4) **Appreciating the Skill to Improve Physical and Mental Harmony**

This part is the most difficult point in the whole process of the traditional practical practice curse. In this part teachers will guide the student to recall the whole process of handicraft skill. The students appreciate the works that they have already made with their individual feature, and students appreciate the cultural essence and the charm of the art of the traditional handicraft. Through the coordination and cooperation with the hand, eye, brain and heart, students would try to feel physical and mental in harmony. At the same time, they can also try to feel skill and technique in harmony. In the process of practice, many of the students choose nature shape as their design topic, which just shows the principle of china's ancient art. This principle is that looking for inspiration in nature, and you will get the essence in the heart. In the course practice process, students see the nature closely and thoroughly, and finally they will reach the harmony of "from human to object, and finally to nature".

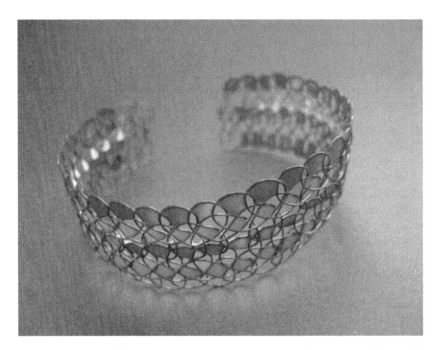

Fig. 4. Modern handicrafts works created by the Non art majors Shan Lu according to Chinese traditional pattern. Photo by Qianhe Man.

In the beginning of learning handicraft, the works of the first time practice tends to be not as their imagination, while with the deepening of practice, the works of students will become better and better. This is not only a skill perfecting process, but also a way to understand the essence of craft. In metal knitting experience course, some students learned to know knitting skills, found a self-owned knitting method and developed their own work. I think such a learning method can also be applied to other subjects [5] (Fig. 5).

The core of the traditional handicraft practice is "designing with creativity" and "practice with creativity". "Designing with creativity" is to cultivate students ability of absorbing traditional handicraft, the students combine their own interests of appreciation to do a second creation, and this progress is cultivating the ingenious heart. "Practice with creativity" is on the basis of the feature of traditional handicraft, and combine their own design ideas to make the idea come to the reality. This is the practice of manual dexterity. Only the students combine the creativity with skill can they realize knowledge and action should go hand in hand, and realize the exploration of traditional handicraft.

The difficult point of the teaching is how to understand the skill and make the body and mental in harmony. This point relates to the summary and understanding of the folk traditional handicraft. Through studying the traditional handicraft itself, we can know its spirits and the philosophy contents. Most of the practical practice courses are stay in the degree of mastering the skill. However, the traditional handicraft practical practice courses need students to rethink their own works and explore the spirits behind the works [6] (Fig. 6).

Fig. 5. Non art majors Shan Lu developed their own knitting skill and made a bracelet. Photo by Qianhe Man.

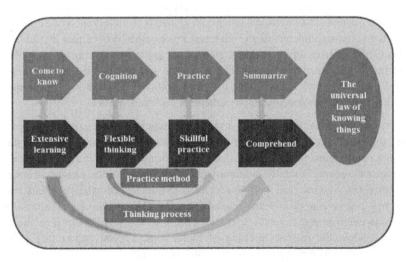

Fig. 6. Analysis of the students understanding and mastering approach things, so as to reveal the rule of knowing things, and then use the rules to education.

5 The Meaning of Traditional Handicraft Practice Teaching in College Quality Education

With the experience of teaching in frontline for years, the writer knows that traditional handicraft course, as a humanistic quality education course, like public foreign language, as well as idea and politics education, belongs to non-academic education towards all college students. The content and teaching method of this kind of course is greatly different with academic course. If this course extracts or copies parts of academic course, students will think the course is too deep to be interesting; while this course is excessive extensive, students will also think the course is generic only, without golden content. Aiming at such specialty of this course, the writer concludes the teaching characters of traditional handicraft practice course, which mainly shows in four aspects: teaching through lively activities, learning to appreciation in lively activities, learning the virtue in the lively activities, and learning to be wise in the lively activities.

(1) **Teaching Through Lively Activities**

As Einstein said, "interest is the best teacher". Interest is the inner impetus to acquire the knowledge, and interesting is the precondition of learning a course. However, whether at home or outside of china, there are many students who choose the elective courses just for getting the full credits. This boring learning mode makes the students feel very tired of the university class. The traditional handicraft course has been set for 12 years and students always have strong interest in this course. Most of the students not only finish the course contents that required by the teacher, but also do some practice after class. We can often see that many students do the practice and apply to take the course not for the credit but for interest. The traditional handicraft course is the rarely motivate course that attract the strong interest of the students. Practice has proven that the traditional handicraft courses are taught through lively activities, exercising an invisible and formative influence on students. The students can learn knowledge in a relaxation and act on his own master. This has the significant practical role in the quality cultivation and personality improvement of college students.

Many people think that college students are adults and their education can be finished without interest guiding, which I disagree. Knowledge learning process should be pleasant and relaxing instead of being just boring and repetitive. The learning experience of students is totally different while the course and the passing rate are the same. Interesting course can help students to remember knowledge points easily, master key points and even learn related knowledge by themselves. Especially in science and engineering universities, students need to deal with lots of data and logic every day, while the interest teaching of humanities, a good opportunity to relax students in body and mind, becomes especially precious.

(2) **Learning to Appreciation in Lively Activities**

Schiller, the father of western aesthetic education, holds that the holistic education depends on a kind of harmony ability. The conception of beauty is the way and method that people pursue spirits harmony. Aesthetic education opens a door for contemporary university students to pursue spirits harmony. Aesthetic education is beauty education, as well as sentiment education and spiritual education. It can not only improve the aesthetic quality of human, but also effect human emotion, taste, temperament and mind, stimulate human spirit and warm human hearts silently.

Traditional handicraft course contains aesthetic education. It not only teaches the students to carry on the traditional ancient handicraft form, but also through multimedia demonstration and material object, the students can learn traditional aesthetic taste and different ethnic aesthetic culture. Therefore, the traditional handicraft practical practice course has special meaning in the aspects of molding character, improving art taste and appreciation ability, and knowing different culture. Traditional handicraft course is closely related to real life and infiltrates practical aesthetic into campus life on multiple levels. Traditional handicraft course is rooted in the deep soil of Chinese excellent traditional culture and has absorbed outstanding achievement of Chinese cultivation. It can help students guiding to establish right aesthetic concept, develop deep national sentiments, motivate imagination and innovative consciousness and widen students' field of vision and mind. Traditional handicraft course combines art experience with logic thinking. In the process of feeling beauty and enjoy beauty, students will develop noble emotion, then deepen their understanding of life by analyzing work in logic thinking.

(3) **Learning the Virtue in the Lively Activities**

The traditional handicraft can not only convey the belief and the values of a society, but also can unite the social spirits and the core value, forming a consistent moral idea. The traditional handicraft as a kind of cultural antecedents, through its patterns and production skill, and the way of wearing and using, it can naturally express and communicate the moral standard of the true, the good, and the beautiful. The students can be moved and then set up the correct outlook of life. From the past to the present, the traditional handicraft with its simple way teaches generation after generation in a simple and unadorned way, and it also has the same positive significance to the contemporary college students' moral education.

Learning the virtue in the lively activities of traditional handicraft course reflects in following aspects:

①. Traditional handicraft course contains the national spirit education. It helps to train students with dignity, confidence and pride, who will defend national dignity, honor, independence, unity and the great unity of all ethnic groups consciously.

②. Traditional handicraft course contains moral character and civilized behavior education. It helps to train students with sound personality and good psychological quality, who can know themselves rightly, have high confidence, be optimistic and have strong self-employment ability, then become prepared to adapt to society and integrate into our society.

③. Traditional handicraft course helps students to establish right professional idea, employment attitude and entrepreneurship attitude, form practical employment view, improve self-employment ability and become prepared to adapt to society and integrate into society.

(4) **Learning to be Wise in the Lively Activities**
The traditional teaching method emphasizes the reading and writing, computing, logic thinking, which make the left brain work heavily and make the right brain leave unused, and therefore will cause the imbalance of the intellectual development. Aesthetic intelligence of the traditional handicraft practical practice teaching lies in controlling the art of right brain, while the practice activities depend on the cooperation of the left and the right brain. During this process, we use the left and right brain at the same time, and mobilize image thinking while do the logic thinking. The teaching effect of this way is great that merely theory teaching cannot reach the effect. The traditional handicraft teaching method can have the essential meaning in helping students' intelligence in developing healthily and steadily.

Therefore, the course of the traditional handicraft emphasizes teaching through lively activities, learning to appreciation in lively activities, learning the virtue in the lively activities, and learning to be wise in the lively activities, which provides a fresher experience way for college quality education, and has valuable practical meaning for college quality education in colleges and universities.

Besides, here is the explanation of the lively activities. It is not a kind of entertainment. It has widely meaning, including pleasant study method, healthy spiritual enjoyment, positive life attitude and peaceful state of mind. In college quality education, the lively activities are very important in students' studying and growing up. In the previous traditional handicraft course, many students enjoyed themselves a lot and were greatly delighted, they forgot the time to go back home, and they cooperated harmoniously. The lively activities in traditional handicraft course turns passive learning into active exploration, turns examination oriented education into evaluation oriented education, and turns competitive relationship into cooperative relationship. As a result, students can finish traditional handicraft course with pleasure and relaxation.

6   Conclusion

In the long run, the traditional handicraft practice course meets the trend of the modern education, conforms to the aim of modern university education, and puts new impetus to college quality education with traditional culture conception. In this age, when the eastern culture meets the western culture, the traditional conception meets the modern conception, and inheritance meets development, it is a problem that needs us think deeply and explore in a long term, which is how to analyze and summary traditional practice experience, understand the teaching idea and spirits of thousands of years, how to teach the essence of the Chinese traditional culture to the younger generation and cultivate the comprehensive talent that suits the trend of the today's society, and how to determine the scientific, rational, adequate teaching method.

References

1. YanPing, L., MingSheng, L.: The exploration of the teaching reform on college art design basic course. Art Des. (Theor.) **11**, 155–157 (2013)
2. Wang, Y.: Liberal education and cultural quality education of university. Educational Criticism of Beijing University, p. 3 (2006)
3. Yan, Y., Peng, Z.: The modern expression of traditional handicraft culture. Ethnic Res. Guizhou. p. 139 (2011)
4. Xi, L., Feng, Z.: Introduction of Aesthetic Education. ShangHai People's Publishing House, p. 112 (2003)
5. Hang, J.: The Idea of Skill. Shandong Pictorial Publishing House, p. 18 (2011)

Elementary Introduction to Traditional Chinese Plant Dyeing Art and Its Inheritance in Modern Times

Fang Tang[✉]

School of Design and Art, Beijing Institute of Technology,
No. 5 Yard, Zhong Guan Cun South Street, Haidian District, Beijing, China
chudu@126.com

Abstract. In the modern era of internet knowledge-based economy, cultural exchange is a global scale, and the distinctive culture of different nationalities is more and more valued by people. Traditional Chinese dyeing and fabric dyeing process has not only encountered unprecedented difficulties but ushered in numerous development opportunities. This paper briefly describes the development process and characteristics of traditional Chinese plant dyeing, analyzes the importance of traditional dyeing technology in modern society, and how modern craftsmen and designers can make constant innovation on the traditional dyeing to adapt to modern market demands and endow it with new vitality.

Keywords: Chinese traditional plant dyeing · Indigo dyeing · Inheritance
Innovation

1 Introduction

Traditional textile and dyeing is a kind of manual skill for human to wear and use. The primary purpose to spin and weave cloth is to keep human bodies from the cold and dyeing technology has developed step by step from the discovery of poplin, hemp and wool for textile printing. The traditional fabric dyeing technology occupies a very important position in the people's daily lives in the ancient times and such dyeing and weaving process as dyeing, printing, painting multicolored, brocade, embroidery emerged during thousands of years of the development process, creating a brilliant traditional Chinese textile culture.

2 Plant Dyestuff Dyeing

2.1 The Emergence and Development of Plant Dyestuff Dyeing Process

Plant dyestuff dyeing is often called "plant dyeing". There is also a pleasant name called "grass dyeing". The history of plant dyeing can be traced back to thousands of years ago. Textile skills are getting more mature and dyeing skills are beginning to develop in the Neolithic period. The emergence of fabric dyeing technology is closely related to the original colored drawing. People have mastered some methods of mineral

© Springer International Publishing AG, part of Springer Nature 2018
A. Marcus and W. Wang (Eds.): DUXU 2018, LNCS 10919, pp. 96–109, 2018.
https://doi.org/10.1007/978-3-319-91803-7_8

dyeing and applied them to pottery as well as fabrics. The Neolithic fabric excavated from archaeology is used to dye red in hematite. Primitive people used natural dyes directly on the skin to draw patterns to decorate the body to express their worship of totem, in order to exorcise and avoid disasters and also found ways to dye the fabric to achieve the same goal. Shifting from the fabric dyeing with witchcraft meaning into the pursuit of beauty, people drew dyes from animals and minerals and plants to decorate fabrics. With the increasing utilization of such dyestuffs as mineral dyes, animal dyes, plant dyes, the colors that can be dyed are more and more abundant. However, compared with animal and mineral dyes, plant dyes have a wide variety and can be cultivated in large quantities, making it a major source of natural dyes. In the Zhou Dynasty, plant dyes have reached a certain scale in varieties and quantities, and special personnel was arranged to collect dyed grass for the use of stained clothing. During the Qin and Han Dynasties, the plant dye was basically used in dyeing process. In the North and South Dynasties, the planting area of plant dyes was enlarged, the variety was enriched and the process of plant dyestuff dyeing was getting increasingly proficient, and the dyestuff could be stored and used for years. During the Sui and Tang Dynasties, a special department of printing and dyeing was set up. Printing and Xie dyeing fabrics were prevalent, and technology was constantly innovating. In the Song Dynasty, because of the use of Xie dyeing fabrics for military supplies, the development of folk dyestuff-dyed fabrics has been suppressed, and till the Ming and Qing Dynasties, indigo has been set up by the government at south of the Yangtze River for the supply of dyestuffs, and the blue Xie fabric has vigorously developed in the folk.

The development of plant dyeing technology in China embodies human creativity and the pursuit of beauty. Plant dye is the most natural staining method, and has a good affinity with natural cotton, hemp, silk fiber with the advantages of soft color, durability and fastness. Plant dyeing fabric has a unique charm, with natural color, quiet and soft temperament and luster and color sense will not change over time. With the change of time, the color and color texture will be more beautiful in addition to the shades of color because of time and use. Therefore, plant dyeing is now attracting increasing attention from designers and craftsmen to inherit and carry forward the traditional process with their modern perspective and aesthetic.

2.2 Plant-Dyeing Process

Monochrome Plant Dyeing

It is found that plant dyes have better color fastness and washable durability than those of mineral dyes in the dyeing process. Some plant roots, stems, leaves, skins, seeds and flowers can be used for dyeing and can be obtained in large quantities. Madder is used to dye red, gardenia for yellow, cirrhotic for brown, tea for Starching and blue grass for blue with color dyed becoming more and more changeable. At the beginning, people used plants to dye when they were immersed in warm water. After repeated practice, people found the steaming and dyeing technology to dye deep colors (Fig. 1).

There is a big problem with plant dyes, that is, most of the plant pigments are easily decomposed and the dyed color fades seriously with no resistance to sun washing, and in the continuous practice, people found that the addition of salt, vinegar, alum can

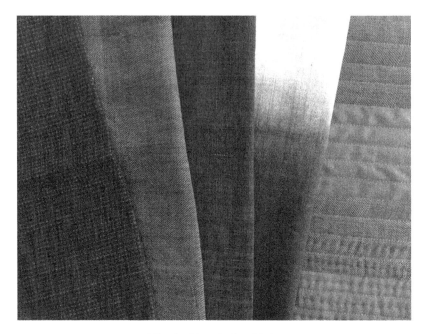

Fig. 1. Plant-dyeing fabric

make the fabric bright and long-lasting and these substances are now known as mordant. The process of dyeing with mordant is called mordant dyeing process. Different mordant has different functions, e.g., vinegar can enhance the effect of red and purple; salt and alum are often used for fixing colors. Some mordant can also let the same plant dye different colors.

Although the plant dyes can dye a rich variety of colors, very few plants can be dyed into green, purple, orange and other colors, especially green. In nature, human eyes are filled with green plants, but green leaves are often dyed by other colors. Plant dyes that can dye red, yellow, and blue are common, so people came up with a set of dyeing methods, that is, red, yellow and blue are chromatically dyed to produce rich colors and this process is called the chromatically dyed process, similar to the colors of the three primary colors in the painting, but the painting is the color adjusted directly to the canvas, and cloth dyeing is first dyed blue, and then yellow, and finally green or first dyed blue, red, and finally purple.

Colorful Polychromatic Plant Dyeing

After being able to use different fabric dyes and mordant to dye a rich single color, people began to pursue the richness of the dyeing of single block fabric, and the dyeing process of re-dyeing and multi-color dyeing began to develop, and the increase of processing means further extended the staining range of plant dyeing. Re-dyeing is to immerse fabric repeatedly into the same dye several times and the color deepens with the increase in the number of immersion and thus the fabric can be dyed at a rich color level by changing the number of times it is dyed. Multi-color dyeing is to immerse the fabric into two or more different dyes to obtain different intermediate color and re-dyeing and multi-color dyeing process enables a richer color with limited staining materials.

Simple and Plain Indigo Dyeing

In ancient China, although people have been able to dye the fabric with rich colors, the color of clothes that people could wear was determined by their social class. Behind the red, green and yellow robe, is the strict feudal hierarchy of the ancient China. Yellow is dedicated to the emperor, red is the color of the aristocracy, but the status of the people in blue continues to decline, and finally to the color of the civilian clothes. Because blue represents the color of the toiling masses, it has the most users and thus blue-dyed and blue-stained clothing began to be seen everywhere in social life, and blue dying became the most common method.

Indigo dyeing has become the most widely used plant dyes and in addition to the social hierarchy of color, the widespread use of cotton in the central plains is also an important reason. The people of all ethnic groups in China's frontier area have been planting and utilizing cotton far earlier than the central plains, while they are planting cotton mainly by silk, hemp and poplin textile. Due to the traffic inconvenience, the cotton textiles are still relatively rare and precious in the central plains in the Han Dynasty. In the Song Dynasty, a large number of cotton textiles were imported into the central plains and cotton cloth were popular in the mainland. People began to grow cotton and learn cotton textile technology. Before the large-scale cotton production, the central plains mainly used hemp and silk to dye various color patterns with small quantity of dyestuff consumption and the patterns are more of embroidery and weaving. The dyeing of cotton cloth was completed by dip method with larger dyestuff consumption. As indigo is easier to obtain than other dyes, it has become the most common and the richest color of national characteristics.

3   Traditional Dyeing Techniques Known as "Xie"

In the early time of china the figured silk fabrics was named as "Xie". Twist-Xie, Wax-Xie, Pinch-Xie and Starching-Xie, are fabric dyeing methods that have been circulated in China. Although there isn't any agreed conclusion concerning the origin of these methods, they are surely developed based on plant dyeing, painting multi-colored, printing and other dyeing process (Fig. 2).

People made their clothing rich and colorful through the re-dyeing and multi-color dyeing, but if the pattern is required for fabric, drawing or printing can be used, and then a brocade and embroidery pattern was created. Brocade and embroidery pattern is rich and luxurious, but very time-consuming and laborious. In order to show status and identity, palace nobles will spend a lot of manpower and resources to weave their garments, creating China's four famous embroidery and fortunei. But the ordinary people do not have the manpower and the financial resources to make the embroidery clothing and at the same time do not satisfy the plain and simple clothing with a hope to wear something decent, so people began to look for the fabric dyeing patterns to make more changes and thus twist-Xie, Wax-Xie, Pinch-Xie, Starching-Xie slowly appeared.

Fig. 2. Plant-dyeing fabric

Because indigo is grown in different places, it is very easy to be collected and refined with strong dyeing effect, and in the period of inconvenient transportation, people tend to find the plant dyeing materials appropriate to local development condition and it has been used to dye blue in many places and thus blue twist-Xie, Wax-Xie, Pinch-Xie and Starching-Xie gradually became the mainstream of fabric dyeing in the fork (Fig. 3).

3.1   Pinch-Xie

Pinch-Xie is to pinch the dyeing fabric with two pieces of woods of the same pattern to achieve the purpose of dyeing patterns, which are more of realism with a variety of auspicious patterns. In the dyeing process, the pattern can't be folded and the adjustment of the closure of the opening on the side of the engraving can enable that the dyeing of different colors reaches the desired stain position, and finally the Pinch-Xie fabric can be dyed. Pinch-Xie flourished in the Tang Dynasty and the Pinch-Xie now we can see from Tang Dynasty is a colorful chromatic Pinch-Xie with a white gap between the overlapping of the color blocks to prevent staining between the color blocks. The production process is similar to that of the modern process with bright colors and symmetrical graphics, which is based on a symbol of auspicious pattern. In the Song Dynasty, dyeing techniques are getting increasingly mature, but the Emperor advocated a simple life to curb the luxury repeatedly and to prohibit the production and use of color dyes, and people are forbidden to wear gorgeous clothes. In the Qing Dynasty, the technology of Pinch-Xie chromatography has new development and there has been a chromatic overprint process more colorful than that of the Tang Dynasty. At

Fig. 3. Pinch-Xie dyeing fabric process

this time, dye printing technology developed with colorful and diverse graphics, whereas Pinch-Xie technology, due to the limitations of color and graphics, faded out of sight and turned into a monochrome dyeing technology in the fork since then. The color printing technology of Pinch-Xie has been extended to the Ming and Qing Dynasties and why has it become a monochrome cotton fabric in modern times, especially indigo dyeing? This may have a great relationship with the easy availability and stability of indigo dyes, and cotton cloth at this time instead of material silk fabrics, became the main fabric, for cotton is particularly suitable for dyeing blue with a more acceptable price (Fig. 4).

3.2 Starching-Xie

Starching-Xie is a kind of traditional dyestuff-dyeing printing process, which is dyed with alkaline anti-staining agent. By using the tung oil soaked bamboo paper, hollow patterns are carved and the mixture of lime and soybean powder is scraped through the hollow pattern plate to the dyed fabric. After the dye powder is immersed in the indigo dye and dyed from shallow to deep color, the dye powder is removed and blue-white pattern appears. The hollow plate can be used for printing the dyestuff and thus the continuous pattern can be formed. This kind of dyeing process uses the hollow cardboard to replace the wood carving board of the Pinch-Xie to dye the pattern. The cardboard carving is easier to carve with varied printing patterns and the process is simpler than wood carving with lower costs and thus Starching-Xie quickly developed into a blue calico. Blue calico became most ordinary people's daily clothing and

Fig. 4. Pinch-Xie dyeing fabric process

household items in the Ming and Qing Dynasties and almost every region has its own blue calico dyeing workshop, and blue calico has become the mainstream of China's blue dyeing industry (Figs. 5 and 6).

Fig. 5. Starching-Xie dyeing fabric process

Fig. 6. Starching-Xie dyeing fabric process

3.3   Twist-Xie

Twist-Xie is also a traditional fabric dyeing process that has been circulated in China for thousands of years. As early as the Qin and Han Dynasties, China has been the producer of twist-Xie technology. This method of dyeing is more prevalent in the Sui and Tang Dynasties due to the development of plant dyes and dyeing processes. Twist-Xie is a kind of high artistic and free anti-staining dyeing method. Traditional twist-Xie is using the line or a simple auxiliary tool to knot, clamp and sew to prevent staining and tightly-tied part of the dye cannot penetrate completely, thus forming a white layered color halo pattern. The mutual infiltration of color is the main characteristics of the twist-Xie and this halo dyeing effect can't be achieved by other printing and dyeing methods. Due to the limitations of the process itself, the color of the twist-Xie is generally relatively simple and a wonderful rhythm and change can be formed by combining the points, lines, and surfaces (Figs. 7, 8 and 9).

3.4   Batik Dyeing

Batik Dyeing, an ancient hand-spinning process, refers to drawing pattern on fabric in advantage of waterproof function of wax to form special patterns after the procedure of dyeing and dewaxing. Batik Dyeing is a flexible and variable dyeing process generated on the basis of multiple dyeing processes such as printing and hui without special requirements on dyeing materials. Cotton, linen and silk can all be used in batik dyeing with plant dyes dominated by indigo, as dark blue highlights the white pattern more. However, batik dyeing faded out people's attention gradually in central China in the Song Dynasty, with beewax replaced by slurry made of bean flour and lime, wax painting replaced by scraping pattern with hollow cardboard and batik dyeing replaced by xi technology that can be copied more easily. Batik Dyeing spread to marginal areas and prospered in ethnic minority areas later. Both the wax and blue dyes are highly accessible in ethnic minority areas with more distinctive national features rendered with traditional techniques of wax painting and waxing. Batik Dyeing techniques such as "Dian La Man" of Miao people and "Yao Ban Bu" of Yao people have become handicrafts handed down from generation to generation in minority areas through long-term preservation and inheritance as symbols of their nations.

Fig. 7. Twist-Xie dyeing fabric with ties on it

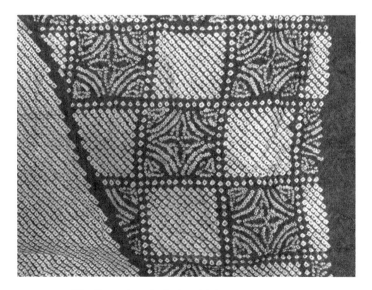

Fig. 8. Twist-Xie dyeing fabric, ties be opened

Fig. 9. Twist-Xie dyeing fabric

4 Plant Dyeing Process and Fabric Dyeing Process in Modern Times

Up to modern times, hand-dyed blue and white cloths, costumes, aprons, headdresses, tablecloths, curtains, etc. have been seen commonly in daily life. Color of each part of dyed clothes people wear varies according to different technical styles of printing, and can be even influenced by the weather. Everyone wears unique clothes with outstanding national characteristics. However, in modern times, the hand-woven and dyed clothes as usual as eating and walking for ancient Chinese are far away from our lives.

The whole process of dyeing and fabric dyeing is dependent on hand-spinning, hand-weaving and hand-dyeing. Dyeing a cloth requires more than 10 processes and such a set of pattern design, printing, dyeing and other integrated art forms, because of the complexity and time-consuming of the process and the singleness of the products, can never adapt to the current market demand. In an efficient modern age, fewer people are engaged in these laborious activity, and only a few of the remaining cloth-dyeing mills continue to work.

4.1 Inheritance of Traditional Fabric Dyeing Technology in the New Era

In modern society, factories use the fastest way to produce products, and people also consume products in the quickest way. With dramatic changes in modern printing and dyeing technology in the passing days, the dyed fabric can't be matched by the previous dyeing method in terms of material and color. But modern dyeing technology also has many disadvantages. In order to pursue color effect, various chemicals used cause water pollution and badly influence human skin. These are the negative effects that are caused by the convenience brought by modernization. Of course, the mention of the drawbacks of modernization is not to emphasize the past is perfect nor to say to go back to the past, but to say in the new era, more efforts should be made to better inherit and carry forward the traditional dyeing process.

Under the influence of modern dyeing technology, many traditional manual dyeing processes have lost, changes occurred in the national characteristics of some ethnic groups and the color of the natural dye was fading away in the earlier days. Because of the convenience and low price of chemical dyestuffs, the minority nationalities in the border area have gradually abandoned the dyeing and processing technology from natural materials, and the disappearance of these technologies often symbolizes the disappearance of some cultures.

However, with the abundance of material life in modern cities, more and more people have begun to realize the problems in life, that is, we lack a sense of intimacy with fabrics that are indispensable in our daily life. The excessively consumed natural resources, the badly damaged ecological balance and increasingly deteriorated living environment have aggregated the problems and some people began to miss the farming era of pastoral life. Traditional handmade products are all derived from the natural environment and coexistence with nature has been emphasized in the production process, endowing the resulting products with a strong human atmosphere, which is exactly in line with people's desire to return to nature.

Some actions to protect the traditional craftsmanship of fabric dyeing have begun and "Pinch-Xie" issued by an editor from Taiwan ECHO of Things Chinese Magazine has set off the trace back of the long-lost dyeing technology and two fabric dyeing private museums have been established in Beijing. Professional handmade artists have set up plant dyeing studios and blue dyeing studios and restored traditional dyeing, hand-woven and hand-dyed technologies to create fabrics of national characteristics and publicize the traditional dyeing process. A number of primary and secondary schools have opened traditional dyeing and fabric dyeing courses to facilitate children's understanding of traditional Chinese craftsmanship and to lay humanistic basis for better inheritance of these skills (Fig. 10).

National government departments have also begun to notice the importance of protecting these traditional techniques, which have been included in the Intangible Cultural Heritage Protection Project. Some traditional handicraft workshops have been revived, and the skills of the old artists with hand-dyed printing have been taken seriously. Wuzhen Hongyuan Thai Dyeing Workshop, Nantong Blue Calico Museum, Wenzhou Blue Xie Museum and other dyeing and printing technology non-heritage projects have been established as a tourist attraction to show people the whole process of traditional dyeing process and market some dyed cloth products to people.

However, the protection and inheritance of traditional technology is a very complex problem, and in modern society, if a traditional technology is only protected and supported by government policy, it is certainly not enough, for pure protection can only make it a non-material cultural heritage to be admired by people. It is necessary to use these traditional techniques to produce products suitable for contemporary generations, pay attention to the development of the art value of the dyeing and fabric dyeing technology and product innovation to endow these technologies with significant market value and to be passed down over thousands of years.

Fig. 10. Modern Xie dyeing fabric

4.2   Innovation of Traditional Dyeing and Fabric Dyeing Process

The emphasis on the inheritance of tradition is to carry forward the unique characteristics rather than the simple and mechanical application. Some contents and forms of traditional plant dyeing and dyeing process have not adapted to the aesthetic demand of people today and more efforts should be made to make the products manufactured by twist- Xie, wax- Xie, Pinch-Xie and Starching-Xie satisfy people's living needs rather than just as tourist souvenirs. We should combine the traditional dyeing handicraft method with the modern design and technology to fully display the taste and individuality of modern people's aesthetic from the color fabric texture, etc. and learn from the useful things of modern technology to enrich and improve the traditional design.

To innovate, we need to know which features of the traditional dyeing and fabric dyeing process need to be retained and which are to be innovated.

Following is the Features that need to be Retained

First, plant dyeing is characterized by the dye oxidation and a rich layer of colors can be formed with local fading fabric. Each piece of work will show different patterns over the years because of different experience. This kind of uniqueness is most suitable for the distinctive characteristics of modern fashion (Fig. 11).

Second, different dyeing and fabric dyeing technologies can form a unique pattern, color halo dyeing and mutual infiltration, superposition with different processes which can never be met by the modern dyeing and fabric dyeing process and which is exactly the human values attached to the products;

Third, all materials of traditional dyeing process are obtained from the nature and the production process will not cause environmental pollution. Thereafter, all the materials can be returned to nature. The advantages and characteristics of these traditional dyeing and fabric dyeing processes must be retained in the process of innovation.

Fig. 11. Modern Xie dyeing bag

Following is the Features that need to be Innovated

First, process techniques should be more diversified to break the limitations of the original process. We can combine the traditional dyeing and fabric dyeing process with other traditional dyeing process, for example, innovation can be made after dyeing by rubbing, painting multicolored, embroidery, quilting and other methods, to create a printing and dyeing aesthetic effect that is different from the traditional and modern process; we can also combine traditional techniques with modern dyeing and fabric dyeing processes to re-process fabrics after traditional processing with modern dyeing and fabric dyeing techniques, which can process unique texture fabrics (Fig. 12).

Second, the pattern color innovation. The new design of patterns, the change of dyeing methods and the use of modern dyeing tools can free the dyeing and fabric dyeing craftsmanship from traditional material constraints to create a rich modern pattern with a variety of styles. The prediction and collocation of fashion color has injected new vitality to the innovation of traditional dyeing process and the traditional hand-dyed products should have new ideas to get in line with the world trends and to cater to young people's pursuit of personalized clothing.

Third, the dyeing technique innovation. Designers continue to incorporate new technology and new techniques into traditional dyeing and fabric dyeing process to imbue the fabric with different texture patterns and colors and be applied to fashion design through the international brand designers.

When mankind entered the Internet knowledge-based economy era and began the cultural exchange of global scale, the traditional dyeing and fabric dyeing process, although faced with the difficulties, witnessed new development opportunities.

Fig. 12. Modern Xied yeing fabric with embroidery

Traditional craftsmanship can serve as a liaison to connect the people of different times, different cultures and different traditions. In today's historical conditions, when people examine and evaluate these cultural traditions from the perspective of modern civilization, traditional craftsmanship as an element delves deep into modern art life to realize the leap forward towards new cultural atmosphere and aesthetic realm, showing a new cultural significance.

References

1. Taiwan ECHO of Things Chinese Magazine, Pinch-Xie, Beijing University Press, Beijing
2. Guyu, Guodazhe, Love the plant dying. Guangxi Fine Arts Publishing House, Guangxi
3. Xin, W., Shu, W.: Blue cloth with design in white. China Society Press, Beijing

Fables – Exploring Natural Ways of Expressing Behavior to Create Digital Simulations

Andrea Valente[1(✉)] and Emanuela Marchetti[2]

[1] Maersk Mc-Kinney Moller Institute, Embodied Systems for Robotics and Learning, University of Southern Denmark (SDU), Odense, Denmark
anva@mmmi.sdu.dk
[2] Media Studies, Department for the Study of Culture, University of Southern Denmark (SDU), Odense, Denmark
emanuela@sdu.dk

Abstract. We are interested in simplifying digital game design and programming for primary school teachers and their pupils. A central problem in this area is how to express knowledge about interactive digital systems in a simple yet powerful enough way, so that new digital games or interactive simulations can be generated automatically by teachers and pupils descriptions. We propose a novel approach that builds on Simon [4] and Schön [5] and the concepts of *simulation* and *repertoire of exemplars*. Instead of looking at programming concepts like conditionals and loops, we draw inspiration from soft methods like rich pictures, and formalisms like concept maps and mobile ambients. In this paper, we define the concept of fables, where a simple fable represents an exemplar and it can be interacted with digitally, as a simulation. A web-based prototype tool is under development, and we are conducting a series of workshops (last semester of 2017 and first semester of 2018) to discuss, co-develop and test our incremental prototype of the fable editor/player. Early tests and interviews indicate that fables are a viable concept with potential applicability in various domains, and that the current prototype is usable enough for further participatory development.

Keywords: Design thinking · Game development · Education
Knowledge management · Visualization

1 Introduction and Motivation

In past projects, we have worked at simplifying digital game design and programming for primary school children and their teachers [1, 2], to empower them and let them learn by creating their own digital games. In line with [13, 19], we found that teachers engage in forms of creative thinking, acting as finders or makers of multimedia applications and playful experience for their own pupils. Teachers tend to explore digital and non-digital solutions made available through the school system or simply the Internet, searching for materials that could be meaningfully contextualized within their class activities. Nevertheless, some teachers would like to address specific needs

© Springer International Publishing AG, part of Springer Nature 2018
A. Marcus and W. Wang (Eds.): DUXU 2018, LNCS 10919, pp. 110–126, 2018.
https://doi.org/10.1007/978-3-319-91803-7_9

or visions for their class, and be able to create ad hoc playful experiences. Hence, as discussed in [1, 2] those teachers experiment with the design of paper-based board games or scripts for role play acts for the pupils, to engage more actively with their learning material. Interestingly, several teachers we interviewed have said that they would recur to designing paper-based games, also because the making of a digital game was seen as too complex for their IT competences. Therefore, in our study we are exploring the making of a system that would empower teachers to develop new games/simulations for their class, leveraging on creative thinking practice, which they seem to master already in their current exploration of paper-based games.

A central problem in this area is how to express knowledge about interactive digital systems in a simple yet powerful way, so that new digital games or interactive simulations can be generated automatically from descriptions created by teachers, pupils, and non-programmers in general. Usual approaches to solve this problem are: provide predefined customizable options (often via a game editor), or turn users into programmers. The latter requires the creation of a special programming language, typically coupled with highly visual and friendly development environments. Although very successful, this approach has problems, the main one being that it takes time for a pupil to be proficient enough to code satisfactory digital games, as discussed in [3]. In our experience the situation is even more difficult if we expect primary school teachers to learn to program digital games, especially teachers with non-technical backgrounds.

We propose to look at a third approach, and in particular we build on Simon [4] and Schön [5], and the concepts of *simulation* and *repertoire*:

- "Simulation, as a technique for achieving understanding and predicting the behavior of systems, predates of course the digital computer" [4].
- "When a practitioner makes sense of a situation he perceives to be unique, he sees it as something already present in his repertoire. [...] The familiar situation functions as a precedent, or a metaphor, or... an exemplar for the unfamiliar one" [5].

The idea that simulation and understanding are related is also supported by research in bounded rationality and naturalistic decision making [6]. In naturalistic decision making a person is said to use a simulation to judge the consequences of possible choices: a mental simulation that acts very much like the exemplars in Schön's repertoire.

For us, the link between simulation and exemplars in a repertoire is the following: when a digital simulation of a real-world situation runs, it generates a sequential story about the situation changing over time. An interactive digital simulation (for example a digital game) will generate different stories each run, depending on the user's interaction. Therefore, a simulation can be said to generate or contain multiple stories, and running the simulation produces an interactive non-linear story. In our previous work [1, 2] we repeatedly encountered non-linearity, when studying how children and teachers express behavior of a system to be implemented digitally. Even with something as simple as digital multiple choice quizzes [9], describing alternatives is perceived as difficult and requiring precise definitions. On the other hand, according to Schön, it should come natural for practitioners to create and maintain their repertoire, and since exemplars must also deal with multiple options and outcomes, handling non-linearity should not be the source of the difficulties we observed. We decided, therefore, to explore natural ways of expressing behavior to create digital simulations, usable by teachers and pupils. Instead of looking at programming concepts like conditionals and loops (such as those in *Computational Thinking*), we draw inspiration from soft methods like *rich pictures* [11], and formalisms like *concept maps* and *mobile ambients* [7, 10]. In this paper, we define the concept of *fables*, where a simple fable represents one of Schön's exemplars. Multiple fables can be composed together to create what Schön calls repertoire.

We are currently implementing and testing a web-based tool to support creation and interactive playback of fables. The playback of fables will be an animated, interactive simulation of the changes that occur in the situation being described, and the user will be able to choose how the fable is progressing, always following one among all possible storylines.

We expect that fables will be used by teachers and pupils to express what they know about a situation or a domain, explicitly and in an objectified way, so that other pupils (and teachers eventually) can *explore* that knowledge by replaying the fables in multiple ways, i.e. interacting with the simulation automatically generated by those fables. If needed, a fable should also be used to generate concept maps or linearized and exported as a slideshow. Moreover, we want teachers to be able to create their own digital simulations within the domains of their pertinence by visually or textually define fables, without the need for them to become programmers.

In the following sections we discuss related work and theoretical background for this study (Sect. 2), present our latest prototype (Sect. 3) and initial findings from testing (Sect. 4); Sect. 5 presents conclusions and future work.

2 Related Work and Theoretical Background

Theoretically our study builds on Schön [5] and his notion of repertoire, and Simons' understanding of simulations [4].

In the book "The Reflective Practitioner", Donald Schön argues that: "a professional practitioner is a specialist who encounters certain types of situations again and again" [5, p. 60]. Different terms are then used in each profession to identify these situations, which could be called: "cases" or accounts, or projects or else depending on the specific profession. According to Schön, as practitioners experience different variations of these cases, they develop "a repertoire of expectations, images, and techniques" drawing from each individual case [5, p. 60]. Through this repertoire, practitioners become able to engage in a reflective conversation with the situation given by new cases, as they build on their repertoire, to reflect on the similarities between the old cases and the solutions applied then, which could inspire new solutions for a newly encountered case.

According to Simon [4] a simulation is a partial reproduction of a phenomenon, in which selected relations between the elements and their dynamics are preserved. So defined, simulations are techniques for "achieving understanding and predicting the behavior of systems" [4, p. 13]. Simulations are based on similarities between two different systems, as one system can be altered so to resemble the other. Computers have contributed to spreading the use of simulations and extended the range of phenomena that can be simulated. According to Simon, an interesting and awkward fact of simulations is that the makers of a simulation can learn something new of the phenomenon that they have reproduced in the simulation, even if they know in depth all the elements of the simulation and their relationships.

Combining the perspective of Schön and Simon, we see Schön's repertoire of cases as a simulative resource, as the construction of the repertoire enables the practitioners to acquire a set of expectations, images, and techniques that, in the terms of Simon, enable the practitioners to predict possible solutions for new cases. In the moment a practitioner engages in reflecting on the new cases, she in fact engages in reflecting on how old cases could be *similar* to the new case, and in simulating in her mind what could happen if one of the old solutions could be applied to the new case.

In our study, we aim at leveraging on the simulative potential of repertoires to create a tool that could enable teachers and pupils to create interactive stories (here called fables) and use them as simulations of specific topics. Hence, following Simon [4], by engaging in interacting and editing fables, pupils and teachers would be participating in the formation of a repertoire of simulated cases, which could foster learning and in-depth reflections, individually and in groups, on the selected topics.

A difficulty we are facing is how to express the behavior of the elements of simulations/games. We intend to face this issue by focusing on the design thinking activity in which teachers already engage when designing paper-based board games and role play scripts. Therefore, in our study we work across disciplines, taking inspiration from studies on design thinking and conceptual formalisms, to shape the logic and workflow for our tool. Regarding the learning aspect, we refer to Donald Schön's concept of reflection in action and repertoire [5], to define our scenario. By design thinking, we refer to "an analytic and creative process that engages a person in opportunities to experiment, create" prototypes, and gather feedback for further improvement [13]. In our scenario, designing thinking would be targeted the design and alteration of learning games and simulations, to be eventually improved with the help and active participation of the pupils. Following [13, p. 336], our scenario approaches design thinking as defined by seven main characteristics: human- and environment-centered concern, ability to visualize, predisposition toward multi-functionality, systemic vision, ability to use language as a tool, affinity for teamwork, avoiding the necessity of choice.

The first characteristic is "human- and environment-centered concern", meaning that designers must focus their intervention in addressing human needs, functional and aesthetic. In our study, look at the needs of teachers and their pupils. The second characteristic of design thinking includes the "ability to visualize", as design practice typically requires visualizations of information and/or of the interactive elements of the specific product. The third is "predisposition toward multifunctionality" and the fourth is "systemic vision", as designers should look at multiple solutions to an issue, shifting in between its overview and details, with the goal of providing *systemic* solutions that address complex issues for different groups of users and stakeholders within specific contexts. In the context of our project, we look at the design thinking in which the teachers continually engage when creating new learning activities for their class, while taking into account the multiple needs of the individual pupils and of the class as a whole. The fifth characteristic of design thinking in [13] is the "ability to use language as tool", as designers should be able to verbally articulate to users and stakeholders the creative process and outcome, where visual information is not obvious or perhaps inadequate. From previous studies (discussed in [1]) we know that language represents a central mode of expression for teachers to create their scripts role play and paper-based board games. Since we intend to leverage on current practices, we strive for a scenario in which language and visualization support each other in enabling teachers to express their creativity through digital media, as they do with paper-based media. The sixth characteristic, "affinity for teamwork", is defined by designers' interpersonal skills enabling them to communicate "across disciplines and work with other people" [13, p. 336]. This is another aspect that we take into consideration in the definition of our scenario, in relation to the role of the teachers as creators of playful experiences. The teachers we have observed and interviewed are engaged in designing playful interdisciplinary learning experiences for groups, leveraging on collaborative and competitive play. Finally, we are critical toward the last and seventh characteristic, called "avoiding the necessity of choice". According to this characteristic, designers should search for "competing alternatives" to land on a final solution which leads to "avoid decision and combine best possible choices" [13, p. 336]. We find this characteristic challenging, as it can be interpreted in an ambiguous way: avoiding decision could refer to how designers create solutions based on best practices, sparing the user from the confusion of having to take decisions among too many choices. This last characteristic can be then related to the principle of simplicity in good design [16], and, in this sense, it has been applied successfully to the design of digital media and games for learning [15]. However, in this project we attempt to empower teachers in becoming more independent in their choice of digital media, for their class, hence, we are more interested in offering more choices instead of reducing them. In this respect, we are rather following [14] in pursue of a democratization of design tools for creating games and simulations for learning: in this way, teachers will not have necessarily to recur to IT experts to create simple digital games and simulations, and retain more authorship and control, as is the case when they work with paper and scripts. In line with Schön [5], our scenario aims at enabling teachers to focus on their *reflective conversation* with learning content and potential game elements (mechanics, roles, possible characters, and tasks) that could enrich pupils' learning experience.

With respect to our goal of finding natural ways to express behavior, we have looked at various formalisms (within theoretical Computer Science, and formal methods) and we selected *mobile ambients* [10] and *rich pictures* [11]. We worked with both in our previous research (see [7, 12]); here we want to take advantage of the spatial metaphor and expressive power of ambients, while dropping most of their formal aspects like typing. In our work with rich pictures we found that when semi-structured data (such as ambients or objects in prototype-based languages) are provided with visual representation, they make for powerful and intuitive tools to represent knowledge, even for non-programmers.

For fables, we want a visual representation (also for direct manipulation in the editor of our prototype) that is spatial, but simpler than a bi-dimensional metric space. Informally, we want fables to be visualized like sticky notes of different sizes, where placing a note on top of another signifies inclusion or part-of (or *stacked* sticky notes). Therefore, diagrams representing fables could be composed of rectangular areas in a metric space, eventually placed one above another, or they could be represented by elements of a grid (with an added dimension for stacking elements, similar to what is called z-index in web pages). Finally, most of the geometrical information could be dropped, leaving mostly inclusion: this would result in tree-like structures, topological in nature since proximity and nesting would still remain. Figure 1 shows the spectrum of possibilities, and we decided to work with trees (Fig. 1 on the right). Interestingly, ambients have a tree-like structure and computation is expressed by creating, dissolving and moving boxes around in the tree.

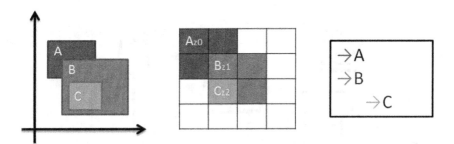

Fig. 1. Range of possibly visualizations: 2D metric space (left), grid with z-index (center), and topological (on the right).

3 The Prototype: An Example, Analysis, Design and Implementation

In this section, we want to define the concept of fables, then look into how a story can be expressed as a fable. The author of a fable should be able to play it back to explore all possible unfolding of the events, and that means that time and choices have to be easy to express in a fable, in a non-technical, natural way. The web-based prototype tool to create, edit and playback fables is called F4BL3s, and it is developed to support the authors by offering textual as well as visual ways to work with fables, leveraging on direct manipulation as much as possible.

3.1 Example of Use: A Ping Pong Match

Consider the following informally defined story. *Alice and Bob are in a room, inside a house, and are playing ping pong. In the room, there is a table and initially Alice has the ball. After Alice serves, Bob has the ball and it is his turn to send the ball back to Alice. Each of them could hit the ball too hard and send it out, which will conclude our story.*

   A text analysis of this ping pong story suggests a spatial metaphor, where people and things inhabit rooms, and where a thing might belong to a person. The unfolding of the story can then be represented by defining the *state of the world* (i.e. rooms and their contents) at a certain time. Actions (such as "Alice serves") bring the world to a new state, where contents of the rooms have changed, and people and things have moved, appeared or disappeared. For us each state is represented by a *slide*, as in a presentation, and many slides constitute a fable. The ping pong story can be turned into a fable manually, following this work-flow (see Fig. 3, top part):

- Chose a title (here it could be "ping pong") for the new fable.
- Define the initial state of the world: i.e. draw a tree with nested rooms, then place Alice and Bob in the same room. Finally, add few things (like the table and ball) so that Alice owns the ball, and the table is in the same room as Alice and Bob (see Fig. 2).

Fig. 2. Informal visualization (This figure uses free icons obtained from www.flaticon.com.) of the first slide of the ping pong story.

- Make a copy of the tree of rooms (i.e. the first slide of the fable) and move the ball from Alice to Bob. Draw an arrow to connect the first state of the world with this new one: the arrow represents an action with label "Alice serves". Draw another action (i.e. arrow) labeled "Bob's answer" that connects the second world tree to the first.

After having defined the "ping pong" fable the author plays it back, deciding interactively step-by-step which actions she wants to perform (if multiple actions are possible for any of the slides), generating a linear sequence of world states. The author can now go back and add a new arrow for the action "Alice serves", expressing the idea that sometimes when Alice serves, she sends the ball out and the game ends. *Non-deterministic* choice (as this situation is called in the ambient calculus) can be easily represented here, simply by defining the playback of a fable in such a way that when 2 actions have the same label the user playing back the fable will not be able to control in which of 2 possibly states the world will end (see bottom part of Fig. 3, in particular the large "Alice serves" arrow going towards Slide2). Sometimes the player will send the user in a state where the ball is moved from Alice to Bob, and other times the ball will *randomly* end out, so neither Alice nor Bob own it anymore. So, in playback the 2 actions will simply be considered a single action with 2 possible, non-deterministic, outcomes.

As we are looking for natural ways of defining fables, incremental definition is very important, since the author should not have to worry about mentally constructing a

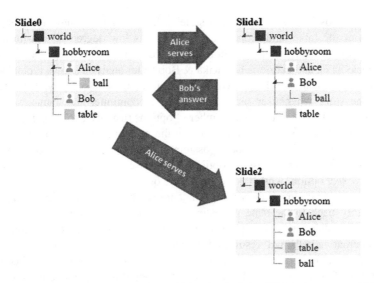

Fig. 3. The ping pong story expressed as a fable with 3 slides. Slide2 shows a world in which the ball is out and the game is over.

complete fable before starting to work on it digitally. We believe that a good digital tool should allow the author to change her mind as well as sketch partially correct fables, and only later go back and finish/fix them. So we could imagine in our example that the author of the "ping pong" fable realizes that she forgot to add a kitchen where Charlie is having tea, so she goes back to the drawings that define the fable, and draws one more room called "kitchen" in all world trees, adding a new person "Charlie" and a thing "tea", owned by Charlie. Playback of the new version of the fable results in a new sequence of world states, all of which also contain the kitchen with Charlie and the tea.

Finally, slides are temporal in nature, but from reading all people, things and rooms in all slides of a fable, we can infer a palette containing a-temporal information. In the case of the ping pong story the palette consists of Alice and Bob (as people), the table and the ball (which are things), and a hobby room (the only room defined in the fable). The palette can be seen as a summary of all elements that can appear in a slide of a fable, hence, the palette will be a valuable part of the F4BL3s editor, helping fable authors to maintain a coherent overview of people, things and rooms across slides in their fables.

3.2   Analysis

To better take advantage of natural ways of thinking and managing knowledge, we want fables to be constrained in various ways. Fables should offer a familiar metaphor, this is why we designed a fable to be a collection of slides, each slide representing the state of the world at a certain time in a story.

We want non-linearity to be present but it should not overwhelm the author, therefore a fable should be an *almost linear* story, with each slide connected to a maximum of 3 possible "next" slides. A slide with no outgoing connections is one of the endings of the fable, and loops are possible. This low degree of non-linearity is consistent with our analysis of other non-linear media, from games like Dragon's Lair to Gamebooks [17], and cartoons like Kika & Bob[1]. Our analysis shows typical patters to describe non-linear storylines: sequence, choice, and end-of-story. Choices, i.e. points in the story when user input is required to continue, are sparse within the narrative and usually present a small number of options (usually 2 to 6, in case a dice is used to decide). In this sense, we are applying the principle of design thinking called "avoiding decision and combine best possible choices" [13, p. 336], as we are still trying to limit the number of possible options for our users. Hence, in many cases, there is a single *correct* option, while taking any of the others brings the story to an end; the end-of-story could be global, terminating the current line of narration, or local, simply bring the story back to the state preceding the choice, to allow the user to explore alternatives. In other cases, multiple options might allow the story to continue, however, the alternative paths will result in different levels of success for the user. Another constraint for a fable is that it should represent a short story. Fables should contain a small number of slides, 10 to 15 by design; with a possibility to define more complex fables by hierarchically composing simple fables together.

As mentioned in the previous section, we want to support incremental definition, so in our F4BL3s tool rooms, people and things can be defined and redefined at any moment during editing of a fable. This is more natural for authors than being forced to define everything at the beginning. However, changes that make the story inconsistent are automatically detected and signaled by the F4BL3s tool. Inconsistencies among slides (e.g. John having an apple in one slide, but there was no apple in any room, in any of the slides before) are allowed but automatically signaled, to support working with partially correct or incomplete fables (i.e. fable drafts).

We require the playback of fables to be digital and multimodal: both a visual animation and a natural-language textual representation should always be available for any fable. For example, the slides of the "ping pong" fable in Fig. 3 can easily be exported as a text in natural language, since all elements have names and actions have labels. In F3BL3s multimodality is supported also by allowing textual definition of fables. The typical work-flow in this case would be:

- Write textual description of a story, as a series of commands in a natural-language inspired DSL as in Table 1 (i.e. a Domain Specific Language [8])
- Compile the textual description and get an automatically generated sequence of slides (i.e. a fable), each with a snapshot of the state of the world at a certain step of the story
- Eventually the fable can be edited manually by redrawing slides or adding action and respective arrows to extend the storyline beyond its original textual description

The DSL language in Table 1 is very simple, and the first line is always the title of the fable. All other lines must start with a room where the story will develop (in analogy to comic books, where the narrating voice often explains where the action

---

[1] Official website: http://www.kikaandbob.com Last visited February 20th 2018.

Table 1. The left column describes the fable to be generated, and the right part shows the palette for the fable.

a ping pong match	Inferred palette
AT hobbyroom, THING table, Alice PICKUP ball	People: Alice, Bob
AT hobbyroom, Alice GIVES ball TO Bob	Things: ball
AT hobbyroom, Bob GIVES ball TO Alice	Rooms: hobbyroom

takes place), and after that a number of statements might follow. Some statements simply state the existence of a thing or a person (e.g. "THING table"), or they could relate people and things (as in "Alice PICKUP ball" or "Alice GIVES ball TO Bob"). Table 1 also shows that the compilation process turning the textual description into a fable automatically infers a palette for the fable. The decision to categorize elements of a fable into rooms, people and things, comes from our desire to base fables upon formal models like mobile ambients. In mobile ambients types are used to restrict the movements and interactions of processes [7]; here we use our 3 categories as a kind of *light typing*. The result is a set of restrictions for the elements of fable: people can be moved from room to room, but things should stay where they are, unless picked up by a person, in which case they can move with the person carrying them. Rooms cannot be moved and exist in the same relative place in the world in all slides, creating a perceptual and cognitive persistence to support authors and users of the fable to navigate (a phenomenon related to memorization techniques like the *method of loci*[2]). Moreover, in our experience we found that metaphorical naming of abstract entities often provides a way to **naturally attach roles** to those entities [20]; in the F4BL3s tool we expect that our categories will help authors and users to easily grasp which affordances are associated to the various elements of their fables.

3.3   Design

In order to implement the F4BL3s tool as a web-based application, we defined an ontology to clarify the relationship among the elements of a fable. The UML class diagram in Fig. 4 states that a fable is simply a collection of slides, and a slide contains a special room called world, and 0 to 3 actions, possibly linking the slide to other slides. The Slide and Action classes are arranged to define a graph data-structure, where slides are the nodes of the graph and actions the edges. The classes for Room, Thing and Person are connected according to the composite design pattern, suggesting that rooms act as containers for other rooms, things and people.

The composite pattern is also central in the definition of objects in object-based languages (like Javascript or Python) and ambients in mobile ambients. In fact, fables share many concepts with these two computational models, as visible in Table 2.

The F4BL3s web-based application has a modular architecture, centered on a single data-type. We started from the fable data-type (Fig. 4), and developed each part of the tool as a standalone web application manipulating the fable data-type, i.e. all webpages

---

[2] Mentioned by Cicero in his: *"De Oratore"*, literally "On the Orator", written circa 55 B.C.

were interoperable by design. This architectural choice made it easy to experiment independently with the individual tools within the F4BL3s web application. For example, we could easily define the first fables by manually writing some data, and could immediately play them back, even if the editor page was still incomplete. The data-centric, modular architecture also made it easy to try out multiple versions of the same page/module, as needed for our user-centered development.

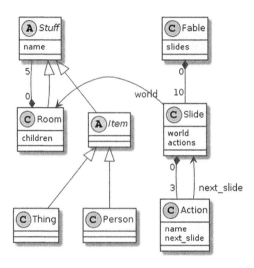

Fig. 4. UML class diagram for F4BL3s. Drawn using PlantText.

Table 2. Comparison among mobile ambients, object-oriented programming and fables' concepts. Concepts on the same line behave similarly.

Mobile ambients	OOP	Fables
ambient literal, type	class	palette of people and things
ambient	object	slide
name	attribute	room
ambient, process	value	people, thing
operation (and reduction semantic)	(short/simple) method	action, going from slide to slide

3.4   Implementation

The F4BL3s prototype is developed as a collection of dynamic web-pages, using Javascript, jQuery, and jsTree to visualize and edit the nested rooms with people and things. The jsTree library is a jQuery plugin especially designed to represent and manipulate trees, it provides many features such as drag and drop, types for the nodes of the trees and even constraints circa which types of nodes can be nested in which other types. Its adoption allowed for a rapid development of the UI in the editor

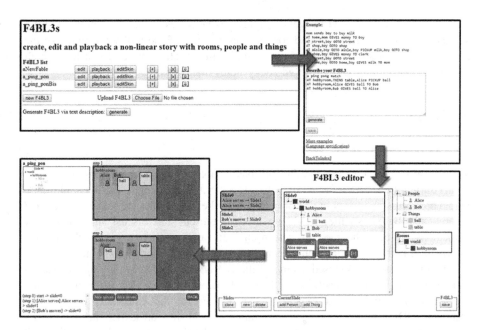

Fig. 5. Navigation diagram of the F4BLEs web application. The blue arrows show a typical workflow: generation of a fable, editing and playback. (Color figure online)

(bottom-right screenshot in Fig. 5), which required the most of our development time so far.

Figure 5 shows a navigation diagram of the 4 main pages of the F4BL3s web application. On the top-left, the main page that works as a dashboard, listing all fables created up to now. Fables can be created, cloned, deleted, downloaded and uploaded from this main page. The current prototype does not allow multiple authors/users, and stores all data locally (using the browser's local storage), however, it should be easy adding a simple user login page and switching to a web-hosted database (like for example mLab's MongoDB) in a few iterations. The screenshot on the top-right of Fig. 5 shows the page for generating a fable from a textual description. Once a fable is created (directly from the main page or via textual generation) it can be opened in the editor (bottom-right part of Fig. 5). The editor page, the most complex page of F4BL3s, is implemented around the MVC pattern, where each fable is a tree of Javascript objects modeled according to the UML diagram in Fig. 4. Operations on the fable data are implemented separately from the data-structure, to simplify JSON-serialization across web-pages. The playback page is visible in the screenshot in the bottom-left part of Fig. 5. The visualization of the slides is different from that used in the editor page: in playback slides look as much as possible like sticky notes, with generic icons and color-coding for rooms, people and things. The playback page lets the user navigate through the slides, by choosing among the (potentially) multiple actions available from each slide. It also offers a rewind button, labeled "back", that allows the user to go back one step and chose an alternative action.

We explored various visualization styles for the slides, which are shown as trees and as sticky notes in Fig. 5, and for the final version of the tool we would like the editor and playback page to have a more uniform visualization, and that the overall visual style is more close to stacked sticky notes than trees.

4   Testing

4.1   Organization of the Tests

We plan to test our concept and the web-based tool with teachers and primary school pupils during the spring semester of 2018. However, we believe that having a minimum viable product is necessary in this project, mainly because fables are rather abstract and theoretically based, so they could be hard to present and discuss in participatory workshops. Hence, the idea of developing an early prototype, designed with the information gathered in previous experiences with school cooperation (such as [2]).

We organized a task-based testing of the F4BL3s prototype in the fall semester of 2017, involving 8 of our bachelor students, all males. They are part of the engineering education in Learning and Experience Technology at the University of Southern Denmark (SDU), hence they know programming and they are experienced in developing e-learning applications together with local schools, teachers and pupils. For us it was a good opportunity to perform usability tests and interview them as experienced users, to collect early impressions and constructive feedback about the prototype and on the idea of fables itself. These students represent a significant sample of our user population, as we aim at developing fables as a metaphor for programming games.

The test was organized at our campus and we divided the students in 3 groups, of 4, 3 and 1 students respectively. The student who took the test alone decided to perform the test from home and write reflections by email. The students who took the test in class were gathered as a focus-group [21] and were sitting with their laptop. The test was conducted as a qualitative evaluation, supported by ethnographic observations and semi-structured interviews, supported by content analysis on video recording gathered during the whole test [22]. In analyzing the videos, we focused our attention on the students' facial expressions and interaction with the system, at the same time we looked at what they were doing on their laptops and took notes on the actions that we considered more interesting in relation to how they were editing their fables. The test started with a 5-min presentation of the fables project, the concept of developing a tool to support non-programmers (as for instance teachers and pupils) in creating their own digital games/simulations, and how fables relate to theories from Schön and Simon. After that the participants were given a few tasks to try out with the tool, starting with generating a fable from a textual description, followed by editing and playing back of the same fable; the last of the tasks was to freely expand the fable, customize it, and eventually alter the sequence of the slides. About thirty to forty minutes were used for the tasks. The last step in the test was to conduct a focus-group semi-structured interview, aimed at discussing problems with the current prototype and collect opinions on the idea of fables in general, as well as suggestions circa the areas of applicability of our tool. The interview took ten to fifteen more minutes. Altogether the tests took roughly one hour for each group.

The first group went through the test exactly as describe above, and none of the participants talked until they finished all tasks, and we got very positive feedback from them afterwards. The second group was less focused on the tasks, and the participants were very quick in getting the point of fables, so they immediately started discussing pros and cons of the prototype, as well as brainstorming on the domains in which they would have like to use fables, or in which they could imagine pupils and teachers using them. The last student, who participated asynchronously and remotely, focused on the usability of the editor, but reported having used circa the same time as the participants physically present at the test session.

The test sessions of the first 2 groups were recorded on camera, and the following interviews were also audio recorded, so we could later perform content analysis and cluster the topics of discussion. The student who participated asynchronously also documented his reflections and sent the data to us via email. In such case, data were gathered applying content analysis on their emails.

4.2 Results and Discussion

Analysis of the test results showed 3 categories in the discussion and feedback: domains of applicability, UI issues, and more general reflections circa the concept of fables.

The first domain suggested was English teaching in primary school, as a foreign language; the argument for that was that F4BL3s are multimodal, and the use of visual and text together should support learning associations between words in another language and images representing the real-world objects. Moreover, fables can easily express typical situations, such as a family at the dinner table, talking about food and kitchenware, which are often used when teaching English to pupils. Another domain that was mentioned was natural sciences. Our students imagined a scenario where a pupil shows what she knows about a forest (for example) by making one as a fable, with animals eating, living, reproducing and dying, plants of various kinds, different rooms representing habitats. The playback of the forest fable can be shown to other pupils for reflection or to a teacher for assessment. In this scenario F4BL3s could be used in class as an interactive alternative to sequential presentations with slides. Some of our students from the second group proposed using fables to represent historical events, or everyday situations from history, like for instance Viking raids. In fact, one of the students started making an example of a story in a Viking village with F4BLEs and that in turn led to interesting reflections on the relation among fables and OOP, where classes and objects are often used to represent the state and evolution of real-world situations. Finally, a student thought of groups playing RPG: fables could help creating the plot for a session of an RPG game, the plot can then be explored digitally using the playback page in F4BL3s.

With respect to the user interface, we received various comments. A few student lamented problems with deleting/inserting slides (in the editor page). We had an interesting discussion about rooms and how changes in them are always automatically reflected in all slides, while adding or changing a thing only affects a single slide at the time. We are happy to see these issues emerging, since fables can be seen as semi-structured data, and when reasoning formally on such structures it is common to use *temporal logic*. For instance, in our ping pong example, the author might decide that Alice had a bag with something inside the whole time as she played ping pong with Bob, and it should be possible to add a bag *thing* to the *person* Alice in all slides, i.e. globally, at all times. To us that suggests that fables could offer a visual way to simplify understanding and thinking in terms of temporal logic, for instance in high-school or university Computer Science courses. We were also glad to observe that none of our participants had problems understanding and taking advantage of the palette.

We collected general reflections on fables in a specific category. A student stated that F4BL3s "feels like OOP in many ways, where slides are a bit like objects, but more visual". Another said: "Nice that is all very visual, but it could actually be even more like a mobile app, with everything drag and drop". There was a request to add an export functionality. The argument was that it would be useful to export the fable as a Scratch program, so that children could use it at school; many primary schools in Denmark have sessions of Scratch programming, or similar visual programming languages. A participant in the first group remarked that if fables could be exported towards other programming languages (e.g. C#) our prototype could effectively be used as a prototyping tool for programmers. Interestingly, these comments seem to point at the need to bridge between the activity of designing and programming games, hence we interpret this comment as suggesting that the students grasped the design thinking aspect of our tool. We find this feedback very encouraging; especially in light of the fact that we are considering an application of fables to the description of game mechanics, for rapid development of simple games to be used in local schools. One of the participants in the second group has relatives who are primary school teachers, he confirmed that most teachers (and pupils too) in his experience are familiar with web and android tools like google slides and Microsoft PowerPoint. This is in line with our data showing that in Denmark many primary schools have laptops, tablets, and often iPads, that can be lent to pupils during classes. Therefore, he argued that the F4BL3s web tool might work better for schools if the editor was re-implemented and made more similar existing presentation tools.

5   Conclusion

We are looking at natural ways of expressing behavior to create digital simulations, for primary school teachers and their pupils. Looking at Simon's simulations and Schön's repertoire of exemplars, we propose a novel approach where authors define a particular kind of non-linear story, using both a text description and/or direct manipulation of people, things and rooms. These stories, called fables, represent Schön exemplars. In line with our previous research, teachers and pupils can *transpose* knowledge from a domain by defining a fable, as well as store, share and demonstrate their fables digitally. In fact, without the need of coding, a fable automatically plays back as a digital interactive simulation of a domain. The concept of *transposition* is discussed in [18].

Results from early tests with a web-based prototype (called F4BL3s) are encouraging. Our students could quickly grasp the idea of fables and could reflect on the implications of defining, editing and simulating real-world situations in primary schools. We consider the test results mainly from a usability standpoint, because the participants are engineers, with programming skills and are used to work and even develop e-learning tools. However, we wanted some validation of our tool before starting the actual user-centered development targeted at teachers and pupils.

We expect fables to be usable in various domains, but the participants to our early test spontaneously proposed even more domains and scenarios of use. Similarities between fables and OOP were highlighted, and we were happy to observe that fables enabled participants to engage in temporal thinking, providing a terminology and visual way to discuss changes in people, things and rooms over time.

We concluded that despite presenting issues with the UI and some functionalities, our prototype is already usable enough to be presented to teachers and school children in coming participatory workshops; moreover, we expect the fables should make sense to them, especially if presented starting from examples grounded in a concrete subject or domain. We are currently organizing a series of participatory workshops to be held in spring 2018, involving local school teachers and their classes, to discuss, co-develop and test the next iterations of our prototype of the F4BL3s web application.

References

1. Marchetti, E., Valente, A.: It takes three - re-contextualizing game-based learning among teachers, developers and learners. In: Connoly, T., Boyle, L. (eds.) Proceedings of the European Conference on Games Based Learning, pp. 399–406. Academic Conferences International (2016)
2. Valente, A., Marchetti, E.: Digital game development for kids, mediated by board game inspired paper prototypes. Accepted for publication, IEE: Information Engineering Express, IIAI (2017)
3. Aivaloglou, E., Hermans, F.: How kids code and how we know: an exploratory study on the Scratch repository. In: Proceedings of the 2016 ACM Conference on International Computing Education Research, pp. 53–61. ACM (2016)
4. Simon, H.A.: The sciences of the Artificial. MIT press, Cambridge (1996)
5. Schon, D.A.: The Reflective Practitioner: How Professionals Think in Action. Ashgate, Aldershot (1986)
6. Klein, G.: The fiction of optimization. Gigerenzer, G., Selten, R. (eds.) Bounded Rationality: The Adaptive Toolbox, pp. 103–121, Dahlem Workshop Reports (2001)
7. Sangiorgi, D., Valente, A.: A Distributed Abstract Machine for Safe Ambients. In: Orejas, F., Spirakis, Paul G., van Leeuwen, J. (eds.) ICALP 2001. LNCS, vol. 2076, pp. 408–420. Springer, Heidelberg (2001). https://doi.org/10.1007/3-540-48224-5_34
8. Fowler, M.: Domain-Specific Languages. Pearson Education, Boston (2010)
9. Marchetti, E., Valente, A.: Quiz-R-Us – Re-conceptualizing quizzes to enrich blended learning in occupational therapy study lines. In: The International Conference of Human Computer Interaction, Lecture Notes in Computer Science, Springer (2018, accepted for publications)
10. Cardelli, L.: Abstractions for mobile computation. In: Vitek, J., Jensen, Christian D. (eds.) Secure Internet Programming. LNCS, vol. 1603, pp. 51–94. Springer, Heidelberg (1999). https://doi.org/10.1007/3-540-48749-2_4

11. Love, S., Gkatzidou, V., Conti, A.: Using a rich pictures approach for gathering students and teachers digital education requirements. In: Little, L., Fitton, D., Bell, Beth T., Toth, N. (eds.) Perspectives on HCI Research with Teenagers. HIS, pp. 133–149. Springer, Cham (2016). https://doi.org/10.1007/978-3-319-33450-9_6

12. Valente, A., Marchetti, E.: Development of a Rich Picture editor: a user-centered approach. Int. J. Adv. Intell. Syst. **3**(3, 4), 187–199 (2010)

13. Razzouk, R., Shute, V.: What is design thinking and why is it important? Rev. Educ. Res. **82** (3), 330–348 (2012)

14. Björgvinsson, E., Ehn, P. Hillgren, P.A.: Participatory design and "democratizing innovation." In: Proceedings of the Participatory Design Conference, pp. 41–50. ACM (2010)

15. Königs, K.D., McKenney, S.: Participatory design of (built) learning environments. Euro. J. Educ. Editor. **52**, 247–252 (2017)

16. Möllerup, P.: Simplicity: A Matter of Design. BIS Publishers, Amsterdam (2015)

17. Costikyan, G.: Where stories end and games begin. Game Dev. **7**(9), 44–53 (2000)

18. Marchetti, E., Valente, A.: Learning via game design: from digital to card games and back again. Electron. J. E-learn. **13**(3), 167–180 (2015)

19. Henriksen, D., Mehta, R.: A beautiful mindset: Creative teaching practices in mathematics. J. Math. Educ. **9**(2), 81–89 (2016)

20. Marchetti, E.: If it looks like a duck. Names as shared signifiers for discussing "cuteness" in healthcare robotics. In: The 9th International Conference on Multimodality, University of Southern Denmark, Odense, Denmark (2018, submitted)

21. Preece, J., Sharp, H., Rogers, Y.: Interaction Design. Beyond Human Computer Interaction. Wiley, New York (2015)

22. Krippendorf, K.: Content Analysis. An Introduction to its Methodology. Sage, Thousand Oaks (2004)

An Exploration of Interaction Design Methodologies for Education: Comparing Professional vs. Educational Approaches, and Investigating the Role of Local Design Cultures

Yichen Wu[✉] and Margherita Pillan[✉]

Politecnico di Milano, Via Durando 38/A, 20158 Milan, Italy
{yichen.wu,margherita.pillan}@polimi.it

Abstract. The connected objects, also named as smart devices, are now very popular and influential in our lives; their design is a hot issue for education in universities around the world, notably, in China, where some universities are updating their programs, and are evolving from traditional Industrial Design to Interaction (IxD) and User Experience Design (UX Design). To this respect, we observed a gap between the IxD and UX Design methods as they are presented in most academic literatures, and the design processes employed in the professional activities; we found this gap as evidence not only in China but also in Western countries. In this context, this research aims to study how to effectively include IxD and UX Design methodologies in the programs of Industrial Design academic courses of an art backgrounded university, so to raise the ability of students to design connected objects, while maintaining the skills that are characteristics of the traditional Chinese design schools. In this research, we use China Academy of Art as the experimental environment as it is a typical art backgrounded university, and due to the cooperation with the authors. Our main focus is on the Chinese design system, and we aim at defining education programs for university courses, so to make them coherent with the professional requirements of the IxD related industry. The results produced in our research have a more general interest since some conclusions we achieved can offer hints for a critical thinking and a theoretical contribution about IxD tools and methods.

Keywords: Design education · Design methodology · Interaction design
User experience design · Connected products

1 Introduction

1.1 Connected Objects as a Considerable Design Topic

The connected objects, also named as smart devices or intelligent products, are objects for personal daily use. Nowadays, we habitually use smartphones to realize social interactions, control appliances at a distance and get information; we employ smart

© Springer International Publishing AG, part of Springer Nature 2018
A. Marcus and W. Wang (Eds.): DUXU 2018, LNCS 10919, pp. 127–147, 2018.
https://doi.org/10.1007/978-3-319-91803-7_10

bracelets to monitor our physical health and other smart products to satisfy our needs, to access remote functions and personalized services. These devices have opened a new industrial product field, and they gradually become a daily necessity, modifying the ways we interact with environments, context and people. They are enabling our life into a new age by the application of the Internet of Things (IoT), Artificial Intelligence (AI), and Information Communications Technology (ICT). Undeniably, the smart objects are changing our surroundings in different directions, showing their value in social, economic and innovation sense [1].

By some reference definitions, connected products are material solutions embedded with processors, sensors, software and connectivity that allow data to be exchanged between the product and its environment, manufacturer, operator/user, and with other products and systems [2]. The introduction of connected objects refers to the development of telecom applications; they provide the touch-points of services through the web and the connection with other connected objects [3].

In 2017, Gartner, Inc. forecasted that 8.4 billion connected objects will be in use worldwide in 2017, and will reach 20.4 billion by 2020. Total spending on endpoints and services were supposed to reach almost $2 trillion in 2017. Regionally, Greater China, North America and Western Europe are driving the use of connected things, and the three regions together represent 67% of the overall IoT installed base in 2017 [4].

By another Chinese report by Analysys.cn, the smart object's market of China reached $52.3 billion in 2016 and was expected to reach $63.1 billion by 2017. It is estimated that by 2019, this market will reach the scale of $85.4 billion [5], (Fig. 1).

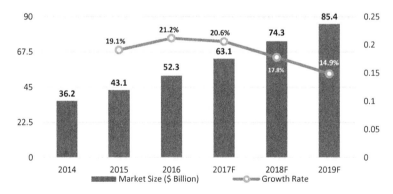

Fig. 1. Chinese smart objects market situation of 2014–2016 and forecast for 2017–2019

In the last decades, China faced a tremendous increase of its production capabilities in several different industrial fields of application and, notably, in the domain of material products including features based on electronics technologies. The analysis of market and crowd-funding platforms shows a flourish of new objects exploiting the properties due to connectivity with the web, which have the potentials to innovate the way of use of traditional objects and to propose new functionalities.

However, in the enormous numbers of the emerging smart/connected objects, only a few between those designed for end-users could be defined as successful from the economic point of view; for instance, until Jan 2018, the success rate for technology-related objects on kickstarter.com is only 19.97%. Furthermore, these data can only be taken as a measure of the interest and attraction aroused by the products, but not as a sign of real success or the quality of the user experience.

A number of different potential factors can be considered as the reasons why of the very high failure rate evidenced for connected products as they are presented on crowdfunding platforms. Most of the so called smart objects present new features, but quite often it is very difficult to predict if the users will consider them as suitable and convenient; furthermore, very often the introduction of electronic components in traditional objects implies critical issues (such as fragility, complex maintenance, need of power supply, compatibility with other technological solutions, high costs compared to traditional products, service/system requirements,...) and the new products require the users to make a cognitive effort to understand the innovative functionalities and the way to access them.

From the point of view of industrial design education, the project of connected objects requires specific skills and cognition in order to understand the functional potentials of digital technologies, to deal with the constraints they impose in the project of physical solutions, to manage the design interactive features and to optimize them with respect to the user experience.

Our research aims to devise an ideal education program for Chinese university students of Industrial Design courses so to provide them with the design methods and tools apt to design connected objects.

During the last decades, a very ample bibliography on this topic have been made available, and our research is deeply grounded in this literature; on the other hand, as the design of interactive and connected products is still a complex and error-prone task, we adopted a critical approach toward literature, and we also performed a research focused on the assessment of professional activities and praxis.

As educators, we believe in the importance of providing the students with tools and methods capable of supporting them in a long-lasting career and design activity. The introduction of Interaction Design methods and UX Design knowledge in education programs produce, as a consequence, a reduction of time and energies dedicated to the knowledge, contents and skills of traditional Industrial Design. On the other hand, in several design schools, we can observe a reduction of the importance attributed to material/physical design to the advantage of non-tangible and non-material values; the international design communities progressively have paid more interest and emphasis to the non-material dimensions of value, and have focused more on the aesthetics of activities, on the act of use [6], on the social and interactive elements of experience.

For these reasons, the introduction of knowledge from the fields of Interaction Design and Design for Experience in education programs is today very important to allow young designers to face the new design challenges; on the other hand, we do believe that material and non-material components of the designed solutions should be considered within a holistic approach focused on experience; in our opinion, the introduction of new contents and the reduction of traditional ones should be carefully evaluated and not simply carried on following trends. We consider our research as a contribution to this respect. The results reported in this paper are based on several activities and, among others, including:

- mapping of IxD design methods in the literature
- mapping of education programs for Industrial Design and IxD
- interviews with young professional Chinese designers and with senior design professors and professionals
- education experiences in Italy and China.

1.2   Connected Object and Design Education

Design methods are a relevant and important issue related to innovation from both the industrial and the education perspectives. Design methods help designers in framing contexts, in understanding needs, potentials and opportunities; in managing the complexity of constraints and goals of the project process; in planning and managing design activities so to match project goals and client needs [7]. In another word, the suitability of a design method is related to the efficiency and effectiveness of the design results, and to the quality and success of the created solutions.

As the institution for training designers, a design university should be a major platform to connect professional designers and industries with academic design researchers and design educators. The training on design methods and tools in education have a direct impact on the future professional design career of students, and on the outcomes of their design activity. University training should provide tools and techniques used in the professional activity for the local and international contexts, but also critical sense and social awareness about the impact of the design choices forming the professional sense and the ethical conscience of the designers. In our research, we consider the training of designers for the project of connected objects as centred in the intersection of different design domains (Fig. 2). Our research aims to investigate how the education programs at university level should be updated so to meet the new requirements of knowledge for the professional activities of designers in China with the international design context, without losing the Chinese cultural characteristics and values provided by the traditional art training. In this paper, we present some results of the research developed in collaboration by the two authors, a Chinese lecturer and an

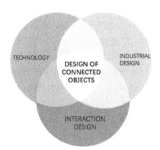

Fig. 2. Our research is at the intersection of design methodology, connected objects and design education

Italian professor, working for two important Design universities in their countries, China Academy of Art (CAA) and Politecnico di Milano (POLIMI).

1.3   Design Issues for the Project of Connected Objects

In the design of traditional material products, the focus of the design process is on form attributes and functional characteristics, but in most cases, functions are steady and consolidated, and innovation is through geometrical features, materials, colours; the innovation of the formal attributes is associated with the generation of new sensorial effects, to new meanings and to the ways functions are embedded into the form. In the design of connected and interactive objects, quite often the functional characteristics of the objects are very innovative, and, actually, design activities and services that are enabled by technological facilities and devices. For this reason, Interaction design methods focus on the user's actions – tasks and goals – and on the modalities of control by interfaces or other solutions; in the design of a new connected object, the design process focuses on motivations, on the cognitive and emotional mechanics and dynamics of user's engagement, and on the reasons why the users should appreciate the service/activity enabled by the product. IxD and UX Design methods propose the use of tools for the project of interactive products including visual representations such as storyboards, mental model maps, customer journeys, and other visual diagrams created for service design. In smart objects, quite often the form has a weak connection with functions or none. In fact, a smart object can be the touch-point for a variety of digital and cloud services, as it happens, for example, with the speaker of Amazon Echo enabling the voice-control of a remote personal agent based on Artificial Intelligence.

In the design of a smart object, the drawings describing the physical appearance of the product must be accompanied by the visualization of the scenarios of use, and on the diagrams describing procedures and flows of actions enabled by the device, with different time scales so to manage best and different modalities of use, including worst and best ones, standard and extreme behaviours. As an instance, a user journey map is a diagram that explores the multiple – visible and invisible - steps taken by users as they engage with the services and functions enabled by a smart object; by drawing activities, designers wonder about the suitability of the activities they enable and manage worst-case analysis, personalization needs, and backend system requirements. In fact, the design of a connected and interactive object is the process of designing user experience and that requires a deep understanding of the real needs from user's perspective, considering contexts, different education, cultural background, expectations and habits. Furthermore, the design of the function requires system representations and service blueprint definition. However, the UX associated to several IoT-based products is in some way off the level expected of mature consumer products [8]. Quite often, innovative products require high investments in service development and communication to make the new objects understood and appreciated; their production, therefore, requires careful strategic planning by the producer.

From another point of view, the design of connected objects is a creative activity aimed at inventing valuable applications of technology so to satisfy the specific need for diverse users; to this respect, products are the physical expressions of the solutions that are substantially non-material and non-tangible, but that require touch point to be accessed. To exploit the potentials of technologies, designers are challenged to invent and envision new scenarios lifestyles and contexts, out of the constraints of present materiality. The invention of innovative smart products can inspire technical development and orient technological innovation; on the other hand, designers inventing new objects should be capable to consider the feasibility of the invented solutions and be aware of the amount of novelty associated to their creations. To do so, a designer should acquire knowledge about the technologies and learn how to cooperate with engineers, so to provide the connective tissue between people and technology; therefore, designers must learn how to investigate what people need and want [9] and develop a social vision of the finalities of the applications of technologies.

Design methodology should support design activities and be adaptable with respect to the social and technical evolutions, so better embrace the changing situations and optimize solutions for human needs and concerns in the evolving contexts.

Finally, we must consider the rapid evolutions of the paradigms of solutions for interactive control of devices: from GUI - Graphical User Interfaces, to the more recent AI-based systems employing voice interaction, we face a continuous change toward more usable products and systems, but it is still impossible to foresee the next generations of smart devices and the kind of design issues that they will impose. The definition of a framework for education in the field of the connected object should consider both material and non-physical dimensions of design. Nonetheless, with the popularity and potentials of the connected objects, the need of designers with specific expertise in this field is an urgent issue for the companies; as such, it became a hot field for design education.

2 The Challenge of Chinese Design Education

2.1 From Industrial Design to IxD in China Academy of Art

Design as a discipline is developing in several different countries with a fast pace that is worth to monitor and analyse. For instance, in China, we count 228 universities offering the Industrial Design programs until 2016 (Network of Science & Education Evaluation in China, 2016), and the number is still rising. Design education programs can be classified into two fields, one referring to science and engineering, and another one founded on arts and humanities; in fact, several art-backgrounded educational institutions founded Industrial Design department since the last decade of 20th century. Our investigation focuses on China Academy of Art (CAA) as a research case, due to academic and education cooperation of the authors.

CAA was founded in 1928, it is a renowned university over the world, beginning with fine arts, and developing a reputation for design these years, after introducing programs related to design in 1986. With the results of the Chinese universities discipline evaluation by Chinese Ministry of Education in 2017, CAA got A+ as the first rank of design discipline with Tsinghua University.

The industrial design curriculum of CAA was founded in 1990, when the Industrial Design was in some way novelty in China education, under the urgency of new professional needs and with little background on local design theories. The Chinese concept of industrial design was defined on the 11th annual meeting of China Association of Industrial Design in 1980; the definition of industrial design was newly revised to mean: it relates to mass-produced products, gives new quality and qualifications to materials, structures, morphology, colour, surface finishing and decoration by training, technical knowledge and visual experience.

Industrial Design education and industry were developed almost simultaneously that time in China. The Bauhaus Academy, founded in 1919, is considered the forerunner of modern design education [10], by the overseas study of the first generation of Industrial Design Chinese experts. Germany was the first country to be studied; with this background, CAA adopted traditional German industrial design methodologies and curriculums, learning from western industrial design system, and developing a successful local interpretation of it. However, in the first decade of its activity, design education in CAA still focused on the form and shape of the products, emphasising the aesthetics point of view as the core and strength of education, coherently with their traditional aesthetic education.

In the late 1970s, though influenced by the international Industrial Design trends, the education programs for the majors promoted by the Ministry of Education in 1979 were named "industrial art design". In 1987, by the revision of the promulgation of the "general university social science undergraduate directory", the Industrial Design was named Industrial Molding Design [11]. From 2002, the Industrial Design Department of CAA started to think about the local culture as a value for product design and, with the foundation of a design school by CAA, "Design of Orientalism" became one of the major education and research theme, for each design department.

In time, between changes and evolutions, a key changing step was the introduction of interaction design studios, indicating a change from traditional product design to the exploration of interactive product design, and from aesthetics of material forms of objects to user experience design. This evolution is oriented to global markets, to the exploitation of traditional Chinese local culture in industrial design, and is a challenge about the suitable education of students so to make them capable of designing both traditional and interactive products, to produce innovation in forms, function and user experience.

As a representative of the art universities, with the single art background, CAA faces a skill-shortage for technology related products. Thus, CAA should evolve the design methods and tools so to include the design of connected objects and better respond to the industry requirements.

2.2 IxD Design Methods and Tools in China Academy of Art

If we make a survey of the existing design literature reporting design principles, methods and tools to design the so called smart or connected products, most references could be framed as western design contributions, being generated in academic or industrial research environments located in Europe and USA, from the pioneering works Norman, "The Design of Everyday Things", to Morgridge, "Designing Interactions", including other cornerstones of IxD the theories: Turner and Benyon, "Designing Interactive Systems: People, Activities, Contexts, Technologies"; Cooper, "About Face"; Saffer, "Designing for Interaction", up to the more recent contributions of Rowland, et al. "Designing Connected Products". On the whole, these references provide a coherent set of knowledge which highlights the importance of conducting user studies; of considering the user experience in its complexity; of designing keeping in mind the emotional and cognitive processes involved in the interaction; of creating mental models so to make explicit the modalities of interaction and the functions, and that give great importance to the prototyping and testing phases.

In the transition from Industrial Design to Interaction Design, design methods and tools applied in CAA were also learned from these western bibliographic references. This is the state of the art; then, in the planning of future design education programs, some questions arise: is the set of knowledge provided by the masters of IxD suitable for academic education in China? Do the design methods and tools proposed by western literature suitable for professional design activity in China? What's the impact of these design methodologies and tools have on Chinese student motivations, skills and cultural preparation? What are the prerequisites of knowledge to obtain an effective education in the field of the IxD? Furthermore, what's the contribution of Chinese design community to the development of a national and international design culture aimed at the development of suitable, sustainable and desirable connected products?

To collect information about these issues, we prepared a questionnaire and collected feedbacks from 132 available subjects from CAA, including 103 graduated students (from less than one year to over five years) and 29 young people still studying in the university (Fig. 3). The questions we asked were in the context of the design methods and tools learned from CAA.

Fig. 3. The number of the samples and the proportion of different graduates

From Fig. 4, we see that how the graduated students consider the knowledge they learned from the university as helpful for their design career; the proportion is scaled up from students of grade two to the five-years graduated; we believe that appreciation of the learned methods increases with the number of design projects participated by the young designers. On the contrary, after working for several years, designers get in touch with new professional methods and tools and prefer them instead of the old ones in the management of their projects. Furthermore, the over five-years graduated refer to education contents provided before the teaching reform since 2012 in CAA.

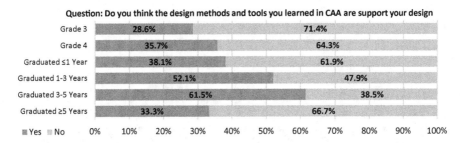

Fig. 4. The proportion of the students' opinion about whether the design methods and tools are useful in their design activities

Figure 5 reports results of the question about which design phase the students think as the most important in a design process. Students realize that User Study is most important indicating that the user experience is becoming the primary concern in the design of innovative products. On another hand, already working as professional express different priorities, and include the concern about user tests. This information can be employed to orient education, so to include user tests as the main teaching.

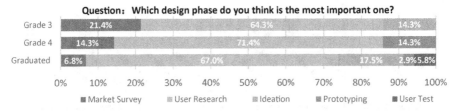

Fig. 5. The proportion of the students' opinion considering the relative importance of design phases.

About the design methods, we compared the most familiar and most useful methods in the student perception. (Figure 6). We can see that the brainstorming is most familiar to students, as well as most useful in their minds; they are also familiar with interviews, case studies and scenarios. The results show differences between familiarity and usefulness. Furthermore, the data show that some methods are considered as helpful but not familiar; the students are still unfamiliar with some methods, such as ethnography and participatory actions.

In the same way, we compared answers about the mastery of tools and their usefulness (Fig. 7), to find the gap between education provided and needs. Through the figure, the highest mastery is on sketching and 3D modelling, as a consequence of the art background of CAA, where design expression is the main educational objectives in the Industrial Design department. However, there is a correlation between the tools the students master better and those they consider as useful, but not a strict coincidence, pointing out the importance of an investigation about the suitability of tools.

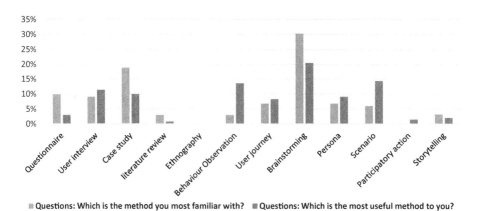

Fig. 6. Most familiar and most useful design methods of the students

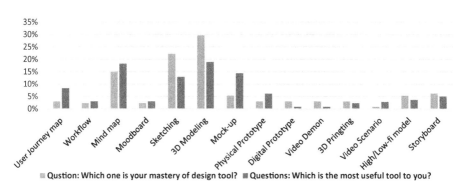

Fig. 7. The comparison between mastery and most useful of the tools to the students

2.3 Investigating the Gap Between IxD, UX Design Methods and Tools in Education and Industry Practice

In addition to the questionnaires given to the students, we carried out interviews with professional young designers working in the field of innovative product design and, notably, on the design of connected objects.

We involved in the survey 42 subjects, including designers working for six kinds of companies, from start-ups to major internet company such as Alibaba. We report here some of the collected information and some comments. And we report the numbers of questionnaires we delivered and the main activity of the interviewed subjects. We asked the interviewed people to refer to one finished project, and we collected information about:

- The approaches they used for user research;
- The main design tools employed in the project;
- The main methods adopted in the project.

The question about the steps the designers most focus on (Fig. 8), we see that the Internet companies indicate A/B tests as important; for start-ups, while every design phase is considered as important, prototyping and testing are the most important ones. Furthermore, private enterprises and design companies focus on the same phases and, with the due distinctions, they adopt the same tools.

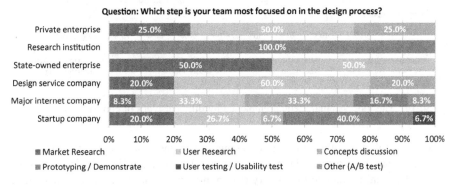

Fig. 8. The design phase that is the main focus for diverse companies

About the survey on tools employed in the design process (Fig. 9), similarly to what emerged in the previous question (Fig. 8), start-ups use several tools including Personas which is instead not as popular in other companies as we expected. User journey maps are a popular tool among these companies as well as 3D modelling.

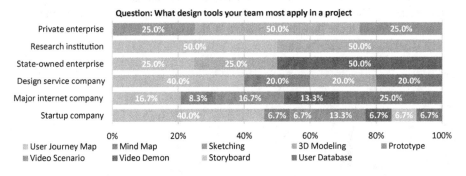

Fig. 9. The most popular design tools applied in diverse companies

Collecting data through the questionnaire, we could verify an inhomogeneous employ of terminologies to indicate design activities and, notably, an uneven interpretation of "ethnography" as an activity to accompany and prepare the innovative design. From Fig. 10 we can see that relatively little resources are dedicated to it; as it emerged from interviews, only major Internet companies use "ethnography" and participatory action. Meanwhile, the major Internet companies prefer to use diverse methods to conduct design.

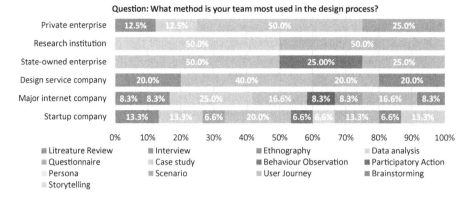

Fig. 10. The most popular method employed by different types of companies in China

We also collected other information showing that the case studies, data collection and analysis are the most popular methods among these companies. What's more, from our investigation it emerged that a very common approach in the design of innovative products is to organize experiments based on developing concepts (rendering) and physical working prototypes to perform evaluation tests and studies, directly involving final users to employ the prototypes or, at least, to express opinions on rendering, so to collect the feedbacks and comments.

We used the collected data to investigate opinions on design methodologies by comparing attitudes of students and professional designers.

From Fig. 11 we can see some phenomena about the adoption and convenience of design methods. The diagram compares case study most popular methods in the professional field, with those that are familiar to students. We can see that in some cases

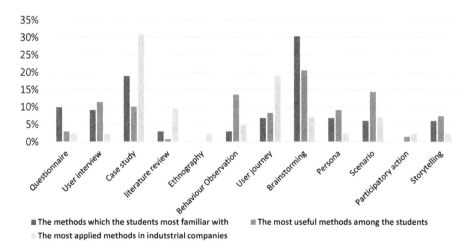

Fig. 11. Design methods: familiarity and usefulness for students in comparison with adoption in industrial companies

students do not perceive as useful as some design tools that are employed in companies. The data give hints about the importance of a better presentation of some design tools to students.

In Fig. 12 we see that the user journey map has the potential to be a suitable tool for education in CAA since there is a gap between the rate attributed to students and its application by professionals. Meanwhile, the video scenarios offer education opportunities for the students in CAA.

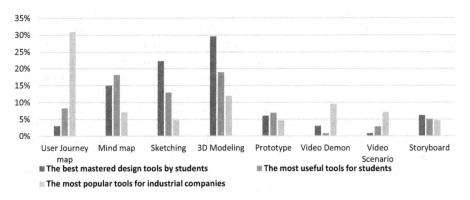

Fig. 12. The comparison among the tools those the students most good at using, the most useful for students and the most popular ones in industrial companies

3   The Experiment of IxD, UX Design Methodologies Exploration

3.1   The Context and Cultural Issues of International Design Educational Experiment

In the last decades, international exchange programs for students and teachers have been vastly encouraged and supported, so producing countless opportunities for collaborations, mutual learning and the creation of main streams of shared knowledge, toward the construction of a global community with no boundaries. However, this doesn't mean that the knowledge learned from the western countries is simply and straightforwardly applied in Chinese academic teaching and in the exertion of the designer's profession. The cultural background, language barriers, different metaphors, and other more ineffable differences make impossible a flat adoption of design methodologies in every context, and we believe that the investigation of the differences developed in the local environment is a source of growth for the international design community. Differences contribute to make every education and design activity very special, and influence the whole didactical process, creating problems but also inspiring situations, stimulating creativity and dismantling old mental frames. As an instance, the basic concepts of "design tools" and "design methods" cannot be given as granted when we translate it from English into a language with a different grammar structure such as Chinese, since some of the terminologies and the related distinctions are defined in Chinese in different ways, and should be redefined when dealing in a multicultural environment involving Chinese designers or students. This is especially true when we deal also with a different disciplinary background, and also with the designers with art background. In IxD, we call as "tools" some conceptual apparatus as Alan Cooper's Personas, while "tools" in common Chinese language is to be thought as a tangible instrument, such as a computer, pen, screwdrivers, not including sketching, persona, scenario, and other basic elements of the design context. Language differences make friction in theoretical conversation about design, introducing involuntary misunderstandings even when all the converser share a common language. More critical, in our experience, is the understanding of some terminologies such as "ethnography" and "empathy", which are in design referred to fields of knowledge, to design methodologies and activities, and to approaches to design for innovation. Empathy supports the design process as design considerations move from rational and practical issues to personal experiences and private contexts [12]. These terms either are not familiar to some Chinese students of design, or they can be interpreted in a very different way from context to context; one reason could be the specific development of Chinese Industrial Design. About design education, most Chinese colleges and universities focus on the basic skills, techniques and knowledge, but have a serious lack of courses on methodology; main focus consists of two parts: one is knowledge and accomplishment, such as craft technology knowledge, mechanics principles, ergonomics, aesthetics, the history of design, etc.; the other is the basis and skills of modelling such as the three-dimensional composition, CAD, renderings and so on [13].

At the same time, there is a gap, in both western and eastern contexts, between the ideal design methods, tools and approaches aimed at innovation as they are taught in universities, and the real activities performed by professional designers in little and large companies. As an instance, in our design activities in collaboration with companies and industries in IxD projects, the time and resources dedicated to preliminary user studies, ethnography and research in the field are very often limited and scarce.

So, in the definition of the contents that should be provided to young design students in China Academy of Art, we found ourselves in the middle of a triangular gap in which extract the set of suitable practical and conceptual knowledge: theoretical IxD and UX Design expertise (with it principles, methods and tools), Chinese traditional industrial design (based on thousand years of Chinese art & craft and on the typical Bauhaus teachings), and modern era professional praxis as it is developed in the China industry system by young designers of innovative products.

3.2   The Survey on the Curriculum in China Academy of Art

In order to produce more knowledge for our research, we performed an education experience in CAA involving students. Before that, we surveyed the curriculum of Industrial Design department in CAA, to analyze the skills and the tools learned by students, so to identify knowledge and skills that can be applied in both Industrial Design and Interaction Design. Here we introduce the survey and present the results with our brief conclusions (Table 1).

Table 1. Used tools of ID and IxD in Industrial Design Department of CAA

	Industrial design		Interaction design
Design & performance	Mechanical drawing Sketching 3D modelling/rendering		
Design & technology	Study models 3D Printing/prototyping		
Design & theory	Literature reading Case study Behavior observation		
Design & professional	Co-creation Process diagrams Role playing	Questionnaire/interviews Prototyping/sketching Brainstorm/mind map Experience map Consumer journey User journey Persona/storyboard/	Scenario Mood board Video demo

From the comparisons, we can observe that there are similar courses for the training on the design skills at performance, techniques and practice, while, at the phase of professional training, there are differences. About the tools, the tables show that students had the experience of using common tools, such as sketching, personas, scenarios and so on. By the comparison of the literature methods and tools in UCD and the current situation in CAA, we found that only half of them are applied in the teaching activities (Table 2).

3.3   An Education Experience in the Design of Connected Objects

Course plan and the practical situation
Our research also included some education experiences and, notably a course in CAA for the students of the Industrial Design program, organized before their graduation final project work. The course involved 26 students, and its object was the design of connected objects as a functional evolution of traditional domestic objects. The entire course lasted eighteen full-time days, and the final delivery was a concept presented through its physical description and a video scenario describing functions and use. We design process refer to IxD literature, and it is reported in Table 3.

With respect to the planned schedule, the survey about existing case-studies and the introduction about connected objects took less time; the user journey analysis was not as smooth as we expected; in the design phase, the definition of functions required an extra day and much revision work with each team.

Table 2. The literature methods and tools in UCD and the current situation of CAA

Typical UCD process	Methods and tools used in a typical UCD process	Actual using ● In use ○ Not use
1. Investigate Vision, goals, objectives		
Identify challeng-es/constraints		
Exist solutions study		
Image	Case study	●
	Mood board	●
User/Audience analysis	User Categories Matrix	○
	Personas	●
	Focus groups	○
	Questionnaires	●
	Expert interviews	○
	Group interview	●
	Individual interviews	●
	In-Context immersion	○
	Task List	●
Task/Purpose analysis	User-Task Matrix	○
	Case study	●
	Function testing	●
	Literature reading	○
Technology analysis	User journey	○
	Scenarios	●
User journey analysis		
	Brief	○
	Card Sorting	○
	Brainstorming	●
	Conceptual/Mental model	●
2. Design	Storyboards, wireframes	●
	Paper prototypes	●
	Shape mockups	●
	Functional prototypes	○
	Participatory/Co-Design	○
	Empathic design	○
	Guidelines reviews	○
3. Evaluation & Test	Usability testing	●
	Interviews	○
	Questionnaires	●
4. Production		

Table 3. The planned schedule and its practical situation

Plan	Course Introduction	Survey of connected objects		Survey of existed cases		User analysis			User journey analysis			Design			Video making		Final exam
Day	1	2	3	4	5	6	7	8	9	10	11	12	13	14	15	16	17	18
Reality	Course Introduction	Survey of connected objects		Survey of existed cases		User analysis		User journey analysis				Design			Video making		Final exam

Methods and tools application in an education experiment

As expected, the research on existing solutions and case studies was carried on by students very efficiently: the Chinese marketplaces offer a very large variety of solutions and products, and a valuable opportunity for students to become acquainted with smart objects (Fig. 13).

Students involved in the course had no previous experience in the field of IxD, and they were not familiar with customer journey analysis. We asked them to produce storyboards as a vivid and intuitive way to describe the interactive and dynamic features of products and to visualize the activities and procedures of their concept since the very begin of the design process. This approach was very effective suitable for the art

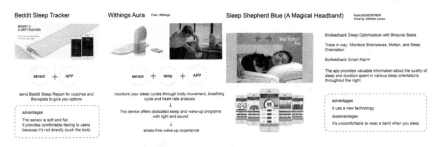

Fig. 13. Case studies from the research of "Sleepod" student team

backgrounded students, due to their ability in sketching and drawing; they created expressive and vivid storyboards to express the use of connected objects (Fig. 14) in just one day. Through the construction of the storytelling, the positive and critical issues related to the interactive features of the products could emerge and be discussed; this helped students in refining and revising the functions and physical characteristics of their concepts.

At the beginning of the design process, we asked the students to produce a creative brief and to consider it as a final agreement about their design goals. We did so to encourage students to become aware of constraints of real design processes, to keep under control the temptation of changing their design proposals, and consider factors affecting design efficiency; this activity was complex for the students with the art background, and it required one more day to improve the briefs. The final brief had to focus mostly on functional features and services, and its use got a positive result for the

Fig. 14. Storyboard (part) of team "IRIGO" and "Streexplore."

students, "It made us work out such a great product in two weeks, usually we should spend four weeks to make a project such as this" was said by one of the students from "Sleepod" team.

Video-scenarios were produced for the final presentation of concepts, and also for preliminary concept evaluation [14]. CAA students had previous experiences in the production of video-storytelling, but they hadn't used or even considered it as a design tool. As a result, due to the artistic background of the students, the presentations produced a variety of languages employed in the presentation of concepts, as they adopted different styles and representation techniques, including not only in real person actions but also different cartoon styles, such as stop-motion animation and low polygon animation (Fig. 15).

The results of the course and the feedbacks

After the course, we discussed the experiment with the teachers in the Industrial Design department, investigating the opportunity to restructure the process of the Interaction Design course, introducing new tools and improving the presentation of others. We also carried out interviews with each student team, and some results are listed here,

Fig. 15. Video scenarios in the course, low polygon animation, stop-motion animation and real person actions

- The biggest difference between this course and others is the design thinking, and we learn something new beyond the fixed approached, some new tools helping us a lot.
- The most useful thing I learned from this course is the arrangement and plan of our design works. It makes me think the design is not only about how to think about the result but also think about the process planning.

- This course helped us start to think about the design process, to make us pay more attention to design methods and tools.

3.4 Learning from Teaching About Design Methodologies

In this education experiment, we tried to understand the impact of the design tools we presented to the students on their capability to manage a design experience. The CAA students could produce new concepts of the connected object in a very short time, and some produced interesting results. Two teams also had produced 3D printing physical prototypes. Their drawing skills compensated the lack of expertise in IxD. Meanwhile, their very strong skills in drawing allowed them to be very effective in the creation of good video-scenarios and prototypes to test concepts and the course provided awareness about the design potentials of their capabilities. The design brief was effective to propose a rational framework for their design activities.

On the whole, we obtained several hints useful in the re-definition of education programs, and also demonstrated the potentials of robust education about drawing.

4 Conclusions

The research we are performing is not based on a statistical data but is effective in revealing phenomena and producing hints for further investigation. Through our discussion and the experiments, we developed the idea that art backgrounded students show an emotional approach to the development of specific solutions and can maintain the focus both on functions and physical forms. With respect to the definition of programs for the students of CAA, we can summarize here some of our findings.

- The creation of international design experiences with teachers coming from other countries is very valuable for Chinese students, and it makes them learning the IxD methods and tools mainly developed by western countries. However, we can learn more by the fast development of China, and there is a knowledge developed by young design professionals and by Internet industries that have a profound influence on the global business. So, we face a challenge on how to reverse this knowledge in education programs.
- Concerning different culture and discipline backgrounds, rational design approaches and emotional art-oriented thinking can rely efficiently on specific tools, for instance, to verify exploit potentials of technologies in innovation. The dedicated literature is effective to learn from science and technology research, while the reference to existing products should be accompanied by critical thinking. While the case study analysis is a key activity in design, it is reductive to rely only on case-study research when aimed at innovation. More attention should be dedicated to blue-sky creative activities.
- With respect to the design expression abilities that are the traditional main contents of art-oriented courses, as in CAA, these abilities show to be very useful also with respect to the design of innovative products since sketching, visually described user journeys, provide the means to produce convincing storyboards; these capabilities

that are straightforward for art students, are suitable for innovation of interaction design approaches. The ability to produce in very short times 3d models and physical prototypes supports an approach based on A-B concept comparisons and tests, that seems to be very convenient for the design profession in China.

- The capability to manage time issues, to reliably plan time-schedule and intermediate deliveries is a very important characteristic of professional designers, and it is not naturally included in the skills of art students. The introduction of design tools such as the creative brief to describe the main features of the object to be designed, its main functional characteristics and innovation values, was quite effective in our experiment and helped the students to understand time and efficiency issues and to indicate possible practical solutions.
- By our research, the gap between the methods and tools applied in professional industry and those included in education programs in China is large; the IxD tools and methods that are applied in Chinese companies are much more than those taught in CAA. A further investigation is, therefore, necessary to understand, for each tool, if its value in education is practical or conceptual, i.e. if it is useful to solve design problems or to introduce design principles. As our final goal is the definition of programs apt to provide young designers with the required skills and theoretical knowledge capable of supporting them in their profession, the analysis of education the suitable education contents must be accompanied to the investigation of real professional activities.

Further development of our research will focus on the how to better foster the Chinese art tradition in the design for innovation of smart, connected objects, to enhance the quality of interaction and user experience.

References

1. Wu, Y., Pillan, M.: From respect to change user behaviour. Research on how to design a next generation of smart home objects from User Experience and Interaction Design. Des. J. **20**(sup1), S3884–S3898 (2017)
2. Kortuem, G., et al.: Smart objects as building blocks for the internet of things. IEEE Internet Comput. **14**(1), 44–51 (2010)
3. Zouganeli, E., Svinnset, I.E.: Connected objects and the internet of things—A paradigm shift. In: International Conference on Photonics in Switching, PS 2009. IEEE (2009)
4. Gartner, Inc.: Gartner Says 8.4 Billion Connected "Things" Will Be in Use in 2017, Up 31 Percent From 2016. https://www.gartner.com/newsroom/id/3598917. Accessed 1 Feb 2018
5. Analysys.: Chinese smart objects industry development special analysis 2017. https://www.analysys.cn/analysis/8/detail/1001082/. Accessed 28 Jan 2018
6. Findeli, A., Bousbaci, R.: L'eclipse de l'object dans les theories du project en design. In: Communication au 6ieme Colloque International et biennale del l'Academie Europeenne de Design EAD – European Academy of Design, Breme (2005)
7. Karjaluoto, E.: The Design Method: A Philosophy and Process for Functional Visual Communication. New Riders (2013)
8. Rowland, C., et al.: Designing Connected Products: UX for the Consumer Internet of Things. O'Reilly Media Inc, Sebastopol (2015)

9. Follett, J.: Designing for Emerging Technologies: UX for Genomics, Robotics, and the Internet of Things. O'Reilly Media Inc, Sebastopol (2014)
10. Du, S.X., Liu, B., Zhang, Y., Lu, J.X.: A Comparative Study of Industrial Design Education at domestic and overseas. Chin. Digit. Educ. **2**, 38–43 (2010)
11. He, X.Y.: The initial stage of Chinese Industrial Design education. Innov. Des. **5**, 11–15 (2010)
12. Kouprie, M., Visser, F.S.: A framework for empathy in design: stepping into and out of the user's life. J. Eng. Des. **20**(5), 437–448 (2009)
13. Liu, G.Z.: Design Methodology. China Higher Education Press, Beijing (2011)
14. Pillan, M., Spadafora, M., Vitali, A.A.: Sketching interactive experiences: video scenario to support imagination and co-design. In: DS 81: Proceedings of NordDesign 2014, Espoo, Finland, 27–29th August 2014 (2014)

Reflecting on Industrial Partnered and Project Based Master Course of 'UX Foundation'

Xin Xin[✉], Wei Liu, and Menghan Wu

Beijing Normal University, Beijing, China
xin.xin@bnu.edu.cn

Abstract. This paper describes the reflection from project based course: 'UX Foundation'. A real project from Philips Lighting was integrated in and played a very aggressive role. This is the first time, students teamed up and do a real project from top company in the world. Series reflections have been listed in this paper, such as students got difficulty in defining target user; got unclear logic relationship between methods; lack of research experience and skills; not thorough understanding stakeholder's requirements; got challenge on briefing the presentation. The purpose of reflecting is to make project based course better in near future.

Keywords: User experience design procedure · Design method
Reflection · Logic

1 Introduction

Beijing Normal University (BNU) is running china's first User eXperience (UX) [1, 2, 3, 5] master program in faculty of psychology. Being educated as user experience researcher, the students have different background. As the first design course, 'UX foundation' plays a crucial role in their educational curriculums in their firs year. In order to equip the students with deign thinking and real project experience, the course brought a project from Philips lighting. The goal was to help students learn and practice user research methods and process.

2 Backgrounds

Beijing Normal University, one of the key comprehensive universities in China, is a renowned institution of higher education known for education science as well as other disciplines in the arts and the sciences. Faculty of Psychology is committed to cultivate both innovative research talents and entrepreneurial talents to build a world-class psychology faculty and support the national development.

The huge demand of psychology discipline in China and the rapid development of master of professional have laid solid foundation for the development of Master of Applied Psychology (MAP) in China. UX master program is one of the direction in MAP, and a first interdisciplinary program in BNU. This program is aiming at training for practical personnel. The curriculum is supported by four parts: psychology, design, technology and business (Fig. 1). Students are from various background: psychology (32%), design (7%), economics (10%), engineering (29%), language (7%), medical science (6%), others (9%).

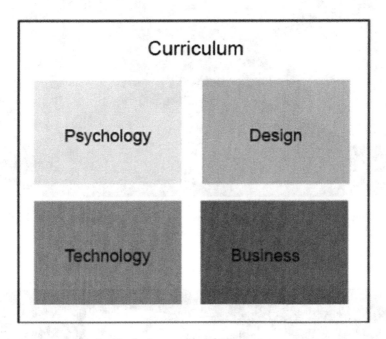

Fig. 1. Curriculum system of UX master program

'UX foundation' is one of the design courses, it has a very important mission to have students have design thinking and knowing well on procedure when they are facing an UX project. Industrial Partners were involved in 'UX foundation' to equip students with UX theory while gaining practical experience in a real project setting, which would provide students with great opportunities to learn and practice in the real world.

Philips is the number one company in lighting globally. The consumer luminaire business entered China few years ago and has been growing rapidly. Philips believes the key in winning the market is through better products and services, which start with innovation.

After a great effort made by the teaching team, Philips decided to set up a project based on low resolution lighting.

3   Approach

3.1   Requirements

69 students were divided into 12 groups, 5–6 students with different background worked together on a design brief assigned by Philips. The project is focus on designing interactive lighting experience with low-resolution facade through mobile

Fig. 2. Lighting reacts to people's movements in the Interference light tunnel in Kolding, Denmark. [10]

Fig. 3. iRiS uses live video to allow people to interact with a media façade [10]

social media. Philips provided project requirement in two key aspects: base on low-resolution technology, interaction controlled by mobile devices, including mobile phone, smart watch, pad and so on. Philips has done many projects in China market, but seldom of them are interactive lighting. Philips want to explore more context, which could utilize low-resolution technology. For example, lighting could reacts to people's movements in the Interference light tunnel in Kolding, Denmark (Fig. 2). Another example is iRiS uses live video to allow people to interact with a media facade (Fig. 3).

3.2 Analysis

Teaching team refined the requirements in four elements (Fig. 3):

- Medium: Mobile device. It emphasized by Philip, as mobile devices are common in people's daily life. Philip wants to explore interaction between personal devices and low-resolution interface.
- Solution: Interactive design. Interactive design can make people engage in interface, there would be more funny and interesting way to solve relation ‘between people and technology.
- Technic limit: Low-Resolution technology. It is suitable for big interfaces for example the façade on building.
- Context [4]. Students should explore users' need in certain context, context and target user must be clear.

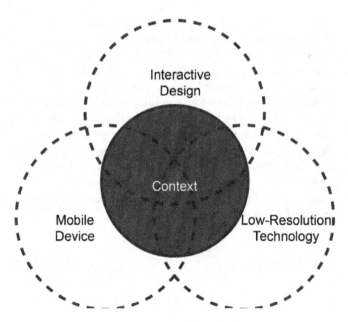

Fig. 4. Four elements in project

Teaching team also clarified the title into goals and research questions to fit the requirements from Philips. These research questions could help students understand the context lucidly:

- What are the motivations, triggers, and insights for interacting with low resolution lighting media? What are the different user segments and user needs, and why?
- What are the main interaction styles between mobile-phone and low-resolution facade? Evaluate various current media, identify the pros and cons.
- What are the best contexts to use Philips low resolution interactive lighting media facade? What are the specific scenarios, and why?
- Given all the previous research and background, what types of interaction styles and functionalities would be designed to create or enhance UX, and why?

4   Settings

This project continued 45 days, although it is an only four-day course. Both teachers in BNU, coordinators from Philips and students paid a lot of time extracurricular. Teaching team were set up by two teachers and 3 senior student assistants. Coordinator team were set up by 3 scientists from developing department in Philips Lighting.

Teaching team designed the procedure before the kick-off meeting, taught the research method on the class, students did project work outside class. Teaching team also set up review time for each group every week, so that make sure each group have right direction and advised students.

Philips experts regularly join the course online and face to face, attend presentation sessions, and provide feedbacks, in order to make sure the end results can provide Philips with key designs and growth opportunities.

To make this industry based project more feasibility, teaching team designed the whole procedure for students, as this was the first time they did an UX project. Basically, the procedure in this project followed a design process, the core process was to find user's needs, transfer them into design opportunities, and finally solve these opportunities via low-resolution technic. This was the first time students discovered the problem and solved the problem for other people. The procedure went through four main stages: defining, context research, analysis and design. And there were many iterations in the process. Teaching team chose basic user research method to be used in this project to guide students. Series of research methods, design methods and business methods were used, such as observing, interviews, collages, user journey map, story boards, logic map and so on (Fig. 4).

5 Findings

As UX is interdisciplinary, cooperation is more important in team working, students with psychological background know research methods well, students with design background know process and visualization well, students with technical background know technology well, and students with economical background are doing well with data analysis and business model. But this was the first time they faced all these aspects simultaneously, they met many barriers during this project (Fig. 5).

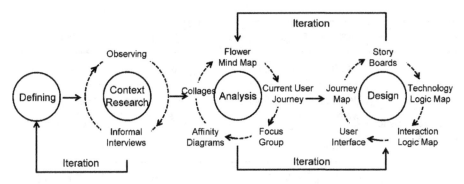

Fig. 5. Process of project

5.1 Difficult to Define a Target User

The first barrier they met was how to define a user. Philips gave a very broad target user group: young people. Students needed to narrow it down in a subdivision group. (Table 1).

Teaching team found there were three problems in this procedure:

- Most of target users were defined by brainstorming but not from desk research and context research. Because they didn't do enough iteration between defining and context research. Another reason is they did a lot document investigation on technic but less on anthropology and sociology, they paid too much attention on technic, but ignored people in the context.
- Exact age was needed in defining target user, but we can see from Table 1, 3 out of 12 groups didn't have it defined. Young people is a large target group, different age group has different lifestyle and experience. There's one group set age group, but didn't narrow down the characteristic, this team had a blurred user, the final plan was normal and had unclear core function, compared to the other group.
- It's better set a rough context when defining target user. Such as Group 5, they set airport as the main context and focused on people who were waiting for flight for a long time. Target user had very clear demand and easy to continue the analysis and design process.

Table 1. Target user defining in 12 groups

	Group 1	Group 2	Group 3	Group 4
Age	28-35 & 4-6	22-25		23-32
Characteristic	Parents and Preschool children	Students in master of applied psychology	Boys in love	
	Group 5	**Group 6**	**Group 7**	**Group 8**
Age	18-30	17-23	16 - 30	16-24
Characteristic	People have waited for the plane for over an hour.	Sociable	Fashionable lifestyle	Seeking for Entertainment
	Group 9	**Group 10**	**Group 11**	**Group 12**
Age			Post 95's	22-30
Characteristic	Business personage	Interns	Road Nerd	Female

5.2   Difficult to Understand Logic Between Methods

This was a challenge for students to use so many methods in one project. Teaching team also had mission of passing on knowledge. Either theory or practice is important in this course. Except method teaching, the best way to let student realize the relationship between methods is learning by doing [6]. Every step is based on the previous result. And any result could find support from desk research and theory.

For example, after passing on the method to do focus group and survey, students had been equipped with basic skills. But they couldn't handle well that the purpose for focus group is to expand interaction opportunities with lighting as qualitative research, and survey would check and verify the result from focus group. Only when they made a mistake, then they could understand why they should use such method, and what they want to get from this method.

5.3   Lack of Research Experience and Skills

Insight is very important for UX research [7], but capability of insight need a lot of experience. For the students from psychology, they have ample experience on psychology method, they might have known interview, questionnaire, observing very well, but usually they follow the procedure step by step. Teaching team found they were absent on sharp insight and find out the motivation behind the behavior. Without a sharp insight and looking back the behavior, they could not dig user's actual demand.

5.4   Not Thorough Understanding Stakeholder's Requirements

In this project, teaching team refined four key elements: Mobile device, Interactive design, Low-Resolution technology and Context. All the elements were crucial in this project. Beginners are easily immersed in their ideal world, but ignore stakeholder's requirement [8].

Low-resolution is the core requirements in this project, it affected the visualization style, and has special feature on screen showing. Although the low-resolution screen couldn't show fine picture, but it could be equipped very large, like the external facade of building, and easy to make interaction realized. User use mobile device to control or interactive with lighting

Group 4 designed a mosaic game in the context of people getting tired in shopping mall. They designed several functions in their low-resolution screen in the beginning, even battery charge. This function deviated seriously with interactive design. Teaching team found primary cause was inefficient focus group, and had a shallow analyze. That leaded to lack of pain points, to enrich their design scheme, they added so many functions. After several iterations, teaching team finally guided them to settle down the function on image interaction.

5.5   Briefing the Presentation

After 45-day's hard working, every team had a lot of original data and source material. A 20-page's report template had been given to students. An under 30-page power point, a video and an 8-minute's presentation was required for the final report.

Students needed to learn how to show the essence and result instead of narrate process, only key information could be shown in the report. All the data and result should be visualized, the story should be shot in a video in any style. Compressing report, making lo-fi prototype, shooting video and cutting, editing and so on, all this work was full of challenge, students must learn expression skills and software in a rapid way.

6   Discussion

This project-based course had produced 12 schemes; Philip Lighting would implement several results. As the first industry project, there were a lot of imperfect, but it's really valuable for both students and teachers.

6.1   Learning from Each Other and Self-learning Is Very Important

As an interdisciplinary program, students have different background, teaching team couldn't ask all students have same skill in a certain level, students need to learn from each other in the project, so that they could enrich their knowledge and prepare for the next project.

Self-learning is another key capacity, time in the class are always limited, explore knowledge by themselves are required to duly recruit knowledge, skills and follow the new technology.

6.2   Learning by Doing

UX program is project based, aiming at practical cultivation. Theory is a support for the project, so bring these theory into practical is more important for students. Learning by doing is a good way to enhance the understanding and experience the knowledge.

6.3   Technical and Requirement Limitation

All the real project has technical conditions to support feasibility. Stakeholders need to consider company culture, business model, cost and benefit to set up requirement limitation, this is what called stakeholders' demand. Students must fulfil all the requirement to let their design come to real. Teaching team should guide students do project in a right direction.

6.4   Keeping Unobstructed Communication with Stakeholders

To make sure doing the project appropriately, having efficient communication with stakeholders is important. Scientists came to class for kicking off, and regularly reviews happened every two weeks, Philips Lighting gave valuable feedback, from technical and design aspect. After each review, groups decided to continue or do one more iteration in stages. All the scientists came to the final presentation to evaluate designs and judge the team working. This two-week review really pushed this project and made a very pleasant cooperation.

6.5   Reflecting

Students did reflection after the project. The reflection focusses on: Desk research is important; Target user should be defined from desk research, and should be narrowed down; make stage target clear to control the overall progress and make sure everyone engaged in the project; toolkits are new for us, but very useful and efficient, we should use it more; from user's point of view (user empathy) [9] is really doable. Teaching team could learn students demand from reflection, then they could prepare the course much better than last year, to push project based course more operability.

The limitations of this course include the short amount of time, insufficient knowledge on interaction design from the students and lack of Usability evaluation.

7   Conclusion

The course successfully ran, stakeholders got ideas, students got to know the normal procedure and research method, teachers got reflections. We have seen this aggressively result oriented target user. Teaching team's finding will implications for the course for next year and will continue the project based course and promote the students to learn and practice in the master program.

Acknowledgements. We thank all students for their enthusiasm and hard work. We thank Xiaoyan Zhu, Xu Zeng and Caijie Yan for their knowledge. We thank Philips Lighting for trust. We thank faculty of psychology in BNU for their support.

The publication of this research project was supported by the Fundamental Research Funds for the Central Universities (No. 01900-310422110).

References

1. Aprile, W., van der Helm, A.: Interactive technology design at the delft university of technology - a course about how to design interactive products. In: Proceedings E&PDE 2011, London (2011)
2. Crowley, T., Milazzo, P., Baker, E., Forsdick, H., Tomlinson, R.: MMConf: an infrastructure for building shared multimedia applications. In: Proceedings of the 1990 ACM conference on Computer-Supported Cooperative Work, pp. 329–342. ACM Press, New York (1990)
3. Greenberg, S., Marwood, D.: Real time groupware as a distributed system: concurrency control and its effect on the interface. In: Proceedings of the 1994 ACM Conference on Computer Supported Cooperative Work, pp. 207–217. ACM Press, New York (1994)
4. Ljungblad, S., Kotrbova, J., Jacobsson, M., Cramer, H., Niechwiadowicz, K.: Hospital robot at work: something alien or an intelligent colleague? In: Proceedings of the ACM 2012 Conference on Computer Supported Cooperative Work (CSCW). ACM Press, New York (2012)
5. Sanders, L., Stappers, P.J.: Convivial toolbox: generative research for the front end of design, pp. 224–225. BIS Publishers (2013)
6. Dufour, R., DuFour, R., Eaker, R., Many, T.: Learning by Doing, A Handbook for Professional Learning Communities at Work. Solution Tree (2006)
7. Karr, A.: UX research vs. UX design. Interactions **22**(6), 7 (2015)
8. Knote, R., Baraki, H., Söllner, M., Geihs, K., Leimeister, J.M.: From requirement to design patterns for ubiquitous computing applications. In: Proceedings of the 21st European Conference on Pattern Languages of Programs, EuroPlop 2016, July 2016
9. Coulton, P., Huck, J., Hudson-Smith, A.: Designing interactive systems to encourage empathy between users. In: Proceedings of the 2014 Companion Publication on Designing Interactive Systems, DIS Companion 2014. ACM, June 2014
10. Lucero, A., Mason, J., Wiethoff, A., Meerbeek, B., Pihlajaniemi, H., Aliakseyeu, D.: Rethinking our interactions with light. Interactions **23**, 55–59 (2016)

The Collaboration Learning in the Interdisciplinary Workshop Based on Design Thinking: A Learning Outcome Perspective

Jun Xu[⊠], Gang Liu, Sicong Liu, and Raoshan Xu

Nanjing College of Information Technology,
Nanjing, People's Republic of China
xujun@njcit.cn

Abstract. Design thinking has been indicated as an approach to improve innovation abilities by focusing on collaborative learning and working. In the past five years, innovation workshops which combined design thinking and interdisciplinary sprung up in China's colleges. In order to explore an effective teaching strategy and improve the teaching effectiveness in these workshops, researchers made learning outcomes based on the five main parts of design thinking, and performed the collaborative task for students. In past teaching practice, the researchers found that students tended to do what they can; few of them were willing to learn what they can't. In this paper, I focus on proposing four learning outcomes to promote students in the multidisciplinary workshop to learn from each other in performing the task together. The four learning outcomes are: a poster of user research, a storyboard, 3 prototypes and a road show. The paper also answers two questions, (1) How to make learning outcomes to deal with cognitive divergences among interdisciplinary students? (2) How to promote collaboration learning effectiveness in interdisciplinary workshops?

This paper introduces a project in which thirty college students, who came from four programs, performed a smart product design task in interdisciplinary groups. The research has two objectives: to experiment the advantages and disadvantages of four learning outcomes in collaborate learning for four specialties students, to reveal the significance of four learning outcomes at interdisciplinary collaborative learning.

In the interdisciplinary workshop, thirty college students came from design, electronic, machinery and software programs. The students were put into five groups based on different disciplines and performed four learning outcomes, which were a poster of user research, a storyboard, three prototypes and a road show. It took eight days to finish the whole task. At the end of the workshop, the students filled in the questionnaire. The data showed that more than the half students thought the four learning outcomes enhanced their learning interest, and promoted their collaborative learning.

The results obtained in this research summarized the advantages and disadvantages of the four learning outcomes and proposed the significance of these at interdisciplinary workshop. The advantages are these outcomes reduced learning difficulties and divergences as well as shorten the collaboration time. The disadvantages demonstrated can't improve the professional abilities and

© Springer International Publishing AG, part of Springer Nature 2018
A. Marcus and W. Wang (Eds.): DUXU 2018, LNCS 10919, pp. 158–168, 2018.
https://doi.org/10.1007/978-3-319-91803-7_12

interdisciplinary collaboration in deeper level. Next the two significances outcomes were, a. it improved interdisciplinary student collaborative abilities by using 4 learning outcomes, b. it provided a visualization method to reduce the difficulties in collaboration learning and provided a model to make self-reflections.

Keywords: Design thinking · The cooperative learning · Learning outcomes

1 Statement of Problem

In 2015, China State Council issued the "Made in China 2025" circular. It set forth the strategic guideline of innovation-driven basic principles clearly. Improving innovative design capabilities, developing various types of innovative design education and stimulating the enthusiasm and initiative of innovative design became a strategic mission across the society. However, what is taught and how to teach innovative courses in colleges has always been bothered teachers. At present, the total number of innovation and entrepreneurship courses in colleges of China are not enough, there are not many public courses, few specialized courses. There is no gradient curriculum system of innovative education (Zheng 2016). The reason is that our country has a long way to emphases on developing innovative thinking, spirit and theories, but slight practice and skills. Education and industry are out of touch (Yan 2015). Faced with questions from academics and practitioners about the quality of innovative ability of college students, we believe that the cultivation of innovative ability based on curriculum should get rid of the traditional teaching logic which deduced practice from theory, and should be come from the action logic of innovative practice. In short, it is teaching knowledge around practice (Xu 2010).

Design Thinking is a methodology which founded on the behavioral studies of architects, designers, and engineers since the 1960s. It is considered as an innovative methodology based on practice and action. The characteristics of innovative activities include learning in innovation, action oriented, multi-disciplinary team facing real problems, and complicated problems without unique solutions, all of which are in line with the characteristics of design thinking.

Several landmark research findings of design thinking show its core features: (1) The solution to the "wicked problem". This formulation was first put forward in the mid-1960s. Design thinking was considered the solution to the extremely complex and multidimensional problems. In a subsequent study, Buchanan argued that design thinking highly integrates and applies domain knowledge to find non-unique solutions to "difficult problems" (Buchanan 1992). (2) User-centered problem solving process. This feature includes two aspects, people-oriented and problem-solving process. The implementation includes "observation, concept, prototype, test" mode (Simon 1996), the five stages of design thinking of Stanford d. school, "Empathize", "Define", "Ideate", "Prototype", "Test", IDEO Design Thinking Phase, "Inspiration", "Ideate", "Implementing", the three-gear design thinking triangle of thinking at Joseph L. Rotman School of Management of the University of Toronto, "empathy and in-depth user understanding", "conceptual visualization", and "Business Design Strategy" (Carlgren 2016).

(3) Multidisciplinary and cross-disciplinary collaboration. As a solution to complex problems, the design thinking emphases on forming a more comprehensive, integrated and in-depth understanding of the problem through the establishment of cross-disciplinary teams including marketing, product development, information technology and customer service. (4) Iteration. Cross considered that the design activity characterized by rapid generation of satisfactory solutions rather than scientific research aimed at obtaining the best solutions to hypotheses (Cross 1982). "The sooner you fail, the faster your success." What is implied in the iteration is the way in which design thinking iterates (Brown 2011). (5) visualization of the results of each stage. The results of all stages of design thinking require visualization, and IDEO puts forward the notion of "making an idea come true" as an effective way to promote deeper thinking (IDEO 2015).

Introducing design thinking into innovative courses in colleges and reconstructing the course structure and implementation methods not only meet the logical starting point of such course development, but also provide an exploratory path for the course reform.

2 Cooperative Learning and Four Learning Outcomes Based Design Thinking

As an educational approach, cooperative learning aims to organize teaching activities into academic and social learning experiences. It has been shown that Cooperative and interdisciplinary learning better prepares students for work and citizenship by developing higher order cognitive skills such as problem solving, critical thinking, and the ability to see multiple perspectives (Lattuca et al. 2004). It can not only provide work abilities training at the capstone level, but at freshman level classes. (Fu 2017)

It has five essential elements, which are positive interdependence, individual and group accountability, promoted interaction, small group skills, group processing. A research conclusion from a literature review showed the context and practices of Cooperative are substantial elements for innovation and open science (Ramírez 2017). From design thinking perspective, learning outcome is a key in teaching and learning practices. In order to arouse the learning motivation of student collaboration, learning activities such as user research, briefing design, brainstorming, storyboard design, team reporting and product roadshow are designed to be completed by each group. In addition, based on 5 steps of design thinking, four key learning outcomes were proposed, that is "a poster of user research", "a storyboard", "3 prototypes" and "a road show".

The poster of user research included photos of the field trip, 3 pain points and 3 solutions. The whole workshop has one story board and prototype in each iteration. At the end of workshop, a roadshow provides a chance for students to present and exhibit their whole works.

3   Collaboration Learning Activities Sequences and Implementation

Collaboration learning is based on a certain learning philosophy or theory, in order to achieve a learning goal, learning activities framework and procedures. The content of collaboration learning is organized according to five aspects of design thinking, "empathy", "define", "Ideate", "prototype", "test" and "reflection". The nonlinear characteristic of design thinking is embodied in the framework design of collaboration learning in three iterations (Fig. 1).

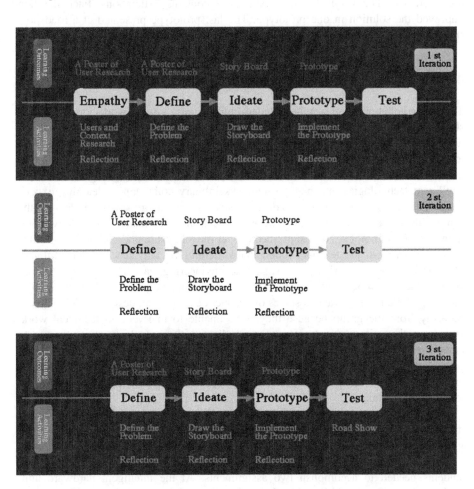

Fig. 1. The layout of collaboration learning based on design thinking

Figure 1 shows the respective positioning and tasks of collaboration learning clearly. In order to deal with divergences which are come from different thinking pattern, knowledge and skills of different discipline students, tutors group developed assignments which students can work together. At the first two parts "empathy" and "define problem" sections, each group completed the user research and context research, determined pain points and solutions. Though students have different thinking patterns and knowledge backgrounds, all of them can work together for the first learning outcomes. In these two part, teachers provide a learning layout and a templet to reduce the difficulties in implementing the learning outcomes, especially for the students who came from design programs. At "creativity" part, students use d story board to tell the story of their product usage. At the last two parts, "prototype" and "test", students use variety of tools and equipment to make prototype and test it by the user feedback. The whole learning experience contains 3 iterations. Each iteration improved the solution in one prototype. The last prototype presented at a roadshow showing the whole process and the usage of the prototype.

4   Details of Learning and Teaching Implementation

The whole collaboration learning included four lectures, a 8-day workshop and a road show. Thirty college sophomores came from five specialties, which were art and design, electronic information engineering, communications engineering, mechatronics, and software engineering. They mixed into five groups. The art design and engineering students numbers ratio was 1: 2. They had mastered designing methods and intelligent technologies, but had no multi-disciplinary collaboration learning experiences. The task of workshop was to design a smart green energy-saving product for the campus they lived. Five instructors were the electronic information technology, communications technology, art design, mechanical model design and architecture. In this lesson preparation, the teachers found that different specialty teachers had different thinking models and working habits, such as engineering teachers were used to considering the technology route, a certain technology or an equipment at the beginngin of the task. While in the advanced stages of product development, design teachers tend to be away from the group because they were unable to intervene in technical work. Based on these issues, instructors group adjusted their teaching arrangements to emphasize less-technical thinking in the "Defining" part, and provided a framework of presentation and roadshow documentation for art design students during "Prototype" and "Test" part. These can promote students learn from each other and improve the learning effectiveness.

The workshop provided five contexts to research. Each group picks one of five by drawing lots, which is library, student dormitory, student canteen, office building and gymnasium.

Prep class had two parts, the basic intelligent hardware and junior design. The students needed to accomplish two assignments. At the intelligent hardware unit, students learn the working principle of intelligent hardware, visual programming methods, sensor types and so on. And at the junior design unit, students learned user-center design concept and the design method from WHAT, HOW and WHY aspect. Students had two tasks in this session: (1) Using visual programming tools, intelligent hardware and sensors to make a flow lamp, then draw a technical roadmap of this lamp. (2) Analyze a product from WHAT, HOW and WHY aspect.

The three iterations in product design students accomplished the learning outcomes three times. In the first iteration, four learning outcomes emphasized on using a poster to show the user research, propose the solution, then used the fist prototype to implement ideas. As there is a general lack of user-based research in engineering backgrounds students, a course survey, reporting exercise, and study materials are provided to students on the campus. After reporting the feedback, students conduct research independently and collect and analyze data according to the requirements of the next day's report and make a poster (Fig. 2).

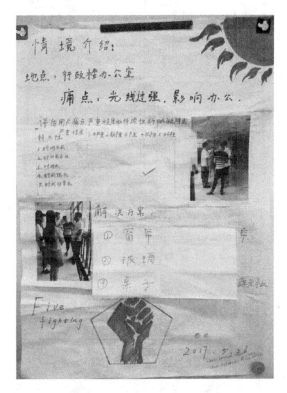

Fig. 2. The first iteration poster

It the second iteration, the prototype is the emphasis on the four learning outcomes. It includes advanced solution and technology. Take the "student dormitories" group as an example. After the first proposal is denied, students think deeply about two issues. One is the user behavior in the student dormitories. What are the pain points? The second is to expand their understanding of the "green", which is physical energy and bio-energy low-consumption lifestyle. After the second scenario research, the team redefines the problem as a solution to the "Understanding the habits of using lamps in the students dormitory." Students draw the storyboard again to show their solution. (Figure 3) Than the team report on the second prototype through a combination of performance and prototype display. This demonstration of learning outcomes facilitates cross-disciplinary collaboration among team members and is of great benefit to the advancement of technologies and solutions in the second iteration.

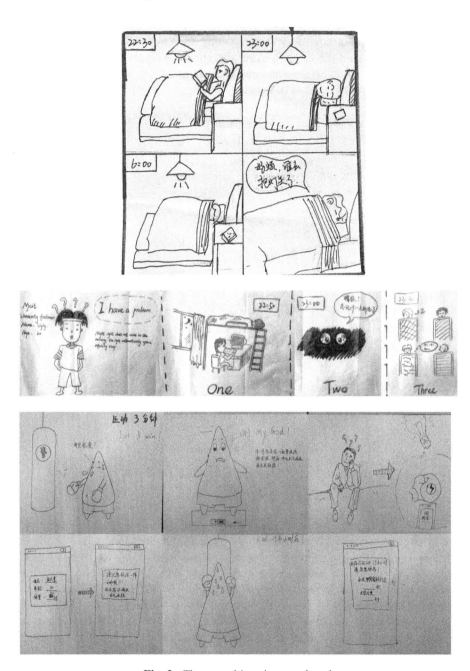

Fig. 3. The second iteration storyboard

Fig. 4. The road show

At the last day of the workshop, each group presented their final prototype in a roadshow (Fig. 4). In order to structure the whole work, tutors group provides a presentation templet for the students, which includes "Introduction of group members", "Brainstorm", "Context research", "Pain point", "Storyboard", "3 prototypes", "Technology road map"and "Posters".

5   Pros and Cons of the Collaboration Learning by Using Four Learning Outcomes in the Interdisciplinary Workshops

After completed of the 8-day workshop, the instructors group made a questionnaire to survey the effective of collaborate learning in interdisciplinary study. Thirty questionnaires were distributed, thirty were recovered, the recovery rate of 100%, of which 100% of valid. In the survey of "do you accept interdisciplinary studies", the proportion of "more accepted" and "very accepted" reached 76.66%. In the five-star rating scale, the students were surveyed on the usefulness of 9 learning contents: "situational research", "user research", "teamwork", "mind mapping", "design geometry", "product design storyboard", "Arduino technology", "Triz innovation theory", and "Model Processing". The data showed that "user research" was considered the most useful, the proportion of "useful" and "very useful" was 73.3%. The proportion of the second-highest "Product Story Edition" was 56.7%. Data showed that more than half of students thought the four learning outcomes helped them complete the workshop task.

Students were asked to rank the learning activates by effectiveness from high to low. The ten learning activities were "brainstorming in teams", "listening to teacher review groups", "attending lectures" and "group report", "combing product interaction with storyboard", "classmates comments", "displaying product design plan with posters", "context research", "doing user interview" and "writing reflective card". In addition to the last "write reflective card" score was significantly low, the other nine scores were above five points (up to ten points), as shown in Fig. 5.

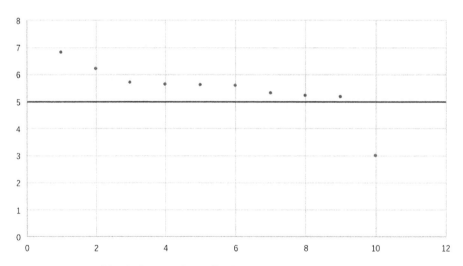

Fig. 5. Scores of the effectiveness of learning activities

All the instructors who we interviewed in the survey considered that the four learning outcomes played a key role in achieving teaching objects. They also thought students' abilities of critical thinking were improved during the creativities from birth to landing in multi-disciplinary learning.

In summary, there were three pros of collaboration learning in the interdisciplinary workshop, which were: a. Improved students' collaborative abilities in using four learning outcomes; b. Provided a visualization method to reduce the difficulties in collaboration learning; c. Provided a model to make self-reflections.

The cons of collaboration learning included two aspects: a. To some extent, learning effectiveness depended on the harmony between the team members; b. It was difficult to improve abilities, technologies and skills deeply in short-term workshop.

6 Conclusion

This paper explored the development of collaboration learning activities by using design thinking in interdisciplinary workshops. The researchers proposed four learning outcomes which were based on the key steps of design thinking, reconstructed the teaching structure, prepared the teaching materials and resources, redesigned learning and teaching activities and implemented it. During the workshop, the researchers made a investigation. The questionnaires and interviews showed that students generally accepted interdisciplinary collaboration. The visualization of the four learning outcomes, which were a poster of user research, a storyboard, 3 prototypes and a road show, improved students' collaborate and self-learning reflection abilities, reduced the difficulty of cross-disciplinary learning. However, it is undeniable that the effectiveness of interdisciplinary collaboration learning relied to some extent on the smooth collaboration among team members. Therefore, how to cultivate a deeper level of professional abilities and inter-disciplinary collaboration across disciplines, how to popularize the teaching mode and improve the coverage and participation are the research directions in the future.

References

Ramírez, M.-S., García-Peñalvo, F.-J.: Co-creation and open innovation: systematic literature review. Comunicar **54**(1) (2017)

Fu, K.: Interdisciplinary learning through design activities uniting fundamentals of engineering curriculum. In: ICED15 (2017)

Miller, P.N.: Is 'design thinking' the new liberal arts? Chron. Higher Educ. (2015)

Carlgren, L., Rauth, I., Elmquist, M.: Framing design thinking: the concept in idea and enactment. Creativity Innov. Manage. **25**, 38–54 (2016)

Huo, X.: Focusing on training Hou Jian innovative educational system. China Higher Educ. **19**, 36–38 (2014)

Jun, X.: A teaching experiment of design thinking based for the innovation course: take DET innovation workshop of nanjing college of information technology for example. Zhuangshi **9** (2017)

An, H.: Innovative education for higher vocational education in the perspective of "All Innovations". Educ. Careers **15**, 81–83 (2016)

Yan, H.: Cultivation of students' creative ability in higher vocational colleges - practice and exploration of "3T" mode. China Vocat. Tech. Educ. **17**, 54–63 (2015)

Yin, B.: Research status and development trend of design thinking. In: Computer Integrated Manufacturing Systems, vol. 19, p. 1166 (2013)

Cross, N.: Designerly ways of knowing: design discipline versus design science. Des. Issues **17**, 49–55 (2001)

Buchanan, R.: Wicked problems in design thinking. Des. Issues **8**, 5–21 (1992)

Simon, H.A.: The Sciences of the Artificial, 5, 61–62,81–101,111. MIT Press, Cambridge (1996)

Cross, N.: Designerly ways of knowing. Des. Stud. **3**(4), 221–227 (1982)

IDEO: Method Cards. https://www.ideo.com/post/method-cards

IDEO: Field Guide to Human-Centered Design

https://dschool.stanford.edu

Jaskiewicz, T.: Prototype-centric explorative interaction design approach. In: Proceeding of 19th International Conference on Human-Computer Interaction, pp. 598–600 (2017)

Dam, R.: What is design thinking and why is it so popular. https://www.interaction-design.org/literature/article/what-is-design-thinking-and-why-is-it-so-popular

Kekan, H.: On maker education and innovation education. Educ. Res. **4**, 12–24 (2016)

Xu, G.: The basic proposition of vocational education curriculum reform in the realization of professional ability. Vocat. Educ. Forum, 4–9 (2010)

Zhang, G.: Positioning and presentation of teaching objectives of integrated vocational education courses. Vocat. Educ. Forum **15**, 76–79 (2013)

d.school: Design Project Guide (2016). https://static1.squarespace.com/static/57c6b79629687fde090a0fdd/t/589ba9321b10e3beb925e044/1486596453538/DESIGN-PROJECT-GUIDE-SEPT-2016-V3.pdf

Wen, Z.: Investigation and analysis of the status quo of innovation and entrepreneurship education in higher vocational colleges. China Vocat. Tech. Educ. (27) (2016)

Brown, T.: Change by Design, 5th edn. Northern Joint Publishing Media (Group) Co., Ltd. Wan Juan Publishing Co., (2011)

Lattuca, L.R., Voight, L.J., Fath, K.Q.: Does interdisciplinarity promote learning? theoretical support and researchable questions. Rev. High. Educ. Fall (2004)

The Advantage of Implementation of Raku Class in Elective Courses at Comprehensive University in China

Bin Zhao[✉]

Traditional Arts and Crafts Department, Arts and Design School,
Beijing Institute of Technology, 5 South Zhongguancun Street, Haidian District,
Beijing, People's Republic of China
253436375@qq.com

Abstract. This paper is to introduce what is Raku and what is the advantage of implementation of Raku class at comprehensive University under interdisciplinary background in China today.

Keywords: Raku · History of Raku · Techniques of Raku
The elective courses · The comprehensive universities of China

1 Introduction

Nowadays, the elective courses of ceramic arts are getting popular at comprehensive University in China because students can easily have the fun of hand-on experience and have a finished ceramic art pieces through this kind of courses. Many students want to get into this type of elective ceramics courses. The conflict between the professional ceramics courses setting and elective courses that students do not have enough time to develop basic skills and this has become obviously in this short study period.

As a kind of fire technique of modern ceramic arts, the making process of Raku is full of the fun, and the final work also presents a unique artistic charm. It presents a unique character which satisfies both the elective ceramics courses setting at comprehensive university and the command of the students in China. Because it has short production cycle to complete quality of works to meet the demand of students who want to quickly get their works. In addition, Raku can be used to produce pottery in the short term, the effect of rich and unique pottery; also can make students participate in the greatest degree in ceramics. The combination of them has not only promoted the extensive and profound ceramic art cultures, but also solved the awkward situation that pottery art encountered of the number of elective courses in Colleges and universities in China.

© Springer International Publishing AG, part of Springer Nature 2018
A. Marcus and W. Wang (Eds.): DUXU 2018, LNCS 10919, pp. 169–183, 2018.
https://doi.org/10.1007/978-3-319-91803-7_13

2   The History of Raku

Raku was come from a type of Japanese pottery, which was traditionally used in Japanese tea ceremonies. Most often in the form of tea bowls. It is traditionally characterized by being hand-shaped rather than thrown. Fairly porous vessels, which result from low firing temperatures, lead glazes and the removal of pieces from the kiln while still glowing hot. In the traditional Japanese process, the fired raku piece is removed from the hot kiln and is allowed to cool in the open air.

In the 16th century, the Japanese tea master Sen Rikyū, was involved with the construction of the Jurakudai[1] and had a tile-maker; named Chōjirō, produce hand-moulded tea bowls for use in the wabi-styled tea ceremony. This technical of made tea bowls root goes back to tri-color glazed ceramics of the Ming Dynasty of China. During the Momoyama period colorful pottery based on this tri-color glazed ceramics came into production in and around Kyoto and Chôjirô was one of the potters practicing such techniques. The old document related to Chôjirô's father, Ameya, initially from China who brought tri-color glazed ceramics techniques from his native country. The oldest ceramic ascribed to Chôjirô is a two-color glazed lion sculpture produced in 1574. His first tea bowl was probably made in 1579. Hideyoshi presented Jokei, Chōjirō's son, with a seal that bore the Chinese character for raku. [1] Raku then became the name of the family that produced the wares. Both the name and the ceramic style have been passed down through the family to the present 15th generation Kichizaemon. The name and the style of ware have become mighty in both Japanese culture and literature [2] (Fig. 1).

In the raku ware tradition, Raku-family members or porters who apprenticed at the head family's studio have been founded branch kilns. After the publication of a manual in the 18th century, raku ware was also made in other studios by other potters or tea practitioners in Kyoto, and around Japan. Raku ware made an important point in the development of Japanese ceramics history because of it was the first ware to use a seal mark and the first to focus on co-operation between maker and patron (Fig. 2).

The familiar technique of placing the ware in a container filled with combustible material is an improved raku practice. Contemporary potters worldwide have modified raku techniques. Raku became popular in western potters with the help of Paul Soldner of American in the late 1950s. American potters remained the normal firing process, heating the pottery quickly to high temperatures and cooling it quickly, but also to make their own style of raku. Warren Gilbertson, who had studied raku in Japan, presented an exhibition of his work at the Chicago Art Institute. He was one of the first to call attention to the making of Japanese raku tea bowls even though his work was largely simulate.

American-style raku is especially the black surface produced by smoking the ware outside the kiln at the end of firing. Other innovations include the quenching of the red-hot vessel in cold water, the production of brilliant and many-colored copper lusters, the forced crackling of the glaze with smoke penetration, the white line halo or ghost image surrounding a black metallic decoration, and the discovery of a copper slip

---

[1] Was a lavish palace constructed at the order of Toyotomi Hideyoshi in Kyoto, Japan.

Fig. 1. Two-color glazed lion, Chôjirô I

Fig. 2. Tea bowl with crane design, raku ware by Ryōnyū (Raku IX) (Source: Encyclopædia Britannica)

that sometimes results in an unusual yellow matte surface. American raku also used shapes rather than the traditional tea bowl. American potters could be more experimental and inventive in making raku than their Japanese counterparts. Furthermore, the speed at which raku could be made allowed spontaneity and opened the way to the creation of new shapes that capitalized on the new freedom from the rigid control of the older utilitarian high-temperature tradition [3] (Fig. 3).

Fig. 3. Raku art works of Paul Soldner (Source: www.paulsoldner.com)

Unlike traditional Japanese raku, which is mainly hand built bowls of modest design; western raku tends to be vibrant in color, and comes in many shapes and sizes. Western raku can be anything from an elegant vase, to an eccentric abstract sculpture. Along some hands build piece, most western potters use throwing wheels while creating their raku pieces [4].

3   The Process of Raku

In the process of learning ceramic art in the west, I have learnt the ceramic art form of Raku, which combines the Eastern and Western cultures, and then mastered the technological essentials of raku after a lot of deep studies and researches. The following that I would like to introduce the process of American style of raku from how to make the clay bodies, glazes and kilns until how to work together to finish the raku firing.

Raku techniques is the most unusual feature, instead of warming and maturing the pottery in a cold kiln, glazed ware is placed in a hot kiln for only about one hour and then removed and forced to cool rapidly at air temperature. The process subjects the pottery to extreme stress and creates unique effects throughout the glaze and, sometimes, in the pottery itself. Because temperature changes are rapid during the raku process, clay bodies used for raku ware must be able to cope with significant thermal stress. The usual way to add strength to the clay body and to reduce thermal expansion is to incorporate a high percentage of talcum, grog, or Aluminum Oxide into the clay body before the pot is formed. I had a test that put the different materials into the Jingdezhen porcelain clay to determine which is best for the thermal shock of raku (Table 1).

As a result, the clay of A, talcum is best material to deal with thermal shock of the Jingdezhen porcelain clay for raku fire. It contributes both mechanical strength, and significantly reduces thermal expansion.

Table 1. Clay bodies added materials test in Jingdezhen porcelain clay

		Jingdezhen porcelain clay
Talcum	A	18%
Grog	B	10%
Aluminum Oxide	C	12%

Actually, people can use any molding techniques or skills to make pottery for raku. People need to pay attention to the connection parts of clay to ensure that they have completely together in the molding process. The works are typically through the biscuit firing temperature (about 800–850°) to ensure that theirs porous and withstand the thermal shock, and to protect the works are not easily broken when they remove from the glowing hot kiln. All the raku works typically glaze fired around 1,000 °C. As the porcelain has long rich tradition in China, there is phenomenon low temperature glazes are not enough used even exclude the of low temperature glazes. On the contrary, many foreign ceramicists are widely used low temperature glazes, and to use them as the prerequisite for raku firing. Although almost any of them can be used in Raku, potters often use specially formulated glazes that "crackle" or craze (present a cracked appearance), because the crazing lines take on a dark color from the carbon with smoke penetration (Table 2).

In theory, any type of kilns can be used for raku firing. It can easily install temperature control equipment for electric kiln, in order to rapidly heat up and keep warm. In the process of firing, it is necessary to open and close the kiln door many times for put in or remove the works, which will cause the heating loss. In fact, using metal pliers to remove hot bodies from an electric kiln has potentially dangerous unless the power is cut off first. The best way is to build a removable kiln for the firing and it will be more convenient for smoking and cooling treatment. In addition, the firing process produces a lot of water vapor and smoke, it is best to raku firing in an outdoor open environment. [5] One aspect that can affect the results is the use of electric versus gas kilns. Electric kilns allow easy temperature control. Gas kilns, which comprise brick or ceramic fibers, can be used in either oxidation or reduction firing. Gas kilns also heat more quickly than electric kilns, but it is more difficult to maintain temperature control [6].

The type and the size of kilns that are used in raku are important in the outcome. Generally the simple self-made outdoor kilns of raku are popular. That kind of kiln is built with about 3 cm thick ceramic fibers, fixation with thick iron wires, rolled into a cylinder. The base is to use firebricks paving a square pedestal and leave two blocks for put two gas-nuzzles in each side of it (Fig. 4).

The construction is more convenient for build an outdoor raku kiln, because of its light and easy handling. The size of the kiln should not big. It is to build a 60 cm high including the cover thickness 13 cm, and diameter of 85 cm to introduce the construction method of the raku (Table 3 and Fig. 5).

First step is to determine the kiln body and the cover size, and use the iron gauze connect a cylinder with a height of about 60 cm and a diameter of about 85 cm. Laying the ceramic fibers inside the cylinder from top and press them until about 15 cm thick. Make the same process for the cover of kiln. Use the electric stove wires for high

Table 2. The elements of Raku glazes analysis

Name of glaze	White Crackle (%)
Chemical components percentage of Raku glaze	Gerstley Borate 65
	Tin Oxide 10
	Nepheline Syenite 15
	Ball Clay 5
	Silica 5

Fig. 4. A simple outdoor raku kiln

Table 3. Materials of building an outdoor raku kiln needs:

1.	Iron gauzes, 700 cm × 60 cm (hole 2 cm or 2.5 cm/thickness 2.5 mm)
2.	Ceramic fibers, 400 cm × 60 cm (thickness 3 cm)
3.	Electric stove wires of high temperature, 400 cm (diameter 2 mm)
4.	Thick iron gauzes, 30 cm (diameter 3 mm)
5.	Thick gloves for each members
6.	3 or 4 Scissors to cut the iron gauzes
7.	Dust masks for each members

temperature to fixed ceramic fibers. In the case of finished paving ceramic fibers, electric stove wires should be cut several parts; each has a length of about 20 cm, and in turn from the inner to the outer of the wall of the cylinder. The electric stove wires fixed on an outer cylinder and wire tight, hide the connector inside, so as they are not hurt hands. Don't forget to make two handles by thick iron gauzes of the kiln in case to remove the kiln in the raku firing procession. In order to make the gas fully burned, to make an opening of 15 cm on the center of the kiln cover (Fig. 6).

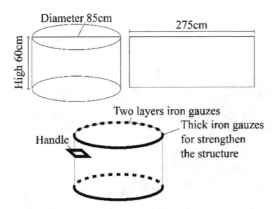

Fig. 5. Sketch map for make an outdoor raku kiln

Fig. 6. Process of make a raku kiln

Use the firebricks to paving a 1-m square pedestal for the kiln. The first layer was carpeted with the firebricks, and the second layers to leave two blocks for put two gas nuzzles in each side of pedestal. In order to reduce the thermal radiation from the kiln body to the ground, we used the kiln pillars to isolate the contact between the kiln body and the ground. The kiln has been finished after operators put the kiln on the bricks and adjusted the position of the gas nozzles (Fig. 7).

It is very necessary to make preparation like ware protective clothing, gloves, and facemask because of high temperature before raku fire. The place of raku firing is better to choose a well-ventilated area, and the water is more convenient. To avoid making mistake, it is better to divide operators the different types of work. Such as some people are in charge of remove the kiln when the temperature were reached, and some in charge of remove the works from the kiln to the chambers, and the other cover the chambers at last.

Fig. 7. Paving the pedestal of an outdoor raku kiln

Take a pottery pot as an example it can be put on any suitable special raku glazes after biscuit firing. This kind of glazes should be fire in the temperature range 900–1000°. However it glazed or not it should carefully fire to the above temperature then holding for a few minutes. If it is a glazed piece, its surface will appear effects like the gloss of melting snow. After waiting for body temperature decrease slightly it can be put into an iron chamber with sawdust, leaves, hairs, pine needles, or other similar combustible substance. Close the iron chamber with cover when it instantaneous burning at this moment. It can cause a strong reduction effect. It also can Use bits of wood or other flammable organic materials such as dead leaves to bury it for reduction reaction. Crack of glazes is a feature raku firing. If you expect this effect, make its more exposure in the air for a few minutes before put the pot into sawdust. As a result, this can increase the effects of glazes crack. The pot is covered up with sawdust sometimes hold in a few minutes, sometimes for an hour even longer until it completely cooling. Immediately put it into the water cooling after take it from the covering. This is to prevent the re-oxidation glaze of the pot. Especially those delicate or closed vessels, it reduces the risk of broken which cooled down in wet sawdust are better than directly cooled in water. When the pot is completely cooled, it can show all colors of glaze surface after cleaning with a metal wire [7] (Fig. 8).

The process is known for its unpredictability, particularly when reduction is forced, and pieces may crack or even explode due to thermal shock. Pots may be returned to the kiln to re-oxidize if firing results do not meet the potter's expectations, although each successive firing has a high chance of weakening the overall structural integrity of the pot. Pots that are exposed to thermal shock many times can break apart in the kiln, as they are removed from the kiln, or when they are in the reduction chamber (Fig. 9).

Raku's unpredictable results and intense color attracts modern potters. Depending on what effect the potters wants, the pottery is either instantly cooled in water, cooled slowly in the open air, or placed in a barrel filled with combustible material, such as newspaper, covered, and allowed to smoke. [8] These patterns and color result from the harsh cooling process and the amount of oxygen that is allowed to reach the pottery.

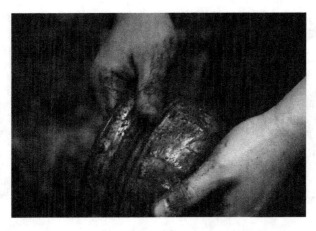

Fig. 8. Wipe ashes and mud with sand to obtain a shining surface

Fig. 9. Reduction process of Raku firing

Water immediately cools the pottery, stopping the chemical reactions of the glaze and fixing the colors. The combustible material results in smoke, which stains the unglazed parts of the pottery black. The amount of oxygen that is allowed during the firing and cooling process affects the resulting color of the glaze and the amount of crackle.

Raku techniques is the most unusual feature: instead of warming and maturing the pottery in a cold kiln, glazed ware is placed in a hot kiln for only about one hour and then removed and forced to cool rapidly at air temperature. The process subjects the pottery to extreme stress and creates unique effects throughout the glaze and, sometimes, in the pottery itself. Reduction firing, in which the hot pottery is placed in a flammable substance to deprive the surface of oxygen, increases the chance aspects and dramatic surface variation of the glaze. Chance and process are the key elements of the raku aesthetic (Fig. 10).

Fig. 10. Process of Raku firing at night

In short, raku has the following characteristics compared with other type of ceramic techniques. The raku works are not vitrified enough it may still absorbed water because of low temperature firing and they are also fragile. The fast reduction reaction make the body absorbing carbon from the burned sawdust not only to present abundant changes of dark tonality to serve as a foil to its glaze but also restore the metallic oxide to pure metal from glaze. Another aspect it also makes the metal oxide in the glaze to be restored into pure metal and assemble with brilliant shining effects on the surface. Because of the rapid cooling, raku firing is easy to produce the crack effect of glaze and is also very good decoration. To mix the low temperature glaze, lead or boron, which is a sort of heavy metal containing poison, is usually blend with other mixtures to reduce the melting point of glaze. Therefore, the raku works cannot be used as food utensils. The time and temperature of reduction of the pot are different, and the combustible organics are also flexible in the iron chamber. They all make the result of raku firing tends to be vibrant, and difficult to imitate.

4   The Application of Raku in Elective Ceramic Courses at Comprehensive Universities in China

In recent years, with the continuous development of Chinese social economy and the improvement of people's living standards, people are paying more and more attention to the protection of intangible cultural heritage. As a traditional Chinese art and cultural category with a long history, ceramic art gradually attracts the attention of people. Moreover, the frequency of using the new-developing digital media is rapid increase of people, which also makes peoples' time and space become narrower and smaller in contact with natural. Ceramic art as a kind of beneficial adjustment and supplement of traditional handicrafts of shows its strong influence gradually.

Under this background, ceramic art practice education has been began to separate from professional ceramic education and gradually enters more and more elective courses of comprehensive universities in China. As an elective course for quality training, these kinds of courses provide opportunities for students whose specializes in other disciplines but they are interest in practical and operational ability in ceramic art and crafts.

However, the practical course of ceramic arts has always been in a marginalized position in the liberal and art category of comprehensive universities. On the one aspect, the administration of universities is eager to acknowledge the status of ceramic art, which has been improved both new-developing art and traditional crafts, as a gimmick to attract students' attention. On the other aspect, the course has deeply troubled by its technological complexity in equipment and personnel settings. At the same time, it as an elective art course full of yearning for a large number of the students from science, liberal and history that have rarely touched in such courses. That lead ceramic art practice course to be embarrassed situation which is many students applied but can only select few of students to access the course (Fig. 11).

Fig. 11. Scenes of the ceramic elective courses in comprehensive university in China

In contrast, most of ceramic art course in foreign countries are establish for students who are in professional occupations and disciplines. There are no phenomena that I have encountered in carrying out ceramic art popularization education in comprehensive universities. For example, a large number of non-ceramic majors students study in elective courses will lead to more waste of materials and energies than professional students. There also exist the problems of disciplines management and so on. They all will increase of teachers' workload and the maintenance of teaching costs.

As I mentioned in previous part of this article, through my practice of raku, I think that raku's unique production and firing process can partly solve the contradictions. It is suitable for carrying out the practice course of ceramic practice at comprehensive universities in China. For example, its requirements of cost for production and firing are lower than other ceramic subjects, so that the range of application of students can scale up. It also could deal with the shortcomings of non-professional students in the aspect of crafts from mastery learning the raku technique. In addition, its equipment is relatively simple and easy to operate, and is benefit for arousing the interest of the students from getting an effective product which is completed fired and has abundant effects very fast.

First of all, raku technique of ceramic art is very suitable for the application of the ceramics practice course in the foundation education because of the limits of the time and the space at comprehensive university.

Raku does not require very high technical level, and it can be made by any forming method or any ceramic techniques to make raku vessel. That conform to the practical conditions of the elective students of comprehensive university who do not have any ceramic art techniques meanwhile they hope to make a pottery from their practical ability. Most of the elective students in comprehensive universities are from majors such as liberal arts or science or engineering. They lack the experience of making ceramics by hands made practice, and do not have much skill for three dimensional design. Most of them hope to grasp the basic skills of making ceramics quickly through short-term training courses to get their works as soon as possible after the class. For example, I had been taught the students from the basic ceramic techniques like throwing and coiling clay to start with their own works. They can use different techniques to make the works, which can reflect the unique style after raku firing. As the students were all first time to make pottery, their works normally thicker than the usual pottery works. In the raku firing, the thicker works has better effects because they could against the thermal shock. That is also one of the reasons the raku firing easily grasped by the beginner of ceramic. Raku also can complete the firing process in a short period of time and students can immediately see the effect. Its rich and unique color effect, which is not only a kind of beautification for the imperfect beginner's defects, but also a powerful assistant to the course of the elective course in the short time and seeing the quick effect.

Secondly, Raku has low requirements for equipment and space conditions. The required equipment and materials of raku: take an example of American Raku kilns; they are generally simple hand-made kilns. Normally are made of fire-resistant ceramics fiber with a thickness of about 3 cm. It is fixed on a coarse mesh wire, rolled or folded into a kiln wall. The base is made of firebricks, and the middle of it is erected the gas nozzle to fire. The main materials is clay, adding some clinker or sagger, applying low temperature glaze fire with low firing temperature, sintering time is also short. These make the raku ceramics elective courses of university have lower investment cost, and also to avoid the environmental requirements of making the best use of everything to avoiding waste. Raku curriculums use simple and practical equipment and open space to attract more students who can get their works in a short time. That is an effective way to coordinate a large number of students with cocka-mamie course arrangement of the elective courses.

Under the premise of all disciplines asking for innovation, ceramic practice teaching should also introduce variety of ceramic techniques. Compared to the high cost, slow effect and non-environmental friendly of "wood fire" and "Salt fire", raku fire has some advantages that are suitable for the application of teaching.

The idea of integrating raku into teaching: The effect of raku works is different from that of Chinese traditional ceramic art works; it may even be an aesthetic way of subverting Chinese traditional ceramic appreciation. Chinese people pursuits the shape of ceramics from rounded and full, regular and symmetry and also the color of the glaze surface feels like jade. The glazes of products which from Yue Kiln, Longquan Kiln, Ru Kiln and Yaozhou Kiln were entire fired though one thousand and three hundred Celsius degrees, and all looked like just take out of the water and desired to drops. Furthermore, raku is a continuation of the Japanese unique contribution for the ceramic arts of worldwide. They use mottled glazes, seemingly random shapes to be harmony with defects and cracks in their low-quality clay. Each pottery of raku seems like just been used for many years, and also it has been broken and old is called "the beauty of wabi-sabi" which come from the Japanese tea ceremony. Just rely on discover and appreciate of the beauty of the vicissitudes of the years which can also be made artificially in raku potteries is not simple. It indeed has opened up a new field of ceramic aesthetics in China. These play a role in good development, demonstration and guidance for the creative thinking of students in various disciplines.

To implement the practice, the teacher needs to guide the students to complete the shape of the form as soon as possible. On the other hand, the teacher should also guide the students to quickly and safely master the skills of raku firing. Therefore, raku is also can practice the students manipulative ability. We had previously described the process of raku with unpredictability. The clay, flame and water of ceramics are interacting with each other in the process of endless changes and effects. In the actual process of operation, students can fully appreciate the happiness of manipulative ability and enjoy the beauty of raku.

We even carried out the practice of combining Raku several times with the elective course of ceramic arts practice at Beijing Institute of Technology in 2017. They were all undergraduate students who came from of different schools of Beijing Institute of Technology include Arts and Design School took part in these elective courses. Also we held a "Raku Workshop" for one time in autumn semester, that cooperation with ceramic artist Powen Liu from the North Carolina State University in the United States. In the Raku workshop, we had taught the students from the basic ceramic techniques like throwing and coiling clay to start with their own works to made two American style Raku kilns until we had raku firing all together at the end of the workshop (Fig. 12).

Fig. 12. Scene of raku workshop in Beijing Institute of Technology, 2017

Get through the raku practice of different majors, I found that most of the students basically reached the effects as the author expected previously. Students were much faster in grasp the process and method of raku, especially interested for the raku firing scenes like to remove the hot pots from the kiln that were unusual atmosphere far from common ceramic firing during process. However, some of the students were still some doubts about the final effects of the raku works. I thought that was still a boundary between different disciplines and professions, and the students were also lack of aesthetic research for ceramic arts. It is required more popularization for aesthetic education of ceramic arts, and to improve the social status for the ceramic arts to contribute the increase of the aesthetic level of the comprehensive universities even for the whole society.

5   The Conclusion

In conclusion, with combining Eastern traditional arts and crafts and Western contemporary ceramic arts, the implementation of raku integrate ceramic arts practice courses at comprehensive universities in China which has significant influences both for the society and education system.

In the aspect of social effect, China has been the largest ceramic country from the ancient times in the world. But ceramic arts and crafts of China have been entered a serious recession since the modern times. In recent years, with the development of the social economy and the improvement of the living standards of the people, ceramic arts has attach importance in category of arts and crafts. The acceptance level of ceramics a sort of handcrafts, and people pay attention to the development of ceramic arts is getting increase. As a useful supplement to Chinese traditional ceramic arts cultures, raku has enriched ceramic views and improved cognition of ceramic arts of people. Ceramic arts education, also belongs to the category of arts and crafts, originally was not popular demand and belonged to marginalize classes in the arts and crafts schools or departments of education system. But in recent years, ceramic arts have been made potential development efforts through all aspects of society. The subject of ceramic arts is indispensable part of arts education, and it is also a useful supplement to training different subjects' students in the comprehensive university. The introduction of raku technique has provided the goal of sustainable development for the elective courses of ceramic arts, and found space and impetus of improvement and innovation for the quality-oriented education at comprehensive universities (Fig. 13).

Fig. 13. A student held her work which just fired from Raku kiln

The prospect of raku technique, combine the advanced teaching and education ideas within the marginal subject of ceramic elective courses, which are applied in the foundation teaching of ceramic arts at comprehensive universities can promote the effect and the status by promoting influence of the liberal and arts colleges in the quality-oriented education. The Raku Workshop that held at the Beijing Institute of Technology will have a good demonstration effects on the ceramic art courses for other comprehensive universities even in some high schools in China. It had been recorded as an enjoyable and beautiful procession from specific documents and exhibitions as example, and generalized to other universities or schools in the nationwide. It will not only solve the practical problems in the quality-oriented education of ceramics arts courses but also economize the materials and energies that are used in ceramic courses. In other words, it indirectly contributes to environmental protection.

References

1. Byers, I.: The Complete Potter: Raku. Series Ed. Emmanuel Cooper, p. 16. B.T. Batsford Ltd., London (1990)
2. The Editors of Encyclopædia Britannica: Raku-ware, December 2017. www.britannica.com/art/raku-ware
3. Soldner, P.: Firing The Raku of American. Ceramic Review, vol. 124 (1990)
4. Jane Malvisi. www.janemalvisi.co.uk. Accessed 05 Nov 2015
5. Zheng, L., Yu, Y., Raku: Ceramic of Jingdezheng, vol. 69, pp. 27–29 (1995)
6. Warshaw, J.: The Practical Potter, a Step-by-step Handbook, a Comprehensive Guide to Ceramics with Step-by-step Projects and Techniques. Hermes House, London (2003)
7. Sun, Z.: Peep at Raku study. J. Nanjing Arts Inst. **06**, 202–204 (2009)
8. Branfman, S.: Raku: A Practical Approach, p. 17. Krause Publications, Iola (2001)

GUI, Visualization and Image Design

Interaction and Animation in Health Infographics: A Study of Graphic Presentation and Content Comprehension

Rafael de Castro Andrade[⊠] and Carla Galvão Spinillo[⊠]

Federal University of Paraná, Curitiba, PR 80060-000, Brazil
ancara@gmail.com, cgspin@gmail.com

Abstract. In the digital environment, newspapers widely use animated and interactive infographics to explain relevant topics such as health information. However, technical features like interaction, animation, and sound can affect readers' comprehension. We address this issue through an analytical and empirical study verifying the effects of animation and interaction on the understanding of health infographics. The procedures are described as follow. A sample of Brazilian newspaper health infographics was analyzed to identify the graphic characteristics of animation, interaction, and presentation of verbal information (written text and audio narration). An infographic representative of the sample was selected to be tested with 50 participants to verify the influence of animation, interaction and verbal presentation of information regarding content understanding, based on the results of the analytical study. The results we found are not conclusive yet, but in this study we identified that the health infographics of the selected sample do not follow the recommendations of prior literature, leading us to question the positive effect of interaction when merged with animation and the negative effect of on-screen text combined with animation or static images.

Keywords: Information graphics · Animation · Interaction

1 Introduction

Infographics is a well-known form of visualization of information, which combines images and texts in a coherent structure [1–3]. It is employed to convey information that is too complex to be represented by text or images only [4], whether explaining facts, processes or how things work. The key aspects of infographics are the arrangement of elements (text, images) in layers of information and the diagrammatic structure that make linear and/or non-linear reading possible [4–6].

Thus, infographic is a graphic representation of information that presents verbal, pictorial and schematic components [2, 4]. The former components regard the use of headings, labels, numbers and captions whether in written or audio text (digital format). The pictorial components regard the use of illustrations, such as drawings, photographs and icons (when in digital format). Finally, the schematic components are those employed to support the verbal and pictorial ones, as for instance, connecting lines, arrows, diagrams, and tables.

© Springer International Publishing AG, part of Springer Nature 2018
A. Marcus and W. Wang (Eds.): DUXU 2018, LNCS 10919, pp. 187–199, 2018.
https://doi.org/10.1007/978-3-319-91803-7_14

When presented in digital form (e.g., online newspaper, e-books, webpages), infographics may make use of technical resources, such as animation, sound, narration and interaction. Such resources are believed to have good acceptance by users [7], promoting content understanding [8, 9], particularly animation. This is considered to facilitate visualization of processes and procedures [10] which are difficult to be shown in static images (e.g., blood circulation), and to reduce cognitive effort [11]. Moreover, combining animation with interaction resources (e.g., play, stop, pause) allows users to focus on particular parts/moments of the animation [11], for instance, by forwarding/backwarding its sequence of content. This may offer users a more immersive viewing/reading experience. In this sense, infographics presenting animation and interaction are of relevance to health communication, as indicated in the study conducted by Arcia et al. [12]. It found positive results in using infographics to communicate information about health treatment and medical procedures.

However, if animation and interaction are over or poorly employed, they may negatively affect understanding and/or cause unpleasant experience to users. This can be perhaps due to drawbacks in the graphic presentation of animation and/or misuse of interaction [8, 10]. Concerning these issues, this paper presents an analytical and empirical study conducted in Brazil on the effects of animation and interaction on understanding newspaper health infographics. A sample of Brazilian newspaper health infographics available in the internet was analysed to identify the graphic characteristics of animation, interaction and presentation of verbal information (written/on screen and audio text/narration). Based upon the results of the analytical study, an infographic representative of sample was selected to be tested with 50 participants to verify the influence of animation, interaction and verbal presentation of information on content understanding. To set the ground, the theoretical rationale of the study is briefly presented next, followed by its methodological procedures, discussion of the results and concluding remarks.

2 Theoretical Background

2.1 Newspaper Animated and Interactive Infographics on Health

Infographics are used in the journalistic field to represent a variety of topics such as entertainment, economics, politics, and health. In Brazil, online newspapers have an important role in communication as a source of reliable information to people. According to a research on Brazilian media communication conducted by the federal government, six out of ten people trust newspaper information [13]. Thus, newspaper may be an effective means to communicated health information to people. Online/digital newspaper infographics can then, aid health education, strengthening preventive actions, mainly in the field of public health [14]. This may prevent unsafe behaviour such as self-medication, that can put at risk the wellbeing of a population [15, 16].

In online newspaper infographics, animations combined with interactive features is said to promote understanding of dynamic information [9], what is particularly relevant to health communication. Several contents on the health field require the representation of movement, as for instance, to explain how the heart pumps blood through the body. Lowe [17] points out that animations demonstrate movement with greater clarity compared to static images, to which movement is not actually showed, but indicated so as to be inferred by viewers/readers.

Animations can have different communication purposes [18]: decorative, attentional, motivational, presentation and elucidation functions. Most health newspaper infographics employ animation with elucidation function to reveal information that cannot be properly perceived in static images (e.g., how a medicine acts in the immunologic system). On the other hand, decorative function of animation in health infographics is not common. Although the decorative function is intended to make animation more attractive, it should be employed with caution (or even avoided), as it may cause distraction and/or deviance from the content explanation.

Regarding the technical presentation of animation, the following aspects were taken into account by Spinillo [7] in an analytical study on animated procedural pictorial sequences:

- Production techniques: computer-generated 2D and 3D representations, stop-motion (photographs) and video-based animation;
- Cinematographic features: these simulate camera movements (e.g., panning, traveling, zoom in and zoom out); transition of scenes (e.g., fade in/fade out, dry cut); and framing planes (e.g., general plane, close);
- Technical effects: these regard resources to emphasize or reveal details of the image (e.g., transparency, magnifying lens effect).

These aspects can be found in newspaper animated health infographics, such as the use of transparency to show internal views of the human body, and the zoom in to call attention to a particular detail of the represented content. It is worth pointing out that even when technical presentation of animation is appropriate, problems in understanding the content may occur. This can be due to deficiencies in the graphic presentation of contents through animation, such as the choice of pictorial style, the representation of visual emphasis, and poor visual hierarchy of textual and pictorial information [7].

Regarding interaction in newspaper animated infographics, this can occur through [6, 19]: (a) linear narrative control (e.g., forwarding and backwarding buttons, scene/segment selections); (b) content controls (e.g., buttons, tabs and links); (c) multimedia controls (e.g., YouTube, Quick Time, VLC); and (d) sensible objects (e.g., mouse over, clicking, dragging). Interaction in health infographics seems to be an important resource as it gives users control over the animation, what is considered to promote content comprehension [8].

2.2   The Cognitive Theory of Multimedia Learning: An Approach to Interactive Animated Health Infographics

The literature on understanding visual representations of information is considerable [20–22]. However, few aim at explaining cognitive processes when one is reading images together with texts, particularly in dynamic representations of contents, such as animations. Taking this into account, the Cognitive Theory of Multimedia Learning -

CTML proposed by Mayer [23, 24] seems appropriate to discuss animated and interactive health infographics.

The main objective of this theory is to improve understanding through content presentation strategies that allow individuals to make better use of cognitive resources to learn. For that, the CTML advocates the combined use of images and words to optimize information processing. The theory is grounded on previous research on information processing models and on learning [25–30], particularly on the Dual Coding Theory [27]. Accordingly, the CTML [24] is based upon the following:

1. The dual channel (visual and auditory) information processing and recording;
2. Limited capacity of these channels to process information;
3. The construction of knowledge as an active process that involves prior knowledge and newly processed information.

Figure 1 shows Mayer's diagram of the cognitive model of multimedia learning, according to the CTML. It presents the following boxes (from left to right): the multimedia presentation (words and pictures), the sensory memory (ears and eyes), the working memory (where the cognitive process actually occurs), and the long-term memory (prior knowledge). The arrows indicate the process flow and related actions (selecting, organizing and integrating). Accordingly, ears and eyes receive word and picture inputs, which are selected and processed as images and sounds interchangeably. They are then, organized into verbal and/or pictorial models integrating prior knowledge. In this regard, Mayer [24] claims that when someone hears the word "cat" s/he might also form a mental image of a cat. The output of this process is the understanding/learning from multimedia presentations.

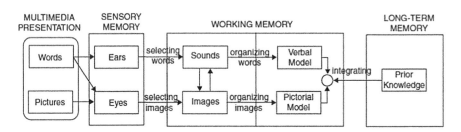

Fig. 1. Representation of the processing model of the Cognitive Theory of Multimedia Learning. Source: Mayer [24]

It is important to point out that when verbal information is presented as graphic text (written text), it will be processed as both visual and verbal inputs, what may increase the cognitive demand. In order to prevent cognitive overloading, Mayer [24] proposed a set of principles to optimize the use of cognitive resources in learning from verbal and visual representations (static and dynamic). These principles are intended to balance presentation strategies, releasing cognitive resources so as to promote understanding. The principles are summarized in Table 1.

Table 1. Principles of the Cognitive Theory of Multimedia Learning. Source Mayer [24]

Principle	Description
Coherence	People learn better when extraneous words, pictures, and sounds are excluded rather than included
Signaling	People learn better when cues that highlight the organization of the essential material are added
Redundancy	People learn better from graphics and narration than from graphics, narration, and on-screen text
Spatial contiguity	People learn better when corresponding words and pictures are presented near rather than far from each other on the page or screen
Temporal contiguity	People learn better when corresponding words and pictures are presented simultaneously rather than successively
Segmenting	People learn better when a multimedia lesson is presented in user-paced segments rather than as a continuous unit
Pre-Training	People learn better from a multimedia lesson when they know the names and characteristics of the main concepts
Modality	People learn better from graphics and narration than from animation and on-screen text
Multimedia	People learn better from words and pictures than from words alone
Personalization	People learn better from multimedia lessons when words are in conversational style rather than formal style
Voice	People learn better when the narration in multimedia lessons is spoken in a friendly human voice rather than a machine voice
Image	People do not necessarily learn better from a multimedia lesson when the speaker's image is added to the screen

Since interactive animated health infographics displayed in digital newspapers are multimedia representations of content, they are within the scope of CTML. Therefore, the abovementioned principles are suitable for interactive animated health infographics, whether for designing them or for analysing their communication effectiveness. Thus, the CTML was adopted to the study presented herein, which is explained next.

3   The Analytical Study of Graphic Presentation of Newspaper Interactive Animated Health Infographics

This topic presents the graphic analysis of a sample of 21 interactive animated infographics selected from Brazilian newspaper websites. The selection was conducted in an intentional and non-probabilistic way, following the criteria for inclusion: (a) simultaneous use of verbal, schematic and pictorial components, (b) display animations, interaction resources, and (c) address health related issues (e.g., development or prevention of disease, the body's reactions to chemicals, injuries). This study aimed at identifying the chief characteristics of the sample so as to determine a representative interactive animated health infographic to be tested in the study on comprehension.

The analysis of the sample considered the variables: animation; menus; verbal, pictorial and schematic components; and elements of interaction. Table 2 shows these variables, and Fig. 2 shows an example of a sample analysis according to these variables.

Table 2. Variables analyzed

Variables	Description
Animation	Nature of the animation (elucidative, decorative)
	Framing (general, open, close and close)
	Apparent technique used in graphic representation (2D, 3D and manipulation of photography or video)
	Scene transition (dry, fading, zoom in/zoom out, slide and overlap)
	Visual effects (flash, transparency, spotlight/highlight, magnifying glass and sound)
	Animation support (video and pop-ups)
Menu	Location of the menu in the infographic (integrate or separated of the infographic)
	Modes of graphic representation (verbal, schematic and pictorial elements)
	Display mode (apparent or hidden)
	Reading aids (numbers, arrows, letters and/or sequence indicators)
	Symbolic elements (semantic marks)
Verbal Elements	Aspects of journalistic text (heading, label, caption and number)
	Emphatic elements (typographic resources, color, size and box)
	Sounds (interface feedback, narration, music, sound effect, and onomatopoeia)
Pictorial/Schematic elements	Emphasis (color and size)
	Views (sectional cut and orthogonal cut)
	Style (photograph, drawing and shadow/silhouette)
Interaction	Occurrence of Interaction (static image, text and animation)
	Interaction elements (narrative controls, video or audio controls, and sensitive objects)

The results of this study were analyzed qualitatively in the light of the Cognitive Theory of Multimedia Learning [24]. This allowed a deeper look at the graphic representation of contents in the interactive animated health infographics of the sample. However, incidence of the variables in the sample was considered to indicate possible graphic trends.

3.1   Main Results and Discussion of the Analytical Study

In general, animation was employed to convey the main health contents of the infographics, drawings style was used to depict the human body and sectional views to show internal parts of the body. The combined use of sectional views and drawings is

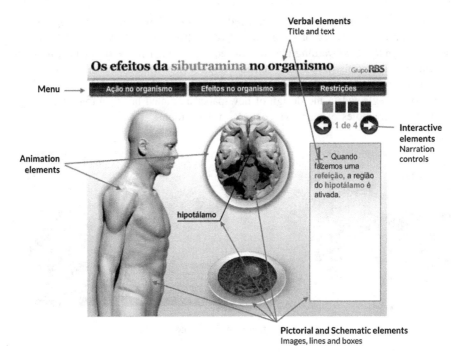

Fig. 2. Example of sample analysis

typical in anatomy illustrations, as those in the medical atlases. The menus were mainly located inside the infographics, showing verbal elements, such as buttons displaying words to indicate different stages of the content of the infographic. The menus also employed schematic elements for narrative control (e.g., arrows, small squares). In addition, schematic elements (lines, arrows) were used to link images to their referring texts (captions, labels). Color was predominantly used to emphasize certain parts of the images/animations to call viewers/users attention.

Most health infographics of the sample presented animation with elucidation function (n = 13), making visible parts/elements which would not be possible for a naked eye. Some infographics (n = 9) also presented animation with decorative function. This may distract viewers from the focus of the explanation [18] and may affect perception and comprehension. In addition, decorative animation does not meet the principle of Coherence of the CTML, which states that irrelevant information should be avoided to promote learning [24].

In general, text was employed predominantly on screen (n = 24) to convey the health contents. Narration occurred in one infographic only, but together with text. This contradicts the Modality and Redundancy principles of the CTML [24]. The former states that narration should be used rather than text on screen, and the latter claims that text together with animation overload cognitive processing as both are visual inputs. Accordingly, the use of on-screen text in animated health infographics may weaken comprehension.

Regarding interaction, it was employed in a limited way in most infographics. There was a predominance of simple narrative controls (n = 12) which only allowed forwarding and/or backwarding the content sequence. Other forms of interaction, such as multimedia controls (n = 2) and sensible objects (n = 6), were hardly employed in the sample. This suggests that the interaction as an aid to learning/understanding [21] seems to be neglected in the design of newspaper animated health infographics. Figure 3 shows examples of narrative controls in the sample.

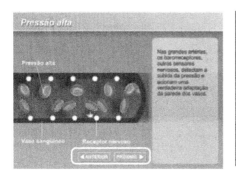 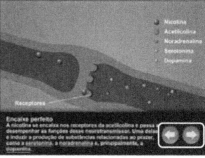

Fig. 3. Narrative Controls in the sample

Based upon the results of the analytical study, an infographic representative of the sample was selected to be tested in the empirical study, which is explained next.

4 The Empirical Study on Comprehension of a Newspaper Health Infographic

As previously mentioned, this study verified the effects of animation, interaction and modes of text presentation (independent variables) on comprehension (dependent variable) of digital newspaper health infographics.

Participants and material
A total of 50 adult participants, male and female, volunteered to this study. Their age ranged from 18 to 25 years old, and their education level was high (graduate and undergraduate). The material tested consisted of the infographic "The effects of sibutramine" (Fig. 4) which was representative of the sample analyzed. It explains the action, effects and restrictions of sibutramine, a controlled prescription drug for obesity treatment.

Five versions of the infographic were developed for testing (Fig. 5): animation and on-screen text (AT); animation, narration and on-screen text (ANT); animation, narration without text (ANWT); interaction, animation and on-screen text (IAT); and interaction, static images and on-screen text (IST).

All versions presented the stages of the "The effects of sibutramine" (Fig. 6): an introduction explaining what the drug is for; the Stage (1) showing where the drug acts

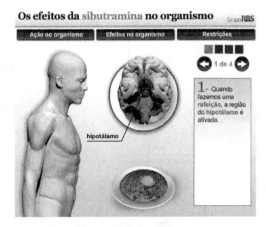

Fig. 4. Infographic "The effects of sibutramine in the body" from the Brazilian online newspaper Zero Hora Source: http://zerohora.clicrbs.com.br/rs/vida-e-estilo/bem-estar/infografico/os-efeitos-ofsibutramine-on-body-35311.html

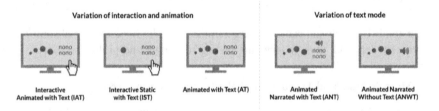

Fig. 5. Versions of the tested infographic

in the body; the Stage (2) explaining what happens in the body and neural system with and without the drug, focusing on the brain centers for hunger and satiety; the Stage (3) showing how these centers are affected by sibutramine and; the Stage (4) explaining the well-being and happiness caused by the drug use.

Procedures
The participants were divided into five independent groups for the testing versions of the infographic. Each participant was asked to view/interact (when pertinent) with the infographic individually and at a time. Afterwards, they are asked to engage in a semi-structured interview about the infographic content. The responses were recorded in video and written notes.

The results were analyzed qualitatively, and numbers were considered to identify trends in the participants' responses. The responses on understanding the infographic content were considered as: Understood (U); Partly Understood (PU), Not Understood or Inadequate Response (NU/IR). When an interview question was not responded by a participant, it was classified as "Not Responded (NR)". To consider an answer as

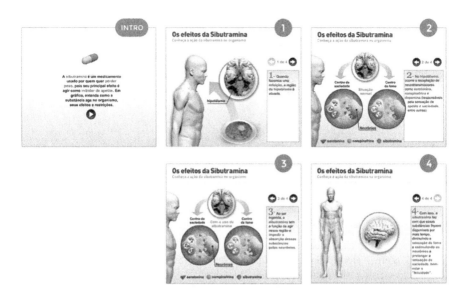

Fig. 6. Stages of the infographic tested

"Understood (U), it should state that sibutramine in the body blocks the absorption of neurotransmitters and, thus, reduces the feeling of hunger and prolongs satiety.

4.1   Main Results and Discussion of the Comprehension Test

A total of 350 responses were provided by the participants, most of them (n = 294) were considered satisfactory, classified as (U) and (PU). By comparing the results across groups, participants who viewed the Animated version (AT) had the highest rate of correct responses (n = 63) and the lowest for not-understanding (n = 7). On the other hand, participants who viewed the Interactive Static version (IST) had the highest rate of responses for not-understanding (n = 16). Table 3 shows the general results.

Table 3. General results

Infographic versions	U	PU	NU/IR	NR
Interactive Animated with text (IAT)	40	14	16	0
Animated with text (AT)	46	17	7	0
Animated Narrated with text (ANT)	44	18	7	1
Animated Narrated Without Text (ANWT)	43	13	12	2
Interactive Static with text (IST)	46	13	11	0
Total	219	75	53	3

The high level of understanding (U and PU) of the Animated version with on-screen text (AT) corroborates the assumption that animation aids to explain abstract/complex contents [4]. For example, participants considered the explanatory animations found in stages 2 and 3, to aid understanding the infographic.

The presence of interaction in IAT and IST versions showed high rates for not understanding (n = 16 and n = 11 respectively). These results seem to oppose studies that indicated the use of interaction enhances understanding [17, 18] as mentioned in the Sect. 2 of this article.

Regarding text presentation modes (on-screen and narration), the results are not in alignment with the Principles of Modality and Redundancy of CTML. The Modality Principle states that narration rather than written text enhances learning when presented together with pictures/animation on screen. However, most participants did not understand the Animated Narrated version Without Text (ANWT), as it presented the highest rates for Not Understood. It is worth mention that this version was visualized about two times by the participants during the test. Regarding the Redundancy Principle, it states that the simultaneous use of narration and text on screen divides attention and may overload the visual channel (written text and animation/images). Thus, narration should again be preferred to written text. Nevertheless, participants' responses may suggest otherwise. The version presenting narration together with on-screen text (ANT) showed a higher level of understanding than the version without on-screen text (ANWT), i.e., narration only. It is worth mentioning that Brazilians are used to read subtitles (on-screen text) in foreign films in television and cinema. This may have influenced their performance. However, as cultural aspects were not investigated, they are beyond the scope of this study.

5   Conclusions and Final Considerations

The qualitative approach adopted to the studies presented herein does not allow generalizations of their results. However, it is possible to draw some conclusions. The outcomes of the analytical study suggest that the Brazilian newspaper health infographics were not in alignment with the principles of the Cognitive Theory of Multimedia Learning [24], particularly the principles of Coherence, Modality and Redundancy. These principles are aimed at improving learning/comprehension of multimedia presentation material.

Nevertheless, when verifying comprehension of the infographic representative of the sample analyzed with Brazilian participants, the results did not fully support the principles of Modality and Redundancy. The versions presenting on-screen text showed better results on comprehension than those without text, except the version in which on-screen text was presented with interaction and animation (IAT). This version showed the lowest rate in comprehension, whereas interaction employed with static images produced the highest rate (IST). These unexpected results may lead to question: (a) the positive effect of interaction employed together with animation; and (b) the negative effect of on-screen text employed together with animation or static images.

Although these results are not conclusive, they indicate the need for further empirical investigation of the effects of animation and interaction on comprehension of newspaper health infographics, particularly regarding the principles of the Cognitive Theory of Multimedia Learning. Moreover, the outcomes could also indicate that cultural aspects may play a part on understanding multimedia material, therefore, worth investigating.

Finally, it is hoped that the outcomes of these studies may contribute to broaden the scope of research on digital newspaper health infographics by considering cognitive aspects of their users/readers from information design perspective.

Acknowledgement. Thanks are due to the volunteers who participated in this study, and to CAPES- Agency of the Ministry of Education of Brazil for a grant to conduct this research.

References

1. De Pablos, J.: Infoperiodismo. Síntesis, Madrid (1999)
2. Lima, R.C.: Análise da infografia jornalística. Master thesis, State University of Rio de Janeiro, Rio de Janeiro (2009)
3. Texeira, T.: Infografia e Jornalismo Conceitos, análises e perspectivas. EDUFBA, Salvador (2010)
4. Lima, R.: O que é infografia jornalística? InfoDesign **12**(1), 111–127 (2015)
5. Fassina, U.: A infografia como recurso comunicacional no processo de aquisição de informação e compreensão de tipografia. Master thesis, State University of Londrina, Londrina (2011)
6. Miranda, F.: Animação e interação na infografia jornalística: Uma abordagem do Design da Informação. Master thesis, Federal University of Paraná, Curitiba (2013)
7. Spinillo, C.G.: Design da Informação em instruções visuais animadas. Curitiba (2010)
8. Tversky, B., Morrison, J., Betrancourt, M.: Animation: can it facilitate? Int. J. Hum. Comput. Stud. **57**, 247–262 (2002)
9. Betrancourt, M.: The animation and interactivity principles in multimedia learning. In: Mayer, R. (ed.) The Cambridge Handbook of Multimedia Learning, pp. 287–296. Cambridge University Press, Cambridge (2005)
10. Höffler, T., Leutner, D.: Instructional animation versus static pictures: a meta-analysis. Learn. Instr. **17**, 722–738 (2007)
11. Lowe, R., Schnotz, W.: A unified view of learning from animated and static graphics. In: Lowe, R., Schnotz, W. (eds.) Learning with Animation. Research Implications for Design, pp. 304–356. Cambridge University Press, New York (2008)
12. Arcia, A., Suero-Tejeda, N., Bales, M.E., Merrill, J.A., Yoon, S., Woollen, J., Bakken, S.: Sometimes more is more: iterative participatory design of infographics for engagement of community members with varying levels of health literacy. J. Am. Med. Inform. Assoc. **23**(1), 174–183 (2016)
13. Brazil Federal Governament: Pesquisa Brasileira de Mídia, Brasília (2016)
14. Macedo, M., Marini, N., Camargo, S., Paz, D., Correia, W., Bueno, C.: Divulgação de saúde na imprensa brasileira: expectativas e ações concretas, http://www.jornalismocientifico.com.br/jornalismocientifico/artigos/jornalismo_saude/artigo5.php
15. Rangel, M.L.: Epidemia e Mídia: sentidos construídos em narrativas jornalísticas. Saúde e Sociedade **12**(2), 5–17 (2003)
16. Luiz, O.C.: Jornalismo científico e risco epidemiológico. Ciência e saúde coletiva **12**(3) (2007). Rio de Janeiro
17. Lowe, R.: Interrogation of a dynamic visualization during learning. Learn. Instr. **14**, 257–274 (2004)

18. Weiss, R., Knowlton, D., Morrison, G.: Principles for using animation in computer-based instruction: theoretical heuristics for effective design. Comput. Hum. Behav. **18**, 465–477 (2002)
19. Cybis, W., Bertiol, A.H., Faust, R.: Ergonomia e usabilidade: conhecimentos, métodos e aplicações. Novatec, São Paulo (2007)
20. Wright, P.: Printed instructions: can research make a difference? In: Zwaga, H., Boersema, T., Hoonhout, H. (eds.) Visual Information for Everyday Use: Design and Research Perspectives, pp. 45–67. Taylor & Francis, London (1999)
21. Ganier, F.: Processing text and pictures in procedural instructions. Inf. Des. J. **10**(2), 143–153 (2001)
22. Maia, T. C.: A representação de dimensões de tempo em instruções visuais e sua relação com imagens mentais de usuários. Master thesis, Federal University of Parana, Curitiba (2008)
23. Mayer, R.: Introduction to multimedia learning. In: Mayer, R. (ed.) The Cambridge Handbook of Multimedia Learning. Cambridge University Press, Cambridge (2005)
24. Mayer, R.: Multimedia Learning. Cambridge University Press, Cambridge (2009)
25. Baddeley, A.D., Hitch, G.: Working memory. In: Psychology of Learning and Motivation, pp. 47–89. Academic Press, New York (1974)
26. Baddeley, A.: Working Memory. Clarendon Press, Oxford (1999)
27. Paivio, A.: Mental Representations: A Dual Coding Approach. Oxford University Press, Oxford (1990)
28. Sweller, J.: Cognitive load during problem solving: effects on learning. Cogn. Sci. **12**, 257–285 (1988)
29. Wittrock, M.: Generative processes of comprehension. Educ. Psychol. **24**, 345–376 (1989)
30. Mayer, R.: Learning strategies for making sense out of expository text: the SOI model for guiding three cognitive processes in knowledge construction. Educ. Psychol. Rev. **8**, 357–371 (1996)

User-Experience-Based Visual Design Study for Carrier Optical Landing-Aid System

Lijun Jiang[1], Yongjie Yao[2], Zhelin Li[1(✉)], Zhen Liu[1], Simin Cao[1], and Zhiyong Xiong[1]

[1] School of Design, South China University of Technology, Guangzhou 510060, People's Republic of China
zhelinli@scut.edu.cn
[2] The Naval Medical Research Institute, Shanghai 200433, People's Republic of China

Abstract. The design idea of Improved Carrier Optical Landing-aid System (ICOLS) has an important impact on the research of carrier landing-aid system. At present, the research on ICOLS in China is mainly focused on the working principle of equipment and technology realization. Although the research on optical and laser application and safety protection technology are relatively mature, the practical application field has not clearly defined the guidance of carrier optics yet formed a complete set of guideline for the visual design. This paper is aimed to investigate the ICOLS systems according to the theory of visual ergonomics, and provide optimization recommendations on optical guidance system for the future development of aircraft carrier. The study gives a brief review of development on optical landing-aid. The optical signal cognitive theory and design principles are analyzed and summarized. A questionnaire survey, observation, and user interview methods were taken to explore the needs of the pilots by asking the information needed at the time of carrier landing. Then, design concept of user-experience-based visual design in line with the existing ICOLS system has been developed, which provides three sets of optical signals in different stages of different distances guided by the basic principles of recognition, and gives the physical properties and optical characteristics' definition. In addition, a simulation software based on PC and flight game consoles has been developed to simulate the optical signal and driving conditions following by a subjective satisfaction survey and a usability test.

Keywords: User experience · Optical landing-aid system · Visual perception Usability

1 Introduction

Landing, with problems such as instable navigation, narrow space to land, short runway, terrible environment, has been the core difficulty of aircraft carrier operation, which is far more difficult than normal airplanes and needs more technique to operate. Pilots in the returning carrier need to specifically control the glissade deviation, center deviation, angle of attack, speed and slope in a short period. According to statistics, the probability of failure of the carrier based aircraft landing at night to reach 15% to 22%,

© Springer International Publishing AG, part of Springer Nature 2018
A. Marcus and W. Wang (Eds.): DUXU 2018, LNCS 10919, pp. 200–217, 2018.
https://doi.org/10.1007/978-3-319-91803-7_15

during the day is 5%. More than half of the accident is mainly because pilots fail to make the right decision or not able to get the information on time while glissading down [1, 2]. Pilot's visual visions is heavily taken up while perceiving the displayed information from panels in a special channel. To solve the problems on lack of location guidance at night, designers usually consider to use the peripheral vision to guide the pilots [3].

The design idea of Improved Carrier Optical Landing-aid System (ICOLS) has an important impact on the research of carrier landing-aid system. At present, the research on ICOLS in China is mainly focused on the working principle of equipment and technology realization. Although the research on optical and laser application and safety protection technology are relatively mature, the practical application field has not clearly defined the guidance of carrier optics yet formed a complete set of guideline for the visual design. By improving optical signal, it may provide the pilot with more visual guidance information and help them with better an early decision-making, and makes the driving task subject to a certain interference.

Persistent light guidance can be taken as an alert task that catches persistent attention, increasing the constant load of the pilots' working memory, which will easily disturb the pilots while driving or making decisions [4]. However, the pilot's visual cognitive processing resources are limited. According to Wickens's multitasking resource allocation theory [5–7], for most optical assistive guidance information, the information specified instruction affects the difficulty of information recognition and processing, and the layout of the information will lead to the transfer of the pilot's visual resources. Therefore, the questions such as how to optimize the optical guidance signal, which kind of guidance should be chosen to improve the pilot's information recognition efficiency and driving performance, are great significance to the ICOLS.

However, currently, the user visual cognitive processing resources to the ICOLS are inadequate in China. The optical signal is the most intuitive and fastest guide mode for the high-speed aircraft when landing on the carrier. The key issues, such as methods for optimizing the optical guidance signal, guidance for improving the user information recognition efficiency and driving performance, are great significance to the contribution to the ICOLS. Designing an optimized visual design for carrier optical landing-aid system based on user experience, such as driving situation and driving needs, could provide safety landing at decision-making level, meanwhile to improve efficiency of landing training activity.

2   Research Method

This paper is aimed to investigate the ICOLS systems according to the theory of visual ergonomics, and provide optimization recommendations on optical guidance system for the future development of aircraft carrier. The study gives a brief review of development on optical landing-aid. The optical signal cognitive theory and design principles are analyzed and summarized. A questionnaire survey, observation, and user interview methods were taken to explore the needs of the pilots by asking the information needed at the time of carrier landing. Then, design concept of user-experience-based visual design in line with the existing ICOLS system has been developed, which provides three sets of optical signals in different stages of different distances guided by the basic principles of recognition, and gives the physical properties and optical characteristics' definition. In addition, a simulation software based on PC and flight game consoles has been developed to simulate the optical signal and driving conditions following by a subjective satisfaction survey and a usability test.

3   Optical Landing-Aid

3.1   Human and Optical Signal Interaction

The process of the pilot using the landing-aid system is a process of information exchange, with the input and output devices used as an interactive media. While glissading, pilots tend to make use of the information outside of vision, such as runway, the nearby marking lines, and the trailing tail to determine the route to the carrier, during daytime and good weather. But only the optical signal can be utilized to guide the route in the night and bad weather. To take the trailer waiting for the route to serve as an example, the carrier-based aircraft in the carrier waiting for the landing instructions issued by the carrier, then leave the Marshall holding pattern for 10 n miles away from the back of the carrier, and continue to raise as high as 1200 feet, putting down landing gear, turning into the Carrier Landing configuration. Travel to 3–4 nautical miles to capture the gliding point, directly into the glide route [8]. The pilot determine their own coordinates and routes and other flight data into the down route by monitoring radar and ground signals, during which the aircraft is landing along a certain slope (usually 3.5°–4°). The aircraft may hit the carrier if the slip slope were too low, and it may let the arresting cable fail to blocking leading the failure of go around, if the slippery slope were too high. When approaching about 0.75 nautical miles, the aircraft landing down to 375 ft, through the view of carrier form, the Fresnel light guide signal and the radio command to determine the landing time. If the landing failed, then go around again and get into the gliding route at 3–4 nautical of the go around route, as shown in Fig. 1.

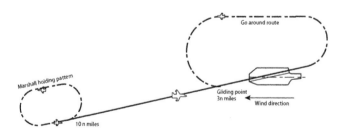

Fig. 1. Stern preparation arrival route.

The information input of whole interactive activity includes five parts: (1) digital information; (2) the external environment vision; (3) other visual information; (4), sound information; and (5) tactility information. The landing process involves visual range, auditory, and tactility, of which each stage is often occupied by more than one channel. According to the Wickensdorf resource processing model [9], the user wants to call two or more channels in the same dimension at the same time. This will inevitably lead to the increase of cognitive load [10].

The pilot can reduce the cognitive load by following several design methods: (1) improving the sensitivity of the target signal, enhancing the user's ability to memorize the signal characteristics, therefore, the pilot can use the intuition to determine the meaning of the guide without accomplishing a complex thinking process; (2) improving the highlight of the target; (3) joining the transient hearing aid in a specific stage to the continuous visual presentation, and reducing the visual resource processing load; (4) reducing the number of propositions.

3.2 Cognitive Principle Based Optical Visual Elements

There are a number of deck lights on the aircraft carrier at night, landing-aid guidance light should align the pilots' cognitive knowledge and pay attention to specific differences of the light. The following parts illustrate factors that affect the identification of optical signals, i.e. lighting color, strobe, layout, and lighting intensity, of recognition optical signals based on the cognitive principle of "the high load or low sensitivity caused by weaken visual tasks", and put forward associated design rules.

Lighting Color. Colors, such as red, green, yellow, and white, are commonly used in the field of lighting color, of which values are based on General Requirements of Lighting Fixtures for Civil Airport (GB/T 7256-2005) or the International Association of Marine Aids to Navigation and Lighthouse Authorities Navigation Guide [11, 12]. In the airport navigation lighting system, the HAPI system for example, the green lights flash for high, while the aircraft is on the slide line, the green lights are steady; when the aircraft is slightly lower the red lights are on, whilst the red lights flash when the aircraft getting lower [13]. Optical guiding should be designed in line with pilots' cognitive habits, otherwise it will cause identification problems [14]. Semantic uniformity and prevent light color interference can improve the light color recognition: (1) in the same system, indicating an azimuth semantics corresponding to the light color should be formed into rules, where two or more light color should not be represented the same meaning; (2) white and yellow color are difficult to be identified from long distance, which should be avoided.

Strobe. Common azimuth lights, warning lights, and other lights' conventional flashing frequency are between 0.75 Hz and 2 Hz. NASA's research on the target light flashing frequency of eye-catching degree studies have shown that 2 Hz frequency is the most easily identified frequency, where fast flicker appropriate frequency is about 2 times as the slow flicker frequency, and 60–120 times/min flicker rate (1–2 times/s) for the highway and the channel can take into account people's ability to identify and available hardware restrictions [15, 16]. In the field of industrial applications, transportation, navigation aviation on the specific function of the light or different light quality of the light rhythm are provided. As a system, it is recommended to use a set of frequencies to distinguish the frequency of fast chatter, or to prefer a higher speed flash.

Layout. As shown in Fig. 2, pilot mainly use the glissading reference angle and the position of the Fresnel light as the reference of glissading of the slope, while use the runway tail line, the runway center line and the tail hanging light as the reference of centering. By visual focusing on the carrier stern and the left side of runway, guidance light is concentrated in the tail and runway edge on the left. The semantics of the "+" or "T" glyphs are the most matched with the mid-down, which is consistent with the basic order of the human eye's search information, and the response mode of flight light. The "+" and "T" form distribution can effectively distribute the slope and centering signals in the range of 15°–20° of the central zone of human eyes, where the human eyes rotates more efficiently [17].

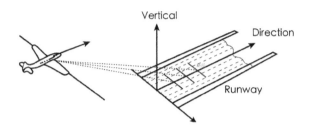

Fig. 2. Visual focus schematic.

The visibility of lighting layout is related to the distance and the human perspective. As the length of the light from the long distance will become shorter, and the larger spacing can form a clear linear effect. While from the distant distance, as the vertical column, horizontal row of the formation of the angle difference getting smaller, parallax changes for the vertical column will be a greater impact. Hence, the "graphical" guide only in a closer distance to play a more intuitive role, and point light can be used for remote guidance.

When the two adjacent lights need to be clearly distinguished, it is important to consider the angle of the view when designing the pitch. Based on the calculation, the deviation angle is very small when flying carrier-based aircraft to do a small increase and fall, which is, the light is not complete offset, resulting in difficulty of identifying the change. When the number of lights is increased, the range of light beams in each light room becomes smaller and the observed light drift is relatively complete when the aircraft is subjected to minor settling at a close range.

The design of the light pitch can be analyzed by referring to the principle of parallax angle that is to determine whether the configuration is theoretically reasonable. Transverse light with a distance of three meters when the theory of the maximum resolution of the line of sight is not more than five nautical miles. According to the analysis, it can be considered to increase the Fresnel lamp room offset slope and the number of lamp rooms, which can get farther resolution of the line of sight, as well as the guidance accuracy and horizontal row. Vertical column guide is limited to close precision guidance by distance. The increase in the guidance of the accuracy of the decline, will affect the observation of information, which the information on the distribution of the two sides of the ship and the middle of the runway extension line area is conducive to the driver's observation.

Lighting Intensity. Light intensity is one of the important factors that affect signal discovery. If the light is too bright, it could hurt the pilot's vision, and consume more energy. Whereas the light is too weak, which will not conducive to the pilot observation. Thus, the lighting system design should consider following two issues:

(1) The design of different lighting intensity system and light source should consider different visible distance. Remote light source should has 10 nautical miles for distance indication. It is difficult to achieve the light group graphics, which has to use monochrome, divergence, and penetrating laser light. Medium-range guidance system should follow the roles of 4 miles and light color recognition. The short-range guidance system is mainly on Fresnel lens light box.

(2) Light intensity adjustment system should be well designed. "Airport lighting equipment configuration and performance requirements" specifies the edge line lights and midline light intensity adjustment range and has five levels: 1%, 3%, 10%, 30% and 100% [18]. Without special requirements, the short-range guide light group can be set to ten light intensity adjustable between 10% and 100%.

4   User Requirement Mining

The ICOLS system is deemed to be able to improve the landing efficiency to pilots. A study on the need of China pilots has been carried out. Figure 3 indicates that the most critical landing time is between 40 s–50 s, when the pilots' attention is mainly focused on angle of attack, the middle runway and Fresnel lights.

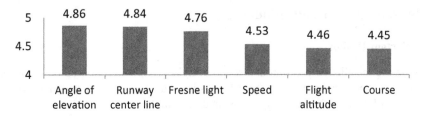

Fig. 3. Information requirement of pilots' attention.

As shown in Fig. 4, before moving into the carrier's route, the pilot mainly focuses on the descending point or the midline of the runway to find the course and determine the target through observing the current pitch attitude and slope, speed, and heading to adjust the flight attitude.

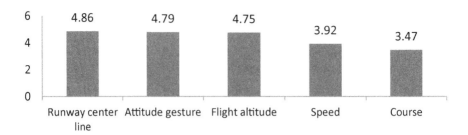

Fig. 4. Information requirements of pilots before entering the downside route.

Based on the analysis of cognitive principles and design principles, the following lessons has been learned for visual design of ICOLS:

(1) Adjusting into the down route is needed when the aircraft carrier is in the range of 10 nautical miles, where instrumentation and radio are the main information sources to the aircraft; When the instrument and radio are failed, which cannot provide precise positioning, lights can guide the carrier to get into the appropriate range of decline.

(2) While at range of 3–4 nautical miles, it can be considered to increase the middle of the guide in the tail, as the carrier is hard to identify. The guide light can help the pilot with successful landing into the appropriate area;

(3) The current efficiency of FLOLS is inadequate, resulting in dangerous landing based on the pilots' own experience at the final landing stage, which causes a high mental load, and unstable operation. Therefore, to improve the efficiency of FLOLS is critical.

5   System Design and Simulation

5.1   System Design

Planning the installation position and scope of light group will be based on the actual situation of the development of optical assisting guidance system and the existing information [19, 20], the design analysis, and user study.

Light Installation Location
Fresnel Lens. IFLOLS and FLOLS are installed in the same location, located on the outer side of the flight deck of carrier, which is about two-thirds of the runway. The lens center is about 4.115 m away from the carrier's side, which uses inertial stability control system to reduce the impact of aircraft carrier roll.

Transverse Band. Installed in the bottom of the carrier below the slope, the center of the yellow and the middle of the runway are aligned, and paralleled to the runway entrance light. The central yellow light beam paralleled to the descending baseline.

Tail Hanging Lights. The lights are installed in the bottom of the carrier below the slope, and extended to the sea to avoid light color interference, which go perpendicular to the runway center line, where the top lights are away from Crossbar center yellow light about 1.5 m–3 m.

The End of the Guide Index. It is installed on the left side of the carrier's runway, parallelled to the runway centerline. One on the runway deck side of the Fresnel lens is in the front of about 76.2 m, the other in the rear of the lens 76.2 m. In order to avoid the runway edge, the distance is greater than 3 m. The specific location can be adjusted according to the carrier model, which is needed to ensure that the beam is paralleled to the descending baseline.

Laser Alignment Indicator. Installed in the center of the transverse light center under the yellow light, the central yellow beam is paralleled to the descending baseline.

Laser Slope Indicator. Installed in the middle of the rear edge of the left side of the beveled deck, the central yellow beam is paralleled to the descending datum.

Light Composition and Scope of Action

Fresnel Lens. The specification of the Fresnel lens design is shown in Table 1. Based on the US military improved light box using 12 light room design, the overall size increased to 72 inches. According to the Fresnel lens parameters, the theoretical Fresnel lens offset can be observed at the theoretical 0.125 nautical miles, and the distance between the Fresnel lens edge and the edge of the reference arm should be over 0.8–0.9 m.

Table 1. The specification of the Fresnel lens design.

Specification item	Fresnel lens
System composition	Aiming lights: a total of 12, the top 10 yellow light room, the following 2 red light room, red light flash 50 times/min (or 60 times/min)
	Auxiliary lights: 7 × 2 base lights, 2 × 2 cut off lights, 4 × 2 flare lights, 3 × 2 auxiliary flare lights, auxiliary light flash frequency 60–80 times (base on the original number)
Size	6.2 m in length
	Aiming light boxes about 1.8 m high, 0.152 m high, 0.152 m wide per light
	Auxiliary light diameter about 0.152 m, spacing 0.152 m (base on the original number, size according to light regulations)
The maximum action distance at night	1 nmi–1.25 nmi
Angle of aiming light emitted beam	Total horizontal viewing angle: ±20°
	Total longitudinal viewing angle: 1.7° (±0.85°) (Yellow light viewing angle 0.13° × 10; red light viewing angle 0.2° × 2)

Transverse and Tail Hanging Lights. The specification of the transverse and tail hanging lights design is stated in Table 2. Transverse light band is a string of bright one-way constant light red spotlight, with the height of 13 m to 19 m. Since the lights are close to the sea, they are easy to damage. It is ensured that the number of lights unremittingly intensive, and also to avoid the impact of individual lighting longitudinal length.

Table 2. The specification of the transverse and tail hanging lights design.

Specification item	Transverse and tail hanging light
System composition	Transverse band: a total of 11 spot lights higher than the runway light intensity
	Tail hanging lights: 1–13 spotlights, always red light
	Yellow light, central, marked as No. 0 light, flash 60 times/min. Never bright out; Green light, right, flicker tail hanging lights flash 60 times/min; Red light, left, flicker lights flash 60 times/min
Size	Transverse light diameter about 0.203 m, light spacing $\geq$ 3.05 m
	Tail hanging light size: 0.203 m, light spacing: 1 m (light size should be based on light regulations)
The maximum action distance at night	3 nmi–4 nmi
Action range	Total longitudinal viewing angle: 5°
	Central yellow flicker light horizontal viewing angle: 0.5° ($\pm 0.25°$)
	Single green or red light horizontal viewing angle: 0.1°

Horizontal light with the middle of the indicator yellow light are always bright and flashing, of which the left side placed five red lights, and five green lights on the right. According to the ICOLS program requirements, 11 lights light up in a continuous manner, theoretically five miles away from the carrier, and the ideal state of the distance between the light edges is 10 feet to form the minimum parallax angle of about 1 arc points. If the view within four nautical miles, the edge of the light should not be less than eight feet.

The End-to-end Slippage Guide Light. The specification of end-to-end slippage guide light is illustrated in Table 3. According to United States end of the slide slope guide light reference to the land-based decline guide way, there is no light when the aircraft is on the decline route. Two lights turn white when the aircraft is slightly higher. As it continue to be higher, the lights begin to flicker. When the aircraft is low, the two lights turn red and blink. However, this red-white lighting color semantic system is inconsistent. The use of red and green strobe lighting system could potentially benefit the lighting color semantic system.

Laser Alignment Indicator. The specification of laser alignment indicator is as shown in Table 4. The LCL is located on the underside of the trailing edge and on the midline extension of the runway. It is a low-intensity pulsed-coded laser that provides an optical sector centered on the slip datum, with a transverse beam angle of about 20° and a beam thickness of 5°. Outside the sector has no lighting zone. The system provides seven modes: red light flashing - red light slow flashing - stable red light - stable yellow light - stable green light - green light slow flash - green light flash. When the pilot is in a signal sector, the falling slope deviation of the baseline $\pm 2.5°$ (1°–6°) are visible to the signal.

Table 3. The specification of end-to-end slippage guide light.

Specification item	End-to-end slippage guide light
System composition	Color-changed blinking spotlights: 2 (red - green)
	Slowly flash 60 times/min, fast flash 120 times/min
Size	Light size: 0.203 m, light spacing: 152.4 m (Lighting spacing and size should be based on carrier size and light regulations)
The maximum action distance at night	3 nmi–4 nmi
Action range	Total longitudinal viewing angle: 20° (±10°)
	No light zone: Offset falls within 0.3° (±0.15°)
	Red light longitudinal viewing angle: 1°
	White fixed light longitudinal viewing angle: 0.4°
	White flicker light longitudinal viewing angle: 1°

Table 4. The specification of laser alignment indicator.

Specification item	Laser alignment indicator
System composition	Yellow light, central, marked as No. 0 light, fixed light
	Green light, right, from left to right marked as No. 1 lights, fixed light; No. 2 lights, flash 60 times/min; No. 3 lights, flash 120 times/min
	Red light, the left side, from right to left marked as No. 1 lights, fixed light; No. 2 lights, flash 60 times/min; No. 3 lights, flash 120 times/min
Size	Laser launcher: 0.97 m long, 0.92 m wide and 0.125 m high, signal source averaging 0.12 m, horizontal distribution; (based on laser line corporation specifications)
The maximum action distance at night	10 nmi
Action range	Total longitudinal viewing angle: 5°
	Total horizontal viewing angle: 20° (±10°)
	Yellow light horizontal viewing angle within 0.5° (±0.25°)
	Red/green fixed light horizontal viewing angle: 0.8°
	Red/green slow flash beam horizontal view angle: 3°
	Red/green flash beam longitudinal viewing angle: 6°

Laser Slide Slope Indicator. The specification of laser slide slope indicator is as shown in Table 5. The laser slippery finger is located on the left side of the carrier and is a low-intensity pulse-coded laser that provides remote slippage information. Indicator signal has five modes: red light slow flashing - stable red light - stable yellow light - stable green light - green light slow flash. There are five modes need to be reduced, such as red flash - lower to rise, red fixed light source - low, amber yellow - on the down route, green fixed light source - high, green flash - higher. When the pilot is in a signal sector, the offset center line within −3°–2° are visible to the signal.

Table 5. The specification of laser slide slope indicator.

Specification item	Laser slide slope indicator
System composition	Yellow lights, the middle, recorded as 0 lights, fixed light
	Green light, right side, from left to right 1 lights, fixed light; 2 lights, flash 60 times/min
	Red light, the left side, from right to left 1 lights, fixed light; 2 lights, flash 60 times/min
Size	Laser launcher: 0.64 m long, 0.92 m wide and 0.2 m high, signal source averaging 0.12 m, the upper left → lower right diagonal distribution; (based on laser line corporation specifications)
The maximum action distance at night	10 nmi
Action range	Total horizontal viewing angle: 5° (−3°–2°)
	Total longitudinal viewing angle: 5°
	Yellow light beam longitudinal viewing angle 0.3° (±0.15°)
	Red fixed light beam longitudinal viewing angle: 0.4°
	Red slow flash beam longitudinal viewing angle of 0.6°
	Green fixed light beam longitudinal viewing angle: 0.4°
	Green slow flash beam longitudinal viewing angle: 1°

5.2   Simulation System

The simulation system is designed to simulate performance of new signal of aircraft landing system to the carrier by restoring the different flight conditions on the current form of signal, which can be recognized by pilots for their cognitive efficiency. The system provides the pilot with visual and dynamic inputs. The software provides the static object model, such as the carrier, the runway mark, the lamp, and the natural landscape. The experimenter can configure the scene element and parameters of driving tasks aligning the needs. In this paper, the virtual simulation environment required for night landing with tasks has three landing phase scenes, i.e. far, medium, and close, as shown in Fig. 5.

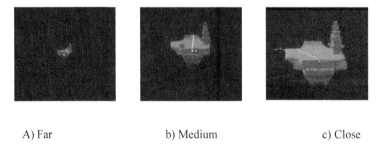

A) Far   b) Medium   c) Close

Fig. 5. Three landing phase scenes during the night in virtual simulation environment.

The experimental simulation data contains the control data during driving task, which is recorded by computer while the pilot is operating, including simulation calculated values, such as driving distance, flight real-time coordinates, pitching operation and tilt angle operation of the original volume, the guidance signal. The performance is determined by factors, such as the completion time of the driving task, and the completion of the situation.

6   Usability Evaluation

6.1   Evaluation Objective and Method

The objective of this section is to evaluate the pilot's perception of the design elements and psychological satisfaction, and to investigate whether the pilot can successfully descend by using the guidance of the optical signal, which guidance has been voted with higher satisfaction. As such the following sections are divided into two parts: (1) Experiment 1: Cognitive tests and interviews to obtain the pilot's presentation of the subjective attitude and understanding, and (2) Experiment 2: Driving task of measurement for obtaining the task of completing the driving process.

A total of six participants (pilots) were selected for driving task test and cognitive investigation test. The participants are about at the same age, and have never participated in such research. They are able to operate the simulation system and equipment after explanation. The test process is designed to encourage them to express their own opinions. Before the start of the test, the participants were told about the general situation of participating in the experiments, and signed an experimental agreement of voluntary participation.

6.2   Evaluation Experiment 1: Cognitive Tests and Interviews

Evaluation Experiment 1: Cognitive Tests and Interviews, is designed for evaluation of signal satisfaction and the use of intention research, which is to find out whether the presentation of the light point is intuitive and easy to read. The experiment process records the signal meaning, subjective attitude value and intention of the participants through the scene presentation and interviews that are focused on their subjective feelings of presented signals.

The LVLA, Crossbar, Fore-After, Droplights and Fresnel lenses are arranged in each system with different presenting approaches. Based on a combination of light color identification, position resolution and frequency comparison, a total of 23 screens for the experiment are in one set.

In order to study whether the guidance of the light array is easy to identify or not, a 1–5 scale has been adopted as following: 1 = Hard to understand, 2 = Not easy to understand, 3 = Moderate, 4 = Clear, 5 = Very clear. The results of the evaluation of satisfaction and use intention evaluation are as shown in Table 6 and Fig. 6.

Table 6. Mean value of experiment 1 results for visual identification level and use intention of LVLA(10 km), Crossbar(5 km), F&A(5 km), Crossbar & LGI(5 km), Crossbar & F&A(5 km), and LCL & LGI(5 km).

	LVLA (10 km)	Crossbar (5 km)	F&A (5 km)		Crossbar & LGI (5 km)	Crossbar & F&A (5 km)	LCL & LGI (5 km)
Identification level	3.50	3.67	2.71 (Red& White)	2.75 (Red& Green)	3.17	2.67	3.33
Use intention	3.0	3.0	0		4.0	0	3.0

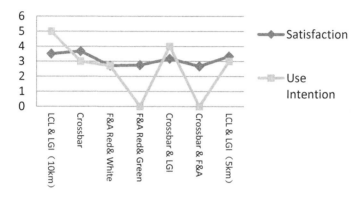

Fig. 6. Mean value of experiment 1 results for user satisfaction and use intention of LVLA, Crossbar, F&A, Crossbar & LGI, Crossbar & F&A, and LCL & LGI (5 km and 10 km).

The results of cognitive tests and interviews indicate:

More than 5 km Away From the LVLA, the LVLA Average Recognition of Satisfaction is Higher, and the Use of Intentions are Relatively High

- Color and flash frequency of the form for performance is relatively simple. The cognitive is no longer a problem, once the pilot is getting familiar with the rules.
- Easy to learn. After the initial explanation, the user is able to quickly and accurately explain the meaning of the signal represented.

The existing problems could be:

- The light perception of the point source is relatively poor. The participants is convinced that the instrument and the radio are more than 10 km, and more brain resources are allocated to the instrument.
- The degree of excursion of the flicker frequency is unclear. Especially during the fast and slow flashing, the pilot has to recall three sets of characteristics of "color" "frequency", and "position", which will negatively affect cognitive efficiency.
- Some pilots thought that the two signals could easily cause confusion without training and memorization.
- The signal should be simple.

Crossbar's Performance is the Highest, but the Participants' Intention is Relatively Little

- Graphical performance is more intuitive than the relatively single signal, which is easy to identify.
- Most of the participants believed that Crossbar is a kind of expression as "vertical Fresnel lights, which is not only has a directivity, but also through the length of the array to determine the".

The existing problems could be:

- A number of visual stimuli are presented more likely to interfere with a line of sight, which waste energy;
- The guide is mainly used for guiding to align the middle of the runway, when a number of lights are hard to be distinguished in a long-distance;
- Some participants suggested that the memory load is too high for identify lights during the landing. However, other participants believed that the problem is due to the color of the light staying same when flashing.

F-A's form of Performance is the Most Recognizable, and the Participants' Intention to Use is the Least

- Instead of using white color, green color is considered to be suitable to represent height, as white color has never used as slope or height.
- Light-free mode could cause confusion of the participants, interrupting cognitive process, and worried about those lights will disturbed the operation.
- Long distance displayed in the vertical column of the display is unclear. It is easy to be confused in the runway with sideline lights in a short distance. One of participant suggested that "lights should be placed as minimum as possible on the deck, as lights can easily interfere and has an impact on judgment of pilot during the night".
- There are too many lights with Crossbar, which will has interference with sight.

The LVLA Medium-Range Guidance is the Most Preferred Approach Followed by Crossbar & LGI

- LVLA guide form is relatively simple and clear. During the actual operation, Crossbar is thought to be too difficult to distinguish.
- The signal of the guide form is constant and stable.

6.3   Evaluation Experiment 2: Driving Task

Evaluation Experiment 2: Driving Task is designed to compare the completion of the driving task and the real-time coordinate measurement for verifying whether the success of the light is guided by the optical signal. The 10-nautical-miles test route has been adopted for waiting for incoming route, since it reduces the impact of flight route on signal identification and can cover all the signals across stages.

Based on the starting speed and distance between the landing route node and each light group during the night, the route for the experiment has three sections, i.e. 180s, 120s and 90s. The experiment takes the utilization of lights as an independent variable, provides fundamental HUD parameters, such as altimeter, speedometer, heading table, pitch scale and distance warning information. As the simulation hardware equipment and the actual aircraft flight facilities could have some discrepancy, the scope of the design range is larger than the light security range. The task flow and scenario scene of simulation for the experiment are shown in Figs. 7 and 8.

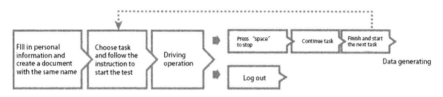

Fig. 7. Task flow chat for Experiment 2.

The results indicate that, when the runway has no auxiliary tips, the participants can complete 58.3% of the tasks by the use of the far and medium light for guiding.

The Situation of Remote Centering and Glissading Task. In the same task range, the optical signal-guided flight can successfully reach the target area in a short time, and the mean value of the completion time is about the same, which indicates that the pilot has a reasonable level of cognition of the optical signal and can understand the meaning of the signal. Most of the participants found the flicker feature during the task, but their tensions make them fail to recognize the difference in frequency, resulting in a light signal that did not give the pilot a clear "quantity" concept like a digital signal.

The Situation of Medium-Range Centering and Glissading Task. The success rate of LVLA mid-range guidance and Crossbar as well as LGI combination could reach 83.3%, while the success rate of Crossbar and Fore & Aft (red and green) is 50%. The finish time of the high success rate are nearly the same. But with the guidance of the LVLA manipulation, the performance is more stable. Crossbar has a good centering effect on close range, but it does exist the problem that it cannot be well known at long distances.

The Situation of FLOLS Glissading Task. The success rate of FLOLS is 67%, and raise to 83% with the number of light rooms increased. The improved Fresnel lights, to a certain extent, do fix the performance of the glissading manipulation.

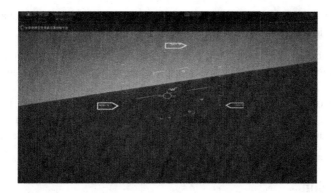

Fig. 8. The scenario scene of simulation for Experiment 2.

6.4   Discussion

Through the two experiments of optical signal form and the task test of guide manipulation for usability evaluation, there are some issues highlighted from the experiments:

- LVLA can be used for assisting the users to complete most of the tasks in far and medium ranges with high efficiency, which achieved a high satisfaction and intention of use from the participants. In theory, the rapid flash can enhance the signal characteristics, however, it did not cause the user's attention, and the processing of the flash frequency occupies the user's cognitive resources.
- Crossbar and LGI combination can facilitate the users completing most of the tasks with high satisfaction of identify. However, under the guidance of Crossbar, its control stability is slightly worse. The users believed that although this kind of display benefits their intuition, but a number of lights interrupt their cognitive process.
- Improved Fresnel lights, to a certain extent, could obtain a better manipulation of performance, which is what the users expected.

Moreover, the results of the experiments help with verifying the hypothesis of this paper, and supporting cognitive principles and design principles:

- Optical signal design should improve the user's ability of memorizing the signal characteristics, unify light color guide rules, and make the design layout reasonable to meet the user's cognitive habits. By the use of a number of colors for lighting, optical signals in different scenes represent their own meanings. Using color scheme for the optical signal and location, can reduce the user's cognitive difficulty.
- The user's cognitive ability and habits should be considered for providing appropriate guidance based on certain stages of the actions. Although Crossbar's performance is aimed at improving the users' intuition, it seems that it has not been proved to be the best method. Users have higher acceptance with pre-use of the guidance, and the habit of using forming into a stable memory, which can facilitate a better results.

Furthermore, the results of the experiments provide insights and challenges to design principles:

- It is wildly believed that signal differences can be improved by implementing proper design method resulting in visibility improvement. Interestingly, the user's cognitive ability and actual situation of the use could be ignored to that.
- The form of the signal should be simplified by minimizing signal features and dimensions. Crossbar factor has not been evaluated for improvement of guidance efficiency due to the lack of time, which follow-up study should cover this issue.

7   Conclusion

This paper presents the general design principle of light color, frequency, layout and light intensity in the design for optical signal, carries on the concept simulation, and obtains the concept of the ICOLS optical guidance system through the exploration of the data survey and the user research. The results indicate that the users can get a better cognitive level and satisfaction in the condition of the color and flashing of the light performed on the glide-slope and centerline guidance in remote and medium distance, especially when the radar communication is disturbed or too difficult to identify landing runway context. Moreover, it would help the pilots with successfully landing in safe area. At the same time, in spite of the pilots could nose down according to the rows of lights on some level, which causes worse satisfaction. Furthermore, the optimized Fresnel lens can improve the satisfaction and the handling stability of drivers. The result can benefit future design iteration and in-depth research.

With the gradual development of China's carrier and maritime aviation field, it is necessary to increase the content and methods for navigation. The development of photoelectric automatic auxiliary equipment is the trend for future development. However, the optical signal guidance, as a kind of application in the specific environment is still essential. It is the direction of the future development to study the optical-aid guidance coping with other related equipment and methods.

Acknowledgements. The authors wish to thank all the people who provided their time and efforts for data collection, especially Xiaoming Zhang who developed the virtual experiments system. This research is supported by the Fundamental Research Funds for the Central Universities 2017ZX013, and the Specialized Science Research Fund from Guangzhou Science Technology and Innovation Commission 201607010308.

References

1. Zheng, Y., Lu, Y., Yang, Z.: Expertise and responsibility effects on pilots' reactions to flight deck alerts in a simulator. Aviat. Space Env. Med. **85**(11), 1100–1105 (2014)
2. Yao, Y., Liu, Q., Wang, Q., Shi, W.: Urgent issues of aviation ergonomics study on carrier based aircraft. Negative **7**(1), 9–10 (2016)

3. Nikolic, M.I., Sarter, N.B.: Peripheral visual feedback: a powerful means of supporting effective attention allocation in event-driven, data-rich environments. Hum. Factors J. Hum. Factors Ergon. Soc. **43**(1), 30–38 (2001)
4. Parasuraman, R.: Memory load and event rate control sensitivity decrements in sustained attention. Science **205**(4409), 924–927 (1979)
5. Teichner, W.H., Krebs, M.J.: Laws of visual choice reaction time. Psychol. Rev. **81**(1), 75 (1974)
6. Wickens, C.D., Carswell, C.M.: Information processing. In: Handbook of Human Factors and Ergonomics, vol. 2, pp. 89–122 (1997)
7. Moertl, P.M., Canning, J.M., Gronlund, S.D.: Aiding planning in air traffic control: an experimental investigation of the effects of perceptual information integration. Hum. Factors J. Hum. Factors Ergon. Soc. **44**(3), 404–412 (2002)
8. Pan, T.: Route Design and Control System Simulation for Carrier-Based Aircraft Approach. Nanjing University of Aeronautics and Astronautics (2014)
9. Wickens, C.D., Hollands, J.G., Zhu, Z.: Engineering Psychology & Human Performance. East China Normal University Press, Shanghai (2003)
10. Wang, Y.: In-Vehicle Secondary Task Study Based on Human-Machine Interactive Simulation. Department of Industrial Engineering of Tsinghua University, Beijing (2009)
11. General Requirements of Lighting Fixtures for Civil Airport (GB/T 7256-2005). http://www.tsinfo.js.cn/inquiry/gbtdetails.aspx?A100=GB/T%207256-2005
12. The International Association of Marine Aids to Navigation and Lighthouse Authorities Navigation Guide. Dalian Maritime University Press, Dalian (1993)
13. Connors, M.M.: Conspicuity of Target Lights: The Influence of Color. National Aeronautics and Space Administration, Washington, DC (1975)
14. Connors, M.M.: Conspicuity of Target Lights: The Influence of Flash Rate and Brightness. National Aeronautics and Space Administration, Washington, DC (1975)
15. National Academies of Sciences, Engineering, and Medicine: Selection and Application of Warning Lights on Roadway Operations Equipment. The National Academies Press, Washington, DC (2008). http://dx.doi.org/10.17226/14190
16. Lewis, J.R.: Handbook of Human Factors and Ergonomics, pp. 1275–1316. Wiley, New York (2006)
17. GJBZ 20272-1995: Layout and Performance Requirements for Airfield Lighting. http://www.zbgb.org/68/StandardDetail2249128.htm
18. Laserline Corporation: Laser Visual Guidance Systems, pp. 1–48, Laser corporation, California (2008)
19. McCabe, M.J.: Landing Signal Officer Reference Manual, pp. 28–52. US Naval Landing Signal Officers School, Washington, DC (1999)
20. Rudowsky, T., Hynes, M., Luter, M., Niewoehner, R., Senn, P.: Review of the Carrier Approach Criteria for Carrier-Based Aircraft-Phase I: Final Report. Defense Technical Information Center (2002). http://www.dtic.mil/dtic/tr/fulltext/u2/a411068.pdf

Aesthetic Experimental Study on Information Visualization Design Under the Background of Big Data

Tian Lei, Nan Ni[(⊠)], Qiumeng Zhu, and Sijia Zhang

School of Mechanical Science and Engineering,
Huazhong University of Science and Technology, Wuhan, China
nanni@hust.edu.cn

Abstract. Information visualization is a pragmatic and artistic means of expression. It is a visual communication art oriented on effective communication that is based on accurate functional claims. Visualization design should follow the principle of formal beauty and combine the content with the form organically to achieve the purpose of disseminating information while entertaining the users with beauty. This article starts with the principle of formal beauty and experimentally studies the influence mechanism of aesthetics on the readability of visualization methods, the accuracy of information delivery and the user's reading experience. This article will propose an effective way to enhance the attractiveness of information visualization and communicate performance from the perspective of formal beauty.

Keywords: Information visualization · Formal beauty principle
Aesthetic experience

1 Background

With the development of Internet and information industry, big data has begun to attract people's attention. Big data has become a disruptive technological revolution in the IT industry.

Information visualization provides an intuitive and effective way for people to learn about industry characteristics, consumer trends and lifestyle through big data. How to allow users to accurately capture the key information without prior learning and seize the logical relationship between the information so as to memorize the information in a better aesthetic experience, is a tricky thing for academics in the industry. This article will explore the influence mechanism of aesthetics on the readability of visualization methods, the accuracy of information delivery and the user's reading experience from the perspective of aesthetics. This article will also seek ways to improve the attractiveness of visualization charts and user reading efficiency by using formal beauty principle.

© Springer International Publishing AG, part of Springer Nature 2018
A. Marcus and W. Wang (Eds.): DUXU 2018, LNCS 10919, pp. 218–226, 2018.
https://doi.org/10.1007/978-3-319-91803-7_16

2 Recent Development of Aesthetic Studies in Information Visualization Design

In some design fields, the influence of aesthetics on design has been widely studied by scholars. For example, Michailidou is dedicated to finding the balance between the attractiveness of web design and users' information loading [1]. In product design, people pay more attention to whether the product can make people feel pleasant when being used. This kind of spiritual delight also relies on the formal beauty of the product appearance [2].

In the field of visualization, some scholars recently have studied the relationship between visualization and task performance and found that appealing visualization charts have led to an increase in the number of participants in the exhibition [3]. Bateman et al. proposed the hypothesis that visual aesthetic enhancements may make them more memorable [4]. Meanwhile, Ying et al. proposed that if the balance between the forms and functions of aesthetics is not achieved so that some gorgeous visualization charts are created while sacrificing its main purpose - the effective transmission of information, the design will deviate from its original intention [5].

Rich graphics and gorgeous colors enable the visual graphics to capture the eye of the audience. While viewing the beauty of visual charts, audiences are also interpreting the meaning and content of visual charts.

From an objective point of view, some scholars think that successful works of art are a combination of science and artistry [6]. Therefore, the visual design needs beauty.

From a subjective point of view, the focus of visualization has shifted from simple usability analysis to user-centered design. It is necessary to understand the process of the users' perceptual thinking to ideal thinking in order to better achieve the "people-oriented design". In everyday life, aesthetics is the spiritual enjoyment sought by all people. Therefore, with the help of visual means, it is a general trend to deliver information clearly and effectively and to bring high-quality aesthetic experience to users.

This shows that aesthetics is affecting people's perception and interpretation of information in an attractive form [7], making information visualization more accessible, easy to remember and easy to disseminate. There are so many kinds of beauty that there is no uniform definition for beauty in the academic world. Pythagoras regarded the harmony caused by the moderation of numbers and proportions as the most beautiful. Aristotle believes that beauty is order, symmetry and the unity of things. This is because, in the long history, different aesthetic conceptions are formed due to the differences in people's geographical location, cultural practices and lifestyle. The formal beauty principle is a kind of sedimentation of human aesthetics for a long time, which is a law summarized in practice. It is an aesthetic object with relative independence [8]. Gorky said formal beauty is "a form that affects emotion and reason, a form of power".

As part of the design, visual design naturally follows the formal beauty principle. However, the improvement in aesthetic quality may weaken the audience's understanding of the visualization chart itself, resulting in a deviation from the design intent.

Therefore, formal beauty can only be fully reflected when it is applied not only as an objective but also as a means to visual design.

We believe that, if the formal beauty principle are integrated into the visual design based on the readability of information and the accuracy of the communication, this information visualization will not only give the user a good reading experience, but also make them easier to understand and remember the content of the information. However, the impact of various laws on the beauty of visual chart has not been studied yet.

Therefore, in order to make more effective use of the formal beauty principle in the visualization design, two experiments are designed based on the formal beauty principle. One is the aesthetic test of users on some particular forms of visualization chart; the other is the aesthetic test of experts on some particular forms of visualization chart. The influence mechanism of aesthetics on the readability of visualization methods, the accuracy of information delivery and the user's reading experience will be studied experimentally. Effective ways will also be proposed to enhance the attractiveness of information visualization and communicate performance from the perspective of formal beauty principle.

3 Experimental Study

The experiment mainly lies in clarifying the influence mechanism of aesthetics on information complexity, comprehensibility, organization, attractiveness, the difficulty of finding data and reading experience. The study is divided into two stages. The stage one is the aesthetic test of users on some particular forms of visualization chart. The stage two is the aesthetic test of experts on some particular forms of visualization chart.

3.1 The Aesthetic Test of Users on Some Particular Forms of Visualization Chart

The experimental independent variables are methods for visualization of information. 24 kinds of common information visualization methods are collected (Table 1) and classified into five categories according to the relationship among the data, which are visualization of single data, visualization of flow relationship data, visualization of contrasted relationship data, visualization of hierarchical relationship data and visualization of logical relationship data. And these methods are used as the level of the independent variables. The controlled variable is the information content and info-graphic color. The experimental material is shown in Fig. 1.

The experimental steps are as follows:

- The subjects are allowed to browse through all the experimental materials first.
- The subjects read the experimental materials one by one and scored the questions corresponding to the dependent variables according to the Five Scaling Method (Table 2).

Table 1. The classification of 24 common information visualization methods.

Single data	Histogram (1)	Hierarchical relationship data	Tree diagram (13)
	Line chart (2)		Circle packing (14)
	Pie chart (3)		Sunburst (15)
	Map (4)		Cube tree map (16)
	Heat map (5)	Flow relationship data	Chord diagram (17)
	Bubble chart (6)		Network diagram (18)
	Scatter plot (7)		Sankey diagram (19)
	Rose figure (10)		Flow chart (20)
Logic relationship data	Time series plot (8)	Contrasted relationship data	Bullet charts (21)
	Parallel coordinate plots (9)		Scatter plot matrix (22)
	Venn diagram (11)		Radar chart (23)
	Clustermap (12)		Boxplot (24)

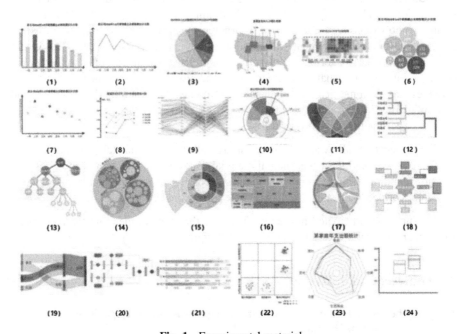

Fig. 1. Experimental material

Table 2. The corresponding variables of the experiment.

Question number	Question
C1	The perception of the complex form of information
C2	Whether the subject is easy to understand the information content
C3	Whether the subject is easy to obtain data
C4	Subjects' perceptions of information forms
C5	The degree of the overall beauty
C6	The degree of color beauty
C7	The degree of shape beauty
C8	The perception of the attractiveness of information forms
C9	Whether it is conducive to reading

25 subjects volunteered to participate in this study with 16 women and 9 men. The 25 people are junior or senior students from university, all of whom are engaged in design industry. And one of them has studied information visualization deeply. They have normal vision during the experiment.

3.2 The Aesthetic Test of Experts on Some Particular Forms of Visualization Chart

This section is mainly for expert evaluation on the information visualization materials selected for the above experiment. Visual communication refers to the design using visual symbols to convey a variety of information [9]. The visualization is the use of graphical means to communicate information clearly and effectively [10]. The two are very similar so that the formal beauty principle in visualization can refer to the formal beauty principle in visual communication. Therefore, the experimental dependent variables are "symmetrical and balanced", "contrast and harmony", "cadence and rhythm" "diversity and unity" [11].

The experimental steps are as follows:

- The subjects are allowed to browse through all the experimental materials first.
- The subjects read the experimental materials one by one and scored the questions corresponding to the dependent variables according to the Five Scaling Method.
- After scoring, the results are discuss and corrections are made.

Six subjects participated in the test. Three of them are women and three are men. All of them are college teachers engaged in design teaching.

4   Analysis and Inference

4.1 Aesthetics of Infographic Affects the User's Reading Experience About the Information

We did a univariate analysis of variance about "The overall sense of beauty", "The perception of the complex form of information", "Whether the subject is easy to understand the information content", "Whether the subject is easy to obtain data", "Subjects' perceptions of information forms", "The perception of the attractiveness of information forms" and "whether it is conducive to reading".

The results show that at the level $\alpha = 0.05$, the infographics of different beauty have significant differences in "Whether the subject is easy to understand the information content" and "The perception of the attractiveness of information forms". The *sig.* are 0.020 and 0.001 respectively (Table 3). This shows that the overall beauty of infographic does affect the subjects' possibility of understanding the information content and perception of the attractiveness of information forms.

Table 3. Tests of between-subjects effect (The overall sense of beauty)

Source	Type III sum of squares	df	Mean square	F	Sig.
Corrected Mod	200.596[a]	36	5.572	3.38	0
Intercept	489.796	1	489.796	297.105	0
C1	1.589	4	0.397	0.241	0.915
C2	19.922	4	4.98	3.021	0.02
C3	10.247	4	2.562	1.554	0.19
C4	3.891	4	0.973	0.59	0.67
C8	32.143	4	8.036	4.874	0.001
C9	4.418	4	1.105	0.67	0.614
Error	242.339	147	1.649		
Total	2016	184			
Corrected total	442.935	183			

Dependent variable: the overall sense of beauty

[a]R Squared = .453 (Adjusted R Square = 0.319)

In order to further clarify which kind of beauty has an impact on the user's cognition, we did univariate analysis of variance using the "shape beauty" and "color beauty" with respect to the above six data. The results are shown in Tables 4 and 5.

Table 4 shows that, the color beauty of infographic, at the level $\alpha = 0.05$, has a significant effect on "The perception of the complexity of the information content", "Subjects' perceptions of information forms" and "The difficulty of finding data". The *sig* values are 0.039, 0.042 and 0.002, respectively. Table 5 shows that, the shape beauty of infographic, at the level $\alpha = 0.05$, has a significant effect on "Subjects' perceptions of the attractiveness of information forms".

This shows that the shape beauty and color beauty of infographic produce different aspects of beauty for subjects. The shape beauty seize the first feeling of the subjects and color beauty provide a greater help for the subjects to extract and understand information later.

Table 4. Tests of between-subjects effect (Color beauty)

Dependent variable: color beauty

Source	Type III Sum of Squares	df	Mean Square	F	Sig.
Corrected Mod	215.359[a]	36	5.982	3.393	0
Intercept	539.894	1	539.894	306.26	0
C1	18.267	4	4.567	2.591	0.039
C2	3.259	4	0.815	0.462	0.763
C3	17.967	4	4.492	2.548	0.042
C4	31.732	4	7.933	4.5	0.002
C8	16.902	4	4.225	2.397	0.053
C9	3.61	4	0.902	0.512	0.727
Error	259.141	147	1.763		
Total	1866	184			
Corrected total	474.5	183			

[a]R Squared = .454 (Adjusted R Square = 0.320)

Table 5. Tests of between-subjects effect (Shape beauty)

Dependent variable: shape beauty

Source	Type III Sum of Squares	df	Mean Square	F	Sig.
Corrected Mod	228.616[a]	36	6.35	3.719	0
Intercept	500.522	1	500.522	293.104	0
C1	5.091	4	1.273	0.745	0.563
C2	12.122	4	3.03	1.775	0.137
C3	11.838	4	2.959	1.733	0.146
C4	9.861	4	2.465	1.444	0.223
C8	24.543	4	6.136	3.593	0.008
C9	6.124	4	1.531	0.897	0.468
Error	249.318	146	1.708		
Total	1866	183			
Corrected total	477.934	182			

[a]R Squared = .478 (Adjusted R Square = 0.350)

4.2   The Aesthetics of Infographic Has a Significant Correlation with Formal Beauty Principle

Taking the shape beauty and color beauty as the X-axis and the Y-axis respectively, the means of the 24 samples on each of the two variables are taken as the coordinates of each sample. We get the distribution of 24 samples in the aesthetic space (Fig. 2). Obviously, chord diagram and circle packing are of the highest beauty. Rose diagram and histogram beauty follow. Parallel coordinate plot are of the worst and bullet diagram ranks the second worst.

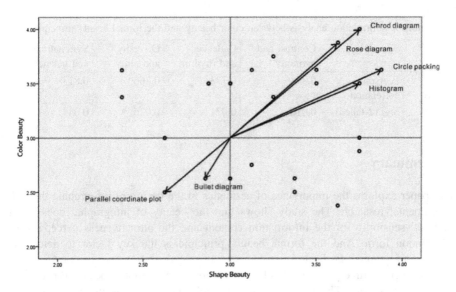

Fig. 2. The distribution of 24 samples in the aesthetic space

Combining the average score in the shape beauty and color beauty of the six samples and experts' score in the form beauty on the six samples, we did the relevant analysis and found:

- The correlation relationship between the shape beauty of the infographic and "contrast and harmony", "cadence and rhythm", "diversity and unity" and "symmetrical and balanced" is significant. And the correlation coefficient is extremely high, with 0.899, 0.890, 0.869 and 0.815 respectively (Table 6).
- Color beauty of infographic only has a significant correlation with "contrast and harmony", "diversity and unity" and "symmetrical and balanced" (Table 7).

This shows that, the formal beauty principle occupies an important position in the aesthetics design of infographic.

Table 6. Correlation analysis between shape beauty and the formal beauty principle

		Contrast and harmony	Cadence and rhythm	Diversity and unity	Symmetrical and balanced
Shape beauty	Pearson correlation	0.899[*]	0.890[*]	0.869[*]	0.815[*]
	Sig. (2-tailed)	0.015	0.018	0.025	0.048

Table 7. Correlation analysis between color beauty and the formal beauty principle

		Contrast and harmony	Cadence and rhythm	Diversity and unity	Symmetrical and balanced
Color beauty	Pearson correlation	0.894*	0.773	0.866*	0.813*
	Sig. (2-tailed)	0.016	0.071	0.026	0.049

5 Summary

This paper explores the importance of aesthetics in the design of infographic through experimental research. The study shows that the beauty of infographic does affect subjects' sensibility of the information content and the attractiveness perception of information form. And the formal beauty principle is the key factor to determine whether infographic has beauty.

However, as time goes, especially in the current era, people's aesthetic needs are constantly changing. The formal beauty principle will gain new understanding and interpretation in the future. Designers need to combine the formal beauty principle with specific issues in the new era and avoid the rigid application of a certain law. The formal beauty principle need to be applied in modern design flexibly in order to better meet the aesthetic needs of users and promote the development of big data era.

References

1. Michailidou, E., Harper, S.: Determining users' perception of web page visual complexity and aesthetic characteristics. University of Manchester (2008)
2. 董莎莉. 信息时代交互美学在产品设计中的应用. 科协论坛(下半月) **10**, 101–102 (2012). (in Chinese)
3. Cawthon, N., Moere, A.V.: The effect of aesthetic on the usability of data visualization. In: Proceedings of the Information Visualization 2007, pp. 637–648. IEEE (2007)
4. Bateman, S., Mandryk, R.L., Gutwin, C., Genest, A., McDine, D., Brooks, C.: Useful junk: the effects of visual embellishment on comprehension and memorability of charts. In: Proceedings of the CHI 2010, pp. 2573–2582. ACM (2010)
5. 熊瑛, 尤斐. 信息可视化与视觉设计. 艺术与设计:理论版 **5**, 40–42 (2012)
6. 肖燕萍. 构图的形式美法则在地图设计中的应用. 测绘通报 **10**, 65–68 (2006). (in Chinese)
7. Bardzell, J.: Interaction criticism and aesthetics. In: Proceedings of the CHI, pp. 2357–2366 (2009)
8. 柯善军, 魏莹. 产品人机界面设计与形式美创造之关系探讨. 包装工程 **27**(3), 159–161 (2006). (in Chinese)
9. 冷德彤. 现代设计中视觉传达的形式美法则的解读. 南京广播电视大学学报 **04**, 79–82 (2008). (in Chinese)
10. 于晖. 数据可视化:科学与艺术的融合之美. 科学艺术 传承创新——科学与艺术融合之路 (2016). (in Chinese)

Color Matching Research Based on Octree-LSD Method and Kansei Engineering: A Case Study of Typical Images of the Grain Rain

Meiyu Lv[1,2] and Hequn Qu[1(✉)]

[1] School of Digital Media and Design Arts,
Beijing University of Posts and Telecommunications, Beijing 100876, China
hequnqu@gmail.com
[2] Beijing Key Laboratory of Network System and Network Culture,
Beijing University of Posts and Telecommunications, Beijing 100876, China

Abstract. This paper proposes a method of extracting colors from natural images scientifically and then coordinating them to apply to corresponding situations. By applying this method, a case study of typical images of the Grain Rain, which is one of the 24 solar terms in Chinese traditional calendar was carried out. The method is as follows: looking for the typical images of the Grain Rain through literature review and social investigation, then taking pictures in the field. Using octree combined with least-significant difference method (octree-LSD method) to original colors, after that, several colors were picked of each image and the degree of beauty of them was also calculated according to the M•Spenser's aesthetic measurement. Only if it comes out that these colors will be qualified on the aspect of aesthetic when combining together, will the next step be carried out which is adopting Munsell Color Harmony Theory to determine the area ratio of each color and gain the color scheme. Last but not the least, using the Semantic Difference method in Kansei engineering to measure the color emotion of each color scheme, then color schemes which will be able to represent the Grain Rain and the application situation of them would be obtained. This method combines scientific calculation methods, western scientific color systems and empirical subjective opinions, which insure that the color schemes obtained by this method can not only be valid but also consistent with people's cognition.

Keywords: Color extraction · Color scheme · Semantic Difference method
Color Harmony Theory

1 Introduction

Since Qin dynasty, Chinese color culture has been continuously improved. Under the influence of Confucianism, Taoism, Buddhism, Chinese color view reflects the idea of the unity of nature and human, which is intuitive, experiential and subjective [1]. On the contrary, the Western have understood, studied and analyzed color in a scientific and rational manner all the time, and they formed scientific color systems by the end of

© Springer International Publishing AG, part of Springer Nature 2018
A. Marcus and W. Wang (Eds.): DUXU 2018, LNCS 10919, pp. 227–246, 2018.
https://doi.org/10.1007/978-3-319-91803-7_17

19th century. Combined with the contents of sociology, imagology and psychology, a series of theories and research methods of color science have been formed.

It is essential to select and apply color in architecture design, landscape design, traffic design, product design, digital design, display design and even personal image design, which indeed should be the fore process of Design. This paper aims to extract color schemes full of Chinese meaning from Chinese local natural and human environment, combining western color theory with the subjective perception from the public. In specific, a complete set of method of color extraction, collocation and application is proposed and applied to the extraction of color schemes from the Grain Rain in northern China, which is one of the 24 solar terms in Chinese traditional calendar.

The object of color extraction, the 24 solar terms in China, is one kind of supplementary calendar which was established in the pre-Qin dynasty and completed in Han dynasty to guide agricultural events [2]. It is a knowledge system formed by observing the anniversary of the apparent motion and getting to know more about the regulation of changes in time, climate, phenology and so on. A large number of custom culture and ritual faith were formed according to the solar terms, which consist of sincere blessing and wishes of Chinese people. Different periods of natural environment and cultural customs will present different colors and feelings. The color schemes extracted form 24 solar terms can be used in package design of related solar terms, physical product design and Internet product design, etc. In addition, they will help to gain the cultural identity of audience and effectively disseminate and promote Chinese culture.

2   Methodology

This method is divided into three steps. The first step aims to obtain materials for color extraction: finding the typical objects by literature review, field research and user research, which can represent the Grain Rain in some perspective. In other words, by which people can intuitively associate with the Grain Rain. Then field research was carried out to take pictures pretty close to the true images. The second step aims to extract colors and match them: colors in the pictures and the count of each color were preliminary gained through octree method, then after matching with the given standard color palette, the standard colors from the picture and their count were obtained through LSD method. According to the count of each color and color distribution in the picture, about 3 to 5 kinds of colors were selected and confirmed that its degree of beauty was qualified through the M•Spenser's aesthetic measurement. Finally, the area ratio of each color could be calculated through Munsell Color Harmony Theory. The third step aims at confirming the emotion words of color schemes: the emotion of color schemes could be measured through the Semantic Difference method in Kansei engineering.

3   Procedure and Results

3.1   Stage One (Obtaining the Materials of Color Extraction)

Literature Review. According to "Huainanzi", the origin of the Grain Rain can date back to Cang Jie creating characters, which was a quite big event [3]. The Yellow Emperor issued a decree at the end of spring and the start of summer, announced that Cang Jie had successfully created characters and called on the world to learn. On that day, it rained unusually and countless grains and rice dropped, therefore, descendants named the day as the Grain Rain, as one of the 24 solar terms. The Grain Rain is the sixth solar term of the 24 ones, which is the last solar term in the spring. As the saying goes, "The snow stops in Qingming, and the frost stops in Grain Rain." It is beneficial for corn crops that the temperature has risen markedly while the rainfall is seasonable during the late spring months, when it is a good time to sow seedlings and grafting. It has been said since ancient times that "rain gives life to all grains" [4].

The ancients have divided Grain Rain into three periods: in the first period, the duckweed starts to grow, for the increasing rainfall. When the second period comes, cuckoos begin to move about frequently to remind people to sow. In the third period, the hoopoes begin to appear on the mulberry. In addition to the typical three periods, it is also time for peony blossoming around Grain Rain, so peony is also known as "Grain Rain Flower" and there is a saying that "Grain Rain is the perfect timing to watch peony" [2].

After reviewing literature and interviewing experts, over 20 kinds of images related to Grain Rain were identified initially, such as duckweed, peony, cedar and so on. They were divided into four types: natural views, farming activities, food culture and folk customs. In addition, the relevant stories, time and location information of each image were collected at the same time.

Questionnaire and Interview. In order to understand the real appearance of images in the modern life, and to understand how the representative images of nature, food, custom of Grain Rain look like in people's views and how do people feel about Grain Rain, questionnaire and interview were designed and carried out.

Questionnaire of Divided Images. There are five parts of the questionnaire: demographic information, images of natural views, foods, customs and overall feeling. Demographics mainly include the participants' gender, age, location information and so on. The images collected in the previous stage were listed separately in the three image categories. Participants were invited to choose one or more images that can represent Grain Rain (they can also add images by themselves). In natural images, participants were asked to select the image and then rank them. Investigation about crops was not included in the questionnaire due to the fact that the general population may know less about it. But there was an open-ended question at the end of the questionnaire in case some participants know crops. In the last part for investigating people's overall feeling, participants were invited to choose representative verse, describe the color of environment and their feeling in Grain Rain.

Interview. In order to investigate the feeling of people whose group was not covered by the questionnaire, such as people aged over 50, and to know how representative people feel about corps in Grain Rain which is not surveyed clearly in the questionnaire, we organized interviews after the questionnaire was completed.

Results. The first part of questionnaire was distributed through the Internet, and 100 valid questionnaires were returned, of which 88 participants were from northern China. A total of 5 participants also from northern China were interviewed. After doing descriptive statistics of the questionnaire and interview data, nine kinds of images that people think can represent Grain Rain were obtained, including rape flower, catkin, cedar, peony, wheat and so on. The analysis summary are as follows (Fig. 1 and Table 1):

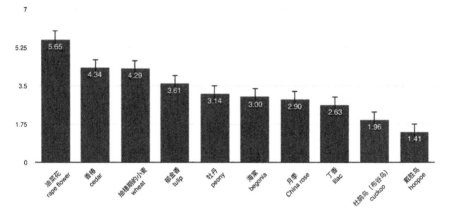

Fig. 1. Rank result of natural views

Table 1. Summary of the first questionnaire and interview

Images	Result from questionnaire	Result from interview	Notes
Cedar	Rank second	Participants know a lot about eating it	In the custom part of the questionnaire, eating cedar ranks first
			In the food part, cedar ranks first except foods not from northern China
Peony	Rank fifth	\	In the custom part of the questionnaire, watching peony was thought to be quite representative
			In the overall feeling of Grain Rain, verse about peony was chosen the most

(continued)

Table 1. (*continued*)

Images	Result from questionnaire	Result from interview	Notes
Catkin	\	Almost every participant has mentioned it	In the open-ended question and description of whole environment, catkin was mentioned quite frequently
Rape flower	Rank first	\	It was planted in the southern China originally, then has been planted in the north for its ornamental value
Wheat	Rank third	\	In the overall feeling of Grain Rain, verse about wheat was chosen many times
Tulip	Rank fourth	\	
Locust tree flower	\	\	In the open-ended question, it was mentioned many times
Cuckoo	\	Some participants have mentioned it, and said they ate it sometimes	The representative animal of Grain Rain
Hoopoe	\	\	The representative animal of Grain Rain

Questionnaire of Images Summary. In the questionnaire and interview described above, representative images were obtained dividedly and there is not a whole representative ranking of them. So another questionnaire was carried out to invite participants to rank the whole images obtained before, then the representativeness and importance of each image will be gained.

The questionnaire was set to ask participants to choose the representative images first and then rank them (Fig. 2).

Results. After distributing it on the Internet, 53 valid questionnaires were returned. The following figure shows the original result (Fig. 3):

From the original data, it is easy to find that the representativeness lists from top to bottom like this: rape flower, catkin, cedar, wheat, cuckoo, tulip, locust tree flower, peony, hoopoe. Considering that most of the participants are ungraduated students, who may know little about peony, and the results of the first questionnaire, interview and the ideas from literature and experts, peony was promoted to the level of more representative (Table 2).

Materials Collection and Arrangement. Field study was carried out during the Grain Rain, after observing the natural views, farm events, foods and customs, lots of pictures of representative images were taken (Fig. 4). Due to the limitation of equipment and environment, a few pictures from professional photographers and Internet were collected as supplements. Then, materials were screened by considering whether its

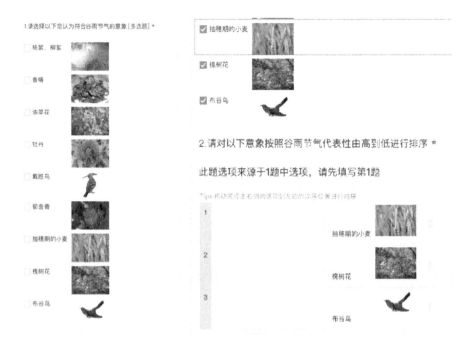

Fig. 2. Questionnaire of images summary

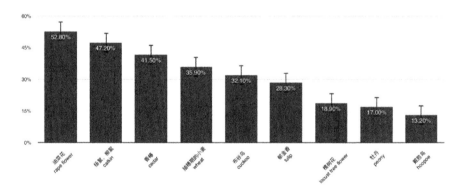

Fig. 3. The result of images ranking

Table 2. Representative images of Grain Rain

	Images
High representative	Rape flower, catkin, cedar, peony
Middle representative	Wheat, cuckoo, tulip, locust tree flower
Low representative	Hoopoe

Fig. 4. Collection of materials (the first row from left to right: cloves, begonia, tulip, peony, the second row from left to right: Chinese rose, rape flower, wheat, cedar)

exposure parameter was reasonable, and whether it is close to the real image. About 5 pictures were chosen to be used in the color extraction.

3.2 Stage Two (Color Extraction and Coordination)

The most widely and often used color extraction approaches, such as K-means clustering, cannot generate color with high level of chroma or extract color that can be a great match to the standard color palette, whose results cannot be used in realistic design [5]. Colors extracted from several pictures of one certain image cannot be merged through these approaches.

The color extraction algorithm can be divided into two steps: initially extracting color (octree algorithm part) and comparing initial colors with the standard color palette (least-significant difference method part). The gray color will be revised as standard color, while the count of each color will come out with each picture so that colors can be merged in the end.

Octree Algorithm. Octree algorithm was created in 1988 at first [6]. Octree is suitable for representing color space, all the colors can be distributed in a cube. In the cube, RGB colors are made as the axes, each of which has numbers from 0 to 255. In this way, each color can be mapped to a certain position in the cube [7]. The structure is suitable for quantifying colors from images, and there are huge advantages of the time complexity and the spatial complexity, as well as the fidelity compared with other methods.

The R, G, B value of color of each pixel form pictures will be obtained, changed to binary numbers and written line by line. The sub-node number of one node will be obtained after arranging RGB channels column by column. Doing this for every pixel in a picture will result in an octree with complete information. For the bottom adjacent leaves, the first seven places of them are same and only the last place is different, in other words, colors represented by these brother nodes will be similar in a certain range. When number of these leaves reaches one certain value, they can be merged to the upper level while preserving the quantity information. After repeating this process, colors will be obtained whose quantity is in a certain range. Due to the uncertainty of color quantity, the range of quantity is specified that no more than 256 colors will be extracted. In this study, the first 64 species of color will be picked for further study.

But there are still some problems of colors extracted by octree algorithm:

a. the quantity of colors cannot be certain
b. it is possible that there are similar colors
c. the colors cannot be used immediately which need to be chosen according to certain situation.

The least-significant difference algorithm will solve these problems.

Least-Significant Difference Algorithm (LSD). By the octree algorithm, the color contained in the picture can be extracted. The color group is not up to any standard palette, although the fidelity of these colors is pretty high, the extracting colors cannot be used directly in the production environment because the colors used in design and production should be based on design guideline and standard palette. The least-significant difference method which will be expressed next, is used to solve such problems.

The color set extracted from the original image by octree algorithm is called the original color group. The color set specified by the design guideline in the production environment is called the standard color group (the Material Design palette was used in this paper, shown in Fig. 5). The aim of the algorithm is to find the extraction color group from the standard color group, which is the most similar to the original color group. The extraction of color groups can ensure that the color of the original picture is similar to the color of the original picture, and it can also ensure that it is standardized. It can ensure the similarity between the extracted color group and the color style of the original image. The extraction color group is also standardized and normalized).

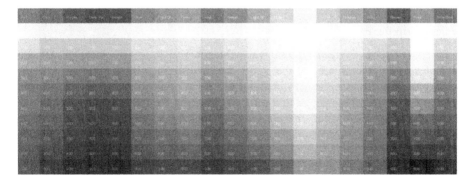

Fig. 5. Material design palette

The LSD algorithm can be divided into three steps: first, calculating the hue of each color in the original color group; second, getting the standard color set which is close to the hue in the standard color group; third, finding out the most similar color between the standard color set and the original color in value and chroma [8].

There are several difficult problems to be dealt with in this method: the first one is how to judge the closest difference of value and chroma in the third step. The usual method, Euclidean distance method will neutralize the difference between two dimensions of color, and the result of color extraction is close to the theoretical distance, but the visual effect shows it is not reasonable. In order to find the color with the smallest difference, we decided to calculate the distance on every dimension, and judge it with the largest distance instead of Euclidean distance. The second is how to deal with the gray color group in the phase of finding the similar color set. Because there is no gray hue, so a guideline has been issued that if the BRG values of a kind of color are too close (the distance between the three values is less than 8), the color is judged to be gray. The third is the classification of standard color groups. Most of the standard color

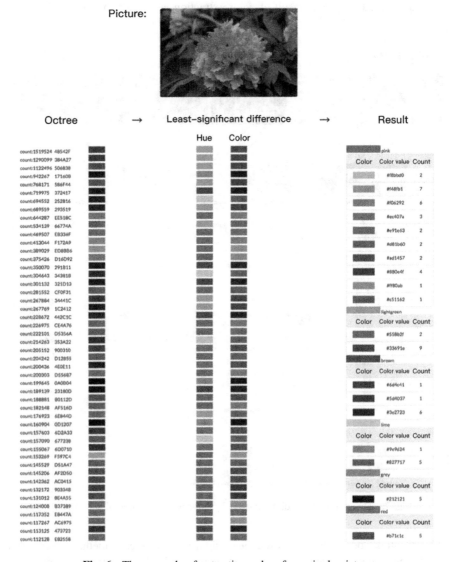

Fig. 6. The example of extracting colors from single picture

palettes are grouped according to hue attributes (such as material design palette), but it performs bad if using this classification directly. There are many colors that are too bright or too low in chroma, though they are quite different from each other in hue, people will consider them very close to white or black. They need to be processed separately. These colors will be filtered out and placed in special high value sets and low chroma sets.

The function of the algorithm was developed based on Web technology. After uploading the picture to the web server, the color extraction results of the picture will be returned. As shown in the Fig. 6:

After extracting colors of all the pictures of each image, the number of the same color was merged to get the result of color extraction, as shown in the Fig. 7:

Peony_pinks

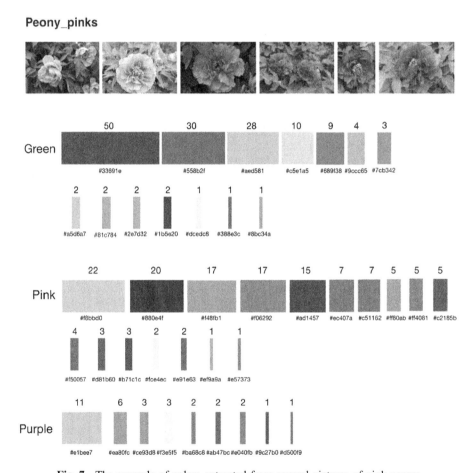

Fig. 7. The example of colors extracted from several pictures of pink peony

In this study, octree combined with least-significant difference method was carried out. This method can generate a great representative of the theme color of the picture as it can ensure the similarity between the extracted color group and the color style of the original image. Also, the color is obtained after matching the given standard colors, so that it can be directly used in the design and development links. Moreover, this method also provides the quantity information of colors in the original materials, which can be acting as the reference for coordinating colors.

Color Selection and Aesthetics Calculation. After preliminarily extracting certain kinds of color, considering the design application, 3–4 colors were selected for color matching from the original result of color extraction (Fig. 8). During the selection process, the quantity information based on the color extraction was taken into consideration, comparative analysis of the image was done, and the most appropriate colors of the image itself would be chosen. Besides, the differences of value, hue, etc. were taken into account.

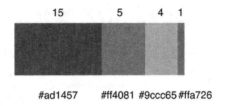

Fig. 8. The example of chosen colors of pink peony

After screening, to make sure these several colors in harness comply with the requirements of aesthetics, M•Spenser's aesthetic measurement was carried out [9]. The aesthetic value should be greater than 0.5. If not, filter the representative color again.

$$M = O/C \tag{1}$$

In formula (1), M is the value of aesthetic, O is the order factor, C is the complexity factor.

This is in agreement with the qualitative opinion that "beauty lies in the unity of diversity", the fundamental principle of beauty in form. But what he has put forward is a quantitative and operable standard of evaluation. The complex factor here means diversity, and the order factor corresponds to unity.

Mencius and Spencer introduced the quantitative formula into the evaluation of color scheme. After experiments, they think that the order factor O has different values whether there is colored hue in color scheme, that is,

$$O = \sum Og \text{ (when consisting of only colorless composition)} \tag{2}$$

$$O = \sum Oh + Ov + Oc \text{ (when consisting of color)} \tag{3}$$

In the formula, Og is an order factor only in a colorless grey combination. Oh, Ov and Oc are all order factors determined by hue difference, value difference or chroma difference when there is any kind of color in color matching. Their values depend on the difference between each color attribute, and all order factors are shown in Figs. 9, 10 and Table 3.

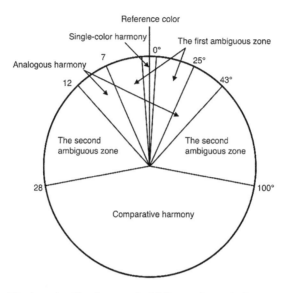

Fig. 9. The hue classification map in M•Spenser's aesthetic measurement

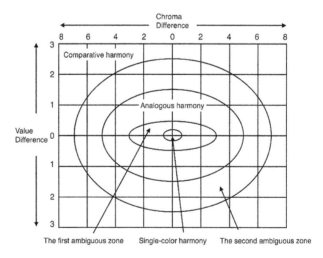

Fig. 10. The value and chroma classification map in M•Spenser's aesthetic measurement

Table 3. The order factors

Order factors	Single-color harmony	The first ambiguous zone	Analogous harmony	The second ambiguous zone	Comparative harmony	Dazzling
Oh	+1.5	0	+1.1	+0.65	+1.7	
Ov	−1.3	−1.0	+0.7	−0.2	+3.7	−0.2
Oc	+0.8	0	+0.1	0	+0.4	
Og	+1.0					

In formula (1), the complex factor C is composed of:

$$C = Cm + Ch + Cv + Cc \tag{4}$$

In formula (4), Cm is the total number of colors in color scheme; Ch the number of color pairs with hue difference; Cv the number of color pairs with value difference; Cc the number of color pairs with chroma difference.

Color Matching. Munsell Color Harmony Theory was carried out to determine the area ratio of each color and gain the color scheme of one certain image [10]. Munsell color system use the value of hue, value and chroma to specify a specific color. In this color system, the same contrast relationship must be shown between the same intervals of color. Color with the same value of value or chroma will perform the same lightness or chroma in the visual sense regardless of any hue. Specifically, the varieties of value and chroma are relevant to the area ratio when matching several colors. The ratio of products of value and chroma of a pair of colors are inversely proportional to their area ratio. There are other key points of Munsell Color Harmony Theory such as: the matching and reconciliation performs the best between colors with the same hue in hue-blending; when doing the chroma-blending in the same hue as the premise, the color number should be controlled and so on. The above points are to provide a theoretical basis for the color collocation.

As an example, change the RGB of 4 colors extracting and screening from pink peony into the value of hue, value and chroma in Munsell color system, they all meet the following formulas:

$$\text{(The value of A} \times \text{the chroma of A)}/\text{(The value of B} \times \text{the chroma of B)}$$
$$= \text{The area of B/the area of A} \tag{5}$$

$$\text{(The value of A} \times \text{the chroma of A)}/\text{(The value of C} \times \text{the chroma of C)}$$
$$= \text{The area of C/the area of A} \tag{6}$$

$$\text{(The value of A} \times \text{the chroma of A)}/\text{(The value of B} \times \text{the chroma of B)}$$
$$= \text{The area of D/the area of A} \tag{7}$$

that is:

$$(\text{The value of A} \times \text{the chroma of A}) \times \text{the area of A}$$
$$= (\text{The value of B} \times \text{the chroma of B}) \times \text{the area of B}$$
$$= (\text{The value of C} \times \text{the chroma of C}) \times \text{the area of C} \quad (8)$$
$$= (\text{The value of D} \times \text{the chroma of D}) \times \text{the area of D}$$

According to the formulas above, the area ratio of 4 colors can be calculated (Fig. 11):

$$S_{A:}S_{B:}S_{C:}S_D = 84 \times 70 \times 48 : 96 \times 70 \times 48 : 96 \times 84 \times 48 : 96 \times 84 \times 70$$
$$= 70 : 48 : 40 : 35$$

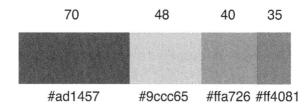

Fig. 11. The example of color scheme of pink peony obtained by Munsell Color Harmony Theory

3.3   Stage Three (Color Scheme Application)

Based on the color image vocabulary from Nippon Color & Design Research Institute, the Semantic Difference method in Kansei engineering was carried out to measure the color emotion of each color scheme [11–13]. 14 emotion adjectives were chosen from the color image coordinates. They are romantic, pretty, casual, dynamic, clear, modern, natural, elegant, chic, old-fashioned, dapper, luxurious, wild and formal (Fig. 12).

The Semantic Difference method in Kansei engineering is divided into several steps. The first step is to find the corresponding antonyms for the existing color emotion words, and form pairs of positive and antonym words (a pair of words is composed of two words in the exist color image coordinates) (Table 4).

The second step is to use color emotion semantic difference scale consisting of the pairs of emotion words to evaluate color schemes. Participants were asked to select one word in the pair and degree that could describe their subjective feelings on a color scheme. For example, one color scheme allows the participants to feel somewhat romantic, in "romantic-rational" pair the score should be "−1"; if making the participants feel very romantic, in "romantic-rational" pair the score should be "−2"; if there is no difference in feeling, "0" should be selected.

53 participants were asked to evaluate all of the color schemes using 5-point scale on the Internet, then their responses were analyzed by carrying out item analysis and

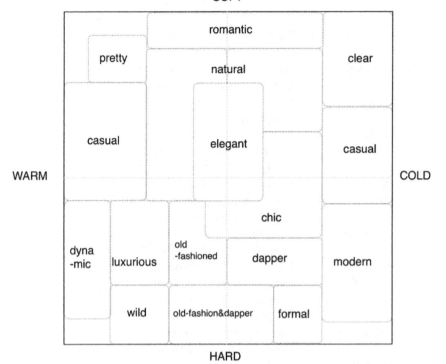

Fig. 12. The color emotion coordinates from Nippon Color & Design Research Institute

Table 4. Pairs of emotion words (original)

No.	Emotion words	
1	浪漫的-理智的	romantic/rational
2	可爱的-厌烦的	pretty/annoying
3	闲适的-烦扰的	casual/disturbing
4	动感的-静态的	dynamic/static
5	清爽的-污浊的	clear/dirty
6	现代的-古典的	modern/old-fashioned
7	自然的-人造的	natural/manmade
8	雅致的-庸俗的	elegant/vulgar
9	精致的-粗劣的	chic/coarse
10	考究的-随意的	dapper/nonchalant
11	豪华的-朴素的	luxurious/plain
12	粗犷的-细腻的	wild/elaborate & delicate
13	正式的-随便的	wild/elaborate & delicate

Table 5. The result of item analysis

		Significance (two-tailed)
romantic/rational	Equal number of variations	0
	Unequal number of variations	0
pretty/annoying	Equal number of variations	0
	Unequal number of variations	0
casual/disturbing	Equal number of variations	0
	Unequal number of variations	0
dynamic/static	Equal number of variations	0
	Unequal number of variations	0
clear/dirty	Equal number of variations	0
	Unequal number of variations	0
modern/old-fashioned	Equal number of variations	0.01
	Unequal number of variations	0.009
natural/manmade	Equal number of variations	0
	Unequal number of variations	0
elegant/vulgar	Equal number of variations	0
	Unequal number of variations	0
chic/coarse	Equal number of variations	0
	Unequal number of variations	0
dapper/nonchalant	Equal number of variations	0
	Unequal number of variations	0
luxurious/plain	Equal number of variations	0
	Unequal number of variations	0
wild/elaborate & delicate	Equal number of variations	0.058
	Unequal number of variations	0.058
formal/informal	Equal number of variations	0
	Unequal number of variations	0

Pearson correlation test, two pairs of emotion words not significant were eliminated. The color image semantic difference scale was optimized.

From this table, it is obvious that significant values of the pair "wild and elaborate & delicate" are more than 0.01, proving that it is not significant and should be removed.

The result of Pearson correlation test shown in Table 5 concurred with the result of item analysis shown in Table 6, the pair "wild and elaborate & delicate" should be removed. The modified pairs of color emotion are shown in Table 7, which were used to evaluate color schemes finally.

Then calculating the score of every color scheme, the emotion words suitable to describe the color scheme would be determined. In addition, it is possible to discovery more situation relevant to use the color scheme. For example, the color scheme extracted from pink peony is relatively lovely and luxurious, kind of romantic, natural and leisurely according the scores, which can be used in packing design of luxurious food or clothing design (Fig. 13).

Table 6. The result of Pearson correlation test

	Pearson correlation	Significance (two-tailed)
romantic/rational	0.415	0.000
pretty/annoying	0.635	0.000
casual/disturbing	0.633	0.000
dynamic/static	0.313	0.000
clear/dirty	0.654	0.000
modern/old-fashioned	0.200	0.003
natural/manmade	0.518	0.000
elegant/vulgar	0.627	0.000
chic/coarse	0.658	0.000
dapper/nonchalant	0.440	0.000
luxurious/plain	0.291	0.000
wild/elaborate & delicate	−0.141	0.037
formal/informal	0.397	0.000

Table 7. Pairs of emotion words (modified)

No.	Emotion words	
1	浪漫的-理智的	romantic/rational
2	可爱的-厌烦的	pretty/annoying
3	闲适的-烦扰的	casual/disturbing
4	动感的-静态的	dynamic/static
5	清爽的-污浊的	clear/dirty
6	现代的-古典的	modern/old-fashioned
7	自然的-人造的	natural/manmade
8	雅致的-庸俗的	elegant/vulgar
9	精致的-粗劣的	chic/coarse
10	考究的-随意的	dapper/nonchalant
11	豪华的-朴素的	luxurious/plain
12	正式的-随便的	formal/informal

Putting color schemes of all representative images of Grain Rain into the color image coordinates, it can be found that color schemes are mainly distributed in pretty, romantic, natural, clear and casual, some of them are distributed in luxurious, chic, dapper (Fig. 14).

As for designing in related fields of Grain Rain, clear and romantic color schemes can be used, such as color schemes from wheat, white peony and white locust tree flower and color scheme, or from purple tulip, rape flower etc.

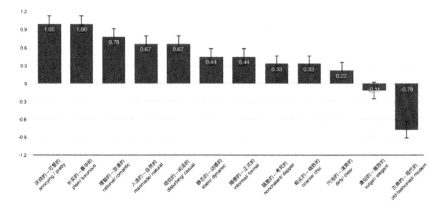

Fig. 13. The scores of the color scheme of pink peony

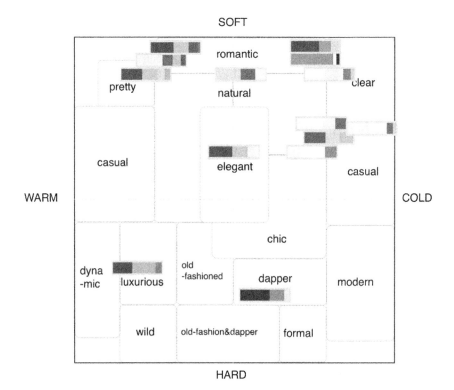

Fig. 14. The color emotion of representative color schemes of Grain Rain

4   Conclusion

The views in this paper are different from China's past subjective and experiential color views and research ideas, but combining western scientific color system, and a scientific method system to extract color schemes from real environment and real things was proposed which includes the acquisition of picture materials, color extraction, harmonization and evaluation. It can be used in even every field to extract the theme color or color matching scheme from any picture material. Especially in the step of carrying out least-significant difference method, the standard palette can be defined as any palette in any industry, which ensures the color schemes extracted can be used in actual production and processing, or meet the display specification in Internet industry etc.

In this paper, M•Spenser's aesthetic measurement and Munsell Color Harmony Theory may be relatively old, but still be able to meet the demand of the method. In the future, it is necessary to explore new aesthetic evaluation methods and new color harmony theory. Then the color schemes obtained by the new theories can be contrasted with the schemes obtained in this paper to see the difference and the quality.

In addition, in the following research participants can be asked to assess whether the color scheme can represent the image or Grain Rain. The research of inviting participants to evaluate the representation of color schemes in graphic design or product design using the color schemes extracted by the method system can also be carried out (using semantic differential method), which will verify the rationality of the extraction and application of color schemes.

References

1. Jiang, C.: Chinese Chromatology. Gansu People's Publishing House, Lanzhou Municipality (2008)
2. Hu, W.: Solar Terms. Harbin Publishing House, Harbin City (2015)
3. He, N.: Huainanzi Collected Explanations, vol. 3. China Publishing House, Haikou City (1998)
4. Liang, Q.: Knowledge of the 24 Solar Terms. Beijing United Publishing Co., Ltd., Beijing (2013)
5. Liu, X., Lu, C., Li, G.: A study on the extraction and reuse of color design. Comput. Eng. Appl. **40**(27), 32–33 (2004)
6. Gervautz, M., Purgathofer, W.: A simple method for color quantization: octree quantization. New Trends Comput. Graph. **36**(5), 287–293 (1988)
7. Sharma, G., Trussell, H.J.: Digital color imaging. IEEE Trans. Image Process. **6**(7), 901–932 (1997)
8. Meier, U.: A note on the power of Fisher's least significant difference procedure. Pharm. Stat. **5**(4), 253–263 (2006)
9. Zhang, X.: Color Design. Chemical Industry Press, Beijing (2003)
10. Zheng, X.: Color harmony theory research. Doctoral dissertation, Soochow University (2013)
11. Kobayashi, S.: Color Image Coordinates. People's Fine Arts Publishing House, Beijing (2006)

12. Hogg, J.: The prediction of semantic differential ratings of color combinations. J. Gen. Psychol. **80**(1st Half), 141–152 (1969)
13. Sakuta, Y., Gyoba, J.: Affective impressions and memorability of color-form combinations. J. Gen. Psychol. **133**(2), 191–207 (2006)

Design of Graphical User Interfaces to Implement New Features in an ATM System of a Financial Bank

Roy Meléndez$^{(\boxtimes)}$ and Freddy Paz

Pontificia Universidad Católica del Perú, Lima 32, Peru
roy.melendez@pucp.edu.pe, fpaz@pucp.pe

Abstract. Actually, many bank customers would like to be able to perform various banking operations from an ATM in such a way that the entire process of long queues is avoided and the waiting time in the transaction process is reduced, which must guarantee the security of the customer's data. That is why, as part of the human-computer interaction course of the PUCP of the master in informatics, it was decided with the support of the BBVA Continental to develop the design project of new operations for its ATMs. For the development of this project, three meetings were considered. In a first meeting, information was gathered with the bank's workers, to be clear about how the operations that are to be designed are being carried out. For our second meeting, the evaluation of the prototypes was carried out in the bank's facilities, for which usability tests were developed. In the last meeting, the improved prototypes were presented according to the breaks recorded in the usability tests. Ultimately, in order to carry out this project, a framework was developed which guaranteed constant interaction with our users and being able to meet all their needs.

Keywords: Human-computer interaction · User-centered design
Graphical user interfaces · Usability · Automatic teller machine

1 Introduction

According to the study carried out by Curran [1], the inconveniences of using an ATM are closely related to the design of the interface, as it is apparently mentioned that many ATM navigation menus are still not as intuitive or as efficient as they could be. In this context, BBVA Continental, which is one of the leading financial entities in Peru, has been showing interest since a few years ago in the development of interfaces with user experience in its transactions.

According to the work carried out by Moquillaza [2], BBVA changed its ATM application a few years ago. In this previous study, the authors determined that the interfaces of their software systems needed improvements in usability. However, there was not much information or methods in the industry to develop usable interfaces for ATMs.

According to the study conducted by Peres [3], it is argued that banks invest more in projects focused on the user and for this purpose considers two necessary methods:

© Springer International Publishing AG, part of Springer Nature 2018
A. Marcus and W. Wang (Eds.): DUXU 2018, LNCS 10919, pp. 247–257, 2018.
https://doi.org/10.1007/978-3-319-91803-7_18

- Usability evaluation.
- Cognitive Inspection.

According to the study carried out by Cooharojananonre [4], two very important aspects are considered to improve the usability of ATMs and reduce their complexity:

- The design of the hierarchical structure of the menu is very difficult to Access.
- Limitation of the number of buttons on the interface screen.

Regarding the usability heuristics that are applied in ATM systems, those mentioned in the Rosenbaum [5] study are considered, which are quite clear and are applied in the same way in transactions such as user control and freedom, prevention of errors and visibility of the state of the system.

According to Van der Geest [6], two aspects must be considered when designing a better user experience:

- Address the user experience as a multi-dimensional construction that includes affective responses to the instrumental qualities of the system.
- Also treat the emotional responses, feelings, and emotions before, during and after the experience of using it.

In this context, BBVA Continental contacted the Pontifical Catholic University of Peru to present its case and requested the improvement of its interfaces. BBVA Continental requested the design of its new banking operations as part of the process of improving the usability of its ATM system. The design should allow the following functions: online check deposit, payment of services and collections for non-customers, the sale of tickets and frequent transactions such as transfer to third parties, payment of services and collections for customers, fast deposit and fast withdrawal.

Later the project was considered as part of the human-computer interaction course of the computer science master's degree. The teacher proposed this project to be developed throughout the course. The final product for the students was to develop a prototype validated by the users.

In order to develop these proposals, the following techniques were considered: metaphors, usability engineering, user profiles, UX story, semiotic engineering, and others.

Finally, for the validation of the prototype, we use the user's tests. Then the design was validated with real users who were classmates and workers of BBVA Continental. This validation allowed for feedback and new information, which was used to improve the prototype.

2 Background

2.1 Human-Computer Interaction

According to the study conducted by Garg [7], HCI is the field of computer science that focuses on the interfaces between humans and computers. It refers to the way in which humans interact with computers and how they provide the user with a pleasant experience.

2.2 Metaphors

According to the study carried out by Abdulhassan [8], metaphors are a conventional approach to user interface design, and he also mentions two reasons to use them:

- You can take advantage of people's knowledge of the world around them by using metaphors to convey concepts and features of the application.
- The recognizable metaphors provide a direct and intuitive interface for the user's tasks.

  It also mentions the benefits of adopting metaphors:

- Makes learning new systems easier.
- It helps users to understand the underlying conceptual model.
- It can be very clever and allow computers and their applications to become more accessible to a greater diversity of users.

2.3 Usability Engineering

According to the study carried out by Chen [9], usability engineering is an advanced methodology of systems development based on psychology. It uses many methods of research in psychology, labor efficiency of human beings, industrial design, man-machine interface, sociology, computer science, statistics, etc. Values human factors in the application of technology also improves the development of the user-centered design.

2.4 User Profiles

According to Granollers [10], we can understand the user profile of an interactive system as a detailed description of the attributes of the users (work, education, usual tasks, age, etc.). These characteristics are usually reflected in ranges of values, and in this way, real users will be within those fields.

2.5 UX Story

According to Gibbons [11], a UX Story is an account of events from the user's perspective; the events in the story show the evolution of an experience.

2.6 Heuristic Evaluation

According to the study conducted by Nielsen [12], the heuristic evaluation is an inspection method, in which 3 or 5 usability experts judge whether each element of a graphical user interface follows the established principles, called heuristics.

2.7   Semiotics Engineering

According to the study carried out by Souza [13], semiotic engineering is defined as a branch of computer engineering focused on the research of communication between designers and users. In semiotic engineering, HCI is a meta-communication process.

2.8   Usability Test

According to the study conducted by Paz [14], the usability test is a usability evaluation method in which a representative number of end users are asked to interact voluntarily with the system. During this test, users must perform a set of predefined tasks using the software product that was tested. While users use the software, usability specialists can identify usability problems through user observation.

3   Case Study: Design of New Functions for the ATM Interfaces of the BBVA Continental Bank

3.1   Purpose of Study

The objective of this work was to design the new functionalities for the ATM interfaces of Banco BBVA Continental. This new interface must meet the following requirements:

- **Checks:** Deposits online, only own checks, one check at a time.
- **Payment of services and collections for non-customers.**
- **Ticket Sales:** Sale of Tickets, with a debit and cash.
- **Frequent Operations:** Transfers to Third Parties, Payment of services and collections, fast deposit and fast withdrawal.

The bank through two meetings held in the classroom provided all the information related to how these operations are performed at the window, and what are their requirements to consider in the design of these functionalities in the ATM interface. In addition, the bank established two main objectives.

- Provide the design of new functionalities that adapt to the needs of the user.
- Apply quality usability tests to obtain good feedback from the user and develop quality prototypes.

3.2   Methodology

The design of the functionality will be based on the user-centered design, according to the topics and techniques developed in the course, in the order shown in the following diagram (Fig. 1):

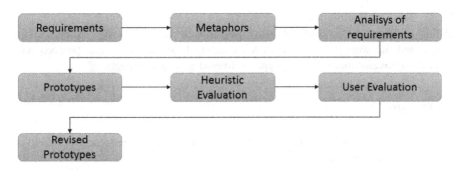

Fig. 1. Steps to make the proposal based on the User-Centered Design Methodology

3.2.1 Requirements
In this first point, we took note of the needs of the users of Bank BBVA Continental where they provided their requirements as a discussion in two meetings held in class.

3.2.2 Metaphors
For the development of the metaphors the following evaluation criteria have been taken into account: Structuring, Applicability, Representation, Adaptability to the domain and Extensibility.

3.2.3 Analysis of Requirements
At this point, we try to find the degree of acceptance that users have with the requirements raised for which was made first of an ethnographic study and then made use of the technical people and user experience stories.

3.2.4 Prototypes
At this point, the prototypes and navigability were designed according to previously identified requirements.

3.2.5 Heuristic Evaluation
For the heuristic evaluation, the methodology was used, which consists of applying the ten basic principles presented by Nielsen [12], in order to find some observations by the evaluating users, an analysis of the results can then be made and determine what their modifications.

3.2.6 User Evaluation
At this point, usability tests were prepared for the users. The result of this point allowed to identify improvements to the proposals and feedback from the users on the functionalities and other related aspects, normally ignored in the design time.

3.2.7   Revised Prototypes

In this last point, we considered both the feedback received by the students of the course and the workers of the BBVA Continental, to analyze it and proceed with several improvements in the prototypes delivered as a first artifact.

4   Results

As mentioned, the methodology described follows the techniques learned and developed throughout the course.

The challenge of this design is to develop and add new features to the automatic teller machines of Bank BBVA Continental. In this sense, an analysis is required of both the requirements of the interested users as well as the needs of the people when interacting with these new functions.

4.1   Requirements

In order to meet the requirements, two meetings took place in class with the BBVA Continental Bank group to consider the details of how the operations currently being implemented in their ATMs are being carried out.

4.2   Metaphors

As previously mentioned in the methodological part, criteria learned and developed in the course were considered to make user interaction with the interface as user-friendly as possible. These criteria are the following:

- **Structuring:** We are considering a set of metaphors of eight elements; the most used functions are on the right.
- **Applicability:** Each of our metaphors is applied when the user requires it, he knows when to apply it because our metaphor is intuitive.
- **Representation:** Our metaphors are associated with text and image, and the user interprets metaphors in a unique way.
- **Adaptability to the domain:** For the user of our domain it will be very easy to associate image and text. Our set of metaphors has been designed from the physical domain.
- **Extensibility:** It could be the case that by including new functionalities in our metaphors, the current structuring of these changed.

The design of the metaphors are shown in the following scheme (Fig. 2):

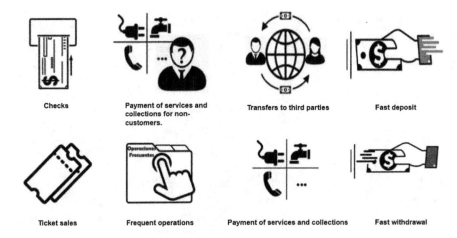

Fig. 2. Design of Metaphors

4.3 Analysis of Requirements

At this point it was considered to carry out an ethnographic study first, then two techniques were used; first, the user profile technique was used to then use the UX Story technique. The following results were obtained from the ethnographic study:

- Users who make check deposits see it convenient to do it by ATM since they would save time instead of doing it through the window.
- The majority of the users who make purchases of tickets, see viable the fact of making a purchase from the ATM as long as it is simple and clear.
- Users over 60 years of age are more distrustful of ATM use due to fear of faults, so they prefer to do their operations directly at the windows.
- The majority of users as one of its most used operations has cash withdrawal, so the option of frequent operations Fast withdrawal; It would be one of the options that could be the most used.

Then, using the user profile technique, the following results were obtained:

- Users between 25 and 35 years of age consider making the check deposit by ATM, in this way they avoid the long queues to be served at the teller window. They also consider buying tickets for ATMs, always and when they have all the clear information about them (hours, prices, seats, etc.).
- In users over 60 years of age, there is a certain degree of mistrust in making purchases through ATMs, but a good number of users are interested in buying tickets in ATM to events because it would save time.

Finally, to complete this step, we considered the UX Story for the functionalities, as shown in the diagram (Fig. 3), the user experience in the realization of the services payment operation.

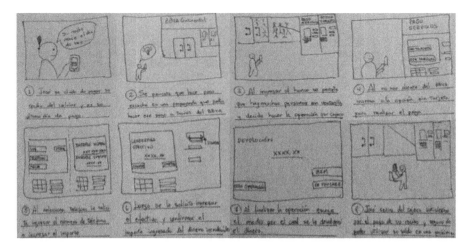

Fig. 3. UX story payment of services

4.4   Heuristic Evaluation

In this stage, colleagues from another group carried out the evaluation of our prototypes in their first version, taking into account the ten principles presented by Nielsen [12], in order to consider them in the redesign of our prototypes. The results of the evaluation were the following:

- On the principle of prevention of errors, the evaluated product presents in its operations several inconveniences that do not allow to go back to the previous step. This possibility has been confused with the action of canceling and definitively leaving the operation.
- About the principle of coincidence between the system and the real world, the product has deficiencies in the definition of the graphics component that allows the selection of options (for example, the distribution of seats on a bus).
- The aesthetic and minimalist design is the principle with fewer associated problems. The product has correctly divided each of the steps in such a way that the user recognizes exactly what is to be done in each one of them. The interfaces are precise, clear and do not present elements that could confuse the user.

4.5   User Evaluation

After considering the changes proposed in the previous stage, the redesign of our prototypes was made, then we proceeded to evaluate these prototypes reviewed by four classmates who will have the role of real users of the system and evaluate the operation of making a quick deposit as also eliminate a fast deposit. The results of this evaluation were the following:

- In task 1, making a fast deposit, users developed activities with delay because they did not easily find the frequent operations option.

- In task 2, delete a fast deposit, users developed activities with delay because they did not easily find the frequent operations option.
- All users considered that the information required in the test was easy to find.
- All users consider that the information obtained has been useful.
- All users agree that the most pleasant thing about the fast deposit operation was its simplicity.

4.6   Prototypes

As a result of the methodology described, the following interfaces were proposed and sent to BBVA Continental. Some of the proposed screens were the following (Figs. 4, 5 and 6):

Fig. 4. Operations for clients (prototype)

Fig. 5. Frequent operations (prototype)

Fig. 6. Deposit of checks (prototype)

5 Validation

For this section, what was obtained in the user test was discussed. In this test, our evaluated were four participants who are students of the course and workers of the BBVA Continental, whose ages ranged between 27 and 30 years. In addition, the test was executed in the testing environments of the Bank BBVA Continental.

In addition, the test was performed individually, where each user had at his disposal an evaluator who accompanied him in the process. The confidentiality agreement and a list of previous indications were also presented to each participant. Each participant agreed and signed the indicated documents.

Subsequently, each participant was given the pre-test questionnaire, which was filled immediately. Next, each participant was given the list of tasks, and some general queries were resolved, immediately after recording the interaction, and the user was left in front of the cashier, and each evaluator took note in the compliance form the tasks, and the breaks that were observed. Finally, each participant was given the post-test questionnaire to complete it with the information requested, which ended the execution of the test.

6 Conclusions and Future Work

At the end of this design, we can conclude that the delivered prototypes allow users to use the system with greater satisfaction.

It was also concluded that it is necessary to follow a process of analysis requirements and interaction design to guarantee a design focused on the real needs of the user.

From the results obtained from the usability test, we can affirm that the majority of the users did the tasks without much difficulty.

References

1. Curran, K., King, D.: Investigating the human computer interaction problems with automated teller machine (ATM) navigation menus. Comput. Inf. Sci. 34–51 (2008)
2. Moquillaza, A., Molina, E., Noguera, E., Enríquez, L., Muñoz, A., Paz, F., Collazos, C.: Developing an ATM interface using user-centered design techniques. In: Marcus, A., Wang, W. (eds.) DUXU 2017. LNCS, vol. 10290, pp. 690–701. Springer, Cham (2017). https://doi.org/10.1007/978-3-319-58640-3_49
3. Peres, R., Cardoso, E., Jeske, J., Da Cunha, I.: Usability in ATMs. In: Proceedings of the 2011 IEEE Systems and Information Engineering Design Symposium, April 2011, pp. 71–75 (2011)
4. Cooharojananone, N., Taohai, K., Phimoltares, S.: A new design of ATM interface for banking services in Thailand. In: Proceeding of the 10th Annual International Symposium on Applications and the Internet, July 2010, pp. 312–315 (2010)
5. Rosenbaum, S.: Creating usable self-service interactions. In: 2010 IEEE International Professional Communication Conference (IPCC), July 2010, pp. 344–349 (2010)
6. Van der Geest, T., Ramey, J., Rosenbaum, S., Van Velsen, L.: Introduction to the special section: designing a better user experience for self-service systems. IEEE Trans. Prof. Commun. **56**(2), 92–96 (2013)
7. Garg, H., Choudhury, T., Kumar, P., Sabitha, S.: Comparison between significance of usability and security in HCI. In: Proceeding of the 3rd IEEE International Conference on "Computational Intelligence and Communication Technology", July 2017, pp. 1–4 (2017)
8. Abdulhassan, R., Massod, M., Hosam, A.: Semiotic differences of macintosh Os X & Microsoft Windows 7 based on metaphors and interpretation. In: Proceeding of the 2nd International Conference on Intelligent Systems, Modelling and Simulation, March 2011, pp. 209–213 (2011)
9. Chen, J., Xuan, Y., Jin, C.: Study on usability engineering of the command and control software design for armored vehicle. In: International Conference on Computer Science and Service System, December 2012, pp. 491–493 (2012)
10. Granollers, T.: Perfil de usuario: técnica PERSONAS. http://www.grihotools.udl.cat/mpiua/perfil-de-usuario-tecnica-personas/. Accessed 20 Dec 2017
11. Gibbons, S.: UX Stories Communicate Designs. http://www.nngroup.com/articles/ux-stories/. Accessed 20 Dec 2017
12. Nielsen, J.: Usability inspection methods. In: Conference Companion on Human Factors in Computing Systems, April 1994, pp. 413–414 (1994)
13. Souza, S.: The Semiotic Engineering of Human-Computer Interaction. The MIT Press, Cambridge (2005)
14. Paz, F., Villanueva, D., Pow-Sang, J.: Heuristic evaluation as a complement to usability testing: a case study in web domain. In: Proceedings of the 12th International Conference on Information Technology – New Generations, June 2015, pp. 546–551 (2015)

Research on the Influence of Multidimensional Display for Users' Concerns

Yingying Miao[1], Weiying Pan[2(✉)], and Bin Jiang[2]

[1] Engineering Training Center, Nanjing University of Science and Technology,
200, Xiaolingwei Street, Nanjing 210094, Jiangsu, China
398991222@qq.com
[2] School of Design Arts and Media, Nanjing University of Science
and Technology, 200, Xiaolingwei Street, Nanjing 210094, Jiangsu, China
1692847688@qq.com, 631603555@qq.com

Abstract. The purpose of the Display Design is to present more information about a product which can help users to understand more about the product, so that get more and more feedback from users to improve the products to meet users' needs.

With the development of multimedia technology, the presentation dimension of modern exhibition design is becoming increasingly diverse. This article bases on the analysis of users' visual attention of different information point under the different dimensions display, to explore the influence of different dimension product shows for user's visual attention. Thus we can provide more accurate and specific application methods for product Display Design, to guide users to know the relevant information of products efficiently. First of all, this article classifies display's dimensional modes of existing Display Design by research. Then, we use smart home coffee machine as the subjects, use 25 to 35 years people as the subjects crowd to carry out this control variable experiment of user's understanding level of the information in different dimensions display. Then, we use the method of mathematical statistics to analyze our experimental data to conclude the effect of user's visual attention for different product information in different dimensions display. We hope It could provide the basis for the targeted application of product Display Design, so that we can use different dimension to give the visitors a better display experience in the future, to improve the effect of Display Design's information delivery.

Keywords: Display Design · User's focus · Character of dimensions
Virtual reality

1 Introduction

With the development of multimedia technology, the presentation of Display Design is becoming more and more diversified. From plane to stereo, from static to dynamic, and from material to non-material, more and more display designers begin to pay more attention to the presentation of interaction's efficiency. The Display Design has aroused a burst of virtual heat, especially in recent years with the maturity of virtual reality technology. Many exhibitions have used 3D simulation technology to replace some

A. Marcus and W. Wang (Eds.): DUXU 2018, LNCS 10919, pp. 258–270, 2018.
https://doi.org/10.1007/978-3-319-91803-7_19

traditional plane information display [1]. But whether 3D visual stimulation is really better than 2D, whether all visual information can be presented by 3D display effectively is still a question which present display designer should consider.

2 The Application of Display Design and It's Current Situation

2.1 The Development Current Situation of Display Design

The opening of the London World Exposition in 1851 opens the history of our world exhibition design develops officially, at the same time, developed countries' research of the theory for Display Design really began. Since then, various types of Display Designs have flourished around the world [2]. With the development of technology and the change of people's consumption concept, the presentation of Display Design is changing constantly. In recent years, with the maturity of multimedia technology and the constantly enrichment of design concept and it's theory, Display Design breaks through the traditional concept of exhibition space fundamentally, and translates it's development mode to consumers as the center of experiential interactive direction [3]. It visual presentation mode also shows a trend that develops from the traditional 2D display to the 3D simulation, from the material to the non-material and from the static to the dynamic.

With the development of Virtual Reality, many enterprises have used 3D simulation display to replace the traditional visual plane to attract consumers' eyeballs. In a sense, the traditional 2D presentation seems to be showing some signs of decline. But because of the visual information of 3D display at present is still in the stage of development, whether it can completely substitute for graphic display status in Display Design is still don't known [4]. So the product's mainly visual information display is still in an integrated use of way, like text display, silhouette display 2D, 2D image display, 3D holographic projection and the physical model display, etc.

2.2 The Application Status of Different Dimension in Display Design

Before the maturity of digital media and modern model making technology, because of the limitation of technology, the Display Design is mainly in 2D way. With the rapid development of multimedia technology, the presentation of design is becoming more and more diversified. From the view of spatial dimension to define the standard point, the current visual information Display Design includes 2D display based on text and 2D silhouette images, 2.5D display based on planar images, and 3D display based on holographic projection and physical object.

(1) Traditional 2D display

The traditional 2D visual information display is a flat display method which completely uses flat frame or text to describe information. It develops for a long time, after the perfection of time it have formed a complete symbol system, and users has a strong recognition for it, so it still has an indispensable status in modern product display. 2D Display Design today is mainly applied in product dimensional specification display, necessary function attribute prompt and so on.

(2) 2.5D display

2.5D display is a visual information display which between traditional 2D display and 3D display. On the visual display, 2.5D is a display way which has the 3D sense but still use plane image to show information. Today, 2.5D display is mainly applied to the display of large area posters, product operation description and so on. Some of the display scenarios that are not provided with physical or virtual simulation also use 2.5D to present description of the product information, such as most current electric business platform mainly use 2.5D graphic to display their products.

(3) 3D display

3D display is a 360° way of display. 3D display can express product information vividly, it provides a richer meaning for the visualization of product information, that will help users to understand the product's visual information carefully [5].

With the development of virtual reality technology, 3D display has begun to replace the physical model with some virtual display now.

3 Dimension and It's Characteristics

Dimension is the number of independent parameters in mathematics. In the field of physics and philosophy, it means the number of independent space-time coordinates. 0 dimension means a point in the world, it don't have length. One dimension usually means a line, it only have length, two dimensions is a plane way, which is formed by length and width (or curve), and three dimensions is a form which 2D form plus height. The environment in which we live is mainly composed of 2D and 3D [6].

Based on the number of different coordinate direction, different dimension shows different level of information, the communication of information of how many there will be differences. In general, the spatial dimension of visual information has the following features:

(1) The larger the dimension base, the information it presents is more and comprehensive.
(2) According to the increase of dimension base, the number of visual information is exponentially increasing.
(3) With the increase of the dimension base, the information it transmits becomes more complex, and users will have greater the psychological and cognitive pressure when they receiving the information.

In addition, because people have different understandings of different dimensions, the application of dimensions in different fields will also be different. In the display of visual information, 2D is the form of conveying information by plane silhouette image which means the pure line and color block or text form in the plane image. And 2.5D is an approximate form which between 2D and 3D, it just like fake 3D, which is actually a kind of 2D in the traditional sense, it is a plane image with three-dimensional sense.

3D is a stereoscopic form, which can show things by a form which with 360 Angle [7]. In this paper, we base on the spatial dimension and the visual presentation in dimension standard, and through user grasp of the visual information quantity and accuracy of the analysis, to explore the influence of user's attention for product's visual information in multi-dimensional display.

4 Experiment on the Degree of the Influence of User's Concerns on Different Dimensions

4.1 Purpose

Because different dimension forms convey different amounts of information when they present different visual information, and they have different advantages and disadvantages when display different types of visual information, so, when we want to show different types of information points, users visual concern extent for different information often occupies an important place. Using different dimension to display different product information in reasonable and guiding users to obtain relevant information efficiently will help Display Design to improve the efficiency of information transmission. In this paper, we explore the influence of different dimensions on users' attention by studying the experiment on the information and accuracy of users in different dimensional products. We hope our experiment could help display designers to find an efficient way which provides users a visual experience with an all-round, multi-angle and efficient visual information display today.

4.2 Subject

Through the investigation and analysis of the current Display Design product category, we found that the products currently displayed are mainly smart home appliances, and the most frequent content of visual information in product display is the product's appearance, material, size and their operation. After analyzing the information of user's usage and the information of these four attributes of design, we select the household coffee machine to be the experimental object. Compared with other household electrical appliances, household coffee machine in the shape, material, size and its operation has relatively more change in the form, so it is easier to sample display information extraction.

By compare the different brands of coffee machine visual information, we decided to choose morphological differences Pitticaffe's next coffee machine, DOLCE GUS-TO's EDG466 coffee machine coffee machine, C - pot's CRM2008-1 as the experiment of three dimensions object extraction experiment sample of products form display which in different dimensions. In the product dimensional display in different dimensions, we decided to select the sample extraction of Pitticaffe - next coffee machine, NESPRESSO's INISSIA C40 coffee machine and NESPRESSO's pixie C60 coffee machine as the experimental object. And in the presentation of product materials in different dimensions, we select NESPRESSO's pixie C60 coffee machine, NESPRESSO's INISSIA C40 coffee machine and c-pot crm2008-1 coffee mechanism for three groups of experimental samples. Finally, when performing the operation of the product, we will select the Pitticaffe's next coffee machine, NESPRESSO's INISSIA C40 coffee machine and NESPRESSO's pixie C60 coffee machine as the sample extraction object (Fig. 1).

Fig. 1. Experiment object

Because a product in a same display has a great difference for the information, to some extent, we do these can reduce the influence of the experimental results which because of users' memory of the subjects.

4.3   Positioning of the Subjects Crowd

In order to ensure the objectivity of our experimental data, the subjects in this experiment should meet the following points: (1) They should be between 25 and 35 years old. (2) They should have the cultural foundation above high school. (3) They should have common sense of home appliances. (4) They should have some spatial imagination. (5) They should have a certain understanding of weights and measures, and also have some understanding of materials. (6) They should have some experience in virtual reality.

Through these conditions, the selection of 20 participants in this experiment is mainly the young teachers and students of a university in Nanjing. In order to reduce the difference in the spatial imagination ability of men and women, the ratio of males and females in this experiment was 1:1.

4.4   Methods and Contents

We based on the experimental psychology theory, divide the experiment three steps' qualitative extraction, classification experiment, and statistics and analysis of experimental samples. The specific experimental steps are shown in Fig. 2.

In the stage of qualitative experiment sample extraction, we mainly use research methods to classify the types of electrical appliances product at the percent. And then, we compare the appearance, size, material and performance of these electrical appliances in this category to selects the experimental subjects (the coffee machine), which has comprehensive differences for the highest percentage. After these, we will use Adobe Illustrator to make the 2D silhouette experimental object, and use camera to make the 2D image production experimental object, and make the two into the same size display board. In order to avoid the influence of the sample size on the user's understanding, the size in multi-dimensional displays is the actual product size. At the

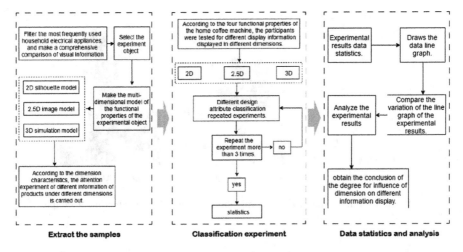

Fig. 2. Experimental procedure

same time, we use 3D software to model the object and use the holographic projection equipment to project the 3D projections. The experimental samples were extracted and produced before the experiment. In order to ensure the subjective interference caused by repeated viewing, different subjects were selected to extract the three dimension samples of this experiment (Figs. 3, 4, 5 and 6).

2D-sketch   2.5D-Photography   3D-simulations

Fig. 3. Multi-dimensional visual display experimental samples of dimensional products

In the stage of "classification experiment", this experiment uses the control variable method to carry out different dimensional visual display experiments on four product design attributes. We will repeat the experiment to observe the user's attention to different dimensions in different lengths of time, and test the accuracy of the user's understanding of information. According to the principle of ergonomics, human memory can be divided into long-term memory and short-term memory. Short-term memory is the behavior which within 60 s, and the information obtained by users is

2D-sketch　　　　2.5D-Photography　　　　3D-simulations

Fig. 4. Multi-dimensional product morphological visual display experiment samples

2D-sketch　　　　2.5D-Photography　　　　3D-simulations

Fig. 5. Multi-dimensional product materials display experimental samples

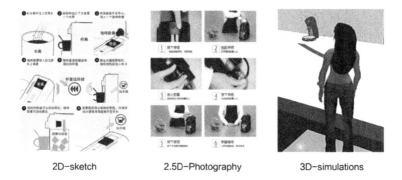

2D-sketch　　　　2.5D-Photography　　　　3D-simulations

Fig. 6. Multi-dimensional product execution operation visual display experiment sample

mostly extensive reading information, more than 60 s is the long time memory, the information acquired by the user is the information after deep learning [8]. Because of it, the two observation times of this experiment were respected 60 s and 120 s (the time used in 120 s include the previous observation).

In the stage of "statistical analysis", we will take the users' accuracy of information acquisition as the evaluation index in the experiment, to calculate the influence of the dimensional visual display on user's attention by demonstrate the statistics of users' accuracy of information acquisition in a certain dimension. In this experiment, we will draw a line chart to analyze the influence of product information in three dimensional visual display for the users' attention and the effect of length of observation time for it.

4.5 Process

The experiment is divided into three basic steps. We will conduct repeated experiments on four product design attributes separately to test the attention of users to a design property at different time in different dimensions. Because this experiment has many steps in fact, so in this paper, we only describe the visual display experiment of product form in three dimensions, the experimental steps of the other three design properties are similar to the following experimental steps. The specific experimental steps are as follows:

Step 1: we ask the experimental participants stood away from the panel (the panel is 1.5 m above the ground) of 0.8 m to observe the 2D samples 60 s, and then, select the product type according to the instruction and select all the basic forms that constitute the product. In order to ensure the accuracy of the experimental results, the experimental subjects were composed of the same number of geometric shapes. When the subjects submitted the test answer, we will ask them to enter the exhibition area, and to observe the 60 s and repeated the above questions again. After these, the first step is completed and we will start the second step.

Step 2: we ask the experimental participants stood away from the panel (the panel is 1.5 m above the ground) of 0.8 m to observe the 2.5D samples 60 s, and then, select the product type according to the instruction and select all the basic forms that constitute the product. After they complete the first answer, they should observe the samples again and repeat to answer the question according to the principle of step 1 (Figs. 7, 8, 9 and 10).

Step 3: we ask the experimental participants stood away from the panel (projection is 1 m above ground) of 0.5 m to observe the 3D samples 60 s, and then, select the product type according to the instruction and select all the basic forms that constitute the product. After they complete the first answer, they should observe samples again and repeat to answer the question according to the principle of step 1.

4.6 Data Statistics

In this experiment, we count the test results obtained from the four design attributes of the family coffee machine in three dimensions. Finally, we obtain 40 user's choice of product attribute perceptions about product form in a variety of dimensional visual display, 137 user's choice of morphological cognition about product form in a variety of dimensional visual display, 40 user's choice of size cognition about product size in a variety of dimensional visual display, 40 user's choice of material cognition about product material in a variety of dimensional visual display, 40 user's choice of execution operation cognition about product execution operation in a variety of

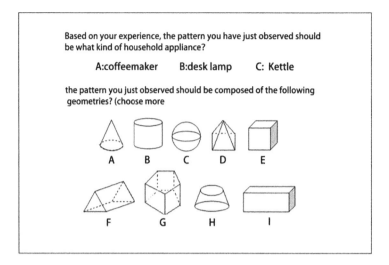

Fig. 7. User's attention test of multi-dimensional product form visual display

Based on your experience, what is the size of the object you think ?

A:1m-1.2m   B:0.5m-0.8m   C:0.3m-0.5m

Fig. 8. User's attention test of dimensional product size visual display

Based on your experience, what kind of materials do you think you have just observed?

A:Plastic, Stainless steel, Wood, Paper
B:Paper, Iron, Paper, Wood
C:Wood, Aluminum, Plastic, Paper

Fig. 9. User's attention test of multi-dimensional product material visual display

dimensional visual display. Because of the paper's limited space, we do not elaborate on the test results of the subjects.

Because the experimental results are not conducive to analyze the user's attention of different design attributes indifferent dimensional visual display. So, we will use the number of results which matched with the actual answer in 20 subjects as the evaluation index of information accuracy. According to the statistics of the correct number of

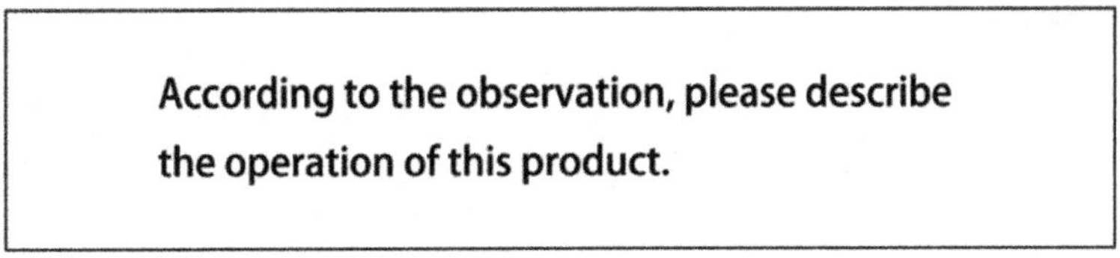

> **According to the observation, please describe the operation of this product.**

Fig. 10. User's attention test of multi-dimensional product execution operation visual display

information which displayed in different dimensions in these two experiments to get its influence on user's attention. In the product morphological experiment, we will calculate the percentage of product morphological cognitive selection results first, and then calculate the number of people who has more than two right choices and the right choices make up more than 60% of the total. In the experiment of product execution, we will only count the experimental results that were able to operate correctly. In order to observe user's attention to different design attributes of the product is displayed in different dimensions better, we will calculate the mean of the two experimental results, and compare it with the two experimental results. The results of this experiment are shown in Table 1.

Table 1. The number of product information obtained by users accurately in different dimensional display.

dimension test	User's attribute recognition for product form of multiple dimensions display			User's form recognition for product form of multiple dimensions display			User's size recognition for product size of multiple dimensions display			User's material recognition for product material of multiple dimensions display			User's operation for product operation of multiple dimensions display		
correct dimension / time	2D	2.5D	3D	2D	2.5D	3D	2D	2.5D	3D	2D	2.5D	3D	2D	2.5D	3D
60s	7	12	19	14	10	9	16	17	16	6	9	11	10	15	17
120s	9	15	19	16	13	12	17	17	18	8	11	13	13	15	18
mean value	8	13.5	19	15	11.5	10.5	16.5	17	17	7	10	12	11.5	15	17.5

4.7 Analysis of Experimental Results

In order to make it easier to observe the impact of different dimension on user's attention, we will draw a line drawing of the above data in this experiment. The results of the user's attention experiment result of the four product design attributes in different dimensions are shown in the Figs. 11, 12, 13, 14 and 15.

After observing the line graph of the experimental results, we can see that the length of time has a little influence on the user's understanding of the visual information in different dimensions. The most affected by time change is the user's attention of visual information for the operation process under 2D silhouette. So we can see that, Compared with other presentations, 2D silhouettes have a low level of attention when it comes to displaying visual information about users' performing operations, so users may need more time to pay attention to this information during presentation.

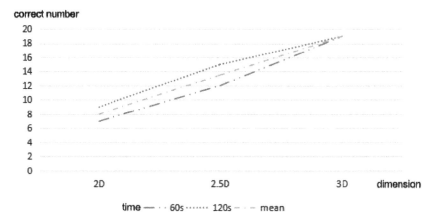

Fig. 11. User's attribute recognition for product form of multiple dimensional display

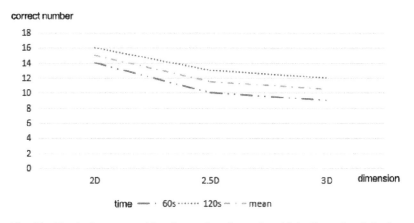

Fig. 12. User's form recognition for product form of multiple dimensional display

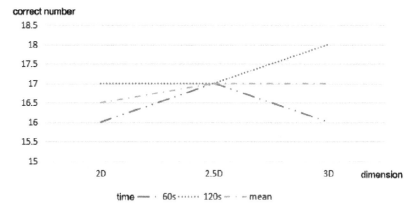

Fig. 13. User's size recognition for product size of multiple dimensional display

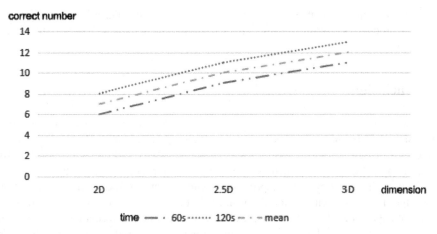

Fig. 14. User's material recognition for product material of multiple dimensional display

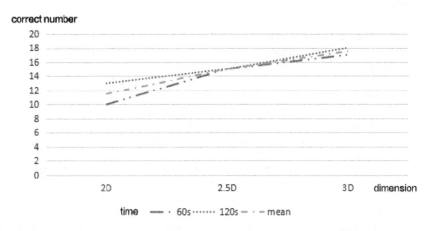

Fig. 15. User's operation for product operation of multiple dimensional display

At the same time, by looking at the mean line graph of the above two experimental results, we can see that, in the terms of product properties display, 3D simulation is easier to present product information to users clearly, 2D silhouette and 2.5D image display have no advantage for it. But in terms of product form display, 2D silhouette images are more likely to show users the basic outline of the product. After comparing these three displays, 2D silhouette shows less disturbing information than the other two dimensions, and users will be more likely to focus on the product profile. In terms of product size display, the display of these three dimensions has no significant influence on the user's attention to the size of the experiment object. In terms of product material display, 3D simulation has a slight advantage over the other two dimensions. By comparison we found that the 3D simulation can show the surface texture of the material more easily, so it is also easier for users to understand this information. In terms of product operation display, the 3D simulation demonstration also has great advantages for it.

5   Conclusion

With the maturity of multimedia technology, the ways of cross-application of various dimensions will be more and more applied in the visual information display of modern products. But how to convey visual information accurately and efficiently to users by using multiple dimensions to increase the user's attention of product and to guide users to obtain relevant information of products accurately and quickly will be a question which the display designers should consider. In this paper, we use the experiment of users' attention on the visual display of some product information in different dimensions to sort out the role of different dimensions in product visual display. We hope these could provide some insight into the design of the future.

References

1. Long, F.: On the three stages of development of exhibition design. Jinan, May 2012
2. Lin, D.: Exhibition Design. Dongbei University of Finance and Economics Press, Dalian, March 2009
3. Wang, J.: The application of visual symbol in Display Design. Northwestern University, Lanzhou, June 2012
4. Zhang, L.: Development and realization of product interaction design platform based on 3d virtual vision. Modern Electronic Technology, Hubei, April 2016
5. Wang, Y., Lu, T.: Based on +Open GL+ES 2d map visualization client design and implementation. Wuhan, September 2013
6. Li, Z., Li, X.: N dimensional vector space and the basis and dimension of the intersection space. Natural Science Paper, Chongqing, September 2002
7. Liao, Z., Liu, X.: EAST assembly simulation of 3d interaction and user interface design. J. Syst. Simul. (2004)
8. Wiker, S.: Ergonomics. In: Li, G., Baker, S.P. (eds.) Injury Research, pp. 139–185. Springer, Boston (2012)

Three Column Website Layout vs. Grid Website Layout: An Eye Tracking Study

Abdallah Namoun[✉]

Faculty of Computer and Information Systems, Islamic University of Madinah,
Medina, Saudi Arabia
a.namoun@iu.edu.sa

Abstract. Research studies have suggested that web viewers scan websites following the F-shaped pattern starting from the top left hand side and moving towards the bottom part of the website. However, this claim is yet to be investigated carefully. The current paper reports on an eye tracking experiment conducted to compare the influence of two popular website layouts, i.e. the three column layout and the grid layout, on information search behavior, user attention and perceived usability. Sixteen participants were recruited and instructed to complete two information search tasks of varying complexity on each layout. The eye tracking metrics showed that the participants did not strictly follow the F-shaped scanning pattern. The column layout exhibited an extensive reading pattern and larger fixation densities than the grid layout. The search tasks seem to inhibit the effects of saliency and visual objects, including pictures and banner adverts, on visual attention. Moreover, participants found the search targets faster in the column layout and favored the column layout over the grid layout. Organizing content within column based web layouts expedites online reading and creates a positive user experience.

Keywords: Eye tracking · Fixation · Visual attention · Column layout
Grid layout · Perceived usability · Perceived aesthetics

1 Introduction

A great deal of eye tracking studies on the web have investigated a myriad of factors that drive the way web viewers allocate their attention on web pages. These factors include page viewing order, individual differences, type of interaction task [19], task difficulty [16], target position [10], and use of images [3, 5]. Little, however, is known in respect to how layouts influence the distribution of visual attention patterns and search performance on websites. Furthermore, the existing findings about viewing behavior determinants are somewhat inconsistent. For example, Nielsen claims that users scan text websites following the F-shaped pattern [18], whilst Shrestha [26] found that this viewing pattern is less prominent in the grid layout where content is organized within a set of grids.

This paper reports on an eye tracking experiment conducted to compare the influence of two popular website layouts, mainly the three column layout and grid layout, on search behavior, user attention and perceived usability. In the three column

© Springer International Publishing AG, part of Springer Nature 2018
A. Marcus and W. Wang (Eds.): DUXU 2018, LNCS 10919, pp. 271–284, 2018.
https://doi.org/10.1007/978-3-319-91803-7_20

layout, the content is organized into three equivalent columns, displayed side by side and running from the top to the bottom of the pages. In the grid layout, the content is organized within a number of blocks, of varying sizes, spanning across the entire web page. These blocks usually have a heading to describe the content. The results of this study are expected to yield a better understanding of users' oculomotor behavior in informational websites.

The current research study makes the subsequent contributions:

- Determine how viewers' visual attention is affected by the organization of content within two common web layouts, i.e. column-based and grid-based layouts, whilst searching for information. In the context of this research, visual attention is measured using heat map densities, fixation count and fixation duration. The focus of this research is viewing patterns within real websites rather than search engine results pages (i.e. SERP).
- Explore how predominant web layouts, i.e. column-based and grid-based, may influence the perceived usability and perceived aesthetics of websites.

The remainder of this paper is organized as follows. Section 2 reviews the major works of eye tracking in websites. Section 3 describes the experimental design of our study. Section 4 outlines the findings. Section 5 discusses the practical implications of the findings. Section 6 outlines the limitations and future directions of this research.

2   Web Eye Tracking Studies

Eye tracking is a modern technique that enables researchers and practitioners to capture and quantify the visual attention of users within graphical user interfaces [23]. In particular, eye tracking devices empower researchers to examine users' ocular behavior with respect to the web elements they look at and the paths their eyes follow. This, in turn, helps identify usability issues arising from a particular interaction [6]. Eye tracking measurements enrich our understanding of locations of interest, duration of gaze, and viewing patterns within the visual field. As such visual attention, captured via eye tracking, has been explored in numerous research areas including web design [4], web search [2], search engine results [17], user experience and design guidelines [1].

Visual attention occurs through two general models, a bottom up model and a top down model [11]. The bottom up model argues that attention to various areas of the visual scene, e.g. an image or a web site, is unconscious and mainly driven by saliency. Saliency is calculated through the combination of several features, such as color and intensity. However, the top down model argues that attention is driven mainly by the goals and interests of the viewer and it is mostly evident when searching for targets. Other forms of attention allocation models are discussed in detail in [11].

Visual attention can be captured and quantified via eye tracking metrics ranging from fixation count, fixation duration, saccades, scan paths to heat maps. These metrics are based on one important concept called fixation. The fixation refers to the maintaining of the eyes on a single area of interest for a typical period of 200 to 300 ms [8]. Fixations signify the cognitive processing of a stimulus, particularly information acquisition. Fixation count is defined as the average number of fixations on a specific area within the page. However, fixation average duration is defined as the length of fixations, measured in milliseconds, on a specific area within the page. Saccades, on the other hand, are rapid shifts that occur between fixations from one area to another and typically last between 20 and 200 ms. However, Rayner [24] suggests that cognitive processing is inhibited throughout saccades. Scan paths encompass fixations and saccades to form the path users follow when exploring or searching for information. Heat maps refer to a thermal map of attention distribution and density across the web pages, with the red areas signifying the highest visual attention [1].

Web search is a popular activity on the web and has therefore received considerable research interest. Eye tracking is used to examine how web viewers browse search results and identify the cues that guide the search behavior [9]. Users' viewing of search engine result pages (i.e. SERPs) follows the golden triangle pattern where reading is more detailed at the top of the triangle and less extensive at the bottom [7]. In search engine result pages, there is strong evidence that users prioritize their attention, and thus their clicking behavior, based on the ordering and relevance presented by the search engine [9].

Related studies assert that users scan text-concentrated websites that implement a list layout, using the F-shaped pattern [18, 27]. In these websites, users pay most of their attention to the top section of the page and read content following the F shape. However, Shrestha [26] and Siu and Chaparro [28] illustrated that the F-shaped reading pattern is less prominent in the SERP grid layout. Hence, the previous results are still inconclusive and more research efforts are required.

Other eye tracking studies investigated several important web aspects. For instance, Resnick and Albert [25] demonstrated that banner blindness is more evident when adverts are placed on the right hand side of e-commerce websites and when users are searching for a target. The use of eye tracking extended to show significant differences in visual attention between males and females when shopping online [12]. Females paid more visual attention to the shopping information parts than males. These aspects, however, are outside the scope of this research.

3 Experimental Design

3.1 Participants

The formal study involved a total of 16 student volunteers (mean age was 24) who had normal vision; 15 participants were male and 1 was female. The participants reported having very good experience searching for information on websites. Participants' level of knowledge and interest about the content presented (i.e. smoking and cancer) within the two layouts were captured in a pre-test questionnaire. The statistical results showed no significant differences in users' knowledge and interest between the tested topics. All participants had no prior encounter with eye tracking devices. In compensation for their time, participants were awarded an Amazon voucher.

3.2 Tasks and Procedure

The experiment utilized a 2 (web layouts) * 2 (task difficulty) within subject design. Specifically, the participants carried out two information search tasks of varying complexity (i.e., easy and difficult) on each web design (i.e., three column and grid layout). In both search tasks, participants were required to scan the contents of the sites to find the answers. In the easy task, the search target was placed on the home page and therefore no navigation was required between the pages. In the difficult task, the search target was placed within a secondary page of the site and would require navigation between pages. The position of the information target was systematically manipulated across the pages to eliminate guessing. Overall, each participant carried out 4 information search tasks, 2 on the column-based design and 2 on the grid-based design. The answers to the search tasks were of equal length in each task type (i.e. easy, difficult) across the layouts and were not guessable by the participants. In other words, the answers were not related to people's general knowledge. The order of web layouts and search tasks were randomly assigned to the participants.

A pilot study including three students was initially performed to verify the experimental setup and search tasks. Minor changes were made to the description of the tasks. The content was reduced to eliminate cluttering from the websites.

During the actual experiment, a repeated measures design was adopted. The participants started by filling out a consent form, as well as an information background questionnaire to collect their knowledge and interest about the topics (i.e. smoking and cancer) being presented within the layouts and information search experience on the web. Next, participants' eyes were calibrated to ensure accurate eye measurements would be captured by the Tobii eye tracker. After the calibration process, the websites were presented on the display, with the home page as the default page. The participants were then given the list of information search tasks and requested to find the answers to these tasks in the designated website. After viewing each layout, they completed perceived usability and aesthetics questionnaires, and ranked the web layouts in order of preference. The eye tracking experiment took approximately 45 to 60 min to be completed.

3.3 Websites and Apparatus

The website layouts under investigation mimicked real websites and contained a variety of content (e.g., menu, paragraphs, images, banner ads, headings). The two websites were systematically designed and developed to structure content within two differing layouts: a three column layout (Fig. 1) and a grid layout (Fig. 2). The content in the three column layout was organized into three equivalent columns, displayed side by side. In the grid layout, the content was organized within a number of blocks, of varying sizes, spanning across the entire web page. These blocks usually have a heading to describe the content.

The two websites contained the same level of complexity, with respect to the number of pages (4 pages on each layout), length of the pages, number of words, paragraphs and design elements used (e.g. large and small images, logo, banner ad, menus, headlines). Moreover, the sites used the same logo (Health & Well-Being)

Fig. 1. Three column website layout (Color figure online)

Fig. 2. Grid website layout (Color figure online)

and hosted content of a similar nature, focusing on health-related topics (particularly smoking, cancer). Both websites used a similar navigational menu placed at the top of the pages. However, the two layouts used different color schemes. The column layout implemented light olive green, whereas the grid layout implemented lime green as a background color.

In essence, this study used eye tracking as a means to collect objective data about fixation patterns and search behaviors. The Tobii eye tracking device 1750 (50 Hz refresh rate), with a 17 in. mounted monitor set to a 1024 * 768 resolution, was used to present the experimental sites and capture the eye movement data, including the fixation count and duration. The viewing order of the two layouts was counter balanced to eliminate any order effects.

3.4 Measurements

Search Performance Metrics. Participants were instructed to complete two information search tasks. Task completion time (in seconds) and task completion rate (%) were calculated and used to compare the information search performance of our participants across the two layouts.

Eye Movement Metrics. The aim of this study is to find out how web users scan the column and grid layouts. To this end, the oculomotor behavior represented by three key eye tracking metrics were collected and analyzed, namely heat maps, average fixation count, and average fixation duration. Heat maps enable to observe the impact of design elements on ocular behavior and compare viewing patterns on different designs [4]. Average fixation count signifies the importance of the areas of interests and design elements being looked at. Average fixation duration signifies the difficulty of task at hand [24]. In this research, we looked for differences in the heat maps between the two layout designs, as well as variations in fixation count and duration.

Post-experiment Questionnaires. Post experiment questionnaires were administered to measure users' perceptions about the website layouts. Users were instructed to rate the perceived usability and aesthetics of the two designs following completion of the search tasks. The questionnaires were adopted from Tactinsky and Lavie [13]. The usability questionnaire focused on measuring ease of use, ease of navigation and orientation, whilst the aesthetics questionnaire focused on measuring the classical aesthetics and expressive aesthetics of the layouts. All questionnaire items used a 7-point Likert scale ranging from 1 = Strongly Disagree to 7 = Strongly Agree.

4 Results

The pages of the two experimental websites were divided into logical areas of interest (i.e. AOIS), represented within rectangles in Figs. 3 and 4. Each area of interest corresponded to a main web element comprising of a logo, menu, image, paragraph, header, or banner ad. The generated heat maps provide an overview of the group ocular behavior in respect to overall fixation density on specific design elements within each layout. Generally speaking areas with red color indicate intense fixations and therefore increased levels of interest from the users [3, 19]. Areas with yellow and green colors however, indicate lower levels of user interest.

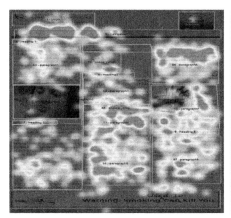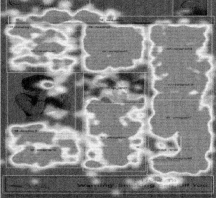

Fig. 3. Fixation patterns (in the form of heat maps) on the home page (easy task) and secondary page (hard task) of the three column web layout (Color figure online)

The heat map analysis (Figs. 3 and 4) illustrated that the viewing patterns on the three column and grid layouts did not necessarily follow the F-shaped scanning pattern in both the easy and difficult task. In the easy task, where the target was placed within the home page, there were smaller fixation densities covering only a small portion of

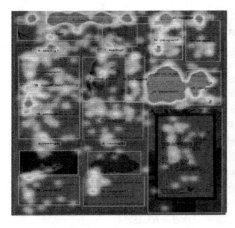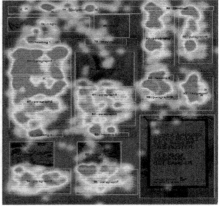

Fig. 4. Fixation patterns (in the form of heat maps) on the home page (easy task) and secondary page (hard task) of the grid web layout (Color figure online)

the areas of interest. These small densities were not always situated at the top left corner. The participants seem to also skip attending to large portions of the text within the home page. Fixations concentrated mainly on the top navigational menu, headings of paragraphs and some relevant paragraphs. These observations suggest that primarily a shallow scanning behavior of information across areas of interest is adopted when the search task is easy. We refer to this as the spotted scanning pattern where viewers read a small set of words deemed relevant to the search target and skip many other words.

In the difficult task, where the target was placed within a secondary page, bigger fixation densities were produced covering a large portion of the text-intense areas of interest. These fixation patterns suggest the adoption of an exhaustive reading behavior by the participants to find the target answer. We refer to this as the deep scanning pattern where viewers are highly motivated to read most of the text in the areas of interest. It is also apparent that the participants allocated less visual attention, in both tasks, to the figures including the logo, pictures and banner ads irrespective of their locations within the website. Therefore, users seem to deliberately ignore looking at pictorial information which created attention gaps within the web layouts. In general, the fixation patterns seem to be driven by the position of the text within the layouts, whilst the search behavior seems to be guided by the text cues.

Comparing visual attention between the two layouts shows that intense reading is more prominent in the three column layout covering most of the text areas of interest. Attention patterns are connected together forming larger blocks of fixations in the column layout such as the rightmost column (Fig. 3). In contrast, the grid layout generated more sparse attention densities across the pages than the column layout, especially as task complexity increased (Fig. 4).

In respect to information search performance, the results were inconclusive (as summarized in Tables 1 and 2). Participants took more time to locate the search target in the grid layout than the column layout when the task was easy (approx. 141 s and 104 s respectively). However, when the search task increased in difficulty no differences were detected in respect to task completion time between the two layouts (186 vs 216 s respectively). Overall, the participants spent more time looking for the search target in the difficult tasks than in the easy tasks (p < .05). However, task completion rate did not differ across the two layouts. Only one participant was unable to complete the difficult task in both layouts.

Table 1. Mean of fixation patterns for layout types during the easy task (*p < .05, **p < .001, repeated measures ANOVA, std = standard deviation)

Web layout	Average fixation count	Average fixation duration (seconds)	Task completion time (seconds)	Task completion rate
Three column	168.25 (std = 103.76)	30.07 (std = 14.24)**	103.78 (std = 63.35)*	100%
Grid	192.78 (std = 64.02)	50.33 (std = 18.50)**	140.96 (std = 89.84)*	100%

Table 2. Mean of fixation patterns for layout types during the difficult task (*p < .05, **p < .001, repeated measures ANOVA, std = standard deviation)

Web layout	Average fixation count	Average fixation duration (seconds)	Task completion time (seconds)	Task completion rate
Three column	456.68 (std = 242.77) **	103.94 (std = 52.51)*	216.86 (std = 134.98)	93%
Grid	314.43 (std = 150.66) **	74.92 (std = 38.88)*	186.09 (std = 92.15)	93%

To gain a deeper understanding of the influence of web layouts on fixation patterns, we analyzed the fixation count and fixation duration. The grid layout stimulated longer fixations than the column layout (50.33 vs 30.07 s respectively), during the easy task (p < 0.001, Table 1). On the other hand, the column layout generated a higher number of fixations than the grid layout (456 vs 314 respectively), during the difficult task which indicates that the column layout incites users to read the text (p < 0.001, Table 2). The participants also fixated on the content of the column layout for a longer time (average of 104 s per page), which may be an indication of complexity.

Overall, the fixation count, fixation duration and task completion time increased in both layouts, as the complexity of the search tasks increased (p < 0.001). In the easy task, there were fewer fixations and shorter fixation durations. In the difficult task, the number of fixations increased and took longer, indicating an intense reading behavior across the areas of interest within the pages, especially in the column layout. These results concur with the findings of Wang et al. [30] who demonstrated that complex search tasks increase the cognitive load of viewers.

Cronbach alpha showed high reliability of the usability and aesthetics scale items, which were used in our study to capture users'overall judgment about the two layouts. The perceived usability construct encompassed four items including ease to use, easy to navigate, easy orientation, and convenient [13]. The participants' rating of the perceived usability showed that the three column layout was deemed as easier to use, easier to navigate, and has an easier orientation than the grid layout ($p < 0.001$, Table 3).

Table 3. Mean rating of perceived usability, perceived aesthetics and general preference (**$p < .001$, repeated measures ANOVA); All scale items were adopted from [13]; Ratings were given on a 7-point Likert scale.

Web layout	Perceived usability (Cronbach's alpha > 0.90)	Perceived classical aesthetics (Cronbach's alpha > 0.90)	User preference (Rank)
Grid	5.28 (0.78)**	4.63 (1.25)**	2**
Three column	5.76 (0.74)**	5.38 (0.86)**	1**

The perceived aesthetics of the two web layouts involved the rating of two dimensions, namely classical aesthetics and expressive aesthetics [13]. Lavie and Tractinsky [13] argue that the classical aesthetics measures the conformance of a website to conventional usability design guidelines, whilst the expressive aesthetics measures the originality and creativity of the web design. The classical aesthetics dimension included five items, namely pleasantness, cleanness, symmetry, clearness and aesthetics. The rating scores of the classical aesthetics showed that the users liked the three column layout over the grid layout despite the longer fixations (Fig. 5).

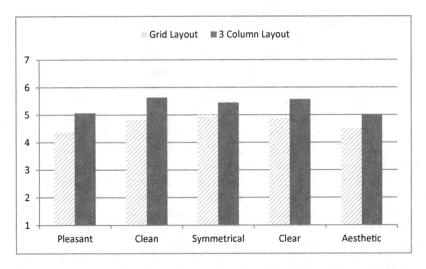

Fig. 5. Average rating of classical aesthetics dimension of the grid and three column layouts

The expressive aesthetics dimension included five items, namely originality, sophistication, creativity, fascination and use of special effects. However, both web layouts were equally favored by the users in respect to the expressive dimensions (Fig. 6). Finally, when asked to rank their preference all participants chose the column layout as their favorite web design.

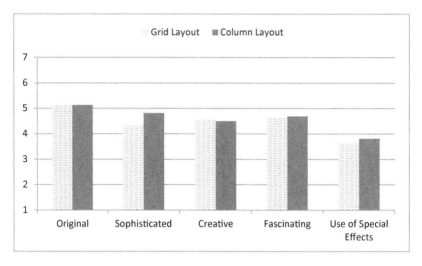

Fig. 6. Average rating of expressive aesthetics dimension of the grid and three column layouts

5   Discussion

This study was conducted to examine the influence of two popular web layouts on users' attention allocation and information search behavior using empirical websites. Contrary to the widespread assumption that web viewers allocate their attention to websites according to the F-shape [18] or golden triangle pattern [7], our heat maps showed that users' fixation patterns were allocated in a different way. In the column layout, attention spread across each of the three columns starting at the top and moving towards the bottom areas of the pages. The column layout encourages users to read text in a detailed manner producing exhaustive attention maps. In the grid layout, attention areas were smaller and distributed across the grids that were placed in different areas of the website. The grid layout encourages partial text reading that involves skipping irrelevant words and sentences in the grid. This implies that attention allocation is not an artifact of a general or common shape but rather the product of the way content is organized within the web pages. The organization of web content is framed within a layout, which our study shows to be the main driving force for attention distribution. This finding confirms the attention model proposed by Sutcliffe and Namoun [29] where structure was identified as one of the key determinants of attention allocation.

Indeed, the F-shaped or triangle viewing pattern may be more applicable when users freely read content online with no particular goal in mind [18]. However, when a search task is assumed, viewing patterns do not necessarily produce an F-shaped attention heat map. In fact, the advocates of F-shaped reading pattern [21] revised their claim in a recent eye tracking study and confirmed that other common scanning patterns exist. Our results do not necessarily contradict the finding that information seekers' scanpaths start at the top left hand corner and move towards the bottom of the page [31]. This study was concerned about the general attention pattern rather than the sequence of attention.

When users were instructed to search for information in the two layouts, they seemed to primarily focus on the top menu items, headings and parts of the paragraphs to find relevant text cues. This approach is well justified in the literature by the information foraging strategy that information seekers adopt to find answers [33]. When the task was varied in complexity users seemed to switch between two reading strategies. In the easy task, they fixated on some areas, which are deemed important and skipped others voluntarily as if they were trying to find some key words related to the designated task. We refer to this as the shallow (non-linear) scanning behavior. In the difficult task, users fixated on most of the text areas of interest exhibiting an extensive reading behavior of almost everything. This resulted in more and longer fixations in both web layouts. We refer to this as the deep (linear) scanning behavior. Moreover, our analysis affirmed that task complexity affects various search determinants such as fixations count, fixation duration, and completion time [16]. In both layouts, task complexity increased the task completion time and resulted in more attention efforts by the users. This indicates that more cognitive load and processing efforts are required by the viewers to find the target when the search task becomes more complex. However, our results are in stark contrast to the findings of Zhou's [32] who found that task type do not have a significant impact on task completion time.

Users ignored looking extensively at the pictorial information, such as logo, banner ads, and figures, which could possibly be an artifact of the effects of top down factors during information search. Previous findings confirmed that top down factors inhibit the effects of saliency and involuntary capture during search tasks [14]. Our findings are consistent with Pfeiffer's [22] who showed that goal-oriented search behavior generates a high number of fixation and refixations and users look at more details in this mode. Moreover, our results showed that users avoided looking at the banner adverts, located at the bottom and right hand side of the layouts. This is in line with the findings of Lee and Ahn [15] that users do not attend to banner ads even when they are animated.

The overall results tentatively suggest that whilst users' goals seem to dominate attention sequence when searching for information, the page layout organizes attention concentration and viewing patterns. However, the organization and position of the content is really what constitutes a layout. The three column layout is found to promote extensive reading behavior and is overall preferred than the grid layout. Users perceived the column layout as more clear and clean than the grid layout.

6 Conclusion and Limitations

In this study, visual attention was measured and compared across column-based and grid-based web designs with the aim of identifying which of the two designs enables more efficient information search performance and attention allocation. Our investigation of eye tracking metrics of 16 participants revealed that information search is faster in the three column layout. This result, however, was significant only when the search task was easy. Users have a stronger preference for the column layout. Remarkably, the F shaped scanning pattern was not apparent across the columns and the grids. Instead, the shape of text areas of interest and position of text within the pages seemed to frame attention fixations. This confirms that the overall web layout has a strong impact on visual attention.

The practical findings of this study imply that designers of information providing websites, such as health and news, may use column based layouts to optimize the distribution of visual attention on their websites and thereby improve the reading performance of users. The three column layout incites readers to scan the web content extensively covering most of the pages. It is also anticipated that organizing content within three columns will create a positive user experience. However, the results show that dividing content into small blocks with headings (i.e. grids) did not improve reading performance. Moreover, when the purpose of the website is to provide information the use of pictures and banner ads may not be beneficial and could in fact be hindering the reading and information search processes.

The herein study recognizes a number of limitations. The two websites used in the experiment employed different color schemes, namely the three column design used light olive green (warm) whilst the grid design used lime green (cool). This color difference might have affected the perceived aesthetics and overall preference towards the two designs. For instance, Pavlas et al. [20] revealed that color tension might impact the perceived aesthetics of websites. Previous studies also showed gender differences in respect to visual attention and attitudes towards e-commerce websites [12]. However, the majority of the participants who were involved in this research were male. Participants' individual traits such as cognitive style and emotions were not considered in our research. Results should therefore be generalized with caution. In the future, we plan to extend our research to investigate other relevant eye tracking metrics such as fixation percentages, saccades, gaze time and scanpaths and explore other popular web layouts.

References

1. Bergstrom, J.R., Schall, A.: Eye Tracking in User Experience Design, 1st edn. Morgan Kaufmann, San Francisco (2014)
2. Cutrell, E., Guan, Z.: What are you looking for? An eye-tracking study of information usage in web search. In: Proceedings of the SIGCHI Conference on Human Factors in Computing Systems, pp. 407–416. ACM (2007)
3. Cyr, D., Head, M., Larios, H., Pan, B.: Exploring human images in website design: a multi-method approach. MIS Q. 33(3), 539–566 (2009)

4. Djamasbi, S.: Eye tracking and web experience. AIS Trans. Hum. Comput. Interact. **6**(2), 16–31 (2014)
5. Djamasbi, S., Siegel, M., Tullis, T.: Generation Y, web design, and eye tracking. Int. J. Hum Comput Stud. **68**(5), 307–323 (2010)
6. Ehmke, C., Wilson, S.: Identifying web usability problems from eye-tracking data. In: Proceedings of the 21st British HCI Group Annual Conference on People and Computers HCI... But Not As We Know It, vol. (1), pp. 119–128. British Computer Society, UK (2007)
7. Enquiro: Enquiro Eye Tracking Study: An In Depth Look at Interactions with Google using Eye Tracking Methodology. http://searchengineland.com/figz/wp-content/seloads/2007/09/hotchkiss-eye-tracking-2005.pdf. Accessed 5 Jan 2018
8. Findlay, J.M., Gilchrist, I.D.: Active Vision: The Psychology of Looking and Seeing, 1st edn. Oxford University Press, Oxford (2003)
9. Granka, L., Feusner, M., Lorigo, L.: Eyetracking in online search. In: Hammoud, R. (ed.) Passive Eye Monitoring, pp. 347–372. Springer, Heidelberg (2008). https://doi.org/10.1007/978-3-540-75412-1_16
10. Guan, Z., Cutrell, E.: An eye tracking study of the effect of target rank on web search. In: Proceedings of the SIGCHI Conference on Human Factors in Computing Systems, pp. 417–420. ACM, San Jose (2007)
11. Hashemi, S.M.R.: A survey of visual attention models. Ciência e Natura **37**(6–2), 297–306 (2015)
12. Hwang, Y.M., Lee, K.C.: Using an eye-tracking approach to explore gender differences in visual attention and shopping attitudes in an online shopping environment. Int. J. Hum. Comput. Interact. **34**(1), 15–24 (2018)
13. Lavie, T., Tractinsky, N.: Assessing dimensions of perceived visual aesthetics of web sites. Int. J. Hum. Comput. Stud. **60**(3), 269–298 (2004)
14. Leber, A.B., Egeth, H.E.: It's under control Top-down search strategies can override attentional capture. Psychon. Bull. Rev. **13**(1), 132–138 (2006)
15. Lee, J.W., Ahn, J.H.: Attention to banner ads and their effectiveness: an eye-tracking approach. Int. J. Electr. Commer. **17**(1), 119–137 (2012)
16. Liu, J., Cole, M.J., Liu, C., Bierig, R., Gwizdka, J., Belkin, N.J,. Zhang, J., Zhang, X.: Search behaviors in different task types. In: 10th Proceedings of the Annual Joint Conference on Digital Libraries, pp. 69–78. ACM (2010)
17. Lorigo, L., Haridasan, M., Brynjarsdóttir, H., Xia, L., Joachims, T., Gay, G., Granka, L., Pellacini, F., Pan, B.: Eye tracking and online search: lessons learned and challenges ahead. J. Assoc. Inf. Sci. Technol. **59**(7), 1041–1052 (2008)
18. Nielsen, J.: F-Shaped Pattern for Reading Web Content (2006). https://www.nngroup.com/articles/f-shaped-pattern-reading-web-content-discovered/. Accessed 1 Oct 2017
19. Pan, B., Hembrooke, H.A., Gay, G.K., Granka, L.A., Feusner, M.K., Newman, J.K.: The determinants of web page viewing behavior: an eye-tracking study. In: Proceedings of the 2004 Symposium on Eye Tracking Research & Applications, pp. 147–154. ACM, San Antonio (2004)
20. Pavlas, D., Lum, H., Salas, E.: The influence of aesthetic and usability web design elements on viewing patterns and user response: an eye-tracking study: In Proceedings of the Human Factors and Ergonomics Society Annual Meeting, vol. 54, no. 16, pp. 1244–1248. SAGE Publications, Los Angeles (2010)
21. Pernice, K.: F-Shaped Pattern of Reading on the Web: Misunderstood, But Still Relevant (Even on Mobile). https://www.nngroup.com/articles/f-shaped-pattern-reading-web-content/. Accessed 2 Jan 2018

22. Pfeiffer, J., Prosiegel, J., Meißner, M., Pfeiffer, T.: Identifying goal-oriented and explorative information search patterns. In: Proceedings of the Gmunden Retreat on NeuroIS, pp. 23–25. Bielefeld University, Gmunden Austria (2014)
23. Poole, A., Ball, L.J.: Eye tracking in HCI and usability research. Encycl. Hum. Comput. Interact. **1**, 211–219 (2006)
24. Rayner, K.: Eye movements in reading and information processing: 20 years of research. Psychol. Bull. **124**(3), 372–422 (1998)
25. Resnick, M., Albert, W.: The impact of advertising location and user task on the emergence of banner ad blindness: an eye-tracking study. Int. J. Hum. Comput. Interact. **30**(3), 206–219 (2014)
26. Shrestha, S.: The effect of search engine results page presentation style on user satisfaction and eye movements. In: SOAR: Shocker Open Access Repository, Publication No. d12039. Doctoral dissertation, Wichita State University (2012)
27. Shrestha, S., Lenz, K., Chaparro, B., Owens, J.: "F" pattern scanning of text and images in web pages. In: Proceedings of the Human Factors and Ergonomics Society Annual Meeting, vol. 51, no. 18, pp. 1200–1204. SAGE Publications, Los Angeles (2007)
28. Siu, C., Chaparro, S.B.: First look in examining the horizontal grid layout using eye-tracking. In: Proceedings of the Human Factors of Ergonomics Society Annual Meeting, vol. 58, no. 1, pp. 1119–1123. Chicago (2014)
29. Sutcliffe, A., Namoun, A.: Predicting user attention in complex web pages. Behav. Inf. Technol. **31**(7), 679–695 (2012)
30. Wang, Q., Yang, S., Liu, M., Cao, Z., Ma, Q.: An eye tracking study of website complexity from cognitive load perspective. Decis. Support Syst. **62**, 1–10 (2014)
31. Zander, K., Hamm, U.: Information search behaviour and its determinants: the case of ethical attributes of organic food. Int. J. Consum. Stud. **36**(3), 307–316 (2012)
32. Zhou, M.: Do online search processes vary by task complexity? An eye-tracking study. Int. J. Soc. Sci. Hum. **7**(11), 698–701 (2017)
33. Pirolli, P.: Rational analyses of information foraging on the web. Cogn. Sci. **29**(3), 343–373 (2005)

Designing a Generative Pictographic Language

Haytham Nawar[(✉)]

Department of the Arts, The American University in Cairo, Cairo, Egypt
haytham.nawar@aucegypt.com

Abstract. The ability to express our thoughts is a very powerful tool in our society. Being able to write is more difficult than being able to read, and this is especially for the Alphabetical languages/scripts. From personal experience, being able to write in Latin/Arabic/Chinese is a lot more difficult than just being able to read them and requires a greater understanding of the language.

We now have machines that can help us accurately classify images and read handwritten characters. However, for machines to gain a deeper understanding of the content they are processing, they will also need to be able to generate such content. The next natural step is to have machines draw simple pictures of what they are thinking about, and develop an ability to express themselves. Seeing how machines produce drawings may also provide us with some insights into their learning process.

In this project/paper, a machine will be trained to learn pictographic scripts by exposing it to a database of selected ancient and modern pictographic scripts. The machine learns by trying to form invariant patterns of the shapes and strokes that it sees, rather than recording exactly what it sees into memory, a simulation of how our brains operate. Afterwards, using its neural connections, the machine attempts to write/construct something out, stroke-by-stroke. A technique that could be applied and used on different platforms, opening the door for a language or means of communication for the future.

Keywords: Generative data · Generative design · Pictographic scripts
Writing systems · Artificial intelligence · Visual communication

1 The Significance of Pictographic Language

1.1 The Origins of Writing

Described by the Swiss designer Adrian Frutiger (1928–2015) as "An early attempt to visualize language and make a record of linguistic discourse", ice-age wall carvings date back to 27,000 to 40,000 years ago. (2006, p. 55). It is said that these drawings were often conveyed along a series of gestures, as a ritual or further elaboration of their meaning. While the drawings serve as a trace of such ancient times, the speech and gestures have long been lost among the years. Moreover, throughout the Sumerian and the Ancient Egyptian periods, the human body was often regarded as a reference point for these drawings, in which men and women featured were distinguished by either drawings of genitalia or full body figures. These significant wall drawings are pictographic signs and can be defined as "proto-writing".

© Springer International Publishing AG, part of Springer Nature 2018
A. Marcus and W. Wang (Eds.): DUXU 2018, LNCS 10919, pp. 285–296, 2018.
https://doi.org/10.1007/978-3-319-91803-7_21

As the evolution of man civilizations progressed, proto-writing systems -featuring ideographic and/or mnemonic symbols- paved the way to the development of today's writing systems. Representation systems of language that utilized visual means ultimately transformed into actual writing, allowing the reader to construct, reconstruct, and derive meaning from a linguistic utterance that is encoded in writing. Writing became a fundamental method of data documentation and information storage, in a tangible sense.

The exact time at which proto-writing developed into true writing systems is greatly debated among scholars. According to recent archaeological research, the origin and spread of writing is quite complex to identify, in which recent findings suggest that proto-cuneiform writing on clay tablets may have existed during the mid-forth millennium BC, in the Middle East. Since clay was inexpensive and famous for its longevity, both pictographic and abstract signs were carved into dampened clay using a reed or stick (Fig. 1).

Fig. 1. Sumerian-proto-writing, clay tablet inscribed with details of food rations, dating from c.3300–3100 BC from southern Mesopotamia.

Studies suggest that the idea of writing gradually spread from a culture to another. The transform of pictograms to ideograms is considered the first stage of development, an effective move from iconic representation to symbolism. The following stage of development was the introduction of the Rebus. A need to communicate a higher level of detail was developed, and hence; the "Rebus" came to mean that the pictographic icon incorporated a phonetic sound associated with the icon.

Scholars acknowledge the independent development of true writing of language in two locales; in Mesopotamia around 3200 BC, and in Mesoamerica around 600 BC. The conventional phase of development from proto-writing to true writing systems of language, suggest the following stages of progression:

1. Pictorial (picture-based) writing system: Glyphs directly represent objects and concepts. In relation to this, the following sub-stages may be distinguished:

   - Mnemonic: Glyphs
   - Pictographic: Glyphs that represent an object or a concept
   - Ideographic: Graphemes (abstract symbols) that represent an idea or concept

2. Transitional system: A grapheme refers to the object or idea that it represents, and the name as well.
3. Phonetic system: Graphemes refer to sounds or spoken symbols, and the form of the grapheme is not related to its meanings. This is explained through the following sub-stages:

   - Verbal: A grapheme (logogram) that represents a whole word
   - Syllabic: A grapheme that represents a syllable
   - Alphabetic: A grapheme that represents an elementary sound.

1.2   Pictographic/Ideographic/Logographic Writing Systems

Writing systems are commonly classified into four categories: pictographic, logographic, syllabic, and alphabetic. Yet, any writing system may feature a combination of some or all of the four categories in varying ranges. Hence, attempting to ultimately classify a writing system might in fact be problematic. In light of this, a writing system is defined as "a complex system". In pictographic scripts, graphemes are iconic images, while in ideographic scripts, graphemes represent concepts and/or ideas, rather than representing a specific word in language. In logographic writing systems, glyphs represent words or morphemes (a meaningful unit of a word that cannot be divided further).

2   Machine Learning

Our lives have become extremely digitally oriented at a very wild pace, ever since the dawn of computers in the middle of last century. Online databases and digital media have been regarded as a substitute for printing on paper as the main method of storing information. Today, all sorts of material, be it numbers, text, images, video, or audio, are stored, processed, and even transferred digitally, thanks to online connectivity. Such great level of digital processing results in an immense amount of data, what we can refer to as a "*dataquake*", is the primary reason behind the prevalent interest in data analysis and machine learning.

For many applications that differ in nature (from vision to speech, from translation to robotics), man was not able to devise sufficient algorithms, despite extensive research dating back to the 1950s. Yet, for all these tasks, data collection was quite easy, and so the current aim is to automatically learn the algorithms from the collected data, substituting programmers with learning programs. This is the fundamental niche of machine learning. Not only has data increased tremendously over the years, but also the extent to which data is successfully transformed into knowledge through machine learning, has significantly advanced.

In essence, machine learning, a branch of artificial intelligence, is a key method of data analysis that utilizes analytical model building. It is based on the core idea of systems/machines are capable of learning from data they are exposed to, accurately identifying and recognizing patterns upon which an algorithm is applied with minimal or almost complete absence of human intervention.

3   Generated Language

In light of the concept of machine learning, the prospect of generating a novel language becomes a certain scenario. Relying on pattern recognition and the theory that computers can learn by merely being exposed to data, without the necessity of being programmed to perform specific tasks, machines can indeed offer mankind a newly developed language (writing system) that is conceived from its processed language(s).

After becoming exposed to a set of characters and/or symbols, a machine becomes capable of independently adapting, learning from acquired computations to produce reliable, repeatable results on a very large scale as it weaves the similarities amongst the data it has been exposed to.

4   Selected Generated Language Projects

4.1   A Book from the Sky 天书: Exploring the Latent Space of Chinese Handwriting (Xu Bing) (1988)

Based on Xu Bing's book titled "*A Book from the Sky*", the project features a huge collection of characters created by a deep convolutional generative adversarial network (DCGAN) that is instructed on a database of handwritten Chinese characters. DCGAN is a form of convolutional neural network capable of learning abstract representations after being exposed to a collection of images. It achieves this by balancing between functioning as a "generator" that fabricates fake images and a "discriminator" that attempts to detect whether the generator's images are authentic. After training, the generator is guaranteed to accurately generate samples of images that are resonant of their originals.

Below is a set of fake images of characters produced by a DCGAN that was exposed to a labeled subset of $\sim$1 M handwritten simplified Chinese characters. The generator was then capable of producing fake images of characters that were not present in the original dataset (Fig. 2).

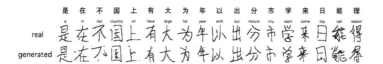

Fig. 2. Generated characters produced by DCGAN.

Xu Bing's Book. The original book upon which this project was built, is created by Chinese artist Xu Bing who featured the styles of fine editions from the Song and Ming dynasties, yet filled entirely with meaningless glyphs that are designed to look like traditional Chinese characters. The book consists of four volumes, forming 604 pages in total, and was printed in a single print run of 126 copies between 1987 and 1991. It was composed incorporating a set of 4,000 characters, which is approximately the number of characters commonly used in modern written Chinese. The characters were engraved into single pieces of movable type made from pear wood, in a style slightly thicker than that of Song typefaces. Firstly, Xu himself typeset samples of the book's pages and then took them to a factory in the village of Hányíng for printing. Workers at the factory then typeset the pages by following a "model book" prepared by Xu as a reference. The book's first public exhibition was in October of 1988, at the Beijing's China Art Gallery (Fig. 3).

Fig. 3. Installation view of *Book from the Sky* (1987–91) in "Xu Bing: A Retrospective" at Taipei Fine Arts Museum, 2014.

4.2 Alphabet Synthesis Machine (2001)

Created by both Golan Levin, Jonathan Feinberg, and Cassidy Curtis, and commissioned by PBS and Art21.org, the "*Alphabet Synthesis Machine*" is an interactive online artwork that allows one to develop and evolve potential writing systems of one's own imaginary civilizations. The software produces abstract alphabet that can be downloaded later as TrueType fonts, and are registered into a complete archive of user creations.

The final products of the "*Alphabet Synthesis Machine*" investigate the liminal boundaries between familiarity and chaos, language and gesture. The project came to be as both an interactive installation and an online tool. From 2001 to 2006, users who visited the website created more than 20,000 abstract writing systems (Fig. 4).

Fig. 4. "Alphabet synthesis machine" project

4.3 Random Radicals: Kanji Machine Learning (2012)

In this project, a machine was trained to learn Chinese characters by being exposed to a *Kanji* (Japanese term for Chinese Characters) database. Similar to how a human brain functions, the machine learned by trying to formulate invariant patterns of the shapes and strokes it is exposed to, rather than merely recording the data in its memory. Then, utilizing its neural connections, the machine became successfully capable of generating characters onto a screen, stroke by stroke (Fig. 5).

Fig. 5. Kanji generated script

six stoned ladies
lonely ghost
wooden food
urban sheep
wood pecker
stop eating lambs
bird hunting
educated horse
listening bird
listerine
new type of wooden house
lucky horse

After acquiring sufficient stroke-level data from the Kanji database, the machine became able to categorize certain strokes together on its own, eventually forming more abstract concepts of basic radicals and components that initially make up the original Kanji language, such as 口, 豆, 辶. Furthermore, the machine also learned to write these radicals in the correct number of strokes, and proper sequence. For instance, 口 must be written featuring three distinct strokes, (丨、㇆, __), in this order, and cannot be drawn at once as a square □ with a single stroke. Despite how one may arrive at a final character after following an incorrect stroke order, the result is also regarded as an incorrect Kanji. Hence, although the machine attempts to construct fake Kanji, it preserves the internal logical order of Japanese Kanji, at both the stroke level and radical level, as it has established a logical pattern about the relative location, and relative sequence to structure its abstract concepts.

Kanji has existed for thousands of years, and hence the writing system has developed numerous branches and divisions. For example, there are two different methods to write 逗, either by using the simplified 辶 or the traditional 辶. Accordingly, the machine also processed the different variations of writing certain Kanji components. The eventual outcome of the machine, is a set of vector lines which suits

Kanji much more adequately than many other recent machine learning image generation methods that are primarily pixel based.

Considering how the ordering of strokes is of fundamental importance to Kanji writing system, using vectors to model the ordered strokes is much more significant than any pixel based generation technique. Remarkably, this approach may pave the way to future developments of facilitating machines to sketch images.

4.4   Asemic Languages

Created by So Kanno and Takahiro Yamaguchi, the project "*Asemic Languages*", directs particular attention towards the form of characters rather than their embedded meanings. Historical civilizations throughout the world have acquired numerous characters as part of their identities, conveying their distinctive culture and history. Accordingly, emphasizing the role of characters as a core means of visual communication and documentation of language, the project features drawn lines that resemble characters but do not hold any meaning.

The project was publicized in 2016 at the international art festival "Aichi Triennale". The design implementation process incorporated a collection of handwritten statements by artists. By learning the handwriting with one writer in each language, the machine collected visual data on the shapes of each character system, as well as the idiosyncrasies of each writer. The lines were generated via a plotter, and written as if they reflect something of great importance, visually deceiving the audience (Fig. 6).

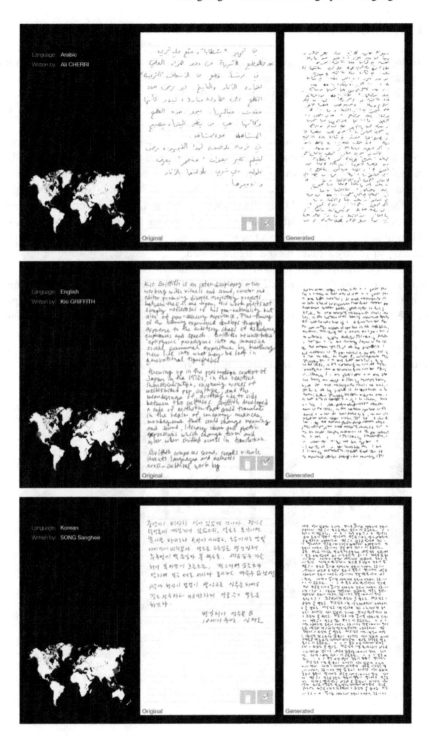

Fig. 6. *"Asemic Languages"* project

5 Project Concept

The pictography existing in all early scripts of mankind is a crucial cornerstone in the theoretical argument of universal iconography common to all writing systems. The fact that all independently derived writing systems came to be as arrangements of pictograms before their evolution into sophisticated forms, serves as evidence to the significant iconographic nature of *writing*, as a notion.

In light of what has been raised and examined above, the aim of my project revolves around the basic idea of introducing a designed pictographic generative language utilizing machine learning. The machine would be exposed to a database of vector-based ancient pictographic scripts, ranging from Sumerian Cuneiforms, Egyptian hieroglyphs, Dongba and Nsibidi symbols, Testerian Catechism scripts, to Chinese characters. By forming consistent patterns of the shapes and strokes it processes, the machine utilizes its neural connections in attempting to produce new pictographic characters, stroke by stroke, onto a digital screen.

Ultimately, by recognizing and grouping similar patterns and pinpointing the similarities amongst these scripts in relation to style of strokes, complexity of figures, and proportions, the machine becomes capable of generating a firsthand pictographic language reflecting the homogenous characteristics of each of the writing systems, combined. Writing systems *created* civilizations, hence; the final result produced, would serve as a unique investigation of the existing, yet unconsciously neglected, relations among the diverse cultures of many civilizations (Figs. 7, 8 and 9).

Fig. 7. Hieroglyphs from the tomb of Seti I, Valley of the Kings, Luxor.

Fig. 8. Detail from a Naxi manuscript, displaying pictographic Dongba.

Fig. 9. Testerian catechism

6 Conclusion

In conclusion, writing systems are instruments of the various languages that have came to exist throughout the long history of mankind. They are considered a historical necessity of the emergence of our countless languages. Accordingly, an investigation of ancient pictographic languages/scripts utilizing machine learning would offer insight into the visual language of the cultures of ancient civilizations, proposing a modern pictographic language of whose traits are drawn by the machine directly from the data it has acquired and processed.

References

1. Alpaydin, E.: Machine Learning: The New AI. MIT Press, Cambridge (2016)
2. "A Book from the Sky 天书 Exploring the Latent Space of Chinese Handwriting." *A Book from the Sky 天书*, Genekogan, genekogan.com/works/a-book-from-the-sky/
3. Bloomfield, L.: Language. University of Chicago Press, Chicago (1958)
4. Chafe, W.: Meaning and the Structure of Language. University of Chicago Press, Chicago (1970)
5. "大卜口 Ml · Design": *Recurrent Net Dreams Up Fake Chinese Characters in Vector Format with TensorFlow|* 大卜口, Studio Otoro, 28 December 2015. blog.otoro.net/2015/12/28/recurrent-net-dreams-up-fake-chinese-characters-in-vector-format-with-tensorflow/
6. Levin, G., et al.: Golan Levin and Collaborators. *Alphabet Synthesis Machine - Interactive Art by Golan Levin and Collaborators*, Golan Levin and Collaborators (2001). flong.com/projects/alphabet/
7. Bing, X., et al.: Tianshu: Passages in the Making of a Book. Bernard Quaritch Ltd., London (2009)

Study on Optimal Parameter Setting of Word Size and Word Spacing in Chinese Text of Desktop-Computer Touch Screen

Yue Qiu[✉], Qian Gong, and Xiaodong Gong

Beijing Institute of Technology, 5 South Zhongguancun Street, Haidian District,
Beijing, China
qiuyue@bit.edu.cn, gongqian_id@foxmail.com

Abstract. The basic text attribute in design of the Chinese human-computer interaction digital interface in the desktop-computer touch screen was subject to quantitative test and analysis by virtue of records of the visual focus, the reaction time, the operation accuracy and other data. This paper firstly pointed out that text is one of the basic elements of the human-computer interaction digital interface, and parameter setting of the basic text attribute is closely associated with the customer cognitive efficiency about the interface. Besides, there are few researches on the relationship between the text attribute of the Chinese interface and the reading performance based on the desktop-computer touch screen. Secondly, this paper presented the testing method of the relationship between setting of the basic text attribute and its influence to the cognitive efficiency. Finally, based on the change of the word size and the word spacing in the text attribute, a test plan was designed to collect, sort and analyze tested data, such as the visual focus, the reaction time and the operation accuracy, and further to study the influence of the text attribute to the cognitive efficiency in the typical operating environment. The test result shows that when the sight distance is about 40 cm, the optimal configuration of the word size and the word spacing of the 27-in. (resolution: 2560px*1440px) desktop-computer touch screen is (16px, 2px). The test method and result can provide reference for related design of the digital interface of the desktop-computer touch screen.

Keywords: Desktop-computer touch screen · Chinese interface
Text attribute · Word size · Word spacing

1 Introduction

The touch screen, as a medium capable of supporting the simpler and more convenient human-computer interaction mode, has been playing its unique advantage in more and more fields in recent years. With the continuous development of the touch screen manufacturing technology and gradual fall in the price, the application of the touch screen has expanded from the handheld devices to the desktop computers and other large-size displays. Currently, most researches on the design specifications of the touch screen interface are based on handheld terminals (like mobile phones) and other small-size screens, while there is hardly any research related about design specifications

© Springer International Publishing AG, part of Springer Nature 2018
A. Marcus and W. Wang (Eds.): DUXU 2018, LNCS 10919, pp. 297–312, 2018.
https://doi.org/10.1007/978-3-319-91803-7_22

of displays of the desktop-computer touch screens. Since the operating environment, the sight distance and the operating mode of the desktop-computer touch screen are different from the handheld small-size terminals, the design specifications of its interface elements cannot simply follow the research results-of the handheld terminals. Therefore, this paper studies the influence of the basic Chinese text attribute (the word size and the word spacing) of the interaction interface on the user cognitive performance and the optimal configuration based on the large-size desktop-computer touch screen through experiments, so as to provide reference for the in-depth study on the design specifications of the display interface of the desktop-computer touch screen in a wider scope in the future.

2   Overseas and Domestic Research Status

Text is one of the most basic elements of user interface design, and nearly all interface products use characters, from error, warning and prompt messages to project introduction, navigation and titles. Design of characters in the interface involves the font, word size, word spacing and line spacing, all of which impact the readability and intelligibility of the text and the availability of information search.

In spite of few researches on the text elements of the interface of the large-scale touch screens, there are some representative research results based on different media, such as paper products, non-touch screen products and handheld small-size touch screens. For example, Legge et al. [1] verified that the English font size influenced the reading cognitive efficiency through experiments; Susana TL Chung thought that the reading speed tended to be stabilized after the font size increased to a certain degree; Fletcher et al. [2] studied the reading cognition from aspects of interface color matching, the view angle, the character structure, the font and the word size, and concluded with the interactive interference between these elements and the cognition efficiency. Moreover, Humar et al. [3] provided a certain design reference for web character design, by conducting a special research of the influence of common color matching and polarity color matching on readability of web texts. The result of their research shows that the strongly contrastive text and background color can quicken the search efficiency and bring positive evaluation for readers.

As to Chinese text elements, Wang and Shao [4] made researches by exploring the physical characteristics, such as the character size, structure, complexity and contrast, and the interactions of these elements, and founded that these elements impact the visual recognition. Liu [5] verified the influence of the font size, the font type and the text spacing on the reading efficiency of patients with maculopathy through experiments. Wang [6] demonstrated by experiments that in mobile phones font size, word spacing, row spacing affect the reading behavior of the elderly and concluded that when size of Chinese characters on mobile phones is 15px*15px (8pt), the line spacing and the word spacing of 6–8px and 2–4px can respectively better improve the readability for the elderly. Zou [7], et al. studied color matching between the brightness of PPT background color and word color, finding that the subjective resolution is higher when the brightness difference between the PPT foreground color and the background color is bigger, and the higher indoor illuminance is helpful for improving the subjective resolution of the PPT. Guo et al. [8–10] discovered that the font, the word size, the line spacing and the Chinese character features of the display and control interfaces of EMU influence drivers' recognition efficiency.

In sum, the overseas and the domestic researches on the influence of the text attribute on the interface reading recognition involve many elements, such as the font, the word size, the word spacing, the line spacing, color matching of the interface, the text structure, the textual carrier, the lighting condition and the circumstance of use, etc. Among all these, the word size is regarded as the most basic attribute in a lot of researches. The referred media are mainly common paper media, electronic products for daily office work and handheld electronic products (like mobile phones). There are few overseas and domestic researches about the influence of the text attribute of the Chinese interface in the desktop-computer touch screen on the cognitive efficiency. Although the research results based on Chinese characters and English letters provide reference for each other and cannot be followed directly due to their difference, the research method and results of the early studies can still provide reference for the study of this paper.

3 Study of Design Elements of Chinese Text Based on Desktop-Computer Touch Screen

This paper explores the optimal setting of Chinese text parameters in Chinese interface based on the desktop-computer touch screen. With two basic text attributes—word size and word spacing as the independent variables, and the black character on a white background as the display environment, this paper provides reference for the study on design specifications of text elements of the Chinese interactive interface.

3.1 Calculation of Sight Distance

When the desktop computer monitor with a large screen size is used, the distance S between the operator and the farthest side of the touch screen can be calculated with the following formula, as shown in Table 1:

$$S^2 = (L_3)^2 - (H_2)^2 - [(L_1 + L_2)/2]^2 \tag{1}$$

$$H_2 = H_1 \cos\theta + H_3 - H_4 \tag{2}$$

According to the current national standard Human Dimensions of Chinese Adults GB 1000-1998 [11], related data of human dimensions can be obtained, as shown in Table 2.

Given the non-specific property of the groups, the design principle of average dimensions of the human dimension data application approach is used, i.e. the 50th percentile human dimension data are used for reference when calculating the relationship between the operator and the touch screen. The result is that the distance between the middle position of the operator shoulder and the farthest side of the display of the touch screen is 48 cm, and the sight distance between the eyes and the screen is about 40 cm (Fig. 1).

Table 1. Definition list of letters used in the calculation formula of the distance between the operator and the touch screen

Parameter	Definition
S	Distance between the operator and the farthest side of the touch screen
L_1	Width of the operational area of the touch screen
L_2	Maximum shoulder breadth of the operator
L_3	Arm length = upper arm length + forearm length + hand length
H_1	Distance between the upper end of the operational area and the bottom of the touch screen
H_2	Height of the touch screen is bigger than shoulder height of the operator
H_3	Height of the workbench
H_4	Shoulder height of the sitting operator + shank height + foot height
θ	Screen inclination

Table 2. Relevant human dimensions parameters

	Male (percentile)			Female (percentile)		
	10	50	95	10	50	95
Height	1604	1678	1775	1503	1570	1659
Upper arm length	294	313	338	267	284	308
Forearm length	220	237	258	198	213	234
Hand length	173	183	196	173	183	183
Sitting height	870	908	958	819	855	901
Cervical vertebra height at sitting position	621	667	701	587	617	657
Eye height at sitting position	761	798	847	701	739	783
Shoulder height at sitting position	566	598	641	526	556	594

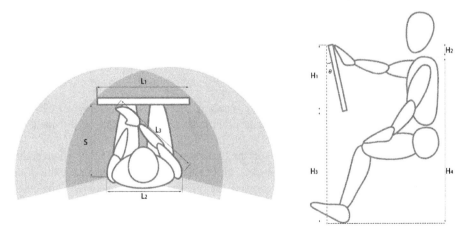

Fig. 1. Simple graph of operator and touch screen of display console (left), and Chart of operation at typical sitting position (right)

3.2   Selection of Font

The several common types of font applied to interface design of the digital products include serif, sans-serif and monospace. The most commonly used Chinese fonts in serif include Song typeface and various derivatives, and the common Chinese fonts used in sans-serif include boldface and various derivatives [12]. Although font selection is affected by the characters of character and the context, the majority of current research results of interface design hold that serif and sans-serif have their own features for continuous reading. Sans-serif shows its advantages in terms of the small-size continuous text, and it is extensively applied to signage, information graphs and screen interfaces. Due to its unique modeling and high identifiability, Serif is mainly applied to titles. This paper chooses the reading context as the study object so that the boldface in Arial is adopted here.

3.3   Calculation of Word Size

The minimum height of characters is calculated with the formula (Table 3):

$$H = 0.0022D + 25.4 * (K1 + K2) \text{ [13]}; \tag{3}$$

Table 3. Definition list of letters in the character height calculation formula

Parameter	Definition
H	Target height (mm)
D	Distance between eyes to the target (mm)
K_1	Importance correction factor: generally 0 is taken, or 0.075 is taken in important conditions
K_2	Illumination and recognition condition correction factor: 0.06, 0.16 or 0.26 is taken in the condition of excellent, good and ordinary illumination, respectively

The calculation results is:

$$H = 0.0022 * 400 + 25.4 * (0.06 + 0) = 2.4 \text{ mm} < 2.6 \text{ mm};$$

Considering that:

1. The word size cannot be smaller than 2.6 mm [13] if D < 500 mm;
2. According to the word size conversion method in the display, the corresponding word size of characters with H = 2.6 mm is 11.15px, and the value of the word size is an even number generally;

Thus, the value of the tested word size takes 12px, 14px, 16px and 18px, and the word spacing chooses 1px, 2px, 3px and 4px. After permutation and combination, the match of the word size and the word spacing is shown as follows (Table 4):

Table 4. 16 types of match of the word size and the word spacing in experiment

Serial No.	Word size	Word spacing
1	12px	1px
2	12px	2px
3	12px	3px
4	12px	4px
5	14px	1px
6	14px	2px
7	14px	3px
8	14px	4px
9	16px	1px
10	16px	2px
11	16px	3px
12	16px	4px
13	18px	1px
14	18px	2px
15	18px	3px
16	18px	4px

In sum, this paper tests the optimal configuration of the word size and the word spacing of Chinese Arial text with black characters and a white background in the display interface of the touch screen through experiments.

The pixel values and physical dimension values of the word size and the word spacing are shown in Appendix.

4 Design of Experimental Scheme

4.1 Design of Experimental Procedures

- Determine the basic influence factors of single-line text reading and operation performance: the word size and the word spacing
- Calculate the man-computer relationship when the touch screen is used;
- Choose the word size and the word spacing according to the interval of the threshold value of the word size during human-computer interaction on the touch screen obtained through the word size calculation formula, and conduct permutation and combination for the word size and the word spacing;
- Design reading questions of the reading text materials, edit the format of the single-line text materials according to configuration of the word size and the word spacing, number these materials, and realize the functions of timing and record options through programming;
- Determine the basic use environment of the experiment and set up a test platform;
- Test the objects with the guide materials and understand the test process;
- Test: Record the reading speed and the answering results through software;
- Experiment ended: Collect and analyze data.

4.2 Subjects

A total of 16 undergraduates at 162–178 cm height, with similar subjectivity in the test experience, educational level and reading ability and normal vision or corrected vision, and speaking Chinese as the mother tongue participated in the test. None of them had contacted the materials used in this experiment.

4.3 Experimental Materials

– Reading materials: 48 long sentences about definitions with about 70 characters and the similar understanding difficulty coefficient. The content of the test text selected in this paper is about definitions of military and politics norms.
– Material editing and processing: place each reading material in the middle of the line and editing them into the single-line text in line with the experimental demand, present one sentence in one interface, and choose the Arial; take one key word or word group from each sentence by aid of the programming language according to the standard of each kind of word size and word spacing corresponding to three sentences, place these key words or word groups at the left, middle and right positions of the sentences, respectively, then divide the 48 sentences into 3 groups (each including 16 sentences with 16 kinds of match between the word size and the word spacing) randomly, prepare the test webpage with each group of materials, collect the corresponding key words to form the corresponding PPT, and display the PPT in the surface as one of the experimental materials (Table 5);

Table 5. Selection of target characters in the test materials

Match	Group 1		Group 2		Group 3	
Word size and word spacing	Position	Character	Position	Character	Position	Character
(12, 1)	Middle	鲜	Right	高	Left	卫
(12, 2)	Left	争	Right	高	Middle	外
(12, 3)	Left	爱	Middle	命	Right	任
(12, 4)	Right	不	Middle	流	Left	采
(14, 1)	Middle	用	Left	用	Right	起
(14, 2)	Left	本	Middle	好	Right	质
(14, 3)	Right	殊	Middle	既	Left	过
(14, 4)	Left	得	Right	以	Middle	间
(16, 1)	Left	务	Middle	民	Right	其
(16, 2)	Middle	或	Left	客	Right	党
(16, 3)	Left	距	Middle	纲	Right	足
(16, 4)	Left	宰	Right	种	Middle	目
(18, 1)	Right	各	Left	告	Middle	予
(18, 2)	Left	迫	Middle	理	Right	议
(18, 3)	Left	用	Middle	采	Right	威
(18, 4)	Right	组	Left	上	Middle	方

4.4   Realization of Material Edit Codes

Material code editing includes 4 parts: the material position in the interface, the basic pattern of materials, the staying time in the interface and option acquisition by the operator, and the countdown during interface transition and buffering, as shown in the below:

(1) The material position in the interface

```
.container1{background:#ffffff;
        width:1078px;
        position:absolute;
        left:50%;
        top:50%;
        margin-top:-90px;
        margin-left:-539px;
        background:#ffffff;}
```

(2) The basic pattern of materials

```
.p{
  font-family:黑体;
  font-size:12px;
  letter-spacing:1px;
  margin-top:9px;
  margin-bottom:9px;}

font-family: boldface;
  font-size:12px;
  letter-spacing:1px;
  margin-top:9px;
  margin-bottom:9px;}
```

(3) The staying time in the interface and option acquisition by the operator

```
<script type="text/javascript" src="jquery-
2.1.1.min.js"></script>
    <script>
        $(function(){
        var time=0;
        setInterval(function(){
    time++;
        },1);
        $("span").click(function(){
                var exp = new Date();
        exp.setTime(exp.getTime() + 1000 * 60 * 60 * 24);
        document.cookie = "time=" + time + "=text=" +
$(this).text()+";expires=" + exp.toGMTString();
                window.location.href ="H1.html";
            })
    })
    function getCookie(name) {
            var strCookie = document.cookie;
            var arrCookie = strCookie.split("; ");
            for (var i = 0; i < arrCookie.length; i++) {
            var arr = arrCookie[i].split("=");
              for(var j=0;j<arr.length;j++)
              {
                if (arr[j] == name)
                  return arr[j+1];
              }
            }
            return "";
        }
    </script>
```

(4) The countdown during interface transition and buffering

```
<script>
var t=3;//set the jump time
setInterval("refer()",1000); /start 1s timing
function refer(){
if(t==0){
location="13.html"; //#set the jump linked address
}
document.getElementById('show').innerHTML=""+t+"";
//display the countdown
t--; //progressive decrease of the counter
}
</script>
```

4.5   Experimental Facilities

(1) Software

- IE or Firefox: Record detailed time and event content (including the reaction time and results) of the test objects during test through JavaScript/html/CSS and other programming languages (Fig. 2);

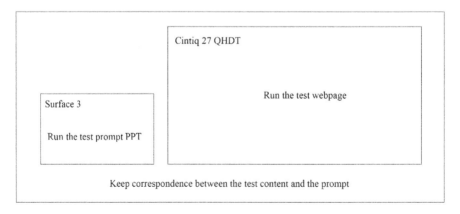

Fig. 2. Setup of the test platform

- QuickTime: Since the above programming displays the reaction time and results but cannot export data, the screen recording software is needed to export the detailed time and event content of the test object during test in the form of video and then collect and record the test result after test;

(2) Hardware

– Wacom Cintiq 27QHD, screen size 27 in. (596.7 * 335.6 mm), screen resolution 2560 * 1440;
– Surface 3;

4.6 Experimental Environment and Test Process

(1) Experimental environment

In the laboratory, temperature was kept at 28 °C. The touch screen was free from interference of the external abnormal light source. The height of the desktop where the touch screen is placed was 72 cm, the included angle between the touch screen and the vertical direction was $10 \sim 20°$, and the sight distance was 40 cm. The touch screen and surface 3 were placed side by side. The height of the desktops and the position of the desks and chairs were fixed to ensure that all the sight distances of the experiment were the same. An absolute quiet environment was maintained during the whole process of the experiment.

(2) Test process

All the test objects were informed with the experimental process in details 1–2 days before the formal experiment. They were also taken to the laboratory to be familiar with the experimental environment, as shown in Fig. 3.

Fig. 3. The real test scene

Each test object received 2 tests, and each test follows the following process:

- Before experiment preparation, adjust the sitting positions, sight distance and view angle of the test objects after they entered the laboratory, and remind them of the experiment content and the issues that need attention in the experimental process;
- Before the formal experiment, guide the test objects to do the group of exercise experiment to help them get familiar with the experimental process and understand the instructions, and then start the formal experiment;
- Start up the experimental facilities, to display the instructions firstly:
- Check the prompt on the surface, and then read a line of words displayed on the touch screen from left to right; click to choose the word as same as the prompt; the finish time and the choice accuracy will be recorded during the experiment; after you are ready, please click to start the test (Fig. 4). (The test assistant will click to change the experiment prompt when the test object waits for page jump. The transition jump time is 3 s, and the test object can check the prompt during the 3 s.)
- Classify and store the experimental data after the test objects finish the test.

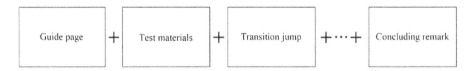

Fig. 4. Stimulus presentation process

- After the test is finished, show sentences with match of 16 kinds of word size and word spacing to the test objects in one interface. The test objects will mark each sentence on the 5-point Likert scale (Fig. 5): 1 point—very poor, 2 points—poor, 3 points—average, 4 points—good, and 5 points—very good.

Fig. 5. Test scene

4.7   Data Analysis and Sorting

This section lists the descriptive statistical results of all dependent variables of the experiment, including the mean and the standard deviation of these dependent variables.

According to Table 6, the mean and the standard deviation of three dependent variables—the completion time of the search task, the operation mistake rate and the readability are calculated in the experiment.

Table 6. Mean and standard deviation of dependent variables of word size and word spacing parameter setting experiment

Experiment prototype: serial No. (word size and word spacing)		Visual search and operation completion time	Operation mistake rate	Readability
(12, 1)	Mean	1.24	0.1	1.4
	Variance	0.26	0.31	0.7
(12, 2)	Mean	1.61	0.0	2
	Variance	0.63	0.0	0.94
(12, 3)	Mean	1.51	0.0	1.8
	Variance	0.92	0.0	0.79
(12, 4)	Mean	1.18	0.03	1.9
	Variance	0.34	0.19	0.88
(14, 1)	Mean	1.11	0.03	2.6
	Variance	0.33	0.19	1.07
(14, 2)	Mean	1.46	0.0	3.4
	Variance	0.79	0.0	0.84
(14, 3)	Mean	1.26	0.0	3
	Variance	1.01	0.0	0.82
(14, 4)	Mean	1.18	0.0	3.1
	Variance	0.94	0.0	0.88
(16, 1)	Mean	1.23	0.0	3.4
	Variance	1.07	0.0	0.52
(16, 2)	Mean	0.93	0.0	4.7
	Variance	0.27	0.0	0.88
(16, 3)	Mean	0.81	0.0	3.5
	Variance	0.26	0.0	0.53
(16, 4)	Mean	1.52	0.0	3.2
	Variance	0.58	0.0	1.32
(18, 1)	Mean	1.03	0.0	4.3
	Variance	0.34	0.0	0.95
(18, 2)	Mean	0.91	0.0	4.3
	Variance	0.17	0.0	0.67
18, 3)	Mean	1.1	0.0	4.6
	Variance	0.45	0.0	0.7
(18, 4)	Mean	0.93	0.03	4.1
	Variance	0.25	0.19	1.1

The result shows that when the match of the word size and the word spacing is (16px, 2px), (16px, 3px), (18px, 2px) or (18px, 4px) in the experiment, the average time needed to complete the task is relatively small. Time consumption for the match of (16px, 3px) is the smallest, followed by (18px, 2px), and then (16px, 2px) and (18px, 4px) with the same performance. As to the operation mistake rate, the match of (18px, 4px) is the only match with operation mistakes. Besides, with respect to the average score of the readability in the 5-point Likert scale, the match of (16px, 3px) and the match of (18px, 4px) are ranked at the last two positions, mainly due to the negative influence of the large word spacing on reading. Moreover, compared with the match of (18px, 2px), the match of (16px, 2px) is accepted by the test objects due to its good readability, and this match can carry more information in the limited space. Therefore, the test result prefers the optimal setting of the match of (16px, 2px).

5   Conclusion and Prospect

This study aims to test the influence of changes in two basic elements of the interface texts—the word size and the word spacing for the human cognitive performance based on the application environment of the desktop-computer touch screen. The 27-in. (resolution: 2560px*1440px) and the approximate 40 cm sight distance are selected to test and compare the human cognitive performance with 16 kinds of match between the word size and the word spacing in Chinese Arial. The conclusion is that in the experimental conditions, after comprehensively considering the elements of visual search and the average value of the completion time, the operation mistake rate and the readability evaluation, the optimal match between the word size and the word spacing is (16px, 2px).

The touch screen is developing towards large scale from the handheld device terminal, but the research on the interface design specifications of the desktop-computer touch screen has not started formally. This research only studies the basic condition of the word size and the word spacing in the text with black characters and a white background. However, the utilization environment of characters is diversified in the practical application. So the experiment scenes and parameter setting should be further enriched in the future, and the studies can cover more conditions. For all this, the research direction, the research methods and the research process of this paper can still provide reference for the study of the text element design specifications based on the Chinese interactive interface of the desktop-computer touch screen.

Appendix

Table of Comparison Between Pixels of Word Size and Word Spacing and Physical Dimensions

See Table 7.

Table 7. Comparison between pixels and physical dimensions in 27-in. touch screen (resolution: 2560*1080)

Word size (px)	Physical dimensions (mm)
1	0.2
2	0.5
3	0.7
4	0.9
12	2.8
14	3.3
16	3.7

References

1. Legge, G.E., Mansfield, J.S., Chung, S.T.L.: Psychophysics of reading. Vis. Res. **41**(6), 725–743 (2001)
2. Fletcher, K., Sutherland, S., Nugent, K., et al.: Identification of text and symbols on a liquid crystal display part III: the effect of ambient light, colour and size. Psychoanal. Psychol. **29** (1), 112 (2009)
3. Humar, I., Gradišar, M., Turk, T.: The impact of color combinations on the legibility of a Web page text presented on CRT displays. Int. J. Ind. Ergon. **38**(11), 885–899 (2008)
4. Wang, Y., Shao, Z.: Stroke frequency and font effects on Chinese character recognition threshold. Psychol. Sci. **1**, 134–136 (2009)
5. Liu, L.: Effects of different word size, font type and text spacing on reading efficiency of patients with maculopathy. Jilin University (2015)
6. Wang, L.: Study on Chinese, South Korean and American elders' information technology acceptance. Tsinghua University (2010)
7. Zou, Y., Zhou, S., Zuo, T., et al.: Study on character-background color matching of PPT design in different illumination intensity conditions. Comput. CD Softw. Appl. **16**, 53–54 (2012)
8. Guo, Z., Li, Y., Sheng, J., et al.: Influence of line spacing of characters on EMU display and control interface on recognition efficiency. J. Railway **34**(12), 31–34 (2012)
9. Guo, Z., Li, Y., Ma, G., et al.: Influence of font size of EMU display and control interface on drivers' recognition efficiency. China Railway Sci. **34**(3), 93–97 (2013)
10. Zhang, J., Wang, X.: Ergonomics and Design Application. National Defence Industry Press, Beijing (2010)
11. Gong, X., Bian, P., Wei, W.: Interactive Design. Hefei University of Technology Press (2016)

12. An, Z., Xu, Z.: Study on key technology of interactive electronic technical manual of complex weapon system. In: The Annual Academic Conference for Outstanding Ph.D. C Candidates of China Association for Science and Technology (2006)
13. UCDChina. UCD Spark Set: Effective Internet product design, mutual information design and user study and discussion. 2/UCDChina. Posts & Telecom Press (2011)

An Improved Model for GUI Design
of mHealth Context-Aware Applications

Mario Quinde[1,2(✉)] and Nawaz Khan[2]

[1] Universidad de Piura, Piura, Peru
mario.quinde@udep.pe
[2] Middlesex University, London, UK
MQ093@live.mdx.ac.uk, N.X.Khan@mdx.ac.uk

Abstract. One of the main challenges of mobile health is using the smaller screens of mobile devices efficiently to show information supporting the health decision-making process. This research proposes a model that can be used to design and evaluate GUIs of mHealth context-aware applications with the aim of ensuring a proper distribution of key information among the screens. The proposed model is then evaluated based on the Health-ITUEM usability parameters description. The results of this evaluation show the attributes related to usability that have been enhanced.

Keywords: Mobile health · GUI design · Usability
Decision-making · GUI · Context-awareness

1 Introduction

The use of smartphones and devices connected to Internet has increased in recent years and it will keep increasing in the future [1–3]. This spread has given users the opportunity to change from software that worked in PC with wired Internet to software that works in mobile devices with wireless Internet.

Mobile technology has brought a new paradigm that has improved efficiency and quality of processes by delivering ubiquitous and user-centered solutions. This is reflected in terms as m-learning, m-health, m-commerce or m-banking [1]. Mobile health (mHealth or m-health) can be defined as a part of eHealth that avoid location boundaries [4] by using mobile devices and wireless communication technologies to support healthcare systems [5]. mHealth provides powerful tools for improving health processes through the use of mobile devices [6].

Table 1 shows relevant benefits that mHealth brings to the main stakeholders involved in the health process: patients, healthcare givers and management staff. The main benefits for patients are empowerment, communities building and learning. Healthcare givers receive benefits from decision-making, communities building and learning. Finally, the main benefit for management staff is the increase of efficiency, accuracy and procedural tracking in their tasks.

© Springer International Publishing AG, part of Springer Nature 2018
A. Marcus and W. Wang (Eds.): DUXU 2018, LNCS 10919, pp. 313–326, 2018.
https://doi.org/10.1007/978-3-319-91803-7_23

Table 1. Benefits of mHealth

Patients	Healthcare givers	Management staff
Empowerment	Decision-making	Efficiency
Communities building		Accuracy
Learning		Procedural tracking

mHealth allows *patients' empowerment* as it increases self-awareness [1,7,8] and self-monitoring [9], which leads to the improvement of patients' decision-making and self-management [10,11]. An example of this is the delivery of support and guidance to patients through mobile devices [12]. Mobile technology also provides ubiquitous communication schemes [13] facilitating the *building of social-communities*. This permits patients to receive feedback and encouragement [11], to share and manage knowledge [11,14], and to receive advice from healthcare givers located around the world [9,10,15]. Mobile devices can also improve *patients' learning process* as it favours the delivery of instructions to react properly to emergencies, to be aware of risks and to improve preventive behaviours [1].

Mobile devices benefit the *decision-making process* of healthcare givers by facilitating the input of patients' data and the reception of targeted health information [5]. This eases the creation of context-aware solutions [14] as a consequence of gathering data from tracking patients and their contexts, and using it to offer recommendations based on well-grounded decision making [3,14]. Healthcare providers benefit from *communities building* in a similar way than patients. The fact that doctors use their personal mobile phones for work issues [16] allows them to perform their activities flexibly by working remotely [17] and to consult with specialists allocated in different places around the world [9]. mHealth also enhances the *learning process* of health workforce because mobile devices have the appropriate technology to offer services that are used to train and increase knowledge of the health workforce [7,18]. Some examples are the use of TB Detext [19] -a mobile application providing health workers with access to up-to-date educational content about tuberculosis-, and the use of PDAs to provide nurses with access to tools and health information [5].

mHealth is improving *efficiency, accuracy and procedural tracking* of healthcare processes. It provides digital ecosystems reducing waste and improving quality [9]. mHealth solutions have been able to engage remote workers, reduce administrative burden, improve the data quality, increase the reliability on records and boost confidence at the point of contact with patient [20]. More specific benefits are: monitoring efficiently patients attributes and environment [1], reducing admissions and readmissions [21], and cutting the cost of care by patients spending more time out of hospitals [9]. Some mHealth solutions that have improved efficiency and quality are applications for consulting information of a patient [22], booking appointments, renewing prescriptions and consulting with healthcare providers [15].

Despite of these benefits, mobile devices still have several challenges to face in order to keep improving health processes [1,3,6,7]. One of the main issues that stops mobile technology from delivering more benefits is the small screen size of mobile devices [5,23]. This is relevant given the complex decision-making environment of health processes [23] and the limited technological background of potential users [10]. Because of this, it is important to find efficient ways of using the screens of mobile devices to show relevant information supporting decision-making [23].

This research contributes to face this challenge by proposing and validating a model that enhances the design of usable Graphic User Interfaces (GUI) of mHealth context-aware applications. The research question answered is how to design usable GUIs of mhealth context-aware applications supporting decision-making. Hence, this work aims to close the gap between the potential benefits of mHealth and the challenge of using efficiently the available space of mobile devices to show information.

The description of the benefits of mHealth shows a strong link between them and the context-aware features that mHealth applications provide. *Context-awareness* (also known as *context-aware computing*) is defined in [24,25] as "*the use of context to provide task-relevant information and/or services to a user*", where *context* is defined as "*any information that can be used to characterize the situation of an entity, where an entity can be a person, place, or physical or computational object*". Because of this link, the proposal of this research will also be analysed from the perspective of context-awareness in order to show the potential benefits that the proposed model could bring to the development of mHealth context-aware applications.

The methodology used to develop this research is shown in Fig. 1. The outcomes of the literature review were used to develop the model and to design the questionnaire. The benefits and challenges of mHealth showed the importance of GUI design when developing mHealth application, and both the Information Supply Chain (ISC) Framework [26] and the analytical model proposed by

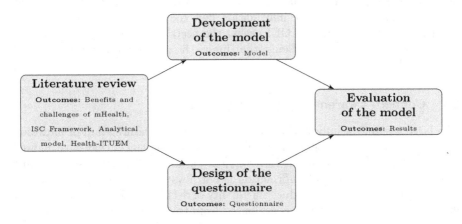

Fig. 1. Methodology process

Varshney [23] set the foundation of the model. The Health IT Usability Evaluation Model (Health-ITUEM) was the basis to design the questionnaire used in the qualitative research that led the evaluation of the model.

This work is divided into the following sections. Section 2 explains the GUI design challenge of mHealth in developing context-aware solutions. Section 3 explains the proposed model and an application example of it. Section 4 describes the evaluation process used to validate the model and shows its results. Section 5 presents a discussion of the results and analyses the model from the perspective of context-awareness. Finally, conclusions are reached in Sect. 6.

2   The Graphic User Interface Challenge of mHealth

The GUI design challenge of mHealth is linked to the smaller screens of mobile devices. It becomes more relevant when is analysed from the health perspective as it directly impacts on quality of health processes [1]. Furthermore, both the complex decision-making environment of health processes [6] and the fact that potential users of mHealth may have a limited technological background [10] make it important to design high-quality GUI of mHealth applications.

Despite this, GUI of mHealth applications are not properly evaluated and tested. The evaluation of GUI mHealth applications is less rigorous than the evaluation of web-based health applications [27]. Moreover, healthcare experts and target users are not included in the development process of these applications [7,8]. To counter this challenge, it is important to develop frameworks enhancing the design and evaluation processes of mHealth applications [18,27]. Besides, it is also critical to use potential users and communities of experts to assess the development of health applications [2,7,18].

Facing this challenge indirectly tackles other mHealth challenges. An appropriate GUI allows to spend less time using the application, which counters the less battery capacity of mobile devices. A proper GUI also decreases the cognitive overload that reduces decision-making capacity [23]. Data integration is another challenge [6] that is faced because a well-designed GUI can be used as a starting point to define the information flow required to develop a mHealth application. Finally, a usable GUI easing the users' adaptation process aids to cope with the IT literacy challenge that limits the number of potential users of mHealth [11].

2.1   Context-Awareness and GUI Design

The large amount of information available and the miniaturization of hardware components are both recognized in [28] as part of the advances that have allowed the emergence of the Intelligent Environment paradigm. Nevertheless, providing users with large amount of information is not always convenient given the fact that cognitive overload can reduce the quality of decision-making and the quality of healthcare services when it is evaluated from the mHealth perspective.

A simple example of cognitive overload is a mobile application tracking the temperature of a house. If this application sends notifications to the users (parents) every time there is a change in the temperature -even for variations of 0.1 °C-, it is highly probable that users will ignore these notifications because the temperature of the house may change several times during the day. This fact may reduce the quality of decision-making as the parents will not be aware of temperature as a consequence of ignoring the notifications. A better scenario is the same mobile application allowing users to set the temperature limits that will trigger the notifications. This approach would be better as the users will be notified only when the temperature changes are relevant for them.

From this point of view, context-awareness is important when is used to reduce the cognitive overload of users in mHealth [23]. In this research, its relevance is analysed from the GUI design perspective of mHealth applications. For this, it is important to highlight that the aim of using context-awareness in this field is to support humans and not to replace them in the decision-making process [23]. Hence, a proper context-aware GUI should provide the right distribution and formatting of the information to show in order to allow users to read the information easily and to make the decision-making process more efficient. In [6], this is explained by saying that the GUIs of mHealth applications should be able to adapt to the cognitive capacity of decision makers and to the necessities of the healthcare professionals involved in the health processes.

3 An Improved Model for GUI Design of mHealth Context-Aware Applications

3.1 Foundation of the Model

The proposed model improves the GUI design of mHealth applications. It is based on both the analytical model for improving decision-making in mHealth proposed by Varshney [23] and the Information Supply Chain (ISC) Framework proposed by Kandl and Khan [26].

Varshney proposes two enhancements for improving quality of decision-making in mHealth. The first one is related to data processing and its aim is to deliver more accurate alerts generated by context-aware solutions. The second enhancement improves GUI design by suggesting how to distribute information among the screens of a mHealth application. With the aim of enhancing decision-making, the author suggests that a mHealth application should show the most important information on the first screens and the least important on the last screens [23].

The ISC Framework of Kandl and Khan supports complex queries by using seven concepts related to integration in the ISC. One of these is the Information Completeness (IC) concept that measures how complete the information for decision-making is. The IC index can be calculated by using Formula 1.

$$IC = \frac{I_p}{I_r}, \tag{1}$$

which represents a comparison between the information instances present in the system and all the information instances required for decision-making [26].

I_p is the number of information instances that are present in the system and I_r represent the number of information instances required for decision-making. For example, to conclude an investigation, information about Sample, Drug, Clinical Issue and Hypothesis must be present. If all required information is indeed linked to the investigation then said information is 100% complete. On the other hand, if Hypothesis is missing the resulting IC is lowered to 75%.

Although the IC can be used to know how complete the information shown by a system is, it cannot be used to measure if the information shown by the system is properly distributed among its screens. This research integrates the IC concept with the enhancement proposed in [23] to show a more comprehensive view on GUI design for mHealth applications.

3.2   Explanation of the Model

The core of the model is Formula 2 that calculates the Information Distribution Index (IDI). This formula is the result of improving the IC for being capable of measuring the distribution of information among the screens of a mHealth application. The IDI is calculated by comparing how the information is distributed among the screens (dividend) and how the information should be distributed (divisor). The result is a real number between 0 and 1 whose interpretation is: the closer to one, the better the information is distributed among the screens of the mHealth application.

$$IDI = \frac{\sum(I_{pi}W_{pi})}{\sum(I_{ri}W_{ri})} \tag{2}$$

It is important to clarify the concept of Information Unit (IU) in order to understand Formula 2. An IU is a specific information that would be shown or not by the mHealth application. Examples of IUs are: weight, blood glucose level and beats per minute (bpm).

I_{pi} is an integer that becomes 0 when IU_i is not shown by the application, and 1 when IU_i is shown. W_{pi} is an adjusted weight representing the importance given to IU_i by the application. W_{pi} will be higher when IU_i is shown on an earlier screen of the application. I_{ri} is an integer that becomes 0 when IU_i is not required for decision-making, and 1 when it is required. W_{ri} is an adjusted weight representing the importance of IU_i in the decision-making process the mHealth application supports. The more important IU_i is in the decision-making process, the higher the value of W_{ri}.

The purpose of using W_{pi} and W_{ri} is making comparable the scale used to define the importance given to the IUs by the application and the scale used to assess the importance of the IUs in decision-making. For instance, an application using 5 screens to show IUs uses a scale of 5 to assess the IUs shown (1 is the value given to IUs shown on the fifth screen, and 5 to IUs shown on the first). If the importance of these IUs in decision-making is assessed by using a scale

of 10 (0 to non-relevant IUs and 10 to the most relevant IUs), both scales will
not be comparable.

W_{pi} is calculated by using Formula 3, where N is the number of screens the
application uses to show IUs. Only screens dedicated to shown IUs must be
included when calculating N (e.g. login or help screens are not included in this
calculation). S_i is the screen number of the mHealth application in which IUi
is shown. If IUi is shown on the first screen, then S_i will be 1.

$$W_{pi} = N - S_i + 1 \tag{3}$$

W_{ri} is calculated by using Formula 4, where E_i is the evaluation given to IUi
regarding its relevance in the decision-making process the mHealth application
supports, and E is the scale used to evaluate the relevance of the IUs in decision-
making. An $Ei - value$ of 0 should be assigned to the non-relevant IUs, while
the highest $Ei - value$ (E) should be assigned to the most relevant IUs.

$$W_{ri} = \left\lceil \frac{E_i N}{E} \right\rceil \tag{4}$$

It is important to consider that if W_{pi} is higher than W_{ri}, then W_{pi} must get
the value of W_{ri}. By doing this, the formula penalizes when an important IU is
not shown on an early screen, but it does not reward when a minor IU is shown
on an early screen. Hence, the IDI does not benefit a mHealth application that
compensates showing important IUs on later screens by showing minor IUs on
earlier screens.

Other consideration to calculate the IDI is that if an application shows IUs
that are not relevant for decision-making those IUs must not be included in the
calculation. Otherwise, the IDI will not be valid. For instance, supposing an
application that supports diabetes self-management shows patient's eyes colour.
If this IU (eye colour) is included in the calculation, the IDI increases as the
dividend is higher. This would be wrong as showing patient's eye colour does not
improve the distribution of important information for decision-making among
the screens of the mHealth application.

The proposed model can be used for two purposes: (a) as an evaluation tool to
assess if the IUs are well distributed among the screens of a mHealth application,
or (b) as a designing tool to provide a guideline on how to distribute IUs among
the screens of a mHealth application that is being designed. Different processes
should be followed depending on the purpose chosen to use the model.

When using the model as an evaluation tool, the process shown in Fig. 2 must
be followed. The first two steps can be performed at the same time, but these
must be completed before beginning the third. The first step aims to define the
evaluation scale (E), the IUs required (I_{ri}) and its level of importance (E_i) in
the decision-making process supported by the mHealth application that is being
evaluated. The evaluation of the IUs must involve expert patients, healthcare
givers and researchers. Including them is considered a good approach to face the
GUI design challenge when creating IT health solutions [2,7,18].

The second step identifies the IUs shown by the mHealth application (I_{pi}), the number of screens dedicated to show IUs (N) and the screen in which each IU is shown (S_i). Finally, the third step is to calculate IDI by using Formula 2.

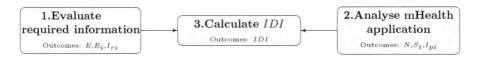

Fig. 2. Process to follow when using the model as an evaluation tool

Figure 3 shows the process to follow when using the model as a designing tool, which is made of three sequential steps. The first step is similar to the first step in Fig. 2. The only difference is that, when using the model as a designing tool, the IUs that will be shown by the mHealth application (I_{pi}) are defined in the first step. These I_{pi} are the same that the IUs required for decision-making (I_{ri}). When using the model as an evaluation tool (Fig. 2), the I_{pi} are defined in the second step.

Fig. 3. Process to follow when using the model as a designing tool

The second step is defining some designing parameters to develop the mHealth application. These parameters will help to define the number of screens the mHealth application will use to show IUs (N). Some examples of these parameters are the fonts and formats that will be used to develop the application. It is recommended to complete Step 1 before beginning Step 2 as knowing the number of IUs the mHealth application will show helps to define N.

The third step is using the IDI to calculate the screen number in which each IU should be shown (S_i). As the objective of this case is to find the best possible distribution, the IDI should be equalized to 1 and, after substituting and clearing the equations related to calculate the IDI, the formula to calculate S_i is the following:

$$S_i = N + 1 - \left\lceil \frac{E_i N}{E} \right\rceil \tag{5}$$

The results of Formula 5 must be used as a guideline to distribute IUs among the screens of a mHealth application supporting decision-making. Other factors must also be considered in the distribution of the IUs among the screens. For example, in [23] it is recommended to show IUs correlated between them on the same screens.

Furthermore, it is also important to explain that the IDI penalizes when an IU is shown on a later screen than the one where it should be shown (S_i), but it does not reward when an IU is shown on an earlier screen than the one where it should be shown. Because of this, the IDI cannot differentiate between an application showing IUs on the screens suggested by the model and an application showing IUs on earlier screens than those suggested by the model.

3.3   Application Example of the Model

This section describes an example to clarify the use of model. The main goal is to show how to use the IDI to provide a guideline to distribute IUs among the screens of a mHealth application supporting diabetes self-management.

Table 2. Results of the application example

i	IU_i	E_i	S_i	i	IU_i	E_i	S_i
1	Blood glucose level	5	1	10	Blood pressure minimum	4	1
2	Urine glucose level	4	1	11	Total cholesterol level	2	3
3	Glucose target	5	1	12	Total cholesterol target	2	3
4	HbA1c level	3	2	13	Low Density Lipoprotein level	2	3
5	HbA1c target	3	2	14	Low Density Lipoprotein target	2	3
6	Fructosamine level	1	4	15	High Density Lipoprotein level	2	3
7	Fructosamine target	1	4	16	High Density Lipoprotein target	2	3
8	Blood pressure (hypertension)	4	1	17	Triglyceride level	2	3
9	Blood pressure maximum	4	1	18	Triglyceride target	2	3

The first step is to evaluate the IUs related to diabetes self-management. The IUs required (I_{ri}) were obtained from the Diabetes UK charity's website [29]. The scale used to evaluate the importance of the IUs in the diabetes decision-making process is 5 (0 to the non-important IUs and 5 to the most important). As the aim of this example is explaining the use of the formula, the evaluation process of the IUs required (I_{ri}) has been simplified. The evaluation of each IU (E_i) was done by interpreting the description provided in the website, without including expert patients, healthcare givers or researchers. The IUs to show in the application (I_{pi}) are the same IUs required for decision-making (I_{ri}).

The second step is to define the number of screens dedicated to show IUs (N). For this example, N is defined as 4. The third step is using Formula 5 to calculate in which specific screen each IU should be shown (S_i). Table 2 shows the results of this application example including the IUs (I_{pi}, I_{ri}), its evaluation (E_i) and the screens where they should be shown (S_i).

4   Evaluation and Results

The proposed model has been evaluated through a qualitative research based on the Health-ITUEM. This evaluation model assesses usability of health IT by evaluating how the technology affects nine concepts linked to usability [27]. These concepts are: Error prevention, Completeness, Memorability, Information needs, Flexibility/Customizability, Learnability, Performance speed, Competency and Other outcomes related to usability. The scenario mapping these concepts for GUI design is shown in Table 3.

Table 3. Scenario mapping Health-ITUEM for GUI design

Health-ITUEM concept	Description regarding GUI design
Error prevention	The GUI facilitates error management (e.g. showing error messages as feedback, supporting error correction and error prevention, etc.)
Completeness	The GUI assists users to successfully complete tasks
Memorability	The GUI aids to remember how to perform task through the system
Information needs	The GUI shows information improving or supporting basic task performance
Flexibility (or Customizability)	The GUI offers more than one way to perform tasks, allowing users to use the system as they wish
Learnability	The GUI makes it easier to learn how to use the system
Performance speed	The GUI allows to use the system efficiently
Competency	Users are confident in their ability when using the GUI of the system to perform tasks

A questionnaire was applied to two samples. The first sample (S_1) was made of 33 students from an Industrial and Systems Engineering undergraduate programme. They had taken and passed a module in which topics related to GUI design were taught and evaluated. The second sample (S_2) was made of 15 professionals that had completed undergraduate programmes related to Software Engineering. All respondents from S_2 had between 3 and 22 years of experiences in the subject and 13 of them had completed or were studying a post-graduate programme related to the subject.

The questionnaire was made of 10 closed questions. Two questions asked how using the model impacts usability and user-friendliness. The other eight questions asked how the model impacts the Health-ITUEM concepts. Hence, the results of the evaluation show if the proposed model improves, does not affect or decreases the Health-ITUEM concepts. Table 4, Figs. 4 and 5 summarize the results of the evaluation process.

All respondents state the model improves Usability, and most of them state the model improves User-Friendliness (S_1: 87.88%; S_2: 93.33%). At least 70% of the respondents of each sample affirm the model improves Error prevention (S_1:

Table 4. Results of the evaluation process

Concept	$S_1(\%)$			$S_2(\%)$		
	Improved	Unaffected	Decreased	Improved	Unaffected	Decreased
Usability	100.00	0.00	0.00	100	0.00	0.00
User-Friendliness	87.88	9.09	3.03	93.33	6.67	0.00
Error prevention	81.82	18.18	0.00	73.33	26.67	0.00
Completeness	87.88	9.09	3.03	93.33	6.67	0.00
Memorability	60.61	27.27	12.12	86.67	13.33	0.00
Information needs	87.88	12.12	0.00	86.67	13.33	0.00
Flexibility	36.36	45.46	18.18	33.33	40.00	26.67
Learnability	81.82	18.18	0.00	73.33	26.67	0.00
Performance speed	72.73	18.18	9.09	100.00	0.00	0.00
Competency	75.76	21.21	3.03	80.00	20.00	0.00

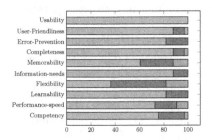

Fig. 4. Results (%) of Sample 1   **Fig. 5.** Results (%) of Sample 2

81.82%; S_2: 73.33%), Completeness (S_1: 87.88%; S_2: 93.33%), Information needs (S_1: 87.88%; S_2: 86.67%), Learnability (S_1: 81.82%; S_2: 73.33%), Performance speed (S_1: 72.73%; S_2: 100%) and Competency (S_1: 75.76%; S_2: 80.00%).

The results also show that respondents do not coincide in confirming that the model improves, decreases or does not affect Flexibility. Moreover, 60.61% of S_1 and 86.67% of S_2 believe the model improves Memorability. All respondents of S_2 agree in affirming the model does not decrease any concept, except for Flexibility (26.67%). Nevertheless, some respondents of S_1 say that the model decreases User-Friendliness (3.03%), Completeness (3.03%), Memorability (12.12%), Flexibility (18.18%), Performance speed (9.09%) and Competency (3.03%).

5   Discussion

According to the respondents, although there is no majority, Flexibility (or Customizability) is the Health-ITUEM concept most negatively affected by the model. The reason why the respondents state this should be further investigated, but this result would be because of the fact that the model assesses the *IUs* for being on a specific screen of the mHealth application. Nevertheless, from this point of view, the model -as a designing tool- can be used to proposed an initial distribution of the IUs among the screens of the mHealth application. Then, this distribution can be altered by the users according to their specific requirements, using a GUI designing approach that allows them to personalise (or customize) the location of the IUs on the screens they want.

The proposed model can also be analysed from the perspective of context-awareness in order to show how it can aid the development of context-aware applications for mHealth. In [24,25], context is defined as *"any information that can be used to characterize the situation of an entity, where an entity can be a person, place, or physical or computational object"*. It can be said that the IU concept is linked to this definition as context is made of IUs *that are relevant to the decision-making process of users*, who in this case are patients or people in charge of them. From this point of view, the model improves the distribution of the IUs that define the context supporting the decision-making of carers and patients regarding their disease. The model defines the *depth of screen* to reach an IU according to the importance the IU has in building the context of patients for a specific disease.

The evaluation of the model shows that it improves the GUI designing process of mHealth applications and it impacts positively on concepts related to usability and user-friendliness. Although the model is mainly targeted to assess the IUs framing the medical dimension of patients' context, the approach can be used to distribute the IUs defining other dimensions of the patients' context. Three main features of context-aware applications are shown in [24]: (1) the presentation of information an services to a user, (2) automatic execution of a service, and (3) tagging of context to information for later retrieval. The use of the model would impact on the first of these features. However, further research should be done to validate the use of the model to distribute IUs building multi-dimensional contexts among the screens of mHealth context-aware applications.

6   Conclusions

This research proposes and evaluates a model supporting GUI design of mHealth context-aware applications. The model directly faces the GUI design challenge and it indirectly faces others: IT literacy, decision-making, data integration and battery duration. It can be used to evaluate if the IUs are well distributed among the screens of an application and to provide a guideline to distribute IUs among the screens of an application that is being designed.

The evaluation of the model was based on the Health-ITUEM and its results show the model improves Usability, User-Friendliness, Error prevention, Completeness, Information needs, Learnability, Performance speed and Competency. Nevertheless, there is less evidence to confirm the model improves Memorability, and there is not enough evidence to know how the model affects Flexibility.

References

1. Nunes, I.L., Simões-marques, M.J.: Exploiting the potential and facing the challenges of mobile devices: application examples. Procedia Manuf. **3**, 807–814 (2015). https://doi.org/10.1016/j.promfg.2015.07.335
2. Samples, C., Ni, Z., Shaw, R.J.: Nursing and mHealth. Int. J. Nurs. Sci. **1**(4), 330–333 (2014). https://doi.org/10.1016/j.ijnss.2014.08.002
3. Fernandez, F., Pallis, G.C.: Opportunities and challenges of the Internet of Things for healthcare: systems engineering perspective. In: 4th International Conference on Wireless Mobile Communication and Healthcare, pp. 263–266. IEEE Press (2015). https://doi.org/10.1109/MOBIHEALTH.2014.7015961
4. Mantovani, E., Quinn, P.: mHealth and data protection: the letter and the spirit of consent legal requirements. Int. Rev. Law Comput. Technol. **28**(2), 1–15 (2014). https://doi.org/10.1080/13600869.2013.801581
5. World Health Organization: mHealth - new horizons for health through mobile technologies. In: Global Observatory for eHealth series, vol. 3 (2011). http://www.who.int/goe/publications/goe_mhealth_web.pdf. Accessed 29 Jan 2018
6. Varshney, U.: Mobile health: four emerging themes of research. Decis. Support Syst. **66**, 20–35 (2014). https://doi.org/10.1016/j.dss.2014.06.001
7. Dinesen, B., et al.: Personalized telehealth in the future: a global research agenda. J. Med. Internet Res. **8**(3), e53 (2016). https://doi.org/10.2196/jmir.5257
8. Schnall, R., et al.: A user-centered model for designing consumer mobile health (mHealth) applications (apps). J. Biomed. Inform. **60**, 243–251 (2016). https://doi.org/10.1016/j.jbi.2016.02.002
9. Isakovic, M., Cijan, J., Sedlar, U., Volk, M., Bester, J.: The role of mHealth applications in societal and social challenges of the future. In: 12th International Conference on Information Technology, pp. 561–566. IEEE Press (2015). https://doi.org/10.1109/ITNG.2015.94
10. Kotz, D., Avancha, S., Baxi, A.: A privacy framework for mobile health and home-care systems. In: Proceedings of the First ACM Workshop on Security and Privacy in Medical and Home-Care Systems, pp. 1–12. ACM, New York (2009). https://doi.org/10.1145/1655084.1655086
11. Almunawar, M.N., Anshari, M., Younis, M.Z.: Incorporating customer empowerment in mobile health. Health Policy Technol. **4**(4), 312–319 (2015). https://doi.org/10.1016/j.hlpt.2015.08.008
12. Danaher, B.G., Brendryen, H., Seeley, J.R., Tyler, M.S., Woolley, T.: From black box to toolbox: outlining device functionality, engagement activities, and the pervasive information architecture of mHealth interventions. Internet Interv. **2**(1), 91–101 (2015). https://doi.org/10.1016/j.invent.2015.01.002
13. Santos, J., et al.: An IoT-based mobile gateway for intelligent personal assistants on mobile health environments. J. Netw. Comput. Appl. **71**, 194–204 (2016). https://doi.org/10.1016/j.jnca.2016.03.014
14. Emmanouilidis, C., Koutsiamanis, R.A., Tasidou, A.: Mobile guides: taxonomy of architectures, context awareness, technologies and applications. J. Netw. Comput. Appl. **36**(1), 103–125 (2013). https://doi.org/10.1016/j.jnca.2012.04.007
15. Grisot, M., Vassilakopoulou, P.: Creating a national e-Health infrastructure: the challenge of the installed base. In: ECIS 2015 Completed Research Papers, paper 63 (2015). https://doi.org/10.18151/7217335
16. Martin, G., Janardhanan, P., Withers, T., Gupta, S.: Mobile revolution: a requiem for bleeps? Postgrad. Med. J. **92**, 493–496 (2016). https://doi.org/10.1136/postgradmedj-2015-133722

17. Turner, C.: Use of mobile devices in community health care: barriers and solutions to implementation. Br. J. Commun. Nurs. **21**(2), 100–103 (2016). https://doi.org/10.12968/bjcn.2016.21.2.100

18. Mechael, P., Sloninsky, D.: Towards the Development of an mHealth strategy: a literature review. The millennium village project (2008). http://www.who.int/goe/mobile_health/mHealthReview_Aug09.pdf. Accessed 29 Jan 2018

19. Labrique, A.B., Vasudevan, L., Kochi, E., Fabricant, R., Mehl, G.: mHealth innovations as health system strengthening tools: 12 common applications and a visual framework. Global Health Sci. Pract. **1**(2), 160–171 (2013). https://doi.org/10.9745/GHSP-D-13-00031

20. Department of Health: National Mobile Health Worker Project: Final Report (2013). https://www.gov.uk/government/uploads/system/uploads/attachment_data/file/213313/mhwp_final_report.pdf. Accessed 29 Jan 2018

21. Bashshur, R.L., et al.: The empirical foundations of telemedicine interventions for chronic disease management. Telemed. e-Health **20**(9), 769–800 (2014). https://doi.org/10.1089/tmj.2014.9981

22. Pereira, A., et al.: Improving quality of medical service with mobile health software. Procedia Comput. Sci. **63**, 292–299 (2015). https://doi.org/10.1016/j.procs.2015.08.346

23. Varshney, U.: A model for improving quality of decisions in mobile health. Decis. Support Syst. **62**, 66–77 (2014). https://doi.org/10.1016/j.dss.2014.03.005

24. Abowd, G.D., Dey, A.K., Brown, P.J., Davies, N., Smith, M., Steggles, P.: Towards a better understanding of context and context-awareness. In: Gellersen, H.-W. (ed.) HUC 1999. LNCS, vol. 1707, pp. 304–307. Springer, Heidelberg (1999). https://doi.org/10.1007/3-540-48157-5_29

25. Dey, A.K.: Understanding and using context. Pers. Ubiquit. Comput. **5**(1), 4–7 (2001). https://doi.org/10.1007/s007790170019

26. Kandl, T., Khan, N.: Information integration of drug discovery and clinical studies to support complex queries using an information supply chain framework. J. Softw. **9**(5), 1348–1356 (2014). https://doi.org/10.4304/jsw.9.5.1348-1356

27. Brown, W., Yen, P., Rojas, M., Schnall, R.: Assessment of the health IT usability evaluation model (Health-ITUEM) for evaluating mobile health (mHealth) technology. J. Biomed. Inform. **46**, 1080–1087 (2013). https://doi.org/10.1016/j.jbi.2013.08.001

28. Augusto, J.C., Callaghan, V., Cook, D., Kameas, A., Satoh, I.: Intelligent environments: a manifesto. Hum. Centric Comput. Inf. Sci. **3**, 12 (2013). https://doi.org/10.1186/2192-1962-3-12

29. Diabetes UK. www.diabetes.org.uk/Guide-to-diabetes/Monitoring/Testing. Accessed 29 Jan 2018

Crack-Free Isosurface of Volumetric Scattered Data

Han Sol Shin[1], Jee Ho Song[1], Tae Jun Yu[2], and Kun Lee[3(✉)]

[1] Department of Information and Communication,
Handong Global University, Pohang, Republic of Korea
[2] Department of Advanced Green Energy and Environment,
Handong Global University, Pohang, Republic of Korea
[3] School of Computer Science and Electronic Engineering,
Handong Global University, Pohang, Republic of Korea
kunlee@handong.edu

Abstract. Isosurface extraction is the method of visualizing multivariate data in three-dimensional space. It is an important process to observe geometrical distribution of iso-value by isosurface extraction. Data obtained by PIC (Particle In Cell) simulation have a characteristic of irregularly distributed volumetric scattered data. Unlike curved surfaces of implicit function, PIC simulation data cannot be represented by continuous function, and each points have no relationship. In such case, isosurface extraction algorithms do not guarantee crack-free surfaces on their results. This paper describes how we get smooth approximation of volumetric scattered data by using a natural neighbor interpolation, and extract a crack-free isosurface on interpolated data.

Keywords: Isosurface · Volumetric scattered data · Data visualization

1 Introduction

Visualization of three- or more dimensional data is a major problem of data visualization field. There are two major categories in way to visualization. One is direct volume rendering, and the other is surface reconstruction. In case of three-dimensional space, the geometrical location of values can be directly represented by x, y, z coordination. Using direct volume rendering, each pixel is examined by light transfer function and their colors are calculated without extracting surfaces. However, deciding color of pixel using light transfer function is expensive computational process. In addition, it is hard to observe the inside structure of value distribution of the dataset. Furthermore, every time the view point and angle changes, colors of pixels should be calculated again.

The other way to visualization is that construct surface on the volume and render it using the method to render general three dimensional meshes. An isosurface, also called implicit surface, is one of the way to construct a surface on volumetric data. It is a surface which has constant value (e.g. density, intensity, temperature) in the three-dimensional scalar field. It is called an isocontour or contour lines in two-dimensional space. Given scalar field f $: \mathbb{R}^d \to \mathbb{R}$ and a constant value $\alpha \in \mathbb{R}$, the

© Springer International Publishing AG, part of Springer Nature 2018
A. Marcus and W. Wang (Eds.): DUXU 2018, LNCS 10919, pp. 327–337, 2018.
https://doi.org/10.1007/978-3-319-91803-7_24

isosurface on the isovalue α is defined by the level set $\{x\,|\,f(x)=\alpha\}$. But since it is just a point set, but not a perfect surface and data cannot be continuous in computer science, an isosurface has to be approximated using specific algorithms. Marching cubes algorithm is one of the widely used algorithm to approximate an isosurface on the volume dataset.

Figure 1 is example of each approach described in previous paragraphs. (a) is direct volume rendered image of laser intensity data, and (b) is its isosurface. Each surfaces of same color have same value.

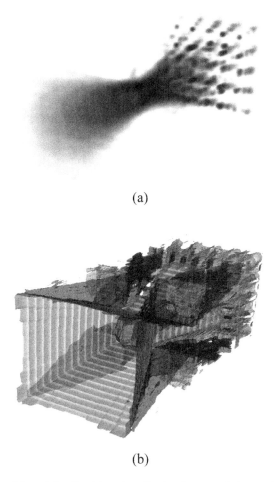

(a)

(b)

Fig. 1. (a) Image of laser intensity data using direct volume rendering and (b) Its isosurface.

2 Problem Description

2.1 Properties of Volumetric Scattered Data

Scattered data has properties of unorganized samples. Each value is located at sparse and irregular position in the space. There are numerous practical examples of scattered data in computer science (e.g. computational fluid dynamics, terrain modeling, etc.). In tri-variate and scalar dependent value case, scattered data can be represented by $f(x_i, y_i, z_i) = F_i, i = (1, \ldots, N)$ where $P_i = (x_i, y_i, z_i)$ are the independent variables and F_i is the dependent variable. In this case, the dataset is called volumetric scattered data.

2.2 Isosurface of Volumetric Scattered Data

Major problem of isosurface is that it is vulnerable to noise of data. Volumetric scattered data is discrete, and not a smooth function, therefore it does not guarantee connectivity of its generated surface. It is even not a surface in many case, because the

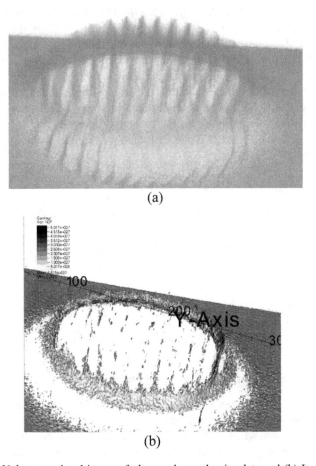

(a)

(b)

Fig. 2. (a) Volume rendered image of plasma charge density data and (b) Its isosurface.

level set of given function and an isovalue is not always a surface. For example, if f is constant function f = α, its level set is all elements of function f's domain when an isovalue is α, but empty set for all the other cases.

Another problem is that data must be organized in cube domain to extract an isosurface using Marching cubes algorithm that is a general method for extracting an isosurfaces of the three-dimensional data. Therefore, scattered data must be interpolated on all vertices of the cubes.

(a) in Fig. 2 is an example of volumetric scattered data and (b) is its isosurface constructed by using Marching cubes algorithm. Constructed surface consist of a lot of disconnected triangles. It is neither good from visual perspective nor easy to get information of geometrical distribution of the isovalue.

3   Related Work

3.1   Marching Cubes

Marching cubes, published in the 1987 SIGGRAPH proceedings by Lorensen and Cline, is famous algorithm for extracting an isosurface of the volumetric data. Marching cubes algorithm is a good choice to construct an isosurface of volumetric data of smooth function. This algorithm use the case table of triangle topology. Each voxel of volumetric data generates an triangle set lying with linearly interpolated point of the voxel's edge using the case table. Each process of generating triangles can be executed independently, so Marching cubes algorithm can be relatively easily accelerated by using parallel computing on multi-core CPU or GPGPU (General purpose graphic processor unit). Figure 3 is the case table of triangle topology, exclusive of symmetric cases.

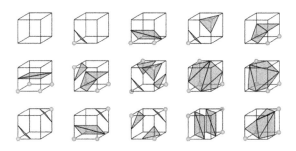

Fig. 3. 15 cases of triangle topology

3.2   Delaunay Triangulation and Voronoi Diagram

Delaunay triangulation is one of the triangulation method that maximize the minimum angle of the generated triangles. A Sliver triangle, which has a long and thin shape, may be inappropriate when used for interpolation or rasterization. In addition, Delaunay triangulation can be extended to three- or higher dimensional triangulation. In three-dimensional case, Delaunay triangulation generates tetrahedrals. Therefore,

Delaunay triangulation can be proper method of triangulation when deciding natural neighbors of the interpolation point. In Fig. 4, there is three ways to triangulate given point set $P = \{p_A, p_B, p_C, p_D, p_E\}$. It can be verified that all the angle of triangles is minimum by all the circumcircle of triangles does not contain any other points except for three points to consist of the triangle. In Fig. 4, (a) satisfies Delaunay triangulation properties, but the others do not.

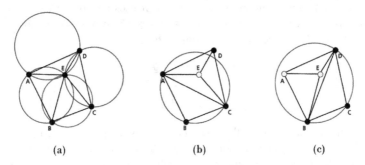

(a)   (b)   (c)

Fig. 4. Delaunay triangulation

Voronoi diagram is the subdivision of the space into Voronoi cells. Voronoi cells represent which point is closest to a position in the space. In other words, Voronoi cells of the point p_i is an influence of p_i in the space. Given point set P and its Delaunay triangulation DT(P), Voronoi diagram of P, VD(P), corresponds to the dual graph of the DT(P). Voronoi diagram can be calculated by connecting the center of circumcircle which is generated by Delaunay triangulation. Figure 5 shows a relationship between Delaunay triangulation and Voronoi diagram.

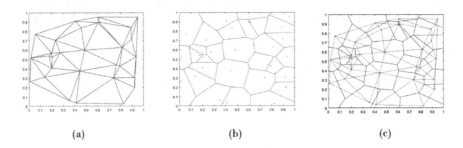

(a)   (b)   (c)

Fig. 5. Relationship between Delaunay triangulation and Voronoi diagram

3.3   Scattered Data Interpolation

Scattered data often approximated to mathematical modeling function to visualization the relationship of each scalar value in the dataset. Scattered data interpolation is the problem that find a function $F(x, y, z)$ which is its dependent variable is an approximated value of given scattered data $f(x_i, y_i, z_i) = F_i$ for a non-given point. There are many options for interpolation method on scattered data. The simplest way of interpolation is Nearest neighbor interpolation. It does not consider a weight of given values but assign same value with its nearest point. This method closely connected to Voronoi diagram. All approximated points in a Voronoi cell has an identical value with the seed point of the cell in Nearest neighbor interpolation.

Another way of interpolation is a weighted average interpolation. A weight can be decided by various terms (e.g. distance based weight). The Shepard's method is one of the basic weighted average interpolation method. It uses an inverse distanced weight for approximation. It can be write in following form where N is the number of points and $p_i, (i = 1, \ldots, N)$ is given point of original function.

$$F(p) = \frac{\sum_{i=1}^{N} \frac{F_i}{\|p-p_i\|^2}}{\sum_{i=1}^{N} \frac{1}{\|p-p_i\|^2}}$$

Considering all the points in the given point set is inefficient for computation. So, many weighted average interpolation methods consider only a neighbor of an interpolated point. Neighbors can be chosen by whether p_i is within a certain distance from an interpolation point. Despite its simplicity, a distance based neighbor has some problems. If points in the data set are not uniformly distributed, distance based method may not work fine. In addition, it is hard to obtain continuous surface even if a data set is uniformly distributed.

4 Voronoi Natural Neighbor Interpolation

Voronoi natural neighbor interpolation offers a good interpolation result with acceptable computational resource. This method resolve two major problems of traditional weighted average interpolation methods; selection of neighbors, and continuousness of surface. It choose neighbor points in which the adjacent Voronoi cells. Given point set P, its Voronoi diagram VD(P) and interpolation point x, insertion of x creates new Voronoi diagram VD(P ∩ {x}). Created Voronoi cell $\mathcal{V}_x$ alters the original Voronoi cells $\mathcal{V}_{p_i}$ which is adjacent to $\mathcal{V}_x$. In Natural neighbor coordinates, new point x represented by weighted summation of its neighbors. A weight can be written following form.

$$w_i = \frac{Area\left(\mathcal{V}_{p_i} \cap \mathcal{V}_x\right)}{Area(\mathcal{V}_x)}$$

Where $Area\left(\mathcal{V}_{p_i}\right)$ represents the area of the Voronoi cell $\mathcal{V}_{p_i}$. The term $\mathcal{V}_{p_i} \cap \mathcal{V}_x$ is a stolen area caused by insertion of x. Voronoi natural neighbor interpolation use this weight w_i for weighted interpolation. Interpolated function $F(p)$ can be represented by this form where N is the number of neighbors. Interpolated function $F(p)$ is continuous everywhere except original point.

$$F(\mathrm{p}) = \sum_{i=1}^{N} w_i F_i$$

(a) in Fig. 6 is the original Voronoi diagram, (b) is newly created Voronoi diagram by insertion of x, and (c) is an overlapped image of previous two images showing weight w_i, which is stolen area of the original Voronoi cell.

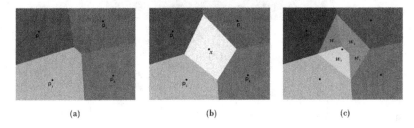

(a)   (b)   (c)

Fig. 6. Voronoi diagram and Natural neighbors interpolation.

5   Results

Experiment was perform by comparing isocontours of three different datasets. First is the original dataset of laser intensity data. Second is the dataset smoothed using Gaussian filter. Last one is the dataset which is down-sampled from original image and approximated to original resolution by using Voronoi natural neighbor interpolation.

The isocontour of original dataset shows many islands, so it is relatively difficult to know intuitively geometrical distribution of isovalues. The second one, Gaussian filtered dataset, shows less islands than previous one, but the range of the value is significantly changed when averaging the values out. In fact, the original dataset's range of value is 4.5e−10 to 6.5501e+03, but the second one is 52.9433 to 2.3670e+03. On the other hand, the isocontour of interpolated dataset shows less islands and modulation does not occur during interpolation process except during down-sampling process.

Figures 7 and 8 are a visualized image of the original dataset and its isocontour respectively. Figures 9 and 10 are images of the Gaussian filtered dataset and Figs. 11 and 12 are images of the interpolated dataset's respectively.

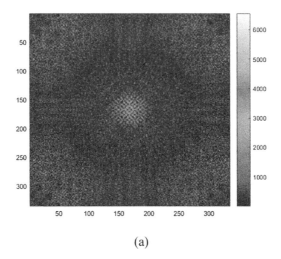

(a)

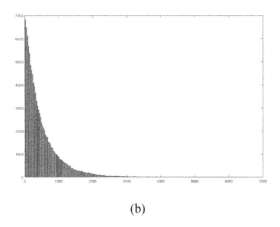

(b)

Fig. 7. (a) Original dataset and (b) Its histogram.

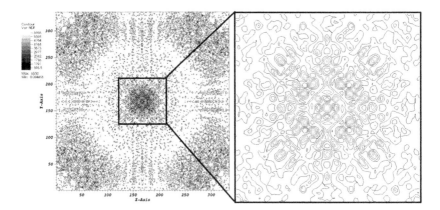

Fig. 8. Isocontour of the original dataset

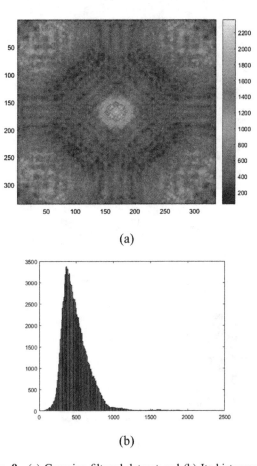

(a)

(b)

Fig. 9. (a) Gaussian filtered dataset and (b) Its histogram.

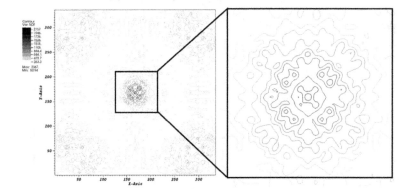

Fig. 10. Isocontour of the smoothed Gaussian filtered dataset.

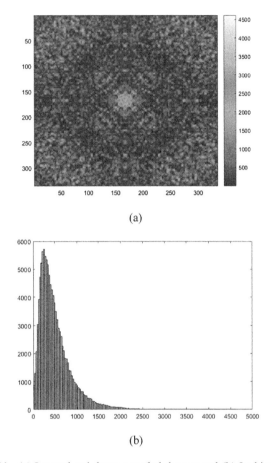

(a)

(b)

Fig. 11. (a) Interpolated down-sampled dataset and (b) Its histogram.

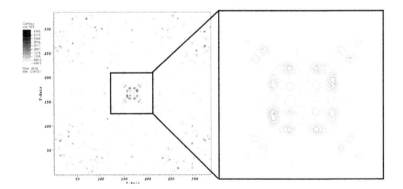

Fig. 12. Isocontour of the interpolated dataset.

6   Conclusions

Scattered data is everywhere in the computer science field. Scattered data is hard to visualize or be analyzed in itself. So reconstruct a surface of scattered data is important issue in computational geometry. This paper showed how to get approximate isosurface or isocontour using interpolation, and described advantages of Voronoi natural neighbor interpolation against other interpolation method. In addition, It showed that problem of using smoothing filter to get less noise isosurface and showed that proposed method solves this problem.

In this paper, uniform down-sampling was used, but it may be valuable to compare the result using other method. In further research, I will compare the result using feature based down-sampling method (like local maximum and curvature) and find proper way to down-sample the original data.

Acknowledgments. This work was supported by the Industrial Strategic technology development program, 10048964, Development of 125 J·Hz laser system for laser peering funded by Ministry of Trade, Industry & Energy (MI, republic of Korea).

References

1. Rübel, O., Geddes, C.G.R., Chen, M., Cormier-Michel, E., Bethel, E.W.: Feature-based analysis of plasma-based particle acceleration data. IEEE Trans. Vis. Comput. Graph. **20**(2), 196–210 (2014)
2. Wenger, R.: Isosurfaces, pp. 1–16. CRC Press, Boca Raton (2013)
3. Telea, A.C.: Data Visualization: Principles and Practice 2nd edn. CRC Press, Boca Raton (2015)
4. Nielson, G.M.: Scattered data modeling. IEEE Comput. Graph. Appl. **13**, 60–70 (1993)
5. Lorensen, W.E., Cline, H.E.: Marching cubes: a high resolution 3D surface construction algorithm. Comput. Graph. **21**(4), 163–169 (1987)
6. Dyken, C., Ziegler, G., Theobalt, C., Seidel, H.-P.: High-speed Marching Cubes using HistoPyramids. Comput. Graph. Forum **27**(8), 2028–2039 (2008)
7. Lee, K.: Visualization of trivariate scattered data interpolation. J. Korea Comput. Graph. Soc. **2**(2), 11–20 (1996)
8. Sibson, R.: A brief description of natural neighbour interpolation. In: Barnett, V. (ed.) Interpreting Multivariate Data, pp. 21–36. Wiley, New York (1981)
9. Boissonnat, J.D., Cazals, F.: Smooth surface reconstruction via natural neighbour interpolation of distance functions. Comput. Geometry **22**, 185–203 (2002)
10. Ledoux, H., Gold, C.: An efficient natural neighbour interpolation algorithm for geoscientific modelling. In: Developments in Spatial Data Handling, pp. 91–108. Springer, Heidelberg (2005). https://doi.org/10.1007/3-540-26772-7_8

Generating an Album with the Best Media Using Computer Vision

Tancredo Souza[1], João Paulo Lima[1,2(✉)], Veronica Teichrieb[1],
Carla Nascimento[3], Fabio Q. B. da Silva[4], Andre L. M. Santos[4],
and Helder Pinho[5]

[1] Voxar Labs, Centro de Informática, Universidade Federal de Pernambuco,
Recife, Brazil
{tantan,jpsml,vt}@cin.ufpe.br
[2] Departamento de Estatística e Informática,
Universidade Federal Rural de Pernambuco, Recife, Brazil
joao.mlima@ufrpe.br
[3] Projeto de Pesquisa e Desenvolvimento CIn/Samsung,
Universidade Federal de Pernambuco, Recife, Brazil
cmpn@cin.ufpe.br
[4] Centro de Informática, Universidade Federal de Pernambuco, Recife, Brazil
{fabio,alms}@cin.ufpe.br
[5] Samsung Instituto de Desenvolvimento para a Informática, Campinas, Brazil
helder.p@sidi.org.br

Abstract. Due to the increase in smartphone usage, it became easier to register memorable moments with a more accessible camera. To ensure a nice capture was made, users often take multiple shots from a scene, later filtering them based on some quality criteria. However, sometimes this may be unfeasible to do manually. To address this issue, this work initially defines relevant characteristics present in a good personal picture or video. We then show how to automatically search for these aspects using computer vision algorithms, successfully assessing personal media based on these aspects. Moreover, we show that it was possible to use this proposed solution in a real-world application, improving the generation of a personal album containing the best pictures and videos.

Keywords: Heuristics · Image · Video · Content analysis
Media description · Album generation

1 Introduction

In recent years, smartphones enabled users to easily register memorable events, being possible to even dismiss the need of a dedicated camera. Pictures and videos from vacation trips, birthday parties or friend meetings are worth keeping to yourself or sharing with others in social network. It is important, therefore, to assure that these records were made properly.

© Springer International Publishing AG, part of Springer Nature 2018
A. Marcus and W. Wang (Eds.): DUXU 2018, LNCS 10919, pp. 338–352, 2018.
https://doi.org/10.1007/978-3-319-91803-7_25

In this sense, users take similar shots from a scene, and afterwards choose the best ones to keep. This evaluation is done by filtering the media based on some personal quality criteria. For example, blurred images, videos with noticeable shakiness or photographs where not everyone appeared in their best pose are often discarded. However, sometimes there is just too much content to analyze, and doing this manually may take too much effort or accidentally cause the loss of media with decent quality.

Personal galleries in smartphones help the users to manage their captures by offering some filters to decrease the quantity of pictures and videos displayed, such as the Apple's Photos[1] app, which filters the content based on specific time periods or locations. While this may help reducing the amount of media to analyze, it is still needed to manually evaluate them. We propose an automatic evaluation method using computer vision that dismisses this manual step, and is able to create an album containing the best pictures and videos.

But how to distinguish a good capture from a bad one? To differentiate high quality shots from bad quality shots is more natural to humans. This means that users without knowledge in photography concepts are able to often determine their preferable picture or video. Figure 1 shows two pictures of a scene as an example.

Fig. 1. Two picture examples. It is clear that the left picture is less pleasant than the right one.

On the other hand, this is more difficult for computers. As stated in [4], challenges in this task include modeling the photographic rules computationally, knowing the aesthetic differences between images from different genres (e.g. night scenes, close-shot object, scenery) and having a large human-annotated dataset for robust testing.

Thus, we organize this work as follows. In Sect. 2 we initially discuss related works that aim to automatically assess the quality of the user's media. Afterwards, we describe in Sect. 3 our developed automatic personal media evaluation, based on searching for a set of important characteristics using heuristics-based and adaptive computer vision algorithms. Section 4 presents the results obtained in datasets of personal pictures and videos. We also emphasize this work's contribution by analyzing its integration to a real-world application, improving the generation of an album containing the user's media with the best quality. Finally, Sect. 5 presents our final considerations to this work and to the prospects of the discussed problem scenario.

---

[1] https://www.apple.com/ios/photos/.

2 Related Work

Over the past years, researchers proposed different ways to automatically assess personal media. We can broadly organize this evaluation into two different approaches [4]: those based on heuristics and those based on adaptive machine learning.

The use of heuristics evaluates a picture or a video based on principles of photography – such as the *rule of thirds* (Fig. 2) – and evaluating high-level semantics like lighting composition, blurring and color.

Fig. 2. The rule of thirds states that the subject of interest should be placed along the indicated red lines. (Color figure online)

Although this achieves good results when tested in a very diverse picture database [6], it only considers the media's visual aesthetics. However, the presence of other people in a personal picture or video matters to the user [3]. As an example, it is often desirable that the people framed are looking at the camera. This means that, in this context, assessing personal media quality does not necessarily imply on strictly following professional photograph rules, because users in some cases may ignore these aspects. In this sense, our work combines a subset of these aspects with the people and scene descriptions when evaluating the quality of personal media.

The machine learning approaches train a model using a dataset of pictures or videos with a human-annotated ground-truth. This model is able to extract information just from the pixels of the input media, learning from that data how to adaptively assess the media's quality. In order to perform a decent training and evaluation of the trained model, the size and diversity of the dataset must be sufficiently large. This, on the other hand, demands significant effort.

To workaround this issue, the work developed in [3] described the construction of a crowdsourced dataset with more than 10,000 images. They annotated the dataset by asking for participants to choose only one picture from random pairs, justifying their choice. With this information, shown in Fig. 3, they proposed a variety of methods for learning human preferences when evaluating photo series. Although having more than 10,000 images collected and annotated, it was still insufficient to successfully train a machine learning model for this task.

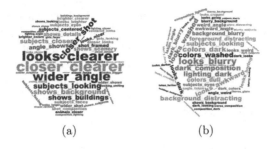

(a)   (b)

Fig. 3. Word clouds visualizing common photo preferences of the participants for (a) preferred photos and (b) rejected photos. Image obtained from [3].

In our proposed work, it is considered not only visual aspects, but also the scene context description, using the presence of the people and objects framed to adaptively perform such media evaluation. Also, we can extend these analyses to personal video quality assessment [8,9,17]. For videos, on the other hand, we can also analyze the scene's *spatiotemporal information*: the information regarding the movement of the framed objects.

3   Photograph and Video Quality Assessment Method

This work lies between these two approaches: the use of heuristics applied to visual features and the use of machine learning algorithms. Searching for visual characteristics is done by applying adaptive computer vision algorithms, which will be detailed in this section.

Our analysis is segmented into four main categories:

- *People Detection*: extracts characteristics of the people framed.
- *Image Properties Computation*: describes the visual aesthetics of the image.
- *Image Content Analysis*: analyzes the context of the picture.
- *Video Processing*: describes the media's spatiotemporal information.

This section will then analyze in more depth each one of these groups, showing which characteristics they analyze and the methods used for searching and describing these aspects.

3.1   People Detection

As previously discussed, it is important to consider the presence of a person in a capture, as it may influence the user's preference. It was observed that, in personal pictures, it is often desirable that the people framed are smiling or with their eyes open. Initially, it is applied a face detector in order to know whether there are faces in a picture. Then, we proceed to analyze these detected faces, describing if their eyes were open and if a smile was visible. We proceed to detail how this work describes these characteristics in an image.

Face Detection. Face detection is done using the SeetaFace [15] method. An overview of SeetaFace Detection is shown in Fig. 4. It feeds its input to a cascade of classifiers, which analyzes a set of characteristics that identify the presence of faces in a picture. Due to its cascade format, the face detector uses the result collected from a given classifier as additional information for the next in the cascade, improving its prediction confidence. As a final output, it estimates the detected faces' bounding box (Fig. 5).

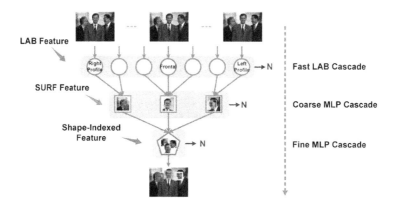

Fig. 4. SeetaFace Detection method overview. Image obtained from [15].

Fig. 5. Faces detected with the SeetaFace method.

Open Eyes Detection. Our developed method for open eyes detection consists of four steps:

- *Face Landmark Detection*: Given the bounding rectangle of a detected face by SeetaFace, we use the method proposed in [18] to obtain the position of the eyes (Fig. 6a).
- *Eye Region Estimation*: For each eye location retrieved by the alignment step, regions centered on these positions are estimated, as illustrated in Fig. 6b.
- *Eye Classification*: This step consists of classifying each region as containing an open eye or not. This is done using an open eyes detector, based on a trained Haar cascade classifier [14]. This makes the regions closer to the detected eyes, as shown in Fig. 6c.

- *Open Eyes Region Estimation*: If any of the face's eyes is classified as open, the detection was considered successful. It is thus estimated the position of the eyes as a final result (Fig. 6d).

Fig. 6. Open Eyes Detection steps: (a) Input faces bounding rectangles (red) and face landmarks estimated by SeetaFace Alignment (yellow). (b) Estimated regions of the left (blue) and right (green) eyes. (c) Refined regions of the left (blue) and right (green) eyes, detected by the Haar classifier. (d) Estimated area of the open eyes (magenta). (Color figure online)

Smile Detection. Given the detected bounding box of a face, we only consider its lower half rectangle for the smile detection, because it is where one expects to find a mouth, as illustrated in Fig. 7a. Then, it is checked if there is a smile inside each region. For this task, another trained Haar cascade classifier is employed for detecting the smiles, returning a rectangle containing the detected smile's location (Fig. 7b).

 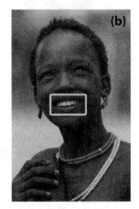

Fig. 7. (a) Only the lower half of the detected face is considered. (b) Refined bounding box for the smile detected by the Haar classifier.

3.2   Image Properties Computation

In images, noticeable motion blur and bad exposure make it difficult to recognize the framed elements or objects (Fig. 8). Thus, we perform the detection of these aspects in a picture.

Fig. 8. Examples of undesirable conditions, such as bad lighting or blurring.

It is worth mentioning that the presence of aspects such as blur or brightness does not imply that the media has bad quality. For example, aspects like blur are not necessarily associated to a bad capture. As shown in Fig. 9, this can be done for artistic purposes. We disconsidered subjective cases like these when performing our media quality evaluation, analyzing these cases just like the others.

Fig. 9. An example of an artistically blurred capture.

Also, since a personal gallery may contain various pictures of the same scene, it is possible that more than one picture has good quality. In consequence, this could cause similar photographs ending up in the generated album. To avoid this, our work proposes the detection of similar images.

Blur Detection. The approach employed for blur detection is based on the Blind/Referenceless Image Spatial Quality Evaluator (BRISQUE) [10]. This technique uses mean subtracted contrast normalized (MSCN) coefficients, which can provide a quantitative description of the image just using its pixels. It was noted that an image exhibits a histogram of MSCN coefficients with a Gaussian like appearance, as shown in Fig. 10. Thus, [10] proposed a statistical relationship between these coefficients, being able to describe the visual aspects of the image using this Gaussian curve, such as blur. A blurred image will cause a characteristic distortion in these values, causing the Gaussian curve to change.

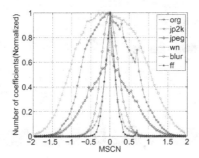

Fig. 10. Histogram of MSCN coefficients as a Gaussian curve. Image obtained from [10].

These curve aspects are used to train a support vector machine (SVM) model by using a set of blurred and unblurred training images. This enables the model to identify if an image is blurred or not, by only considering these mentioned aspects.

Exposure Detection. Exposure detection is inspired by the Zone System [1], which assigns numbers from 0 through 10 to different brightness values for an image - where 0 represents black, 5 middle gray, and 10 pure white. These values are known as zones, and are illustrated in Fig. 11.

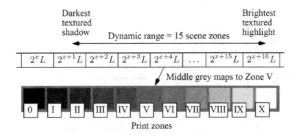

Fig. 11. The Zone System. Image obtained from [12].

This information is used to estimate a value related to the overall illumination of the scene, called the scene's *key value* [12]. This key value is then used to classify an image as underexposed (very dark), illuminated neutrally or overexposed (very bright). Figure 12 shows that underexposed images have a lower key value, images with neutral illumination are associated with intermediate key values and overexposed images present a higher key value.

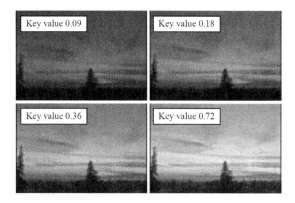

Fig. 12. Different image exposures and their corresponding key values. Image obtained from [12].

Similar Images Detection. Our similar images detection algorithm is based on perceptual hashing [16], which only uses the information of the pixels. An overview of the similarity detection is shown in Fig. 13.

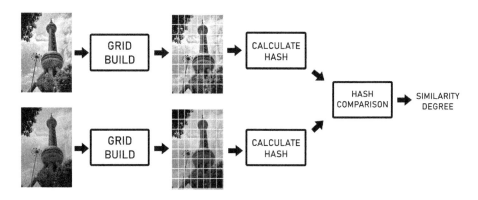

Fig. 13. Blockhash perceptual hashing method overview.

The two input images are, initially, segmented into grid blocks. By segmenting the images using a grid, it is able to make a more specific comparison of the two inputs, increasing the robustness of the technique. Afterwards, we use a hash to assign an individual binary code for each block, creating a representation of that image as an array containing only 0s and 1s.

Finally, given the two binary codes of the input images, we calculate their similarity degree by estimating how much they differ, using hamming distance. Thus, it is expected that similar images will have a high similarity degree.

3.3 Image Content Analysis

For humans it is possible, as an example, to identify that a photograph is related to a party by recognizing balloons, a cake, party hats, etc. (Fig. 14). In this sense, this work enables understanding the scene's context based on the objects captured. Using object detection, it is possible to use the classes of the detected objects to obtain this context information.

Fig. 14. Party pictures or videos often presents distinctive objects.

Object Detection. The approach adopted for object detection is based on the YOLO system [11]. The process performed by YOLO is described in Fig. 15.

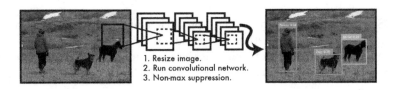

1. Resize image.
2. Run convolutional network.
3. Non-max suppression.

Fig. 15. YOLO (1) resizes the input image to 448×448, (2) runs a single convolutional network on the image, and (3) thresholds the resulting detections by the model's confidence. Image obtained from [11].

Using a single convolutional neural network, it segments the input image into various regions. Each region is associated with a probability of containing an object of some class (e.g. dog, car or bicycle), as shown in Fig. 16.

After increasing its confidence in its predictions, this method finally considers the object classes with the highest probabilities and outputs the corresponding bounding boxes for each object class detected.

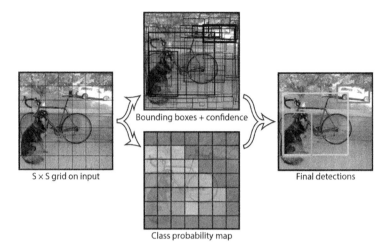

Fig. 16. YOLO divides the image into an $S \times S$ grid and for each grid cell predicts bounding boxes, confidence for those boxes, and class probabilities. Image obtained from [11].

3.4   Video Processing

All of the previous analyses for images can be extended to video frames. This is done by analyzing each individual video frame and averaging these characteristics for the whole video. We, therefore, combine an individual frame analysis along with the media's spatiotemporal information. By describing the stableness of the video, we can estimate if a video is shaky or steady. In this section, we detail the detection of what is called hand shakiness.

Hand Shakiness Detection. The approach employed for hand shakiness detection is based on the method proposed by [17]. This technique uses the frame's *optical flow* information, which is the structure of the movement between two consecutive frames. Figure 17 shows a visualization of this structure.

Fig. 17. The optical flow of a scene.

Since only the motion of the camera describes the video's movement stableness, it is expected that framed objects moving in the scene should not be considered. It is then necessary to distinguish the movement of the objects from the movement of the camera itself. As proposed by [17], extracting the frame's optical flow information from its border area addresses this issue, increasing the robustness of this method (Fig. 18).

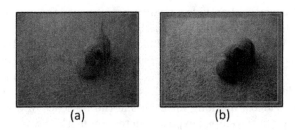

(a)   (b)

Fig. 18. Extracting the information from the (a) entire area may cause false alarms, whereas reducing to the (b) border area may provide a more robust analysis. Image obtained from [17].

Finally, we describe the video's shakiness using its optical flow information. In unstable videos, the movement direction changes very frequently [8]. Also, if the amount of movement is very significant, this results in a perceptual shaky recording. Using the optical flow of the video, it is possible to perceive the changes in the camera's movement direction.

Thus, we intuitively define the hand shakiness degree calculation as: *If the direction of the movement changed between two frames, then how much did it change?* For a video, we accumulate the hand shakiness degree and average it to obtain an estimation for each frame. A shaky video will have a higher average value of hand shakiness, whereas a more steady one will have a lower average value.

4 Evaluation

4.1 Dataset

Since this work aims to assess the quality of personal media, our own dataset is composed of pictures and videos that would belong to a personal gallery. As discussed before, these captures register, for example, vacation trips, birthday parties, etc. The images and videos from our evaluation dataset were manually annotated. This annotation described the presence or absence of some particular characteristics (e.g. blur, smile, underexposed, shaky video, etc.). Our dataset was then segmented into groups regarding their visual aspects.

Training Datasets. The adaptive machine learning models (blur, face and object detectors) require a dedicated dataset to train their respective neural networks. The BRISQUE model for blur detection was trained using the CERTH Image Blur dataset [7]. The SeetaFace and YOLO models for face and object detection were made available by the authors as a previously trained model, which were used in our work.

Evaluation Datasets. For video quality assessment, the public availability of evaluation datasets containing personal recordings is scarce. To address this issue, a dataset called CERTH VAQ-700 [13] was made available, containing hundreds of personal videos useful for evaluating automatic video quality assessment techniques. However, it was not very clear in the dataset's annotations if a video was considered shaky or steady. Thus, we manually selected and annotated a subset of these videos, marking for each one the presence or absence of hand shakiness. Finally, the developed exposure detection method was evaluated using the ImageCLEF 2011 dataset [2] and the YOLO object detector was tested in the MS-COCO 2015 dataset [5].

4.2   Implementation

This proposed solution was implemented in C++ using the computer vision library OpenCV. The testing execution times were obtained using a computer with an Intel Core i7-5500U @ 2.40 GHz processor and 16 GB RAM.

4.3   Results

It was calculated a score for each technique, determining how effective the algorithm was in its task when tested on a dataset segment (0 means complete inaccuracy and 1 is perfect accuracy). Table 1 shows the scores obtained when executing our techniques in the described set of images and videos, along with the average execution times per image/video frame for the developed methods.

Table 1. Final results in the evaluation dataset.

Media description	Evaluation dataset	Data amount	Score	Execution time
Face detection	Ours	180	0.9013	1.40 s
Open eyes detection	Ours	180	0.8425	1.93 s
Smile detection	Ours	180	0.7724	1.42 s
Blur detection	Ours	69	0.6818	1.21 s
Exposure detection	ImageCLEF 2011 [2]	8000	0.1934	0.17 s
Similar images detection	Ours	51	0.7246	0.37 s
Object detection	MS-COCO [5]	20288	0.4400	4.62 s
Hand shakiness detection	CERTH VAQ-700 [13]	50	0.9340	0.30 s

4.4   Real-World Application

All the proposed methods, except for object and hand shakiness detection, are currently integrated to a Windows application available worldwide. It was perceived an improvement over existing functionalities, generating a more agreeable album containing the user's best pictures and videos. While this emphasizes this work's contribution, it also shows the efficient optimization of the developed solution, dismissing the need of significant computational power to use it.

5   Conclusion

This work proposed an automatic approach for personal media evaluation, using computer vision. We conducted an initial discussion about important media characteristics that are often more perceivable to the layman users. This set of visual aspects was then searched in the users' pictures and videos by adaptive computer vision algorithms. It was possible to improve the application's album generation functionality of a real-world application, only including the agreeable best quality media, emphasizing this work's contribution.

However, as experimentation shows, there is still room for improvement. One can argue that there are subjective cases, where it is not that easy to decide, for example, if a picture was artistically blurred or if a video had a shaky movement. In our scenario, we decided to dismiss these more complex cases, because, as discussed before, quality assessment is already harder to computers than to humans. We showed that, instead of using deep features only recognizable computationally, it is possible to provide to computers a more natural understanding of the scene. Giving a sense of scene context to a machine makes its media evaluation more similar to the analysis made naturally by humans. Thus, we believe that it is possible to make much more future progress in this direction.

Acknowledgements. The results presented in this paper have been developed as part of a collaborative project between Samsung Institute for Development of Informatics (Samsung/SIDI) and the Centre of Informatics at the Federal University of Pernambuco (CIn/UFPE), financed by Samsung Eletronica da Amazonia Ltda., under the auspices of the Brazilian Federal Law of Informatics no. 8248/91. The authors would like to thank the support received from the Samsung/SIDI team. Professor Fabio Q. B. da Silva holds a research grant from the Brazilian National Research Council (CNPq), process #314523/2009-0.

References

1. Adams, A.: The Negative: Exposure and Development Basic Photo 2, vol. 98. Morgan and Lester, New York (1948)
2. Bosch, M.: Imageclef experimental evaluation in visual information retrieval. Inf. Retr. **1**, 4 (2016)
3. Chang, H., Yu, F., Wang, J., Ashley, D., Finkelstein, A.: Automatic triage for a photo series. ACM Trans. Graph. (TOG) **35**(4), 148 (2016)

4. Deng, Y., Loy, C.C., Tang, X.: Image aesthetic assessment: an experimental survey. IEEE Sig. Process. Mag. **34**(4), 80–106 (2017)
5. Lin, T.-Y., Maire, M., Belongie, S., Hays, J., Perona, P., Ramanan, D., Dollár, P., Zitnick, C.L.: Microsoft COCO: common objects in context. In: Fleet, D., Pajdla, T., Schiele, B., Tuytelaars, T. (eds.) ECCV 2014. LNCS, vol. 8693, pp. 740–755. Springer, Cham (2014). https://doi.org/10.1007/978-3-319-10602-1_48
6. Luo, Y., Tang, X.: Photo and video quality evaluation: focusing on the subject. In: Forsyth, D., Torr, P., Zisserman, A. (eds.) ECCV 2008. LNCS, vol. 5304, pp. 386–399. Springer, Heidelberg (2008). https://doi.org/10.1007/978-3-540-88690-7_29
7. Mavridaki, E., Mezaris, V.: No-reference blur assessment in natural images using fourier transform and spatial pyramids. In: 2014 IEEE International Conference on Image Processing (ICIP), pp. 566–570. IEEE (2014)
8. Mei, T., Hua, X.S., Zhu, C.Z., Zhou, H.Q., Li, S.: Home video visual quality assessment with spatiotemporal factors. IEEE Trans. Circuits Syst. Video Technol. **17**(6), 699–706 (2007)
9. Mei, T., Zhu, C.Z., Zhou, H.Q., Hua, X.S.: Spatio-temporal quality assessment for home videos. In: Proceedings of the 13th Annual ACM International Conference on Multimedia, pp. 439–442. ACM (2005)
10. Mittal, A., Moorthy, A.K., Bovik, A.C.: Blind/referenceless image spatial quality evaluator. In: 2011 Conference Record of the Forty Fifth Asilomar Conference on Signals, Systems and Computers (ASILOMAR), pp. 723–727, November 2011
11. Redmon, J., Divvala, S., Girshick, R., Farhadi, A.: You only look once: unified, real-time object detection. In: Proceedings of the IEEE Conference on Computer Vision and Pattern Recognition, pp. 779–788 (2016)
12. Reinhard, E., Stark, M., Shirley, P., Ferwerda, J.: Photographic tone reproduction for digital images. ACM Trans. Graph. (TOG) **21**(3), 267–276 (2002)
13. Tzelepis, C., Mavridaki, E., Mezaris, V., Patras, I.: Video aesthetic quality assessment using kernel support vector machine with isotropic gaussian sample uncertainty (ksvm-igsu). In: 2016 IEEE International Conference on Image Processing (ICIP). pp. 2410–2414. IEEE (2016)
14. Viola, P., Jones, M.: Rapid object detection using a boosted cascade of simple features. In: Proceedings of the 2001 IEEE Computer Society Conference on Computer Vision and Pattern Recognition, CVPR 2001, vol. 1, p. I. IEEE (2001)
15. Wu, S., Kan, M., He, Z., Shan, S., Chen, X.: Funnel-structured cascade for multi-view face detection with alignment-awareness. Neurocomputing **221**, 138–145 (2017)
16. Yang, B., Gu, F., Niu, X.: Block mean value based image perceptual hashing. In: International Conference on Intelligent Information Hiding and Multimedia Signal Processing, IIH-MSP 2006, pp. 167–172. IEEE (2006)
17. Yang, C.Y., Yeh, H.H., Chen, C.S.: Video aesthetic quality assessment by combining semantically independent and dependent features. In: 2011 IEEE International Conference on Acoustics, Speech and Signal Processing (ICASSP), pp. 1165–1168. IEEE (2011)
18. Zhang, J., Shan, S., Kan, M., Chen, X.: Coarse-to-fine auto-encoder networks (CFAN) for real-time face alignment. In: Fleet, D., Pajdla, T., Schiele, B., Tuytelaars, T. (eds.) ECCV 2014. LNCS, vol. 8690, pp. 1–16. Springer, Cham (2014). https://doi.org/10.1007/978-3-319-10605-2_1

Study of Chinese City "Portrait" Based on Data Visualization: Take City Dashboard for Example

Xueting Tong[✉] and Zhanwei Wu

Media and Design Institute, Shanghai Jiaotong University, Shanghai, China
{tongxueting,zhanwei_wu}@sjtu.edu.cn

Abstract. The purpose of this study is to consider the case study summarizes the characteristics of urban dashboard, and with the help of literature research to analyze the necessity and difficulties of urban dashboard design in China at this stage. In the second part of this paper, we give a brief overview of smart city and urban dashboard, summarize the importance of data visualization in the construction of smart city, and emphasize the outstanding performance of using urban dashboard in this data to better serve the public contribution. Then the third part of this article based on the previous study of the city dashboard, summed up the six characteristics of the dashboard. And through six typical urban dashboard cases to explain these six characteristics in detail. In the fourth part of this article, we propose the possibility and difficulty of designing the urban dashboard of China considering the national conditions of Chinese characteristics. In the fifth part of this article, we summarize and prospect the research work done so far.

Keywords: Smart city · City dashboard · Chinese city

1 Introduction

Urban dashboards enable the visualization of key data from the city's operational core system, making the city's service system feel sensible. The construction of an urban dashboard will contribute to the construction of a smart city, better serve the public, satisfy the needs of the public and enhance the quality of life of the public. The ultimate goal is to promote harmonious social development and efficient allocation of urban resources.

2 Related Research

2.1 Smart City and City Dashboard

The migration rate of urban population in the world is increasing at an alarming rate. According to experts, by 2050, 70% of the world's population (more than 6 billion people) will settle in urban areas. In the past 10 years, the concepts of "digital city", "big data city", "smart city" and "smart city" have become a heated topic in academia

© Springer International Publishing AG, part of Springer Nature 2018
A. Marcus and W. Wang (Eds.): DUXU 2018, LNCS 10919, pp. 353–364, 2018.
https://doi.org/10.1007/978-3-319-91803-7_26

and social media. The construction of smart cities provides a new way of thinking for the transformation of cities in twenty-first Century. "Smart city" is actually a more advanced form of "data city". The degree of openness of a city affects the intelligence of the city, and ultimately determines the convenience and livability of urban life.

According to Pike Research's research on smart cities, the market for smart cities was valued at $100 billion by 2020. The application of smart city is very extensive, such as smart energy, intelligent transportation, intelligent building, intelligent education and so on. Microcosmic includes community, health care, hotel management, aviation, retail, entertainment, waste disposal and other industries. It is an inevitable choice for the construction of China's smart cities to construct a data center system based on large data to run the city. It is the inevitable choice for the construction of China's smart cities [1]. On the basis of the construction and development of smart city building in different areas of data resources to fully integrate and use general data, information process of an industry or a region can be divided into two stages, the first stage is digital, it includes information sensing, computing, storage, transmission and control network and digital; the second stage is intelligent, is the higher stage of digitization, introduces the concept of intelligent, digital into various forms of sensible [2]. According to this theory, urban digitalization can be divided into two stages: the digital city (Data City) and the intelligent city (smart City). The management and service of cities are continuous, and there will be huge amounts of data generated. The characteristics of these big data are large capacity, variety, high speed and high value. These data will reflect the characteristics, laws and changes in the process of urban operation. The opening and sharing of these urban data will greatly affect the pace of the construction of intelligent cities. A lot of data are collected by citizens and government agencies, which are becoming more and more open to public use. Through the analysis of these data, the intelligent city management can provide the decision-making basis, and can provide new insight for the service system of the intelligent city. Data visualization is a common means of data analysis. Visualization technology is a theory, method and technology to transform data into graphic or image form to screen and interact with each other based on computer graphics and image processing technology. The main features of data visualization technology are interactivity, multidimensional and visibility [3].

Using data visualization method, we can better connect and share these data and information, enhance the presentation effect of data, facilitate users to observe data in a more intuitive way, and find hidden information in data, and effectively use data. Data visualization is a scientific and technological research on the form of visual representation of data. To sum up, the city dashboard based on data visualization came into being.

2.2   The Value of City Dashboard

City dashboards need to integrate different platform data and different business data in urban operation process, including data collection in municipal, police, transportation, power, business and other fields. Combining with the geographic information system, monitoring camera images and GPS data, building three-dimensional data and many other types of data, a comprehensive display of the status of city operation, including:

the characteristics, economic vitality of tourism, transportation, public security, human services, entertainment and culture, environmental sustainability, citizen participation in governance in areas such as [4]. Control the city dynamics in a full range. The city dashboard is a summary and summary of various indicators of urban operation, showing the overall operation of the city and guiding the healthy, scientific and intelligent operation of the city. Through the management of urban operation signs, we can monitor the objects of urban operation and management, excavate the inherent laws of urban development, and provide a deep insight for urban life [5].

Which section of the city is congested? How many cultural activities are going on? Where is the construction in the construction? You can get to know your city in real time through the city dashboard. There are two forms of dashboards in the city: dashboard, which is a part of control and command center, or citizen participation, which allows public and urban workers to explore urban data. The former tends to focus on a specific system, such as monitoring internal traffic or safe cities, and the city system of the command center [6]. The dashboard of the city converts data into accessible information, information search and use. It is a carrier tool to directly communicate with users and help users to make decisions. As the collected vital signs from a macro perspective to research and control of the body, through the data and information collected in the monitoring of the city, on the data and information analysis form the overall judgment on the situation of the city, take effective measures to dispose of the city operating problems of the specific situation, the city is always in good condition, for monitoring and early warning, scientific analysis and objective evaluation of city operation, auxiliary decision-making, so as to improve city environmental protection, intelligent transportation, emergency command, infrastructure, public security and other aspects of the comprehensive management level. We have summed up the importance of the city dashboard. The dashboard can not only create good local democracy, but also provide opportunities for learning. A dashboard is simply a way of presenting a source of knowledge to understand and handle the complex reality of cities [7].

3   Case Studies on City Dashboard

The city is made up of many elements. The dashboard displays these elements as the following categories: transport, environment, statistics, economy, community, culture and security. The goal of a city dashboard is to present all the data, graphics, and other results in the most readable way. Through the rich interactive query function, the gorgeous data display form, the visual effect of film and television level, help urban managers improve the efficiency of urban management. In order to achieve the comprehensive management of city comprehensive status. Based on the comprehensive analysis of dashboards in dozens of foreign countries, we summarize the six characteristics of city Dashboards: recording, connectivity, sensing, interaction, adaptation, and integration. We will give a detailed illustration of each of the features of the dashboard.

Record

The first step of the process of city data visualization is to record all kinds of large data produced in the process of city operation. The sources of these data can be roughly divided into three categories: orientation, automation, and voluntary [8]. Through all kinds of sensing devices and application systems, data can be recorded throughout the whole process, and then provide data basis for subsequent services, and provide support for analysis and decision making. The next picture is a city dashboard on London's daily real-time situation. For example, you can see information on the "dashboard", such as the weather and the running state of the subway station. In this corner, there are cameras and their network. In addition, there are a series of data, such as market operation and so on. This series of data will give users a good overview of the city. They can know what is happening in the city from any angle, and these data are continuously uploaded (Fig. 1).

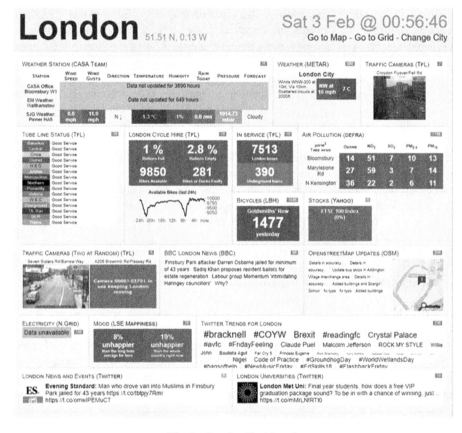

Fig. 1. London Dashboard

Connectivity

Connectivity means connecting and interworking. The Dublin dashboard is exactly the feature of connectivity.

Through the ubiquitous devices (street lights, video monitoring probe, LED, network camera, touch screen, wireless network, microphone, camera, sensor, infrared detector, mobile phone, computer), collected from different departments of data integration, city instrument panel to create a seamless connectivity, users can use the city whenever and wherever possible dashboard. This concept will be connected to separate from the physical space, and the use of personal computer or mobile device screen using in any place, through all kinds of APP better divergence of city services, so that we can more easily share the same vision information in scattered population, regardless of who is to expand public officials and technical personnel, or all residents of the city. But the current problem is that the number of APP is too large and needs to be further integrated to promote "connectivity" (Fig. 2).

Sensing
It is an important link in the process of city data visualization to understand all kinds of large data produced in the process of city operation. Through all kinds of perceptual technology, we can fully perceive the city environment, understand the social relationship, quickly discover the trend, and deal with the complex relationship. In order to achieve this goal, it is necessary to start from the foundation, that is, to collect the data fully through the perceptual technology and the means. This is an Irish Kirk dashboard. You can see that these dashboards are starting to add some practical functions, which can guide people to perceive real-time data. Some simple diagrams can also be used to translate data and visualize the trend of data development so that users can better understand the characteristics of data change. This is a positive exploration of the city dashboard. This information is captured with sensors and city maps, and can get real-time data updates, directly control the overall situation and respond to the problems in time (Fig. 3). Without this processing of the data, we really can't perceive the real time and the details that are happening at different locations.

Interaction
Interaction defines the content and structure of the communication between two or more interactive individuals, so that they cooperate with each other. Interaction includes two aspects. From a microcosmic point of view, it is possible to query the data you want to know at any time and need more practical means of inquiry. For example, Leeds city dashboards can use various ways of interaction such as point selection, adding, zooming and narrowing, to achieve good user experience and provide rich presentation and interactive functions. From the macro perspective, the overall environment of man-machine interaction can be realized in such a system, users use the behavior of Leeds city the dashboard itself is the city, a variety of intelligent devices and combine into an organic whole, and analyze the situation of the city found that the real-time response service city takes place in real time (Fig. 4).

Adaptation
The dashboard is the city data visualization, the real time display of the city intelligence index, to help the government to simplify the process of identification from the problem to the solution. Based on all kinds of basic information, including the information of perception and recording, it provides users with accurate and personalized urban data services. A reasonable and effective dashboard design should be investigated in a

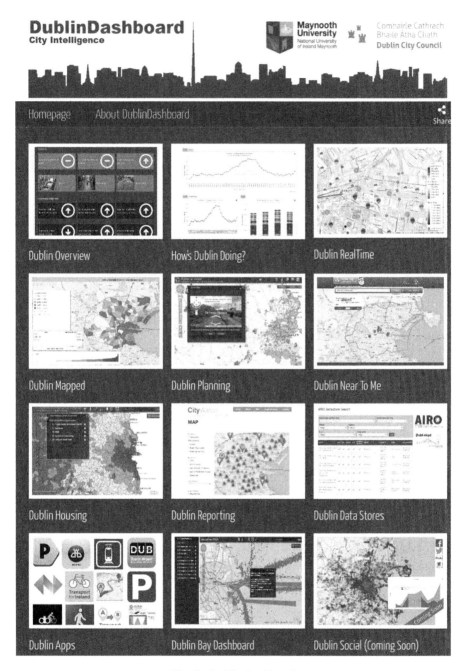

Fig. 2. Dublin Dashboard

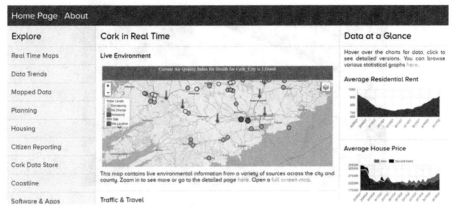

Fig. 3. Cork Dashboard

Fig. 4. Leeds Dashboard

comprehensive way, providing customized products and services based on local characteristics and needs of citizens. The Glasgow dashboard is a typical case of the user's self - customization. The "passive service" of the city dashboard is transformed into "active service". It allows users to customize their dashboards according to subway, catering, entertainment, news and other modules, giving users more freedom to choose independently, which is loved by users (Figs. 5 and 6).

Fig. 5. Glasgow Dashboard

Fig. 6. Glasgow Dashboard

Integration

It will open and integrate all kinds of information, resources and services collected during the dashboard process, so as to provide better information services for users. Based on the coordinated integration of urban data, the work efficiency is enhanced and the satisfaction of the citizens is improved. San Diego City dashboard for different departments in the field of data, mixed data and many departments, need to observe and analyze from different angles, the data according to the theme, systematically presented, for city managers to master the rules and significance of data in different dimensions, to understand the city running situation. Through the case of San Diego can be seen, along with the rise of the network of the city, people pay more and more attention from all aspects of collection, processing and analysis can realize the precise management of all areas of city data, realize the accurate and convenient city life service, data service to embody the people-oriented (Fig. 7). With the city dashboard as the carrier, the data will be fully integrated, excavated and utilized, and the new dynamic mode of the city will be more and more knowable and controllable [9].

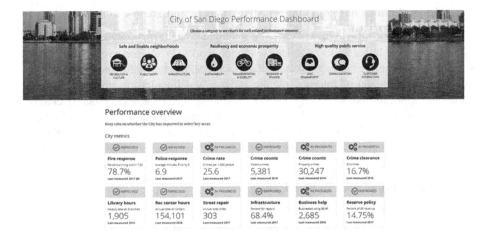

Fig. 7. San Diego Dashboard

4 The Efforts to Design Chinese City Dashboard

4.1 The Necessity of Building Dashboard in China's Cities

(1) China is actively building smart cities

Since the concept of intelligent city has been put forward, the enthusiasm for construction in all parts of our country has been constantly rising. At present, 290 cities have been selected for the pilot of the national intelligent city, which will bring convenience to the life of the urban residents. After several years of construction, the intelligent city is changing from planning to reality in our country. It is expected that in the year of this year, the number of intelligent cities in China is expected to be more than 500. Industry forecasts, with the development of local smart cities, the scale of the market will be expected to expand to hundreds of billions of yuan, or even trillion yuan.

(2) **China is opening a lot of data gradually**

Chinese after nearly thirty years development, government departments and business system data reserves have been very mature, in Chinese, the most complete, most large and the core data, the accumulation of a large number of governments at all levels and the public life and production related data, such as: meteorological data, financial credit data, data and power data and gas data, tap water data, traffic data, passenger safety data, criminal case data, housing data, customs data entry and exit data, tourism data, medical data, education data, environmental data, is the largest holder of government social data on how these sleeping through data fusion, to extract key data analysis, mining, and use real for the city manager, city control situation, The real realization of the intelligent city, the government has begun to work, China's big data enterprises are also working for it.

(3) **The continuous development of infrastructure and science and technology**

In recent years, urban basic design and intelligent data technology have developed rapidly in China. In particular, wireless sensor networks (WSN) are widely used in the intelligent management and control of urban facilities, safety, traffic and environment. With the development of Internet, mobile Internet and Internet of things, the connotation and application of smart city are more and more abundant, and gradually change all aspects of people's life. Based on the data visualization form of the city dashboard, we can help build a channel between the public and the public data, so that people can conveniently and simply use open data to explore and explore, so that the value of these public data can be exerted.

(4) **Urban services need to be upgraded**

The wisdom city of China is the pursuit of building a world - class Intelligent City, which is based on strengthening the city supervision and service and completing the construction of information infrastructure. The urban service in China emphasizes the needs of the people's livelihood, and takes people as the core and the needs of the people's livelihood as the starting point. Urban dashboards can quickly find the trend of urban data development and deal with the problems of complex cities. Therefore, the introduction of urban dashboards in China can help Chinese cities build public platforms and effectively improve the quality of public services and the efficiency of public services.

4.2   The Difficulties Faced by China in Building the City Dashboard

(1) **Social participation is not enough**

A lot of data are collected by citizens and government agencies, which are becoming more and more open to public use. Users use the dashboard process to fully display the open content and form of urban data, and can provide personalized customization. To mobilize users' participation in the development of city dashboards from bottom to top will help encourage public participation in urban dashboard research, improve residents' understanding of urban services and maximize public interest, thereby enhancing community stickiness and vitality. As rob and others pointed out, dashboards need to provide new solutions on the basis of understanding the needs of cities, but there is confusion or reduction of the reasons why it is difficult to perceive or simulate [10].

(2) **There is a regional imbalance in infrastructure and development**

The gap between urban and rural areas in China is huge, and the development gap between cities is also large. Different data visualization construction targets are set for different regions of the same town. For the metropolis with high urbanization, such as Beijing, Shanghai and Guangzhou, smart city construction is more emphasis on further improvement of the existing infrastructure network and public services, combined with the development of the new generation of IT industry, promoting the coordinated development of urban and rural areas. For a relatively low level of urbanization, more emphasis should be laid on consolidating the foundation of urban construction at the present stage, such as infrastructure construction and capital investment, so as to lay a solid foundation for subsequent urban data collection and processing.

(3) **Lack of relevant visualizations**

In the face of the challenge of information explosion, almost everyone is exposed to various forms of information visualization. Through data visualization, we can create a channel between public and public data, so that people can conveniently and simply use open data to explore data, so that the value of these public data can be exerted. Professional designers and developers can understand how people read, understand, explain and distinguish the visualization of various forms, and puts forward how to improve the technology innovation management scheme to consider from the user's point of view, to help government departments to monitor the city service status, forecast the development trend of city services. However, the number of talents and universities in China is relatively small, and the lack of talents has become a major reason why China has not yet developed its own dashboard.

5   Conclusion and Future Work

In the future city dashboard can also have more and better, for example, the establishment of city children lost face recognition system, classification of garbage city better, monitor the recovery process of waste batteries, avoid pollution two;,,,, park trees growth are all can be uploaded to the cloud data visualization, perceived the intersection of the vehicle at the intersection of the sensor; improve the efficiency of traffic intersection; provide the city near the city parking information, and choose an optimal route to the public, and real-time navigation etc. The city dashboard will be an indispensable foundation for the future collection, perception, visualization, processing and sharing of big data regardless of whether it supports government decision-making or urban services. Take the city dashboard as the carrier, based on the data visualization, and show the society through the innovative way, and optimize the service function of the city.

There is no doubt that the construction of smart cities is a huge and complex project, and we believe that the city dashboard will make a better life in the city. However, more efforts and efforts are needed to try to link China's urban service needs with dashboard tools. Many of the problems involved are waiting for people's further thinking and answers.

References

1. Zhen, F., Qin, X.: The application of big data in the research and planning of intelligent city. Int. Urban Plan. **29**(6), 44–50 2014
2. Li, W.: Several key technical problems on the intelligent transformation of "digital city". Global Finance **6**, 72–78 (2015)
3. Ren, Y., Yu, G.: Research and development of data visualization technology. Comput. Sci. **31**(12), 92–96 (2004)
4. Elmaghraby, A.S.: Visual data analytics for an event city. In: Ajman International Urban Planning Conference Aiupc 7: Planning for Event City (2015)
5. Piovano, L., Garrido, D., Silva, R., et al.: What (Smart) Data Visualizations Can Offer to Smart City Science, 96. Social Science Electronic Publishing (2014)
6. Mcardle, G., Kitchin, R.: The Dublin dashboard: design and development of a real-time analytical urban dashboard. In: ISPRS - International Archives of the Photogrammetry, Remote Sensing and Spatial Information Sciences, vol. III-4/W1, 19–25 2016
7. Kitchin, R., Lauriault, T.P., McArdle, G.: Urban indicators and dashboards: epistemology, contradictions and power/knowledge. Reg. Stud. Reg. Sci. **2**(1), 43–45 (2015)
8. Kitchin, R.: The real-time city? Big data and smart urbanism. Geojournal **79**(1), 1–14 (2014)
9. Kitchin, R., Maalsen, S., Mcardle, G.: The praxis and politics of building urban dashboards. Geoforum **77**, 93–101 (2016)
10. Kitchin, R., Lauriault, T.P., Mcardle, G.: Knowing and governing cities through urban indicators, city benchmarking and real-time dashboards. Reg. Stud. Reg. Sci. **2**(1), 6–28 (2015)

Metacity: Design, Data e Urbanity

Nelson J. Urssi[✉]

Centro Universitário Senac, São Paulo, Brazil
nelson.jurssi@sp.senac.br

Abstract. The Technologies of information and communication in all instances of our daily life change the way we live and think. Urban, ubiquitous, locative, multimedia and interconnected computing generates a large amount of data, resulting in an abundance of information about almost everything in our world. In order to redesign our urban life, it is considered the development of more accessible interfaces made in locative applications (geoapps), optimizing queries to society and making participation more accessible and more direct in the project. The research is based on the study of information and media experience in the urban environment. This article composes the body of studies of the UrbeLab group in the research program of the Centro Universitário Senac in São Paulo. The research aims to extend design process in the cities and to collaborate with the practice of creative and collaborative project involving communities. It presents UrbeLab research, through case studies, urban explorations and interviews, where we can observe our present contemporary condition. The city updated in real time is an urban informational ecosystem of new and infinite possibilities of interfaces and interactions.

Keywords: City · Experience · Complexity

1 Urban Status

The cities permeated by personal, vehicular and environmental sensors acquire sentient characteristics. A citizen-sensitive city can work with individualized day-to-day strategies. The article discusses the role of cities in the complexity of our lives, the interrelationship of physical equipment (hardware), symbolic models (software) and usage patterns (applications), and the design challenges for this global ecosystem of information.

The increasing use of computing has altered our relationships with the city, each connection and each generated data, a new reading of the urban environment. Everything we do leaves a trail, our digital trail. In this ocean of data is our complete profile. Where we live, where we go, what we buy, what we said... everything is recorded and stored forever, be it a smartphone, computers and cars, refrigerators, thermostats, pressure and weight meters, or even tolls and parking lots are designed to be data generators. Cities with control and security systems, intelligent architectures and the use of mobile devices by their citizens can be configured in real time. For architects, urban planners and designers, how we can present or transform data into information can give a new status to what we know of cities.

A. Marcus and W. Wang (Eds.): DUXU 2018, LNCS 10919, pp. 365–378, 2018.
https://doi.org/10.1007/978-3-319-91803-7_27

When analyzing data and found that there are poles erased in a certain region of the city and that this region has increased crime or even when you monitor their weight, pressure or heart rate by means of wearable devices that allow to establish parameters of good health, you realize that you are using data intelligently. In these examples we can have the dimension of optimized use of information and thus prioritize existing resources to take care of things that have efficiency. We can see the city as a responsive organism, an environment responsive to our needs for new ways of living.

A few weeks before the H1N1 virus appeared in the headlines, Google engineers published a work in Nature that caused commotion among health officials and computer scientists. The authors explained how Google could "predict" the spread of winter flu in the United States, not only nationally, but in specific regions and even states. The company got this forecast when analyzing the most searched terms on the internet. Because Google receives more than three billion searches per day and saves them, the company had a lot of data to work with. (Mayer-Schönberger 2013)

People who have connected devices have become information producers for the system. If before our access was by the desktop computer, today is increasingly mobile. We turn an individual node into the network. The internet was what was missing for all sensors and devices to communicate. We build a global brain that has new functions and access it primarily with mobile devices. The important aspect in looking at the data is that it broadens our senses and increases our ability to perceive the world.

The multiplication of the original space by the networks and the intense flow of data causes the interweaving of physical spatial and digital environments. The idea of excess space constituted by the abundance of information provokes the idea of global shrinkage and of no places (Augé 1994). The city permeated by information becomes fluid space and without limits what redefines the way we live. The human activities cover different aspects of urban space and generate data of different categories: geographic, demographic, economic and social. We never measured so much, everything we do in everyday life is measured and produces huge amounts of data. If we could see them continuously we could observe the city in its nuances. Urban technologies make the city an observable medium of great importance to understand our time. And netnography is an ethnographic process in digital networks, it is an interpretative method of research where we study interactions and experiences that manifest themselves in information and communication technologies, in our clipping, manifestations mediated by urban computing, geomedia and geoapps.

The netnography (Kozinets 2010) proposed in this research uses observation and participation of social interaction mediated by geoapps; analysis and creation of data; definition of immersion contexts and experiences of urban life. It adopts qualitative field research, laboratory activities and interviews, both in physical and digital environments, considered in a multispace of flows, on the relations between users, space and information mediated by urban computing. We focused on the possible modes of interaction generated by mobile devices (geomedia) and applications (geoapps) that allow an increased understanding of the urban environment.

The researches were carried out in three stages - locative, contextual and experiential - identified and evaluated based on the understanding of the use of technology in urban space as support and instrumentation to everyday situations as actions of going (and coming) from one place to another, locating in the world, do something specific, talk and think about it, collaborate and socialize. These contexts are aligned with processes of evaluation of interactions and usability (Preece, Rogers; Sharp 2007) in which we must consider the ecology formed by user, system and activities, especially in the urban environment, focusing on the challenges that involve the trinomial design, information and technology in the development of 'objects' that can be accessible and usable by anyone to perform tasks involving human cognition.

1.1 Bigdata

Data is continuously generated in volume, variety and speed at different levels. The idea of bigdata has been established with the evolution of methods and systems that shape unrelated or unstructured data. The algorithms allow to organize massive volumes of data processing them according to objective needs such as organization, analysis, synthesis and presentation for its use and possible decision-making in terms of its management.

In essence, bigdata relates to forecasts. Despite being described as a branch of computer science called artificial intelligence it is more specifically an area called "machine learning". This idea is misleading, the bigdata has nothing to do with trying to "teach" a computer to "think" as a human being, rather it is about applying mathematics to huge amounts of data in order to predict probabilities. (Mayer-Schönberger 2013, p. 8)

The bigdata allows us to collect petabytes of data which uses algorithms to analyze what we had never observed. According Joi Ito (Smolan 2014), "Before we had the idea, we wrote it and it became knowledge. The bigdata is the opposite. We have a lot of data that we only saw when we looked at it." It's like trying to analyze something around us but it has structures and patterns that are invisible without the right instruments. All of these data increase our ability to understand our surroundings.

A number of innovations in preparing end user data for bigdata have emerged in recent years, such as Tableau, Microsoft Excell and Qlik Sense, data processing tools that have reduced the time and complexity of preparing data, especially important in the world of large data when dealing with a variety of types and formats. In recent years, visualization instruments have evolved to be able to process a huge amount of data in this way we can observe complex systems in operation - patterns and facts impossible to be seen otherwise and recreate them in any format, practically everything is measurable and quantifiable.

Increased data-processing capacity, incorporated and accessed throughout urban infrastructure, will make this experience somewhat unrestricted in the future. We innovate in the use of video 4k–8k, virtual and augmented reality, the internet of things and multitasking applications. A much more consistent computing experience of the city that can create new forms of interaction, services and information, on demand and in real time (Fig. 1).

We estimate that by 2020 the volume of data will be 40 ZB, to get an idea, if we add all the sand grains of the planet and multiply by 75, would give 40 ZB of information. All data processing over the past two years has outpaced data processing for the last 3000 years. The greater the volume of information, the greater the problems we

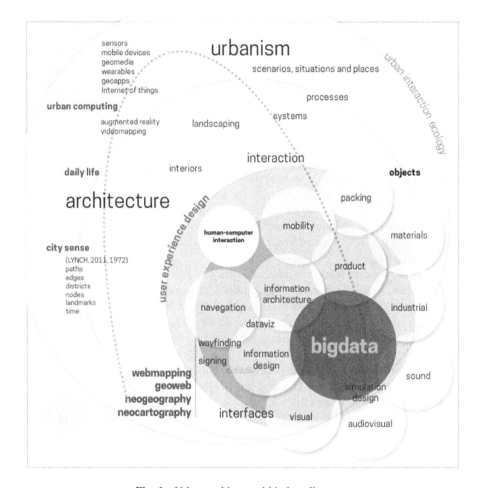

Fig. 1. Urban ambient and bigdata diagram.

will have to solve. Every powerful tool has a shadowy side everything that changes the world is able to change for worse or better is not a one-way street (Smolan 2014).

This is not to say that we can observe all this information, we are still seeing the tip of the iceberg. Most of the data may not make sense until they are interpreted and, thus, we create a narrative. It's almost an investigation to try to trace the traces of the data to the concrete fact. We need to connect everything to make sense and observe the meanings of our existence.

We are witness a world that moves from linear development. A world in disruption. Global warming can already be measured. If we exhaust the planetary ecosystem, there will be a collapse. The economic crises will be increasingly generated by the bigdata. Diversity and inequality appear to be the faces of the same coin. We need to act, the tools we have will enable this. The organizations can analyze their own data in a particular context for new ideas and make decisions that enhance productivity and efficiency. In the context of city management, visualization initiatives are enabling companies and governments to intelligently manage their assets by providing a more comprehensive and skilled supply of information.

1.2 Space as Information

Throughout the last decades, the planet has acquired different levels of information about the activities that develop on its surface. Numerous layers of information have been established without a global project for its implementation, but which profoundly affect our lives. Traditional cartographic tools are no longer adequate to observe this complexity. Each of its urban aspects generate information that can help us to understand our daily life.

One of the most basic information in the world is, well, the world itself. But most of the time, the area was never qualified or used in the form of data. Geolocation of nature, of objects and people clearly constitutes information. The mountain is there: the person is here. But to be useful, this information needs to be transformed into data. Mapping locations requires a few prerequisites: a method for measuring all square centimeters of Earth's area, a standardized way of doing this measurement, and an instrument capable of monitoring and recording data. Quantification, standardization, collection. Only then can we store and analyze the location not with a place in itself, but as given (Mayer-Schönberger 2013, pp. 59–60).

From the relation between space and objects as a place constructed by looking at an environment configured by information, the city presents itself as an environment of research and analysis of its forms of representation. Historically the union between landscape and perspective, space and representation, related geography to the act of signification. The prefiguration of the built space appeared with the perspective in the Quattrocento and evolves to the present day with the software of 2D drawing and 3D modeling. The evolution of design - from perspective to digital simulation - materialized by the evolution of technical and technological instruments shifted our constructive paradigms to a new conception of urban space, production and the possibilities, not only of representation, but also of the autonomous creation of the environment as concept. These devices, as communication and exploratory instruments, enabled the visualization of the distinct moments of creation, implantation and documentation of the project, helping the understanding of space as a support for reflection and creation. Thus, the construction and manipulation of a three-dimensional model develop and enhance the understanding of the environment as a means of making and evaluating real proposals built by the information. Surfaces and shapes are now transformed into indexed instances of interaction materializing into a new landscape, the digital landscape. A natural path for spatial creation, digital simulation lies between information, the synthesis of images and spaces, allowing the development of sophisticated exploration and analysis skills of interactive and immersive environments. The simulation of informational aspects in the urban environment is the possibility of developing prototypes of experiences that may show us new forms of city uses.

An updated version of The Image of the City (Lynch 2011) for contemporary cities is characterized by real-time information that broadens the different aspects of our urbanity mediated by the classic concepts of imaginability and readability with primordial issues. (Offenhuber and Ratti 2014)

Information in the twentieth century was all over town, signs and messages, sounds and images, news and orientations, facts, projections and abstractions, a relational multispace. From the telegraph, radio, television and billboards, the 21st century made the information permeate all the space made the city a mediascape. A system that approaches the concept of hypertext in which each of these elements - physical, sensory and digital - can define other forms of connection and specific and individual path. The city in the information age - the media city - has become a reflection of mediated and idealized thinking, as a set of languages that de-automates and alters our senses. The relationship between urban space and information technology allows the possibility of simultaneous readings that broaden the idea of the city as a place of stimulation of cultural production.

The urban landscape is amplified by the informational flows of each of us in a hypertextual and hypermedia cartography. This annotated city is the urban environment with quality of language and movement, expresses the way people use space in many media. When people note the city with their individuality, become agents (stakeholders) of his life active, participatory and collaborative manner. They expand the conceptions of presence, time and space, constructing new realities that provide the current urban fabric, possible places, imaginary and habitable. And it is this new cartography that allows to map a city not only to represent it, but also to give meaning to it.

We may have another perception of this environment with urban computing, all these possibilities of reading the city naturally migrate to the digital medium. With mobile devices, the individual can get information about their environment in addition to traditional graphical forms of representation such as maps of regions or neighborhoods or even the subway. Digital maps allow interaction and sharing of information which helps you experience the city as a learning environment.

The city presents itself as the sum of individual and plural dimensions, a complex experience constantly updated by the use of computing. The annotations generated by geolocated personal assistants (geoapps) show us the city as we experience it, from its individualization. The individualization of these references corresponds to the transformations of time and space in relation to the individual who, as the perceptual center of the world, becomes a reference for interpreting urban life. This accumulation of digital traces captures the daily pulse of the city, an accurate and organic result of urban life, in a city of countless authors. Such information allows people to understand and use the city intelligently and cognitively.

We create and provide information about ourselves and relate it to local information by building a new urban cartography that can give us fresh looks for the place we live. The reading of the urban fabric provides the physical, meaningful and technological interaction that is configured as a fragmented space, full of meaning and information, building at the same time a real and fluid place where we construct our contemporaneity.

The capture and subsequent representation of this information through annotations and mappings, both concrete and rhetorical, should consider the notions of scale and amplitude to capture the accuracy of this insertion. The bigdata allows us to discover patterns when we point these resources to our daily lives and to ourselves. The various levels of information is a qualifying action that considers the city as an environment composed of the architectural and media infrastructure and the various urban flows. Considering the physical space plus digital information levels, we believe that the individual atmosphere in the city is set from the access to information, as a fluid and momentary place.

1.3   Urban Interaction Ecosystems

We can understand a city physically by the characteristics of its space based on the demarcation of relevant places like monuments, buildings, squares and gardens or by means of the tracing of its streets and avenues. Increasing the imaginability of the urban environment means facilitating its visual identification and structuring. The isolated elements - paths, boundaries, landmarks, nodal points and regions - are the building blocks in the process of creating firm and differentiated structures on an urban scale. (Lynch 2011, p. 106) Lynch established that a city can be identified and understood by elements that make up the structure of its spaces such as paths, boundaries, landmarks (natural and edified), crossings and regions. These elements of architectural, visual and environmental orientation with the design and organization of structured landscapes are largely responsible for a highly readable and understandable urban environment.

Lynch is credited with the term wayfinding for a spatial orientation or navigation system, a project that involves several visual and spatial elements such as maps, street numbers, directional signs, and other elements he called ' wayfinding devices '. We can also add the scents of the city such as aromas of restaurants and cafes, aromatic plants and flowers or even carbon monoxide in high traffic vehicular routes, useful to people's navigation. Systems such as these primarily refer to techniques used by blind or visually impaired people as they move from one place to another independently and safely. This terminology was developed by the five main elements of architectural guidance, cited above. Later Lynch added the Time (1972) among these five initial elements allowing us to observe the unfolding of other fluid elements such as urban flows.

Wayfinding is derived from many design disciplines like architecture, landscaping, urbanism, topography, geography, among others. It is the organization and communication of our dynamic relationship in space and in the environment, a system that must meet all users. Designing such a system should develop a plan that will take you from your location to your destination, connecting and arranging spaces through architectural signs and graphics in a safe, unboundaries environments. These projects encompass, in addition to signage, architecture, landscaping, lighting, landmarks and guiding points. They are divided into two categories: guidance and navigation. Guidance is the ability to position with respect to an environment and mobility the ability to safely move, detecting and avoiding obstacles and other potential hazards.

Guidance and navigation systems need to take into account how people with different capabilities interact with the built environment. For the 'Principles of Universal Design' it is necessary that the constructed spaces be adaptable for all, these principles show that the inclusive design can accommodate people with varied abilities. The 'Universal Design Principles' (Lidwell et al. 2003) can be applied to evaluate existing projects, guide the design process and citizens about the characteristics of environments, objects and products most suitable for use. If we follow these principles, we will have a design of great value inclusive with high usability for all and without the need of adaptation or specialized design.

We can consider four main areas in the design of an orientation system: architectural clues, visual communication, auditory communication, tactile communication and four main categories of orientation elements: identification, reinforcement, orientation and destination. In general terms, a wayfinding system enables us to know where we are, where we move, how to get there or recognize our destiny, all done safely and independently.

Systems of guidance and space navigation are validated by the way users experience the communicational elements in the displacement of a point A to a point B, usually they are composed by maps; panels; directories; signals; color coding; floor and bedroom numbering; buildings and sites; interior and exterior views; auditory instructions; built and natural landmarks; logical progression of spaces. We were able to extend this system by adding digital information through the use of geomedia and geoapps during netnographic investigations, which defines a more complete ecosystem of urban information. With urban computing, design should assist users in solving space problems by providing consistent, constantly updated clues.

If we consider that digital information is not always available for viewing by people, can we devise a strategy to guide us through the city permeated by this information? How do we navigate and interact with information in urban space? How can geomedia change the design of information in space? An urban system with characteristics can be exploited through its transport systems, utilities, geographic patterns, historical structures such as information flows and thus provide answers to potential queries even before users have to ask help or even indicate where users should not go. We will increase the viewers of data generated by geomedia changing or increasing a physically signaled space.

The city of the 21st century is an interactive and sentient environment (Shepard 2011). Its spaces are experienced as a meeting place of cultures and communities that reflects modular structure where physical, digital, presential and virtual systems can merge. Through these technological combinations are formed territories that consist of information flows at the intersection between physical and digital city (Lemos 2008). This environment as a place of use, information and everyday interface (Shepard 2011) gives urban interaction levels characterizing themselves as an urban informational ecosystem.

The city as an interface, an immersive and multimedia environment, is composed of people and objects with different levels of interaction. This experience expands our perception and the very language of architecture and design, communication and urbanism. From urban space to the urban informational environment: complexity acts as the main idea in the construction of narratives of the city. This urbanity is the result of a kaleidoscope of geographic, ethnohistorical, sociocultural, and technological diversities, defined by innumerable informational layers that create a constant interaction flow between our body and various urban contexts, our current experiences.

In order to understand the conception of this urban informational ecosystem, consider the data generated by urban computing, in particular the use of the mobile and locative devices previously studied, and the possible user interfaces. The forms of visualization of information in the urban environment, and consequent construction of an ecosystem, are conceptually derived from the urban interaction ecology articulated in Vassão (2008), the mobile and locative experiences in Lemos (2008) the data and its tangibilization in Ishii (2016), our nomadic condition in Beiguelman and La Ferla (2011), and the construction of meaning in Santaella (2010).

As a living text, cities are becoming a great book where at every connection they are rewritten with new data. An environment in which information can be accessed in a customized way according to the needs of this user-citizen. With the data generated daily we have the opportunity to experience our daily lives in other ways. This geo-media user can find any type of information related to their specific environment. An information system that can guide us through the city giving information in real time where we are, the best way and time of arrival or what happens around us. Urban cameras and sensors, geoapps like GoogleMaps, ARsense or Urbotip, have expanded the information of the urban environment to allow us to think about a new perspective on the city (Offenhuber and Ratti 2014). A communication system that harnesses the data generated collaboratively in personal (sensor citizen), urban (cameras and sensors) and social (social network data) levels. A succession of strategic clues - physical and digital - that activate our sensory system formed by visual, audible, tactile and olfactory elements that establish active urban interfaces.

The city permeated by computing urban allows us to create new everyday interfaces. It is the fabric urban transformed in an urban ecology of interactions (Vassão 2008). And the information accessed in real time transform the city in an Metacity, the idea of a city updated by citizens in each connection, an environment daily sensitive that allow new forms of use and design (Fig. 2).

If a traditional system provides information to users such as correct direction, origin and destination, location and orientation within a building or in an external environment, with a guidance system can we anticipate potential situations or hazards (and escape safely in case of emergence), to obtain additional information about where we are, to search for historical content, to identify alternative paths or to define customized approaches to information. How can we note daily life in the great global center, the dematerialization of socio-economic-cultural exchanges and the consequent alteration of human activities in urban space? The geomedia and geoapps are our measuring instruments, annotation and location to give our everyday journey to the requirements we use the city in amplified form.

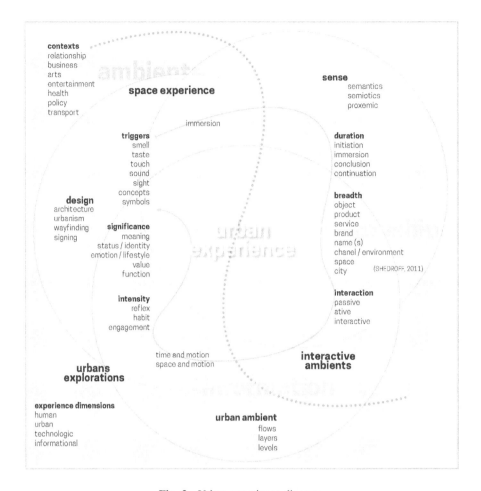

Fig. 2. Urban experience diagram.

2 Metacity

Our everyday imaginary has deconstructed the relationship between the sensory and the individual utilitarian by presenting the contemporary space as an informational system in this fluid and potential reality. The verification of the informational status of cities allows us to discuss the exercise of design for new and potential urban experiences. The areas of project knowledge were brought into question when modern thinking was deemed limited to meet the longings of contemporary societies. Natural domain of engineering, architecture, landscaping, urbanism, the city by the designers look can be thought of at levels customized for the individual, community and society, citizens and city dwellers. For design, the balance between several areas of knowledge and practice allows us to create conditions for change. Design can unite heterogeneous fields of thought by redesigning processes with each new data, with each new information. Thus, we must reinvent our conceptions of city with tools of perception, design and interaction of an extended urban environment.

Adapting to uncertainty (Morin 2000) is to be prepared to act with quality in the projective process in a qualifying environment that allows the observation of the urban world in its latent state. This social experience allows us to incorporate into the projective processes the continuous learning of the history and experience of the community involved by the make-use-interact of a space in eternal change. The urban environment may seem out of the reach of a designer, but its projective process can approach the themes of the city in depth, because part of its performance and training, broad and general, is attentive to the individualities of people. People incorporated into the project are at the heart of the process, generating more accurate decision support. The radicant quality (Borriaud 2011) of the condition of its inhabitants permeates the urban environment of a volatile nomadism materialized as accessible information at any time and place of its human history.

Designers add value when working on an urban scale. Although the design has helped create the world we know, projects like the iPhone or Google search algorithm have the desire to make it simple and easy to use something unknown and complex. Urban design encompasses important issues for the city on a different level, its proximity to market, people, and citizen's everyday issues, enabling it to address certain issues from a different perspective.

Although the way to organize and construct the information continues with the modern basis of thought, the forms of expression, the digital tools, both hardware and software, have allowed to work in a more fluid and much more open design. Common projective methods, such as problem solving, prototyping and use testing, can be applied to help cities empower urban agents to increase infrastructure, governance, and quality of life.

Uncertain, unpredictable or turbulent environments call for a better understanding of their hidden dynamics, tendencies, and structures (Pizzocaro 2000). When designing for cities, we will certainly face a number of challenges to overcome. Design can help simplify objects and services, products that are easier to understand, more accessible and more relevant to our daily lives.

Redesign everything, the whole city, its objects and processes. When design operates in a world expanded by digital media, interfaces can venture beyond the physical space and technology, as well as the urban individuality itself. No more interaction between user and computer, but between many people and a common environment. We can act on several project fronts, whose construction of meaning and the structuring of new experiences will form this new reality. If our interactions in the city are mediated by networks, devices and applications, they acquire an expanded sense of human culture. The look is for the planet, but with urban eyes (Fig. 3).

The design of this city requires that we articulate different levels of knowledge by making the intellectual limits less rigid and the contents more accessible. This complexity cannot be experienced from within the boundaries of disciplines. It is experienced precisely at the intersections of various disciplines and fields of knowledge. From space to environment: the city is composed of narratives by the informational complexity, interaction, navigation and usability in its construction. In this sense, we can point out that design joins these processes of change capable of eliminating the

Fig. 3. Metacity, design, data and urbanity diagram.

boundaries between the natural and social sciences and the technological sciences. Design in its most basic form, the act of designing, can meet what we want in a city. In the environment, innovation involves variables, not restricted to the market: it articulates processes, supplies, materials and technologies (Pizzocaro 2000).

There is a great accumulation of technologies and we do not know where cities can go. What is expected of people's action is the occupation of this urban environment. From the metadata to the information we can use the sensing of the urban fabric to better understand our world, organizing, visualizing and articulating the knowledge of each person on Earth. The goal is to build new, instantaneous looks, enabling multiple observations of the bigdata contained in urban environments.

What else do we want to discover out of our lives from subsidies? In this urban environment, where geographical references and time are relativized, spaces fragment and regroup momentarily in environments in which human culture is modified by building our urbanity.

The urban structures keep all the necessary information so that we can attend to the questions that are presented, they are places of action and reflection of its own original design added to the bigdata. The idea of Metacity incorporates the city as a propositional environment of diversified everyday realities, as a space in perpetual process of multiplication and expansion of its layers of meaning. Metacity is the environment of projective explorations that uses abundant urban data as a source and is permeated by information. It is the city whose physicality is increased by information flows to the intense technological evolution.

Metacity is what we imagine for our cities in the near future. An urban space, continuous and interlaced with information, new materials and projected forms; reflection and exercise of design for an urban informational ecosystem, whose object is the soaked space by the bigdata, shared at every moment and of political action. It is the opportunity for us artists, designers, architects and engineers to imagine an enlarged and responsive daily life for our personal needs. Metacity as our second nature is an urban process that is just beginning.

References

Augé, M.: Não Lugares. Introdução a uma antropologia da supermodernidade. Editora Papirus, Campinas (1994

Bourriaud, N.: Radicante – por uma estética da globalização. Martins Fontes, São Paulo (2011)

Beiguelman, G., La Ferla, J. (org.): Nomadismos tecnológicos. Editora Senac, São Paulo (2011)

Ishii, H., Nakagaki, K., Vink, L., Counts, J., Windham, D., Leithinger, D., Follmer, S.: Materiable. http://tangible.media.mit.edu/project/materiable/. Accessed 30 July 2016

Kozinets, R.V.: Netnography. Doing Ethnographic Research Online. Sage Publications, Los Angeles (2010)

LEMOS, André. Mobile Communication and New Sense of Places: a Critique of Spatialization in Cyberculture. São Paulo, Galáxia, n°16, December 2008

Lidwell, W., Holden, K., Butler, J.: Universal Principles of Design. Rockport Publishers, Inc. (2003)

Lynch, K.: A imagem da cidade. Martins Fontes, São Paulo (2011)

Lynch, K.: What Time is this Place?, MIT Press, Cambridge, MA (1972)

Mayer-Schönberger, V.: Big Data: Como Extrair Volume, Variedade, Velocidade e Valor da Avalanche de Informação Cotidiana. Elsevier, Rio de Janeiro (2013)

Morin, E.: Os sete saberes necessários à educação do futuro. Cortez&Unesco, São Paulo (2000)

Offenhuber, D., Ratti, C.: Decoding the City. Urbanism in the Age of Big Data. Birkhäuser, Basel (2014)

Pizzocaro, S.: Complexity, uncertainty, adaptability: reflections around design research. In: Durling, D., Friedman, K. (org.) Doctoral Education in Design: Foundations for the Future. Staffordshire University Press, London (2000)

Preece, J., Rogers, Y., Sharp, H.: Design de interação: Além da interação homem-computador. Tradução: Viviane Possamai. Porto Alegre: Bookman (2007)

Shedroff, N.: Designing Meaningful Experiences. AIGA CT (2011)

Shepard, M.: Sentient City: Ubiquitous Computing, Architecture, and the Future of Urban Space. The MIT Press (2011)

Smolan, S.: The Human Face of Big Data. Ebook/Application. Against All Odds Productions (2014)

VASSÃO, Caio A. Arquitetura Livre: Complexidade, Metadesign e Ciência Nômade. Tese de doutorado, USP (2008)

Smart Systems in Emergency Wayfinding: A Literature Review

Elisângela Vilar[✉], Francisco Rebelo, and Paulo Noriega

Faculdade de Arquitetura, Centro de Investigação em Arquitetura,
Urbanismo e Design, Rua Sá Nogueira, Universidade de Lisboa,
Polo Universitário, Alto da Ajuda, 1349-055 Lisboa, Portugal
elipessoa@gmail.com,
{frebelo,pnoriega}@fmh.ulisboa.pt

Abstract. Wayfinding difficulties may lead people to avoid places; it also can make them late for important occurrences such as business meetings or flights, which may cause loss of opportunity and money. Additionally, as settings grow in dimension and complexity, emergency evacuation emerges as a key problem, and wayfinding becomes a matter of life and death. Thus, a large concentration of people, with different degrees of familiarity with the building, motivations, and anxieties, should be able to satisfy their needs in a network of paths leading to different destinations, even when, during an emergency, they face doubtful situations created by the incongruence between the architecture and the signage system. In this context, the present paper is focused on a theoretical review on emergency evacuation process and signage systems in order to explore new paradigms on emergency wayfinding into complex building. Considering the evolution of technology in terms of availability, cost and ease of use, this paper discusses the use of traditional and new wayfinding system considering some established theories such as the "cry wolf" and the "learned irrelevance" theories.

Keywords: Smart systems · Smart buildings · Wayfinding
Emergency evacuation · Signage

1 Introduction

With buildings becoming increasingly larger and more complex, the needs of the occupants in terms of accessibility and safety have also significantly increased. Buildings use is now so diversified that sometimes facilities combine the functionalities of a variety of structures such as airports, hotels, shopping center areas, public transportation terminals, apartments, and offices. Additionally, emergency situations and wayfinding generally are not the main focus for developing such facilities, and many times, such as in interventions in historical buildings, renovations and changes in buildings use, conflicting situations between information given by architecture and the available signage system may appear during an emergency.

Wayfinding difficulties may lead people to avoid places; it also can make them late for important occurrences such as business meetings or flights, which may cause loss of

© Springer International Publishing AG, part of Springer Nature 2018
A. Marcus and W. Wang (Eds.): DUXU 2018, LNCS 10919, pp. 379–388, 2018.
https://doi.org/10.1007/978-3-319-91803-7_28

opportunity and money. Additionally, as settings grow in dimension and complexity, emergency evacuation emerges as a key problem, and wayfinding becomes a matter of life and death.

During an emergency into complex buildings, evacuation time is a key factor, and design effective wayfinding systems that reduce this time is a challenge for architects, designers and safety planners. According to some authors (D'Orazio et al. 2016; Kobes et al. 2010a; Vilar et al. 2014a; Vilar et al. 2013), wayfinding systems success are influenced by environmental and individual aspects such as, signs design, and location, presence of light/smoke and architectural configuration of the space, people's attention and perception. So, effective wayfinding systems can be more complex than only using static exit signs in pre-defined points. According to Bernardini (2017), human behavior, individual's response and Human-environment interactions seem to be underestimate by the current approaches for wayfinding systems. Thus, a large concentration of people, with different degrees of familiarity with the building, motivations, and anxieties, should be able to satisfy their needs in a network of paths leading to different destinations, even when, during an emergency, they face doubtful situations created by the incongruence between the architecture and the signage system.

In this context, this paper will present new trends in emergency wayfinding systems, mainly considering the use of technology to overcome some limitations presented by the current available systems, through a theoretical perspective.

2 Emergency Evacuation

According to Abdelgawad and Abdulhai (2009) emergency evacuation can be understood as the movement of people from a hazard area to safe destinations. This movement is made via specific routes which should be part of an evacuation plan. Thus, emergency evacuation can be defined as the process of wayfinding in stressful situations, which should be assisted by environmental information, such as definition of escape routes, signs and maps.

Considering this, three distinct analytical dimensions can be referred to the emergency evacuation behavior: the physical location of the evacuation; the existing management of the location; and the social psychological and social organizational characteristics impacting the response of persons and collectivities that participate in the evacuation (Santos and Aguirre 2004). The physical location can be understood as the total environment, from the hazard area and its configuration until the safe zone, considering the evacuation routes. The management refers to procedures, and controls deployed at evacuation, including support devices (from signs to technology-based emergency guidance).

For a successful emergency evacuation plan, these three dimensions should be aligned in order to provide congruent support to evacuees. An example of the problem with this three dimensions' misalignment are conflicting situations created when environmental characteristics contradict safety signs information. Previous studies (e.g., Vilar et al. 2014b; Vilar et al. 2013) shown that when buildings' architectural elements act as environmental affordances, they can interfere with occupants' behavioral compliance with emergence egress signs, decreasing the efficiency of the egress signs and, consequently, increasing the probability of injuries.

Some authors (Kobes et al. 2010b; O'Connor 2005; Purser and Bensilum 2001), divide the evacuation process into two main categories, which comprise:

- Pre-movement process: comprised by Cue validation/Recognition phase and Response phase;
- Movement process.

Purser and Bensilum (2001) stated that the pre-movement process begins when an alarm is triggered or at a cue, and ends when the occupant starts his/her travel to the exit or to a safe place. The cue validation/recognition phase begins at an alarm or cue and ends with occupant's first response. So, it is the awareness of danger by external stimuli. During this phase, occupants continue with their pre-alarm activities. The response phase is the response to danger indicators. It begins at the first response and ends when the occupant's travel to an exit begins. It is a decision-making period during which occupants carry out a range of activities, such as investigating the situation, alerting others, fighting fire. Thus, this process depends upon hazard detection, provision of warnings, response of warnings (pre-movement phase), and pre-egress behavior (e.g., collecting belonging, seeking information, choosing an exit).

The movement process starts when the occupant's travel to an exit begins and ends when the occupant leaves the building or find a safe place. In order to analyze this process, it is necessary to take into account the occupants flow patterns through the escape routes, and the time required for the occupants to travel to a safe place (Purser and Bensilum 2001).

Bernardini (2017) argues that, in general, evacuating people are considered as moving fluid particles by regulations about fire safety, as well as by work health and safety, and problems are solved by simply increasing number and width of evacuation paths and exits. Author also point that other widely considered approaches are related with objective measures of correlating evacuation paths width and pattern's flow and the evacuation time in function of pedestrian's movement speed and path length.

According O'Connor (2005), for many years evacuation time was considered the basic measure to evaluate fire protection systems. However, when human behavior is considered, many basic assumptions about occupant's behavior with little or no basis in behavioral literature have been made by engineers, architects and designers. O'Connor (2005) gives as example the often-cited assumption that occupants' automatically and immediately evacuate a building upon the sounding of the fire alarm system. Considering this, in last years some authors (e.g., Gamberini et al. 2003; Gamberini et al. 2015; Mantovani et al. 2001; Vilar et al. 2013) have studied the human behavior during emergency evacuation to incorporate this dimension into the prediction models, evacuation plans, and in the design of the emergency signage.

Additionally, since 2009, guidelines from European fire safety (2009) included the Available Safe Egress Time (ASET) and the Required Safe Egress Time (RSET), introducing the performance-based fire safety engineering design of buildings (ASET > RSET). So, all building occupants have to be able to evacuate the place in conditions of not-exceeded tenability criteria om the building itself. According to the guidelines from European fire safety (2009), ASET is "calculated time available between ignition of a fire and the time at which tenability criteria are exceeded in a specific space in a building" and RSET is "calculated time required between ignition to detection and the time at which the evacuation is completed". So, ASET is mostly related with buildings features and fire characteristics, and RSET essentially considers human behavior and Human-environment interactions, including actions performed during pre-movements and movement phases (D'Orazio et al. 2016).

3 Support Systems for Indoor Emergency Wayfinding

Traditionally, static signs are the main support system for emergency evacuation used in buildings. They are a symbol-based type signs consistent with the International Organization for Standardization's (ISO) 3864-1 (ISO 2002) standard. According to Duarte et al. (2010), efforts have been done in order to harmonize ISO and American National Standards Institute (ANSI) Z535 (2002) standards, thus text panels are also being inserted on ISO signs.

The emergency exit signs are usually made of paper, metal or plastic (Duarte et al. 2010), and must be placed where necessary (mainly on decision points) to inform people about the escape routes during an emergency. Nowadays, several types of emergency wayfinding systems can be found, such as: reflective signs, photo luminescent (PLM) signs, electrically illumined signs, interactive wayfinding systems, acoustic wayfinding systems. Mostly, these systems applications are punctual (mainly placed at intersection points and exits), however continuous systems applications are also found (D'Orazio et al. 2016).

Signage is an important issue during wayfinding process (Conroy 2001) as it optimize people's performance in finding their way in both, everyday (Vilar et al. 2014a) and emergency situations (Mantovani et al. 2001). However, some studies have been done to investigate the efficiency of emergency exit signs, and findings suggests that static signs generally have low compliance rates, mainly when the built environment presents doubtful route-choices (i.e., exit signs pointing to corridors with lower illumination levels versus a corridor more illuminated).

Some studies have been done to examine the effect of dynamic features in signs on behavioral compliance during work-related task and an emergency egress (e.g., Nilsson 2009; Duarte 2010; Duarte et al. 2010; Duarte et al. 2014). According to Nilsson (2009), flashing lights at emergency exits, as a dynamic feature, can potentially optimize evacuation of buildings. The design aspects of flashing lights at emergency exits, namely the color of the light source, the aspect of the light and the location of the light are very important aspects to consider when designing emergency exit systems. In this way, Nilsson (2009) pointed that dynamic signage with flashing lights should have green color and lights should be placed at both sides of the exit sign. Findings of a study conducted by Duarte (2010), suggested that, for un-cued signs, dynamic presentation produced higher behavioral compliance than static ones.

According to Wogalter (2006), in a research about behavioral compliance with signs, mainly with technology support, dynamic ones can be more effective than the traditional solutions because of some features that make them more noticeable and more resistant to habituation. These features can be related with some dynamic attributes, such as availability only when necessary, use of flashing lights and sound.

Some studies have been done in order to verify the effectiveness of the emergency signage systems used into complex buildings nowadays. In researches that investigate evacuation times in buildings, Shih et al. (2000), in a VR-based study, and Xie et al. (2012), in a real world experiment, verified that in some situations people followed routes that were different from those indicated by the egress signs and, generally, regardless the presence of signs and smoke, they tried to return the direction they entered the building. The influence of the environment over behavioral compliance with exit signs was also found by Tang et al. (2009). In their study using VR, they reported that when participants were faced with seemingly contradictory information in the form of both an exit sign and an exit door, almost half of the persons choose to proceed through the door rather than follow the directions posted on the sign. The results of a previous study (i.e., Vilar et al. 2014c) revealed worrying low rates of compliance with static ISO-type exit signs (about 30%) for the first decision point, with an increment of the compliance along the route. It happens due to the fact that some architectural features can overlap the exit signs, influencing people's wayfinding decision in a stressful situation (Vilar 2012).

Additionally, according to Bernardini et al. (2016) in situations like Architectural Heritage, fire safety regulations approaches generally suggest structural interventions to improve the occupants' level of safety, mainly related with changes in building layout, increasing corridor's width and number of exits, and introduction of fire-proof elements. Authors argue that this type of change represents a conflict between heritage preservation and fire safety regulations, which can affect occupant's level of safety. An alternative could be using smart active systems, that are activated when emergency occurs.

3.1 Smart Systems for Emergency Wayfinding

Authors have suggested alternatives considering the use of technology for helping people during emergency wayfinding. They are smart active systems, based in a match between occupants' behavior and characteristics, and environmental conditions. Smart active systems can control, for instance, doors that open and close when activated during an emergency, and technology-based signs that can be dynamic, adaptable and/or interactive. They can be available on building site, such as sensors and dynamic signs or portable equipment used by occupants of the building, such as smartphones and augmented reality devices. A review of these systems is available on Ibrahim et al. (2016). Some authors (e.g., Wogalter and Mayhorn 2006; Wogalter and Mayhorn 2005; Mayhorn and Wogalter 2003; Smith-Jackson and Wogalter 2004; Wogalter and Conzola 2002) described how this technology can produce better warnings and signs, however there are few information about their application for emergency wayfinding systems.

According to Lijding et al. (2007), smart signs are based on small computers that can be incorporated on the environment, providing users with customized context-aware guidance and messaging to support wayfinding tasks in complex buildings. Authors present a pilot study with a prototype of a smart sign which was tested on the Zilverling and Waaier Buildings of the University of Twente. For the test, 21 persons, unfamiliar with the building, were separated in two groups (control and experimental), and both were asked to perform wayfinding tasks. Control group used traditional signs and experimental group used smart signs to help during two wayfinding tasks. Results shown a significant reduction in the time needed to conclude the wayfinding tasks, as well as a significant improvement in the perception of learnability, helpfulness, efficiency and satisfaction level in comparison to the traditional signs.

Thus, smart systems can be designed as an interactive system that deliver safety information directly to users' portable devices based on environmental information acquired by sensors. The fact that they allow information only to be delivered when needed could explain their higher effectiveness when compared to traditional emergency, corroborating McClintock et al. (2001) theory about learned irrelevance. These authors, argued that the reason why people generally do not notice emergency exit signs is because they are seldom used. According to Baker (1976), learned irrelevance is the inability to effectively respond to previously irrelevant information. McClintock et al. (McClintock et al. 2001) argued that learned irrelevance can impact human behavior in emergencies into buildings as it can cause occupants to ignore safety information (e.g. exit signs) that is available and they can see every day but never use. These authors tested an alternative design for emergency exit using blue flashing lights combined with European Back-lit emergency exit sign. The proposed design was compared with others through a questionnaire-like survey. Responses revealed that the proposed design was preferred amongst the participants and had the highest attention capturing ability.

According to attention theory (Wickens and McCarley 2008), dynamic signs such as those used in smart active systems, can be more effective to catch peoples' attention due to their salience. Duarte et al. (2014) argued that exit signs could benefit from those dynamic features reported by Wogalter (2006) because when in emergency there is stress that might tie up attention capacity. In stressful situations, people tend to narrow their attention, thus salience could make smart signs more noticeable, and then more effective than traditional static ones. Results from a study conducted by Duarte et al. (2014) using Virtual Reality-based methodology, shown that dynamic exit signs produced better egress performance than static ones. Participants viewing dynamic signs had higher compliance rates, spent less time, covered shorter distances, and took fewer pauses in the during a virtual complex building evacuation.

According to Breznitz (1984), the effectiveness of a warning system depends significantly on its credibility. Each false alarm reduces the system effectiveness due to the fact that for the future similar alerts may receive less attention, losing credibility and creating a false alarm effect, also called by the author as "cry wolf" effect. Unfortunately, in many situations, emergency systems such as smoke detectors on hotels, fails on detecting real dangerous situation, being activated by, for instance, cigar smoke. A person who had an experience like this might perceive a future threat as less intense and might elicit weaker fear reactions. Breznitz (1984) agued that this person may reduce his/her willingness to engage a protective behavior. Smart active systems could be an alternative to decrease the false alarm effect. An example could be customized information delivered directly to occupants of a complex building during a fire. In this case, verbal message could be sent to directly to occupants alerting them that the emergency is real (or it is not an emergency simulation). Other example could be cue validation through a smart system, in which occupants could be alerted that there is a real hazard if system won´t detected protective behavior from the occupant.

The smart system presented by Gorbil and Gelenbe (2011) is an autonomous emergency support system based on opportunistic communications to support emergency evacuation. According to the authors, it was done considering low-cost human wearable mobile nodes allowing the exchange of packets at a close range of a few to some tens of meters with limited or no infrastructure. In this way, their proposed emergency support system uses opportunistic contacts (oppcomms) between wireless communication portable devices to gather information regarding the current situation and disseminate wayfinding messages to promote safe evacuation. Their solution is target for densely populated places, as node density, as stated the authors, plays an important role in the effectiveness of oppcomms. This solution was implemented and tested in a multi-agent distributed building evacuation simulator, considering two situations: a three-floor large office building, modeled based in a real building, and in a 5 km^2 area of Fulham district of London. Results shown that the proposed smart system perform better than un-informed shortest path routing, and evacuation system based on static signs.

Targeting the architectural heritage issue, Bernardini et al. (2016) proposed a behavioral-based smart system that could monitor Human behaviors (mainly considering how people move) and related analyses in the evacuation process (e.g. slowing down along paths, paths blockage), suggesting the "best" evacuation path to occupants depending on their effective behaviors. According the authors, considering behavioral aspects, mainly in cases where pedestrian density effects could be more representative (e.g., narrow paths or complex layouts) could increase the system effectiveness. They tested their smart system considering an historical Italian-style theatre as case-study and compared an existent emergency wayfinding system with a smart system. The available wayfinding system was a traditional punctual one, composed by photoluminescent standard directional signs hung at the wall and placed at directional intersections. A freeware fire evacuation simulator was used to implement the new solutions (algorithm and effects, in terms of choices, on occupants). Results presented a lower evacuation time when the proposed smart system is used, with an increment for the use of secondary exits. Authors pointed out the benefits of using such system, mainly considering architectural heritage, due to the fact that with its use, no structural change is necessary, avoiding the lack of architectural characteristics of historical places.

4 Conclusions

Studies suggest that smart active systems can be more effective than traditional ones to direct people to safe places into complex buildings (e.g., Gorbil and Gelenbe 2011; Lijding et al. 2007; Vilar et al. 2014c). These smart active systems are mainly based on context, such as the weather and emergency situations, like fire or medical needs, and can also consider users' characteristics, such as mobility limitations, health conditions. Their main goal is to optimize routes and safety communication to increase occupants' level of safety. Smart active systems are able to inform occupants about new routes considering human behavior during the emergency wayfinding, allowing people to avoid, for instance, blocking paths. They can also be personalized delivering the information according to users' needs.

Their effectiveness has been analyzed and evaluated mainly using building evacuation simulators (e.g., Gorbil and Gelenbe 2011; Bernardini et al. 2016) with only few prototypes being tested in real-world buildings (e.g., Lijding et al. 2007). Some authors have studied particular features of smart active systems, such as the dynamism (e.g., Duarte 2014) and availability when necessary (e.g., Vilar et al. 2014a) considering virtual reality-based methodologies, and results shown high behavioral compliance rates. However, although some patents of emergency smart systems can be found, there are still few applications of these systems into real buildings.

It is a matter of fact that the development of these systems requires a multidisciplinary approach. In this way, to ensure users safety in emergency situations, safety design should consider an interdisciplinary approach, implicating experts in several fields of knowledge, namely safety engineering, architectural design, signage design, ergonomics and human factors, psychology and technology.

Acknowledgements. This research is supported by FCT grant n. SFRH/BPD/93993/2013.

References

Abdelgawad, H., Abdulhai, B.: Emergency evacuation planning as a network design problem: a critical review. Transp. Lett. Int. J. Transp. Res. **1**, 41–58 (2009). https://doi.org/10.3328/TL. 2009.01.01.41-58

Almeida, A., Rebelo, F., Noriega, P., Vilar, E., Borges, T.: Virtual environment evaluation for a safety warning effectiveness study. Procedia Manuf. **3**, 5971–5978 (2015). https://doi.org/10. 1016/j.promfg.2015.07.692

Baker, A.G.: Learned irrelevance and learned helplessness: rats learn that stimuli, reinforcers, and responses are uncorrelated. J. Exp. Psychol. Anim. Behav. Process **2**, 130–141 (1976)

Bernardini, G.: Fire safety and building heritage: the occupants perspective. Fire Safety of Historical Buildings. SAST, pp. 7–43. Springer, Cham (2017). https://doi.org/10.1007/978-3-319-55744-1_2

Bernardini, G., Azzolini, M., D'Orazio, M., Quagliarini, E.: Intelligent evacuation guidance systems for improving fire safety of Italian-style historical theatres without altering their architectural characteristics. J. Cult. Herit. **22**, 1006–1018 (2016). https://doi.org/10.1016/j. culher.2016.06.008

Breznitz, S.: Cry Wolf: The Psychology of False Alarms - S. Breznitz - Google Livros. Lawrence Erlbaum Associates, Inc., New Jersey (1984). https://books.google.pt/books?hl=pt-PT&lr= &id=lxwLVy16wqoC&oi=fnd&pg=PR2&dq=cry+wolf+Theory&ots=BIvM4NcC5M&sig= D6V175lXGqVrtncQ9Djp1nBpZog&redir_esc=y#v=onepage&q=crywolfTheory&f=false

CFPA-E Guideline n° 19:2009 F.: Fire safety engineering concerning evacuation from buildings. CFPA Europe, Zurich (2009). http://www.cfpa-e.eu/wp-content/uploads/files/guidelines/ CFPA_E_Guideline_No_19_2009.pdf

Conroy, R.: Spatial Navigation in Immersive Virtual Environments. Faculty of Built Environment (Vol. Doctor). University of London, London (2001)

D'Orazio, M., Bernardini, G., Tacconi, S., Arteconi, V., Quagliarini, E.: Fire safety in Italian-style historical theatres: How photoluminescent wayfinding can improve occupants' evacuation with no architecture modifications. J. Cult. Herit. **19**, 492–501 (2016). https://doi.org/10.1016/J.CULHER.2015.12.002

Duarte, E.: Using Virtual Reality to Assess Behavioral Compliance with Warnings. Technical University of Lisbon, Lisbon (2010)

Duarte, E., Rebelo, F., Teles, J., Wogalter, M.: Behavioral compliance in virtual reality : effects of warning type. In: Kaber, D.B., Boy, G. (eds.) Advances in Cognitive Ergonomics, pp. 812–821. CRC Press/Taylor & Francis, Ltd., Boca Raton, Florida (2010) http://www.safetyhumanfactors.org/wp-content/uploads/2011/12/312DuarteRebeloTelesWogalter2010.pdf

Duarte, E., Rebelo, F., Teles, J., Wogalter, M.S.: Behavioral compliance for dynamic versus static signs in an immersive virtual environment. Appl. Ergon. **45**(5), 1367–1375 (2014). https://doi.org/10.1016/j.apergo.2013.10.004

Gamberini, L., Chittaro, L., Spagnolli, A., Carlesso, C.: Psychological response to an emergency in virtual reality: effects of victim ethnicity and emergency type on helping behavior and navigation. Comput. Hum. Behav. **48**, 104–113 (2015). https://doi.org/10.1016/j.chb.2015.01.040

Gamberini, L., Cottone, P., Spagnolli, A., Varotto, D., Mantovani, G.: Responding to a fire emergency in a virtual environment: different patterns of action for different situations. Ergonomics **46**(8), 842–858 (2003). http://www.informaworld.com/10.1080/0014013031000111266

Gorbil, G., Gelenbe, E.: Opportunistic communications for emergency support systems. Procedia Comput. Sci. **5**, 39–47 (2011). https://doi.org/10.1016/j.procs.2011.07.008

Ibrahim, A.M., Venkat, I., Subramanian, K.G., Khader, A.T., De Wilde, P.: Intelligent evacuation management systems. ACM Trans. Intell. Syst. Technol. **7**(3), 1–27 (2016). https://doi.org/10.1145/2842630

ISO: ISO 3864-1 graphical symbols — safety colours and safety signs. J. Acoust. Soc. Am. **130**(4), 2525 (2002). https://doi.org/10.1121/1.3655080

Kobes, M., Helsloot, I., de Vries, B., Post, J.: Exit choice, (pre-)movement time and (pre-)evacuation behaviour in hotel fire evacuation — behavioural analysis and validation of the use of serious gaming in experimental research. Procedia Eng. **3**, 37–51 (2010a). https://doi.org/10.1016/J.PROENG.2010.07.006

Kobes, M., Helsloot, I., de Vries, B., Post, J.G.: Building safety and human behaviour in fire: A literature review. Fire Saf. J. **45**(1), 1–11 (2010b). https://doi.org/10.1016/j.firesaf.2009.08.005

Lijding, M.E.M., Meratnia, N., Benz, H.P., Matysiak Szóstek, A.: Smart Signs Show You the Way. I/O Vivat, **22**(LNCS4549/4), 35–38 (2007). https://ris.utwente.nl/ws/portalfiles/portal/6873918

Mantovani, G., Gamberini, L., Martinelli, M., Varotto, D.: Exploring the suitability of virtual environments for safety training: signals, norms and ambiguity in a simulated emergency escape. Cogn. Technol. Work **3**(1), 33–41 (2001). https://doi.org/10.1007/pl00011519

Mayhorn, C.B., Wogalter, M.S.: Technology-based warnings: improvising safety through increased cognitive support to users. In: 15th International Ergonomics Association Congress, pp. 504–507 (2003)

McClintock, T., Shields, T.J., Reinhardt-Rutland, A.H., Leslie, J.C.: A behavioural solution to the learned irrelevance of emergency exit signage. In: 2nd International Symposium on Human Behaviour in Fire, Boston, MA, pp. 23–33 (2001)

Nilsson, D.: Exit choice in fire emergencies : influencing choice of exit with flashing lights. Dept. of Fire Safety Engineering and Systems Safety, Lund University (2009)

O'Connor, D.J.: Integrating human behaviour factors into design. Fire Prot. Eng., pp. 8–20 (2005). https://c.ymcdn.com/sites/www.sfpe.org/resource/resmgr/FPE_Magazine_Archives/2000-2009/2005_Q4.pdf

Purser, D., Bensilum, M.: Quantification of behaviour for engineering design standards and escape time calculations. Saf. Sci. **38**(2), 157–182 (2001). https://doi.org/10.1016/S0925-7535(00)00066-7

Santos, G., Aguirre, B.E.: A critical review of emergency evacuation simulation models NIST workshop on building occupant movement during fire emergencies. In: NIST Workshop on Building Occupant Movement during Fire Emergencies, pp. 25–50 (2004)

Shih, N.-J., Lin, C.-Y., Yang, C.-H.: A virtual-reality-based feasibility study of evacuation time compared to the traditional calculation method. Fire Saf. J. **34**(4), 377–391 (2000). https://doi.org/10.1016/S0379-7112(00)00009-6

Smith-Jackson, T.L., Wogalter, M.S.: Potential uses of technology to communicate risk in manufacturing. Hum. Factors Ergon. Manuf. **14**(1), 1–14 (2004). https://doi.org/10.1002/hfm.v14:1

Tang, C.-H., Wu, W.-T., Lin, C.-Y.: Using virtual reality to determine how emergency signs facilitate way-finding. Appl. Ergon. **40**(4), 722–730 (2009). https://doi.org/10.1016/j.apergo.2008.06.009

Vilar, E.: Using Virtual Reality to Study the Influence of Environmental Variables to Enhance Wayfinding within Complex Buildings. University of Lisbon (2012)

Vilar, E., Duarte, E., Rebelo, F., Noriega, P., Vilar, E.: A pilot study using virtual reality to investigate the effects of emergency egress signs competing with environmental variables on route choices. In: Marcus, A. (ed.) DUXU 2014. LNCS, vol. 8519, pp. 369–377. Springer, Cham (2014a). https://doi.org/10.1007/978-3-319-07635-5_36

Vilar, E., Rebelo, F., Noriega, P.: Indoor human wayfinding performance using vertical and horizontal signage in virtual reality. Hum. Factors Ergon. Manuf. Service Ind. **24**(6), 601–615 (2014b). https://doi.org/10.1002/hfm.20503

Vilar, E., Rebelo, F., Noriega, P., Duarte, E., Mayhorn, C.B.: Effects of competing environmental variables and signage on route-choices in simulated everyday and emergency wayfinding situations. Ergonomics **57**(4), 511–524 (2014c). https://doi.org/10.1080/00140139.2014.895054

Vilar, E., Rebelo, F., Noriega, P., Teles, J., Mayhorn, C.: The influence of environmental features on route selection in an emergency situation. Appl. Ergon. **44**(4), 618–627 (2013). https://doi.org/10.1016/j.apergo.2012.12.002

Wickens, C.D., McCarley, J.S.: Applied Attention Theory. CRC Press (2008). https://www.crcpress.com/Applied-Attention-Theory/Wickens-McCarley/p/book/9780805859836

Wogalter, M.S.: Thnology will revolutionize warnings. In: Proceedings of the Solutions in Safety through Technology Symposium. American Society of Safety Engineers, Scottsdale (2006). http://www.safetyhumanfactors.org/wp-content/uploads/2011/12/294-Wogalter-2006.pdf

Wogalter, M.S., Conzola, V.C.: Using technology to facilitate the design and delivery of warnings. Int. J. Syst. Sci. **33**(6), 461–466 (2002). https://doi.org/10.1080/00207720210133651

Wogalter, M.S., Mayhorn, C.B.: Providing cognitive support with technology-based warning systems. Ergonomics **48**(5), 522–533 (2005). https://doi.org/10.1080/00140130400029258

Wogalter, M.S., Mayhorn, C.B.: The future of risk communication: technology-based warning systems. In: Wogalter, M.S. (ed.) Handbook of warnings, pp. 783–794. Lawrence Erlbaum Associates, Inc. (2006)

Xie, H., Filippidis, L., Galea, E.R., Blackshields, D., Lawrence, P.J.: Experimental analysis of the effectiveness of emergency signage and its implementation in evacuation simulation. Fire Mater. **36**(5–6), 367–382 (2012). https://doi.org/10.1002/fam.1095

Interactive Visualization of People's Daily

Xiaohui Wang[1(✉)], Jingyan Qin[1(✉)], and Dawei Li[2(✉)]

[1] School of Mechanical Engineering,
University of Science and Technology Beijing, Beijing, China
wangxh14@ustb.edu.cn, qinjingyanking@foxmail.com
[2] School of History and Civilization, Shaanxi Normal University, Xi'an, China
dw-li11@outlook.com

Abstract. As the number of documents grows larger and larger, it becomes more and more difficult for people to make sense of it all. People's Daily is the official newspaper of Chinese Communist Party Central Committee, which has a decisive guiding role for the Chinese mainland politics in different periods. In this paper, we develop an interactive visual analytic system to represent 1,365,802 documents of People's Daily from 1946 to 2003, in order to help analysts examine them more quickly and dig out potential information more efficiently. It is an easy-to-use system, which provides four distinct views of document visualization, including document view, calendar view, storyline view and query view. Besides, abundant human-centered interactions and text visualization techniques are adopted to improve user experiences. Experiments verify the usability of the system. Some discoveries about the change and development in Chinese society are found by using the system.

Keywords: Interaction · Text visualization · People's Daily
Data mining

1 Introduction

Information visualization is the study of transforming data, information and knowledge into interactive visual representations [1]. For large collection of data, information visualization is a good method for data overview and mining. The visualization system has been widely used in many fields, such as chemistry [2], engineering [3], public service [4].

People's Daily is the official newspaper of Chinese Communist Party (CCP) Central Committee. On July 1 in 1946, Chairman Mao personally wrote the Chinese headline for People's Daily. In 1992, People's Daily was named as one of the top ten newspapers in the world by UNESCO. As the mouthpiece of CCP and Chinese government, People's Daily does not only actively promote the policy advocacy of CCP and Chinese government and disseminate information in all fields at home and abroad, but also record the change and development in Chinese society. In addition to providing the outside world with direct information

© Springer International Publishing AG, part of Springer Nature 2018
A. Marcus and W. Wang (Eds.): DUXU 2018, LNCS 10919, pp. 389–400, 2018.
https://doi.org/10.1007/978-3-319-91803-7_29

about the CPC's policies and opinions, the editorial of People's Daily reflects the views of the CPC Central Committee on the handling of the incidents.

Because People's Daily has a decisive guiding role for the Chinese mainland politics in different periods, many political watchers at home and abroad usually go through the essays in People's Daily to find the true meaning of the CPC Central Committee's wishes and some of Chinese unique political messages. So in this paper, we download the documents of People's Daily from 1946 to 2003 and dig out more useful information about CCP, Chinese government and society through the visualization research.

The objective of our research is to build an interactive visual analytic system to help investigators better review, analyze, understand and explore data. The challenge is how to clearly show the huge document collection and effectively explore the data to find the insightful patterns. We design the system from four distinct perspectives, called views, including document view, calendar view, storyline view and query view. The four views cooperate to provide various analytic tasks in different levels of data, and combine with convenient interactions to offer a more easy-to-use tool. In these views, some text visualization techniques are adopted to the system, such as summarizing a single document, showing the words and topics, creating storylines.

The main contributions include:

- An interactive visual analytic system is developed to investigate the data of People's Daily from four distinct views. Human-centered interactions and text visualization techniques are appropriately adopted to increase the usability of the system and improve user experiences.
- Some discoveries about the change and development in Chinese society from 1946 to 2003 are found by using the proposed system.

The rest of the paper is organized as follows. Section 2 gives related work. Section 3 shows the data collection and processing. Section 4 describes the design of four visualization views in the system. Section 5 illustrates the experimental results. Section 6 finally draws the conclusions and future work planned for the system.

2 Related Work

2.1 Text Visualization

Text visualization techniques regarding their design goals can be largely divided into five categories: revealing content, exploring document corpus, visualizing document similarity, visualizing sentiments and emotions of the text, and analyzing various domain-specific rich-text corpus [5]. Visualizing the content of a text document, a few documents, and even hundreds of thousands of documents is essential for overview of large text data, which is one of the most important tasks in text visualization. From the different levels of details, showing content of documents can be from the following aspects: summarizing a single document, showing the words and topics, detecting events, and creating storylines [5]. Many studies on exploring document corpus are query-based techniques so that users can retrieve the data based on their interests [6].

In this paper, some of these visualization techniques are adopted for our proposed interactive system, such as summarizing a single document, showing the words and topics, creating storylines, query-based document exploring.

2.2 Interactive Visualization System

The interactive visualization system has been used to many different fields, such as chemistry [2], engineering [3]. A visual analytic system Jigsaw represents documents and their entities visually from multiple coordinated views [13]. Shi et al. presents an interactive visual system for exploring complex flow patterns of Public Bicycle System [4]. A system architecture called Reactive Vega provides the robust and comprehensive treatment of declarative visual and interaction design for data visualization [14].

In this paper, we present an interactive visual analytic system to explore the change and development in Chinese society from People's Daily data.

3   Data Collection and Processing

We download 1,365,802 documents in People's Daily from May 1946 to December 2003 from the website [7]. Each document is textual, in Chinese natural language, and in loose narrative format. News, stories and reports are the main types of the documents with a few paragraphs.

We organize these documents in Json files according to the published time, and each Json file uses published month as its name, such as '194605.json', includes all the documents published in this month. Each data item in the Json file contains four parts: url, title, published time and original content. There are 692 Json files in total.

The number of documents in each year is shown in Table 1. From the statistics, we can see that there are tens of thousands of documents a year on average. In other words, there are dozens of documents or more than a hundred documents a day on average. So the data is a very comprehensive source on historical events.

For Chinese texts, word segmentation is the first step for text analysis. We use Jieba (Chinese for 'to stutter') toolkit for Chinese text segmentation [8]. The algorithm is to generate a directed acyclic graph (DAG) composed of all possible Chinese words in the sentence, then by using the dynamic programming to find the maximum probability path to find the maximum segmentation based on word frequency combination. For unregistered words, an HMM model based model and Viterbi algorithm are built based on Chinese word formation.

Besides, the keywords are automatically extracted, and the documents to be extracted can be any combinations of the downloaded documents, such documents in one day or one year. The TF-IDF based keyword extraction algorithm [15] is adopted in this system.

Table 1. The number of documents in each year.

Year	#	Year	#	Year	#	Year	#	Year	#	Year	#
1946	5954	1956	23821	1966	12538	1976	12583	1986	34345	1996	38688
1947	10773	1957	25374	1967	9461	1977	12991	1987	33397	1997	35645
1948	8247	1958	28074	1968	9364	1978	13603	1988	34298	1998	35799
1949	19023	1959	23993	1969	10342	1979	17779	1989	31074	1999	36463
1950	20169	1960	23929	1970	11762	1980	27708	1990	32783	2000	36399
1951	14504	1961	22608	1971	10908	1981	28898	1991	34774	2001	37248
1952	13397	1962	17887	1972	14537	1982	28934	1992	38446	2002	36431
1953	12820	1963	16047	1973	15029	1983	31889	1993	37562	2003	44955
1954	14035	1964	17028	1974	12984	1984	32440	1994	35321		
1955	15659	1965	16724	1975	13543	1985	35024	1995	39791		

4 System Design and Implementation

4.1 Overview

The interactive visual analytic system is a web based system to represent documents visually in order to help analysts learn about the content more effectively. The system visualizes the data from different aspects through various distinct views as follows.

- **Document view.** Document view is a single document summarization. Users can select one document, the system gives the word cloud and keywords automatically extracted from the document.
- **Calendar view.** Calendar view presents a quick overview of documents in one year or one month.
- **Storyline view.** Storyline view demonstrates the keywords in time series to explore the process of the events.
- **Query view.** Query view provides a word-based document search function.

Specially, the four views focus on the data in different levels and cooperate to provide various analytic tasks. Convenient interactions are combined with these four perspectives to provide a more easy-to-use tool for obtaining a more comprehensive understanding of data. The detail for each view and interactions will be described in the following subsections.

4.2 Document View

The document view, shown in Fig. 1, is a single document summarization. There are four parts in the document view interface. The left part is the selection area, users select one day, then the document list shows all the documents published in that day. After users select one document, three visualization perspectives of

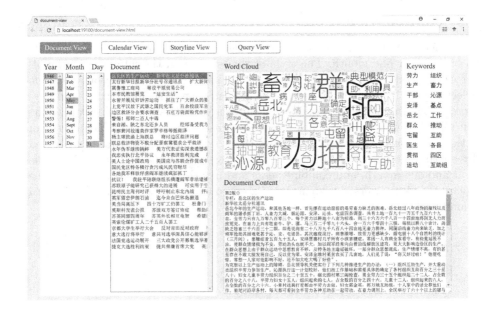

Fig. 1. The document view.

a document (word cloud, keywords and original content) are illustrated on the right parts.

Word cloud [9] is one of the most popular and intuitive techniques for word visualization, which shows a bag of words with different sizes and colors that summarize the content of the input document and packed together without any overlap. The higher the frequency of a word is, the larger its font size is. Color is used to distinguish different words for easy recognition. There are different types of word cloud based on various packing methods, such as Wordle [10], Radcloud [11]. In this paper, we use the word cloud toolkit [12], which is a little word cloud generator in Python. The input of the word cloud toolkit is the segmentation results by the Jieba toolkit [8].

The part of keywords provides a more intuitive view of the document. 20 Keywords are automatically extracted from the document content by the TF-IDF based keyword extraction algorithm [15].

The visualization results cannot replace the documents. If the users find the interests from Word Cloud and keywords, in most cases they want to read the original document content carefully to learn more about it. So we present the document content in the right corner.

In the word cloud part, users can zoom in or zoom out to review the details. If users hover over a keyword, all of this keyword in the original content are highlighted to give users an intuitive view.

4.3   Calendar View

The calendar view, illustrated in Fig. 2, presents a quick overview of documents in one year or one month. The style of the selector on the interface is a familiar calendar showing years and month. The users can click the year, then the selected year is highlighted and the right part shows the word cloud and keywords generated by all the documents in this year. Besides, if the year on the left selection area is double clicked, the month selector is shown. Then users can select one month, the right part shows the word cloud and keywords generated by all the documents in this month. Besides, users can select more than one year and one month, and combine years and months anyway. As same as in the document view, users can zoom in or zoom out to review the details in Word Cloud part.

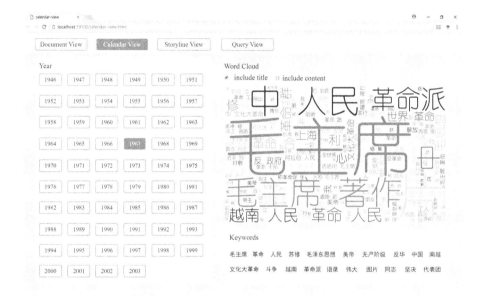

Fig. 2. The calendar view.

In Fig. 2, the year 1967 is selected, the word cloud and keywords are generated by all the documents published in 1967. The word 'Chairman Mao' is in the biggest size and also the top one keyword. Besides, from 'Zedong Mao', 'Revolutionaries' and 'the Great Proletarian Cultural Revolution' in Word Cloud and Keywords, we can infer to the ear of Great Proletarian Cultural Revolution in China. Chairman Mao got started the Great Proletarian Cultural Revolution from May, 1996 to October, 1976, which was the most volatile and disastrous stage in China. In People's Daily in 1967, the words 'Zedong Mao' and 'Revolutionaries' occurred frequently, which illustrated that the Great Proletarian Cultural Revolution becames the very important political event in China.

The calendar view provides a very quick and easy-to-understand method to find potential interests. To achieve this purpose, users can only choose by years and month as the unit in this view. If users are interested with keywords of one year or one month, they can jump to the document view to review the detail. Furthermore, if users want to customize any time period, the storyline view provides this function.

4.4 Storyline View

The document view and calendar view give the whole view for any time periods. Sometimes, users want to explore the process of the events. For this purpose, the storyline view is designed, shown in Fig. 3, which demonstrates the keywords in time series. Users can customize the time period and select the analytic target. The analytic target can be the title, the content or the both. This view supports different scales of keyword visualization, such as year, month or day. The users can zoom in or zoom out to switch to different scales. Under the time point in the storyline visualization, top 20 keywords extracted from the document titles or contents based on the selected analytic target in the given time period are shown.

One keyword can be selected by hovering over it, then the bottom box immediately shows all the document titles in which the analytic target contains the keyword. Users can double click the item in the bottom box, then the word cloud, the keywords and the original document content are popped up in a floating window. When the mouse clicks the storyline view window, the floating window disappears.

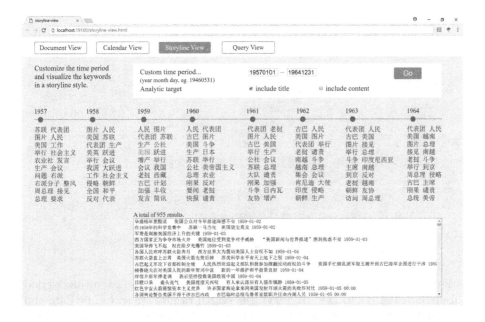

Fig. 3. The storyline view.

For example, in Fig. 3, the time period is set from Jan. 1, 1957 to Dec. 31, 1964. The analytic target only includes titles. The keywords of the eight years are shown in the storyline. The storyline results show the keywords by unit 'year' as the visualization scale first based on the selected time period and the space on the interface. Users can zoom in the storyline area to review the details. By hovering over the keyword 'United States' under the year 1959, there are a total of 955 documents which contain the keyword. The bottom box shows the titles and published dates of all the 955 documents.

4.5 Query View

The query view, shown in Fig. 4, provides a word-based document search function. The search options contain time period, sort type and search target. The time period can be anytime and custom range. Any time is from May 1946 to December 2003. The search results are sorted by relevance or by date specified by the sort type. The search target sets the search range, including titles or contents. The search result demonstrates the document title, the published date and part of the content. For each result, users can view the original document content by clicking the title whose font color is a little dark blue.

Fig. 4. The query view.

For example, in Fig. 4, the search item is 'Chairman Mao', the time period is from Jan. 1, 1947 to Dec. 31, 1954, the search results are sorted by date and the search target only includes titles. There are 1,557 search results, which are listed in the main area of the interface.

5   Experiments

In the experiments, we invited a few teachers and students in China School of History and Civilization to use the system. We just tell them the link of the system and let them to find the interest point. In addition to testing the functionality of the system, we want to test the ease use of the system, so we do not demonstrate the function and operations. Using the proposed system, many CCP and Chinese government policies toward the political, economy, culture and so on from 1946 to 2003 are found.

5.1   Case Study 1: Chinese Economic Policy Analysis

The first case is an example of Chinese economic policy analysis by using the document view of the visualization system.

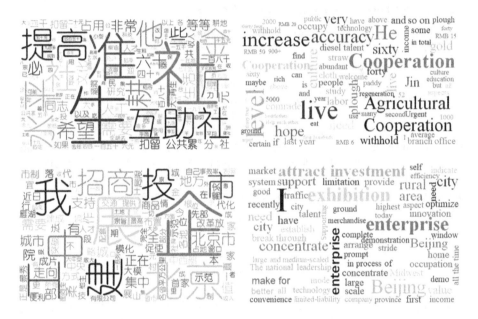

Fig. 5. The word clouds of two documents. The top one corresponds to the document published in Feb. 2, 1958. The bottom one corresponds to the document published in Nov. 26, 1992.

Two typical documents are chosen. The first one is 'new problems arising from the great leap forward in agricultural production' published in Feb. 2, 1958. The second one is 'the operation of the market mechanism to all parts of the country merchants' published in Nov. 26, 1992. The word clouds of the two documents are shown in Fig. 5.

From the top word cloud in Fig. 5, we find that the word 'Agricultural Cooperation' is the interest point. The Agricultural Cooperation from 1956 to 1958 was a part of Chinese socialist system of public ownership and the Planned Economy, in which agricultural lands, machines and other production materials belong to the agricultural collectives. Most of the Agricultural Unions profits is taken away by government. The personal consumption of farms are allocated according to his work.

From the bottom word cloud in Fig. 5, we find that there were many enterprises from the rural areas of China which sought to attract the capital investment in Beijing in 1992. This phenomenon tells us that the rural areas were included into the system of Socialist Market Economy at this time. But, in 1950 s there was not any enterprises in the rural areas, because CCP and Chinese government implemented the Agricultural Cooperation Policy and prohibited the Market Economy. So, we can see the changing of CCP and Chinese government in economic policies and the rural areas from 1950 s to 1990s by the two documents.

5.2 Case Study 2: Foreign Policy Analysis

The second case is an example of foreign policy analysis by using the storyline view.

From the storyline view, we find the keyword 'Suxiu' from January to December of 1969. Figure 6(a) is a screenshot of the storyline from January to September of 1969, users can zoom in and zoom out to switch to different visualization scales. 'Suxiu' literally is Soviet Revisionism, which refers to that Nikita Khrushchev criticized Stalins doctrine and put pressure on China in 1960 s after he became the Premier of the Soviet Union. Since then, the relationship between Soviet Union and China has deteriorated, and the Socialist Alliance has ruptured. So Soviet Union was called 'Suxiu' in People's Daily in 1960s, by which we can find the change of relationship between Soviet Union and China.

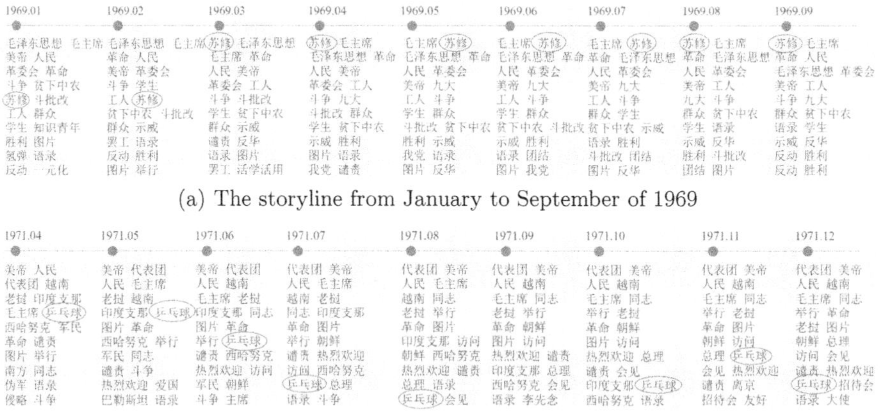

(a) The storyline from January to September of 1969

(b) The storyline from April to December of 1971

Fig. 6. The storylines.

From the storyline view shown in (b) of Fig. 6, we find the keyword 'Pingpong' from April to December in 1971. From April 10 to 17 in 1971, American Pingpong team was invited to China, which was the first official activity between America and China after the establishment of People's Republic of China and considered as symbol of ice breaker. After then, America and China have established the formal diplomatic relation. So we can find the important events of international relations and the change of international relations by the keywords in these storylines.

6   Conclusion

In this paper, we build an interactive visualization system for exploring the text data of People's Daily. First, we download 1,365,802 textural documents in People's Daily from May 1946 to December 2003. Then, we design the visualization system from different aspects through four distinct views. Convenient interactions are combined with these four perspectives to provide a more easy-to-use tool. Finally, experiments verify the usability of the system. By using the system, some history events about the change and development in Chinese society from 1946 to 2003 are shown clearly.

In the future research, more computational linguistics analysis techniques can be applied to the system. For example, the topics of the documents are automatically extracted and analysts can digest the development from different perspectives such as politics, economics, military and culture. Besides, the pictures in these documents can be collected and image processing techniques are adopted to enrich the analysis. All of the above are fruitful fields for future work.

Acknowledgment. This work was supported by the National Natural and Science Foundation of China (61602033), Science and Technology Plan Project of Beijing (Z171100001217009) and the Social Science Fund of Beijing (16YTC027). This work was also supported by the State Scholarship Fund of China.

References

1. Liu, S., Cui, W., Wu, Y., Liu, M.: A survey on information visualization: recent advances and challenges. Vis. Comput. **30**, 1373–1393 (2014)
2. Pettersen, E.F., Goddard, T.D., Huang, C.C., et al.: UCSF Chimera a visualization system for exploratory research and analysis. J. Comput. Chem. **25**(13), 1605–1612 (2004)
3. Upson, C., Faulhaber, T.A., Kamins, D., et al.: The application visualization system: a computational environment for scientific visualization. IEEE Comput. Graph. Appl. **9**(4), 30–42 (1989)
4. Shi, X., Yu, Z., Chen, J., Xu, H., Lin, F.: The visual analysis of flow pattern for public bicycle system. J. Vis. Lang. Comput. **45**, 51–60 (2018)
5. Cao, N., Cui, W.: Overview of text visualization techniques. Introduction to Text Visualization. ABAI, vol. 1, pp. 11–40. Atlantis Press, Paris (2016). https://doi.org/10.2991/978-94-6239-186-4_2

6. Kucher, K., Kerren, A.: Text visualization techniques: taxonomy, visual survey, and community insights. In: 2015 IEEE Pacific Visualization Symposium (PacificVis), Hangzhou, China, pp. 117–121 (2015)
7. People's Daily. http://paper.people.com.cn
8. Jieba: Chinese text segmentation toolkit. https://github.com/fxsjy/jieba/
9. Kaser, O., Lemire, D.: Tag-cloud drawing: algorithms for cloud visualization. arXiv preprint cs/0703109 (2007)
10. Viegas, F.B., Wattenberg, M., Feinberg, J.: Participatory visualization with wordle. IEEE Trans. Visual. Comput. Graph. **15**(6), 1137–1144 (2009)
11. Burch, M., Lohmann, S., Beck, F., Rodriguez, N., Di Silvestro, L., Weiskopf, D.: Radcloud: visualizing multiple texts with merged word clouds. In: 2014 18th IEEE International Conference on Information Visualisation (IV), pp. 108–113 (2014)
12. Word cloud toolkit. https://github.com/amueller/word_cloud
13. Stasko, J., Gorg, C., Liu, Z.: Jigsaw: supporting investigative analysis through interactive visualization. Inf. Visual. **7**, 118–132 (2008)
14. Satyanarayan, A., Russell, R., Hoffswell, J., Heer, J.: Reactive vega: a streaming dataflow architecture for declarative interactive visualization. IEEE Trans. Visual. Comput. Graph. **22**(1), 659–668 (2016)
15. Blei, D.M., Ng, A.Y., Jordan, M.I.: Latent Dirichlet allocation. J. Mach. Learn. Res. **3**, 993–1022 (2003)

Multimodal DUXU

Scanner for Visually Impaired People

Juan Felipe Almada$^{(\boxtimes)}$, Regina De Oliveira Heidrich,
and Ana Paula Steigleder

Universidade Feevale, Novo Hamburgo, Brazil
{juanfa, rheidrich, anapaulas}@feevale.br

Abstract. This project involves a multidisciplinary professional team from different areas of expertise such as Physics, Mathematics, Electronic Engineering, Computing, and Design. It aims to develop a desktop scanner that besides scanning a book or a document can also read texts aloud. The scanner will operate without being connected to any devices. This work is based on the Inclusive Design and User-Centered Design approaches. The Inclusive Design Toolkit was designed by a group of researchers from The Cambridge University Engineering Design Centre. The key design issues were solved through successive cycles of exploring needs, creating concepts, and evaluating options, guided by the project management, analyzed by the qualitative methodology of the study case. The diversity of users encompasses a range of capabilities, needs, and aspirations. The developed product allows the user to handle the scanner sitting on a chair, since the equipment will be placed on a desk, facilitating the performance of the task. As a result, the usability evaluation was presented in the software and product interface development. It is intended to present the development phases of the product to users who are visually impaired. Based on the studies presented in this article, the product is aimed to develop a simple, intuitive interface that allows blind and low vision users to easily access all the necessary resources needed to use the desk scanner.

Keywords: Inclusive design · Cognitive ergonomics · Interaction
Visual

1 Introduction

According to data from the 2010 Census, more than 35 million Brazilians present some type of visual impairment, with more than 6 million being totally blind or presenting severe difficulties to see, Oliveira [1].

This project involves a multidisciplinary professional team from different areas of expertise such as Physics, Mathematics, Electronic Engineering, Computing, and Design. It aims to develop a desktop scanner that apart from scanning a book or a document, can also read texts aloud. The scanner will operate without being connected to any devices.

Despite several initiatives by the Brazilian government to reduce the gap between disabled and non-disabled people, solutions to increase the autonomy of the visually impaired people and facilitate their access to information, entertainment, education, and

© Springer International Publishing AG, part of Springer Nature 2018
A. Marcus and W. Wang (Eds.): DUXU 2018, LNCS 10919, pp. 403–413, 2018.
https://doi.org/10.1007/978-3-319-91803-7_30

work are still lacking. Also according to the 2010 Census, almost half of Brazilians with 65 years or more - 49.8% - presented some degree of visual impairment (Oliveira, [1]).

The quality of life of the blind person is directly linked to the possibility of being able to promote the development of their individual potentialities. Therefore, the development of assistive technologies targeting this public becomes critical to enable their inclusion in the school setting. According to the ADA concept, Assistive Technology is defined as "a full range of equipment, services, strategies, and practices designed and applied to decrease the functional problems faced by individuals with disabilities" (Cook and Hussley [2]).

The Technical Assistance Committee - CAT1- of the Ministry of Science and Technology of Brazil approved and recognized, on December 14, 2007, the concept of Assistive Technologies. It is an interdisciplinary area of knowledge that encompasses products, resources, methodologies, strategies, practices, and services that aim to promote functionality, related to the activity and participation of people with disabilities or reduced mobility, targeting their autonomy, independence, quality of life, and social inclusion.

Assistive Technology is considered a broad concept and can be a key element in the promotion of Human Rights since it provides to disabled people the opportunity to achieve autonomy and independence in various aspects of their lives (Secretary of Human Rights of the Presidency of the Republic [3]).

Disability is the absence or diffusion of a psychic, physiological or anatomical structure. Physical disability causes a disadvantage, resulting from a commitment or disability, which limits or impedes the motor performance of a particular person (Fernandes et al. [4]). Radabaugh [5] defines: "For people without disabilities technology makes things easier. For people with disabilities, technology makes things possible".

2 Development

2.1 Visual Impairment

According to the World Health Organization (WHO/WHO), "blindness is the inability to see." The blind person lives in a world different from the world of the seer because he (she) is devoid of sight, light, and color. For Blanco [6], it is a world in which the information received by the other senses assumes a higher importance. Thus, blindness is defined, in a clinical (Bruno [7]) or legal sense (Lima et al. [8]), as visual acuity equal to or less than 0.05, with the best optical correction (Lima et al. [8]), and a visual field of less than 20° (Bruno [7], p. 7). In the educational sense, blindness is the total loss of sight, reaching the null projection of light (Bruno [7]; Blanco [6]) "or minimal residue of vision that leads the person to need the Braille system [or computers and their functionalities] as a means of reading and writing." (Lima et al. [8], p. 6).

According to Julião et al. [9] vision is responsible for providing information for the sensory organization, understanding the surrounding world, and giving meaning to objects, concepts, and ideas. Therefore, the loss of visual capacity implies the limitation of information and knowledge that favors motor development, perceptive, and emotional response, causing adversities to the individual and collective nature, affecting the quality of life, occupational restrictions, and self-esteem. These factors may also limit the exercise of citizenship.

In this way, Santos [10], points out that the universalism we want today is the one that seeks to provide human dignity. Taking this into account, the differences arise and must be respected. "We have the right to be equal when difference makes us inferior and the right to be different when equality mischaracterizes us. Hence the need for an equality that recognizes differences and a difference that does not produce, feed or reproduce inequalities." (Santos [10], p. 56).

2.2 Similar

The analysis of similar products to the one presented in this article was carried. Figure 1(a) shows the Scandock flatbed scanner, which does not need to be connected to a computer to be used. The structure of the product presents a light appearance and great handling convenience. The user must attach his smartphone to the scanner frame to capture the images. The document to be scanned must be inserted into the aluminum base of the product, which has a slope of three degrees. In the aluminum base, there is a silicone film, offering greater adherence to the document to be scanned and preventing folds. The two rods positioned on the sides, right and left, evenly distribute the light on the document to be scanned with eight small LED lamps being inserted in these rods in order to distribute the light needed for scanning. The maximum format for scanning is 22 × 31 cm. The materials used for the manufacturing of this product were aluminum and polymer, according Scandock [11].

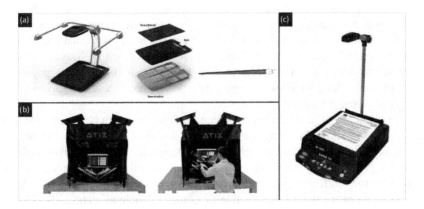

Fig. 1. Pictures of similar products. Source: Modified by Scandock; Atiz; Freedom Scientific [12].

Another scanner that was analyzed was the Book Drive Pro, by Atiz (Fig. 1b). It is a desktop scanner with a larger size (130 cm in height, 144 cm in width, and 138 cm in depth). This scanner needs to be connected to a computer to be used. One of its differentials is the V-shaped glass base, which according to the developers, solves the typical problem of curvature of books at the time of scanning, called The Warping. This glass attached to the open book at an angle of 120°, leaves its pages free of curvatures, thus facilitating their scanning. Two cameras are used for scanning, one for the right page and other for the left. The image capture is done at the same time for both pages, with up to 800 pages being captured per hour. The maximum format for scanning is 42 × 61.5 cm (ATIZ [12]).

The Sara CE, (Fig. 1c) by Freedom Scientific, is capable of automatically detecting when a new page is exposed to the camera. In order to perform voice read, this scanner needs to be connected to a computer. The keyboard is large, with tactile keys that are easy to memorize. This scanner is able to read up to 18 languages and presents other features such as increasing text size for low vision, changing the background color, adding more space between letters, etc. (Freedom Scientific [13]).

3   Materials and Methods

The present work used the case study methodology as the qualitative approach to analyze all the gathered information since this is a multifaceted in-depth investigation of a single social phenomenon. The case study is usually conducted in great detail and is often based on the use of various data sources (Feagin et al. [14]).

The qualitative research was carried out from a selection of data collection, based on the fragmentation and extraction of everything that might be useful to the analysis and always examining the value of each piece of information acquired through both the documental bibliographic research and the case study approach.

Regarding design, we have used the concepts of Inclusive Design and User-Centered Design. The British Standards Institute [15] defines inclusive design as "The design of mainstream products and/or services that are accessible to, and usable by, as many people as reasonably possible, without the need for special adaptation or specialized design". The inclusive design does not suggest that it is always possible (or appropriate) to design a new product to address the needs of the entire population. Instead, inclusive design guides an appropriate design response to the diversity presently found in the population.

The 'Design for all' and 'Universal design' philosophies both have the same literal meaning. These philosophies originated from the design of the built environment and websites. In the context of product design, both 'Design for all' and 'Universal design' approaches, pragmatically accept that it is not always possible for one product to meet the needs of the entire population. Nevertheless, these approaches maintain that all mainstream products should be accessible to as many people as technically possible.

The Inclusive Design defined by Clarkson et al. [16], is characterized by verifying and questioning the project decision in order to include or exclude people. The inclusive design underscores the importance of the contribution provided by the awareness of the diversity of users for the development of the project. It covers the range of abilities, needs, and aspirations of the users and seeks to reach as many people as possible, as shown in Fig. 2.

User observation is about uncovering what people really want, what they really need, and what they really do. Observing actual behavior is vital because people often

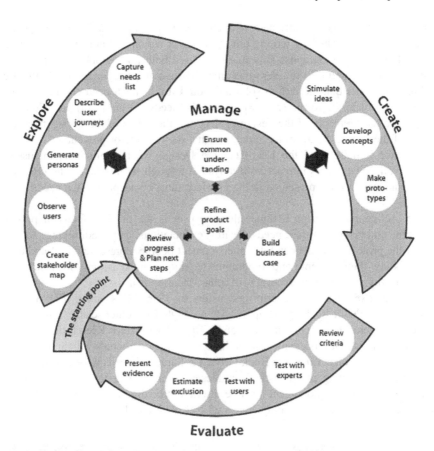

Fig. 2. Diagram of the inclusive design method. Source: Developed by Clarkson et al. [16].

struggle to clearly articulate their real needs because they have poor awareness of their own habits and practices, change what they say depending on what they think the interviewer wants to hear, and cannot imagine all the possible alternatives to the current situation. Focusing on the needs of the real user helps the design team to avoid overloading the product with every feature they want or think the users want. User observation helps with other exploring activities, as well as with refining the product goals. It should be complemented with other methods to uncover user needs, such as interviews, questionnaires, diary methods and focus groups. Anthropometric, ergonomic and capability data can also supplement user observation providing insight into the diversity of users.

A user journey is a step-by-step description of his(her) interaction with a product. It also describes what the user does immediately before and after using the product, as this provides some context for use. It should consider the purchase, initial use, getting support, and dealing with the end of the shelf life of the product, as well as the 'normal' product use. A user journey helps the design team to understand the user experience and helps to ensure that the needs list is complete.

User journeys should ideally be constructed by 'Observing users' (see above). The journeys can be described by writing down each user action and are further enhanced by the addition of photographs. This study has used both photographs and films.

A needs list is used here to refer to a comprehensive and categorized list of the user and business needs that the design solution should fulfill. Each need can be captured with a statement in the form. The purposes of the needs list are to (a) provide a link between the requirements of the design project and the needs of the users; (b) prioritization of the needs, based on the outcomes that they enable or prevent.

We have initially used the User-Centered Design when a blind person used a scanner with voice. Users interact with a system through its interface. The concepts, images, and terminology presented in the interface must be adapted to the needs of the user.

The user-centered design assumes that the user is the primary focus of product realization, and prioritizes their needs, desires, expectations, and conditioning. At each stage of the project, designers and designers consult people representative of end users to get to know them in depth and to combine technique and sensitivity for results that create empathy and identity, according Avellar, Duarte [17].

The user experience was performed using the Sara-PC scanner (Fig. 3). This scanner is 25 cm wide by 35 cm deep and 3.5 cm high. Like other scanners, it converts printed documents to voice using the 5645 Optical Character Recognition (OCR). Another feature is that this device also digitalizes Braille documents, which might later be converted into voice. Like Atiz Book Drive, the Sara - PC needs to be connected to a computer. Its operating mechanism resembles a common scanner, where the cover must be opened and the document must be inserted to be digitized for later conversion into voice. The size of the scanning area is 21.5×29.7 cm (Freedom Scientific [13]).

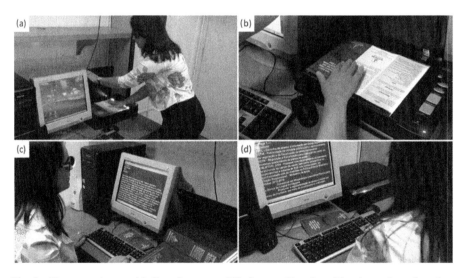

Fig. 3. User experience with Sara Scanner – PC. Source: Developed by the authors, based on the research performed (2016).

In Fig. 3(a) the user lifts the cover and inserts the document in the scanner. Before this, it was necessary to fit the device to locate the cover and buttons for the drive. Then, in Fig. 3(b), the user adjusts the document in the scanner tray. In both procedures, the previous skill of the user helped in the execution of the task, but an unprepared PCD would have difficulties to perform it. In Figs. 3(c) and (d), the user can be observed using the software that performs the text-to-speech conversion and scanning different materials, encyclopedia, and spiral, which present greater difficulty for the image capture performed by the device.

4   Results

The first prototype of a desktop scanner was crafted, based upon which the researchers involved in this project set the initial parameters for the development of the product. The prototype was divided into two parts, the base and the top (a). The top has a structure with two mirrors forming a 45° angle, providing the adequate support for the placement of the materials to be scanned avoiding the warping effect. The size of the top is X cm height, X width, and X cm depth. The dimensions of the base are 53.5 cm height, 80 cm width, and 56 cm depth, with doors on both sides to facilitate the handling of the internal equipment. Two LED plates (dimensions C x L) (amount of lumen) were placed inside the base (b) as the light source. These lights a "mirror bed", angulated in 45°, being therefore parallel to the top glass that will receive the images to be captured. In addition to that, there are two cameras that perform the image capture in a synchronized way, of the materials put under the top. Both the base and the top of the prototype were painted with black automotive paint to avoid light refraction providing, therefore, a proper setting for image capture.

This initial format allowed all angulation tests for the image capture to be performed. After the use of successful algorithms for better calculation, the team responsible for the design, ergonomics, and testing with users developed a new design (Fig. 4).

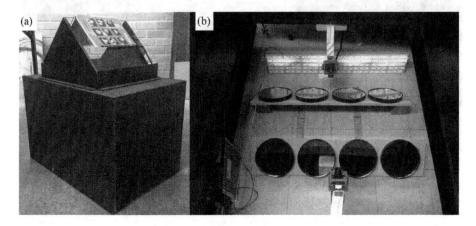

Fig. 4. Prototype. Source: Elaborated by the authors, based on the performed research (2017).

After the technical issues and the required parameters for the adequate image capture were solved, the process of developing the desktop scanner was started through the analysis of the similar products found in the market. The initial parameters for the process of creation and prototyping of the scanner were set. After performing a brainstorm with the team involved in the project, the initial ideas were represented through drawings. The product developed enables the user to handle the scanner seated in a chair, since the scanner will be placed over a desk, which will facilitate its operation. The user will remain seated during all the process since the support that will receive the book/document presents a slope of 10°, which allows the total control of the process. The defined rounded and organic shapes provide the project with a harmonic proposal that allows the user to "embrace" its structure enabling them to reach the buttons positioned in the right and left sides of the device (Fig. 5).

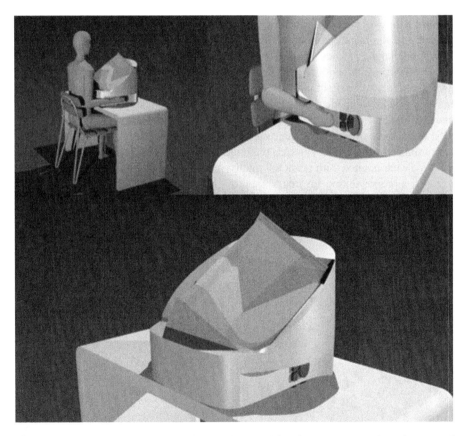

Fig. 5. New layout of the scanner. Source: Elaborated by the authors, based on the research performed (2017).

The top of the prototype is 50 cm wide, 31 cm high and 45.5 cm deep. The shape resembles a pyramid with a 45-degree angle. Two 42.7 × 33 cm glass slides were inserted at the top of the pyramid, which will have the function of accommodating the book or the material to be digitized. This format is suggested since it will likely eliminate the reading and scanning problems due to the spine bending, wire-o (binding type), and spirals that attach the sheets of these materials.

The team has also designed buttons with the functions on/off, enter, cancel, line, skip the line, and repeat line, all of them in Braille and with different textures. The buttons present simple and easily understandable forms following the regulations of the Associação Brasileira de Normas Técnicas, NBR 9050 that establishes the criteria and parameters for accessibility projects. The button design started from the creation of a grid through the Illustrator software. The grid refers to a set of lines and shapes used to

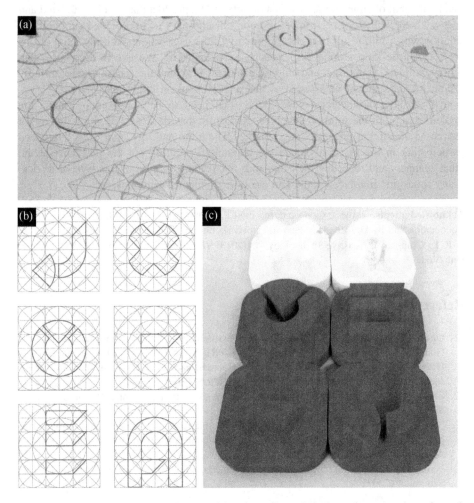

Fig. 6. Button details. Source: Elaborated by the authors, based on the research performed (2016)

sort and structure the graphic elements of a creation. According to Samara [18], the grids might be free, organic, and rigorous, introducing an order and facilitating the development of a layout. Tondreau [19], highlights that the grid maps a plan for the entire project. In this case, the grid served as a basis to create a family of buttons that were later printed in a 3D printer.

Several options of designs have been tried out (Fig. 6(a)). After analyzing their shapes and lines, one option of each button was selected to be vectorized using the Illustrator software, as shown in Fig. 6(b), and later modeled in the Rhinoceros software for 3D printing (Fig. 6(c)).

5   Conclusion

The final result obtained up to now is a prototype of a product that will be validated and later adapted. The work performed by a multidisciplinary team provided simplicity of solution which will result in higher autonomy to the user. The great differential of this project of a desktop scanner with speech is its low cost. We live in a country with serious political, economic, and cultural problems in which the access to education by disabled people should be assisted so that a true inclusion might take place.

This project has detected some points that need to be improved to enable the implementation of the solution developed and, from that, develop a proposal that might overcome the similar products in the market. The blind and low sight users have been participating in the proposals since the beginning, pointing out the problems of the other scanners and reporting their demands about the operation of this type of device. Many times this involves simple and easily implemented solutions.

Acknowledgments. Project sponsored by FINEP - Public Call CTI/SECIS/FINEP/FNDCT Cooperation and by Universidade Feevale, Novo Hamburgo, RS, Brazil.

ICT - Company - Assistive Technology - 01/2013. Vocalizer F2: Developing a Desk Scanner with Voice.

References

1. Oliveira, M.L.B.: Cartilha do Censo 2010 – Pessoas com Deficiência. Secretaria de Direitos Humanos da Presidência da República (SDH/PR)/ Secretaria Nacional de Promoção dos Direitos da Pessoa com Deficiência (SNPD)/ Coordenação-Geral do Sistema de Informações sobre a Pessoa com Deficiência; Brasília: SDH-PR/SNPD (2012)
2. Cook, A.M., Hussey, S.M.: Assistive Technologies: Principles and Practices. Mosby, St. Louis (1995)
3. Secretaria de Direitos Humanos da Presidência da Republica. http://www.pessoacomdeficiencia.gov.br/app/sites/default/files/publicacoes/livrotecnologiaassistiva.pdf. Accessed 10 Dec 2017
4. Fernandes, A.C., et al.: Medicina e Reabilitação: princípios e prática. Artes Médicas, São Paulo (2007)

5. Radabaugh, M. P.: Study on the Financing of Assistive Technology Devices of Services for Individuals with Disabilities -A report to the president and the Congress of the United State, National Council on Disability, Março (1993)
6. Blanco, M.A.N.: Deficiencia Visual. III Congreso la atención a la diversidade en el sistema educativo. http://campus.usal.es/~inico/actividades/actasuruguay2001/10.pdf. Accessed 10 Oct 2017
7. Bruno, M.M.G.: Deficiência Visual: reflexão sobre a prática pedagógica. Laramara, São Paulo (1997)
8. Lima, E.C., Nassif, M.C.M., Felippe, M.C.G.C.: Convivendo com a Baixa Visão: da criança à pessoa idosa. Fundação Dorina Nowill para Cegos, São Paulo (2007)
9. Julião, C.H., et al.: A deficiência visual e o processo de construção da cidadania: um estudo no Instituto de Cegos do Brasil Central de Uberaba. Revista Família, Ciclos de Vida e Saúde no Contexto Social (2013)
10. Santos, B.S.: Reconhecer para libertar: os caminhos do cosmopolitanismo multicultural. Introdução: para ampliar o cânone do reconhecimento, da diferença e da igualdade. Rio de Janeiro: Civilização Brasileira (2003)
11. Scandock. http://www.scandock.com. Accessed 12 May 2016
12. ATIZ: Book Drive Pro. http://pro.atiz.com. Accessed 13 May 2016
13. Freedom Scientific. Sara CE. http://www.freedomscientific.com/Content/Documents/ProductFlyers/SARA_CE_Flyer.pdf. Accessed 20 May 2016
14. Feagin, J., Orum, A., Sjoberg, G.: A Case for the Case Study. The University of North Carolina Press, Chapel Hill (1991)
15. British Standards Institute (2005) standard BS 7000-6:2005: 'Design management systems - Managing inclusive design - Guide' defines inclusive design and provides guidance on managing it. It can be purchased from the BSI website. Cetindamar, D., Phaal, R., Probert, D.: Understanding technology management as a dynamic capability: a framework for technology management activities. Technovation, **29**(4), 237–246 (2009)
16. Clarkson, P.J., et al.: Inclusive Design: Design for the Whole Population. Springer Science & Business Media, Heidelberg (2013)
17. Avellar e Duarte: Design Centrado no Usuário. http://www.avellareduarte.com.br/layout/design-centrado-no-usuario/. Accessed 11 June 2017
18. Samara, T.: Grids: construção e desconstrução. Tradução: Denise Bottmann. Cosac Naify, São Paulo (2007)
19. Tondreau, B.: Criar Grids: 100 fundamentos de layout. Tradução Luciano Cardinali. Editora Blucher, São Paulo (2009)

The Role of Dialogue User Data
in the Information Interaction Design
of Conversational Systems

Heloisa Candello$^{(\boxtimes)}$ and Claudio Pinhanez$^{(\boxtimes)}$

IBM Research, São Paulo, Brazil
{heloisacandello, csantosp}@br.ibm.com

Abstract. Designers face several challenges when designing information for conversational systems. In this paper, we discuss those challenges in the context of Information Interaction Design and the role of conversational data to address them. Using an actual study performed prior to the development of a financial chatbots adviser, we identified a set of common issues which led to 18 design recommendations. We categorize those recommendations according to the disciplines they are related (Information Design, Interaction Design, and Sensorial Design). The guidelines were employed by the actual developers of the system, simplifying considerably the development, and show the importance of actual user conversational data in the design process of conversational systems.

Keywords: Conversational interfaces · Dialogue systems · Chatbots
User experience

1 Introduction

The rapid progress of natural language processing in the recent years, fueled by notable advances in Artificial Intelligence and Neural Networks, made the construction and deployment of conversational systems and machines not only possible, but a reality on the fingertip of any smartphone user. However, understanding how to design compelling and useful experiences for such systems is still in its infancy, with very limited theoretical frameworks to support it. In this paper, we explore some of those design issues under the perspective of Information Design.

Information design investigates the organization and presentation of data to result in meaningful information. Shedroff [19] claims that while Information Design primarily focuses on the representation of data and its presentation, the emphasis in Interaction Design is on the creation of compelling experiences. Those experiences are shaped by people perceptions in context, making the sensorial design also a valuable topic of tailoring people's communication. *Information Interaction Design* is the intersection of the disciplines of Information Design, Interaction Design and Sensorial Design [19]. Those three disciplines are essential to design compelling user experiences with conversational systems. We expect that conversational interface design also may benefit from the intersection of those disciplines.

© Springer International Publishing AG, part of Springer Nature 2018
A. Marcus and W. Wang (Eds.): DUXU 2018, LNCS 10919, pp. 414–426, 2018.
https://doi.org/10.1007/978-3-319-91803-7_31

We define conversational interfaces as computational systems which interact with humans through dialogues. Such machines or systems are known by various names such as virtual personal assistants, intelligent assistants, chatbots, and cognitive advisers. There are two primary types of conversational interfaces, the ones where the user input is through audio and the ones where it is via text.

In this work, we focus on the challenges of designing interactive information for text-based conversational systems. First, we show technical challenges and unveil how conversational systems are usually built. Then, we discuss the design of the verbal messages supported by users studies and data collected before the development of prototypes of the actual system. We show that the user data highlights issues and not only provide design recommendations for conversational interfaces creators but also structures the programming of such systems. The challenges we present here are tailored by the three disciplines: Information Design, Interaction Design and, Sensorial Design. We consider essential those perspectives to shape effective conversational experiences with conversational machines (Fig. 1).

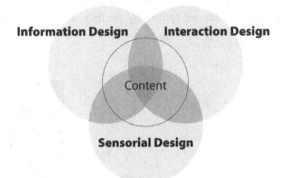

Fig. 1. Information Interaction Design. [19] illustrates the combination of the three categories that compose Interface Design. Illustration source [19].

2   Technical Limitations in the Design of Conversational Systems

Information interactive design for current conversational systems presents many challenges. Challenges such as bots being too responsive, not understanding utterances, lack of personality consistency, and giving too many options in the form of buttons for users are some of the issues affecting negatively the user experience. Some of those challenges are connected to the limitations and particularities of the technology currently employed. In most cases, the information flow of chatbots is tailored manually by developers using framework tools which structure the conversation quite rigidly. Those frameworks are used by designers and developers to build the content and structure of a possible conversation in detail, often using rule-based paradigms. Examples of commercial conversational frameworks and API platforms are Facebook's *wit.ai*, *IBM's Watson Conversational Services*, *Microsoft's LUIS*, *Amazon's Lex*, *Google's Conversation APIs*, and as well as an increasing number of systems provided by startups.

In many ways, the technology behind most of today's commercial deployments is not too different from the one used by the early chatbots [24]. But the first key dimension in differentiating capabilities of different technologies and platforms refers to whether the dialogue is driven by the user, known as *user-initiative*, by the computer, known as *system-initiative*, or by both, or *mixed-initiative* [27]. It is therefore essential that the needs of the application and the interface, regarding the initiative, match the capabilities of the platform.

But independently of whether the user or the system has the initiative, most conversational systems today are built using an *intent-action* approach. The system is created by defining a basic set of user and the systems utterances and how they should match to each other. In user-initiative systems (for example, typical Q&A systems), groups of questions from the user are mapped into a single answer from the systems, sometimes with some variations. The term *intent* is used to describe the goal of the group of questions, so the basic task of the conversational platform is to identify the intent of a given question written or spoken by the user, and then output its associated answer or *action* (Fig. 2).

Fig. 2. An example of template-based system. IBM Watson Conversation Service. Designers of chatbots create a list of user intents, which are associated with an answer. Nowadays, designers may test the intent matching in real time and fix any possible discrepancy.

In system-initiative systems, the designers and developers of the conversational system have to provide sets of typical user answers for each question the system is going to make. Based on the *intent* of the answer of the user, an *action* is often produced with the help of primary natural language parsing technology to help extract by the system needed information such as numbers, choices, etc. Notice that in both cases, as well as in mixed-initiative systems, the users' utterances always have to go through a process of matching with a set of available examples (often mistakenly called as "intents") for that context. The *intent matching* is often the most important source of problems in the development of conversational systems, due to the complexity and difficulty of analyzing natural language.

Many different technologies and platforms can be used for intent matching. A conventional approach is to use *template-based* systems in which the intent is determined by the presence of manually defined terms or groups of words in the user utterance. When the template matches the utterance, the associated intent is identified. Template-based systems, although often the simplest way to start developing a conversational system, suffer from two critical problems. First, it is hard to capture in simple templates the many nuances of human language. Second, as the number of templates increases, typically beyond one hundred or more, it becomes complicated to track the source of errors and debug the system successfully.

An alternative approach which is gaining increasing popularity is to use *machine learning-based* intent recognizers. In this approach, the conversational system developers provide a set of examples in natural language for each intent and use machine learning (ML) techniques to train an automatic classifier that is used in the run-time. Different types of classifiers can be used, such as *Bayesian networks, support vector machines (SVM),* and the currently popular *deep neural networks (DNN).* The main differences, advantages, and properties of those technologies are beyond the scope of this paper. Suffice to say that often the critical element of success when using machine-learning based intent recognizers is the quality and comprehensiveness of the data set provided to the ML classifier. Designers should not underestimate the importance of the often time-consuming task of collecting and organizing the training dataset.

An alternative method of creating conversational systems, still in the research stage, bypasses the definition of the intent-action sets and uses a large corpus of real dialogues to learn from the scratch how the conversation system should behave [21, 18, 25]. Notice that some of those works use corpora with hundreds of millions of conversations samples, or, conversely, very narrow domains, so this is an approach can only be applied with current technology to particular cases which meet those constraints.

Most of the communication expressions between conversational machines and humans consist of words and statements verbalized or in written mode. Conversational systems, popularly named chatbots, are in their essence verbal-based and supported by visual elements such as emoticons, pictures, and sometimes even action buttons. Most often than not, each chatbot's response is manually created by the designer or developer. They face an array of challenges not only to design of the conversational verbo-visual elements which reflect the personalized expression of the machine but also how to do this while obeying the constraints of the implemented algorithms and classifiers and handling the on-the-fly identification of context and user intentions. Understanding how those platforms work help and limit designers to create the conversation flow is important, since in practice the generated conversations are characterized by "moment-by-moment management of the distribution of turns" [22].

Those are some of the central concerns designers should keep in mind to battle the very common problem of conversation breakdowns. Conversational systems built using intent-action rules have, by the way they are built, clear limits on their ability complex dialogues and utterances beyond the programmed scope. On the one hand, humans are experts to understand implicit interactions in a certain domain while machines struggle to keep up with it [9]. Ideally, understanding the conversation context and real-world knowledge should be part of chatbots repertories, but the reality of today's technology is that most conversational systems are very limited and easily broken. This challenge is even more prominent when more than one bot and a person is part of the same conversation. Turning-taking and governance of the conversation are vital elements to group conversation flows, and the same might be true when machines take part in group conversations. General rules have been created by designers and developers to guide chatbots behavior inspired by human conversation social rules [16, 7, 17], but they are still quite limited.

In the rest of the paper we discuss how some of those design challenges can be more effectively tackled with the help of collecting user conversational data before the system is developed. Based on the utterances and patterns detected, it is possible to simplify the design and deployment process considerably. Notice that performing user studies prior to system's development is a practice rarely used in the field.

3   User Data as the Design Guide of a Conversation System

Collecting natural human conversation data to understand the conversation dynamics is a way to build machines which reflect what users expect. Conversation logs can be used as a resource to simulate conversations and can be grounded in fieldwork studies. Although the main concentration of bot expression is textual, it is paramount to understand contextual clues (voice tone, facial expressions, environmental sounds, and utterances) which are only able to be collected in the field. As humans, the context where those conversations are situated matter and the actors in the same discussion affect the way people react with information. Enriching user studies with video and semi-structured interviews help to understand why specific questions were made to machines. Several design activities may help on collecting user data to understand the dynamic of the conversation. Some techniques such as *Wizard of Oz* technique [1, 3, 12, 13, 26], *Roleplaying* [8, 15, 23], and *Magic thing* [5, 9] may assist designers in investigating user interaction with conversational systems.

In this section, we describe a Wizard of Oz study which highlighted important challenges for designers to consider. Based on this study we exemplify challenges related to specific user issues and in the next section provide some design recommendations for overcoming those.

This study belongs to a series of user studies [1] with potential users with the limited financial knowledge. Those studies belong to a wealth management project where multiple chatbots are governed to provide investment advice to users. [2].

We conducted a Wizard of Oz study to understand human-machine conversation patterns, to map typical user's reactions to financial assistant answers, and to collect data with real user questions to build the first system corpus. Fifteen participants were invited to test a "the first version" of an intelligent financial adviser dialogue which could answer questions related to two kinds of investments: savings accounts and a fixed-income investment called CDB (Bank Deposit Certificate). Following a typical Wizard of OZ protocol, the participants believed they were interacting with a functional system. The participants were remote and each session took approximately 30 min. The main data gathered were notes and audio and video recordings (screen captures). Participants were young adults (26 to 43 years old), highly educated and high-income bracket. All the participants described themselves as not interested or not keen on finances, particularly investments. All the participants answered positively to the consent form document, allowing us to use the data gathered.

3.1 Procedure

Participants were recruited by a snowball sampling and invited to be part of the remote study. The sessions started with demographic questions and questions of their financial investment experiences. Following that, they shared their screen with the researcher and started interacting with the chat mock up, the supposed Intelligent Financial adviser (Fig. 3).

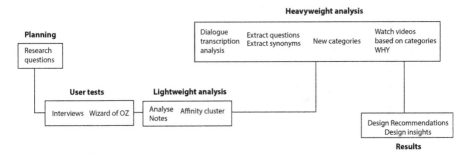

Fig. 3. Experiment procedures.

A human operator, who was not the same as the researcher facilitating the user session, answered their questions using a protocol. The human operator used a small table of content to answer the questions. The table was composed of 36 small paragraphs extracted from popular financial websites. The content relied on investment definitions, pros (return) and cons (risk) of two types of investments. Every table cell had a label (e.g. interest, safety, minimum value) to help the operator find the questions quickly during the sessions. The human operator could use sample answers in case she did not have an answer (*1. I don't know; 2. Ask again please; 3. I don't have enough information*). In the end of the session, the facilitator asked the participants to give their impressions about the system and disclosed the true identity of the intelligent system.

3.2 Data Gathering and Analysis

Lightweight and heavyweight analyses were the approaches to analyze the data [6]. The lightweight analysis consisted in an affinity cluster extracted from notes and offered guidelines for the main categories to look for in the audio transcriptions. The main categories emerged from the data were: User reactions; Investment questions; Improvements; Technical issues; Communication issues; Conversation flow breakdowns. In the heavyweight analysis, the *Nvivo* software was used to analyze the data. Notes, chat transcriptions and videos were analyzed. Categories from the affinity cluster phase were used as a base to analyze chat transcriptions and video transcriptions. Videos were mainly a source for understanding why people asked some questions to the financial adviser, allowing us to investigate how users structured their interaction during the study. For example, sometimes people repeated a question, or rephrased a question before writing the question and not always they typed what they wanted to know. Some reactions and contextual information were only possible to gather from watching some sessions again (Fig. 4).

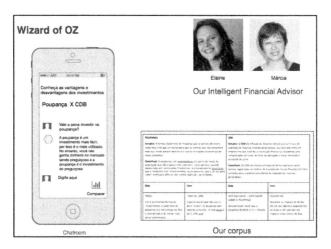

Fig. 4. This figure illustrates the components of a Wizard of Oz technique applied to collect user questions in the finance context. A chatroom environment, two researchers simulated the agent and a preliminary corpus in the table. Researchers simulated the agent and only used the content of the table to answer users.

3.3   Findings

In a previous paper [1], we described shortly the design process and how the results of this experiment impacted the development team. Here we present the main findings uncovered by this study which show typical issues designers of chatbots face. We classify those findings into 5 main categories, illustrating typical results obtaining from running user studies before system development starts. Those categories guided the elaboration of design recommendations, discussed in the next section, which were used by the development team for the actual construction of the conversational system.

Question Categories and Intent Definition. The study highlighted the main topics and questions potential users expected to be answered by a conversational investment adviser. The questions collected were organized in topics and illustrated by a visual taxonomy for each investment type (Fig. 5). Emerged topics from the study helped classifiers to recognize the user questions grouped into user intents and connect suitable answers to user intents. Overall 125 questions were gathered which provided the first corpus for the financial adviser (see examples in Table 1).

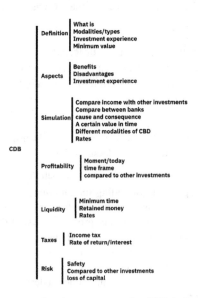

Fig. 5. Example of a taxonomy for CDB investment.

Essential Non-answered User Questions. It was also possible to detect information which participants expected from the system. Essential information not answered relied on participants asking for real-time value investment calculation; meanings of acronyms; a comparison between investments; and the system not answering questions about itself: *(P8) If it was you, which investment would you invest? (P5) Did you understand my question?* and generic questions such as *(P7) What is the best choice for investment?* Rarely participants asked out of scope questions; it might be because of the presence of a researcher facilitator observing their interactions.

User Perceptions of the Nature of the Chatbot Expression. The set of questions used by the human operator in the experiment had a neutral tone, which helped to identify in which degree participants expected the system biased the answers. Several participants verbalized their concern on how to communicate with this machine. Should it be formal or informal tone the questions? Should it understand acronyms of not? Should it understand punctuation? Showing transparence of how to communicate was essential for participants. It might be that some of the participants' concerns could be minimized by personalizing the chatbot answers, for example the tone of the utterances.

Identification of Context-Free and Contextual Issues. While performing the lightweight and heavyweight analysis we noticed issues that were connected to investment decisions and content specific and other context-free issues. We defined context-free

Table 1. Examples of categories and questions extracted from the study.

Categories	Sample question
Definition	What are the types of CDB?
Advantages and disadvantages	What are the advantages to invest on CDB?

conversation what might be extracted as ordered phenomena from conversational materials which would not turn out to require reference to one or another aspect of situatedness, identities, particularities of content, or context. [16]. Both types of issues are described in Tables 2 and 3.

Table 2. Context-free design recommendations classified by aspects of Information Design (ID), Interactive Design (IXD) and Sensorial Design (SD).

	Context-free - Information Interaction design recommendations
01	**The system cannot appear to be hiding information.** (ID) Participants felt the system showed what it knows by short pieces of textual information, and they wanted a complete information (pros and cons) to decide
02	**The system must be prepared to be tested. Repeated questions may have a more complete answer and new information.** (SD) Participants asked repeatedly for more information because they were not satisfied with the first answer, some thought the system did not understand them, others because they want to test the system.
03	**The system could help users to ask new questions.** (IXD) Participants did not know if the machine would understand them, they had trouble formulating sentences. Others did not have a basic knowledge of investments that would give ideas of what to ask.
04	**Basic information is expected.** (ID)(SD) Participants expect the system to know what they know at least.
05	**The system must engage the participant in the conversation**. (SD) (IXD) After moments of silence, or after the system answers a question not always the users kept asking. If the system asks: *Any more questions?* – and repeats prompt phrases of engagement, it would improve the flow of the conversation
06	**The system should identify the context of the question.** (IXD) (SD) Participants did not always include the name of the investment in the question, especially when the previous questions were related to an investment
07	**People expect the system to respond as a person even knowing that it is not a person** (SD) Questions allocated to the system were not answered to participants. The system reacted as *I don't have enough information*
08	**The system should introduce itself as being a machine**. (ID) (IXD) Participants were informed that they were talking to a machine by the researcher. Participants verbalized many concerns of how the system understand utterances and punctuations
09	**Consider the ambiguity of words.** (ID) (SD) Words may have double meanings. For example: rate is related to profitability rates or interest rates

Table 3. Contextual design recommendations classified by aspects of Information Design (ID), Interactive Design (IXD) and Sensorial Design (SD).

	Contextual (Finance) - Information Interaction design recommendations
10	**Showing evidence of real time value calculation** (IXD) (SD) Only four participants did not ask the system for a simulation with numbers
11	**Savings account should be used as a baseline for comparison.** (SD)(ID) (IXD) Participants had previous experience with Savings accounts, and often asked for comparing Savings to other investments
12	**The system should provide better information than bank managers.** (SD)(ID) People do not like to ask managers and often do not understand what the manager is talking about
13	**The system should have a visualization to compare the data.** (ID) Participants felt lack of visual presentations and tables to compare investments
14	**The system should give priority or weight to information related to loss.** (SD) Participants find more decisive the information that showed how much money will be lost than other kind of information such as: Minimum Application or Income

Reflections on Verbal Design Interaction. From the design activity, several reflections on how to conduct the next stage of the design emerged. Those are displayed as self-reflection questions: (a) What could be strategies to open spacesfor collaboration between man-machine in the decision making? (b) How a chatbots using text expression can help people to ask what they really want to ask? (we often saw that participants in the experiment rephrased or changed the questions verbalized to the researcher before typing); (c) How to better present and compare investments using dialogue?

4 Recommendations for Design of the Conversational System

Eighteen (19) design recommendations emerged from this study. Those were classified by strength of confidence and evidence accompanied by issues that occurred in the experiment. This rating scale was inspired by the scale applied in [20] work. The list of design recommendations accompanied by correlated issues and strengths was made available for the development team as an internal wiki page.

The recommendations were rated according to the level of confidence and organized into two groups: *Context-free* (Table 2) and *Contextual Design* (Table 3) recommendations. The Information Interaction Design recommendations are described in bold, followed by user issues observed in the study. Fourteen design recommendations for conversational interfaces were classified by aspects of three disciplines: Information Design (ID), Interactive Design (IXD) and Sensorial Design (SD).

We also classified each recommendation accordingly by the perspective of our collected data from the experiment participants. For instance, Sensorial aspects were classified in respect to verbalized participant feelings - expectation, frustration, confusion, satisfaction [19]. Information design aspects were the ones considering organization, presentation and/or text structure [14]. Interaction design aspects were concerned of action, control, feedback, learning, balancing, engagement and conversing [4]. Some of the issues and recommendation fall into more than one of those three disciplines.

Context-free design recommendations posts challenges for Information designers, claiming legibility and transparence of information (01); literacy (04); personalization (08) and understanding (09). From the Interaction design perspective engagement with the system (03, 05), contextual reference (06), and interaction actions (02, 08). Participants also shaped their interaction in sensorial ways felling compelling to repeat their questions when not satisfied with answers or not felt understood by the system (02, 09). Expectation of machine-like behavior and lack of engagement were identified as important issues to considerate too. (05, 07). We expect that those design recommendations be useful for other intelligent conversational advisers in other areas.

Information Interaction design recommendations for similar financial advisers rely all 5 into the aspects of Sensorial design. (10, 11, 12, 13) were connected to expectations and previous experiences with financial products or bank manages. Moreover, the user sense of comparison with well-known investments, such as Savings, may assist to shape trust and reliability on this context. The last recommendation (14) is also supported by the loss aversion element present in the Prospect Theory [11]. The participants need and expectation for real time simulation and comparison of the investments influenced on the interaction design experience (10). Information designers should consider how to shape utterances based on previous user knowledge and experience (11, 12), with the aim of effectiveness and clarity of information. Visualizations and pictures are supported by conversational systems nowadays and are more suitable representations for comparing data than text (13).

5   Final Remarks

In this paper, we described technical and information interaction design challenges to create conversational interfaces and how using conversational data collected from users can help designers to face them. We exemplify with data captured from an experiment with real users which enriched and gave strength to design recommendations used by a development team of a conversational financial adviser. Fourteen design recommendations pointed out issues designers of conversational systems should consider also in other contexts. The lens provided by the three disciplines Information Design, Interaction Design and Sensorial design helped to shape and unveil our findings. We hope other designers may benefit from this study and apply the Information Interaction Design recommendations described here on similar conversational projects.

References

1. Candello, H., Pinhanez, C., Millen, D., Andrade, B.D.: Shaping the experience of a cognitive investment adviser. In: Marcus, A., Wang, W. (eds.) DUXU 2017. LNCS, vol. 10290, pp. 594–613. Springer, Cham (2017). https://doi.org/10.1007/978-3-319-58640-3_43
2. de Bayser, M.G., Cavalin, P., Souza, R., Braz, A., Candello, H., Pinhanez, C., Briot, J.-P.: A Hybrid Architecture for Multi-Party Conversational Systems. arXiv:1705.01214 [cs] (2017)
3. Dow, S.P., Mehta, M., MacIntyre, B., Mateas, M.: Eliza meets the Wizard-of-Oz: blending machine and human control of embodied characters. In: Proceedings of the SIGCHI Conference on Human Factors in Computing Systems, pp. 547–556. ACM (2010)
4. Dubberly, H., Pangaro, P., Haque, U.: ON MODELING What is interaction?: are there different types? Interactions **16**, 69–75 (2009)
5. Forlizzi, J., Battarbee, K.: Understanding experience in interactive systems. In: Proceedings of the 5th Conference on Designing Interactive Systems: Processes, Practices, Methods, and Techniques, pp. 261–268. ACM, Cambridge (2004)
6. Goodman, E., Kuniavsky, M., Moed, A.: Observing the User Experience: A Practitioner's Guide to User Research. Elsevier, Waltham (2012)
7. Grice, H.P.: Logic and Conversation, pp. 41–58 (1975)
8. Iacucci, G., Iacucci, C., Kuutti, K.: Imagining and experiencing in design, the role of performances. In: Proceedings of the Second Nordic Conference on Human-Computer Interaction. pp. 167–176. ACM, Aarhus (2002)
9. Iacucci, G., Kuutti, K., Ranta, M.: On the move with a magic thing: role playing in concept design of mobile services and devices. In: Proceedings of the 3rd Conference on Designing Interactive Systems: Processes, Practices, Methods, and Techniques, pp. 193–202. ACM (2000)
10. Ju, W.: The design of implicit interactions. Synth. Lect. Hum. Centered Inform. **8**, 1–93 (2015)
11. Kahneman, D.: Thinking, Fast and Slow. Macmillan (2011)
12. Kerly, A., Bull, S.: The potential for chatbots in negotiated learner modelling: a Wizard-of-Oz study. In: Ikeda, M., Ashley, Kevin D., Chan, T.-W. (eds.) ITS 2006. LNCS, vol. 4053, pp. 443–452. Springer, Heidelberg (2006). https://doi.org/10.1007/11774303_44
13. Martelaro, N., Ju, W.: WoZ way: enabling real-time remote interaction prototyping & observation in on-road vehicles. In: Proceedings of the 2017 ACM Conference on Computer Supported Cooperative Work and Social Computing, pp. 169–182. ACM, New York (2017)
14. Pettersson, R.: Information design theories. J. Vis. Literacy **33**, 1–96 (2014)
15. Pinhanez, C.: Computer Interfaces to Organizations: Perspectives on Borg-Human Interaction Design. arXiv:1712.03012 [cs] (2017)
16. Sacks, H., Schegloff, E.A., Jefferson, G.: A simplest systematics for the organization of turn-taking for conversation. Language **50**, 696–735 (1974)
17. Searle, J.R.: Speech Acts: An Essay in the Philosophy of Language. Cambridge University Press, Cambridge (1969)
18. Serban, I. V. S., Sordoni, A., Bengio, Y., Courville, A., Pineau, J.: Building end-to-end dialogue systems using generative hierarchical neural network models. In: Proceedings of the 30th AAAI Conference on Artificial Intelligence (AAAI-2016) (2016)
19. Shedroff, N.: Information Interaction Design: A Unified Field Theory of Design. Information Design. MIT Press, Cambridge (2000)
20. Shneiderman, B., Leavitt, M.: Research-Based Web Design and Usability Guidelines. Department of Health and Human Services, Washington, D.C. (2006)

21. Sordoni, A., Galley, M., Auli, M., Brockett, C., Ji, Y., Mitchell, M., Nie, J.-Y., Gao, J., Dolan, B.: A neural network approach to context-sensitive generation of conversational responses. In: Proceedings of Human Language Technologies: The 2015 Annual Conference of the North American Chapter of the ACL (2015)
22. Suchman, L.: Human-Machine Reconfigurations: Plans and Situated Actions. Cambridge University Press, New York (2007)
23. Wagner, G.: Exploratory and Participatory Simulation. In: Proceedings of the 2013 Winter Simulation Conference: Simulation: Making Decisions in a Complex World. pp. 1327–1334. IEEE Press, Piscataway (2013)
24. Weizenbaum, J.: ELIZA—a computer program for the study of natural language communication between man and machine. Commun. ACM **9**, 36–45 (1966)
25. Weston, J. Dialog-based Language Learning. arXiv preprint arXiv:1604.06045 (2016)
26. Yu, Z., Nicolich-Henkin, L., Black, A.W., Rudnicky, A.: A Wizard-of-Oz study on a non-task-oriented dialog systems that reacts to user engagement. In: Proceedings of the 17th Annual Meeting of the Special Interest Group on Discourse and Dialogue, pp. 55–63 (2016)
27. Zue, V.W., Glass, J.R.: Conversational interfaces: advances and challenges. Proc. IEEE **88**, 1166–1180 (2000)

User Interaction for Guided Learning Supporting Object Recognition in Service Robots

Jan Dornig, Yunjing Zhao, and Xiaohua Sun[✉]

College of Design and Innovation, Tongji University, Shanghai, China
jandornig@gmail.com, ginzhao@foxmail.com,
xsun@tongji.edu.cn

Abstract. Under current technical conditions, robots often have difficulties or make errors in object recognition due to the complexity of the scene or the particularity of the object to be recognized. It is necessary for users to provide input or guided training for the robot during the recognition process. However, most of the input methods commonly used by researchers, is limited to using mouse and keyboard to mark outer and inner edges of the object on the screen. We introduce in this paper a survey of possible actions and input methods for designing human robot interactions supporting guided learning in object recognition. Specifically, we analyzed key factors and procedures in analyzing typical object recognition and proposed human robot interaction methods appropriate for each type of obstacle.

Keywords: Human robot interaction · Interaction design · Guided learning
Object recognition

1 Introduction

Object recognition plays a key role in the functioning of service robots, enabling the robots to perceive and interact with its surroundings. Research in object recognition of robots has seen rapid progress in recent years. Methods such as RGB/RGBD semantic segmentation [1] and SLAM [2] have been developed and widely tested in laboratory and real-life conditions. However, these methods often require manual labeling of large pre-defined datasets, which differs from the case of service robot's actual environment of use. The layout and content of such environments are mostly unknown, with many objects not covered by the dataset. Moreover, the complexity of the environments also poses a problem for effective object recognition in real-life scenarios.

One method currently used to overcome this problem is to adopt guided learning techniques- preparing a robot to receive additional, ongoing input from humans at a later stage during use. This method has been proven to be effective by extended research under laboratory conditions, but there are still problems hindering its real-world application and we have to differentiate between how end-users will interact with a robot and a situation that is fully controlled by researchers in a lab. The actual users of the robot lack the expertise and experience in utilizing complex interfaces to

© Springer International Publishing AG, part of Springer Nature 2018
A. Marcus and W. Wang (Eds.): DUXU 2018, LNCS 10919, pp. 427–436, 2018.
https://doi.org/10.1007/978-3-319-91803-7_32

accurately provide the information needed. This calls for designing of more natural, user-friendly interfaces and means of interaction. However, the way that users interact with the robot can be unpredictable and often multimodal, complicating the development of robots that are able to adaptively learn object recognition from user interaction.

In this paper, we aim to look at key parts of the interaction between human users and service robots and derive a framework by analyzing the situation and matching the appropriate reactions and interaction possibilities. The outcome will serve as a tool for designers and engineers to help develop service robots that are able to take advantage of user input to perform guided learning in its environment of use, while doing so in a natural, user-friendly way.

2   Recognition Obstacles

In order to deal with the recognition problems and determine corresponding interactions to support guided learning, we first start to analyze the kinds of recognition obstacles that the robot may encounter. A thorough analysis and prediction of most possible situations from which difficulties may arise will contribute to the effectiveness of the counter-actions that may follow.

The possible recognition obstacles can mainly be divided into five categories as below [3–7]:

O1. Object Similarity. It refers to the situation when there is an object which is similar to the target object and the robot is confused by these two objects. This confusion can stem from objects that are very similar, like an apple smartphone and an apple iPod, to point out an extreme case [3]. To situations where there are multiples of the same object but only one of them is referred to [4].

O2. Difficult to Distinguish from Surroundings. It includes different cases, the first one is that the color of the target object is similar to its surroundings, which makes the target object blend into the surroundings. The robot cannot find or cannot identify the particular shape. The second one is that the edges of the target object are complex and or blurry, such as hair, and the robot is unable to mark the edges successfully. Similarly, transparent objects like glass can appear in a way that is extremely difficult to process. Reflections and shapes appear in the object and distortions happen through the shape.

O3. Partially Occluded. If the target object is occluded partially by surroundings, especially when key elements are occluded, it can be difficult or impossible for the robot to identify the object [5].

O4. Change in Objects. When the feature of the target object has changed significantly over time, the robot is not likely to be able to identify it. For example, a flower, once bright and blooming, will become withered in several days. Then the color and shape of the flower will be totally different. It is hard for the robot to recognize it as the same flower or object as recorded before. Additionally, current image processing algorithms often show shortcomings with objects that are rotated [6], so if the algorithm and training data doesn't account for that, an object that is found later on laying on the floor instead of standing up, might be also difficult to recognize.

O5. Missing Knowledge/Understanding. The user might refer to objects in a particular way that the robot has not yet learned. Relationships between the user and the object and general context information of an object like *"my* cup" or "the *3 o'clock* pills" have to be taught to the robot. This personalization can also include regional colloquial names for objects [7].

Further obstacles exist in relation to the spoken word – misunderstanding of pronunciations can lead to many mistakes and is still an issue in natural language processing. Ambiguity in language, words that are the same but refer to different objects and can only be differentiated through context, are an issue. This paper considers this to be out of scope for the issue discussed here since it's a stage prior - understanding commands, no matter what it refers to.

3   Instructional Actions

After summarizing the possible recognition obstacles that the robot will encounter, we are attempting to list the instructional actions for guiding the robot to learn. These actions are selected considering both physical and digital means, which can deal with the recognition problems effectively. The specific instructional actions are as follows [8–11]:

A1. Point at the Target Area. When the robot cannot distinguish the target object and another similar but different object, the user can point at the target object to let the robot know which the correct one is. This can be done over visual information that the robot provides, a sort of first person view, or for example use existing data like a map of the room, to point to the location of the object [8].

A2. Mark the Edges of the Target Area. A common procedure to help with image and object recognition is to help the robot understand the outline of an object – differentiating object and background. The user can help the robot to mark the edges of the target for the robot to collect the data of the target object and identify it more precisely [9]. The action can include different operations for editing the selected area, such as moving points and zooming.

A3. Move the Target Object. The user can move the target object by hand and show it to the robot clearly from all angles, enabling the robot to collect the data of the object more effectively. Besides, if the target object is hidden by surroundings, the user can also pick it up and show it to the robot, and then the robot can be aware of the existence of the object.

A4. Define the Target Object. When the user aims to let the robot know what the target object is, can help to define the object for easier identification [10, 11]. The user can input information that further define the object and its current state like the color, position, size, material, shape, etc. Additionally, the user might have to tell the robot about certain relationships and context attributes, *"my* cup", that cannot be known to the robot before or are too difficult to reliably perform. For example, if the robot cannot recognize that the present withered flower and the past blooming flower are the same object, the user is supposed to define the withered flower as "the same", letting the robot know they are the same object and remember it.

4   Operation Modality and Medium

Every user's instructional action requires an operation medium in order to be conveyed to the robot. Even when performing the same instructional actions, a change in medium can influence the whole interaction process. Here we list possible operation mediums and modalities to use in constructing corresponding interactions between robot and human. They can be divided into several categories:

M1. Robot's own Screen. It refers to the screen equipped on the robot. The robot can display the photo of target object and surroundings on this screen, and then the user can perform the actions like pointing at the target object or mark the edges of it.

M2. Robot's own Projector. The robot is able to project its recognition area on the physical target object. The user can edit this area through other input methods and make like gesture or screen input.

M3. Screen-Based Device. It refers to devices such as smart phone, iPad and laptops, which are independent from the robot and use a screen. They can be very helpful for more detailed input, loosing ambiguity of interpretation of the medium that might occur in voice and gesture-based input. Screens are well suited for displaying visual information like the first-person view of the robot or maps and let the user act on that.

M4. Augmented Reality Device. It refers to the AR device like HoloLens or AR applications in Smartphones. Using AR with the robot would require a shared physical and digital environment. In a sense, it is comparable to two people using a HoloLens which are able to see the same holograms. Large amounts of information could be communicated in a user-friendly way like that. The human can also use the various input methods of the devices to input further information in form of commands or even 3d data like defining volumes.

M5. Voice. The user can directly instruct the robot via voice commands. It is convenient for the user to define the target object via voice but might be difficult for the robot to interpret.

M6. In-air Gesture. The user instructs the robot only by gesture without any other assistant equipment. For example, the user can just point at the target object by finger and let the robot remember it. This method can only be used if it's ensured that the robot is reliably able to recognize such gestures as pointing to an area a couple meters away can be quite ambiguous.

M7. Physical Action and Assistant Tools. The user can use some assistant tools such as labels and laser pointers. He or she can attach a label on the target object, making it easy for the robot to recognize it. As for the laser pointer, the user can use it to point at the target object, providing a more direct way than gesturing with the convenience of not having to physically walk around the room.

5   Obstacle, Action, Interface Analysis

After considering instructional actions and operation mediums for dealing with recognition obstacles and guiding the robot to learn, in order to design the interactions for different recognition obstacles, we are analyzing which actions and modalities are suitable for each recognition obstacle. First, it is necessary to list the possible combinations of actions and modalities as below (Table 1).

Table 1. Possible combinations of actions and media.

	M1	M2	M3	M4	M5	M6	M7
A1. Point at the target area	✓	✓	✓	✓	✓	✓	✓
A2. Mark the edges of the target area	✓	✓	✓	✓		✓	✓
A3. Move the target object							✓
A4. Define the target object	✓		✓	✓	✓		✓

For *A1. Point at the target area*, it is possible for the user to perform this action based on any media. Because the user can click at the target area on any digital device, and includes *M1. Robot's own screen*, *M3. Screen-based device* and *M4. Augmented Reality device*. The user can do it by gesturing, *M6. In-air gesture*. For *M2. Robot's own projector*, the user can also point at the physical target object first, which can be detected by robot's camera. Then the robot will project the recognition area on this object, so this action is feasible via the media of the projector. Although for *M5, Voice* the interpretation has to be stretched a bit and overlaps with *A4, Defining the object*, as the user is able to select the target object via descriptions like "the left one", verbally pointing. Finally, the user can point at the object with the aid of some physical assistant tools like the laser pointer, which demonstrates *M7. Physical action and assistant tools* is also possible.

Similarly, for *A2. Mark the edges of the target area*, the gesture and every digital device seem to be possible. The user can also use the laser pointer or other tools to mark edges. However, *M5. Voice* is hardly possible, although you could direct the robot to follow an object outline by directing it, we don't see this implemented are user-friendly in any robot at the current time.

For *A3. Move the target object*, it can only be realized by physical action. *M7*.

As for *A4. Define the target object*, most means can provide additional information apart from *M6 In-air gesture*, gesturing and *M2 Robot's own projector*, since it's mainly an output medium.

Then we can analyze the suitable combinations of actions and modalities for each obstacle as below (Table 2).

In order to cope with *O1. Confused by another similar object*, first we should select the correct target object, which requires *A1. Point at the target area*. Secondly, we need

Table 2. Suitable actions and media for recognition obstacle O1.

	M1	M2	M3	M4	M5	M6	M7
A1. Point at the target area	✓	✓	✓	✓	✓	✓	✓
A2. Mark the edges of the target area	✓	✓	✓	✓		✓	✓
A3. Move the target object							✓
A4. Define the target object	✓		✓	✓	✓		

to show the difference between two objects to the robot and mark it, so this includes *A2. Mark the edges of the target area* (mark the key feature of the target object) and *A3. Move the target object* (show from all angles). Finally, we are supposed to let the robot know what the marked feature or object is and how to recognize it, which requires *A4. Define the target object*. So all the combinations are suitable for it.

As for *O2. With difficulty in marking edges*, what we need to do first is to mark the edges of the target object, and then let the robot know what the target object is. If the target object is hidden, we should pick it up and show it to the robot. Therefore, it is not necessary to point at anything, and *A1. Point at the target area* is not suitable for it (Table 3).

Table 3. Suitable actions and media for recognition obstacle O2.

	M1	M2	M3	M4	M5	M6	M7
A2. Mark the edges of the target area	✓	✓	✓	✓		✓	✓
A3. Move the target object							✓
A4. Define the target object	✓		✓	✓	✓		

To address the problems caused by *O3. Partially occluded*, we should instruct the robot to recognize it through the exposed part of the target object. We can mark it, a feature of it, or move the object (Table 4).

Table 4. Suitable actions and media for recognition obstacle O3.

	M1	M2	M3	M4	M5	M6	M7
A1. Point at the target area	✓	✓	✓	✓	✓	✓	✓
A2. Mark the edges of the target area	✓	✓	✓	✓		✓	✓
A3. Move the target object							✓
A4. Define the target object	✓		✓	✓	✓		

Similarly, with *O4. Object has changed*, we need to find the unchanged feature that can demonstrate that they are the same object, and then mark it for the robot. Finally, we should define the object. It requires *A2. Mark the edges of the target area* and *A4. Define the target object* (Table 5).

Table 5. Suitable actions and media for recognition obstacle O4.

	M1	M2	M3	M4	M5	M6	M7
A2. Mark the edges of the target area	✓	✓	✓	✓		✓	✓
A4. Define the target object	✓		✓	✓	✓		

For *O5. Missing Knowledge/Understanding*, when the robot misses some knowledge about the target object, the user is supposed to show the object to the robot and provide more information about it, which includes *A3. Move the target object* and *A4. Define the target object* (Table 6).

Table 6. Suitable actions and media for recognition obstacle O5.

	M1	M2	M3	M4	M5	M6	M7
A3. Move the target object							✓
A4. Define the target object	✓		✓	✓	✓		

It is not necessary that the user has to use all suitable actions to deal with a single recognition obstacle. On the contrary, during guided learning, we aim to instruct the robot with the least interaction effort, in order to optimize the user experience and improve the robot's learning efficiency.

6   Interaction Process

With the overview of possible obstacles, counter-actions and ways to interact, we can attempt outlining a process for the human-robot interaction with the goal to engage the user productively. In further research, this process must be tested, refined and overall validated.

There are in general two situation where a guided learning project will be triggered. In the case of a robot entering initially a new environment, it might be a standard procedure to take part in an extensive setup process, where the human figuratively introduces the new space to the robot. An example would be a newly bought or rented service robot being welcomed in the residence of a customer. This particular situation might be accompanied by a professional "robot-handler" but in any case, we assume that either the professional, the customer or both together would engage in the introductory setup process. In this initial stage, the robot would start scanning and identifying objects in the household while the present people would input the necessary data for the robot to start handling its assigned task. This can be specific information about the rooms that the robot will occupy as well as important objects and chores that need to be handled and taken care of. It is likely that during this process the first problems of object recognition occur and in the same vein since guided learning already happens because object relationships that could have not been known before are now introduced to the robot.

The second situation occurs during the regular use of the robot. Similarly to the setup process, the ongoing human-robot interaction might carry some elements of guided learning. Each time new tasks are introduced, and objects referred to, the robot will attempt to understand the instructions to its best ability. If the ambiguity in the occurring situation is very low, the robot might be able to infer already from part of the interaction about what it is needed to do. In the case the robot's prediction was correct, it can regard the rest of the interaction as additional input and extract for example object specific names or relationships from this. A person could call the robot to "bring me my bag" and indicate an area with only one bag. In this moment the robot would add the information that this is the person's personal bag and recall this information the next time the object is referred to and can act on it even without the same clear indication of location.

While this naturally occurring learning moments will be crucial to enable an intelligent and fluid use and interaction of the robot, it will be necessary to create a defined process to handle the situation for when errors occur. In the setup process as well as during the latter use, the robot will undeniable run into problems with translating instructions into action. In these moments, we propose the following steps could be considered to arrive to an adequate solution in terms of situation handling as well as solving the problem.

1. **Error occurrence.** It is possible that the robot itself realizes a lack of information hindering the fulfillment of a request or the failure to recognize an expected object. The information of error occurrence can also be sent to the robot by the human when they notice that the robot is making a mistake. In general, this means the robot has encountered one or more of the object recognition obstacles.

2. **Error identification.** After noticing that an error is occurring, the robot should attempt to analyze the cause of the error. It might be able to point to low confidence in the understanding of an instruction or the inability to match the instruction to any object in his surroundings.

   In the case that the human triggered the error notice, the robot might be able to take a second chance on accomplishing the task. The error notice itself might add enough information to enable a better understanding of what was the initial request like when two similar objects were present. Overall, in the scenario that the human informs the robot of the error, the robot would ideally restart the last task with the information that this object was the wrong one and see if it can solve it now, or be programmed to await further instruction from the user in that moment.

3. **Obstacle Communication.** The robot needs to convey the right information to enable a productive user interaction. The design of the robot and it´s system should provide it with the ability to communicate which part of the current task leads to interruption. For example, the robot might be able to identify a range of objects that fit the instruction and ask the user for a relatively simple clarification or share its own current view to the human, transmitted through the discussed media use.

4. **User Instruction.** In the fourth phase, the main part of guided learning takes place. The human acts on the given information. The user will take steps as discussed in the *Instructional Actions* section to deliver additional input to the robot or manipulate the surroundings to enable recognition on the part of the robot. The

choice of action will be foremost based on the encountered obstacle and secondly on the available input methods. Ideally a simple interaction can solve the problem but if the problem persists, the interaction might cycle through a set of possible solutions asking consequently more information and help from the user.

5. **Learning Feedback.** Lastly, the robot should confirm the newly learned information with the user. It should clarify to the human what happened and in case, what new information has been added to the database. This serves the purpose of avoiding learning something wrong, which could lead to greater complications later on. This feedback could be supported by knowledge graph representation.

7   Conclusion

Human-Robot interactions are composed of several key factors which provide a significant influence on the exploration of suitable interaction methods. A design solution identified on one aspect is not guaranteed to be a good solution for all aspects of the use scenario. Analyzing a scenario from multiple key factors can associate them into an integrated view which is a way to discover hidden problems and opportunities [12]. In this paper we analyzed the key factors (1) Obstacles (2) Actions (3) Media and came to propose a generalized process supporting guided learning for solving object recognition errors. With this information, we aim to provide a basis for designing successful guided learning interactions. Further research on detailed scenarios will be necessary and should involve additional key factors to complete the design. We suggest including the following factors: (4) User- mobility and capabilities (5) Environment- public, private (6) Human-Robot distance derived from the Design Information Framework [13].

Acknowledgments. This paper was supported by the Funds Project of Shanghai High Peak IV Program (Grant DA17003).

References

1. Gupta, S., Girshick, R., Arbeláez, P., Malik, J.: Learning rich features from RGB-D images for object detection and segmentation. In: Fleet, D., Pajdla, T., Schiele, B., Tuytelaars, T. (eds.) ECCV 2014. LNCS, vol. 8695, pp. 345–360. Springer, Cham (2014). https://doi.org/10.1007/978-3-319-10584-0_23
2. Ekvall, S., Jensfelt, P., Kragic, D.: Integrating active mobile robot object recognition and SLAM in natural environments. In: Proceedings of IEEE/RSJ International Conference Intelligent Robots and Systems, pp. 5792–5797 (2006)
3. Shectman, E., Irani, M.: Matching local self-similarities across images and videos. In: IEEE International Conference on Computer Vision and Pattern Recognition, pp. 1–8 (2007)
4. Shi, G., Xu, T., Luo, J., Guo, J., Zhao, Z.: Alleviate Similar Object in Visual Tracking via Online Learning Interference-Target Spatial Structure, 19 October 2017. Published online
5. Gao, T., Packer, B., Koller, D.: A segmentation-aware object detection model with occlusion handling. In: IEEE International Conference on Computer Vision and Pattern Recognition (CVPR), June 2011

6. Khurana, K., Awasthi, R.: Techniques for object recognition in images and multi-object detection. Int. J. Adv. Res. Comput. Eng. Technol. (IJARCET) **2**(4), 1383 (2013)
7. Darrell, T.: Overcoming Ambiguity in Visual Object Recognition. UC Berkeley Berkeley EECS Department & International Computer Science Institute (ICSI) (2010)
8. Chao, F., Wang, Z., Shang, C., Meng, Q., Jiang, M., Zhou, C., Shen, Q.: A developmental approach to robotic pointing via human–robot interaction, **283** (2014)
9. Anderson, H.: Edge Detection for Object Recognition in Aerial Photographs, February 1987
10. Cantrell, R., Schermerhorn, P., Scheutz, M.: Learning actions from human-robot dialogues. In: RO-MAN 2011, pp. 125–130. IEEE (2011)
11. Lauria, S., Bugmann, G., Kyriacou, T., Bos, J., Klein, E.: Training personal robots using natural language instruction **15**, 38–45 (2001)
12. Lim, Y., Sato, K.: Development of design information framework for interactive systems design. In: Proceedings of the 5th Asian International Symposium on Design Research, Seoul, Korea (2001)
13. Lim, Y.-K., Sato, K.: Describing multiple aspects of use situation: applications of Design Information Framework (DIF) to scenario development. Elsevier Ltd. (2005)

Designing Behaviors to Interactively Interlace Natural Language Processing, Text to Speech Procedures and Algorithmic Images

Tania Fraga[1,2(✉)]

[1] Institute of Mathematics and Arts of São Paulo, São Paulo, Brazil
taniafraga.pesquisa@gmail.com
[2] University of Brasilia, Brasília, Brazil

Abstract. This article presents the artwork **Interlace** and its related application, **#ELIZA_Interlacements,** as a case study. Both are works in progress aiming to develop and explore an interface with ELIZA, a natural language processing software using text to speech – TTS – procedures interweaving them with algorithmic images. ELIZA was modeled as a pseudo Rogerian 'psychotherapist' and was created between 1964 and 1966 at the MIT Artificial Intelligence Laboratory by Joseph Weizenbaum. ELIZA is a very simple program but it is still quite entertaining and thought provoking. The new application created using ELIZA aims to design behaviors that interactively interlace natural language processing, with text to speech procedures, entwining algorithmically generated images with dialogues of ELIZA and the public. By interweaving images with onscreen dialogues obtained with 'talks' to ELIZA it is possible to experiment the visual poetic potential of such explorations and their immanent relations. These visual poetic results point to a potential symbiotic relationship between man and machine. This experimental artwork shows different aspects of the poetic, aesthetic and technical characteristics of the explored object for art and design aims. The application's interface is being developed using the IDE Processing. Autonomous bots, represented as images processed in real time are presented interactively with the dialogs in a graphic interface that will be shown in big projected screens in *site specific* installations and performances.

Keywords: Computer Art · Algorithmic art · Virtual reality
Natural Language Processing (NLP) · Text-To-Speech (TTS) · ELIZA

1 Introduction

The action of making art is, and should always be, an act of opening the doors of perception, of showing new poetic and aesthetic characteristics, of unveiling sensitive organizations, of fighting stereotypes, of magnifying sensory aspects, and of intensifying the cognition of the lived instant. Thus, by emerging at the level of consciousness these actions can engender space-time configurations allowing changes and transformations due to the weaving of human actions with computer percepts.

The quoted application explores such field of possibilities using ELIZA [1], a natural language processing software [2], text to speech – TTS – procedures [3], and interweaving them with algorithmic images. ELIZA was modeled as a pseudo Rogerian 'psychotherapist' and was created between 1964 and 1966 at the MIT Artificial Intelligence Laboratory by Joseph Weizenbaum. It was firstly developed by K. M. Colby aiming to make a software that would pass the Turin Test. The Turin Test is a procedure presented in 1950 by the British mathematician Alan Turin intending to be a test "about the possibility that the machine would think reasonably" [4], p. 5. ELIZA is a very simple program but it is still quite entertaining, thought provoking, and works with such exit that it can fool users for some time.

By interweaving images with onscreen dialogues obtained with 'talks' to ELIZA it is possible to experiment the visual poetic potential of such explorations and their immanent relations as can be seen in Figs. 1, 2 and 7. These visual poetic results point to a potential symbiotic relationship between humans and machines and this experimental artwork shows different aspects of these characteristics for art and design aims. The application's interface is being developed using the IDE Processing [5]. Autonomous bots represented as images processed in real time are presented interactively with the dialogs in a graphic interface that will be shown in big projected screens in *site specific* installations and performances, see Figs. 3 and 4. Sometimes, the resultants dialogues are hilarious, which is a characteristic we intend to improve.

The application is based on the existing Java ELIZA code implemented by Hayden [6], see Figs. 5 and 6, which was reimplemented to fulfill the goals of the present artistic research as it was defined by Busch in [7]. Analyzing a few dialogues one can say that the application unravels the program behind them. One might even realize while talking to ELIZA that they are performing a monologue and not a real dialogue. Such approach opens a field of inquiries that can not be focused here. But it would be very interesting to see some of these philosophical questions debated elsewhere.

Any uncompromising and aimless 'conversation' carried out with a program as simple as ELIZA points to the potential aspect of more natural forms of interaction exploring the relationship among humans and machines. Probably, with the development of natural language programs, text to speech, artificial intelligence as defined by Norvig [8], Brain Computer Interfaces (BCI) as described in [9–13] and with the development of quantum computing as presented by Penrose [4] we may foresee the day when one will establish much more complex dialogues with machines. Maybe then it will be possible to clarify hazy aspects of our own cognitive process, as well as the act of thinking or creating as it is extensively discussed by Baum in [14].

By reflecting on the processes involved in designing behaviors for such interfaces one can show how ideas and actions engender each other during the creative process. In Computer Art, actions related with the designing of behaviors and the programming computational interfaces give artists a broad field of choices.

The central role of computers for the genesis of Computer Art is an approach extensively developed by Caillaud in [15]. The resultant emerged realities widen frontiers, leaving us to foresee new conceptual models that will expand the linear field of verbal languages, extending them into new horizons. In this way, poetic articulations between natural, artistic and computational languages will also be amplified. The computational technology, when used for poetic and aesthetic exploration opens new experimental fields to artists, architects and designers who are thus immersed in a totally new territory. At the present moment, this approach allows the emergence of a

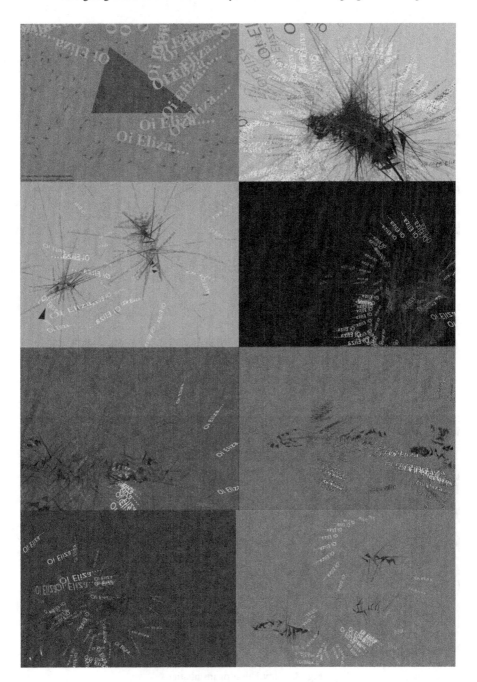

Fig. 1. Preliminary on screen dialogues

melting pot of potential transformations for the art field. How artists, architects and designers will use this potential is a wide battleground for speculations.

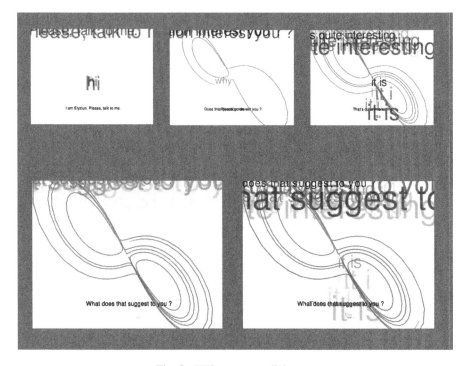

Fig. 2. TTS on screen dialogues

Fig. 3. Simulation of installations

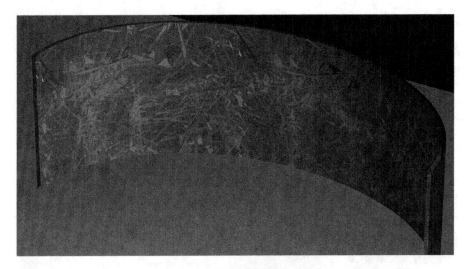

Fig. 4. Simulation of installations

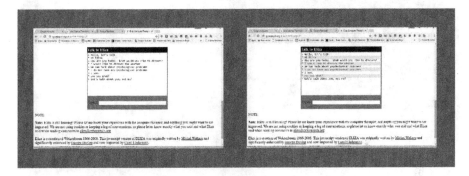

Fig. 5. Online dialogues with ELIZA

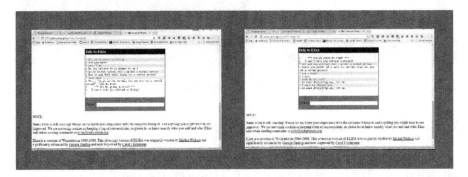

Fig. 6. Online dialogues with ELIZA

2   Methodology

This article aims to show the art research in development for the interactive computer artwork **Interlace** and its application, **#ELIZA_Interlacements** as a case study. It reflects upon the poetic, aesthetic and technical aspects involved in such a study. It applies a methodology of successive approximations to the desired goals described in detail in [16]. The transdisciplinary intersection of art, architecture and design with computer science and mathematics has enabled the development of the present investigation. They allow the establishment of a fundamental set of strategies to formulate new dialogues and actions, enabling the future production of the artwork and its complementary products. The new formulated dialogues expand ELIZA's repertoires which was also translated into Portuguese, see Fig. 7.

Fig. 7. On screen Portuguese dialogues

3   Results and Discussion

As it was stated by David Norman the present time is a time of co-evolution of humans and computers [17]. In times such as these it is possible to observe that some groups in society, having a dystopic point of view, fear that humanity will lose power and independence. To fight such stereotypes the author has been developing hypothetical symbiotic systems among humans and machines, aiming to accomplish an anti catalytic effects over such ideas as can be seen in [9–13]. **Interlace** is one of such projects. As it was said before, **Interlace** aims to establish dialogs with the public using a customized Java application to achieve a symbiosis among humans and computers. The former ELIZA's dialogs were broadened in order to include new sets of questions and reflections amplifying their previous characteristics.

Kaku analysing computers says that, although digital computers are inspired in our brains they are not analogous to it [18], p. 90. Digital computers are modeled using an intellectual model created by the mathematician Alan Turing in 1936-37, a subject Roger Penrose discuss in [4] pp. 31–80; this model is denominated as 'Universal Turin Machine' and is also intensively discussed by Eric Baum in the book 'What is thought?', a book that is "largely an attempt to spell out the details and ramifications of strong Artificial Intelligence (AI)" [14], p. 6. The conceptual 'Universal Turin Machine' proposes an input for data, a processor that will manipulate these data and an output for the transformed data. Such machine can realize a staggering amount of calculations, something only very few humans can achieve. But there is no universal algorithm to decide when a 'Universal Turin Machine' will stop its calculations and this is considered by mathematicians as proof that not all problems can be solved by such machines [4], p. 68.

By the other side, human brains are able to renew, constantly, their own circuits using a distributed net system of sensory organs within the body. This system do parallel processing and is able to establish connections by modes until now unexplained by sciences. Modes we call intuition or inspiration. Roger Penrose tells that these modes are related to non probabilistic problems (NP) that can not be computed by 'Universal Turin Machines' [19], p. 104. Meanwhile one can perceive that it is possible to trace analogies among these modes; metaphors and analogies usually provoke ambiguities and, therefore, provide very interesting materials to be experimented from an artistic point of view. The art field propitiates the environment for such experimental works to be formulated. The present one aims to explore such materials. As it was said before the result can be hilarious, a characteristic intensified by the use of a masculine computer voice. Such characteristics allow the establishments of bounds with the public and therefore will be explored.

ELIZA follows a script which creates a set of possible choices for the answers it provides; answers that are, in general, other questions or provocative statements that instigate more questioning and reflections. The present set of collected questions, statements and reflections turns ELIZA in a much more believable agent which, except for its voice, makes its artificial characteristic much harder to be detected than it was in its previous version.

From poetic and aesthetic viewpoints, human-machine symbiosis are vectors pointing to the solutions we intend to reach: human minds affecting machine processes which answer as if they are changing their own behaviors. Therefore, the artwork looks for ways to integrate, interdependently, human and machine processes in such a way that they result in symbiotic process.

In the 50's, looking for ways to establish a partnership among humans brains and computers, J. C. R. Lickleder developed a mode of interaction he called as 'symbiotic relationship'. Lickleder defined symbiosis as "a state found in Nature in which two or more organisms act in complementary ways to achieve survival" [17], p. 3. It would be a natural mode of interaction in which the final result could be a harmonic fusion among humans and machines for the combined development of tasks. He thought that we could have much more interesting results if we combined these two systems [17], pp. 22–23. Researching such symbiosis some questions arise: Will these systems be able to interpret the environment and to communicate among themselves in different ways? Will human-machine symbiosis allow better interpretation and communication among these systems?

Looking for answer to these questions we have to consider this mode of interpretation and communication within the context of Computer Art projects. Therefore, it is important to highlight that these projects have strong aesthetic and poetic goals. Goals that are essentially based on a set of elements such as:

- the public and the artists with their natural environment, sociocultural backgrounds, and their own modes of perception;
- the computational devices and their programs with their specific types of perception through sensors.

Due to the different manners in which humans and machines perceive their environment, these perceptions must be considered accordingly. "Perception provides agents with information about the world they inhabit." Perceptions in machines are mediated by sensors which are "anything that can record some aspect of the environment and pass it as input to an agent program" [8], p. 863.

Otherwise, in humans the sensory system works simultaneously integrating several sensations. For example, the sensations of heat and cold may be influenced by other factors such as colors or previous sensations. If someone puts a hand in very cold water and after in normal water this last one may be perceived as hot. This does not happen with machines.

Humans are curious, unquiet, eager to learn diverse things in order to fulfill any lack of knowledge they have, and they are also able to react in unforeseen situations.

Computers are semiotic machines programmed to do something and, in general, they do not work well under unexpected situations. Therefore, both have different characteristics and implicit behaviors that need to be studied separately.

Machines do not tire because they are constantly subjected to perceptive stimulus. But humans and machines age; the materials of the latter may become old, oxidized, their rubber and plastic parts may brake and their screws may lose tightness to quote just a few problems that may arise. Different modes of lights and sounds, permeating an ambient, may provoke very different perceptions either in humans or in machines sensors. Signs and signals may also give diverse environmental evidence either to humans or to machines. This is because both have very different patterns of perception and behaviors for the acknowledgment of data.

Humans communicate intentions, share expressions and emotions that command actions. They provoke answers and may be unpredictable. Machines are predictable. The combined actions of these two systems point to a moist media development as it is defined by Ascott [20], pp. 333–335. Moist media mixture wet biological systems with dry computer systems; and this is the kind of approach the present art research project aims to develop.

4 Conclusion

As it was said in the Introduction any uncompromising and aimless 'conversation' carried out with a program as simple as ELIZA points to the potential aspect of more natural forms of interaction exploring the natural language and test-to-speach (TTF) procedures to achieve a better relationship between humans and machines. In Computer Art the creative process for creating them is related to actions of designing behaviors and programming computational interfaces, actions that give artists a broad field of choices.

Nowadays, around the world, there are many artists and groups interested in similar approaches. It goes beyond the present article to point to such endeavors. But, as examples, we quote a few authors in Brazil who are studying them. Debora Gasparetto states that there are more than one hundred Brazilian groups experimenting with digital technology [21]; Fragoso, Venturelli and the author's collected data due to the organization of exhibitions in Brasilia since 1987 show a staggering amount of researches by computer artists as can be seen in [22–24].

To widen the topic from outside Brazil it is interesting to talk about researches such as the one formulated by the Portuguese Eduardo Miranda who developed, at the University of Plymouth in the United Kingdom, a brain-computer device that allows individuals with severe disabilities to play music using only data achieved from their own brain [25]. Another stimulating approach is the research developed by the Chilean group EMOVERE that uses physiological parameters achieved trough sensors attached to their bodies to deliver data from the body of each performer to devices used in spectacles [26].

As shown by these few examples the computer technology used for poetic and aesthetic exploration is opening new experimental fields to architects, artists and designers. By reflecting on the processes involved in designing behaviors and interfaces for such artworks one can show how ideas and actions engender each other during the creative process.

These new symbiotic realities widen the art domain, leaving us to foresee new conceptual models expanding the linear field of verbal languages, extending them into new frontiers. In this way, poetic articulations between natural, artistic and computational languages are also amplified. It is up to artists, architects and designers, in the coming years, to expand the field of Computer Art by bringing space-time, non-linearity, multiplicity, among many others relations, to the artistic research field. By symbiotically integrating computational environments with perceptions of the body in order to explore multimodal articulations and transductions one may also expands the conceptual, cognitive, poetic and aesthetic horizons.

Acknowledgments. Customized software in Java (Processing IDE); Programmers: Pedro Garcia and Tania Fraga; Conception, implementation, Graphic interface, Interactive project, Photos and images: Tania Fraga; Mathematician consultant: Donizetti Louro.

References

1. ELIZA. https://www.cyberpsych.org/eliza/#.WaBd1iiGO03. Accessed 04 Dec 2017
2. Natural Language Processing. https://machinelearningmastery.com/natural-language-processing/. Accessed 04 Dec 2017
3. Text-to-speech. https://play.google.com/store/apps/details?id=com.google.android.tts&hl=en. Accessed 04 Dec 2017
4. Penrose, R.: A mente nova do rei. Campus, Rio de janeiro (1993)
5. Processing. http://processing.org. Accessed 04 Dec 2017
6. Hayden, C.: https://github.com/codeanticode/eliza. Accessed 04 Dec 2017
7. Busch, K.: Artistic research concept. Artistic Research and the Poetics of Knowledge (2014). http://www.artandresearch.org.uk/v2n2/busch.html. Accessed 06 Oct 2017
8. Norvig, P., Russel, S.J.: Artificial Intelligence. Prentice Hall, Englewood Cliffs (2003)
9. Fraga, T.: Caracolomobile: affect in computer systems. AI Soc. J. Faustian Exch. **28**, 167–176 (2013). http://www.springerlink.com/content/d8u21638134u834g/export-citation/,vol21. Accessed 06 Oct 2017
10. Fraga, T.: Por trás da cena: produção de espetáculos com cenários interativos/Behind the scene: production of spectacles with interactive scenarios. In: Garcia, I.H. (ed) Estética de los mundos possibles/Aesthetic of Possible Worlds, pp. 183–198. Pontifícia Universidad Javeriana, Bogotá (2016)
11. Fraga, T.: Exoendogenias/Endogenously. In: Costa, M.C.C. (ed.) A pesquisa na Escola de Comunicações e Artes da USP/Research at the School of Communications and Arts from USP, pp. 46–66. ECA, Sao Paulo (2012)
12. Fraga, T., Donizetti, L., Pichiliani, M.: Experimental art with brain controlled interface. In: Human Computer Interfaces Proceedings, HCI 2013, Las Vegas (2013)
13. Hirata, C.M., Pichiliani, M.C., Fraga, T.: Exploring a brain controlled interface for emotional awareness. In: Proceedings of SBC, SBSC 2012, Sao Paulo (2012)
14. Baum, E.B.: What is Thought?. MIT Press, Cambridge (2004)
15. Caillaud, B.: La creation numerique visuelle. Europia, Paris (2012)
16. Fraga, T.: Artes interativas e método relacional para criação de obras/Interactive arts and relational method for artworks creation (2006). http://taniafraga.art.br/arquivos_pdf/ArtesInterativasMetodoRelacionalParaCriacaoObras.pdf. Accessed 06 Oct 2017
17. Norman, D.: O design do futuro/The Future of Design. ROCCO, Rio de Janeiro (2010)
18. Kaku, M.: A Física do Futuro. ROCCO, Rio de Janeiro (2012)
19. Penrose, R.: A Mente Virtual. Gradiva, Lisboa (1997)
20. Ascott, R.: Telematic Embrace. University of California, Los Angeles (2003)
21. Fraga, T.: 21st Century Brazilian Computer Art (2014). https://www.youtube.com/watch?v=nVjmgROEp5A. Accessed 01 Nov 2017
22. Gasparetto, D.A.: O "curto-circuito" da arte digital no Brasil. Edição do autor, Santa Maria (2014)
23. Fraga, T., Fragoso, M.L.: 21st Century Brazilian (Experimental) Computer Art. In: CAC.3 Proceedings, Europia, Paris (2012)
24. Venturelli, S.: Arte Computacional. UnB, Brasilia (2017)
25. Eduardo Miranda's BCI device to play music. http://www.abledata.com/product/bci-music. Accessed 14 Nov 2017
26. Emovere Group. http://www.emovere.cl/en/. Accessed 14 Nov 2017

Speech Communication Through the Skin: Design of Learning Protocols and Initial Findings

Jaehong Jung[1], Yang Jiao[1], Frederico M. Severgnini[1],
Hong Z. Tan[1(✉)], Charlotte M. Reed[2], Ali Israr[3], Frances Lau[3],
and Freddy Abnousi[3]

[1] Purdue University, West Lafayette, IN 47907, USA
{jung137, jiao12, fmarcoli, hongtan}@purdue.edu
[2] Massachusetts Institute of Technology, Cambridge, MA 02139, USA
cmreed@mit.edu
[3] Facebook Inc., Menlo Park, CA 94025, USA
aliisrar@fb.com, flau@fb.com, abnousi@fb.com

Abstract. Evidence for successful communication through the sense of touch is provided by the natural methods of tactual communication that have been used for many years by persons with profound auditory and visual impairments. However, there are still currently no wearable devices that can support speech communication effectively without extensive learning. The present study reports the design and testing of learning protocols with a system that translates English phonemes to haptic stimulation patterns (haptic symbols). In one pilot study and two experiments, six participants went through the learning and testing of phonemes and words that involved different vocabulary sizes and learning protocols. We found that with a distinctive set of haptic symbols, it was possible for the participants to learn phonemes and words in small chunks of time. Further, our results provided evidence of the memory consolidation theory in that recognition performance improved after a period of inactivity on the part of a participant. Our findings pave the way for future work on improving the haptic symbols and on protocols that support the learning of a tactile speech communication system in hours as opposed to the much longer periods of time that are required to learn a new language.

Keywords: Haptic speech communication · Memory consolidation
Phoneme

1 Introduction

For a very long time, individuals with hearing impairments have utilized various visual and touch-based methods for speech communication such as *sign language* and *fingerspelling*. Individuals who are both deaf and blind, however, use a natural (i.e., not assisted by man-made devices) method called *Tadoma* that relies solely on the sense of touch. In this method, the "listener" places the hand on the speaker's face, and in the absence of any visual or auditory information, feels the articulatory processes

© Springer International Publishing AG, part of Springer Nature 2018
A. Marcus and W. Wang (Eds.): DUXU 2018, LNCS 10919, pp. 447–460, 2018.
https://doi.org/10.1007/978-3-319-91803-7_34

(e.g., mouth opening, air flow, muscle tension and presence/absence of laryngeal vibration) associated with speech production (Fig. 1). The Tadoma method is a living proof that speech communication through the skin alone is entirely achievable, as established by past research on Tadoma and other natural speech communication methods [1]. Inspired by the Tadoma method, electromechanical devices have been developed to study and replicate the cues produced by a talking face that are crucial for speech reception by Tadoma users [2]. Experimental results on one such device, the Tactutor, demonstrate an information transmission rate of 12 bits/s, the same rate that has been established for speech communication by Tadoma users [1, 3]. Despite such promising results in the laboratory, however, there are still no commercially-available communication devices that can be used by people who are deaf or deaf-and-blind for speech reception at a level that is comparable to that shown by Tadoma users. The challenges are manifold. First, a talking face is a rich display and require actuators that can deliver a wide range of sensations including movement, vibration, airflow, etc. Second, such communication devices should be wearable, or at least portable. Third, the input to such devices should ideally be processed, as opposed to raw, acoustic signals for consistent conversion of sound to touch. Fourth, the mapping between speech sounds and haptic symbols needs to be designed such that it is easy to learn and retain. Last but not the least, a significant effort is expected of any individual who wishes to learn to use such a communication device.

Fig. 1. The Tadoma method of speech communication. Shown are two individuals who are both deaf and blind (on the left and right, respectively) conversing with a researcher (center) who has normal vision and hearing. (Photo courtesy of Hansi Durlach)

With the recent development in haptic display and speech recognition technologies, now is the time to give it another try to develop a wearable system for speech communication through the skin. In our research, we use an array of wide-bandwidth actuators for presenting "rich" haptic signals to the skin on the forearm. The display portion of our system is wearable but still tethered to equipment that has yet to be miniaturized. We assume that speech recognition technologies are available to extract phonemes from oral speech in real time, and therefore use phonemes as the input to our system. We have designed and tested a set of distinct haptic symbols representing phonemes of the English language. The present work focuses on the exploration of training protocols that facilitate the learning of phonemes and words in hours as opposed to days or weeks. Our initial results with six participants have been very promising. In the rest of this paper, we present the background for our approach followed by methods and results from one pilot study and two experiments. We conclude the paper with guidelines for effective learning of speech communication through the skin via man-made systems.

2 Related Work

There is a long history of research on the development of synthetic tactile devices as speech-communication aids for persons with profound hearing loss (e.g., see reviews [4–6]) that continues to the present day [7–9]. From a signal-processing point of view, many devices have attempted to display spectral properties of speech to the skin. These displays rely on the principle of frequency-to-place transformation, where location of stimulation corresponds to a given frequency region of the signal. Another approach to signal processing has been the extraction of speech features (such as voice fundamental frequency and vowel formants) from the acoustic signal prior to encoding on the skin. For both classes of aids, devices have included variations in properties such as number of channels, geometry of the display, body site, transducer properties, and type of stimulation (e.g., vibrotactile versus electrotactile).

A major challenge in the development of tactile aids lies in encoding the processed speech signals to match the perceptual properties of the skin. Compared to the sense of hearing, the tactual sensory system has a reduced frequency bandwidth (20–20,000 Hz for hearing compared to 0–1000 Hz for touch), reduced dynamic range (115 dB for hearing compared to 55 dB for touch), and reduced sensitivity for temporal, intensive, and frequency discrimination (see [10]). The tactual sense also lags behind the auditory sense in terms of its capacity for information transfer (IT) and IT rates [3]. For example, communication rates of up to 50 words/min are achieved by experienced operators of Morse code through the usual auditory route of transmission, compared to 25 words/min for vibrotactile reception of these patterns [11]. Taking these properties of the tactual sense into account, certain principles may be applied to create displays with high IT rate. One such principle is to include as many dimensions as possible in the display, while limiting the number of variables along each dimension.

Another challenge is present in the need to provide users with adequate training in the introduction of novel tactile displays. Compared to the structured training and many years of learning associated with the Tadoma method, most tactile aids have been evaluated within the context of relatively limited exposure in a laboratory setting. Recent advances arising out of the literature in language-learning [12] and memory consolidation [13] offer insight into improved approaches for training that may be applied to the use of a novel tactile speech display. Results from a multi-modal, game-based approach to language learning have shown that observers are able to learn to categorize auditory speech sounds when they are associated with the visual stimuli needed to perform the task. In addition, studies of learning suggest that following exposure to a new task, the initial memories associated with this task may be further consolidated by activations of these memories during periods of wakefulness and sleep. Thus, learning can occur between the laboratory sessions with no explicit training involved.

Based on the literature, we explored several strategies of facilitating learning and training such as breaking up training time into smaller intervals, sounding a phoneme/word out while feeling the corresponding haptic symbols, and keeping the task doable but challenging at all times.

3   General Methods

3.1   Participants

A total of six participants (2 females; age range 20–30 years old) took part in the present study. All were right handed with no known sensory or motor impairments. The participants came from diverse language backgrounds. While all participants spoke English fluently, only one was a native English speaker. Other languages spoken among the participants included Korean, Chinese, Tibetan, Hindi and German. Most of the participants also received early childhood music training including piano, clarinet, violin and percussion.

3.2   Apparatus

The experimental apparatus consisted of a 4-by-6 tactor array worn on the non-dominant forearm. The 24 tactors form four rows in the longitudinal direction (elbow to wrist) and six columns (rings) in the transversal direction (around the forearm). As shown in Fig. 2 below, two rows (i and ii) reside on the dorsal side of the forearm and the other two (iii and iv) on the volar side. The tactor positions were adjusted so that the rows form straight lines and the columns are evenly distributed

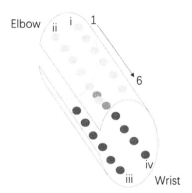

Fig. 2. Illustrations of tactor layout in the experimental apparatus

from the elbow to the wrist. The tactors were attached to a sleeve via adjustable Velcro strips. The sleeve was then wrapped around the forearm with a snug fit to ensure good contact between the tactors and the skin.

A wide-bandwidth tactor (Tectonic Elements, Model TEAX13C02-8/RH, Part #297-214, sourced from Parts Express International, Inc.) was used as the actuator. It has a flat frequency response in the range 50 Hz to 2 kHz with a resonant peak close to 600 Hz. A MOTU audio device (MOTU, model 24Ao, Cambridge, MA, USA) was used for delivering 24 channels of audio waveforms to the 24 tactors through custom-built stereo audio amplifiers. A Matlab program running on a desktop computer generated the multi-channel waveforms corresponding to the haptic symbols for phonemes, presented a graphic user interface for running the experiments, and collected responses from the participants.

With this setup, the tactors can be driven independently with programmable waveforms and on-off timing. The stimulus properties include amplitude (specified in dB sensation level, or dB above individually-measured detection thresholds), frequency (single or multiple sinusoidal components), waveform (sinusoids with or without modulation), duration, location, numerosity (single tactor activation or multiple tactors turned on simultaneously or sequentially), and movement (smooth apparent motion or discrete salutatory motion varying in direction, spatial extent, and trajectory).

The participants sat comfortably in front of a computer monitor. They wore a noise-reduction earphone to block any auditory cues emanating from the tactors. The participants placed their non-dominant forearm on the table with the volar side facing down. The elbow-to-wrist direction was adjusted to be parallel to the participant's torso. The participants used their dominant hand to operate the computer keyboard and mouse (Fig. 3).

Fig. 3. Experimental setup

3.3   Phoneme Codes

English words are pronounced by a sequence of sounds called phonemes [14]. Table 1 shows the IPA (international phonetic alphabet) symbols of the 39 English phonemes used in the present study and example words that contain the corresponding phonemes. The list consists of 24 consonants and 15 vowels.

Table 1. The thirty-nine (39) English phonemes used in the present study.

IPA symbol	Example word	IPA symbol	Example word	IPA symbol	Example word	IPA symbol	Example word
/i/	meet	/U/	hood	/k/	key	/ʒ/	azure
/ei/	mate	/ʌ/	hut	/p/	pay	/tʃ/	chew
/u/	mood	/OU/	boat	/t/	tea	/dʒ/	jeep
/aI/	might	/ɔI/	boy	/b/	bee	/h/	he
/ae/	mat	/aU/	pouch	/g/	guy	/r/	ray
/ɑ/	father	/d/	do	/f/	fee	/l/	lie
/ɔ/	bought	/m/	me	/ʃ/	she	/j/	you
/ɛ/	met	/s/	see	/Θ/	think	/n/	new
/ɝ//ɚ/	bird	/w/	we	/v/	voice	/ŋ/	sing
/I/	bid	/ð/	the	/z/	zoo		

Vibrotactile patterns using one or more of the 4-by-6 tactors were created, one for each phoneme. The mapping of the phonemes to haptic symbols incorporated the articulatory features of the sounds, balanced by the need to maintain the distinctiveness of the 39 haptic symbols. For example, place of articulation was mapped to the longitudinal direction so that the wrist corresponds to the front of the mouth and the elbow the back of the mouth. Therefore, the consonant /p/ was mapped to a 100-ms 300-Hz pulse delivered near the wrist (front of the mouth) whereas the consonant /k/ was mapped to the same waveform delivered near the elbow (back of the mouth). Their voiced counterparts, /b/ and /g/, were mapped to the 100-ms 300-Hz pulse modulated by a 30-Hz envelope signal delivered near the wrist and elbow, respectively. The modulation resulted in a "rough" sensation that signified voicing. Details of the phoneme mapping strategies and the resultant haptic symbols can be found in [15].

3.4   Intensity Calibration

In order to control the perceived intensity of vibrotactile signals at different frequencies and different locations on the forearm, signal amplitudes were calibrated in two steps in Exp. I. First, individual detection thresholds were taken at 25, 60 and 300 Hz for the tactor on the dorsal side of the forearm near the center (row i, column 4 in Fig. 2). A one-up two-down adaptive procedure was used and the resulting detection threshold corresponds to the 70.7 percentile point on the psychometric function [16]. Signal amplitudes were then defined in sensation level (SL); i.e., dB above the detection threshold at the same frequency. In the present study, signal amplitudes were set to 30 dB SL for a clear and moderately-strong intensity.

Second, the perceived intensity of the 24 tactors was equalized using a method of adjustment procedure. A 300-Hz sinusoidal signal at 30 dB SL was sent to the tactor used in the detection threshold measurements (see the black tactor in Fig. 4). The participant selected one of the remaining 23 tactors, say the upper-left tactor in Fig. 4, and adjusted its vibration amplitude until the vibration felt as strong as that of the black tactor. This was repeated for all the tactors. The equalization results for one participant are shown in Fig. 4. The numbers below each tactor indicate the signal amplitudes in dB relative to the maximum amplitude allowed in the Matlab program for a 300-Hz vibration at 30 dB SL. For example, this participant's detection threshold at 300 Hz was –54 dB relative to the maximum allowable amplitude. The amplitude for the black reference tactor was therefore at –24 dB for a 30 dB SL signal. The number –23 below the tactor in the upper-left corner indicates that its amplitude needed to be 1 dB higher than that of the black tactor to match its strength for a signal at 30 dB SL. In other words, the skin near the elbow under this tactor was slightly less sensitive than the skin under the black tactor. Generally speaking, the skin on the dorsal side was more sensitive than that on the volar side and the wrist area was more sensitive than the elbow area.

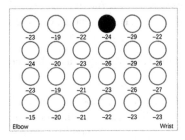

Fig. 4. Tactor intensity equalization

3.5   Data Analysis

The experiments reported in this paper consisted of learning and testing of phonemes through individual haptic symbols and words through sequences of haptic symbols. Test results were organized as stimulus-response confusion matrices where each cell entry is the number of times a haptic symbol was recognized as a phoneme label. Table 2 below shows an example of a confusion matrix for a 6-phoneme stimulus set. As was typical of most tests, a majority of the trials fall on the main diagonal cells (i.e., correct answers). Therefore, the results could be well captured by the percent-correct

Table 2. An example confusion matrix for a 6-phoneme recognition test. Each cell represents the number of times a haptic symbol is recognized with a phoneme label

		Phoneme labels (responses)					
		/m/	/d/	/s/	/ei/	/u/	/i/
Haptic symbols (stimuli)	/m/	9	0	0	0	0	0
	/d/	0	5	0	0	0	0
	/s/	0	0	7	0	0	0
	/ei/	0	0	0	5	0	0
	/u/	0	0	0	0	13	0
	/i/	0	0	0	1	1	9

scores (48/50 = 96%) and the error trials /i/→/ei/and /i/→/u/. Therefore, in the rest of the paper, we report the percent-correct scores and error trials for each test.

4 Pilot Study: Learning of 6 Phonemes and 24 Words

The purpose of the pilot study was to gain initial experience and insight into the learning process. One participant (P1) practiced and learned phonemes and words over a period of 21 days and took detailed notes. Within the 21 days, 4 days fell on a weekend, there was a break of 3 days after the 5th learning day, and a break of 2 days after the 11th learning day. Thus, there were a total of 12 experimental sessions.

Learning Materials. The materials included 6 phonemes and 24 words made up of the phonemes. The six phonemes were /i/, /ei/, /u/, /d/, /m/, and /s/. The words consisted of 10 CV (consonant-vowel) words (e.g., may, see) and 14 CVC (consonant-vowel-consonant) words (e.g., moose, dude).

Time Constraints. The learning and testing was self-paced. The participant took a break whenever needed.

Procedure. The following list shows the tasks performed by P1 over the 12 learning days. For each task, he practiced first with an individual phoneme (or word), then with a random list of phonemes (or words), followed by a recognition test. The numbers in parentheses indicate the total time spent on each learning day.

- Day 1–3 (20, 10, 15 min): 6 phonemes;
- Day 4–7 (5, 5, 5, 17 min): 10 CV words;
- Day 8–11 (5, 24, 5, 30 min): 14 CVC words;
- Day 12 (24 min): test with all 24 words.

Results. Participant P1 achieved a performance level of 200/200 (correct-trials/total-trials) with the 6 phonemes on Day 3, 198/200 with the 10 CV words on Day 7, 200/200 with 7 of the 14 CVC words on Day 9, 200/200 with the remaining 7 CVC words on Day 11, and 198/200 with all 24 words on Day 12.

Insight Gained. The results of the pilot study indicate clearly that participant P1 was able to learn the 6 phonemes and 24 words almost perfectly after 165 min. He intuitively progressed from easier to harder tasks, each time learning and testing himself before moving onto more difficult tasks. Since the task was highly demanding, it was challenging for P1 to maintain a high level of concentration after about 20 min. Therefore, it was necessary and more productive to spread the learning and testing over many days instead of spending a long time continuously. Furthermore, P1 found that his performance did not deteriorate after a 3-day gap between Day 5 and Day 6.

Encouraged and informed by the results of the pilot study, two experiments were conducted. Experiment I tested four new naïve participants with 10 phonemes and 51 words. Experiment II tested one more naïve participant with the full set of 39 phonemes and tested the memory consolidation theory explicitly.

5   Experiment I: Learning of 10 Phonemes and 51 Words

5.1   Methods

Four new naïve participants (P2-P5) took part in Exp. I. Each participant spent a total of 60 min to learn 10 phonemes and 50 words made up of the 10 phonemes.

Learning Materials. The ten phonemes included the six used in the pilot study and four more: /w/, /ð/, /k/, /aɪ/. The words consisted of the 24 words used in the pilot study plus 27 additional words (13 CV and 14 CVC words).

Time Constraints. The learning time was capped at 10 min on each day, with no break. The design ensured that each participant could maintain full concentration during the time spent learning the phonemes and words, and took advantage of memory consolidation by spreading the one-hour learning period over multiple days.

Procedure. The following list shows the tasks performed by each participant over the six learning days. On each day, the participant practiced for 5 min, followed by a test with trial-by-trial correct-answer feedback for another 5 min.

- Day 1 (10 min): 6 phonemes;
- Day 2 (10 min): 24 words made up of the 6 phonemes;
- Day 3 (10 min): 4 new phonemes learned, all 10 phonemes tested;
- Day 4 (10 min): 27 new words;
- Day 5–6 (10, 10 min): all 51 words.

5.2   Results

The results in terms of percent-correct scores are shown in Fig. 5. Due to the fact that the participants reached near-perfect performance level on Day 3 (10 phonemes) and Day 6 (51 words), we do not report the few error trials. The results are organized by day (and cumulative training time in min). Data for the four participants are shown in different color patterns.

Several observations can be made. First, it was relatively easy for the participants to learn the phonemes. Performance was near perfect on Day 1 (6 phonemes) after 5 min of learning and on Day 3 (10 phonemes) after 5 min of learning 4 new phonemes. Second, the transition from phoneme to words took some getting used to, as seen comparing the results from Day 1 (6 phonemes) and Day 2 (24 words made up of the 6 phonemes). This indicates that additional learning was required in order to process phonemes delivered in a sequence. Third, despite the initial "dip" in performance on Day 2 and Day 4 when the participants transitioned from phonemes to words, word-recognition improved quickly as seen in the rising performance from Day 4 to Day 6. The most significant improvement occurred with P5 who reached 62.5%, 77.5% and 97.5% correct from Day 4 to Day 6, respectively. Finally, regardless of individual differences among the four participants in earlier days, all participants succeeded in identifying the 51 words with very few errors by the end of the 60-min period.

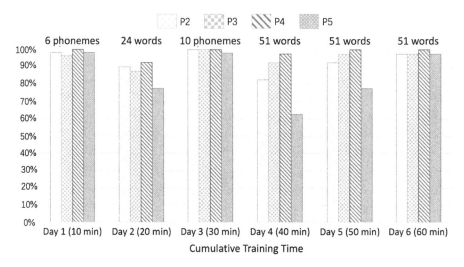

Fig. 5. Results of Exp. I (10 phonemes and 51 words)

Compared with the pilot study, participants in Exp. I learned more phonemes and words in less time. This is probably due to the strict control of learning time per day in order to maintain a high level of concentration on the part of the participants. In addition, the mapping from phoneme to haptic symbols was improved based on the feedback from P1 in the pilot study. The new haptic symbols were more distinct and easier to learn than those in the pilot study. The continued improvement from Day 4 to Day 6 for all participants, especially P5, led us to speculate that memory consolidation may have played a big role in the learning process. We therefore designed Exp. II to explicitly test the effect, if any, of memory consolidation. We also used Exp. II to test whether all 39 phonemes could be learned and how long the learning process would take.

6 Experiment II: Learning of 39 Phonemes

6.1 Methods

The objectives of Exp. II were to (1) test memory consolidation explicitly, (2) gain experience and insight into learning all 39 phonemes, and (3) record the time it takes to learn the phonemes and the attainable performance level. One new naïve participant (P6) took part in Exp. II for a total of 14 consecutive days, including the weekends.

Learning Materials. All 39 phonemes shown in Table 1 are included in Exp. II. The 39 phonemes were divided into 8 groups. In addition to the first two groups (containing 6 and 4 phonemes, respectively) that were used in Exp. I, an additional 6 groups of phonemes were created with 5 new phonemes per group except for the last group that contained 4 new phonemes.

Time Constraints. As in Exp. I, the learning time was capped at 10 min on each day, with no break. The participant took detailed daily notes on his observations afterwards.

Procedure. For testing the memory consolidation theory, the participant always ended a day and began the next day with the *same* test, except for Day 1 when there was no test at the beginning of the day. The participant then spent 3–4 min on learning new phonemes and the rest of the 10 min on testing all phonemes learned so far, with trial-by-trial correct-answer feedback. In addition, the participant sounded out a phoneme during the learning phase. The learning plan is shown below, with the total number of phonemes learned/tested each day clearly marked (Fig. 6). The participant had to achieve a percent-correct score of 90% or higher before he could move on to the next group of new phonemes. As shown below, the participant was able to learn one group of phonemes per day during the first 8 days, and was tested with all 39 phonemes from Day 9 to 14.

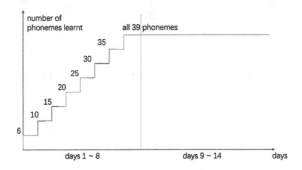

Fig. 6. Learning plan for Experiment II

6.2   Results

The results are presented in two parts. We first show the percent-correct scores for phoneme recognition from Day 1 to Day 8, including the test conducted on Day 9 that repeated the last test on Day 8 (Fig. 7). It is clear that when the same test was conducted again the next day, the performance level either remained the same or improved. This provides a clear evidence for the memory consolidation theory in the sense that performance improved (with the exception of Day 6 to Day 7) after a period of activities not related to phoneme learning. A second observation is that the participant had no difficulty learning between 4 to 6 new phonemes a day, presumably due to the highly distinctive haptic symbols and the easy-to-learn mapping from phoneme to haptic symbols.

Starting on Day 9, the participant was tested with 4 runs of 50 trials on all 39 phonemes for six consecutive days. The daily percent-correct scores from the 200 pooled trials are shown in Fig. 8. Overall, P6 was able to maintain a high performance level (93.8% ± 3.8% correct).

A stimulus-response confusion matrix was constructed from all 1200 trials (50 trials/run × 4 runs/day × 6 days) to examine the most-confused phoneme pairs. The following is the list, in order of descending number of confusions:

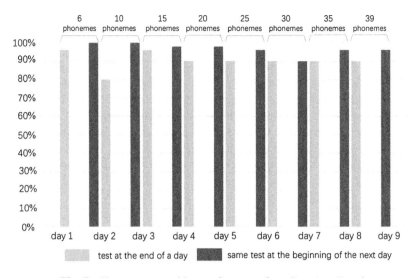

Fig. 7. Phoneme recognition performance from Day 1 to Day 9

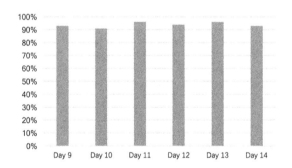

Fig. 8. Daily phoneme recognition scores from Day 9 to Day 14

- /t/with /k/(9 times);
- /ae/with /l/(8 times);
- /b/with /d/(4 times);
- /g/with /d/(4 times);
- /i/with /z/(4 times);
- /t/with /p/(4 times);
- /u/with /ai/(3 times);
- /g/with /m/(3 times);
- /n/with /h/(3 times).

The rest of the errors occurred twice or less and are not listed. The confusion pattern served to guide further refinement of the design of haptic symbols.

7 Concluding Remarks

The present study offers evidence to support the claim that speech communication through the sense of touch is an achievable goal. The participants received speech information (phonemes and words) presented on their forearm through a sequence of haptic symbols encoding phonemes. The results of Exp. I show that four naïve participants were able to recognize 51 words in 60 min. The results of Exp. II show that all 39 English phonemes could be learned in 80 min. We demonstrated memory consolidation in Exp. II by showing an improvement in phoneme recognition performance when the participant P6 was tested a day after he learned the phonemes.

Several guidelines can be provided based on the experimental results and the insights we have gained from the present study. First, the learning time should be limited to 10 to 20 min per session. It was difficult for participants to maintain full concentration after 20 min. Second, it might be helpful for the participant to sound a phoneme out as the haptic symbol was delivered to the forearm although we did not collect data to prove that. Third, the task difficulty should be carefully managed so that the participant is challenged but able to make progress. Last but surely not the least, the results of Experiment II provide evidence for learning that occurred between laboratory sessions when the participant was not being trained. Therefore, we recommend spending a short period of time (e.g., 10 min) per day and taking advantage of memory consolidation for further improvement of learning outcome. Furthermore, the benefit of memory consolidation did not appear to be impacted when learning sessions were interrupted by one or more days.

In the future, we will continue to improve the haptic symbols to further reduce errors in phoneme recognition. We will also compare different learning strategies such as reversing the order in which phonemes and words are introduced to the participants. Our ultimate goal is to develop a haptic speech communication system for people with all levels of sensory capabilities.

Acknowledgments. This work was partially supported by a research grant from Facebook Inc. The authors thank all participants for their time and dedication, and Keith Klumb for project management.

References

1. Reed, C.M., Rabinowitz, W.M., Durlach, N.I., Braida, L.D., Conway-Fithian, S., Schultz, M.C.: Research on the Tadoma method of speech communication. J. Acoust. Soc. Am. **77**, 247–257 (1985)
2. Tan, H.Z., Durlach, N.I., Reed, C.M., Rabinowitz, W.M.: Information transmission with a multifinger tactual display. Percept. Psychophys. **61**(6), 993–1008 (1999)
3. Reed, C.M., Durlach, N.I.: Note on information transfer rates in human communication. Pres. Teleoper. Virtual Environ. **7**(5), 509–518 (1998)
4. Reed, C.M., Durlach, N.I., Braida, L.D.: Research on tactile communication of speech: a review. In: American Speech-Language-Hearing Association (ASHA) Monographs Number 20, May 1982, 23 p. (1982)

5. Reed, C.M., Durlach, N.I., Delhorne, L.A., Rabinowitz, W.M., Grant, K.W.: Research on tactual communication of speech: ideas, issues, and findings. Volta Rev. **91**(5), 65–78 (1989). Monograph entitled "Research on the use of sensory aids for hearing-impaired people," N.S. McGarr, Editor

6. Kirman, J.H.: Tactile communication of speech: a review and analysis. Psychol. Bull. **80**, 54–74 (1973)

7. Yuan, H., Reed, C.M., Durlach, N.I.: Tactual display of consonant voicing as a supplement to lipreading. J. Acoust. Soc. Am. **118**(2), 1003–1015 (2005)

8. Israr, A., Reed, C.M., Tan, H.Z.: Discrimination of vowels with a multi-finger tactual display. In: Proceedings of the Symposium on Haptic Interfaces for Virtual Environment and Teleoperator Systems, pp. 17–24 (2008)

9. Novich, S.D., Eagleman, D.M.: Using space and time to encode vibrotactile information: toward an estimate of the skin's achievable throughput. Exp. Brain Res. **233**, 2777–2788 (2015)

10. Verrillo, R.T., Gescheider, G.A.: Perception via the sense of touch (Chap. 1). In: Summers, I. R. (ed.) Tactile Aids for the Hearing Impaired, pp. 1–36. Whurr Publishers, London (1992)

11. Tan, H.Z., Durlach, N.I., Rabinowitz, W.M., Reed, C.M., Santos, J.R.: Reception of Morse code through motional, vibrotactile, and auditory stimulation. Percept. Psychophys. **59**(7), 1004–1017 (1997)

12. Wade, T., Holt, L.L.: Incidental categorization of spectrally complex non-invariant auditory stimuli in a computer game task. J. Acoust. Soc. Am. **118**(4), 2618–2633 (2005)

13. Karni, A., Dudai, Y., Born, J.: The consolidation and transformation of memory. Neuron **88**, 20–32 (2015)

14. Ecroyd, D.H.: Voice and Articulation: A Hanbook, pp. 63–87. Scott Foresman & Co Publisher, Glenview (1966)

15. Reed, C.M., et al.: A phonemic-based tactual display for speech communication. IEEE Trans. Haptics (2018, in preparation)

16. Levitt, H.: Transformed up-down methods in psychoacoustics. J. Acoust. Soc. Am. **49**(2B), 467–477 (1971)

Evaluating Tangible and Embodied Interactions for Intercontinental Educators, Researchers, and Designers

Wei Liu[(✉)]

Beijing Normal University, Beijing, China
wei.liu@bnu.edu.cn

Abstract. This study presents evaluations conducted with a working prototype in a lab setting. The goal of these evaluations was to both evaluate the prototype and to find out what effect a new interactive work tool can have on the cross-geographical designers' interaction behavior. By evaluating the tangible and embodied interactions we also evaluate what was found before in theory and practice. Through the evaluations, we found that the prototype supports users in experiencing designerly type of interactions and in enhancing computer supported cooperative work activities. The overall evaluation was positive with some valuable suggestions to its user interactions and features.

Keywords: Tangible interaction · Design evaluation · User experience
CSCW · Context of use

1 Introduction

Collaboration requires individuals working together in a coordinated fashion, towards a common goal. Accomplishing the goal is the primary purpose for bringing a team together. We help facilitate action-oriented design teams working together cross-geographical distances (i.e., between China and USA) by providing tools that aid communication, collaboration and the process of problem solving. Additionally, collaborative platform may support project management functions, such as task assignments, time-managing deadlines and shared calendars. The artefacts, the tangible evidence [7, 8] of the problem solving process and the final outcome of the collaborative effort, require documentation and may involve archiving project plans, deadlines and deliverables. This would create a more sustainable working and living environments, which is in line with the theme of future ways of co-working and social innovation. By integrating international design resources and the most advanced information technologies (e.g., cloud computing), we aim to achieve a real-time, remote, collaborative and digital product service system from a designer-centered perspective. This product service system is called Digital Collaborative Design Platform [5], which includes a set of technological toolkit, intellectual property databases, an easy-to-use cross-border digital prototype and a collaborative design network. This platform connects professional design laboratories geographically spread around the

© Springer International Publishing AG, part of Springer Nature 2018
A. Marcus and W. Wang (Eds.): DUXU 2018, LNCS 10919, pp. 461–471, 2018.
https://doi.org/10.1007/978-3-319-91803-7_35

world, and supports co-design through seamless digital and physical computer supported cooperative work (CSCW) collaborations.

This study was set up to evaluate the tangible interaction designs [6, 14, 17] of the prototype. The objective of the study was to evaluate the contributions of such interactions on new ways of co-designing and co-working. The research question is: How are the interactions of the new design experienced? A controlled lab evaluation was conducted to evaluate if novel functions and its interactions can be experienced by the users when interacting with the prototype. The focus of this study was to see if we succeeded in enabling designerly type of interactions [10].

2 Designerly Type of Interactions

The starting point of this research was formed by the research questions as listed in the introduction. In the remainder of this section, the author discusses what answers were found.

2.1 'What Are Generation Y Styles of Interaction in Home Life and Office Work?'

In our previous work of studying user interactions in the work contexts [4, 5], we identified a number of typical designerly type of interactions, which are further refined below:

- **Integrating IT and Life:** they regard IT as an integral part of their lives. They spend considerable amounts of time interacting with digital technology. They easily communicate with others and access information quickly and instantaneously. They use personal computers, surf on the Internet, watch DVDs, play video games and use mobile phones more often than any other generation. They spend fewer amounts of time reading offline magazines and newspapers than any other generation. They integrate IT into life, as well as bring life into IT. A more intimate understanding of how they lead their lives is becoming part of designing how IT is offered.
- **Connecting through Mobile Technology:** mobile phones mean much more than just talking. They spend a great amount of time using mobile devices to search for information on the Internet, listen to music, text messaging, instant messaging, communicate on social network sites and interact in virtual communities.
- **Working Socially and Collaboratively:** they are a social and collaborative workforce. They prefer working as a team to accomplish independent tasks as they use the skills, knowledge and resources of team members to satisfy individual needs. Self-actualization and a balanced work and personal life are considered essential. Therefore, they want to have more control in doing their work with the freedom to execute the task in their own way and eventually leave a personal mark on the work. They are eager to communicate, work with personal preference, being in control and being more productive and creative than any previous generation.

- **Multitasking:** by using technology, they have trained themselves in the ability to handle more than one task at a time without feeling overwhelmed. They are used to multitasking, they can also manage what and when things should be done. Even more, they look forward to the challenges of performing and completing several tasks at the same time.
- **Balancing Life and Work:** they strive for flexibility and balance in their day-to-day life. They want to work, but they do not want 'work to be their life'. They have a higher value on self-fulfillment. They feel that they deserve the freedom to work fewer hours while still taking jobs that are challenging. They want to work flexible and have the ability to do part time jobs, or even leave the working environment temporarily when there is a need from their friends and family. As an example, they may want to work at home one day per week to take care of their children.
- **Sharing:** they write and talk openly about themselves and friends both online and offline. Compared with older generations, they like to show off their taste, always looking for new ways to entertain themselves, to spend more time having fun with friends and family. They are much more influenced by what they perceive to be trendy and fresh than other generations, they are also more willing to try new things, they value peers' advice, and they are inclined to seek for input from friends and family.
- **Learning:** they are always seeking for new knowledge and are eager to learn new technologies both in work and life. They want to try out all kinds of new product interactions, which they can learn very fast based on their previous and similar use experiences. They do not like to fall behind of modern technologies. Instead, they like to pursue state-of-the-art (digital) interactive products and exchange their learning experiences with their peers.

To accommodate these interactions, we went through five stages to design the Digital Collaborative Design Platform prototype: (1) product service system analysis, (2) collaborative design, (3) research on computer supported cooperative work (CSCW) model, (4) user experience research, and (5) product service system design. Recommendations were given to design and develop interactive collaborative design platforms in the work context.

3   Method

In this evaluation participants were invited to a laboratory setting. The researchers controlled the evaluation procedure and observed the reaction. Previous researchers [2, 3, 9] recommend the researchers do not get involved in performing the user interactions but remain passive observers, watching, listening to and documenting the ways of interacting, and then drawing conclusions from it. This study underlines two essential characteristics: (1) it is a purposeful, systematic and selective way of evaluating interaction; (2) it focuses more on the behavior than on the perception of the participant. To reach out a variety of participants with different backgrounds and expertise, the evaluations took place in our institute. A portable video camera was pointed at the table and the participant to record all user interactions.

4 Participants

30 participants were involved in this study. There were18 male and 12 female participants. Their ages were between 19 and 70. Their professions concentrated mostly in the field of designers, engineers and students: 6 participants worked in industry, 14 in academia, 8 were students and 2 were unemployed. They had different educational backgrounds: design (18), engineering (8), management (3) and other (1). Their educational levels varied: undergraduate (12), graduate (7) and PhD (11).

5 Video Scenarios

The prototype was designed as a Y-shaped structure in order to get the best line of sight and the interaction relationship, its software interface was developed at our institute [5]. See Fig. 1 for an impression.

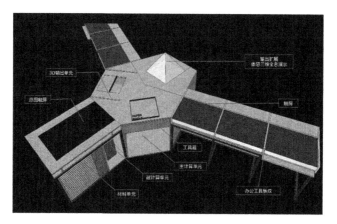

Fig. 1. The Y-shaped structure and the interface design logic of the Digital Collaborative Design Platform prototype

To assist the participants to experience the prototype as much as possible, video scenarios were created to introduce the eight main functions of the prototype [11, 13, 18]. Figure 2 shows the screenshots of the video scenarios. The eight functions are as follows:

- **Collaborative Annotation:** designers can design together by canvas synchronization. This function supports real-time sketching and some essential aspects of design drafts exchange.

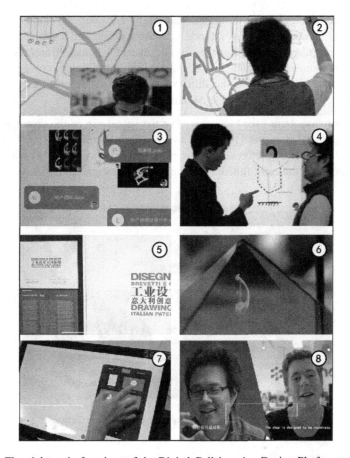

Fig. 2. The eight main functions of the Digital Collaborative Design Platform prototype

- **Backtracking:** designers can find each step of the design process and the corresponding file information based on the timeline.
- **Multi-Index Category:** designers can quickly sort files and upload them to the cloud server. Backtracking and Multi-index Category, these two functions can clearly find the achievement ownership and protect the intellectual property rights of designers.
- **Post-It:** designers can use post-it to transfer and share files in real-time more conveniently and faster.
- **Material Library and Instant Printing:** designers from different design backgrounds can take advantage of the huge cloud material library and patent library to get a steady stream of inspiration.
- **3D Model Projection:** After the sketch modeling, designers can improve the design through the holographic projection. Designers have an intuitive seeing and analysis of the model by 3D printing. Finally, the design can be produced and manufactured by many trades co-operation.

- **Documents Integration:** designers can view and edit all kinds formats of third-party documents such as Autodesk, Adobe, Office and so on.
- **Instant Language Translation:** by online instant language translation systems, different languages no longer hinder the smooth and efficient cross-geographical design work. When holding the different languages conference, this system can instantly translate and display the contents to all clients.

The participants were asked to experience the actual use of the prototype and the detailed tangible interactions [19]. Key user-platform interactions (see Fig. 3) were demonstrated by videos, pictures and described by key words [15, 16] when the participants experience the eight functions of the prototype. Some examples are as follows:

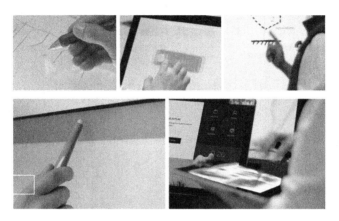

Fig. 3. Examples of the key user-platform interactions

- The participant taps the screen twice to adjust the screen size when they edit the design shape by the electronic pen.
- The participant uses the slide gesture to drag the file to the Whiteboard area.
- When the participant uses the Post-It, they can click the screen by single finger to open the file.
- The participant uses the electronic pen to slide along the timeline to find the step of the design process.
- The participant transfers files to others by throwing them in/through the air.

6   Procedure

Each evaluation took about 30–40 min per participant, during which they went through the following steps [1, 12]:

1. The researcher verbally introduces the project background in brief and the definition of tangible interaction.

2. The researcher explicitly introduces and demonstrates the eight functions of the Digital Collaborative Design Platform.
3. The participant is asked to try out each user-platform tangible interaction with the prototype.
4. The participant is interviewed to explain in what ways the new design is related to the tangible interaction and where they succeed and where not.
5. The participant views the recorded video and describe the detail of the tangible interaction in each scenario.

Round up discussion and reflection on the ways the new design would improve (or not improve) the cross-geographical co-working.

7   Results and Analysis

Data from the study were:

- Observations of participants interacting with the prototype, e.g., recorded in videos and notes.
- Selected remarks by participants recorded noted as quotes.
- Answers by participants of the evaluation of interaction experience, such as the weakness and problem they face to in the testing stage under working context.
- Analyses result is concluded from of the user feedbacks with sorting.
- Transcripts of use satisfaction rate from the evaluations.

7.1   General Analyses

In order to get the objective user observation record, the researchers set up an observation principle that includes three steps. Firstly, classifying different roles of participants and observing the reactions when the researchers show them the introduction video and the guidance of the prototype. According to the backgrounds and relationship of stakeholders in the real design development projects, participants are divided into four types of roles, they are crossing-geographical designers, suppliers, developers and project manager. And then, recording the using situations and experience after the researchers giving them a collaborative design task in the working context. Next, collecting user experience feedbacks from in-depth user interviews. That means whether the prototype has smooth interaction process, the flexible information communication abilities, or easily-used and friendly designed interfaces and so on.

The observations and interviews results were organized into three aspects that include the usability, the accessibility and the interactivity. First of all, three participants described that they had difficulties to find the interface of backtracking function accurately under the collaborative discussion context. Because repeated discussions and collaborative sketch are the most common feature in design development activities, therefore, when designers show the product sketches or models, other participants usually need to back to the front process if they had better suggestions or opposite opinions. However, the interfaces exploded the disadvantage of information communication, and it would adversely affect the discussion or concept generation. This description from users indicated that the logic of usability and user-friendliness of interface design are both vital for cross-geographical collaboration platform.

Other feedbacks belong to the aspect of accessibility. The participants felt confused when they tried to choose the project entrance interface to start a collaborative online conference. On one hand, because of several ongoing projects are arranged on the same page and the same operation level. On the other hand, the information structure and interfaces for different roles of users have no clear distinction that has influenced the smooth use experience for different roles. Different levels of accessibility for users should be seen as an indispensable feature of interface development.

On the aspect of interactivity, most participants gave positive feedbacks. They reflected that the cross-geographical collaborative interactions are user centered design outcomes. The participants described that this platform broke the traditional barrier of time, space and language for the conceptual phase of multinational design project. The interaction behaviors of tapping for quick view, dragging to integrate documents backtracking with electronic pen to check every process of sketches and the multi-screens linkage for collaboration modification on different terminal equipment were greatly beneficial to improve work efficiency. Comparing with other input peripherals (i.e., keyboards, joysticks and mice), these gestures are natural behaviors. They can enable the instant operations without the limitation of space and different size screens. Above user observations indicate that effective tangible interaction gestures and the instant backstage feedbacks are the core user experience in the real collaborative work context.

7.2   Evaluation of Tangible Interactions

Following results were found regarding the user feedbacks after testing eight core interaction functions of the Digital Collaborative Design Platform.

- **Collaborative Annotation:** this interaction can be achieved by backstage recording of any drawing operation command on the main whiteboard. All the participants approved this user centered interaction can improve the cross-geographical concept generation quality greatly. But there are still interaction weaknesses like the function area settings of interface design or the lack of gestures diversity. All these weaknesses can lead to unavoidable mistakes. Improvement suggestion from participants is adding operational gestures like sliding, tapping, swiping or dragging to distinguish different interaction commands.
- **Backtracking:** the participants found it was easy to cause mistakes because the speed of the interaction gesture is difficult to control. This function is the most high frequency interaction behavior during the ideas generation process, and the feature is using electronic pen to backtrack on the timeline. So the tangible interaction way needs to adjust the position of the bottom, and the interaction command also needs to take into different gestures in order to offer accurate and easy-used interaction experience for users.
- **Post-It:** every participant can sent design ideas to the main whiteboard by this function, and the participants also had the ability to classify the information and sort

out useful direction for project concept generation. The core of using experience is the readability and operability of interactive instruction.

- **Multi-Index Category:** the participants could only get basic information like titles, authors and date from the preview when they tested the Multi-index Category function with tapping the function area. Different tangible gestures like dragging the documents icons for more previews or swiping to close present interface should be considered to enhance the category experience.
- **Material Library and Instant Printing:** researchers found the problem of sight out of focus was obvious under the working context because the prototype was dependent on the large-size touch screens, so more compact arrangement for operation panel should be taken into interface design. It also indicated the accessibility of interaction behaviors.
- **Model Projection:** the core problem of multi-screens linkage interaction is the accuracy. When participants tried to swipe in the air above the screen of personal equipment to main whiteboard, they found the accuracy and response speed are not satisfactory. It indicates the improvement of tangible trigger mechanism.
- **Documents Integration and Instant Language Translation:** although the participants gave positive feedbacks of these two interaction and functions, documents compatibility and information stratification were still the challenge for backstage technology support.

8 Discussion

The results of this study indicate that the prototype and its tangible user interactions would fit into user needs and the co-design context. From analyzing the evaluation feedbacks, guidelines are concluded which set up a paradigm for other cross-geographical collaboration challenges.

8.1 Usability

The tangible interactions should fit into user habits and the guidelines. It should set up different ranges of control limits and trigger mechanism (such as sliding, tapping, dragging, swiping on the air, etc.) for reducing interaction mistakes in the co-design context. Interface design should consider the instructive and suggestive interaction gestures. Instructive interaction means the tasks and guides for users to enable them understand how to control interaction commands and the operation procedure. Suggestive gesture means using design effects like lighting, colors stratification or renderings to guide them use the tangible interactions. Instructive gestures could be efficient for users to grasp the interaction behaviors, and suggestive gesture experience is more smooth and user-friendly.

8.2   Accessibility

It is worth to build a flexible mechanism for information transmission and feedback. Such platform should ensure instant and effective response for tangible interaction in the collaborative work context. It means the diversity of feedback actions should be applied to interface or instruction design. Like changing of colors, sounds or vibrations to let users know if the present situation is suitable for interactive gestures or if the tangible interaction command is succeed.

8.3   Interactivity

Collaborative operation requires the interaction experience fits into multipoint using scenario. Like using PQ Labs Multi-Touch SDK to integrate the gestures into whiteboard system to achieve the backtracking and repetition of collaborative modification function. This requires tangible interactions with dynamic gestures. Accuracy is the core of gestures, it includes movements, sliding direction, multi-point gestures and other features. On the other aspect, interactivity needs the tolerance of user differences for multi-terminal (subscribers') equipment, which means tangible interactions have inclusive ability for the mistakes within a reasonable range.

9   Conclusions

This study shows that the functions and its tangible interactions implemented in the Digital Collaborative Design Platform prototype are experienced well. The primary contribution of this work to the existing knowledge domain is the understanding of how novel interactions can support designerly ways of interacting and co-working cross-geographically.

By carefully choosing evaluation methods and controlling the evaluation procedure, we have been able to verify key functions and interactions for. If researchers and designers would make designs that appeal to designerly type of interactions, contexts, tasks and people, the approach of designing tangible interactions are recommended. Although the present study focuses on work tools only, a similar approach may be valid for other forms of (computer supported interactive) tools, applications and services.

References

1. Buxton, B.: Sketching User Experiences: The Workbook. Morgan Kaufmann, San Francisco (2014)
2. Koskinen, I., Zimmerman, J., Binder, T., Redström, J., Wensveen, S.: Design Research Through Practice, 1st edn. Morgan Kaufmann, San Francisco (2011)
3. Kumar, R.: Research Methodology: A Step-by-Step Guide for Beginners, 2nd edn. Sage Publications, Thousand Oaks (2005)
4. Liu, W., Pasman, G., Taal-Fokker, J., Stappers, P.J.: Exploring 'Generation Y' interaction qualities at home and at work. J. Cogn. Technol. Work 16(3), 405–415 (2014)

5. Liu, W., Lou, Y.: The Sino-Italian collaborative design platform: designing and developing an innovative product service system. In: Rau, P.L.P. (ed.) CCD 2014. LNCS, vol. 8528, pp. 766–774. Springer, Cham (2014). https://doi.org/10.1007/978-3-319-07308-8_73
6. Locher, P.J., Overbeeke, C.J., Wensveen, S.A.G.: Aesthetic interaction: a framework. Des. Issues 26(2), 70–79 (2010)
7. Löwgren, J.: Articulating the use qualities of digital designs. In: Aesthetic Computing, pp. 383–403 (2006)
8. Martin, F., Roehr, K.E.: A general education course in tangible interaction design. In: Proceedings of the ACM Conference on Tangible Embedded Interaction (TEI), pp. 185–188. ACM Press, New York (2010)
9. Norman, D.A.: Emotion and design: attractive things work better. Interactions 9(4), 36–42 (2002)
10. Øritsland, T.A., Buur, J.: Interaction styles: an aesthetic sense of direction in interface design. Int. J. Hum. Comput. Interact. 15(1), 67–85 (2003)
11. Pasman, G., Boess, S., Desmet, P.: Interaction vision: expressing and identifying the qualities of user-product interactions. In: Proceedings of the International Conference on Engineering and Product Design Education, pp. 149–154 (2011)
12. Paton, M.: Qualitative Research and Evaluation Methods, 3rd edn. Sage Publications, Thousand Oaks (2002)
13. Preece, J., Roger, Y., Sharp, H.: Interaction Design: Beyond Human-Computer Interaction, 2nd edn., pp. 181–217. Wiley, New York (2007)
14. Ross, P.R., Wensveen, S.A.G.: Designing aesthetics of behavior in interaction: using aesthetic experience as a mechanism for design. Int. J. Des. 4(2), 3–13 (2010)
15. Sanders, L., Stappers, P.J.: Convivial Toolbox: Generative Research for the Front End of Design, pp. 224–225. BIS Publishers, Amsterdam (2013)
16. Stappers, P.J.: Teaching principles of qualitative analysis to industrial design engineers. In: Proceedings of the Conference on Engineering & Product Design Education (2012)
17. Wensveen, S.A.G.: A tangibility approach to affective interaction. Doctoral dissertation. Eindhoven University of Technology, Eindhoven (2005)
18. Whyte, W.: Advancing scientific knowledge through participatory action research. Sociol. Forum 4(3), 367–385 (1989)
19. Zimmerman, J., Forlizzi, J., Evenson, S.: Research through design as a method for interaction design research in HCI. In: Proceedings of the ACM SIGCHI Conference on Human Factors in Computing Systems (CHI). ACM Press, New York (2007)

Research on Conversational User Interface in Financial Scenario

Lei Wang[1,2] and Song Liu[1,2(✉)]

[1] Beijing Normal University, Beijing, China
lei.wang@bnu.edu.cn, soso539@126.com
[2] Rongqi (Beijing) Creative Design Co. Ltd., Beijing, China

Abstract. This paper describes the usage of conversation user interface in financial scenario. In 2017, intelligent voice interaction has attracted a lot of attention from researchers. Intelligent voice provides a natural means of interaction. In financial scenario, users have to input and click in order to interact with the graphic interface when they use mobile banking applications. Conversational user interface based on intelligent voice technology provide feasibility to simplify the interaction between user and the application. The paper lists "transfer accounts" as a research case to show the process how the conversation interface should be used in this scenario. The research is aimed to explore richer possibilities in the future.

Keywords: Conversation user interface (CUI) · Intelligent voice
Voice user interface · Financial scenario · Transfer accounts

1 Introduction

Conversational user interface (CUI) is a kind of interface mode based on the chat window, which is different from the graphical user interface and natural interaction mode. The conversation interface can provide the entrance for intelligent voice, but also carries pictures, controls and hypertext forms [2, 3, 5, 7]. For complex financial service scenario, the conversation interface combines both the voice user interface (VUI) and graphical user interface (GUI) for the user to promote the overall interaction flow, in order to realize the user tasks [1, 4].

2 Background

2.1 More Natural Way of Interaction

Conversational interface based on intelligent voice technology provides a natural form for people to communicate with technology [6, 19]. From CLI (Command-line interface), to complicated GUI (Graphical User Interface), people have been searching ways to understand and communicate with machine for about thirty years (Fig. 1). Human brains are fundamentally considered that the source of speech is human. It is the first

© Springer International Publishing AG, part of Springer Nature 2018
A. Marcus and W. Wang (Eds.): DUXU 2018, LNCS 10919, pp. 472–482, 2018.
https://doi.org/10.1007/978-3-319-91803-7_36

time which people use their own way to interact with machine. That means conversational interface can be considered as a much more natural way than GUI [8, 10, 12].

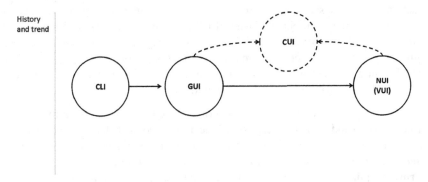

Fig. 1. History and trend

CUI is a transition from GUI to a VUI (Fig. 1). It is at the in the form of dialog [9, 17]. The form of dialogue weakens the way of accessing and operating the main information. It would bring not only the interface change but also the process alternation.

2.2 The Feasibility

Technology and human recognition system provide the feasibility for conversational interaction. Voice interaction technology has developed rapidly. People have the requirement that the machine is able to understand themselves as human beings, or be their real assistant. At present, more than one Technology Company has announced that their voice recognition rate is up to 97% [9, 11, 15]. In the other hand, the booming Social Networking Services (SNS) make conversational interface familiar with the users than any time in the history [18].

2.3 The Improvement of Experience

For a long time, the GUI has been used as an intermediary for people to interact with software. There are a lot of interactive logic and control rules in GUI, which cost users a lot of learning costs. Compared with the graphical user interface, conversational interface based on intelligent voice technology has a unique advantage [13]. People don't have to look for the function they want among a big list. The voice user interface (VUI) should lead the whole task to reduce operation steps. At the same time, the graphical user interface (GUI) also provides the visual advantages complementary at the key touch-point. This is definitely a huge improvement in the user experience.

3   Process

Conversation user interface (CUI) is aimed to shorten the task flow and optimize user interaction with the system [16]. CUI provides the obvious advantage experience, but at the same time the open characteristic of CUI would lead to personalization of the user flow. Rather than a fixed step of GUI era, CUI design requires the user experience designer to predict user intent and create task-driven scenarios.

Establishing a financial scenario requires integration of the financial service characteristics. The following should be paid attention:

- **Security.** It includes user account security and environmental security. Account security is included in the security of the user account behavior, such as login, transact etc. Environmental security includes the judgment on environmental interference, whether it is safe for trading in this environment.
- **Professional.** Unlike other Fibo as personal assistant, CUI applied in financial scenarios should be designed with strong user intent. Therefore, rigorous logic and perfect feedback mechanism are necessary.

The core element of CUI is the scenario-based dialogue, which is task-driven and focuses on what users say and how chatbot responds. Therefore, the design process could be concluded as below (Fig. 2).

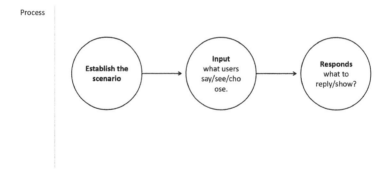

Fig. 2. Process

3.1   Establish the Scenario

"Transfer the remittance" in mobile banking have been chosen example for exploratory conversational interaction [14]. And the intelligent system provides the conversational financial service was name "Fibo".

The scenario provides the following conveniences for the change of CUI.

- The instructions issued by the user is clear and simple, which could be summarized in terms of "Verb plus object".
- It is a High frequency use function in mobile banking.
- The normal interaction flow is less than or equal to three.
- The number of modifiable or edited items could be controlled.

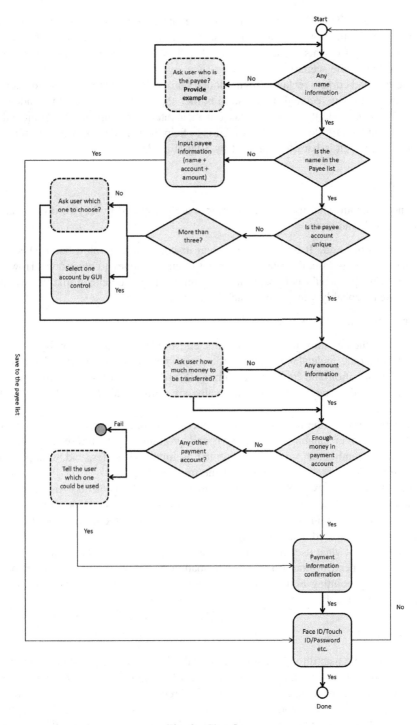

Fig. 3. Chat flow

Compared to the GUI, users interact with the interface by pointing or clicking, VUI provide a "query to answer" flow for the users. If someone (A) wants to transfer money to someone (B) from his/her account, the chat flow below (Fig. 3) shows the possibilities of the whole scenario.

The rounded corners rectangles with dotted border show where VUI would happen. The rounded corners rectangles with solid border show where GUI would be added to help. VUI is to guide the user to speak out their intent, and turn it into command in order to push the task flow. However, GUI is to help the user dealing with complicated information, which is hard to represent by VUI (Fig. 3).

3.2   Input

Utterance is about what users say. Utterances are composed by keyword commands, natural speech and slot.

Keyword Command. It is what users intent to do, such as book a hotel, check the weather etc. In this case, the intent of user is to transfer money to other ones. However sometimes people would not speak out their intent. The people said that "I owe jack $500" might probably want to pay back by money transfer.

Natural Speech. Such as filler words.

Slot. Slot is the key information point extracted from the user instruction by the NLU. The NUL module understands the specific requirements of user instructions through this key information and its Value definition (Slot-Value). In this case, the slots are payee name and money amount.the slot-value are corresponds to "jack" and "$500" (Fig. 4).

However, one of the most important aspects is defining the range of what people might say. Human language is extensive and profound. In this case, the intent of "Transfer the remittance" could be presented as follow. Transfer,send,remit,pay,wire could be used to express the meaning of the transfer (Fig. 5).

The utterance showed above is aimed to extend built-in intents. Also providing examples of utterance could help to ensure a good experience. One-shot utterance including the key command and slot could lead the user to the destination. One-shot example is always used as a start (Fig. 6).

Input is about what user communicate with the GUI shown in the dialogue box. In this case, user need to confirm payee information by browsing list and select payee account list by pointing option. The dialogue box carry the view and control for the users' eyes and hands.

3.3   Respond

CUI responds the user through text to speech (TTS) and GUI dialogue box. Designers write a good answer scripts, played through the TTS engine into speech. The response brings the user the most intuitive experience. GUI reflects the personality of the product through interactive design and visual design, while VUI is a personalized through the emotion and speech organization. To set the VUI personality in financial scenario

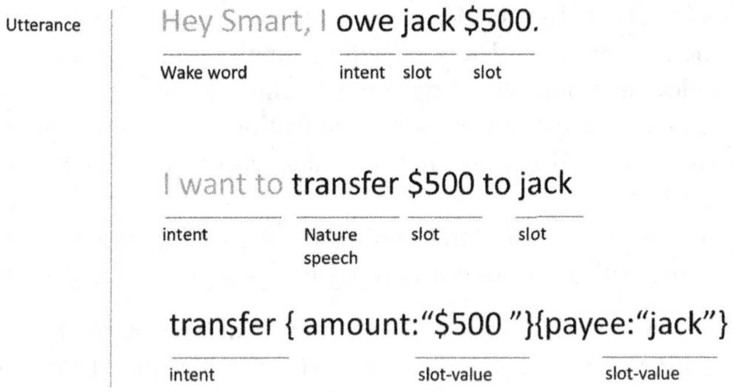

Utterance

Hey Smart, I owe jack $500.

Wake word   intent slot   slot

I want to transfer $500 to jack

intent   Nature   slot   slot
          speech

transfer { amount:"$500 "}{payee:"jack"}

intent   slot-value   slot-value

Fig. 4. Utterance

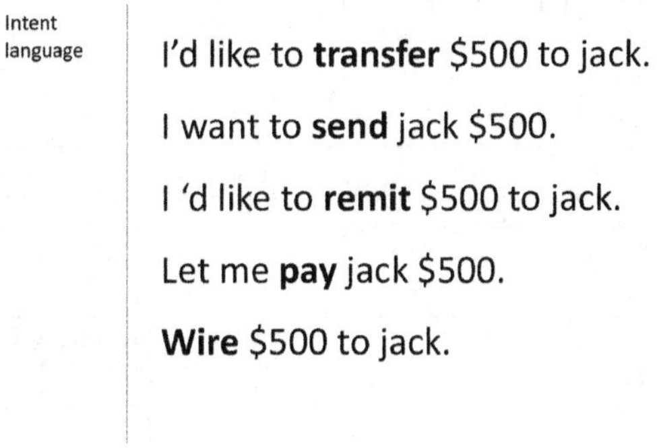

Intent
language

I'd like to **transfer** $500 to jack.

I want to **send** jack $500.

I 'd like to **remit** $500 to jack.

Let me **pay** jack $500.

Wire $500 to jack.

Fig. 5. Intent language

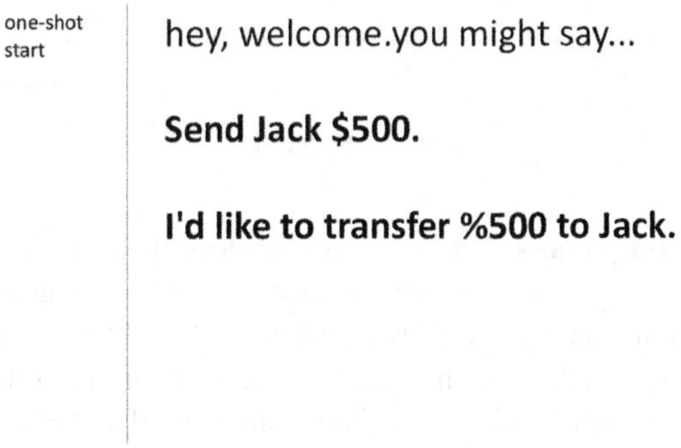

one-shot
start

hey, welcome.you might say...

Send Jack $500.

I'd like to transfer %500 to Jack.

Fig. 6. One-shot start

needs to be based on in-depth user research. Through users' persona to insight the social need. It also needs to integrate the character of financial product, such as professional, reliable, etc.

The design of CUI requires the designer to predefine several types of responses that might arise in the conversation. The whole dialogue design is much like the design of movie script, which help users to complete tasks through query and answer.

At the same time, the research pays more attention on the touch-point which GUI should be applied. The CUI carries GUI as dialog box form to make sure the whole process in immersive environment.

There are three Key nodes in "transfer the remittance" scenario. These key nodes would produce different touch-point according to the user's account status.

- **Payee list.** The payee who is not in the list means that payee information including name and account should be newly created. There is no shortcut for inputting a long string of card Numbers, unless the payee account is mapped as an email address or cellphone Numbers. If the form of the account information is mapped as contact information, the scenario should provide VUI branch flow aimed to get the information from users' contact list (Fig. 7).

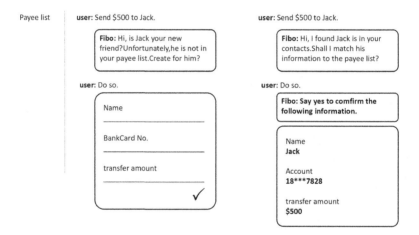

Fig. 7. Payee list

- **Payee account uniqueness.** If the payee has more than one account in the payee list, the system should ask the user to choose one. If the utterance includes the feature information such as XYZ bankcard, which could be tagged by system, the step of payee account selection should be omitted. Otherwise, GUI selection control is recommended to apply for users' easy choosing if there are more than three accounts (Fig. 8).
- **Payment account balance.** If the payment account balance is insufficient, other accounts which balance is sufficient should be matched to the process. The system should ask user to confirm the alternation. If the payment account is unique, the transfer amount less than the balance should be recommended to help to continue the process (Fig. 9).

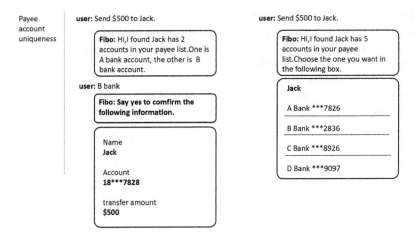

Fig. 8. Payee account uniqueness

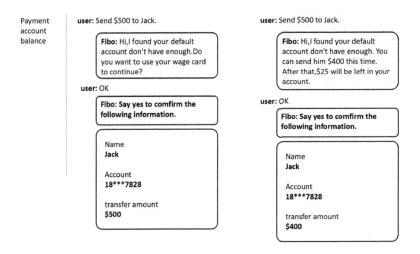

Fig. 9. Payee account uniqueness

4 Design

In this case, two session processes have been selected in this scenario to carry out the high fidelity prototype design (Fig. 9). The design follows the following principle:

- Maximize the entrance of voice
- Enhance content presentation
- Use clear and simple graphical interface controls, form styles to improve interaction efficiency.

The first session choose the one-shot session. The whole conversation is brief. GUI dialogue box is used in the penultimate step for confirmation for the transaction. With the development of biometric technology, users will no longer rely on graphical user interface to verify signatures in the future.

The second session choose the payee account adulteration session. The conversion is composed of wise response and simple control. Compared to the traditional GUI process, only one point for the option is involved in the whole process (Fig. 10).

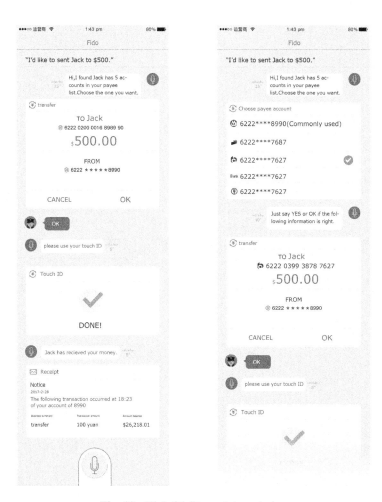

Fig. 10. High fidelity prototype design

The element of CUI is dialogue box. The process of different session could be considered as the combination of different boxes.

5   Conclusion

CUI connects the graphical user interface and natural user interface. By using social scene with user familiar with, through the intelligent voice technology which help users to think and do users want, with interesting dialogue the CUI build up tasks-driven scenario. CUI have succeed in shortening the process and optimizing the user experience.

The mission driven, immersive, single-threaded elements of financial service has a good match for the CUI experience. Based on the research on CUI for financial services scene provides a practice to explore the intelligent voice commercial market.

In the future, CUI may evolve or disappear with technological innovations. But it's still worth exploring the method of a natural interaction.

Acknowledgement. We thank all my fellows for their enthusiasm and hard work. We thank Zhang Ning for her knowledge. We thank Wei Liu, Xin Xin, and Di Zhu for their support. We thank ICBC D&R center for their support. The publication of this research project was supported by the Fundamental Research Funds for the Central Universities (No. 01900-310422110).

References

1. Aprile, W., van der Helm, A.: Interactive technology design at the Delft University of Technology - a course about how to design interactive products. In: Proceedings of the E&PDE 2011, London (2011)
2. Archer, B.: The nature of research. J. Codes. **2**, 6–13 (1995)
3. Arvola, M.: Interaction design qualities: theory and practice. In: Proceedings of the NordiCHI 2010, pp. 595–598. ACM Press (2010)
4. Klemmer, S.R.: The future of user interface design tools. In: Extended Abstracts on Human Factors in Computing Systems, CHI 2005, pp. 2134–2135. ACM (2005)
5. Liebenberg, L., Steventon, J., Brahman, N., Benadie, K., Minye, J., Langwane, H., et al.: Smartphone icon user interface design for non-literate trackers and its implications for an inclusive citizen science. Biol. Conserv. **208**, 155–162 (2016)
6. Giraudet, L., Imbert, J.-P., Bérenger, M., Tremblay, S., Causse, M.: Erratum to "The neuroergonomic evaluation of human machine interface design in air traffic control using behavioral and EEG/ERP measures" [behav. brain res. 294 (2015) 246–253]. Behav. Brain Res. **300**(5), 246 (2016)
7. Grudin, J.: The case against user interface consistency. Commun. ACM **32**(10), 1164–1173 (2017)
8. Princen, J., Bradley, A.: Analysis/synthesis filter bank design based on time domain aliasing cancellation. IEEE Trans. Acoust. Speech Signal Process. **34**(5), 1153–1161 (2003)
9. Al-Tamimi, A., Lewis, F.L., Abu-Khalaf, M.: Model-free Q-learning designs for discrete-time zero-sum games with application to H-infinity control. In: Control Conference, vol. 43, pp. 1668–1675. IEEE (2015)
10. Khaitan, S.K., Mccalley, J.D.: Design techniques and applications of cyberphysical systems: a survey. IEEE Syst. J. **9**(2), 350–365 (2015)
11. Esselman, P.C., Allan, J.D.: Application of species distribution models and conservation planning software to the design of a reserve network for the riverine fishes of northeastern mesoamerica. Freshw. Biol. **56**(1), 71–88 (2015)

12. Arora, S., Arora, G., Lakshminarayan, R., Brown, G., Frid-nielsen, M., Mok, C., et al.: Hierarchical drag and drop structure editor for web sites. US, US8935602 (2015)

13. Bianchi, A., Corbetta, J., Invernizzi, L., Fratantonio, Y., Kruegel, C., Vigna, G.: What the app is that? Deception and countermeasures in the android user interface. In: Security and Privacy, pp. 931–948. IEEE (2015)

14. Marcus, A.: Universal, ubiquitous, user-interface design for the disabled and elderly. HCI and User-Experience Design. HIS, pp. 47–52. Springer, London (2015). https://doi.org/10. 1007/978-1-4471-6744-0_7

15. Bailey, M.: Interaction design: beyond human-computer interaction 2002(4), pp. 369–378 (2011)

16. Kolko, J.: Introduction-thoughts on interaction design. Thoughts on Interaction Design, pp. 96–97 (2010)

17. Cooper, A., Cronin, D., Noessel, C., Reimann, R.: About face: the essentials of interaction design. Mental Neurol. **18**(1), 1 (2014)

18. Xin, X., Zhou, W., Li, M., Wang, H., Xu, H., Fan, Y., et al.: Innovation design in personal center interface of mobile application. In: Marcus, A., Wang, W. (eds.) International Conference of Design, User Experience, and Usability. LNCS, pp. 310–323. Springer, Cham (2017). https://doi.org/10.1007/978-3-319-58637-3_25

19. Bruce, M., David, K., Bryan, R., Ian, R., Jonathan, D., Anne, M.C.: Multi-modal assessment of on-road demand of voice and manual phone calling and voice navigation entry across two embedded vehicle systems. Ergonomics **59**(3), 344–367 (2016)

Research on Interaction Design
of Somatosensory Games Based on User
Experience - A Case Study of Cervical Spine
Health Somatosensory Games

Zhi Wang[✉] and Yangshuo Zheng[✉]

School of Art and Design, Wuhan University of Technology,
Wuhan 430070, China
18717126101@163.com, zhengyangshuo@163.com

Abstract. Internet medical is a new application of Internet technology in the medical field. With the human-computer interaction technology-oriented, people-centered experience design more reflected in the Internet medical industry. More traditional medical devices, more now is to promote the use of new science and technology as relying on the combination of user-centered service design concept to solve the patient's physical illness. Therefore, based on the experience of somatosensory game, this article will focus on the service design and practice of cervical spondylosis medical services, and makes bold prediction on the intelligent closed-loop feedback-based health management information exchange system of internet medical data. In the traditional rehabilitation medical treatment, there still exist many problems such as asymmetric information between doctors and patients, unbalanced supply and demand between rehabilitation physicians and patients, and the status quo. Based on the innovation of man-machine interaction mode, the amusement and sports of somatosensory game medical treatment are continuously improved, and the interaction between somatosensory and user interaction is also more and more. Driven by this, somatosensory games provide more choices and support for medical rehabilitation. By using somatosensory devices instead of traditional rehabilitation exercises, Internet medical services can provide huge benefits in terms of medical costs and alleviating the imbalance between supply and demand help. At the same time relying on somatosensory game as a media point of contact to better reflect the user in the course of easy to learn, friendly and entertaining, patients experience through somatosensory gaming experience have contributed to the medical service system design forward.

Keywords: User experience · Somatosensory game design
Cervical health care · Interactive design

© Springer International Publishing AG, part of Springer Nature 2018
A. Marcus and W. Wang (Eds.): DUXU 2018, LNCS 10919, pp. 483–497, 2018.
https://doi.org/10.1007/978-3-319-91803-7_37

1 Introduction

1.1 Game Therapy Design Thinking Brings New Ideas to Healthy Exercise

Social progress and scientific and technological development have changed people's original way of life, speeding up the pace of work, bringing many conveniences and laying down many hidden dangers for people. The incidence of chronic diseases caused by unhealthy lifestyles has been increasing year by year, trend. The 2014 Global Report released by WHO shows that the number of deaths due to chronic diseases was 38 million in 2012 and is expected to reach 53 million in 10 years. An about 6 published live reports in 2017 show that chronic diseases cause 40 million deaths annually, Equivalent to 70% of the world's total deaths. Chronic diseases include sub-health and strain of cervical spine. According to WHO's "Spinal Cord Injury from an International Perspective," this new WHO report provides an overview of the experiences, prevention, care and personal experience of spinal cord injury among those with spinal cord injury The best available evidence. Men are most likely to develop spinal cord injuries 20 to 29 years of age and above, while women at greatest risk are 15–19 years of age and 60 and older. The study showed that the risk of adult men and women at least 2:1 ratio. Spinal cord injury results in lower enrollment and economic participation, and children with spinal cord injuries are less likely than their peers to enroll in school and less likely to stay in school even if they enroll. Adults with spinal cord injury face similar barriers to participation in socioeconomic life, and the unemployment rate for adult patients worldwide is above 60%. Spinal cord injury is accompanied by huge personal and social costs. Many of the outcomes associated with spinal cord injury are not caused by the disorder itself but by the lack of access to adequate healthcare and rehabilitation services and the lack of access to community life due to physical, social and policy environment barriers. This shows that cervical health has seriously endanger the normal life. The main object of this article is the crowd of young college students who are often referred to on the Internet as nowadays. In such people, a series of degenerative changes have taken place in people's body posture, such as sedentary, lack of exercise, late sleep and other bad habits. There have been many bad body posture problems, but also led to a variety of body imbalances

1.2 Game Therapy Design Thinking Brings New Ideas to Healthy Exercise

Driven by such environmental effects, auxiliary tools for rehabilitation work have emerged. Aids for rehabilitation include various categories, both physical types and virtual types. Compared with the physical type, the virtual scene interactive rehabilitation training belongs to a new type of treatment behavior, using computer graphics and image technology, the use of infrared scanning of the human body, the patient exposure and a virtual environment, combined with different patients themselves Problem, the computer has a variety of training games corresponding to the treatment, the patient need only according to the changes in the screen scenarios and prompts to imitate and respond to a variety of actions to maintain the screen in the scene mode to continue until the final completion of training objectives. This interactive learning feedback of virtual situation can not only improve the rehabilitation efficiency and reduce the disability rate, but also enhance the patient's initiative and participation, in line with the concept of modern rehabilitation medicine, and bring a new direction for the design of medical rehabilitation.

1.3 Game Therapy Design Thinking Brings New Ideas to Healthy Exercise

Game therapy, also known as game therapy or game-assisted therapy, as the name suggests refers to the game as a therapeutic medium or carrier of an intervention. It is based on the human brain plasticity theory and functional reorganization theory as the basis for research, entertainment therapy for the purpose of the game activity. It has gone through three stages of development: psychoanalytic game therapy, structural game therapy and humanistic game therapy. The applicability of game therapy The crowd first used in children. Children's game therapy is mainly through the game of children's inherent anxiety psychology manifested in the interaction with the game therapist to increase awareness of individual behavior and emotions, thereby enhancing children's courage to face difficulties, challenge the difficulty of ability to promote Children's personal development. Game therapy originated in psychoanalysis. Sigmund Freud, a famous Austrian psychologist and psychoanalytic pioneer, pioneered the use of games to treat children's mental illness (Fig. 1).

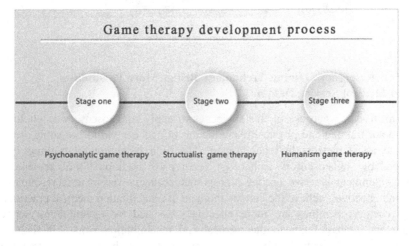

Fig. 1. Game therapy development process

Nowadays, game therapy is widely used in the treatment of depression in children, which lays a corresponding theoretical basis for the game therapy of multi-aging sports. In order to reach a certain therapeutic result and establish a persuasive user experience, in order to achieve the goal of the user, interactive guidance and behavior guidance need to be implemented step by step. In the entire guidance process, users may lose their user status or mood Product patience and tolerance, then game therapy design can be very good attention to stimulate people through the game to achieve their ultimate goal. Game therapy design in today's social life is also numerous cases, such as the game "Peter Shut up" is a treatment for stuttering children's games, children in the game by way of talking to the game, in the game with the game characters Communicate with each other, complete corresponding tasks arranged in the game, score and record the children after the end of the game, and the corresponding learning status of the children will be reflected in the parents' cell phones, so that the children and parents can work together to overcome the children Language defects (Fig. 2).

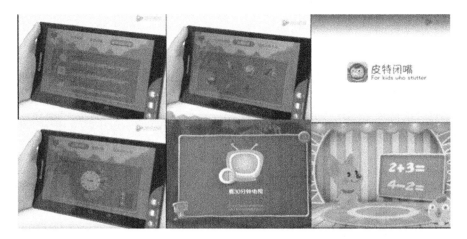

Fig. 2. Game screenshots

1.4   Somatosensory Gaming Technology Brings More Possibilities to Medical Service Design

The main research purpose of this subject is to apply somatosensory technology to active motor training and physical rehabilitation of patients and to use somatosensory games to assist patients in rehabilitation. The limb rehabilitation training system developed by somatosensory technology can replace traditional limb rehabilitation training equipment and save a series of costs such as manpower, material resources and space and effectively relieve the current shortage of rehabilitation medical practitioners in our country, Families are more effectively assisted by rehabilitation services, bringing more possibilities to the medical and rehabilitation work, alleviating the asymmetry of doctor-patient information, helping patients to heal their own treatments, and seeing themselves in constant circular and reciprocal training Rehabilitation medical progress.

2   Research Backgrounds

2.1   Research Status of College Students' Physical Health

In recent years, due to sedentary, the body appears cervical pain, frozen shoulder, obesity, muscle strain and other sub-health disorders are increasingly plagued ordinary college students. Modern lifestyles make people's lives more comfortable, but bad habits also make people's body posture a series of degeneration. Long-term past will cause deformation of the body joints, triggering functional disorders and other issues. Modern ordinary college students, comfortable lifestyle, poor eating habits, the overall poor self-control, fitness awareness is weak, confused at the same time, often stay up late to play online games, mobile phones anytime, anywhere, a variety of body posture problems also will come. There are some serious problems in the daily living habits of ordinary college students. For example, they have to go to bed late and exercise time is too short, they are sedentary for a long time, and their understanding of their attitude is not clear enough and they have not got enough attention from themselves. These factors are all potential factors that affect the health of college students. The author in China Known online search "cervical spine" a total of 305 academic articles. There are 230 periodicals, 21 dissertations, 25 conference papers. there are 183 categories of medical and health care, 43 science and education, 6 industrial technology, and only 1 in each category of economy, literature, art and biology (Fig. 3).

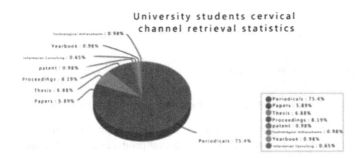

Fig. 3. University students cervical channel retrieval statistics

2.2   Research Status of Somatosensory Game Design

Somatosensory game refers to the use of the body to feel the video game. Different from the PC game controller or keyboard mouse to control the game, somatosensory game is a new type of video game.

The difference between somatosensory games and online games lies in the fact that the users can participate in the game as far as possible without being affected by the location, the time or the weather. For example, the user wants to go out and play today and experience the helplessness of the weather. The restriction is not good The user's travel, the user desperation can only choose to indoor activities, such online games has become a choice, but most online games are still sitting in front of a long time in front of the computer, for a long time to maintain the position of not only the user Of the cervical spine injury, but also contrary to the user initially wanted to play outdoor activities, so the experience of the game in this not only became an indoor game has also become a new way to experience the movement.

The somatosensory game The author is mainly divided into four categories, racing categories: racing, running, etc., the confrontation categories: boxing, baseball, etc., leisure puzzle categories: music and dance, pets, drama, other sports categories: yoga, aerobics, Mental exercise and so on (Fig. 4).

Fig. 4. Somatosensory classification game screenshots

3 Theoretical Exploration

3.1 Experience the Design Thinking for the Game-Oriented Treatment

The range of user experience is not limited to the visual and auditory levels, but also includes touch, taste and more. Many of the actual product cases in life are showing us the importance of experience design so that sustainable design concepts are constantly innovating and breaking through. In game design for therapeutic purposes, user experience design requires us to observe the user in more detail. Because the user is not only the user of the product, he has another identity that is the patient and needs to think about the user from two identities Experience design. Therapeutic game experience design strategy is based on the experience of game therapy in the design of thinking-oriented role, so that each patient's specific situation to complete the program design, dig deep pain points and needs. In order to meet the immersive experience and emotional experience of young people in the treatment of the game, mobile touch screen game design experience should start from what aspects of the study? Next, I will be further analyzed from the perspective of "five levels of user experience design".

3.2 Design of Cervical Vertebrae Health Somatosensory Game for College Students

For the undergraduate cervical vertebrae health somatosensory game experience design, can be based on the "user experience design of the five levels", combined with several major game design module to experience the design of the dimension. In general, game design requires game planners and designers to have a thorough division of labor and cooperation in game visual arts, game interaction, game planning, and game business models. Through the previous analysis of "five levels of user experience design", I will be the game design and several major modules corresponding and related (Fig. 5).

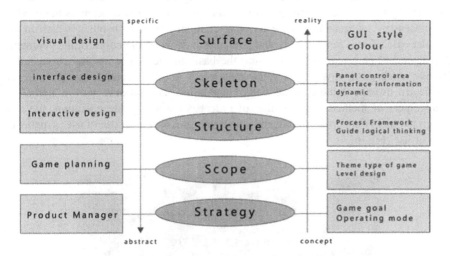

Fig. 5. Five levels and the link between the game

a. Strategic level: product goals and user needs

The strategic layer needs to find out the needs of users when using somatosensory games through pre-market, user research and brainstorming, and how to ensure the medical treatment needs during the game so as to formulate corresponding design directions and design goals. In order to rehabilitation fitness for the purpose of the virtual body therapy game products first and foremost is the product development goals and user needs to participate in the game. The goal is divided into two major content (product goals, user goals) Product objectives: developers hope that the expected value of game products and product development. Target users: emphasize the main product service crowd, and ordinary somatosensory game difference, the medical type of somatosensory game in the entertainment at the same time to ensure that to a certain extent, to do the role of physical training. Therefore, the initial formation of the product in terms of the strategic level is more need to target (including products and target users) and user needs analysis.

b. Scope layer: functional sections and content design

Through the design of the strategic layer, the goals and requirements of the somatosensory game product can be clearly defined, and transforming the user's needs into the functional blocks actually required in the product is the work that needs to be clearly defined in the scope layer. Product features of the plate and each plate in the content design is the core content of the product.

The "digital arrangement" follows the ease-of-use, functionality, and content of the user experience in game functionality. Ease of use in the user experience refers to the simple level of use of the product to quickly understand the usefulness of the product's functionality and use. Functional refers to the functional design of the product to meet the needs of users. Content refers to the accuracy of the information and structure provided by the product. Somatosensory game products more important is the need to somatosensory game and exercise the way combined with each other, which in the product ease of use, functionality and content have a clear direction. In the "Numeric Arrangement" game, in order to ensure the basic medical needs of the cervical and lumbar vertebrae to move together, the game needs to be designed so that the user can frequently use the lumbar spine before and after. The product uses a numerical arrangement of methods, the number of orders is a very simple operation, the user begins to quickly understand the game's final purpose, the clever use of user experience ease of use (Fig. 6).

Fig. 6. "Digital arrangement" screenshots

c. Structure layer: Information architecture and interaction design

Information architecture refers to the product content of the information in a series of related analysis, organization and design, the required information accurately presented information structure. Simply put, is the user from point A to point B need to go through what steps, through the structural layer of the boot design to help users to achieve the goal.

Interaction design, you need to understand the psychological and behavioral characteristics of the target user, dedicated to the completion of two objectives of usability and ease of use. In the process of human-product interaction, we need to achieve these usability goals, which are safe, effective, easy to learn, and interesting to use, and have corresponding emotional and experiential features to make users feel happy, happy, inspired, or emotionally charged Meet and so on. Interaction design here not only refers to the interactive design of the process, but also includes the design of modular interactive sports, the action is completed at the same time be able to get the appropriate score in the game, allowing users to interact when using somatosensory games more deep move, the demand for treatment gradually eased, more immersive sense of the game. In the somatosensory game "Sitting bingo", after the correct number is completed, the numbers are crossed off, proving that they have been used correctly, and that the prompt tone is displayed correctly. These subtle interactive design behaviors, which minimize medical seriousness and add to the fun and immersive gameplay, also reinforce more realistic and effective interactions between users (Fig. 7).

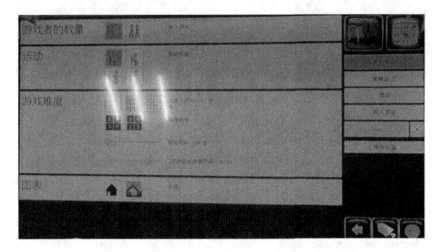

Fig. 7. Game screenshots

d. Framework layer: interface design and information design

In the interface next to the user shows the image of sitting immediately, always remind the user's sitting status and standing up. In the user error or the camera failed to identify the player user, the screen will display prompts to help users adjust their stance and standing point in time to successfully complete the game. In the game, if the number of players correctly identify the appropriate number of picture crossed out, if the number of get the number aircraft does not match the numbers in picture, the player can remain in place, waiting for the countdown beep to restart shaking Number appears new numbers. In the entire game interface tips of these information need to appear to help game player users to successfully complete the related game operation therapy. In the entire game interface effectively communicate between users and products presented, with value, to reach the user's satisfaction, to the user a sense of reliability. The accuracy and accuracy of the information in the product interface design can better help users understand the product, the trust of the product, so as to better help the product content and function of the extension (Fig. 8).

Fig. 8. Game screenshots

3.3 Research Status of Somatosensory Game Therapy Products

The author interviewed a local hospital in Wuhan, a top three field hospital for field research, for rehabilitation subjects involved in somatosensory game patients interviewed. Most patients currently exposed to somatosensory game products are in patients with dyskinesia in the upper and lower limbs. Somatosensory games more games are based on the main treatment of hemiplegia, motor blockage in patients with neurological use, exercise types are also divided into six categories, namely sitting upper limb training, standing balance training, walking training, upper limb training, shoulder Neck training, cognitive training, daily life ability test training. The doctor will adjust the corresponding exercise work according to the patient's physical activity and training items. Next, 1–2 games will be taken in each category for usage analysis and product barrier analysis to pave the way for the design of somatosensory game products for future cervical health care (Table 1).

Through the game analysis, the six categories of somatosensory sports games are targeted at patients with different conditions, mainly for hand and foot inconvenience, after a car accident or stroke and other diseases plagued rehabilitation training. The basic simple operation treatment is satisfied, but the difficulty level and difficulty of the game are not fulfilled, and the difficulty and the operation and play are relatively simple. There is no uniform requirement for professional modular action. At the same time, the standard of the action still needs external medical staff to help to adjust.

Table 1. Game analysis

Game type	Name	Sports mode	Advantages and disadvantages	Difficulty
Upper and lower limb training	Sitting bingo	Sit down - stand - sit down	Exercise mode is more common, exercise lumbar	1
Balance	Hamster	Forward - back - left pan Variety of sports patterns, choose the size of sports venues	Training mode is aimed at patients with balance problems, such as rehabilitation training after a car accident, limb rehabilitation training for stroke patients	3
Walking	Collect flowers	Forward - back - left pan	Training model for car accident patients, stroke patients. Add difficult interference in the game, there are interference items collection activities, in order to improve patient acquisition speed. The difficulty of the game options are limited	2
Shoulder	Take the golden egg	Neck and neck movement	The difficulty of the game is limited, the activity area is relatively narrow, can only be moved by hand, easily lead to shoulder stiffness	3
Cognitive training	Number arrangement	Waist strength training Before - after - left - right	Single game mode, exercise user's waist power exercise. The game is less difficult for normal users	1
Daily life training	Image sorting	Arm strength, walking exercise, cognitive ability	The beginning of the game will give the correct picture sequence, after scrambling by the user self re-collage	3

On the other hand, the fun of the game, the beauty of the screen is relatively lacking. Most of these somatosensory sports games are functional and functional products. In the game the picture requirements are relatively simple, there are many problems for the treatment of patients, you need a variety of games for treatment, the main way to game therapy is more diversified is the need to strengthen such games, and add the story of the game, Easier to help users adhere to complete.

4   Design Exploration

4.1   User Research

In order to tap the emotional needs of users in cervical health care somatosensory games, this design has taken a questionnaire survey and in-depth method of user research. For the crowd of users mainly for 18–30-year-old user groups, mainly with undergraduate and graduate academic backgrounds of knowledge-based youth groups.

Table 2. Document investigation

Problem	Option	Statistical results
Do you understand somatosensory games?	1 never heard of 2 heard, no contact 3 contact the relevant game	18.64% 32.2% 49.15%
Which of the following types of somatosensory games you will try?	1 racing categories: racing, running and so on 2 confrontation categories: boxing, baseball and so on 3 leisure puzzle categories: music and dance, pets, drama category 4 other sports categories: yoga, aerobics, mental exercise and so on	57.63% 61.02% 57.63% 35.59%
Do you think somatosensory games can be used as a way of fitness?	1 Yes 2 No	86.44% 13.56%
Do you have an experience when you have finished your day's work and study?	1 head left and right, up and down, tilted 45 degrees rotation obstruction 2 head twisting with a slight impact sound 3 dizziness headache, difficulty concentrating 4 limbs weakness, appear numb leg phenomenon 5 palpitation, a slight vomiting 6 neck stiffness, pain 7 None of the above	51.72 55.17% 48.28% 24.14% 12.07% 48.28% 13.79%
For cervical health you have a detailed understanding of it	1 a very detailed medical understanding 2 slightly know one or two, understand the related cervical exercises 3 not yet 4 other	5.17% 37.93% 55.17% 1.72%

The questionnaire was distributed and filled in using the image of the online questionnaire. Questionnaires were delivered from two aspects of cognition of somatosensory games and awareness of cervical spine care. A total of 137 questionnaires were received. Table 2 shows the answers to some of the representative study questionnaires.

Through some of the questionnaires can be summarized as user research:

1, somatosensory game therapy market has a vast space, most students are willing to buy and use somatosensory games for the treatment of cervical products, and that has a certain value.

2, in the interview and exchange, found that most users have a sense of recreational body somatosensory game, more emphasis on the screen requirements, entertainment is also required better, for the medical class somatosensory game less involved, it is not exposed Professional somatosensory game.

3, in life, students are more willing to spend time to touch the somatosensory game, to enhance physical activity, but related to cervical spine treatment expertise has not been enough to learn and expand, there are some limitations.

4, players are more willing to multiplayer games, to play with their friends and roommates. If you can learn in ordinary life after classmates with non-regular use of somatosensory game movement is considered to have been a good exercise mode.

4.2   Experiments Outcomes

From the above questionnaire survey, we can draw some directions for improvement. From the five levels of user experience described earlier in this article, we can explore deeper and more systematically the design and study of cervical spondylosis in somatosensory games in the future.

a. the strategic level - product goals and user needs

Through just the questionnaire survey, the purpose of the user needs to be clear, the user's needs can be better understood in future somatosensory game iteration and innovative design exploration. In the face of different student groups, we can better face the design group, make the product's goal decision.

b. the scope of layers - functional sections and content design

In the range of layers of the plate design, according to the user's social needs, incentives, cooperation, increase the difficulty of the game, time mode control, multi-dimensional mind map for game design to help users can exercise in the usual holy lake In the exercise of cervical exercise.

c. the structure layer - information architecture and interactive design

The interaction between late-stage product design and the plot is also a way to exchange feelings between the user and the product. In the exchange of sports on the medical health care activities of the cervical vertebra so as to achieve the goal of the product, cervical care somatosensory game design.

d. the framework layer - interface design and information design

Throughout the design of visual design in the game accounted for the main position in the previous figure you can see the beauty of the article in the article pictures and information management problems in the iterative innovation process, the interface information integration and dispersion need to think, But also need to use the usability test for the user to complete the appropriate design ideas back to the card. The interactive research on the operational experience and emotional experience of the product seeks to achieve the product's usability, ease of use and friendliness.

5 Conclusion

The topic of cervical health status, combined with today's increasingly serious outdoor pollution and the rise of somatosensory games, somatosensory game to prevent and treat cervical spondylosis feasibility and significance are discussed. First of all, the author of the current status of scientific development of the cervical spine to investigate and understand the doctor and patient information imbalance, college students lack of knowledge of cervical health. Secondly, through the five levels of user experience design, it analyzes how the five levels in the game are reflected, and adds the design of the game in the actual hospital. According to the actual product design and the case analysis method, which performed. Through quantitative research to investigate white-collar workers on their own cervical spondylosis cognitive status and their perception of somatosensory game, and through qualitative research to analyze the rehabilitation exercise hospital existing somatosensory game mode of motion, and the advantages and disadvantages of the game and evaluation of the difficulty. After that, I carried out the interactive design elements of somatosensory game, and summarized the principle of interactive design of somatosensory game and the design strategy of somatosensory game of cervical vertebra health according to the five levels of user experience design for the psychological needs of undergraduates, and provided the follow-up design for somatosensory game model Suggestion.

Acknowledgements. This paper was supported by the research project from Chinese National social science fund "4D evaluation model research and application of information interaction design (16CG170)".

References

1. Emergency medical teams: minimum technical standards and recommendations for rehabilitation. [EB/OL] Geneva: World Health Organization; 2016. Licence : CC BY-NC-SA 3.0 IGO
2. China Industrial Information Network, Report on the Operation Situation and Investment Strategy of China Rehabilitation Medical Market from 2017 to 2022. [EB/OL] (2017)
3. Liang, Q.: The Research of Experience Design Based on Play Therapy—Taking The Mobile Touch Screen Game of the Quasi Aged As An Example, Jiangnan University, June 2016

4. I-research, 2015 Chinese Host Somatosensory Game Research Report [EB/OL] (2015). http://report.iresearch.cn/report/201509/2460.shtml
5. Garrett, J.J., Fan, X.-Y.: The Elements of User Experience. China Machine Press, Beijing (2008)
6. He, Z.: Intelligent Health Promotion Service System For Chronic Diseases Exercise Intervention, University of Science and Technology of China (2016)
7. Corbin, C., We, G.: Concept of Physical Fitness: Active Lifestyle for Wellness. McGraw-Hill, New York (2003)
8. Shih, J.L., Hsu, Y.: Advancing adventure education using digital motion-sensing games. Educ. Technol. Soc. 19(4), 178–189 (2016)

Research on Application of Gesture Recognition Technology in Traditional Puppet Show

Mu Zhang[✉] and Zhanjun Dong

Shandong University of Art and Design, No. 02, Nineteen Floor, Unit 1,
Building 5, No. 187, Jingliu Road, Huaiyin, Jinan, China
153962234@qq.com

Abstract. This article uses gesture recognition technology to study the culture, structure and performing form of traditional Chinese puppet show. It aims at annotating traditional culture by using new media art language. Taking "Puppet" as an example, this article summarizes the characteristics of controlling the marionette under gesture recognition technology as well as the binding point design in both traditional way and new technology by analyzing the characters. Through communication and interviews with the inheritors of the intangible cultural heritage, this paper discusses the new and old performing form and controlling features. This research lowers the threshold of learning puppet show, and puppet show fans only need to use simple operations to perform complicated movements. The cost of learning the puppet show decreases because of HCI. This article annotates the traditional meaning of gesture control under new technology background by comparing the new and old controlling form.

Keywords: Traditional culture · Gesture recognition · Puppet show
Puppet · New media art

1 Introduction

Puppetry, a special form of dramatic art, is a common art form in all over the world. As an inheritance of intangible cultural heritage, puppetry has left a deep impression in human history and culture. The forms of puppetry vary in different parts of the world, but generally they undergo the process of transition from religious worship performances to entertainment. For example, Italian dramatist Fligny explored puppetry of ancient Egypt along the Nile Valley. In his book "History of Puppet", he proposed that the priests controlled the puppet to induce blind faith among the public, suggesting that religious worship endowed puppet with life. Besides, in the description of Greek historian Herodotus, the priest stepped onto the altar in the music along with the puppet and used dramas, songs and dances to entertain the God [1]. The ancient Chinese puppet shows began in Han Dynasty and enjoyed a rapid development in Tang Dynasty. Gradually the shows gave birth to various and different art forms. Among various branches, the marionette, as a representative branch, has passed down until today.

© Springer International Publishing AG, part of Springer Nature 2018
A. Marcus and W. Wang (Eds.): DUXU 2018, LNCS 10919, pp. 498–512, 2018.
https://doi.org/10.1007/978-3-319-91803-7_38

Marionette, also known as line puppet or hanging puppet, is made up of board, lines and puppet. The principle is that the puppet is maneuvered by the lines so as to make corresponding movements, which imitates human actions and creates vivid dramatic scene [2]. The puppet, similar to anatomic human body, is consisted of head, belly, limbs, etc. Among all kinds of puppetry, the performance of marionette is closest to humanity. Puppetry is a kind of art form relying on human control of the puppet. During the performance of marionette, the performer binds lines into the joints of the puppet and with the help of the board, the lines are maneuvered by the performer so as to make the puppet present different movements. Therefore, the performer should not only use his hands in balance to make sure the puppet moves flexibly, but also use fingers to move the puppet's limbs.

During the process, whether the performer can control the lines proficiently and know how to bind the lines well are keys to the flexibility of marionette [1]. Nowadays people live a fast-paced life, fans of puppetry have little time to learn cumbersome practices or study skills and principles of binding lines. Besides, decrease of performers overtime leads to gradual disappearance of puppetry, the intangible cultural heritage. By studying the operating characteristics and skills of traditional puppetry, we apply gesture recognition technology to puppetry performance. In doing so, not only puppet operation is simplified, but also learning cost is reduced. In this article, we choose Leapmotion, a gesture recognition hardware to help users learn puppetry easily. Puppets can present sophisticated movements with a few simple gestures. In addition, this study not only combines traditional puppetry culture with contemporary culture under the new technology, but also explores traditional cultural expressions in the new media environment by studying operating modes of two ages (Fig. 1).

Fig. 1. Marionette

2 Technical Theory and Background

Gesture recognition technology is based on computer science and was first born in the 1980s and 1990s. This technique explains human gestures through pattern recognition. Initially, this research is focused on development input of special hardware. For instance, B. Thomas developed his own digital glove in 1993. When users put on the glove, the computer can not only read the position of their hands immediately, but also detect whether their hands stretch and even the direction of the fingers. Though the technology has realized the purpose of input, the experimenter must wear hardware devices and natural Human–Computer Interaction cannot be achieved. Therefore, in the following research, developers began to focus on non-labeling gesture recognition technology, which can capture location and shape of hands without wearing devices. In 1994, Gaowen et al. of Harbin Institute of Technology proposed the capture and recognition of hands under a static and complex background. In May of 1995, they proposed the capture and recognition of hands under a dynamic and complex background. In the 21st century, gesture recognition technology has enjoyed a rapid development and presented tremendous scientific research and commercial value in robot control, automatic navigation, interactive education as well as healthcare, etc. With the intensive research of gesture recognition and promotion of related products, hardware devices based on non-labeling gesture recognition technology spring up like mushrooms and gradually enter into public life (Fig. 2).

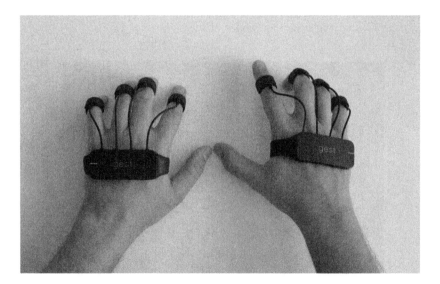

Fig. 2. Digital glove

2.1 Three Types of Gesture Recognition Technology

Gesture recognition technology is divided into three types, namely two-dimensional space hand recognition, two-dimensional space gesture recognition and three-dimensional space gesture recognition. The former two is mainly different from the latter in space. In two-dimensional space gesture recognition technology, computer-captured information includes width in horizontal line as well as height in vertical line (X and Y in geometry) and this space only extends in the two-dimensional scope [6]. On the other hand, computer-captured information using three-dimensional space gesture recognition technology includes length, width as well as height (X, Y and Z in geometry). In this case, we apply three-dimensional space gesture recognition technology.

Gestures and Actions. Three-dimensional space gesture recognition technology uses special hardware to collect in-depth information instead of single common camera because the latter is unable to provide in-depth information. At present, there are three kinds of hardware around the world, namely Structure Light, Time of Flight and Multi-camera [4]. Three-dimensional space gesture recognition system solves depth problems, which enables hands to move freely within the recognition area. Fortunately, there is no need for users to wear any devices to be recognized. In addition, the technology has high accuracy, large scope as well as various HCI modes, and therefore, UX is highly improved.

2.2 Principles and Characteristics of Leapmotion

In this case, we choose Leapmotion, a hardware developed by Leapmotion company. This hardware mainly takes Multi-camera recognition technology, which captures images with various cameras at the same time. The principle is similar to compound eye insect [5]. By comparing with the difference among images captured by cameras in different angles, the technology calculates in-depth information in order to form a three-dimensional image (Fig. 3).

For example, the principle of dual camera is based on geometry to calculate in-depth information as described in the figure. Camera 1 and camera 2 take two pictures of different angles respectively at the same time in the same environment. This process simulates the principle of human eyes. We can calculate the distances between the object and cameras if we can find out the location of the object as parameters of the two cameras and their relative location are known (Fig. 4).

The hardware demand for Multi-camera is lowest among all three-dimensional gesture recognition technology. Besides, extra special devices are not required as the technology is totally relied on computer vision algorithm. As a result, the Leapmotion is smaller and cheaper than many other hardware. It is convenient for users to carry and install [5].

Fig. 3. Leapmotion

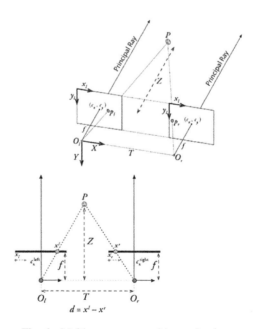

Fig. 4. Multi-camera recognition technology

3   Case Study

This study is based on a social science research project of Shandong Province called "Research on Integration and Development of Excellent Traditional Culture in Shandong Province and New Media". The case is "Puppet", which includes a large number of traditional elements of Laixi puppet show. According to our investigation, Laixi county of Shandong Province is one of the birthplaces of Chinese puppetry with important research values. Our research is divided into four phases. The first phase is investigation and research. Our members went to Laixi county of Shandong Province for data collection and artists' interviews. The second phase is data aggregation and culture studies. By referring to artistic features of Laixi puppetry, we study characters, binding as well as stage in the puppet show. The third phase is HCI theoretic research. During the second phase, we have been looking for reasonable hardware support. Therefore, we can sketch the model, solve the problem of HCI and programming. The last stage is for the perfection of the technology. We combine the puppet and the stage, install sensor and single-chip microcomputer, look for BUG problems in the program in order to make the technology perfect and practical. In the following part, this article will present specific content of this study stage by stage.

3.1   Preliminary Research

Our group arrived in Laixi county, Shandong Province from 15th to 20th, April, 2016. We not only explore the local puppetry history and puppet making, but also communicate with inheritors of intangible cultural heritage. During our research, we have found out that Laixi puppet mainly uses characters from the Peking opera such as male role, female role, painted face, clown, etc. to represent different characters in different stories. The eyes, ears, nose and mouth of the puppet can move. The most three important operations of puppet show are how to lift up the puppets, rotate the stick as well as make the puppet move flexibly. During the interview with Laisheng Wang, an inheritor of intangible cultural heritage, we knew that a tremendous puppet was unearthed from the wooden-chambered tomb of Western Han Dynasty in Daishu village of Laixi county in 1978, which has attracted significant attention in the archaeology field both at home and abroad. The puppet, composed of 13 sections of wooden limbs, is 193 cm high. Its joints can move so as to sit, stand or kneel. The puppet from the tomb is by far the earliest and largest wooden puppet, which was regarded as the most famous Chinese puppet. The discovery is also a proof that Laixi is the birthplace for puppetry. In addition, after interviewing with Yang Zhang, a puppet show performer, we have had a general understanding of making puppets. A puppet is composed of a head, a body, hands and clothes. First of all, the artisan designs a puppet model and then makes a clay mold according to the drawing. Secondly, the artisan repeatedly pastes newspapers onto the mold before taking down the dried newspapers (form a cardboard), which has formed the shape of a puppet. Thirdly, the artisan fills mud into the cardboard that becomes smooth and sturdy after polishing. This process is commonly known as puttying. At last, the artisan draws eyes, eyebrows, mouth, etc. on the cardboard. If making a gimmick puppet, the artisan needs to leave two holes on its head in order to put Ping-Pong as eyes. In addition, it also takes some time to make the operating stick, clothes as well as accessories. Therefore, it takes at least months to make a puppet [1].

3.2 Research on Puppet Show and Binding Skills

During the performance of marionette, there are four basic binding skills. The first is to control the lines to make the puppet move. The second is to clear up the lines so they are in perfect order. The third is to clamp the unused lines timely during the performance. The fourth is to prepare lines for the next movements. Due to years of performance, the performer has gradually developed various skills such as lifting, rubbing, twisting, hooking, shaking, turning, spotting, swinging, dialing, buckling, turning, etc. [1] For instance, lifting can make the puppet nod or bow. In certain area, the artisan will put lines into special body parts of the puppet. For example, the artisan links lines with his belly button of the clown, the laughing role has lines in his hip, and Monk Sanhua has lines in his shoulders. What's more, there are lines to control the fan when the puppet is performing a fan dancing and there are also lines to control the crutch when the puppet needs to be on crutches. Therefore, special characters are able to make special movements in different shows due to this kind of special lines. As a result, though line-controlling skills become increasingly complicated, artistic performance becomes more vivid. Lines to lift up the puppet are different in numbers, but there are six basic lines put in the limbs and body of the puppet.

We take "uproar in heaven" in "Journey to the West" as an example. The main puppet character is Monkey King, one of the most famous Chinese mythological figures who looks like a monkey and is called "stone monkey" because he was born from a stone since the creation of the world. The artisan put 10 lines in the head, wrists, elbows, hip, ankles and knees respectively in order to present his moving features.

3.3 Research on HCI Technology

After a preliminary investigation and research, we decide to use gesture recognition technology to realize HCI. The final work is mainly composed of 6 parts, which are PC,

ARDUINO single-chip microcomputer, two stepping motors, LEAPMOTION sensor, the puppet and the stage.

First of all, we connect LEAPMOTION and single-chip microcomputer to the PC. LEAPMOTION and ARDUINO will establish a communication link after we program LEAPMOTION by using UNITY3D. During the process, we need to set two gestures in order to operate the two stepping motors. Opening the right hand and making a fist are two gestures we choose so as to lower the error. When the right hand is open, stepping motors rotate clockwise. On the contrary, stepping motors rotate anticlockwise when the right hand makes a fist. Unity3D is a comprehensive game tools and a professional game engine that allows players to make 3D videogames, realize architectural visualization or make real-time 3D animation. By using the software, we can program various HCI-based hardware such as LEAPMOTIN, KINECT depth camera as well as TOBII eye tracker. Virtual games or hardware machinery can therefore be controlled by the hardware. Unity3D uses C# language to program and the code scrip is as follows (Fig. 5):

Fig. 5. Unity3D programming

```
using UnityEngine;
using System.Collections;
using System.Threading;
using System.IO.Ports;

public class SerialPortTest : MonoBehaviour
{
    //Setup parameters to connect to Arduino
    public static SerialPort sp = new SerialPort("COM3", 9600, Parity.None, 8,
StopBits.One);
    //public static SerialPort st = new SerialPort()
    public static string strIn;
    public string message;
    float ww = 0;
    // Use this for initialization
    void Start()
    {
        OpenConnection();
        // InvokeRepeating("kk", 1, 2);
    }
    /*
    void kk()
    {
        sp.Write(ww.ToString());
        ww += 0.01f;
    }
    */
    void Update()
    {
        //Read incoming data
        //   strIn = sp.ReadLine();
        // print(strIn);
        //You can also send data like this
        //   sp.Write("2");

        if (Input.GetKey(KeyCode.A))
        {
            sp.Write("1");
        }
    }
    //Function connecting to Arduino
    public void OpenConnection()
    {
        if (sp != null)
        {
```

```
      if (sp.IsOpen)
      {
        sp.Close();
        message = "Closing port, because it was already open!";
      }
      else
      {
        sp.Open();  // opens the connection
        sp.ReadTimeout = 50;  // sets the timeout value before reporting error
        message = "Port Opened!";
      }
    }
    else
    {
      if (sp.IsOpen)
      {
        print("Port is already open");
      }
      else
      {
        print("Port == null");
      }
    }
  }
  void OnApplicationQuit()
  {
    sp.Close();
  }
}
```

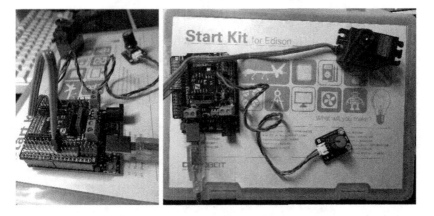

Fig. 6. Arduino connection

Secondly, we connect two stepping motors to Arduino single-chip microcomputer. Single-chip microcomputer and stepping motors will establish a communication link after we program single-chip microcomputer by using PC. So far we have completed setting up hardware operating system. Users can then control stepping motors by using LEAPMOTION. ARDUINO uses C++ language to program and the code scrip is as follows (Fig. 6):

```
const int PUL = 2; //PUL+ 接Pin 2, PUL-接GND
const int DIR = 3; //DIR+ 接Pin 3, DIR-接GND
const int PUL1 = 4; //PUL+ 接Pin 2, PUL-接GND
const int DIR1 = 5; //DIR+ 接Pin 3, DIR-接GND
boolean isWork= false;

void setup() {
pinMode(PUL, OUTPUT);
pinMode(DIR, OUTPUT);
pinMode(PUL1, OUTPUT);
pinMode(DIR1, OUTPUT);
Serial.begin(9600);
}

void loop() {
 if (Serial.available() > 0) {
     char incomingByte = Serial.read();
     switch(incomingByte){

case '0' :
if(isWork){
 break;
 }
   //===========逆时针转向：
   digitalWrite(DIR, HIGH);
   digitalWrite(DIR1, HIGH);
   delay(5);
   GenPulse(1000, 500);
     //===========顺时针转向：
   digitalWrite(DIR, LOW);
   digitalWrite(DIR1, LOW);
   delay(5);
   GenPulse(1000, 500);
  break;
 case '1':
if(isWork){
 break;
 }
```

```
//============逆时针转向：
  digitalWrite(DIR, HIGH);
  digitalWrite(DIR1, HIGH);
  delay(5);
  GenPulse_(1000, 500);
    //============顺时针转向：
  digitalWrite(DIR, LOW);
  digitalWrite(DIR1, LOW);
  delay(5);
  GenPulse_(1000, 500);
 break;
   }
 }
}
void GenPulse(unsigned int PulseNum, unsigned int Feq) { //PulseNum：步数
isWork==true;
for (unsigned int i = 0; i < PulseNum; i++) { //Feq：频率
digitalWrite(PUL, HIGH);
delayMicroseconds(500000 / Feq);
digitalWrite(PUL, LOW);
delayMicroseconds(500000 / Feq);

}
isWork ==false;
}
void GenPulse_(unsigned int PulseNum, unsigned int Feq) { //PulseNum：步数
isWork==true;
for (unsigned int i = 0; i < PulseNum; i++) { //Feq：频率
digitalWrite(PUL1, HIGH);
delayMicroseconds(500000 / Feq);
digitalWrite(PUL1, LOW);
delayMicroseconds(500000 / Feq);

}
isWork ==false;
}
```

Thirdly, we connect the puppet to stepping motors by lines in order to maneuver puppet's movements. Due to the limited number of experimental equipment, only two stepper motors are used during the process. We use lines to connect hands and feet of the puppet to the two stepping motors respectively. The operating principle is as follows. When the user opens his right hand, PC detects its shape through LEAP-MOTION and then sends the information to ARDUINO single-chip microcomputer. In this occasion, the two stepping motors rotate clockwise, which leads to the downside

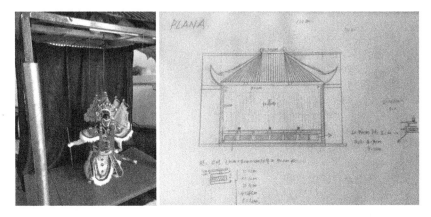

Fig. 7. Stage drawing

movement of puppet's hands and feet. On the contrary, when user's right hand makes a fist, the two stepping motors rotate anticlockwise, which leads to the upside movement of puppet's hands and feet (Fig. 7).

At last, we use wood to set up the stage. The stepping motors are installed on the roof of the stage. By controlling the length of the lines, the puppet can suspend in the air. During the performance, the user only needs to put his right hand in front of the stage can he control the puppet's movements with different gestures (Fig. 8).

Fig. 8. Structure

3.4   Research on Cultural Inheritance of Puppetry

The main task of the experiment is to study the cultural relationship between gesture recognition technology and traditional marionette show. During the millennium of traditional puppetry performance, performers maneuvered puppets with their hands, a form that has Chinese traditional features and connotation. The hands have become a bridge between new and old culture. Puppet show artists control puppets by using various skills such as lifting, rubbing, twisting, hooking, shaking, turning, spotting, swinging, dialing, buckling, turning, etc. The operation has become an integral part of puppetry culture because of various gestures and perfect cooperation of performer's two hands. In this experiment, we still use two hands to control the puppet, which inherits the traditional acting media. The two gestures in the experiment, opening hand and making a fist, are similar to rubbing and twisting in the traditional performance. The old and new operating method is in contrast with each other from a cultural perspective. In future study, we will add more hardware devices and gestures (Fig. 9).

Fig. 9. Live demo

3.5 User Experience and Feedbacks

We have conducted surveys among users of different groups in order to evaluate the prospect and market value of gesture recognition technology. 15 experimenters, ranging in age from 18 to 50, have taken part in our small-scale symposium. They also have different careers such as college students, university teachers, business owners and puppetry artists. The questionnaire includes the following main points. First, we ask them to write down their understanding of traditional puppetry. Second, we ask them whether they have ever used similar products. Third, we ask them whether the operation is practical and convenient. Fourth, we ask them what aspects of cultural inheritance we should pay attention to in our work. We hope that we can gain some suggestions for improvement from this survey.

In the symposium, we elaborated the concept, research process, operating methods, etc. to the experimenters. They can have the opportunity to participate in the interactive process and use gesture technology to perform puppet shows. During the meeting, we encouraged attendees to discuss in detail the various issues they encountered in the interactive experience and to gain a thorough understanding of interactive modes. In order to increase the practicability of the concept, we also hope that the participants can provide more ideas on integrating new media and traditional culture as well as HCI in this field in the future.

3.6 Findings and Conclusion

According to our results, most experimenters focused on HCI and hardware and they have provided a lot of positive feedbacks. On the one hand, students speak highly of the interactive experience because of the simple operating method and decreased time cost of learning. Business owners hope that accuracy of hardware recognition can be improved. On the other hand, puppetry artists and teachers has given their opinion on the relationship between HCI modes and cultural inheritance of puppetry. In their opinion, the experiment has not only established a connection between new media and traditional culture, but also basically realized mutual communication between two ages and two cultures. However, the connection is rather simple. In the future, we hope that we can have further study in this field, especially in finding out more breakthrough points to establish connections between new media and traditional culture.

3.7 Conclusion

In this study, we prove that gesture recognition technology can be applied in the field of puppetry. It can not only reduce user's learning time and improve operating experience of the puppet performance, but also play an active role in publicizing traditional puppetry culture. In the cultural field, cultural features are not missing in the puppet show that uses gesture recognition technology. On the contrary, the technology has played a significant role in cultural inheritance. This experiment interprets the traditional cultural significance of gestures under the background of new technology and builds a bridge between new media art and traditional culture.

References

1. Wang, K., Liu, K., Zhang, X.: Puppet Show 3. China Society Press, Beijing (2007)
2. Wang, Y., Yu, F.: Puppetry. Jilin Publishing Group Co. Ltd., Changchun (2013)
3. Wei, L.: History of Chinese Puppet Show. Cultural Relics Publishing House, Beijing (2007)
4. Zhang, S.: Non-labeling Gesture Recognition based on Vision, p. 6. Jilin University Press, Changchun (2016)
5. Wang, W.: Leapmotion: Application Development on HCI. Xidian University Press, Xi'an (2015)
6. Wang, Y., Gao, Y.: The world's most advanced gesture recognition technology [EB/OL] (2018). https://www.leiphone.com/news/201502/QM7LdSN874dWXFLo.html

HRI Design Research for Intelligent Household Service Robots: Teler as a Case Study

Shujing Zhang[1], Jingyan Qin[1(✉)], Sha Cao[1], and Jinhua Dou[2]

[1] School of Mechanical Engineering, University of Science and Technology
Beijing, Beijing, People's Republic of China
qinjingyanking@foxmail.com
[2] School of Computer and Communication Engineering, University of Science
and Technology Beijing, Beijing, People's Republic of China

Abstract. This paper analyzes the human-robot interaction (HRI) design based on artificial intelligence technology. Combined with the needs of artificial intelligence technology, this paper summed up the new characteristics of human-robot interaction which include high dimension, high tolerance, complex scenario merged with context awareness computing, consciousness awareness computing and emotion awareness computing. Take Teler, a household robot of Robotics Interaction Lab in Intel Labs China as the reference case, the paper analyzes the methods and characteristics of household robotics human-computer interaction. Multi-channel information input portal, parallel interactive framework and multi-sensory collaborative feedback are the new interaction design requirements. The paper summarizes the advantage and disadvantages of robot-human interaction in artificial intelligence field, sorts out information classification and information processing. In this paper, we present three human-robot interactive relationships which include passive feedback, proactive learning and active feedforward, and maps the three relationships with accurate command interaction, semi-opening dialog interaction and opening dialog system interaction. The three types of HRI associate with the different mental model, interaction model, information architecture, interactive behavior logic, information visualization and interface design. The paper presents the new method of interaction design for household robot context-awareness interaction and use the case Teler AI household service robot human-robot interaction design to verify the user experience targets and usability targets.

Keywords: HRI · Artificial intelligence · Household service robots
Interaction design · Information design

1 Introduction

With the great development of AI technology such as deep learning, natural language processing, computer vision, changes have taken place in the field of HRI. AI impacts and creates a new sense and influences the interaction design method, flow processes, perception mental model, interactive technology and interactive interface presentation ways in a disruptive innovation [1]. Intelligent robot, as a main research and application field in AI, is defined as mechanical creature which can take the function autonomously [2].

© Springer International Publishing AG, part of Springer Nature 2018
A. Marcus and W. Wang (Eds.): DUXU 2018, LNCS 10919, pp. 513–524, 2018.
https://doi.org/10.1007/978-3-319-91803-7_39

Compared with ordinary smart devices such as smart phone, wearable devices, intelligent robots have the better capacities of cognition, perception and movement in the physical world. Due to this, intelligent robots have become the focus of technical and design researchers. Current research in robotics is driven by the goal to achieve a high user acceptance of service robots for private households [3].

Service robot is defined as robots that performs useful tasks for humans or equipment excluding industrial automation applications. Service robots are categorized according to personal or professional use. A personal service robot is a service robot used for a non-commercial task, usually by lay person [4]. In this paper, our research object is intelligent household service robot, which is referred as personal service robot worked in some domestic environments with the capability to function autonomously. Designing a service robot also contains service design process, in this paper we focused on sorting out the interaction logic, interaction model, information architecture, etc. from the perspective of interaction design and Information design of Human-Robot Interaction.

Human–Robot Interaction (HRI) is a field of study dedicated to understanding, designing, and evaluating robotic systems for use by or with humans [5]. The disciplines such as robotics, computer science, and design, among others are focusing on Human-Robot Interaction [6]. In the process of HRI, robot must make good use of sensors, artificial intelligent and electromechanical part to complete information collection, recording, processing and feedback.

In this paper, we take Teler the second-generation household service robot (the first-generation is Inin) developed by Robot Interaction Lab of Intel Labs China as a case study. Teler is a tablet robot based on Intel® RealSense™ technology. Teler can establish model of people based on multi-modal information, is able to autonomously find target person in the environment, and follow the target from multiple directions under real, complicated conditions. Tablet Robot could implement indoor location and navigation by its "Visual SLAM" capabilities based on Intel® RealSense™. With proper visual, graphic, and audio algorithms, Teler could also detect face, human body and hand gesture, and work as a teaching assistant, in-home exercising partner, etc. The robot can learn behavior patterns for user profiling.

Although intelligent robots possess the hardware and software technology advantages, the computational context, user context, physical context, temporal context and social context [7] which robots' artificial intelligence need to deal with are quite complex. In the multiple target users interacting in real time complex and ever-changing domestic environments, how to complete the collection and process of user information through HRI design, collecting information through contextual perception, processing and feedback information through artificial intelligence technology, so as to bring users a better interactive experience is the problem we want to solve.

Motivated by the aforementioned issues, the necessity and possibilities that the intelligent household service robots need the Human-Robot Interaction Design is indisputable. And it is necessary to tightly integrate design with development phases. The objective of our research is to sort out the new features of HRI with artificial intelligence technology. And present the interaction design method which can construct the HRI model and information architecture under the influence of HRI autonomy and initiative of human-robot interaction relationship.

The main contributions include:

- Summarized the differences and features of HRI with or without AI intervention.
- Sort of three types of human-robot interaction: accurate command interaction, semi-opening dialog interaction, opening dialog system interaction.
- Taking Teler, as a case study, explains how we design an intelligent household service robot.

2 Related Work

2.1 Service Robot

Personal service robot can also be classified by application areas such as domestic servant robot, automated wheelchair, and personal mobility assistant robot etc. The basic composition of an intelligent household service robot can be briefly summarized as: the mechanical and electrical structure, sensors and artificial intelligence, which can be understood as a combination of movement, cognitive and cognitive capability. Several researches are focusing on build an assistant robot in elderly care such as Nursebot [8], Care-o-Bot [9], PALRO [10]. Others such as Pepper [11], FABO [12] etc., look much more like a companion robot at home which provide entertainment, companionship, and emotional support.

Styliani Kleanthous etc. use questionnaires and in-depth interviews to explore the elderly users' preferences and requirements on service robot's personality, appearance and interaction [13]. Angela Giambattista etc. examined the recognition of emotions being expressed by a service robot in a virtual environment (VE), and by universities students [14]. Weijane Lin and Hsiu-Ping Yueh investigated the personal space and the attitude that child patrons possessed under a specific context of library [15].

The study was distinct from previous studies of service robots, we focus on analyzing the interaction logic, interactive behavior pattern, interaction model and information architecture from the perspective of interaction design and information design of household service robot.

2.2 Human-Robot Interaction

Scholtz and Goodrich [5] summarize five attributes that affect the interactions between humans and robots. One of the five attributes is autonomy which is a means of supporting productive interaction. Tom Sheridan [16] classified the level of autonomy (LOA) into 10 scales, from entity being completely controlled by human (computer offers no assistance; human does it all) to the completely autonomous (computer decides everything and acts autonomously, ignoring the human). Autonomy is implemented using techniques from control theory, artificial intelligence, signal processing, cognitive science, and linguistics [5]. The development of AI technology such as deep learning, natural language processing, computer vision help increasing LOA of HRI. Therefore, in addition to fully autonomous systems, service robot statistics include systems which may also be based on some degree of human-robot interaction (physical or informational) or even full tele-operation [17]. In this context, human-robot interaction can be considered as human intelligence interacting with artificial intelligent actively and passively. The interaction includes exchange of information, materials, energy through user interfaces. Moreover, Scholtz [18] provided 5 roles that robots can assume in HRI: supervisor, operator, mechanic, peer, and bystander. He presents the HRI model to each role according to Norman's HCI model. Michael and Alan [5] add 2 roles into this list: mentor and information consumer.

With literature review and comparative study, we choose Scholtz and Goodrich's books (total citations 635), and Tom Sheridan's paper (total citations 518) as the core references for our research object. We choose LOA theory as HRI classification basis for intelligent household service robot. Besides, HRI relationship is a major determinant for interaction model and information architecture in HRI design. So, in this paper we analyze the HRI relationships and initiative human-robot interaction, at the same time, we take human-robot dialogue mechanism into consideration. The paper analyzed the human open dialogue mechanism and robotic closure loop mechanism, correspondingly classified the HRI into three types: accurate command interaction, semi-opening dialog interaction, opening dialog system interaction. In this paper, we focus on constructing HRI interaction model and information architecture for semi-open dialogue interaction.

3 New Features in HRI

In this section, we discuss the differences and features of HRI with or without intervention of artificial intelligence shown in Table 1.

In the HRI without artificial intelligent invention, the autonomy of HRI is relatively low. The communication medium often uses a contact-based user interface such as graphic user interface, requiring point–to-point and end-to-end mapping. Due to this, the HRI process requires accurate information input to make sure the robot can accomplish the task. The information generated in point–to-point mapping is inherent information which is relatively complete and accurate with small-size quantity. The sequential processing method doesn't have the ability to deal with noise information. Therefore, the tolerance and affordance of HRI system is low spectrum. There is no self-learning and optimization in this repetitive and modeled HRI. The interaction objects involved are usually people and robot, mainly dealing with low-dimensional physical space information. The final information output and feedback speed are near-time.

With the intervention of artificial intelligence, there are many new features in HRI. The autonomy is relatively higher and the design focuses on building multi-modal interfaces 4. Therefore, the information architecture and interaction framework appeared to be peer-to-multi or multi-to-peer. The information type contains both inherent information and impromptu information. Robot can accomplish some prediction and deal with new information based on AI technology such as knowledge graph and machine learning etc. Information such as text, sounds, images, behavior, depth, speed, are often intertwined together. Interaction process also results in a large number of incomplete, vague and noisy information input. Depending on time

Table 1. HCI contrast with or without AI.

Features	HRI without AI	HRI with AI
Autonomy	Low	High
Interaction medium	Point–to-point, end-to-end mapping Contact-based user interface	Peer-to-multi or multi-to-peer Multimodal interfaces
Information input	Complete, accurate command	Incomplete, vague and noisy dialog
Information type	Inherent information	Inherent information Impromptu information (based on knowledge graph etc.)
Information processing	Sequential processing	Parallel processing
Tolerance	Low	High
Affordance	Low	High
Information environment	Physical space (Low Dimension)	Physical space (Low Dimension) Cyberspace (High Dimension)
Output and feedback	Near-time	In-time Real-time

synchronized parallel processing, non-repetitive and non-modal human-robot interaction can be undertaken. Robot can self-optimize based on user experience information, knowledge and learning. Interactive objects extended to human, robots and environments. HRI interaction design often deals with the information both from physical and cyberspace. And the output and feedback information can be in-time even real time.

4   Three Types of HRI

In the development process of artificial intelligence, the guidance change from the symbolism and connectionism into the cognitive science. Robots gradually get the abilities to imitate human thinking pattern, learning method perception and cognitive pattern. Once robots have similar human thinking and cognitive pattern, the human-robot dialogue mechanism, human-robot interaction methods and HRI relationship changes correspondingly: from closed-loop, command and passive HRI to semi-opened, proactive or active HRI. New relationship of human-machine master-slave algorithm leads to new HRI relation, we need to build a new interaction model based on the new interaction relationship correspondingly.

As shown in Fig. 1, according to the three initiative relationship of human-robot interaction which include passive, proactive, active, we classified HRI into three types: accurate command interaction, semi-opening dialog interaction, opening dialog system interaction. And their interaction features in interaction initiative, robot role in HRI, HRI relationship, information input mode and the AI type is showed in Fig. 1.

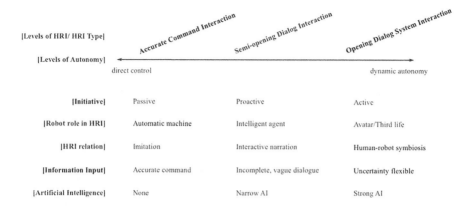

[Levels of HRI/ HRI Type]	Accurate Command Interaction	Semi-opening Dialog Interaction	Opening Dialog System Interaction
[Levels of Autonomy]	direct control		dynamic autonomy
[Initiative]	Passive	Proactive	Active
[Robot role in HRI]	Automatic machine	Intelligent agent	Avatar/Third life
[HRI relation]	Imitation	Interactive narration	Human-robot symbiosis
[Information Input]	Accurate command	Incomplete, vague dialogue	Uncertainty flexible
[Artificial Intelligence]	None	Narrow AI	Strong AI

Fig. 1. Three types of HRI and their interaction features in interaction initiative, robot role, relation, information input and the AI type.

4.1   Accurate Command Interaction

In the accurate command interaction, robot can be defined as an automatic machine that passively interact with human user. Robot can only accomplish actions according to human user's accurate command in some specific context.

As shown in Fig. 2, interaction process is driven by humans to start and robots' inner interaction build up the close-loop self interaction model. Users input complete and accurate instructions information through user interfaces, and robots use the hierarchical paradigm to receive sensors sending single-sense information, task planning units generate accurate execution instructions, and action parts execute the specific and precise commands, finally make the robot complete the operation and feedback. User's command information input and robot's feedback form the peer-to-peer mapping relationship. The interaction logic and process occupy the time and algorithm space, the feedback is single-threaded and non-interactive response, consequently the mapping is not flexible and agile transformation with the changing environment. HRI is lack of agile rapid interaction to deal with the impromptu information and surprising computing which is out of the predesigned program. The current robots only can imitate humans thinking mode and interaction relationship under the fixed design interaction logic. The robots first receive the perception from different sensors and cognition from the perception data by the guidance of human-like interactive behavior logic. The media and interaction logic are the information architecture and mental models which are predesigned by designers, engineers and users.

Norman's HCI model in Fig. 2, clearly illustrates the cycles that the user may go through. Identified a goal, formulated an intention, then selected an action that seems appropriate to accomplish the goal, the system feedback is examined and evaluated by the user [18]. Therefore, robot's operating instructions are precise and suitable for the task of carrying out the sequence process. The path and goal of carrying out the task are relatively clear, so once there is ambiguity or error in the instruction information, the interaction tasks will deviate from the original Human-Robot Interaction target or even terminate.

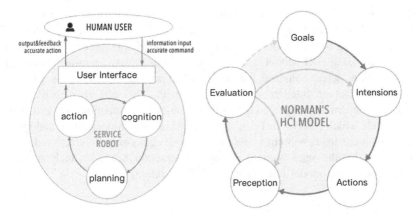

Fig. 2. Accurate command interaction process and Norman's HCI model

4.2   Semi-Opening Dialog Interaction

Household service robot interacts with the smart home or multiple users and needs to identify different multiple information owners through computational context, user context, physical context, temporal context and social context. The context awareness is full of complexity and uncertainty and needs the gray computing, triangulation and AI technology to take the flexibility and openness from the humans into consideration for HRI interaction design. We communicate through languages, gestures, facial expressions and six senses to form the open-structured and dialogue interaction without clear goals in the human-human interaction. Machine learning from human-human interaction behavior and logic, HRI interaction design constructs the flexible interaction model and form the interactive and cooperative human-computer interaction relationships. It makes the human-machine principal and subordinate relationship much more flexible initiative and the interaction model be optimized or adjusted according to the change of the situation. The semi-opening dialogue interaction model transform from the changing situation and liberate HRI interaction design from the pre-designed scenario design methodology. In semi-opening dialogue interaction, robot can be defined as an intelligent agent that can proactively interact with users who own the human intelligence. Robot can accomplish multiple task during having dialog with human user through multimodal interfaces in some basic scenario.

As shown in Fig. 3, interaction process of semi-opening dialogue interaction mostly driven by humans, robots can also initiate proactive interactions based on context awareness, conscious awareness, and emotion awareness with AI technologies. In this context, the principal and subordinate relationship of human-computer interaction is determined by the situation. HRI is not fixed and flexible with the open-source impromptu information support for open-node human-machine interaction loop from the dialogue mode. Semi-opening dialog interaction model supports not only the representation of the artificial intelligence of symbolism and connectionism under the support of the closed loop of the robot machine language, but also embed a semi opening dialogue structure formed by artificial intelligence under the support of brain cognitive science. The semi-opening dialogue create new information through quantified self and generated contents from humans and build the living information architecture which is continuously semi-opening knowledge frame. Each phase in semi-opening dialog HRI Model, such as goals identification, intentions formulation, actions selection, perceptions and feedback evaluation, can be defined as a key node that users with Human Intelligence can interact with. The semi-opening dialog HRI model forms the structure based on the fixed human-robot interaction loop and also has the open mode which receive the open source contents from human-robot dialogue, the transformation creates new human-robot interaction relationship. Interaction design for robots guided by the semi-opening dialogue interaction needs to analyze the new characters for mental model influenced by artificial intelligence.

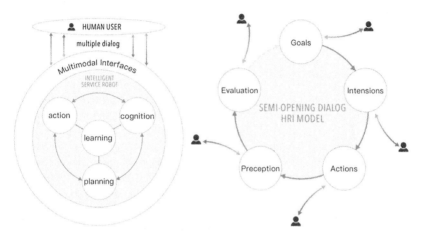

Fig. 3. Semi-opening dialog interaction process and new HRI Model

4.3 Opening Dialog System Interaction

In the opening dialog system interaction design, robot can be considered as an avatar or the third life. Robot have complete autonomy and dominance in the Human-Robot interaction process. In this context, relying on strong AI technology, robot can deal with the uncertainty flexible environment of the input information. Therefore, HRI interaction design intends to achieve the human-robot symbiosis goal. Strong or universal AI influences the interaction logic, interaction model and information architecture prominently and generally in the near future.

5   Case Study and Verify the Interaction Design Targets

In this section, we use the case Teler AI household service robot human-robot interaction design to verify the user experience targets and usability targets.

5.1   Multi-channel Information Input Portal

At the beginning of design process, considering the intelligent robot must accomplish interaction tasks facing multiple family members in a complex domestic environment. AI techniques such as deep learning and context computing require robot to collect as much information as they can about robot itself, user and environment. Therefore, we need to design a multi-channel information input portal so as to ensure that robots record hundreds of millions of pieces of information during interaction with humans, obtain information through non-focused information gathering for subsequent information processing and output.

Human beings use five channels of "eyes, ears, nose, tongue and body" to perceive the surrounding world's "color, sound, scent, flavor and touch". Among these channels, the nose, tongue and the body can be defined as three non-perceived information entrances. And the other three are perceived information entrances. Currently, in the filed of service robot. In addition to visual, auditory information input, other information input methods are not widely developed and applied. Due to this, at the beginning of designing Teler's hardware (see Fig. 4), we choose Intel® RealSenseTM (RGBD camera), hearing sensor to complete the visual and auditory information collection of user and environment. In addition, Teler can rely on its' touch screen tablet graphic interface and mechanical input such as mouse and keyboard to get user' accurate command information input.

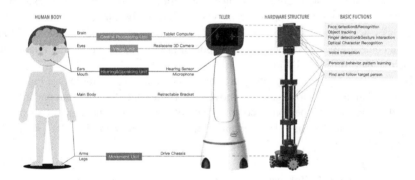

Fig. 4. Teler's hardware structure and basic functions

The information an intelligent household service should gather can be divided into two types: inherent information and impromptu information. The inherent information here mainly refers to the user's identity information, such as age, gender, height, name, voiceprint, fingerprints, passwords. They are fixed, infrequently changing, pre-set information, usually input through the non-perceived information entrance and then be recorded. Impromptu information, due to its uncertainty, unpredictability, is the problem to be solved in the process of HRI. Therefore, by designing the interaction behavior and the fault tolerance of information input in advance, we input a large amount of user data before interaction and increase the affordance of robot perception information through machine learning. When new users or noise users appear, the user can be quickly modeled and locked by inputting user information features in the early HRI process.

As shown in Fig. 5, Teler's find and follow target person function. At the early process of HRI, the user information such as age, sex, proportion of head and shoulder, and color of clothes is collected through RGBD camera. Then the user behavior patterns are established through a variety of visual and auditory information so that the user can be followed in 360 degrees. If there is interference from others, the robot will not be disturbed.

Fig. 5. Teler-Follow Target person function (Intel, 2016)

5.2 Parallel Interactive Framework

The intervention of artificial intelligence makes the semi-opening dialog interaction possible. In the mean time, the accurate command interaction is also indispensable for a household service robot. Therefore, we need the parallel interactive framework to make sure robot can respectively map different types of information into different interaction frameworks according to the computational context, user context, physical context, temporal context and social context. Correspondingly, the initiative of HRI relation can also be changed during HRI process.

Teler's "Personal behavior pattern learning" function is an example (see Fig. 6). By detecting facial information, gesture, movement route and the environment information, Teler can predict personal potential activity based on the context awareness technology. After mining the personal pattern, Teler can interact with user preoperatively.

5.3 Multi-sensory Collaborative Feedback

The processed information needs to be output again to the user by the robot, which we call the process of feedback. The user can judge whether the interaction is valid, accurate and natural through feedback. The new changes in AI make the input and output occur at about the same time. With AI and interaction design, we can transfer multi-channel information input porta into multi-sensory collaborative feedback not only providing timely and effective feedback, but also makes the best use of the hardware. Education assistant based on optical character recognition and finger recognition (see Fig. 7). Teler can judge the correctness of handwritten mathematical formulas and translation the English word. The result of the judgment and translation is fed back to the user through various channels such as projector, sound effect and screen image information.

Know user's needs instead of simply follow

"Detect": Facial information, gesture, voice commands, text infomation and so on.
"Predict": Possible movements, needs and anything unexpected in nearby surrounding.
"Interve": Take reasonable actions to stop accidents, or to provide required helps.

Fig. 6. Personal behavior pattern learning (Intel, 2017)

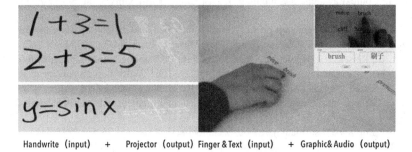

Handwrite (input)   +   Projector (output) Finger & Text (input)   + Graphic& Audio (output)

Fig. 7. Education assistant: Math formula and English translation (Intel, 2017)

6   Conclusion

The paper comparative researches the human-robot interaction design with and without artificial intelligence and AI technology supported HRI interaction design transform from the open source information input and interaction model changes. In the three types of human-robot interaction, semi-opening dialog interaction model has the compatible abilities which include computer accurate command interaction and human's communication opening dialog system interaction. Finally, the paper takes Teler as a case study to explains how to design an intelligent household service robot by using of semi-opening dialog interaction model, logic, mental model and information architecture. Strong or universal intelligence transform the interaction model into the living open source or even the living open information structured model, it also changes the interaction design methodology in a disruption way.

Acknowledgement. The intelligent household service robot Teler is a research project supported by Intel Labs China. We accomplish the HRI design with programmers, mechanical designers and other colleagues in Robot Interaction Lab in 2017. Dr. Peng Wang, Xiaobo Hu and all the research team members are greatly appreciated for the big data computing and human-robot interaction technology.

References

1. Jingyan, Q.: Impaction of artificial intelligence on interaction design. Packag. Eng. **28**(20), 27–31 (2017)
2. Murphy, R.R.: Introduction to AI Robotics. MIT Press Bradford Books, Cambridge (2000)
3. Wrede, B., Haasch, A., Hofemann, N., et al.: Research issues for designing robot companions: BIRON as a case study. In: Proceedings of IEEE Conference on Mechatronics & Robotics, pp. 1491–1496 (2004)
4. ISO 8373: Robots and robotic devices - Vocabulary; 2012[EB/OL]. http://www.iso.org/iso/iso_catalogue/catalogue_tc/catalogue_detail.htm?csnumber=55890. Accessed 02 Feb 2018
5. Schultz, A.C., Goodrich, M.A.: Human-robot interaction: a survey. Found. Trends® Hum. Comput. Interact. **1**(3), 203–275 (2007)
6. Breazeal, C.: Designing Sociable Robots. MIT Press A Bradford Book, Cambridge (2002)
7. Gu, J.: Context awareness computing. J. East China Norm. Univ. (Nat. Sci.) **2009**(5), 1–20 (2009)
8. Matthews, J.T.: The nursebot project: developing a personal robotic assistant for frail older adults in the community. Home Health Care Manage. Pract. **14**(5), 403–405 (2002)
9. Graf, B., Reiser, U., Hägele, M., Mauz, K., Klein, P.: Robotic home assistant Care-O-bot® 3-product vision and innovation platform. In: 2009 IEEE Workshop on Advanced Robotics and its Social Impacts (ARSO), pp. 139–144. IEEE, November 2009
10. Palro Garden. http://www.palrogarden.net/palro/main/framepage.html. Accessed 26 Jan 2018
11. Pepper. http://www.softbank.jp/robot/special/pepper/. Accessed 26 Jan 2018
12. FABO. http://www.efrobot.com/homeEnjoy.jsp. Accessed 26 Jan 2018
13. Kleanthous, S., Christophorou, C., Tsiourti, C., Dantas, C., Wintjens, R., Samaras, G., Christodoulou, E.: Analysis of elderly users' preferences and expectations on service robot's personality, appearance and interaction. In: Zhou, J., Salvendy, G. (eds.) ITAP 2016. LNCS, vol. 9755, pp. 35–44. Springer, Cham (2016). https://doi.org/10.1007/978-3-319-39949-2_4
14. Giambattista, A., Teixeira, L., Ayanoğlu, H., Saraiva, M., Duarte, E.: Expression of emotions by a service robot: a pilot study. In: Marcus, A. (ed.) DUXU 2016. LNCS, vol. 9748, pp. 328–336. Springer, Cham (2016). https://doi.org/10.1007/978-3-319-40406-6_31
15. Lin, W., Yueh, H.-P.: The relationship between robot appearance and interaction with child users: how distance matters. In: Rau, P.-L.P. (ed.) CCD 2016. LNCS, vol. 9741, pp. 229–236. Springer, Cham (2016). https://doi.org/10.1007/978-3-319-40093-8_23
16. Sheridan, T.B., Verplank, T.L.: Brooks.: Human and Computer Control of Undersea Teleoperators. Human & Computer Control of Undersea Teleoperators (1978)
17. International Federation of Robotics(IFR): Service Robot-Defination and Classification WR 2016 [EB/OL]. https://ifr.org/img/office/Service_Robots_2016_Chapter_1_2.pdf. Accessed 02 Feb 2018
18. Scholtz, J.C.: Human-robot interactions: creating synergistic cyber forces. In: Schultz, A.C., Parker, L.E. (eds.) Multi-Robot Systems: From Swarms to Intelligent Automata, pp. 177–184. Springer, Dordrecht (2002). https://doi.org/10.1007/978-94-017-2376-3_19

Mobile DUXU

Skeuomorph Versus Flat Design: User Experience and Age-Related Preferences

Nils Backhaus[1]([⊠]), Anna Katharina Trapp[2], and Manfred Thüring[2]

[1] Group 2.3 Human Factors, Ergonomics, Federal Institute for Occupational
Safety and Health, Berlin, Germany
backhaus.nils@baua.bund.de
[2] Cognitive Psychology and Cognitive Ergonomics,
Technical University Berlin, Berlin, Germany

Abstract. The "right" design of graphical user interfaces (GUI) may help to provide positive user experience and to support users in dealing with the complexity of technological artifacts. We compared two design strategies for GUIs: skeuomorph and flat design. For this purpose, two interface versions of a smart phone operating system (flat and skeuomorph) were created. Since skeuomorph design uses metaphors from the non-digital world, we expected that it is preferred by elderly users (digital immigrants) compared to young users who might choose the modern flat design (digital natives). To test this assumption, we conducted a study ($N = 24$) with younger and elderly users by combining a standardized usability testing scenario, a user experience questionnaire (meCUE), and a half-standardized interview. Our results indicate that there is a significant difference between the two age groups. Elderly users showed a preference for skeuomorph design whereas the younger generation favored the flat design. Practical consequences and theoretical implications of these findings are discussed on the basis of the CUE model (Components of User Experience).

Keywords: Skeuomorph design · Flat design · User experience
CUE model · Hygienic and motivational factors
Graphical user interfaces (GUIs) · Preferences · Age

1 Introduction

Digitization has changed our daily life more than any other technological or industrial revolution before. The digital world becomes increasingly complex and humans are often confronted with straining systems they cannot fully understand. Therefore, designers are striving to improve user experience (UX) and to reduce complexity by creating interfaces that are easy to comprehend und intuitive to use. Adherents of two opposite design strategies argue about what is the "better design" to reach that goal: skeuomorph or flat [1]. As will be shown in the following, both strategies have a number of assets and drawbacks.

© Springer International Publishing AG, part of Springer Nature 2018
A. Marcus and W. Wang (Eds.): DUXU 2018, LNCS 10919, pp. 527–542, 2018.
https://doi.org/10.1007/978-3-319-91803-7_40

1.1   Skeuomorph Versus Flat Design

The term **skeuomorph** is derived from the Greek words *skeuo* (container or tool) and *morph* (shape or gestalt) and originated from the arts and crafts [2, 3]. Skeuomorph design can be characterized as adding features and properties to digital products or artifacts that are not necessary for their functionality [4], e.g. faux-wooden bookshelves in iBooks (iOS 6). Skeuomorph design transfers characteristics of objects from the physical world into the digital GUI [5] to generate a feeling of familiarity and to increase the perceived value of products [6]. If one knows an item from the real world, one might interact faster and more intuitively with its counterpart in the digital world. Skeuo-morphism goes in hand with a more realistic design and uses metaphors and affordances. Therefore, it is often considered as self-explanatory and easy to use [7], and it has been shown to improve the hedonic quality of products [4]. Adding unnecessary aspects, however, may lead to cluttering and thus increase users' cognitive and visual load as well as the loading time of the device – both reducing its usability. Furthermore, some researchers argue that the advantage of the real-world metaphor may not work for younger generations of 'digital natives' as they are not familiar with the real-world archetypes [8], such as the floppy disk serving as a symbol for saving files.

Flat design can be seen as the counterpart of skeuomorphism. Flattening GUIs means to refrain from real world elements [5, 9]. The success of flat design started with the revolutionary redesign of operating systems (OS), e.g. Microsoft 8 and Apple iOS 7 [10–12], where the interface was reduced to the essential. 3D effects, shadows, lights, texture, and many other non-functional features were removed. Flat design "empha-sizes a minimalist design language of flat colors and an overall digital-native mentality" [10, p. 4]. This minimalistic approach has a lot of advantages with respect to loading times [13]. Furthermore, it is mostly regarded as clean and pure [11] following the less-is-more zeitgeist and, doing so, fostering consistency in visual design [13]. Anyhow, users from an older generation are not that familiar with flat designs and may miss the metaphors and affordances they got accustomed to.

As these arguments show, the pros and cons for each design strategy might be related to the user's age. Therefore, elderly users may have other design preferences than younger users and may experience both design strategies differently.

1.2   Design and User Experience

UX is closely linked to design aspects because it involves "a person's perceptions and responses that result from the use or anticipated use of a product, system or service" [14]. Hence, UX comprises two important factors, the perception of non-instrumental qualities, (such as visual aesthetics, haptic quality, identification, or stimulation), and the perception of instrumental qualities (like usability, functionality or usefulness) [15–17]. The interaction of these different aspects is illustrated by a number of models in UX research, such as the Components of User Experience model (CUE model, see Fig. 1; [15, 18, 19]). The CUE model describes UX as the result of interaction char-acteristics that are impacted by system properties, user characteristics, tasks, and the context of use. With respect to the present study, it must be noted that the model does not regard the user's age as a factor of influence per se. Instead, individual features, such as knowledge, attitudes and habits that are typical for users of a particular age or generation are considered to impact the usage of a system. The resulting interaction characteristics frame the user's perception of non-instrumental (hedonic) qualities and instrumental (pragmatic) qualities. Both perceptions are closely linked to emotional reactions during the interaction with the artifact, and together these three components impact the overall judgment of the system and its future usage (or non-usage).

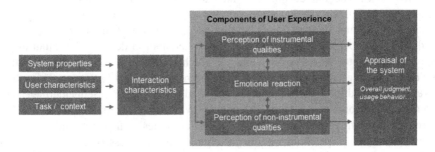

Fig. 1. CUE model (based on [15, 18, 19]).

All three UX components can be linked to the two design strategies. The perception of visual aesthetics, for instance, is an important aspect for both, flat and skeuomorph design. Do users prefer a minimalistic style ('less is beautiful') or do they appreciate ornaments and décor? Depending on their liking and prior experience, users' aesthetic impressions may be different for the two designs. As to pragmatic qualities, users might perceive a skeuomorph interface as cluttered since the data-ink ratio is much smaller compared to a flat one [20]. Consequently, the minimalistic approach might have advantages for usability and efficiency [21]. Flat design, however, may lead to a loss of information that users value and regard as helpful [13]. Moreover, it refrains from 3D shapes and is therefore less affordant [1]. Since affordances make controls more self-explaining and support their intuitive usage, they can improve users' interaction with a system [22–24]. Emotional reactions might also differ for the two design styles: Familiar items from the real world might be linked to memories and therefore elicit emotions during the interaction [20, 25]. Furthermore, a physical look-and-feel can be stimulating and therefore may be considered as aesthetically pleasing [26]. Again, there are pros and cons for both design strategies and each may have advantages as well as disadvantages for the generation of positive UX.

2   Related Work

In response to the shift from skeuomorph to flat design, the implications of both design strategies for UX and HCI have been studied in different contexts, e.g. for the design of operating systems and websites, with respect to automotive assistance systems, as well as for symbols and icons in general.

2.1 Empirical Comparison of Skeuomorph and Flat Design in UX

Several researchers tested the effect of skeuomorph and flat design in the context of mobile operating systems. Oswald and Kolb [7] conducted a survey immediately after the preview of Apples release of iOS7 in June 2013 in order to capture the initial responses to the paradigmatic shift from skeuomorph to flat design. A relatively young sample (M = 27 years) of smart phone users (91%) had to compare iOS6 (skeuomorph) and iOS7 (flat). The flat design was rated as more fun and childlike whereas the skeuomorph design was rated as more serious and grown-up. In a follow-up study eight months after the first sample, the authors observed a change of judgment. The "new", flat design was now rated similar to the "old", skeuomorph design. The initial difference was interpreted as a "novelty effect", which resulted from comparing a radical new design to an established design that had been around for a long time. This effect, however, vanished after the participants got used to the change. Schneidermeier and colleagues [11] conducted a study to compare Windows 7 (skeuomorph) and 8 (flat, metro design) with respect to usability (i.e., effectiveness, efficiency and user satisfaction). Windows 7 performed better in terms of effectiveness (task success score), efficiency (number of clicks and completion time), and overall satisfaction. However, the authors conclude that this effect might vanish with growing experience and exposure to the flat interaction style, which is in line with the results of the study by Oswald and Kolb [7].

In summary, both studies show how former experience with design features and systems can influence the experience and subjective usability of common users. But how do experts, especially designers, value the skeuomorph and flat strategy? Page [27] surveyed 274 design students about their preferences for using them in practice and found that the majority favored the minimalistic approach. However, they also saw a benefit in combining both. This combination is named "skeuominimalism" and "provides a methodology for the development of learning objects in mobile design education" [27, p. 131].

Such a combination was applied by Wu and colleagues [5]. They designed three versions of an interface for a navigation system: one strictly skeuomorph, another strictly flat, and a third one "skeuominimalistic" as a combination of both. Forty-five students interacted with all versions of the interface in the laboratory. Emotions, UX and the perceived artificiality of the design were assessed with respective questionnaires. While the skeuomorph version received the lowest UX ratings and artificiality judgments, the moderate version was rated highest and the flat version ranked second. Moreover, the two rating scales correlated strongly with each other (r = .8). According to the authors, artificiality had a large significant positive effect on judging UX. The flat design which was considered as more artificial led to a higher UX rating in contrast to the skeuomorph design. However, the study used a rather young sample (M = 23.67, range 20–27 years) what might have influenced the strong preference for the moderate respectively flat design version of the interface.

Differences between skeuomorph and flat design have also been shown for visual search. In an eye-tracking study [28], several icon types were compared (line-drawing, metro, flat, and skeuomorph design). Skeuomorph design showed the longest average total task time and the longest time to first fixation as well as the longest average fixation duration and the highest average visit frequency. The authors conclude that there is a relationship between visual complexity and search efficiency. The more complex the icon design, the longer it took the participants to find the correct item. Skeuomorph design was by far the least efficient design strategy in this study.

Pelet and Taieb [21] evaluated the layout of a mobile ecommerce website. Results showed that the flat layout led to higher ease-of-use and intention-to-use ratings. In addition, users of the flat interface were more willing to order something as well as to revisit and recommend the site. However, the authors conceded that more research has to be conducted regarding preferences of the ageing population in order to make internet applications universally acceptable.

Li, Shi, Huang, and Chen [25] analyzed the difference between the two design strategies by comparing flat and skeuomorph symbols for graphical user interfaces. The authors discuss advantages and disadvantages for both, skeuomorphism and flat design. On the one hand, skeuomorph symbols are more familiar to users and thus enable them to infer the represented functions faster and more easily. On the other hand, they are shaped by the culture they come from, making it hard for users with a different cultural background to understand their meaning. Moreover, skeuomorph symbols tend to be rather complex which may lead to overloaded and unclear interfaces. However, the authors also argue that flatly designed symbols can "escape their function" if they are too planar. They conclude that skeuomorphism has social significance and is related to personality and emotions. It enables unique experiences, but is also complex and culturally biased.

2.2 Design Preferences and Age

An important factor for the UX of different GUIs seems to be the user's age. The term *Digital Natives* was coined by Prensky [29] in 2001. He described a new generation that grew up in the digital world of modern information and communication technologies, like smart phones and computer games. On the opposite, previous age groups were described as *Digital Immigrants*. Their analogue selves had to adapt to the digital world due to social pressure or changes in their working environment (e.g., with the advent of personal computers) [7]. However, Digital Immigrants grew up with analogue technologies, like telephones with keypads or even rotary dials. They remember how it felt to lift the receiver to answer a phone call, and they used floppy disks to save and exchange digital data files [30]. As metaphors referring to the analogue era, the appearance of such devices is transferred into the digital age by the symbolic language of skeuomorph interface design.

Cho and colleagues [31] analyzed the impact of skeuomorph app icons on elderly users. A conjoint analysis showed that a higher degree of realism increased the aesthetic satisfaction and improved the understanding of the icons in this age group. The advantage was even bigger for novice users among the elderly. The results indicate that the experience with analogue counterparts of digital app icons augments the acceptance of the technology and the comprehension of the underlying functions. These findings are in line with the results of an investigation by Blaynee and colleagues [32]. The authors conducted a UX diary study with 25 elderly participants (age $\geq$ 65 years) and concluded that skeuomorphism was a way to enable older persons to relate to the design. They argued that the shift to flat design makes it harder for the elderly to access digital technologies since affordances are removed and the familiarity with analogue technology is impaired.

The effect of flat icons on elderly users was also tested by Sha et al. [33]. In an experimental study, 24 participants (age $\geq$ 60 years) had to recognize icons in a visual search task and were asked to report their satisfaction with them. The icons were all flat but differed in color. They were either multi-colored or monochromatic. The task consisted of the presentation of a target icon and its recognition after a short interval. The two color conditions significantly influenced the required time for recognition: the monochromatic items were identified more quickly. The subjective data revealed that monochromatic items were rated as more concise, easier to remember, but less beautiful. Even though the study used flat icons only, it emphasizes the importance of UX in this context. It shows that perceptions of instrumental and non-instrumental qualities are neither always in line with each other, nor are they necessarily affected in the same manner. Taken together, the studies by Cho et al. [31] and Blaynee et al. [32] show that elderly users tend to prefer the skeuomorph design, as it increases satisfaction and improves the perceived non-instrumental qualities. However, Sha et al.'s [33] results indicate, that superfluous information (e.g. multi-coloring of icons) can impair the instrumental qualities of a device.

Although the three studies provide a valuable gain of knowledge, they have a shortcoming. They are restricted to elderly persons and lack the comparison with other age groups (younger users, respectively *Digital Natives*). Such a comparison was made by Robbins [34], who studied the preferences for flat and skeuomorph design in three age groups (younger: 13–26, middle: 27–45, old: 46 and older). While he found a preference shift for the middle agers towards flat design, both the younger and older groups were almost evenly distributed on the two design strategies. However, the results were only reported descriptively without testing for significant differences. Furthermore, the study did not look at the underlying mechanisms that might have led to the preferences of the age groups. Zhang and colleagues [26] also used an experimental approach to compare skeuomorph and flat designed icons. Over all participants, there was a slight preference for skeuomorphism. Again, an age effect could be obtained. Adults (age > 30 years) and children (age < 15 years) showed a tendency towards skeuomorphism, whereas participants in the medium age category ($15 \geq$ age $\geq$ 30 years) showed a preference for flat design. However, the differentiation between the age groups appears as questionable in both studies since they only investigated rather young samples.

Summing up, it seems that the preference for a GUI is influenced by age-related user characteristics and the design strategy. Elderly users are often less familiar with modern technologies and more accustomed to the original archetypes that are metaphorically used in skeuomorph design. The younger generation, in contrast, might not be that familiar with skeuomorph design elements [8] and seems to appreciate minimalistic GUIs in a flat style. According to the CUE model, differences in preferring one design type over the other should be rooted in differences of the UX between the two age groups. Hence, an interaction effect of age (young vs. old) and design (skeuomorph vs. flat) should occur in an experiment which investigates preferences as well as components of UX.

3 Empirical Study

To test the interaction hypothesis, an experiment with a mixed-methods approach was conducted in which both age groups (young vs. old) and two design strategies (flat vs. skeuomorph) served as independent variables. In case of an interaction effect, the younger group should prefer the flat design while the older group should favor the skeuomorph design. Moreover, differences for perceived instrumental qualities (usability, usefulness), non-instrumental qualities (aesthetics, status) as well as emotions (positive, negative) should occur that are in line with the respective preferences.

3.1 Participants

$N = 24$ persons participated in the study[1]. All of them were assigned to one of two groups according to their age. All members of the "young" group had used a personal computer regularly before the age of eighteen ("*digital natives*" [29]). Each group consisted of twelve participants. The demographic structure is presented in Table 1. Participants received no gratification for taking part in the experiment.

Table 1. Demographic structure of the sample (M – Mean, SD – Standard Deviation)

Group	Sample N	Gender N_{Male}/N_{Female}	Age M (SD)
Young	12	6/6	24 (*3.30*)
Elderly	12	6/6	50 (*10.78*)
Total	24	12/12	37 (*15.23*)

3.2 Material

Versions. Two high-fidelity versions of a smart phone OS were especially designed for the study using Axure RP Pro. They were presented on a Samsung Galaxy S4 smart phone. Each version showed eighteen typical apps on its home screen; six of them were functional for user testing (weather forecast, notes, contacts, documents, alarm clock and settings). The versions were equipped with the same functionality, but differed in design (skeuomorph vs. flat, see Fig. 2).

UX Questionnaire. To assess the UX variables, six scales of the German version of the meCUE questionnaire ([36], see also http://www.mecue.de) were used: usability, usefulness, aesthetics, status, positive emotions, negative emotions. Each scale consists of three items (except for positive and negative emotions with six items). All items employ a bipolar seven-point-Likert scale ranging from "strongly disagree" (1) to "strongly agree" (7). The scales are theoretically based on the CUE-model (see Fig. 1)

---

[1] According to [35] with a sample size of $N > 23$ participants large effects ($\eta_p{}^2 \geq .14$) can be found with a power of $1-\beta = 0.9$ (for $\alpha < .05$, two-tailed).

and the items used in this study are listed in the appendix (German and English version, see Table 3).

Fig. 2. Exemplary Screenshots of the Smart Phone OS Versions (left side: flat, right side: skeuomorph).

Paper-Based Stimuli. To assess the general preference for flat or skeuomorph design, the following materials were created and printed on cardboard or paper: (a) eleven pairs of icons (taken from the flat and skeuomorph version in Fig. 2), (b) a screenshot of each complete GUI (see also Fig. 2), and (c) 23 positive attributes, such as 'precious', 'stylish', 'professional', 'novel', etc. (adopted from [16]). The cardboard icons and OS versions served to inspire verbal responses in the qualitative interview at the end of the experiment.

3.3 Procedure

After filling in a consent form and questionnaires for assessing demographics, technological experience, and personal innovativeness (as control variables), participants completed a number of tasks embedded in a typical usage scenario (calling a friend, finding and opening a file, making notes, setting the alarm). All tasks were accomplished with both, the flat and the skeuomorph OS version on the smart phone. The order of tasks was counterbalanced over all participants and blocked for each version. During the interaction, the screen was recorded and participants' verbal comments were taped. After the tasks, everyone filled in the meCUE questionnaire for each version. Then the screenshots on cardboard were presented and the participants were asked which one they would like to use more often (design preference). Subsequently, the printed app icon pairs were shown and everybody had to select one icon of each pair (flat vs. skeuomorph) to indicate his or her preference. Finally, the verbal attributes had to be assigned to one of the two screenshots. The selected icons and attributes were discussed with the interviewer in a half-standardized interview to investigate the reasons for the preferences. The whole study lasted approximately one hour.

3.4 Experimental Design and Statistical Analysis

The two independent variables were represented by the factors "design strategy" (flat vs. skeuomorph, within subjects) and "age" (elderly vs. young, between subjects). The combination of both factors resulted in a mixed 2×2 experimental design. Since only interaction effects were expected (see Sect. 2.2), we focus on the interaction effect of both factors but also analyze the main effects in a 2×2 mixed ANOVA for the dependent variables (i.e., the UX scales of the meCUE questionnaire). F- and p-Values are reported for significant differences, the effect size is quantified by partial eta squared (η_p^2). According to [35], $.01 \leq \eta_p^2 < .06$ corresponds to small, $.06 \leq \eta_p^2 < .14$ to medium, and $\eta_p^2 \geq .14$ to large effects.

The preference for one of the designs was a dichotomous (binary) dependent variable which can be represented in a 2×2 contingency table ("age" x "preference"). We analyzed it with Fisher's exact test and report p-Values and the Odds Ratio (OR) as effect size. According to [37], $1.5 \leq OR < 3.5$ corresponds to small, $3.5 \leq OR < 5.0$ to medium, and $OR \geq 5.0$ to large effects.

4 Results

4.1 Quantitative Results

Interaction effects supporting the hypotheses for UX were found for aesthetics ($F(22,1) = 4.836$, $p = .039$, $\eta_p^2 = .180$), status ($F(22,1) = 4.683$, $p = .042$, $\eta_p^2 = .176$), and positive emotions ($F(22,1) = 4.349$, $p = .049$, $\eta_p^2 = .165$). Neither for usability and usefulness (instrumental qualities), nor for negative emotions significant interactions were detected. Both groups rated usability as well as usefulness very high and negative emotions very low. A main effect for design could be found for usefulness ($F(22,1) = 4.760$, $p = .040$, $\eta_p^2 = .178$), where the flat design was rated more useful than the skeuomorph design in both age groups.

The overall preference of the flat vs. skeuomorph OS version was influenced by age. Fisher's exact test revealed significant differences ($p = .045$, $OR = 6.410$) between the two groups as to the favored design. Elderly users chose the skeuomorph version (83.3%) more often compared to the younger group which preferred flat design (58.3%). In order to explain these effects, personal innovativeness was found to be a significant predictor of these preferences ($F(1,22) = 7.86$, $p = 0.010$, $\eta_p^2 = .263$). Younger respondents showed a larger amount of personal innovativeness which may reflect a mediation effect. No gender effects were observed ($Fs < 1$, $ps > 0.05$).

4.2 Qualitative Results

To analyze the qualitative data, the audio recordings were transcribed and sorted into hierarchical categories following the Content Analysis according to Mayring [38].

The frequencies of comments for the most prominent categories of interest are listed in Table 2.

Table 2. Frequencies of comments per category by elderly and young participants.

Categories	Elderly	Young
Reduction to the essential (flat design) is good	1	10
Skeuomorph is easy to understand	6	8
Skeuomorph is more trustworthy because it reminds of the atmosphere in the living room (wooden shelves)	6	2
Flat is more trustworthy because it shows its paces	0	8
Skeuomorph seems to be more sophisticated and is therefore better	3	7
Preference is a matter of habit	5	2

For the icons and interface versions, respondents of both groups stated that they regarded the skeuomorph icons and GUI as easy to understand. Many participants regarded the design preference as a matter of habit and experience with different systems. One respondent from the elderly group said "Flat would be OK as well, if I used it more often. Then I would get accustomed to the flat icons".

Users expressed the wish that "personal" apps, which are linked to precious memories (e.g. notes or a photo gallery), should be more realistic and creative. Common apps without personal significance (e.g. a calculator), however, should be designed in a clean and functional fashion.

5   Discussion

In this study, we investigated how flat and skeuomorph design strategies affect the UX and preferences of young and elderly persons. The results regarding preferences showed that elderly participants more often favored the skeuomorph version, while younger participants more often favored the flat one. According to the CUE model, preferences should coincide with particular differences in UX. Hence, there should be differences in the perceptions of product qualities and emotions between the two age groups which fit their distinct preferences.

Regarding the perception of non-instrumental qualities (e.g. visual aesthetics, status) and positive emotions, the two design strategies affected the two age groups differently; ratings of visual aesthetics, status and positive emotions were higher for the flat design and lower for the skeuomorph design in the younger group compared to the older group. Interaction effects were neither found for instrumental qualities (usability, usefulness), nor for negative emotions.

The effect pattern of the experiment is also in line with the two factor approach of hygiene and motivating factors [39]. Studies have shown that both may affect UX in a certain manner [40, 41]. Usability and usefulness can be characterized as hygiene factors. While their absence leads to dissatisfaction, negative emotions, and withdrawal, their presence is not sufficient to generate satisfaction, positive emotions or acceptance. On the other hand, motivating factors, such as an aesthetical and innovative design, have the potential to create satisfaction, positive emotions, and acceptance, but their lack does not necessarily lead to negative effects.

Referring to our results, both age groups seem to agree about the hygienic aspects, but not about the motivating factors of the two design versions:

- Neither for usability and usefulness, nor for negative emotions a significant interaction occurred. This appears as reasonable if both instrumental product qualities functioned as hygienic factors because they did not interfere with the solution of the tasks. Indeed, both age groups considered the usability and usefulness of the two versions as so high that the according ratings even suggested a ceiling effect. This result goes in line with comments in the interview; both elderly and younger participants stated that "skeuomorph is easy to understand". At least for our study it seems that the skeuomorph elements and metaphors were not outdated enough to be incomprehensible for members of the younger generation.
- For visual aesthetics, status, and positive emotions an interaction effect was found which matched the difference in preferences between the two age groups. Contrary to the younger participants, the elderly ones rated the UX components these components higher for the skeuomorph version. These different appreciations of the non-instrumental qualities might have acted as motivating factors, which influenced both age groups so that their preferences diverged. Results of the interview give a first hint on some of these factors. Trustworthiness as well as aesthetic aspects, such as sophistication and reduction to the essential, seem to matter in that respect, but more research is required to clarify their role.

As stated before, age is probably not an influence factor per se in this study. Instead, it can be regarded as a placeholder for a number of user characteristics, such as knowledge, habits and tastes, which are typical for persons of the same generation. In particular, age may covary with familiarity. While the younger generation is not well accustomed to many of the analogous objects used in skeuomorph metaphors, the older generation grew up with them. Moreover, younger users of technology might be more flexible and open to innovations compared to elderly ones [42]. This aspect is also reflected by the mediation effect of personal innovativeness in our study. On average, older users take longer to adapt to technological changes [43] - although this effect may vanish over time [11].

To summarize, age related user characteristics might have been responsible for the revealed differences in UX and preferences between both groups. This interpretation is also supported by the qualitative findings in our experiment. Especially, familiarity seems to be a key factor for the differences that occurred. Many older respondents stated that the skeuomorph design appeared to them as better and more trustworthy because they were familiar with the physical objects which served as metaphors in the skeuomorph version. Across both age groups, respondents furthermore agreed that design is a matter of habit. Most users appear to be creatures of habit, which may influence their acceptance and preferences with respect to the two design strategies.

Another qualitative finding concerns the connection between the purpose of an application and its design. Skeuomorph design was especially appreciated for personal, individual applications. For example, respondents preferred more embellished design for applications related to memories (like photo galleries) and minimalistic design for functional apps (like calculators). This finding may prove as important in the debate about both design strategies, since it not only supports the attempt to combine both [27], but also hints at when to employ which of them. When checking specific information (e.g., temperature, time of day), or reading a virtual book, designers should minimize animations, textures, and patterns to a minimum in order to decrease access costs and to improve readability and accuracy [1]. On the other hand, hedonic or non-instrumental applications may benefit from skeuomorph design elements that are aesthetically pleasing and stimulating [25]. To find the "right design" means to select the appropriate design strategy for a use case and a user group. A composition of different elements from both designs may be a good way to combine the advantages and neutralize the disadvantages of flat and skeuomorph strategies [9]. After all, minimalistic design always runs the risk of losing information, which might be necessary to interpret the semantics of a GUI: "Simplification is great if you don't lose information and after all, flat doesn't necessarily imply non-skeuomorphic elements" [13, p. 368].

The results of this study have several implications for research and practice. With respect to the CUE model, age-related user characteristics were found to be vital for UX. To account for the consequences of the aging population and the demographic change, designers of GUIs should take the familiarity and habits of elderly generations explicitly into account. Especially when designing personal applications which might be associated with positive emotional memories, this can help to provide positive experiences and to prevent users' reservation and rejection. To accomplish this, designers must reveal users' real-world and digital metaphors and include them in their concepts. More qualitative and quantitative research is therefore required to discover users' mental representations, semantic interpretations, and personal preferences. User-centered strategies, which feedback such empirical insights into the design process, seem especially suited for this purpose.

Additionally, our results strengthen the idea of a two-sided approach of UX dimensions based on hygiene and motivating factors. This approach should be further distinguished and analyzed in different contexts and use cases. It seems that the motivating element is by far more individual than the hygienic component. Since the "right" design heavily depends on the user group, following the GUI principle "know thy user" seems to be extremely important, especially when it comes to age-related knowledge, habits and preferences. Design strategies must be adjusted to these aspects to ensure satisfaction and positive experiences for all age groups.

Acknowledgements. We thank Meike Schröder who contributed significantly to this paper and conducted the data collection during her Master Thesis.

Appendix

Table 3. meCUE questionnaire items (German and English), see also http://www.mecue.de, 7-point-likert scale, German: "lehne völlig ab, lehne ab, lehne eher ab, weder noch, stimme eher zu, stimme zu, stimme völlig zu", English: "strongly disagree, disagree, somewhat disagree, neither agree nor disagree, somewhat agree, agree, strongly agree".

Scale	Original German items [36]	English translation [18]
Usability	1. Das Produkt lässt sich einfach benutzen 2. Es wird schnell klar, wie man das Produkt bedienen muss 3. Die Bedienung des Produkts ist verständlich	1. The product is easy to use 2. It is quickly apparent how to use the product 3. The operating procedures of the product are simple to understand
Usefulness	1. Die Funktionen des Produkts sind genau richtig für meine Ziele 2. Ich halte das Produkt für absolut nützlich 3. Mithilfe des Produkts kann ich meine Ziele erreichen	1. The functions of the product are exactly right for my goals 2. I consider the product extremely useful 3. With the help of this product I will achieve my goals
Aesthetics	1. Das Produkt ist kreativ gestaltet 2. Das Design wirkt attraktiv 3. Das Produkt ist stilvoll	1. The product is creatively designed 2. The design looks attractive 3. The product is stylish
Status	1. Das Produkt verleiht mir ein höheres Ansehen 2. Durch das Produkt werde ich anders wahrgenommen 3. Meine Freunde dürfen ruhig neidisch auf das Produkt sein	1. The product would enhance my standing among peers 2. By using the product, I would be perceived differently 3. My friends could be quietly envious of this product
Positive emotions	1. Das Produkt beschwingt mich 2. Das Produkt entspannt mich 3. Durch das Produkt fühle ich mich ausgeglichen 4. Das Produkt stimmt mich euphorisch 5. Das Produkt beruhigt mich 6. Durch das Produkt fühle ich mich fröhlich	1. The product exhilarates me 2. The product relaxes me 3. The product makes me feel happy 4. The product makes me feel euphoric 5. The product calms me 6. When using this product, I feel cheerful
Negative emotions	1. Das Produkt macht mich müde 2. Das Produkt nervt mich 3. Durch das Produkt fühle ich mich erschöpft 4. Das Produkt frustriert mich 5. Durch das Produkt fühle ich mich passiv 6. Das Produkt verärgert mich	1. The product makes me tired 2. The product annoys me 3. When using this product I feel exhausted 4. The product frustrates me 5. The product makes me feel passive 6. The product angers me

References

1. Gu, B.: East meets west on flat design: convergence and divergence in Chinese and American user interface design. Tech. Commun. **63**(3), 231–247 (2016)
2. Bollini, L.: Beautiful interfaces. From user experience to user interface design. Des. J. **20** (sup1), S89–S101 (2017)
3. Blitz, J.H.: Skeuomorphs, pottery, and technological change: skeuomorphs, pottery, and technological change. Am. Anthropol. **117**(4), 665–678 (2015)
4. Blackwell, A.F.: The reification of metaphor as a design tool. ACM Trans. Comput.-Hum. Interact. **13**(4), 490–530 (2006)
5. Wu, L., Lei, T., Li, J., Li, B.: Skeuomorphism and flat design: evaluating users' emotion experience in car navigation interface design. In: Marcus, A. (ed.) DUXU 2015. LNCS, vol. 9186, pp. 567–575. Springer, Cham (2015). https://doi.org/10.1007/978-3-319-20886-2_53
6. Lakoff, G., Johnson, M.: Metaphors We Live By. University of Chicago Press, Chicago (2003)
7. Oswald, D., Kolb, S.: Flat design vs. skeuomorphism–effects on learnability and image attributions in digital product interfaces. In: Proceedings of the 16th International Conference on Engineering and Product Design Education, Twente (2014)
8. Hou, K.-C., Ho, C.-H.: A preliminary study on aesthetic of apps icon design. In: 5th International Congress of the International Association of Societies of Design Research (2013)
9. Shahid, S., ter Voort, J., Somers, M., Mansour, I.: Skeuomorphic, flat or material design: requirements for designing mobile planning applications for students with autism spectrum disorder. In: Proceedings of the 18th International Conference on Human-Computer Interaction with Mobile Devices and Services Adjunct, New York, NY, pp. 738–745 (2016)
10. Zhou, A.: Cybernetics and human-computer interaction: case studies of modern interface design. In: IEEE Conference on Norbert Wiener in the 21st Century, Boston, MA, pp. 1–6 (2014)
11. Schneidermeier, T., Hertlein, F., Wolff, C.: Changing paradigm – changing experience? In: Marcus, A. (ed.) DUXU 2014. LNCS, vol. 8517, pp. 371–382. Springer, Cham (2014). https://doi.org/10.1007/978-3-319-07668-3_36
12. Gross, S., Bardzell, J., Bardzell, S.: Skeu the evolution: skeuomorphs, style, and the material of tangible interactions. In: Proceedings of the 8th International Conference on Tangible, Embedded and Embodied Interaction, New York, NY, pp. 53–60 (2014)
13. Stickel, C., Pohl, H.-M., Milde, J.-T.: Cutting edge design or a beginner's mistake? – a semiotic inspection of iOS7 icon design changes. In: Marcus, A. (ed.) DUXU 2014. LNCS, vol. 8518, pp. 358–369. Springer, Cham (2014). https://doi.org/10.1007/978-3-319-07626-3_33
14. ISO 9241-210, Ergonomics of human-system interaction, Part 210: Human-centred design for interactive systems. International Organization for Standardization, Geneva (2010)
15. Thüring, M., Mahlke, S.: Usability, aesthetics and emotions in human–technology interaction. Int. J. Psychol. **42**(4), 253–264 (2007)
16. Hassenzahl, M.: The interplay of beauty, goodness, and usability in interactive products. Hum.-Comput. Interact. **19**(4), 319–349 (2004)
17. Hassenzahl, M., Tractinsky, N.: User experience - a research agenda. Behav. Inf. Technol. **25**(2), 91–97 (2006)

18. Minge, M., Thüring, M., Wagner, I., Kuhr, C.V.: The meCUE questionnaire: a modular tool for measuring user experience. In: Soares, M., Falcão, C., Ahram, T.Z. (eds.) Advances in Ergonomics Modeling, Usability & Special Populations, vol. 486, pp. 115–128. Springer International Publishing, Cham (2017)

19. Minge, M., Thüring, M.: Hedonic and pragmatic halo effects at early stages of User Experience. Int. J. Hum.-Comput. Stud. **109**, 13–25 (2018)

20. Pandab, P.: Ingredients of Good Design: Affordance, Emotion and Complexity (2013). https://www.researchgate.net/publication/266899536

21. Pelet, J.-É., Taieb, B.: From skeuomorphism to flat design: when font and layout of m-commerce websites affect behavioral intentions. In: Martínez-López, F.J., Gázquez-Abad, J.C., Ailawadi, K.L., Yagüe-Guillén, M.J. (eds.) Advances in National Brand and Private Label Marketing, pp. 95–103. Springer International Publishing, Cham (2017)

22. Jung, H., Wiltse, H., Wiberg, M., Stolterman, E.: Metaphors, materialities, and affordances: Hybrid morphologies in the design of interactive artifacts. Des. Stud. **53**, 24–46 (2017)

23. Norman, D.A.: Emotional Design: Why We Love (or hate) Everyday Things. Basic Books, New York (2005)

24. Pucillo, F., Cascini, G.: A framework for user experience, needs and affordances. Des. Stud. **35**(2), 160–179 (2014)

25. Li, C.F., Shi, H.T., Huang, J.J., Chen, L.Y.: Two typical symbols in human-machine interactive interface. Appl. Mech. Mater. **635–637**, 1659–1665 (2014)

26. Zhang, X., Wang, Q., Shi, Y.: Contrastive analysis on emotional cognition of Skeuomorphic and flat icon. In: Zhao, P., Ouyang, Y., Xu, M., Yang, L., Ouyang, Y. (eds.) Advanced Graphic Communications and Media Technologies, pp. 225–232. Springer Singapore, Singapore (2017)

27. Page, T.: Skeuomorphism or flat design: future directions in mobile device User Interface (UI) design education. Int. J. Mob. Learn. Organ. **8**(2), 130 (2014)

28. Xi, T., Wu, X.: The influence of different style of icons on users' visual search in touch screen interface. In: Rebelo, F., Soares, M. (eds.) AHFE 2017. AISC, vol. 588, pp. 222–232. Springer, Cham (2018). https://doi.org/10.1007/978-3-319-60582-1_22

29. Prensky, M.: Digital natives, digital immigrants part 1. Horizon **9**(5), 1–6 (2001)

30. Oksman, V.: Young people and seniors in finnish 'Mobile Information Society'. J. Interact. Media Educ. **2006**(2), 2 (2006)

31. Cho, M., Kwon, S., Na, N., Suk, H.-J., Lee, K.: The elders preference for Skeuomorphism as App icon style. In: Proceedings of the 33rd Annual ACM Conference Extended Abstracts on Human Factors in Computing Systems, New York, NY, pp. 899–904 (2015)

32. Blaynee, J., Kreps, D., Kutar, M., Griffiths, M.: Collaborative HCI and UX: longitudinal diary studies as a means of uncovering barriers to digital adoption. In: Proceedings of British HCI 2016 Conference Fusion, Bournemouth, UK (2016)

33. Sha, C., Li, R., Chang, K.: Color affects the usability of smart phone icon for the elderly. In: Duffy, Vincent G. (ed.) DHM 2017. LNCS, vol. 10287, pp. 173–182. Springer, Cham (2017). https://doi.org/10.1007/978-3-319-58466-9_17

34. Robbins, W.H.: Design Practices in Mobile User Interface Design. California Polytechnic State University, San Luis Obispo (2014)

35. Cohen, J.: A power primer. Psychol. Bull. **112**(1), 155–159 (1992)

36. Minge, M., Riedel, L., Thüring, M.: Modulare evaluation von Technik. Entwicklung und Validierung des meCUE Fragebogens zur Messung der user experience. In: Grundlagen und Anwendungen der Mensch-Technik-Interaktion. 10. Berliner Werkstatt Mensch-Maschine-Systeme, Berlin, pp. 28–36 (2013)

37. Chen, H., Cohen, P., Chen, S.: How big is a big odds ratio? interpreting the magnitudes of odds ratios in epidemiological studies. Commun. Stat. - Simul. Comput. **39**(4), 860–864 (2010)
38. Mayring, P.: Qualitative content analysis: theoretical foundation, basic procedures and software solution, Klagenfurt (2014)
39. Herzberg, F.: Work and the Nature of Man. Crowell, New York (1966)
40. Tuch, A.N., Hornbæk, K.: Does Herzberg's notion of hygienes and motivators apply to user experience? ACM Trans. Comput.-Hum. Interact. **22**(4), 1–24 (2015)
41. Backhaus, N.: Nutzervertrauen und – erleben im Kontext technischer Systeme. Technische Universität Berlin (2017)
42. Gilly, M.C., Zeithaml, V.A.: The elderly consumer and adoption of technologies. J. Consum. Res. **12**(3), 353–357 (1985)
43. Pohlmeyer, A.E.: Identifying Attribute Importance in Early Product Development. Technische Universität Berlin (2011)

My Best Shirt with the Right Pants: Improving the Outfits of Visually Impaired People with QR Codes and NFC Tags

Sílvio José Vieira Gatis Filho[✉], Jefté de Assumpção Macedo,
Marília Moraes Saraiva, Jean Elder Araújo Souza,
Felipe Borba Breyer, and Judith Kelner

Informatics Center of Federal University of Pernambuco, Recife, Brazil
{sjvgf,jam4,mms5,jeas,fbb3,jk}@cin.ufpe.br

Abstract. In our daily lives, some situations demand a dress code. Those circumstances may cause issues to the visually impaired people (VIP), mainly when they need to select a specific outfit. This study considers the importance of visual references on fashion and presents a solution to help VIP during the process of picking the proper clothing with awareness of their look. We explored technologies from the Internet of Things (IoT), such as Near Field Communication (NFC) combined with Quick Response (QR) Codes, in an assistive context. The project goal is to develop a cloth matching and an audio description system. This way, VIP may recognize the parts of an outfit and also combine such pieces. To give information about the apparel's data, we attached an NFC tag and a QR code on the clothing tag. Our set up uses an Android application, to scan the QR Codes with the garment data. We also used a prototyping board to read the NFC tags, providing feedback about the clothing combinations. To measure the effectiveness of our solution, we conducted a pilot test with a group of visually impaired users (VIU). The procedure consisted of asking them to pick clothing from a garment rack, with a specific purpose in mind, and then check if they fit the requested dress code. The volunteers were positive about the audio description and the clothing matching system feedback. The participants suggested a few adjustments to the system, and they would recommend our solutions for other VIU.

Keywords: Visual impairment · Accessible clothing tags · Clothes matching
NFC · QR code

1 Introduction

The act of dressing up may involve graphics choices and references. For example, when a person attends to a specific occasion, such as a costume party, or either following a dress code at work. Those situations may cause issues to the visually impaired people (VIP), particularly, when they need to select an outfit. Besides, the textile industry usually present useful instructions in the printed labels, and those are not accessible to the VIP community, which suffers from not noticing features, such as color, texture and other graphical elements from the apparels.

© Springer International Publishing AG, part of Springer Nature 2018
A. Marcus and W. Wang (Eds.): DUXU 2018, LNCS 10919, pp. 543–556, 2018.
https://doi.org/10.1007/978-3-319-91803-7_41

In the last years, the popularization of the Internet of Things (IoT) and the growth of the electronic prototyping tools, such as the Arduino boards, and other sensors and actuators, have given strength to a crescent presence of connected devices in our lives. The IoT gave us the possibility to enhance the everyday activities and even our environment. With these features, it is possible to improve ordinary objects, like clothing, helping people to deal with inherent disabilities, such as blindness. Smart objects can provide information that otherwise would go unnoticed in our routine, expanding our senses. Hence, the use of these interactions in an assistive context can help people to overcome their impairments.

This research introduces a system to aid the VIP community to deal with clothing visual information. Our concern is to provide data which otherwise the visually impaired user (VIU) would not have access by either touching or feeling the apparel's fabric.

Our concept uses connectivity to provide data on the visual elements of each garment piece. In that way, VIP may recognize the parts of an outfit and also combine such pieces. For example, the system would recommend to the user when selecting suit pants that match with coat. To make this possible, we empowered clothing items with QR Codes and NFC tags.

QR Code is a barcode pattern, readable by anyone with a smartphone; it either can store data information or redirect a user to a specific web address. The NFC is a wireless form of communication between devices; it works by approximating two devices, one emitting a short field of radio frequency and another with an antenna capable of picking up this signal. The NFC technology is getting popular in everyday objects, thanks to its application in services such as electronic tickets, and virtual wallets with smartphones.

This study primary objective is to explore the possibilities of QR Codes and NFC tags as interactive tools providing autonomy for VIU to dress up with visual awareness of their look. Making "How connected objects can help VIP to gain autonomy in the act of dress up?" our research question. Our contributions are our design process, that enabled the creation of our concept and our findings with the VIP community. We hope to encourage other studies and the community to think about the users with visual impairments in the future.

In this paper, we discuss related works, with approaches to help VIP to perceive the visual aspects of the clothes. In the methodology section, we describe our design process and methods, explaining the project choices, and the development of our prototype, and how we tested it. Further, this paper presents our proposal, describing our solutions, and the Usability Test section, where we describe our pilot test. Finally, this study ends with the discussion and the conclusion sections.

2   Related Work

Marco Conti et al. defined the Internet of People (IoP) [1] as a human-centric paradigm to the Internet, thanks to the relation between Human-Computer Interaction (HCI) and IoT. The IoP paradigm discusses the concept that understanding humans is essential for the structure of internet with multiple connections between people-operated gadgets and devices.

Blind and visually impaired people rely on different senses to comprehend the world around them. Accordingly, with Lefeuvre et al. [2] it is vital to designers understands how these people discover and interact with new products.

In their article, Lefeuvre et al. introduced the "Loaded Dice," a tool designed to present possibilities from connected devices, composed of two cubes filled with sensors and actuators. Their goal was evaluating how VIP could collaborate with ideas and solutions, of IoT products, acting as co-designers after experiencing the Loaded Dice. Authors claimed that their tool and methodology helps VIP to understand better how devices can work, and Designers to comprehend how to develop better solutions for VIP. Although we have not followed the co-design and workshops models, we agree that user-centered design is a compelling practice when working with concepts and generation of alternatives with VIP. In our case, contact with the community was also fundamental to the project.

In the Paper "Current and future mobile and wearable device use by people with visual impairments" [3], the authors consider that Visually Impaired People do not rely on visual cues in screen guided interactions. For this reason, connected wearables are an exciting solution to VIP interacts with devices like tablets, smartphones or computers. In the paper, the researchers developed a wristband using e-textiles materials. Their wearable emerged from a co-design process with VIP. One concern of their focus group was the appearance of the prototype, accordingly to their standards, the ideal design is discrete, to avoid social awkwardness by signing the need for a particular device, and the device has to attend fashion requirements, becoming attractive to use. Thus, it is interesting to observe that user comfort is a requirement for the creation and adoption of assistive technologies. We have adopted this concept in our project.

About visual impairment and clothing information, the study "Recognizing Clothes Patterns for Blind People by Confidence Margin based Feature Combination" [4], developed a method of cloth texture pattern analysis through computer vision. It classified the clothing texture by organizing into four major categories: "stripe," "lattice," "special," and "patternless," and translate this information into audio for VIP. The article also describes technical details of the image processing algorithm. One of the co-authors, Shuai Yuan, also published the short paper "A System of Clothes Matching for Visually Impaired Persons" [5], with a clothing match system for VIP. Yuan's work uses a camera and image processing to compare two pieces of fabric and points if their texture and color match. This system captures the clothing with a camera, process with an external computer, returning feedback through audio.

Regarding Yuan's matching system, it results does not cross information considering clothing utility. Additionally, it only demonstrates that some aspects of tissues are equal, while there are situations with clothing that fabrics can be different but still combine. For example, a white cotton shirt and a blue jeans pants are a classic fashion combination of distinct kinds of fabrics and colors. To deal with this gap, we proposed a system that turns simple aspects of two garment pieces, e.g., color, texture, size, and kind, in data. Both cloth data is analyzed, and then, the system crosses these characteristics to return information about the combination to the user.

Another project with clothing combination suggestions is the Smart Wardrobe System [6]. According to the authors, the project target is two kinds of people, busy entrepreneurs, and color blind people. It uses Radio Frequency Identification (RFID) tags, to register and track apparels in a wardrobe. The user needs to attach an RFID reader to the wardrobe and a tag in the garment piece, after registering it in the system with the system's software. The Smart Wardrobe's main idea is to manage apparels from its software, which indicates the best choices based on the user mood, color or style of the day. This solution has some interface issues since it relies on visual elements; it is not friendly for VIP users. Besides, the software clothing, color, texture, and materials combination is very subjective. Regarding the focus on blind people, the Smart Wardrobe System has the flaw of being too much dependent on subjective factors and in a screen interaction to deal with clothes. We propose a more VIP friendly interaction, with clothing data-based feedback.

Another aspect that conferred several solutions was the feedback techniques, while some researchers designed solutions with audio feedback, others preferred tactile feedback. *"Touch and #Tag"* [7], for example, is a system to organize and store garments by styles, sizes, and functions. The researchers developed a tactual tag system that permits to VIP to classify and store their clothing, e.g., a social shirt would receive a tag and a casual shirt another. Their approach has the advantage to not rely on external digital gadgets to provide feedback, but it has some issues. First, in our opinion, the authors designed a tactile icon system that could demand a high learning curve for the user. Second, the tag is not attached to the cloth; it works more like a wardrobe sign and mapping. These problems can cause cognitive overloading for the user, Lefeuvre et al. [2], for example, had some misinterpretations with tactile icons for VIP during the development of the Loaded Dice, and the Touch and #Tag is also vulnerable to those misinterpretations.

Apart from these considerations, the Touch and #Tag seems to deliver value after an adaptation period, since its cloth tags system has information about clothing appearance, which usually isn't accessible to VIP. Commonly, tags appear at certain spots on cloth fabrics and could transmit more information about the apparel itself, becoming an assistive resource for VIP, with the application of some technologies and techniques.

The researcher Ringland [8], listed possibilities to make cloth tags a primary source of information to VIP. Her article included four solutions to improve the tags. The first was an alternative using ordinary cloth buttons of different form and sizes to pair clothing pieces and act as indicators of color and texture. The second solution is the use of braille tags with text information about the piece.

Ringland also contemplated the use of QR codes as a third solution and RFID/NFC tags as the last suggestion. The author suggests using these technologies can bring benefits for VIP because it can store information and the description of the clothing pieces. She also considers that VIP has some difficulties with QR Codes, due to the necessity to scan the code with a camera, while washable RFID/NFC tags had an elevated price. Regarding the current popularization of the NFC technology in smartphones, and the improvements in the accessibility software in their operational systems, we think that those adverse conditions for using either NFC or QR Codes are currently in mitigation process.

3   Methodology

During the development of this research, we analyzed studies related to IoT and visual impairment fields, to better understand the human factors behind the connections related to VIP interaction with connected devices. We searched in the scientific literature, studies that investigated IoT as assistive technology, by mapping related design solutions. After this analysis, we conducted a brainstorming session, which defined the general theme of VIP and clothing. Hence, we went back to digital libraries to search specific articles about the subject.

Therefore, our development stage, we listed our design principles and made our product concept, then we designed the prototypes and the user test scenario.

3.1   User-Centered Design Based Method

To reach our proposal, we conducted a method based on the User-Centered Design practices, considering the final user as the most crucial factor of our project. We consulted the VIP community at two local institutions, the Pernambuco's State Blind People Association (APEC) and the Blind People Institute "Antônio Pessoa de Queiroz" (BPI), both in Recife City, Brazil.

During the visit at the Blind People Institute, we had the opportunity to perform informal interviews with four VIPs. The content of the interviews swirled through questions about habits involving clothes, from how they organize clothing at home, to questions about how to choose outfits to get out.

In our design process, we did not only make assumptions of how VIP would like a system to help them dress up; the interviews gave us important data before brainstorm sessions, and we had the convenience to evaluate our prototype with VIP participation. Unlike some participatory design practices, such as reported in other related works, as Loaded Dice [2] or the Wearables article [3]. The VIP did not take part assuming the role of co-designers of our projects, but we delivered user-driven solutions, always in touch with the local VIP community.

Our prototypes had to be fully accessible to the VIP public, providing regular feedback by our focus group. Our research also consulted the accessibility guide published by the Samsung Research Institute for Informatics Development (SIDI) [9], to design the prototypes.

3.2   Brainstorming Sessions

We conducted two classic brainstorm sessions, where we briefed the participants about the research matter, with a synthesis of the interviews at the Blind Institute, and collaborated with ideas. No visually impaired people attempted to participate directly in the process.

The first brainstorm session occurred after the first search about VIP and IoT at the literature, and it resulted in our research focus to help VIP to deal with visual information on clothes. The second session happened after a new search at the literature and the interviews with VIP at the Blind Institute, and it resulted in the insights of our two proposals for the VIP community, the audio description application, and a clothing combination system.

3.3   Proposals

The first solution selected from the brainstorm round was the idea to translate cloth description into audio. To make it possible, we attached QR codes into clothing tags and created a smartphone application that reads QR Codes and provides means to a VIP user scan a piece of cloth and obtain an audio description.

Our second solution was to create a clothing matching system, where the user would compare two garment pieces and obtain positive or negative feedback about the outfit combination. To realize such task, the user must pick a piece of clothing at a time, so we developed our idea with an NFC module.

3.4   Usability Test

To evaluate our solutions, we performed an exploratory usability test with two volunteers, a thirty-year-old woman with low vision (V1), and a thirty-eight-years-old blind man (V2); both recruited at the APEC Institution, which also, was the usability test location.

We evaluated our proposals with a usability test setup consisted of a garment rack with six pieces of clothing, all attached to NFC tags and QR Codes, as displayed in Fig. 1. Our script consisted of an interview, two tasks, and a post activities interview.

Fig. 1. Test scenario and a t-shirt with an NFC tag and a QR Code.

We have conducted a semi-structured interview with the participants, before starting the testing sessions. This interview aimed to collect details about the user's behavior when using smartphones, and data about how they manage garments in their daily lives.

After the interview, the volunteer performs the pilot test activities. The first task was to combine an outfit by reading clothing tags with the NFC Module. To complete the task, the user had to pick a piece of cloth from the garment hack, scan the tag with the NFC Reader, then pick the second piece of clothing and repeat the scanning process to hear the feedback about the clothing combination.

The second task was to pick a proper outfit for a social event. To complete the task, the volunteer had to pick a piece of clothing from the garment hack and use our android application to scan the QR code attached to the clothing and hear its description to decide to pick it or not.

Before the activities, we instructed both volunteers about the concepts and functions of the technologies involved in the prototypes. We also authorized them to make comments or to ask questions about the procedures during the execution of the tasks.

At the end of the activities, we realized the second interview to evaluate the user's satisfaction and to gather qualitative feedback from them. To measure the user's contentment with the experience, we asked if the volunteer would introduce our prototypes to their routines and if they would recommend our devices to others.

Three members of the research group managed the pilot test. The interviews and activities with the prototypes were duly recorded and filmed by one of the researchers, while a second researcher was responsible for taking field notes, recording comments and observations. The third researcher conducted the operations, interviewing the participants, explaining the procedures and answering questions about the activities.

4   Results

Our informal talk at the Blind People Institute and the brainstorm session with our advisers led us to two alternatives, which generated the evaluated prototypes at the pilot test with VIP users.

4.1   Prototype 1: "Eu Visto" Application

The first solution from the brainstorm rounds was the idea to translate cloth description into audio, with a brief description of the clothing aspects. To realize such task, we designed the concept of an accessible smartphone application with a QR Code reading feature. With our app the VIU would scan the QR Code attached to the cloth tag, using the android phone camera, obtaining a brief description of the garment appearance and details about it. The application would gather information from an online database, with all tags description content.

Our application adopted a very clean aesthetics, with black and white assets to guarantee a high contrast application, considering VIU with low vision. For this first version, we designed our prototype with the QR Code scanning function, as displayed in Fig. 2. All screens are compatible with the talkback function, the screen reader from Google Android Operational System. The first version of the app is called "Eu Visto," which means "I Wear" in Portuguese.

In our concept, the printed QR Code is an address to an online database, and every address contains four underlying parameters: Type, Size, Texture, and color. When the

Fig. 2. "Eu Visto" application final screens.

user scans the QR Code address, it downloads the information to the smartphone, which translates the parameters to audio through the talkback function. All parameters refer to universal aspects in clothes. Type referees to cut and seam accordingly to function. Size refers to the measuring unit present in the cloth tag, the texture parameter refers to the pattern displayed, and the color parameter describes predominant colors in the garment. With these four characteristics, it is possible to describe a piece of cloth in a very distinct way; we can say that a basic t-shirt, for example, is casual, small, without textures, and white.

The structure of the application "Eu Visto," uses the "zxing" library, and two activity screens, one for camera activation, and other for the screen's audio description. The talkback function works by reading everything settled at the application "Context Description." This way, everything settled in the application, has also to be set in the Context Description, in order to the talkback function returns the screen-reading audio. Thus the smartphone reads the QR Code and returns the cloth characteristics, which the talkback function converts to audio description.

4.2 Prototype 2: Cloth Matching System with NFC

We designed an additional module exploring NFC communication. This module can aid the VIU in checking if the selected pieces would match. The user would choose a piece of cloth for the top, and another for the bottom, i.e., a shirt and pants. Then, using the application, reading the NFC tags of both pieces, so that the system will provide recommendations on the combination.

This module is viable due to the possibility of writing data in the NFC tags. In our concept, each label will store significant characteristics of the clothing, its kind, color, texture, and size, same aspects from the QR Code lecture. Thus, when the user read the label of two distinct pieces, with the NFC module, it would send the signal, trough Wi-Fi connection, to the system application. Then the data comparison from both tags would be processed in an external computer or smartphone.

We mounted our prototype on an Arduino mega board, equipped with a buzzer, and an NFC/RFID PN532 module, emulating an accessory that people would have near to their wardrobes, as displayed in Fig. 3. The buzzer's audio was the feedback component of our system. For our prototype, we set the buzzer to beep three short beeps when the combination was right and to execute a long beep for wrong combinations.

Fig. 3. Clothing combination prototype with the buzzer and the NFC/RFID PN532 module.

4.3 Usability Test Results

The first step of our pilot tests was the recruitment. We conducted the usability test with two subjects recruited in loco, at the APEC institution. We gathered two users, V1, with severe low vision since birth, and V2 with a total loss of vision, also from birth.

The first stage of our procedure were semi-structured interviews, which revealed us that our volunteers are familiar with smartphones; both used Android devices and the talkback function for years.

We asked both users about their habits with garments, general questions related to how they choose an outfit and organize their wardrobes. V1 declared that her low vision allows some autonomy in organizing clothes, but she has problems at stores. During shopping, she suffers to consult clothing labels and to verify visual elements on pieces, such as words or phrases. V2 stated that he buys and organizes garments by tissues styles, such as polo shirts because it usually has specifics kinds of tissue, texture, and design. He revealed to consulting his wife about visual elements in cloth and uses some cues, like embroidery symbols, to memorize which cloth is that. He also consults his wife before leaving home to know if his outfit is acceptable. Curiously, at the interview, V2 admitted not to know if the shirt he was using had a graphic pattern.

After the entry interviews, each participant executed the usability tasks in less than 5 min. They did not experience any problem completing the desired tasks. However, they had some issues with the audio feedback of the buzzer. The volunteers had trouble to understand if the garment combination was right or wrong at the first time, in a misinterpretation of the buzzer's beep.

When using the application and QR codes, both users had enjoyed using the audio description feature. Still, V2, in Fig. 4, who is blind, had issues. For example, at the first try, the user held the device in an incorrect position, requiring assistance. However, after instructions, the user could read the labels without assistance.

Fig. 4. Volunteer 2 testing our android application.

After the activities, both users declared that would use our solutions in their routines, and that would recommend it to others. V1 also stated that clothing tags with audio description could make a big difference in VIP routines, and observed how this approach could help herself at shopping. V2 gave more feedback about the clothing combination system. He said that it is an interesting concept since it can prevent VIU from going out with the wrong clothes combination. V2 also said that his nine-year-old daughter, who is also blind, would take benefit from both solutions, since, according to him, she is vain and likes doing errands independently.

5   Discussion

During the research, we gathered relevant information about how VIP deal with visual aspects in clothing. Our methodology allowed us to analyze state of the art and understand how researchers project solutions for VIP with IoT technologies.

The research process allowed us to consider the needs of VIPs and comprehend that the lack of vision of our targeted audience is not a problem for the requirements of our system, but an element that is part of the specificity of our users. Blindness does not define them; it is a personal characteristic. Therefore, the access of the blind to our proposals must be the same as those of the full-sighted. This article session discusses our research process and the experience of evaluating prototypes with VIU.

5.1   A System to Aid VIP Deal with Visual Information on Clothes

During the research stages, our user-centered design-based method led us to data that permitted brainstorms, prototypes, and evaluation with VIP. Our interviews at the Blind People Institute revealed intriguing factors about their routines; we understood that is essential to blind people to map their clothes since its earning through storage, up to day usage. Besides, sometimes they have to ask for help from a person with clear sight for aware how their outfits look.

We understand that VIP have a different perception of their surroundings, and this reflects on how they interact with applications and products. For this reason, we defined design concepts and came up with a solution that enables people with visual disabilities to be aware of their clothing and their look. These concepts gave us the opportunity to create a cloth matching alternative, different than Yuan's system [5] or from the Smart wardrobe [6]. Also, we could advance at the Ringland's [8] study of possibilities to use QR Code and NFC tags for aid VIP.

After the brainstorm session, we came up with these two objectives, to provide cloth's visual elements audio description and to create a system of clothing match. Therefore, we designed two prototypes, an android application that uses the smartphone camera to read QR Codes, and the NFC module that provides feedback about the clothing combinations. We separated the QR code and NFC modules to evaluate the VIP abilities to interact with each technology, like different products evaluation. Furthermore, we decided to compare how the local public, used to solutions using smartphones, would fare interacting with an application and a screenless device.

We developed the application for Android because, at APEC and the Blind People Institution, most of the blind people use Android phones. The primary objective of our application evaluated the interaction between the VIU and the QR Code reading and audio description feedback, so we elected these features as essential requirements for our first prototype. During the software development stage, we considered other functions for the application's first version, such as create, store and edit QR Codes. However, this number of functionalities started to accumulate on screen, making these features costly and burdensome for the user. In the end, we decided to cut it, for keeping the design clear as possible for the user, as displayed in Fig. 5.

Fig. 5. Prototype (left) and final version (right) of the application.

From our point of view, the clothing match system device should be an independent gadget, so we mounted an external device with the Arduino board, the NFC/RFID module, and the buzzer. The reason we picked NFC instead of RFID was the NFC's low frequency. In our idea, the clothing pieces reading must occur in order, so this low frequency helps to prevent simultaneous readings, forcing the user to operate one reading at the time. We created the feedback pattern with the buzzer because it is compatible with for the Arduino board setup. Also, it can emit different tones in a programmable order, which permitted us to create a pattern for wrong and right combinations.

Regarding the clothing data, we proposed a system with four common aspects of clothes because it was a simple way to summarize clothing description. Hence, the conversion of these characteristics of clothing to data inputs is not a hard task. We can compare these inputs with data from other pieces. Thus, the four topics structure works for the audio description and the system of clothing match, making possible to both solutions share the same database.

5.2 Evaluation with Visually Impaired Users

The usability test procedure revealed some interesting aspects of the context of VIP and clothing. Our two volunteers, with distinct degrees of blindness, helped us to understand how deal with visual data in fashion can be a burdensome task for VIP. The first round of interviews demonstrated that our volunteers experience different issues for picking and buying clothes. V1, with low vision, pointed that even with a sight degree that makes it possible to her organize and combine apparels, it is hard dealing with garments at stores since she cannot read labels or have to come very close at garments to understand details. While V2, totally blind, relies on apparel's format, cut and tactual tissue textures to organize a clothing management system, supported by his wife. This behavior reminded us the studies about wardrobe organization.

During the task execution, the users demonstrated the ability to operate the systems. V1 did not have any issue in manipulating devices, while V2 had issues in point correctly at the QR Codes. However, after some training, he dealt with the smartphone camera independently, without any other trouble, founding the application interesting. Regarding the clothing matching system, the feedback from the buzzer was an issue for both users. Even with our previous explanation about the audio feedback from the buzzer, both users misunderstood its feedback at the first time. After scanning both tags, they listened to the three beeps confirming a right combination and declared their choices as wrong. They only realized the buzzer functioning after trying another combination and listening to it a second time. Perhaps the buzzer's sharp, mechanical sound has confused the volunteers.

The user's response to the audio description was better than beeps from the buzzer. It is interesting to observe because they did not have any trouble in operating the clothing match system, only to comprehend its feedback. With the QR Code, the scenario is almost reverse, the volunteers comprehended the feedback from the application. However, V2 has issues with its operation.

About the volunteer's feedbacks, in our opinion, the enthusiasm of both users during the interviews after the tasks, biases their answers. They were less comfortable to realize negative critics to some aspects of the evaluation, like the buzzer feedback, or difficulties related to the Smartphone camera. However, even so, their feedback was essential to our conclusions about the prototype performances.

We found that the audio description feature is fascinating for both volunteers. V1 was happy to realize differences from a casual to a social shirt, and V2 pointed that discover the color of a suit jacket is a prominent feature. Their feedbacks demonstrated to us that the awareness of dressing an outfit is indeed a significant form of self-expression.

About the Clothing matching system, V1 was less impressed from its feedback and functionality. We think that she has a degree of sighting that is enough to make it possible to combining clothing. Meanwhile, V2 was very impressed with the possibilities of the solution, since many tissues are very similar regarding tactual textures, but have a completely different visual pattern. These diverse reactions from our volunteers demonstrated to us that maybe the cloth matching system is more relevant to blind users than it is for people with low vision.

The usability test served to analyze interactions of volunteers with our solutions; We consider our results to be interesting to the community and recognize the potential impact that these features can make in the lives of VIP. The systems were efficient in giving awareness of the pieces of clothing for VIP, although we recognize the necessity of some adjustments. The test with QR Codes evidenced that many VIP might have trouble using this technology independently. A future solution, merging both approaches, integrating the audio description feature to NFC tags may be a better approach for the future, since the number of devices with this technology is increasing, and the NFC tags can perform both the audio description and clothing matching tasks.

6   Conclusion

During the development of this research, we reached two different approaches to help VIP deal with visual aspects of clothing. We build up two proof-of-concept solutions over user-centered design principles, reaching an android application that translates QR codes in apparel audio description, and a system of garment matching based on NFC reading and data comparison. With our solutions, VIU can not only have complete awareness of their looks but also, combine and compare different pieces of clothing.

We designed prototypes for each concept and tested them at APEC a blind people local institution, with two volunteers, one with severe low vision and another blind from birth. Both users had no problem completing the usability test tasks. However, they had issues with some assets of our solution.

We found that our prototype is ready to use by the blind, with some training before assimilating all functions. Based on the outcomes, we believe that an NFC only solution, with the same audio description of QR Codes, would be better for VIP. Our next steps are to integrate the NFC module into the mobile application and perform more analysis with VIP people.

Acknowledgments. We would like to thank the APEC institution, which gives us space and helped us to recruit the volunteers of our user test scenario. Moreover, to the researchers at the Networking and Telecommunications Group (GPRT) and Virtual Reality and Multimedia Research Group (GRVM) at the Federal University of Pernambuco (UFPE), for the helping us with the NFC Module and for letting us use their laboratory structure.

References

1. Conti, M., Passarella, A., Das, S.K.: The Internet of People (IoP): a new wave in pervasive mobile computing. Pervasive Mob. Comput. **41**, 1–27 (2017)
2. Lefeuvre, K., Totzauer, S., Bischof, A., Kurze, A., Storz, M., Ullmann, L., Berger, A.: Loaded dice: exploring the design space of connected devices with blind and visually impaired people. In: Proceedings of the 9th Nordic Conference on Human-Computer Interaction, Article No. 31. ACM, New York (2016)
3. Ye, H., Malu, M., Oh, U., Findlater, L.: Current and future mobile and wearable device use by people with visual impairments. In: Proceedings of the SIGCHI Conference on Human Factors in Computing Systems, pp. 3123–3132. ACM, New York (2014)
4. Yang, X., Yuan, S., Tian, Y.: Recognizing clothes patterns for blind people by confidence margin based feature combination. In: MM 2011 Proceedings of the 19th ACM International Conference on Multimedia, pp. 1097–1100. ACM, New York (2011)
5. Yuan, S.: A system of clothes matching for visually impaired persons. In: Proceedings of the 12th International ACM SIGACCESS Conference on Computers and Accessibility, pp. 303–304. ACM, New York (2010)
6. Goh, K.N., Chen, Y.Y., Lin, E.S.: Developing a smart wardrobe system. In: Consumer Communications and Networking Conference (CCNC). IEEE, USA (2011)
7. Hsu, T-Y., Li, Z-Y., Lin, H-Y., Liou, Y-H., Tsai, C-L.: Touch and #Tag: improving clothing experiences of people with visual impairment. In: Proceedings of the 2016 CHI Conference Extended Abstracts on Human Factors in Computing Systems. ACM, New York (2016)
8. Ringland, K.: Accessible clothing tags: designing for individuals with visual impairments. In: CHI EA 2013: CHI 2013 Extended Abstracts on Human Factors in Computing Systems. ACM, New York (2013)
9. Mobile Accessibility, Guide to the Development of Accessible Mobile Applications. http://www.sidi.org.br/guiadeacessibilidade/en/index.html#inicio. Accessed 05 Feb 2018

Design of Smartphone 9-Key Keyboard Based on Spelling Rule of Pinyin

Xiaodong Gong[✉] and Maoqi Liu

School of Design and Arts, Beijing Institute of Technology,
Zhongguancun South Street 5, Haidian, Beijing, China
hildagxd@bit.edu.cn, liumaoqi2132@qq.com

Abstract. Currently, the layout of the smartphone 9-key keyboard is that 26 Latin letters are sequentially distributed on the 1st to the 9th keys according to the alphabetical order, which is irrelevant to the spelling rule of pinyin. This paper, based on the study and conclusion of the spelling rule of pinyin, designs a layout mode of the 9-key keyboard that can meet the Chinese input demand by combining the analysis of usability of different areas of the smartphone interactive interface. Moreover, the new layout mode is compared with the existing keyboard layout by comparing the finger movement distance during Chinese input, and the Chinese input efficiency of the new layout mode is verified. This paper provides new possibility for realizing diversification of the human-computer input interface of the mobile terminal in the future and better meeting the demand of Chinese input users, especially the elderly users.

Keywords: Pinyin · 9-key keyboard · Human-Interaction design
Chinese input · Input efficiency

1 Introduction

The existing keyboards of smartphone platforms with Chinese input include the 26-key keyboard (the full keyboard) and the 9-key keyboard. Each keyboard contains 26 Latin letters, and the layout is shown as follows.

Compared with full key input, the 9-key keyboard is a more frequently-used keyboard input mode [2, 3], mainly due to its good fault tolerance. Compared with the 26-key keyboard, the number of keys of the 9-key keyboard is smaller, so each key has a bigger occupation in the same sized mobile phone screens. Taking the iFly input keyboard of the iOS 10 system of the 4.7-in (diagonal line) iPhone 7 as an example, the size of a key of the 26-key keyboard is 4.9 mm*6.7 mm while that of the 9-key keyboard can be as large as 12.7 mm*8.5 mm, as shown in Fig. 1. According to the study data of the MIT laboratory, the average fingertip size is 8–10 mm [4], and key operation is generally not simple fingertip touch. Therefore, the large key area ensures that the 9-key keyboard has better fault tolerance, because users can see the keys more clearly and avoid misoperation easily. This feature of the 9-key keyboard is important for the elderly users with poor eyesight and users with thick fingers, and it is also the reason why the 9-key keyboard is more suitable for the smartphones with small sized screens.

© Springer International Publishing AG, part of Springer Nature 2018
A. Marcus and W. Wang (Eds.): DUXU 2018, LNCS 10919, pp. 557–574, 2018.
https://doi.org/10.1007/978-3-319-91803-7_42

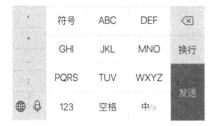 

iFly pinyin 9-key keyboard of ios   iFly pinyin 26-key keyboard of ios

Fig. 1. 9-key keyboard and 26-key keyboard [1]

However, some problems still exist in the layout mode of the 9-key keyboard:

The Layout Does Not Reflect the Spelling Rule of Pinyin. In the 9-key keyboard, the 26 Latin letters are distributed on the 1–9 keys in the sequence of A, B, C, D, E, F, G, H, I, J, K, L, M, N, O, P, Q, R, S, T, V, U, W, X, Y and Z. This layout ignores the spelling rule of pinyin. For example, for users [5] of small sized mobile phones and accustomed to operating with one hand, the letter V with a small use frequency in Chinese input appears in the key within the comfortable operation area of the mobile phone interface, while the letter N with a high use frequency is put in the key within the operation area difficult to operate. Considering the large difference between pinyin input and English input, this keyboard layout mode has obvious limitation for Chinese input and influences the input efficiency during human-computer interaction.

The Existing Layout Mode has no Function of Initial Associating Inputting. When using the 26-key keyboard, users can input common word groups simply by inputting initials. For example, to input "到处 (daochu)", users only need to input initials D and C and then choose the word group "到处 (daochu)" from the options. However, the initials and the finals are always on the same key in the 9-key keyboard. For example, both the final A and the initials B and C are on key 2, and both the final E and the initials D and F are on key 3. Thus, the 9-key keyboard does not support fast associating inputting through initials like the 26-key keyboard in most cases.

In sum, the 9-key keyboard has better operation fault tolerance due to its large key area and it is more suitable for the smartphones with small sized screens. However, the existing layout of pinyin letters of the 9-key keyboard does not take the spelling customs of pinyin into full consideration. With the development of the human-computer interaction technology, it is certain that the keyboard design will break through limitation of the existing mode and provide more diversified selections for different customer demands, thereby improving the human-computer interaction efficiency and user experience. Thus, based on consideration of the use rules of pinyin and the human-computer interaction comfortableness, this paper designs a 9-key keyboard layout mode that can meet the Chinese input demand, hoping to improve the Chinese input efficiency and meet the demand of the elderly users and Chinese users.

2 Research Method

(1) Summarization and conclusion of the spelling rule of pinyin: functions of different letters of pinyin were analyzed, and the letters were divided into groups according to the functions.

(2) A new letter layout mode of the 9-key keyboard for Chinese input was designed based on the above rule by combining the human-computer interaction operation hot area.

(3) Human-computer interaction efficiency verification: based on the general method of keyboard efficiency verification, this study built a distance matrix according to the finger movement distance of the operator, and compared the new letter layout mode and the existing layout mode, so as to verify whether the human-computer interaction efficiency is improved during Chinese input.

3 Study of Spelling Rule of Pinyin

3.1 Use Frequency of Pinyin Letters

Figure 2 shows statistics of the use frequency of pinyin letters. According to the statistics table:

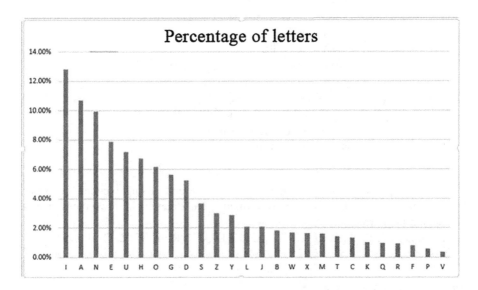

Fig. 2. Statistics of use frequency of pinyin letters [6]

1. The use frequency of vowels A, E, I, O and U which are generally used to form finals in pinyin is high, and one reason is that the final component is necessary for utilization of pinyin.

2. Apart from the vowels A, E, I, O and U, three consonants N, H and G also have a high use frequency. The reason is that N and G are the only two consonants that can form finals, and H can be combined with other letters to form initials.

3.2   Initials and Finals

Initials and finals are the most basic components of Pinyin. Pinyin contains 21 initials and 34 finals, as shown in the following table [7] (Tables 1 and 2).

Table 1. Table of initials

b玻	p坡	m摸	f佛	d得	t特	n讷
l勒	g哥	k科	h喝	j基	q欺	x希
zh(ẑ)知	ch(ĉ)吃	sh(ŝ) 诗	R日	z资	c此	s思

Table 2. Table of finals

	i |衣	u |乌	ü|迂
a啊	ia|呀	ua|蛙	
o喔		uo|窝	
e鹅	i.e.|耶		üe |约
ai哀		uai|歪	
ei诶		ui (uei) |威	
ao熬	iao|腰		
ou欧	iu(iou) |忧		
an安	ian|烟	uan|弯	üan|冤
en恩	in|因	un(uen) |温	ün|晕
ang昂	iang|央	uang|汪	
eng鞥	ing|英	ong(ueng) |翁	iong|雍

(Note: letter ü is substituted by Latin letter V in the existing input methods).

Considering that the input method layout uses the unit of single letters, this paper, by combining the forming rule of pinyin, divided the 26 letters into two types, named initials and finals respectively:

21 initials: B, P, M, F, D, T, N, L, G, K, J, Q, X, R, Y, W, Z, C, H and S

6 finals: A, E, I, O, U and V

3.3   Cacuminals and Velar Nasals

Cacuminals and velar nasals are common syllable combinations of pinyin, as shown in Table 3:

Cacuminals zh, ch and shi are formed by Z, C and S and H, respectively. These three cacuminals are also the only three initials formed by two letters.

Table 3. List of cacuminal and velar nasal combinations

Z, S, C, H	zh-,ch-,sh-
N, G	-ang,-eng,-ing,-iang,-iong,-ong,-uang

In nasal finals, the finals with –ng tails are velar nasals formed by finals N and G. The finals with –n tails are alveolar nasals.

In the letter combinations of pinyin, there are many combinations of two finals, such as ai and i.e. From the list of finals in Table 2, it can be seen that nasal finals are the only compound finals with initials. Velar nasals are the only nasals formed by combinations of initials, and use of initials must be combined with finals in other conditions. The extensive utilization of nasal finals in pinyin leads to the high use frequency of N and G.

3.4   Combinations of Initials and Final

Apart from initials Z, S, C, H, N and G which form cacuminals and velar nasals, there are 14 initials left. The list of combinations of these initials and the finals is as follows (Table 4):

In this paper, the 14 initials except Z, S, C, H, N and G were called independent initials. The following figures show the data statistics condition of combinations between these 14 independent initials and the finals. (Note: Dots in Figs. 4 and 5 are center points of the bar graph, and they reflect whether the combinations between the initials and AEI or between the initials and OUV have more combination possibilities.) (Fig. 3).

According to the above statistical data, the following rules can be obtained:

(1) The number of syllable combinations of letters F and W is relatively small, and there are also few syllable combinations between them and finals AEI and OUV. Generally, the number of syllable combinations of letters D and L are the most, and their combinations with finals AEI and OUV are also the most. Thus, we can consider putting F and W on the key relatively far from the finals but putting D and L on the key close to the finals.

(2) There are many syllable combinations between letters B, P and M and finals AEI, but fewer between letters B, P and M and finals OUV. There are few syllable combinations between letters K and R and finals AEI, but relatively more between letters K and R and finals OUV. Thus, we can consider putting B, M and P on the key relatively close to the finals AEI, but D and L on the key relatively close to the final OUV.

(3) The quantity of combinations of letters J, Q and X is basically the same, and their positions on the keys can be further analyzed by combining their use frequency.

Table 4. List of combinations of initials and the finals [8]

Initial	Combinations with AEI	Combinations with OUV	Total
J	-i,-ia,-i.e.,-ian,-iang,-iao,-iu,-iong,-in,-ing| 10 kinds	-u,-ue,-un,-uan|4kinds	14
Q	-i,-ia,-i.e.,-ian,-iang,-iao,-iu,-iong,-in,-ing	10kinds	-u,-ue,-un,-uan|4kinds	14
X	-i,-ia,-i.e.,-ian,-iang,-iao,-iu,-iong,-in,-ing	10kinds	-u,-ue,-un,-uan|4kinds	14
K	-e,-en,-eng,-a,-an,-ai,-ao,-ang |8kinds	-ong,-ou,-u,-ua,-uo,-un,-ui,-uai,-uan,-uang	10kinds	18
T	-e,-eng,-a,-an,-ao,-ang,-i,-i.e.,-ian,-iao,-in,-ing |12kinds	-ou,-ong,-u,-uo,-un,-ui,-uan| 7kinds	19
P	-a,-ai,-an,-ao,-ang,-ei,-en,-eng,-i,-i.e.,-ian,-iao,-in,-ing	14kinds	-o,-ou,-u|3kinds	17
Y	-a,-ao,-an,-ang,-i,-ian,-in,-ing |8kinds	-ou,-ong,-u,-ue,-un,-uan	6kinds	14
L	-a,-ai,-ao,-an,-ang,-e,-ei,-en,-eng,-i,-i.e.,-ian,-iang,-iao,-iu,-in,-ing|17kinds	-ou,-ong,-u,-ue,-uo,-un,-uan,-v|8kinds	25
B	-a,-ai,-ao,-an,-ang,-ei,-en,-eng,-i.e.,-i,-ian,-iao,-in,-ing	14kinds	-o,-u|2kinds	16
W	a,ai,an,ang,ei,en,weng |7kinds	o,u|2kinds	9
R	-ao,-an,-ang,-e,-en,-eng |6kinds	-i,-ou,-ong,-u,-uan,-ui,-un,-uo| 8kinds	14
M	-a,-ai,-ao,-an,-ang,-e,-ei,-en,-eng,-i.e.,-i,-iu,-ian,-iao,-in,-ing |16kinds	-o,-u,-ou	3kinds	19
F	-a,-an,-ang,-ei,-en,-eng |6kinds	-o,-ou,-u	3kinds	9
D	-a,-ai,-ao,-an,-ang,-e,-ei,-en,-eng,-i,-ian,-iao,-i.e.,-in,-ing,-iu|16kinds	-ou,-u,-uan,-un,-uo,-ui| 6kinds	22

(Note: dia and biang are hardly used in daily life and their use frequency in written texts is very small).

(4) Compared with the above initial letters, there is no obvious inclination between combinations of letters T and Y and the finals AEI or OUV. The positions of T and Y on the keys can be further analyzed by combining their use frequency.

In sum, this research divides pinyin letters into the initials and the finals, and summarizes the following rules: (1) Except V, the other 5 finals have a high use frequency. (2) The utilization of the initials includes 2 conditions: (1) independent utilization of the initials: generally, there are very few combinations between F and W and the finals, or between F and W and AEI and OUV, respectively; generally, the syllable combinations between D and L and the finals are the most, and the combinations between D and L and the finals AEI and OUV respectively are also the most; there are many syllable combinations between letters B, P and M and the finals AEI but few between letters B, P and M and the finals OUV; there are few syllable combinations between letters K and R and the finals AEI but relatively more between letters K

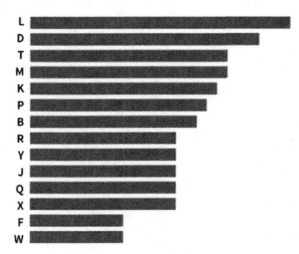

Fig. 3. Total quantity of possible combinations of syllables of the 14 independent initials in the descending order

Fig. 4. Quantity of combinations between the independent initials and AEI in the descending order

and R and the finals OUV; (2) combined utilization of the initials: since the initials H, N and G can be combined to form cacuminals zh-, ch- and sh- and velar nasals –ng, these three initials are very frequently used in pinyin.

Fig. 5. Quantity of combinations between the independent initials and OUV in the descending order

4   Design of 9-Key Keyboard Layout Based on Use Rule of Pinyin

4.1   Analysis of Existing 9-Key Keyboard

As shown in Fig. 6, keys of the existing 9-key keyboard are distributed in 3 rows and 3 lines, with the 26 Latin letters distributed on the 9 keys in the sequence of A, B, C, D, E, F, G, H, I, J, K, L, M, N, O, P, Q, R, S, T, V, U, W, X, Y and Z. There are 3–4 letters on each key. Generally one of the nine keys is reserved as a functional key which is used for symbol input, switching of the input methods and line feed, such as key 1 in Fig. 6.

1	2ABC	DEF3
4GHI	5JKL	MNO6
7PQRS	8TUV	WXYZ9

Fig. 6. Schematic diagram of layout of the existing 9-key keyboard

According to the positions of the keys and their relations with surrounding keys, this paper numbers the keys in sequence, including 1 center key (key 5), 4 side keys (keys 2, 4, 6 and 8) and 4 corner keys (keys 1, 3, 7 and 9). The center key is located at the center of the keyboard, adjacent to the 4 side keys and forming diagonal lines with the corner keys. The distance between the center key and all other keys is short. The side keys are located on four sides of the keyboard, adjacent to the center key and 2 corner keys and forming diagonal lines with 2 side keys. The distance between each side key and the 3 keys on the opposite sides is far. The corner keys are located at 4 corners of the keyboard, with each one adjacent to 2 side keys and forming diagonal lines with the center key. The distance between each corner key and the other 5 keys is far, as shown in Fig. 7.

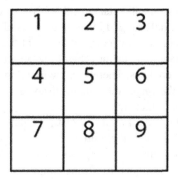

1	2	3
4	5	6
7	8	9

Fig. 7. Schematic diagram of keyboard number

4.2 Layout of Finals

The above analysis indicates that finals are a necessary part of pinyin combinations, and also the pinyin letters with the highest use frequency. Thus, the finals should be put on the keys that enable the finals to be combined with other letters on surrounding keys more conveniently. The distance between the center key and all others is short and the center key can be well coordinated with the surrounding keys. Besides, the existing researches show that key 5 has the best operation performance [9] in terms of the reaction time and the correction rate. Thus, in the new keyboard layout, the first step is to put the finals on the center key and one side key, as shown in Fig. 8.

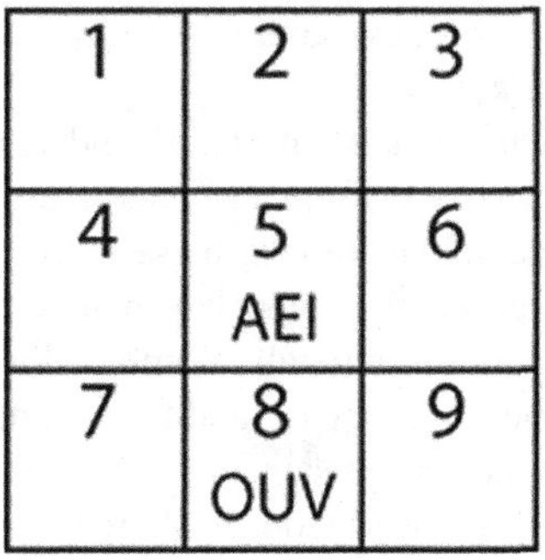

1	2	3
4	5 AEI	6
7	8 OUV	9

Fig. 8. Layout of keys AEI and OUV

The layout of concentrated distribution of finals on the center key and one side key has the following advantages:

(1) According with the use logic of pinyin and reducing the operation burden. The concentrated distribution of finals realizes clear division of the final zone and the initial zone in the keyboard. Users can input Chinese characters according to their logical thinking of inputting initials first and then finals. The explicit division of the initial zone and the final zone relieves the trouble of searching in the whole keyboard area when looking for letters, thereby significantly reducing the visual search and attention burden.

(2) Reducing the finger movement distance and improving the input efficiency. There are a lot of compound finals formed by combinations of the finals, such as "来lai" and "怪guai". After adopting concentrated layout of the finals, the click operation which needs long-distance finger movement before changes to double click and click operation at adjacent keys. Therefore, the input operation becomes faster and more convenient and the finger movement distance of users is shortened, which helps improve the input efficiency.

(3) Making the application of the initial associating inputting method possible. After the finals are separated from the initials in the layout, the initial associating inputting method which can only be applied to the 26-key keyboard now can be used in the 9-key keyboard, thereby further improving the input efficiency.

Furthermore, the analysis of the letter use frequency indicates that compared with O, U and V, the use frequency of the finals A, E and I is higher. Therefore, this paper puts A, E and I at the center key and O, U and V at the side key adjacent to the center key, to form the keyboard layout containing the AEI key and the OUV key shown in Fig. 8 (The key where letters A, E and I are distributed is called the AEI key in this paper, et cetera).

4.3   Layout of Commonly-Used Initials

After the AEI key and the OUV key are determined as the above mentioned, the side keys having the closest linkage with the final zone are key 4 and key 6 which are adjacent to the AEI key and in diagonal relations with the OUV key. Thus, the initials with the high use frequency can be distributed at these two keys. Besides, since the number of letters on each key of the existing keyboard is generally 3–4. Four letters can be distributed on each of these two keys, and this can realize the maximal utilization of the convenience of these two keys.

The above analysis indicates that H, N, G, D and L are initials with a high use frequency and many combinations. Moreover, since letters Z, C and S are generally combined with H to form cacuminal initials, these three letters are also incorporated into initials and are distributed on the same key with H, which can facilitate input. Similarly, since letters N and G are generally combined to form the velar nasal final, these two letters are put on the same key to facilitate input. Thus, the other commonly used initials D and L can be put on the same key with N and G, i.e. H N G D L Z C S ==== ZCSH NGDL. The keyboard layout is shown as follows, in Fig. 9:

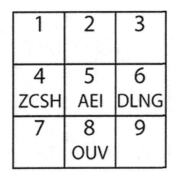

Fig. 9. Schematic diagram of layout of main initials

4.4 Layout of Other Initials

The other 12 letters and the blank key have to be distributed on the left 5 keys, including 1 side key and 4 corner keys. Among the 4 corner keys, 2 corner keys adjacent to the OUV key are closer to the final zone, so they can be combined with the finals more conveniently. The other 2 corner keys are relatively farther from the finals. Considering that a blank functional key is generally reserved in the 9-key keyboard and this key has a smaller use frequency compared with the letter keys, so that one corner key far from the final key can serve as the blank key. Thus, key 1 is temporarily set as the blank key.

Key 2 is the last side key. It is close to the AEI key but relatively far from the OUV key. Thus the initials with fewer combinations with OUV but more combinations with AEI are distributed on key 2. From the above analysis, it can be seen that there are more combinations between initials B, P and M and the finals AEI but fewer combinations between initials B, P and M and the finals OUV. Thus the letters B, P and M are distributed on key 2.

The corner key 3 is far from the final zone so that the letters with fewer combinations with the finals can be distributed on key 3. From the above analysis, it is known that the number of combinations between F and W and the finals is the smallest, and there are few combinations between F and W and the finals AEI and OUV. Thus, it is suitable to distribute F and W on key 3.

The 7 letters left are J, K, Q, R, T, X and Y. According to analysis of Figs. 4 and 5, there are fewer combinations between K and R and the finals AEI but more between K and R and the finals OUV; while there is no obvious inclination in the number of the combinations between J, Q, X, T and Y and the finals AEI or OUV. Thus, K and R can be temporarily distributed on the corner keys 7 and 9. The use frequency of letters shows that the use frequency of Q is relatively small, so it is temporarily distributed on the corner key 3. The final keyboard layout is shown in Fig. 10.

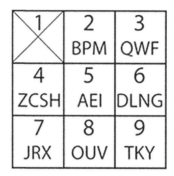

Fig. 10. Layout of 9-key keyboard designed for Chinese input

4.5   Layout Adjustment

(1)   Adjustment according to use frequency of letters

Considering that,

(1) P is the initial with the smallest use frequency, now it is put on the side key 2 close to all other keys.
(2) If operated with one hand, the corner key 3 is one of the most inconvenient keys in the keyboard. However, currently W on this key has a high use frequency, and "我(wo)" is used frequently in practical Chinese input. Thus, we should consider adjusting W to the position close to the letter O.
(3) The use frequency of Q on the corner key 3 is higher than that of P, so it can be adjusted.
(4) The corner keys 7 and 9 are convenient. While among the letters Y, J, X, T, K and R, the use frequency of R is small, so it can be adjusted.

Finally, W and R are exchanged, and P and Q are changed. The new layout is as follows (Fig. 11):

	2	3
1	BQM	PRF
4	5	6
ZCSH	AEI	DLNG
7	8	9
JWX	OUV	TKY

Fig. 11. Keyboard layout after fine adjustment according to the use frequency

In addition, there are another 4 keyboard layout methods according to different positions of the OUV key. The ZSCH key and the DLNG key, the JWX key and the TKY key, and the blank key and the PRF key have similar convenience, so they can be exchanged.

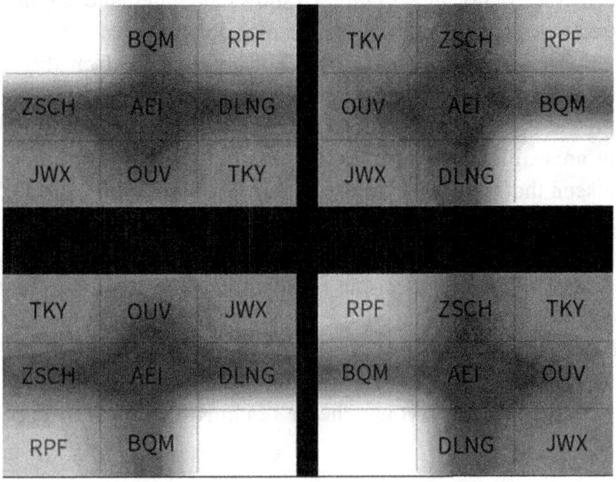

	BQM	RPF		TKY	ZSCH	RPF
ZSCH	AEI	DLNG		OUV	AEI	BQM
JWX	OUV	TKY		JWX	DLNG	
TKY	OUV	JWX		RPF	ZSCH	TKY
ZSCH	AEI	DLNG		BQM	AEI	OUV
RPF	BQM				DLNG	JWX

Fig. 12. Other equivalent layout schemes

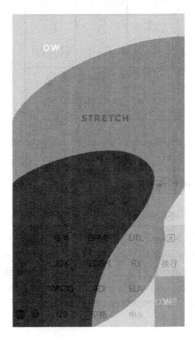

Fig. 13. Schematic diagram of singe hand operation hot area

(2) **Layout adjustment according to interactive hot area**

When using mobile phones, 67% of user use right hands, and 49% of them hold mobile phones through one hand [10]. It is believed that if the keyboard layout is convenient and reasonable for single hand operation, there will be no problem for two hands operation. Thus, this research finely adjusts the keyboard layout based on the single hand operation in the interactive hot area. Figure 13 shows the schematic diagram of the thumb operation hot area when the operator holds the mobile phone with one hand.

The schematic diagram of the operation hot area is based on the 326 ppi 4.7-in iPhone 6 screen with 1334 * 750 pixel resolution. The dark area is the comfortable natural area, and the operation difficulty increases with shallowing of color. The light grey area is the area difficult to operate. Combining the key distribution of the keyboard, it can be seen that the line of keys on the rightmost of the keyboard and the side keys on the bottom of the keyboard are in the area relatively difficult to operate.

To improve the operation comfortableness and convenience of the keyboard, the keys which are less frequently used can be distributed in the light color area. In the keyboard layout scheme of this paper, the keys less frequently used include the blank key, the BQM key and the PRF key. Thus, the second layout mode in Fig. 12 is the optimum scheme.

In sum, the final keyboard layout scheme obtained is shown in Fig. 14:

1	2	3
TKY	DLNG	PRF
4	5	6
OUV	AEI	BQM
7	8	9
JWX	ZCSH	

Fig. 14. The final keyboard layout scheme

5 Efficiency Verification

5.1 Explanation of Verification Method

The common method of keyboard comparison is to build an evaluation model, quantize the keyboard input operation and evaluate the operation efficiency of the keyboard with the appropriate evaluation function [11, 12]. Calculating the time needed to quickly move to a target based on the Fitts's Law and then conducting comparison and design is an important method of the human-computer interaction field [13, 14]. The common form is:

$$T = a + b\log_2(1 + D/W) \tag{1}$$

Where,

T—The average time for finishing movement Constants a and b reflect the inherent attribute of the equipment
D—The distance between the starting point and the target center
W—Target size

The Fitts's Law reflects that in a certain equipment condition, when the movement distance for operation is shorter, the operation time needed is shorter; when the target size is bigger, the operation time needed is shorter. This research builds the evaluation model of the 9-key keyboard on this basis.

5.2 Building of the Evaluation Model

In the Chinese input process of smartphones, the operator's input behavior can be summarized to be formed by two movements:

(1) Click the keys: for this operation, since there is no key process in the keyboard of the smartphone platform, the finger movement distance is very little in the click operation. Thus, time consumption of this movement is very short;
(2) Fingers move to the next key: the finger movement operation refers to the process that the finger leaves the current key and moves to the next key to be clicked. In this process, if the current key and the next key are the same one, the finger only needs to operate with double clicks. This omits the movement of the finger for a certain distance and simplifies the input process.

This section builds the analog test function based on the input operation actions, and tests the existing keyboard layout and the redesigned keyboard layout through the operational program. Furthermore, the input efficiency is verified by comparing the finger movement distance in the input process.

When comparing the typing time of these two kinds of keyboards, it is assumed that the length of the character string input by the user is n, the time for the finger to press on the key is T_0, the key reaction time is T_1, and the time for the finger to move from one letter to the adjacent one is $T_{xy}(x < n-1, y < n)$, then the time for inputting the character string

$$T = T_0 * n + T_1 * n + T_{12} + T_{23} + \ldots \ldots T_{(n-1)(n)}. \tag{2}$$

Assume that the finger movement speed is $V * W_{xy}$ (V is the average speed and W_{xy} is the weight of the influence of different finger operations on the speed) and the distance of adjacent two letters on the keyboard is $S_{xy}(x < n-1, y < n)$, then

$$T_{xy} = S_{xy}/(V * W_{xy} *) \tag{3}$$

The test of typing time is largely affected by the subjective conditions of the test objects, and measurement of T_0, V, T_1 and W_{xy} may be different for the test objects in different periods and with different equipments. Thus, to highlight the key points and simplify the test, it is assumed that the finger movement speed of the test objects at any time with any action is the constant, and in the condition of the same key reaction time of mobile phones, the test of typing time can be simplified to comparison of the finger movement distance $S = S_{12} + S_{23} + \ldots\ldots + S_{(n-1)(n)}$ during typing. Hence, the verification method of this research is simplified to comparison of the finger movement distance when typing with these two kinds of keyboards.

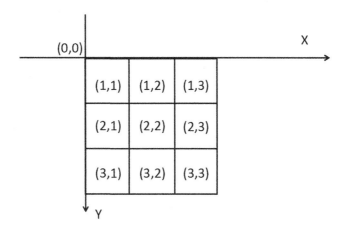

Fig. 15. The layout of the -key keyboard in the XY coordinate system

The layout of the 9-key keyboard is set in the XY coordinate system, and each key has its coordinate, as shown in the following figure. To simplify the complexity of distance calculation, each key of the 9-key keyboard is viewed as a square model (Fig. 15).

This paper writes the distance calculation program based on the above evaluation model. In the program, the coordinates of the 26 letters in the coordinate system are recorded according to the keyboard arrangement. When the user inputs the character string, the distance S_{xy} of two adjacent letters in the character string is calculated $S_{xy} = |(X_y, Y_y) - (X_x, Y_x)|$; the final distance S is calculated by adding all the S_{xy} and then is output. If S is smaller, it means the finger movement distance is shorter, i.e. the typing time is smaller; vice versa.

For example, to input a simple short sentence "我爱北京天安门wo ai bei jing tian an men", the operator presses 9-6-2-4-2-3-4-5-4-6-4-8-4-2-6-2-6-6-3-6 on the orignal keyboard in sequence; the total distance is $10 + 9\sqrt{2} + \sqrt{5}$, approximately 24.96. While on the redesigned keyboard, the operator presses 7-4-5-5-6-5-5-7-5-2-2-1-5-5-2-5-2-6-5-2 in sequence; the total distance is $11 + 4\sqrt{2}$, approximately 16.66.

The letter input path and the program calculation results are shown as follows (Fig. 16):

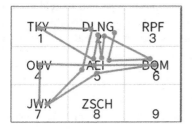 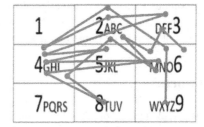

Fig. 16. Schematic diagram of the letter input path

Additionally, some other texts are tested, to compare the distance of these two kinds of keyboards. The results are shown as follows (Table 5):

Table 5. List of test results

Text source	Original keyboard	New keyboard	Optimization degree
Prose: Moonlight over the Lotus Pond (Number of words: 1,349)	5217.44	3408.36	34.67%
Xinhua net: How the Graphene industry breaks the ice and sets sail (Number of words: 1,785)	7072.67	4828.18	31.74%

According to the test result, the finger movement distance during Chinese input can be reduced by over 34% under the new keyboard layout. Therefore, compared with the existing keyboard, the new keyboard layout remarkably improves the Chinese input efficiency.

6 Conclusion

This research focuses on redesigning a Chinese input oriented 9-key keyboard layout scheme applied to the existing smartphone platforms according to the use rule of pinyin. Theoretically, the new layout mode can reduce 30%–40% finger movement distance of the operator, thereby improving the keyboard efficiency and realizing more efficient Chinese input. At the same time, the layout design provides possibility for the application of the initial associating inputting method and improves the efficiency of Chinese input through the small-screen electronic equipment.

With the development of the human-computer interaction technology, the keyboard design is bound to break through the existing mode, to provide more diversified selections for users with different demands. The keyboard design scheme of this paper can make full use of the advantages of the 9-key keyboard and create better human-computer interaction experience for Chinese input users and the elderly users.

The practical application of the keyboard layout scheme needs learning and adaptation of users. The transition process still needs further test, study and discussion.

References

1. 2017 Apple Inc.: iPhone 7Technical Specifications [EB/OL]. www.apple.com/cn/iphone-7/specs/. Accessed 15 Apr 2017
2. Liu, B., Miao, F., Liu, R.: Research of keyboard finger-write input method for mobile phone. Appl. Res. Comput. **27**(9), 3422–3424 (2010)
3. iiMedia Research: 2015–2016 China Mobile Input Method Annual Research Report [EB/OL]. www.iimedia.cn/40374.html. Accessed 03 Apr 2017
4. Dandekar, K., Raju, B.I., Srinivasan, M.A.: 3-D finite-element models of human and monkey fingertips to investigate the mechanics of tactile sense. J. Biomech. Eng. **125**(5), 682–691 (2003)
5. Biqiang, L.: Research and Implementation of Intelligent Input Method for Mobile Phone Based on Smartphone OS. Harbin Institute of Technology (2006)
6. GOUKI: The use frequency of pinyin letters for Chinese character input with pinyin [EB/OL]. www.zhihu.com/question/23111438/answer/31580566. Accessed 15 Apr 2017
7. Institute of Linguistics, CASS: Xinhua Dictionary (the 11th version), 677–678 (2011)
8. Baidu Baike: Pinyin syllables [EB/OL]. http://baike.baidu.com/link?url=ZK71i0kg2uTYG GGhQpAASNBGRxIFeAURrIbt0Kh02q67PZI_5TG6j_y-KeEF-t1b-FwIhHr2FubLO835RP_Aj3uNKruHHG4o3K-thZwhUKzOV5CtatUAKhvjh_V8dGYZ Accessed 15 Apr 2017
9. Canqun, H.: Ergonomics Study of Thumb-Based Chinese Mobile Keyboard Layout. Faculty of Science, Zhejiang University (2009)
10. Hoober, S.: How-do-users-really-hold-mobile-devices [EB/OL]. www.uxmatters.com/mt/archives/2013/02/how-do-users-really-hold-mobile-devices.php. Accessed 05 Jul 2017
11. Junlin, Z., Yong, C., Hongyi, W.: Layout comparison and optimal design of the standard keyboard. Comput. Syst. Appl. **21**(4), 254–258 (2012)
12. Canqun, H., Xiujie, W., Liezhong, G.: Studies on text input methods of mobile keypad. Sci. Technol. Rev. **30**(1), 76–79 (2012)
13. Liang, C.: Study on Availability of Interaction Technology Behind Handheld Devices. University of Electronic Science and Technology of China (2015)
14. Tong, Z., Wenhu, Y., Xining, Z.: An analysis of mouse operation in graphical user interface environment. Appl. Psychol. **9**(3), 14–19 (2003)

The Research of User Experience of Mobile Products in Intelligent Age

Xinwei Guo[(⊠)] and Jingyan Qin

School of Mechanical Engineering,
University of Science and Technology Beijing, Beijing, China
guoxinwei@ustb.edu.cn

Abstract. Recalling the previous information revolution, big data, cloud computing and the Internet of things has become a phenomenon characterized by obvious features, the bearing of technology has become an important support for economic development in the era of intelligence, mobile products are still the core media for people to access information. This paper studies the design cases and academic theories of today's classic mobile products through the methods of literature review and case study, and explores the features and corresponding design methods of mobile products in the era of intelligence. Based on the traditional design method, this paper analyzes the new characteristics of the user experience of mobile products in the intelligent era, and proposes the use of artificial intelligence technology to provide users with personalized services, while using the big data thinking to give play to the traditional design thinking to take into account the product's commercial value and social value theory. So as to realize the harmonious coexistence between man and nature, intelligence and emotion. This is equally the ideal of high growth in the era of information civilization.

Keywords: User experience · Mobile product · Interaction design

1 The Arrival of the Intelligent Era

With the development of information economy, the channels for users to access information have changed from unity to complexities, the way from the active search information in the past to the current precision push, and the tools have also been upgraded from "software + hardware" to "cloud computing + big data".

The Fourth Industrial Revolution is a new technological revolution based on Internet industrialization, industrial intelligence and industrial integration as well as artificial intelligence, clean energy, unmanned control, quantum information technology, virtual reality and biotechnology [1]. The richness of the media in this channel has diversified our quest for information into exploration in multidimensional data space, and at the same time we have looked forward to the flexibility and precision of information.

The main characteristics of the intelligent era are the integration of technologies, the elimination of the boundary between the physical world, the digital world and the biological world. Design has always been an important promoter of the development of human civilization and an important driving force in leading the industrial revolution. However, in the new era, the concept of design and product is being redefined as we need new ways and means of thinking to help upgrade and transform traditional industries in order to further adapt and lead the new industry structure and user's consumer demand.

2   Features of Mobile Products in Intelligence Age

2.1   Intelligent Service

Intelligence is an essential feature of mobile products in the intelligence era. Along with the rapid development and application of big data, cloud computing and Internet of Things, various intelligent Internet information products can be found everywhere in life, which greatly enriches and improves people's lifestyles.

Intelligent speech interaction is a new generation of interactive mode based on speech input. It can get feedback results by speaking. Most of the traditional voice interaction are the question and answer form. In the iOS system, users can use Siri to start the famous Chinese application WeChat, and turn the voice into the text and send it to a designated contact. These actions are artificial intelligence technologies such as speech recognition, semantic analysis, and speech generation system (see Fig. 1).

Fig. 1. Siri in iOS

Another case of intelligence service is iOS system album features. Album based on intelligent scene recognition and face recognition to classify all the photos again, the system can automatically integrate elements of similar photos. At the same time, the memory function in the album can help users wake up the memory. This function can provide based on the map or on different identity display, accompanied by playing the form of music (see Fig. 2).

Fig. 2. Album in iOS

With the development of intelligence, the pace of information processing is getting faster and faster, and the rapid response and elaborate management of the system are required to help human beings to complete more preset work or unnecessary labor. Therefore, the design and development of products need scientific decision-making based on the analysis of data, and thus the requirements for the development of intelligent products are also promoted. Intellectualization of product and services will lead to a revolution in life, work and thinking [2].

2.2 Combination of Software and Hardware

From the rise of computers in the 1980s to the development of the mobile Internet in the 1990s, the design we talked about during this period mainly focused on the research of interface design and the interaction of users and interfaces. By the second decade of the 21st century, the development of big data, the Internet of Things, and artificial intelligence has made everything interconnected. The combination of users, systems, data, and items makes the network connection more relevant and valuable. In the smart era, the diversity and richness of products such as smart hardware, smart phones and wearable devices have changed from the interaction of software to the combination of software and hardware. The essential change is the product concept and design object Change [3]. In particular, traditional mobile products require a combination of hardware bearer, system service and physical product. Deep integration of software and hardware products increasingly obvious trend. Under this trend, our description of the characteristics of mobile products needs to provide services in all aspects based on the traditional interface design and interaction design and hardware assistance.

2.3   Naturally Multimodal Collaboration

The "(human positively) input – (computer passively) output" interaction pattern can be date back to the early 1940s, since than keyboards and pointing devices such as light pen, mouse and touchscreen have been the primary modality of human-computer interaction. The old efficient texting and clicking method "forced" many "designers" create tones of great things (e.g., Vi/Vim or GUN Emacs text editor, X window server, mouse, tablet/digitizer, Light pens, CAD, space ball/trackball, joystick) (see Fig. 3).

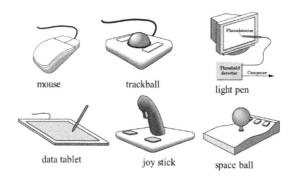

Fig. 3. Physical interactive devices

If the information age is the initial stage of the development of the information economy. The current smart era is the stage of upgrading. Each business cycle naturally enjoys its own design paradigm. We look back at the information age from the interaction between people and the interface; and in the intelligent age, we are seeking the balance point between human perception and all things. From the linear interaction of "input-output-input" of the traditional Human-machine interface to the multi-dimensional closed-loop interaction of people, people to objects, people to systems, people to data. The design center of gravity also shifts from the standardization of the study of logic of human machine interaction turns to the acquisition of human perception, the transfer of data from emotion and the research on the emotional expression of the system.

3   The Characteristics of User Experience of Mobile Products in Intelligent Age

3.1   Lower Threshold and More Efficient Mode of Experience

With the development of artificial intelligence technology, the development of machine learning, image recognition, AR/VR technology and so on, more and more in-depth analysis of the needs of users, understanding of things, complex problems, more efficient and lower cost interactive mode. The user's learning cost is reduced, the operation and feedback are more efficient, and the user's experience path is shortened to a certain extent. Constantly powerful machine-assisted ability to effectively liberate the user's brain, makes people better focus on decision-making and creativity. For example, the dramatic increase in the accuracy of biometrics enables unprecedented security, speed, and convenience in authentication such as payment, and voice interactions play a significant role in a contextualized experience as they can handle multiple tasks at one time; Tools AI help users to solve the tedious data analysis, processing and other operations, so that it can focus on communication, creative creation [4].

Luka is a picture-book-reading robot that can interact with children. Children can quickly recognize the picture book by placing the picture book in front of it. Flip the picture book and read it automatically to the children. In addition, Luka will interact with children, make laughter, be spoiled, and make different expressions according to different states (see Fig. 4).

Fig. 4. Luka

3.2   Stronger Sense of Participation Experience

Most of the success of the Internet economy depends on the aggregation. The success of Tencent stems from the aggregation of social resources. The success of Baidu stems from the aggregation of Internet information. Alibaba succeeds in the aggregation of commodity resources. Recall that we are familiar with the "Wikipedia", "Baidu Baike," "Baidu know" and so on, are in fact the majority of users at any time in any place of data aggregation.

"Xiao Ai" is a smart interactive voice product, which designed and produced by Xiaomi company. Since its birth in March 2017 has developed rapidly. Xiaomi official announced that only 10 months' time equipped with "Xiao Ai" accumulated more than 10 million smart devices as of January 2018. As for the smart speakers designed and manufactured in China, users can also participate through the "Xiao Ai Training Program" (see Fig. 5). Through the user's self-training, "Xiao Ai" can become more intelligent, users can attach it to their personality, and these individualities after the nuclear review into everyone's smart speakers, so we can be "Xiao Ai" as A collective creation of products.

Fig. 5. Xiaomi smart voice interactive products

To achieve the similar human-human voice conversation result in human-computer interaction field, people need to teach computer to learn what human say and mean, also why they say it and why to me, and finally what do we both know, things I should say in response to human being [5, 6].

Intelligence era data is obtained from the user and then serve the user. Each of us is the consumer of information and the producer of information. Each time we enter, every search, every selection will be the next user's data source. We introduce user engagement into the design process so that users are aware that they themselves are the subject of design services, which in itself expands the user's understanding of how to create value for themselves and at the same time reinforces the user's satisfaction of the self-creating value capabilities sense.

3.3   Expand Brand's Commercial Value Through Social Experiences

US information interaction design expert Szeto Fu in the "Experience Design" book, for the first time gives the definition of experience design in 2001: "Experience design integrates the participation of consumers into the design, that is, the enterprise takes service as the "stage" and the product as the "property", the environment as a "scenario", so that consumers feel in the course of business experience a beautiful experience."

Every year before the Spring Festival, Alipay will distribute red envelopes on New Year's Eve through the activities of collecting five FU (see Fig. 6). Users can scan "Fu" characters directly through the AR, and can also use the AR to scan their friends' "Five FU" gestures. The same can be achieved through social networks. In addition, many brands also joined in this activity, users can scan physical products through the AR, such as Starbucks coffee cups, Coca-Cola bottles, as shown. Alipay looks forward to passing on the word "blessing", a symbol of Chinese culture that is familiar to friends all over the world. It is not translated into LUCK, but "FU".

Fig. 6. Alipay set red envelopes in the annual Spring Festival before

The widespread application of group socialization has already become the key to product design and brand value acquisition in this era. The essence of community thinking is that people, emotions, spirit and values are highly connected. People of the same values and hobbies will be connected together to form a specific network, and even become a basic lifestyle of this era. Social relationship-based marketing has inherent advantages in user and consumer insights and analytics, so we can free up more effort to move from system flow design to human representation through products and to enhance customer experience in the Internet Economy era, And the interface presents a double match based on the user's mental model fit the design of the natural to achieve the original purpose of the enterprise.

4   User Experience Design Method of Mobile Products in Intelligent Age

4.1   With Artificial Intelligence Technology to Provide Users with Personalized Service

In the process of mining user needs, the use of artificial intelligence technology, can better reflect the characteristics of thousands of people, reflecting the definition of personalized needs. Alibaba Luban artificial intelligence system can be based on product themes and consumer characteristics, product images will be personalized presentation. Ads served in the "Double 11" Shopping Festival shows different content for different users. On average, each sub-venue needs to launch 30,000 image mate-rials, and a total of 400 million-volume materials has been produced during the double 11, equivalent to about 8,000 posters per second. At the same time, Luban's system analyzes the user's purchasing preferences to customize the service content and match specific content to specific groups of people. In addition, the system can help designers to solve the problem of material management and creative design by analyzing data such as advertisement position, time and place.

In the era of intelligence, the intelligence level of the machine is enough to provide us with personalized service, turning all the people facing the same software into a system that automatically adapts to different users and presents different interfaces to realize the brand's development strategy. In the ever-changing and rapidly evolving context, the user experience's role can not be confused. The essence of design is to find the problem - analyze the problem - solve the problem, we should keep the learning state like the deep learning algorithm, and use the scientific product design method to analyze the problem calmly and intelligently. Combined with knowledge in the fields of natural sciences, social sciences, philosophy, anthropology, computer science and cultural communication, and constantly accumulating and innovating in practice.

4.2   Employing Big Data Thinking Empowers Traditional Design Thinking

Traditional design thinking refers to the designer in the design process to use the thinking patterns and methods. DESIGN THINGKING was first put forward in the book "design thinking" by Peter G. REWE. David Kelly, a professor of mechanical engineering at Stanford University, founded D.school and introduced design thinking as a theoretical foundation for teaching in 2004. Design thinking process contains empathy, define, ideate, prototype and test five steps (see Fig. 7).

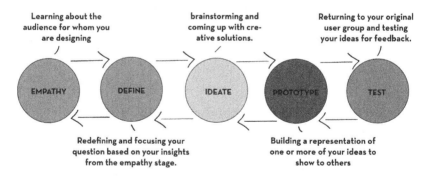

Fig. 7. Designing thinking

Under the smart era, the ability of applications such as machine learning, image recognition and data computing is greatly improved, which can greatly enhance the performance of the entire product development cycle. The traditional design thinking is usually through observation and interview and other means to obtain user data, and through the prototype design with a certain user test or A/B test, to constantly debug to improve the product. And we take advantage of big data thinking to eliminate this one-sided approach and provide everyone with a tailored experience. Deepening to the typical behaviors and defects in the personal level, the user's actions are guided by the context [7]. We first assemble disorganized data, filtered, filtered and processed. And then use the big data to find common rules, and applied to each specific user, and ultimately passed to each specific application [8] (see Fig. 8).

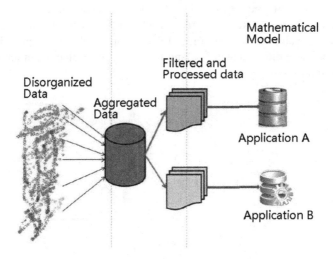

Fig. 8. Big data collection, processing and modeling process

Anil Jain, IBM Watson vice president, put forward the 5 V features of big data: Volume, Velocity, Variety, Value, Veracity, [9] These features are exactly the same challenges as the transition from traditional mobile products to modern smart mobile products. The essence of big data thinking lies in the use of more scientific and rational way to define and refine the user's pain points and needs, with the design thinking to provide more in line with and exceed user expectations of products and solutions. Designers no longer design based on the user's active feedback, but rather through the detection of large data flow of user behavior, with the relevant technology and model for statistical analysis, mining potential data value to guide product design [10].

4.3 Product Design Should Take into Account the Commercial Value and Social Value

Human value is no longer simply a matter of owning experience, but rather trans-forming experience into free-flowing data. The technical bearer of the intelligent era enriches our contacts with the information connection and at the same time put us in an anxiety of information explosion. According to Herbert Marcuse, a philosopher in the United States, "technology, as a tool, can both reinforce human power and enhance human vulnerability." Data can only be translated into information as it flows, and information must after breaking the reorganization can reserve for knowledge. In the changing times of the information age in the industrial age in the farming era, from the visual beauty to the functional beauty to the aesthetic experience, our focus is on the change from usefulness to usability. The author believes that in the data age, usability has been unable to meet the potential needs of users. Whether traditional Internet products, or smart wearable devices and even artificial intelligence robots, the user's requirements for the product is no longer "executive", replaced by "perception." The user experience design is a bridge to connect all things, to connect the data and the senses of the media, to connect the data and emotional channels.

The Harvard Business Review (HBR, 1998) mentions the trend of experiential economy and its value model (see Fig. 9) and mentions that the better the product experience, the more differentiated it is and the greater the value it can gain from this development trend.

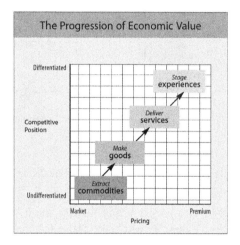

Fig. 9. The progression of economic value

Good experiential design promotes people's pursuit of truth, goodness and beauty by expanding human cognition of themselves, helping to re-recognize themselves, making people more kind-hearted, more broad-minded and more positive and optimistic. We need to keep thinking about where to keep the traditional design approach and when artificial intelligence needs to play a role in it. Therefore, we need to follow the design principles of user experience and user experience that are based on sociology, psychology and economics in product design. We should always cautiously and carefully choose ways and scenes of experience to provide more opportunities for people to fulfill their social responsibilities and create social values through proper guidance and contagious "self-actualization" opportunities rather than to show their desires to individuals blindly pursue. It is necessary to eliminate unequal and effective use of information, balance information for design purposes, and try to achieve a more optimal distribution of social values while paying attention to the issue of human nature [11].

5 Conclusion

This paper studies the design cases and academic theories of today's classic through the methods of literature review and case study, and explores the features and corresponding design methods of mobile products in the era of intelligence. Based on the traditional design method, this study analyzes the new characteristics of the user experience of mobile products in the intelligent era, and proposes the use of artificial intelligence technology to provide users with personalized services, while using the big data thinking to give play to the traditional design thinking to take into account The product's commercial value and social value theory. So as to realize the harmonious coexistence between man and nature, intelligence and emotion.

Each period has its dominant design and artistic paradigm. Science and technology also have an important influence on this process. The arrival of the smart era, the design mission is very important. Our research on design also advanced from the traditional research methods of human-computer interaction to the interaction between human and data, the interaction between human and emotion, the interaction between human and society and the interaction between human and nature. Good design is to empower human beings, make life easier. It is the design goal that we have been pursuing through the integration of people and data, intelligence and emotion, nature and society through wisdom solutions. The harmonious coexistence of man and nature, intelligence and emotion is also the ambitious ideal of the development of information civilization.

References

1. Marr, B.: Why Everyone Must Get Ready for the 4th Industrial Revolution. Forbes (blog). Accessed 12 Dec 2016
2. Viktor, M.: Big Date Era: Great Changes in Lifework and Thinking. Zhejiang People's Publishing House, Hangzhou (2013)
3. Ke, M.: Research on product design thinking and methods in internet and intelligent times, 38(18), 166–170 (2017)
4. HJUX. https://mp.weixin.qq.com/s/eS8S9BDL2C1vYQ5T-r6r7A. Accessed Feb 2018
5. Shneiderman, B.: Designing the User Interface: Strategies for Effective Human-Computer Interaction. Pearson Education, India (2010)
6. McNeill, D.: Gesture and Thought. University of Chicago Press, Chicago (2008)
7. Zhiyong, F., Yuyao, Z.: Design innovation in the age of artificial intelligence. Chin. Art, 56–61 (2017)
8. Jun, W.: Intelligence Era, Beijing, p. 164 (2016)
9. Jain, A.: The 5 vs of Big Data. http://www.ibmbigdatahub.com/blog/why-only-one-5-vs-big-data-really-matters. Accessed 19 Mar 2015
10. Xi, T., Zheng, X.: Iterative innovation design methods of internet products in the era of big data. Packag. Eng. 37(8), 1–4 (2016)
11. Zhilong, L.: From the design life style to the significance of design life - an analysis of the development mode and design potential of information social experience design. Ind. Des. 2017(01), 66–68 (2017)

Comparative Study on the Usability of Navigation Style in Iteration Process of Mobile Software

Canqun He[✉], Jiafeng Gu, Zhangyu Ji, and Xu Yang

College of Mechanical and Electrical Engineering,
Hohai University, Nanjing, China
hecq@163.com

Abstract. Based on the summary analysis of the development rules of mobile App iteration process, this paper selected six popular mobile phone software whose main navigation styles are iterated from drawer navigation to tabbed navigation, conducted a usability test of six old and new version software through the eye movement experiment, and compared the usability differences before and after the change in navigation style to study which navigation style is more suitable for mobile phone software. It carried out a comparative analysis of the usability of six old and new version software based on task completion rate, task loss degree, the completion time of search task (gaze time), the number of fixation points in browsing task, the time of entering ROI for the first time in browsing task and the time of triggering ROI for the first time obtained from the experiment, combining participants' subjective satisfaction questionnaires and in-depth interview after the experiment. The results showed that the use of tabbed navigation software is better than that of drawer navigation software, and the usability difference caused by this navigation style is not related to the software type. In addition, this paper summed up usability problems in navigation design according to the experimental results, and provided a reference for interface designers and interaction designers to choose the navigation style and design interface.

Keywords: Software iteration · Information architecture · Navigation style
Eye-track experiment · Usability

1 Introduction

The rapid development of Mobile Internet has promoted the rapid rise of mobile APP application industry. By the end of 2016, the total number of applications in Apple's APP stores had reached 2.93 million [1], and the Android Market had provided dozens of applications for downloading services. The normal life cycle of a software needs to undergo user need analysis, product conceptual design, information architecture design, interface interaction design and product usability assessment [2]. In order to meet the demands of consumers, mobile softwares have to undergo an iteration and updated process after being put on the market. In the software iteration process, users often reflect that the new version of the software is inferior to the old one, so it becomes a

© Springer International Publishing AG, part of Springer Nature 2018
A. Marcus and W. Wang (Eds.): DUXU 2018, LNCS 10919, pp. 586–602, 2018.
https://doi.org/10.1007/978-3-319-91803-7_44

focus that designers need consider how to make use of usability assessment to find a nice design, to grasp the correct design trends and to continuously improve the software usability in the iteration process.

In the iteration process, the software involves an iteration of information architecture, interface interaction, and so on. In recent years, some scholars began to pay attention to the usability research of information architecture and interaction design. Ku [3] (2009) etc. found that websites with a wide range of information architecture and natural atmosphere can relieve users' pressure and improve the usability of websites. They [4] also studied the influence of touch input mode and navigation style on the usability of ecological education system, and found that tabbed navigation with long touch had more superior usability. Minghui and Liming [5] studied the usability of information architecture in the early stage of digital library development by introducing the framework of usability design based on software architecture, and verified the impact of each indicator of information architecture on usability characteristics and attributes by examples.

After the literature review, it is found that there are a lot of research on the framework layer such as information architecture [6, 7] and interface interaction design [8, 9] in recent years while the research on the availability of mobile devices mainly focuses on the presentation layer such as interface layout [10, 11], icon design [12–14], interface details [15–17]. The research of information architecture is lacking. Due to the relatively mature website usability research, there is a reference for the research of other objects. Therefore, the study of the usability of mobile devices will gradually shift to the research of the framework layer.

Navigation design is an important part of the interface interaction design, and the choice of the appropriate navigation style can help users quickly switch freely and improve efficiency in the use of mobile devices. In this study, we summarized the iteration process of eleven commonly used mobile phone Apps. Nine of them are based on changes in the navigation style, among which six are iterated from drawer navigation to tabbed navigation and are iteration of first class navigation style. It can be seen that designers are increasingly inclined to tabbed navigation when designing. In order to explore whether this design trend is scientific and reasonable, we selected six popular mobile phone software whose main navigation styles are iterated from drawer navigation to tabbed navigation to compare usability difference before and after the change of navigation style, summarize the applicability of the two navigation styles, and verify the rationality of design rules. At the same time, we put forward some targeted suggestions to improve the usability of existing navigation by comparing the usability problems of two navigation styles.

2 Experiment Design

This study mainly evaluated the impact of navigation style on usability. In order to ensure the validity of experiment, we controlled irrelevant variables (such as interface layout, font size, color, navigation architecture, etc.) through the following ways: firstly, Axure was used to eliminate the impact of other factors and secondly, experiment tasks were set up strictly to ensure usability differences caused by different navigation styles.

2.1   Experiment Task

The experiment tasks mainly included purposeless browse task and purposeful search task. According to the complexity of the software structure, time allocation for purposeless browse was different, but the same browsing time was guaranteed for two different versions of the same software. Purposeless browse task mainly helped users familiar with the software, eliminate user anxiety. At the same time, the participants were surveyed about the degree of discovery and use of different navigation icons when using the software. Purposeful search task mainly determined the search efficiency of the participants, that is, whether they can quickly find the task entry and switch effectively.

2.2   Experiment Participants

The 38th China Internet statistics report by CNNIC [18] shows that the age distribution of Chinese Internet users is dominated by 20–29-year-old users, which accounts for about 30% of the total number of users. Therefore, this study selected similar age groups of students as participants, and participants with the same level of experience were screened out through the questionnaire to understand the user's frequency of use and familiarity of six software to avoid the effect of differences in participants' level of experience on the experiment. At the same time, all participants are with normal vision or corrected visual acuity, colorless, weak, etc.

There are 12 objects (6 software * 2 versions) and the experiment is divided into A and B groups. Group A is the same kind of software namely community reading software and group B is different kind of software (Fig. 1). Each group contains 10 participants, half male and half female.

Fig. 1. Experiment objects

2.3   Experiment Equipment

The experiment equipment consists of Tobii X120 desktop eye tracker, eye tracker mobile test stand, Microsoft LifeCam Studio camera and two 5.5-in. redmi Note2 Phone (Fig. 2).

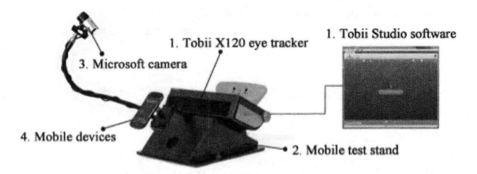

Fig. 2. Experiment equipment

2.4 Experiment Process

The experiment required 2 experimenters. Experimenter A is responsible for debugging the experiment equipment, recording the experiment operation of participants to prepare for the interview after the test and experimenter B is responsible for guiding the participants to complete the pre-test and post-test questionnaires, explaining usability tasks and assisting participants to complete the eye movement test including answering questions raised by participants.

2.4.1 Experiment Preparation Stage

Experimenters should not only ensure that the connection of experimental equipment is normal, the experimental software is installed in place and the speed of experimental environment is well, but also explain the purpose, processes and precautions of this experiment to participants. At the same time, about one minute was given to participants to be familiar with the mobile phone used in the experiment to prevent them from misuse due to being unfamiliar with the experiment equipment.

2.4.2 Eye Movement Experiment Stage

(1) The first task of the experiment is to browse the experiment software, whose time is counted by experimenter A. Participants can freely browse the software within specified browsing time, and the eye movement data will also be added into the result analysis (Fig. 3).
(2) After participant browse, the interface returns to the main interface. Experimenter A reads the task 2 to participant and ensures that the participant knows experiment tasks well. Then the experiment starts.
(3) The maximum completion time for each task is 30 s, and experimenter B records time. When the time reaches 30 s, the experimenter B stops timing and the task is marked as a failure.
(4) All the experimental tasks of a software are completed by repeating step (2) and (3).
(5) Phone A is replaced by phone B and tasks of another version of the same software are completed by repeating the above steps.

(6) Participant fills the satisfaction test questionnaire.
(7) All tasks of six software are completed by repeating the above steps.

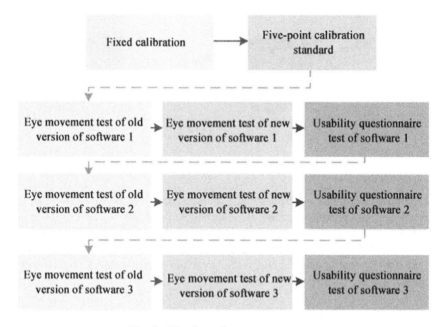

Fig. 3. The flow of eye movement test

In order to avoid the influence of learning effect on the experiment results, the test sequence of phone A and phone B and the experimental sequence of the three software on the same device are random in the experiment.

2.4.3 Post-test Interview Stage
Interview is divided into two parts. (1) Review and think aloud. Participant and experimenter together reviewed the experiment process of eye movement video. Experimenter asked questions and the participant answered. (2) In-depth interviews. Experimenter A had a in-depth interview with the participant according to the record results. The experiment ended after the interview.

3   Analysis of Experiment Results

The eye movement data obtained from the experiment were recorded and exported by Tobii Studio software. The remaining data were recorded by experimenter and written by participants. All data were analyzed by SPSS software.

3.1   Effectiveness Indicators

3.1.1   Task Completion Rate

Task completion rate (Table 1) refers to the proportion of participant who completed the experiment independently in all participants in each task, and the task completed under the tips of experimenter was not counted as task completion.

Table 1. Search task completion rate in the experiment (%)

	Task 1	Task 2	Task 3	Task 4
Old Zhihu	60%	100%	90%	100%
New Zhihu	100%	100%	100%	100%
Old DGtle	100%	100%	90%	100%
New DGtle	100%	100%	100%	100%
Old NetEase news	100%	90%	90%	
New NetEase news	100%	100%	100%	
Old Amazon	60%	90%	80%	100%
New Amazon	100%	100%	90%	100%
Old Youdao cloud notes	90%	100%	40%	100%
New Youdao cloud notes	100%	100%	100%	100%
Old path	100%	90%	100%	90%
New path	100%	100%	100%	100%

The results showed that in the 23 tasks of the old version of software using drawer navigation, 12 tasks were not completed by all participants while only one task of the new version of software using tabbed navigation were not completed by all participants. It can be seen that task completion rate of the old version is far lower than that of the new version. There are several main reasons for unfinished tasks according to the task analysis that the completion rate was lower than 90%. Firstly, participants did not find a drawer navigation icon, or clicked the navigation icon and then searched only in the first level navigation list without entering the secondary navigation, which led to the failure of the task. Secondly, the level of the target is deeper and the participants who did not finish the task were lost in more secondary and tertiary classification. Thirdly, icons are too scattered and the target entrance is not in the main navigation. Fourthly, the secondary navigation is not obvious and can not be directly observed. Fifthly, the poor layout of the page caused that participants had no illusion of content below. Among the above reasons, all but one was caused by page layout, the remaining tasks were not completed due to insufficient navigation design.

3.1.2   Lostness

Lostness [19] is a unit of measurement which measures participants' effectiveness in finding targets during the completion of a search task and is often used to evaluate the efficiency of navigation and information structures. Lostness can be calculated using the following formula:

$$L = \mathrm{sqrt}\left[(N/S - 1)^2 + (R/N - 1)^2\right] \qquad (1)$$

Note: N refers to the number of different pages visited when the task is completed. S refers to the total number of pages visited when the task is completed and the pages that are repeatedly visited are marked as the same page. R refers to the minimum or optimal number of pages that must be visited when the task is completed.

The calculated participants' average lostness of the different versions of six software was shown in Fig. 4. An optimal lostness score should be 0, and when the lostness score is greater than 0.5, the user will have a markedly lost profile.

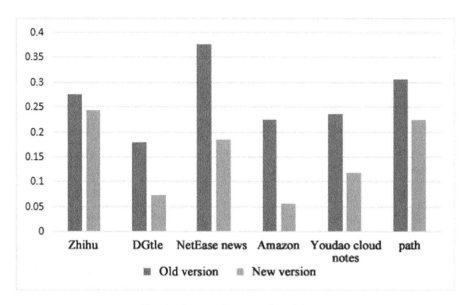

Fig. 4. Average lostness of participants

Significance test of lostness of new and old versions of software was carried out (Table 2). The results showed that there was significant difference (P < 0.01) in the lostness of the old and new version of Netease News, Amazon and Youdao cloud notes. The difference (P < 0.05) in the lostness of DGtle software was significant while there was no significant difference between Zhihu and path. During the experiment, it is found that when using the new version of tabbed navigation, participants were more inclined to try to find more targets by keeping clicking because of the lower cost of mistakes, so the number of click was more. On the contrary, participants were more inclined to look for, confirm the target and then click because of the high cost of mistakes when using the old version of drawer navigation. Therefore, the non-significant difference in lostness of Zhihu and path software was caused by the above reasons to a certain extent.

Table 2. Comparative analysis of lostness of Old and New software

	Mean difference	Standard deviation	95% confidence interval		F	p
			Old version	New version		
Old Zhihu - New Zhihu	0.032	0.260	0.200	0.105	0.286	0.594
Old DGtle - New DGtle	0.103	0.179	0.115	0.100	4.213	0.043[*]
Old NetEase news - New NetEase news	0.190	0.256	0.159	0.134	9.561	0.003[**]
Old Amazon - New Amazon	0.167	0.289	0.207	0.083	24.177	0.000[**]
Old Youdao cloud notes - New Youdao cloud notes	0.118	0.327	0.230	0.108	15.709	0.000[**]
Old path - New path	0.083	0.242	0.168	0.123	2.416	0.124

3.2 Efficiency Indicators

This study selected the following four factors as the efficiency indicators for usability evaluation, namely, the completion time of search task (gaze time), the number of fixation points in browsing task, the time of entering ROI for the first time in browsing task and the time of triggering ROI for the first time.

3.2.1 Task Completion Time (Gaze Time)

During the experiment, the participants were asked to observe the screen when the task began and stop observing after completing the task. After the experiment, the experimenter used Tobii studio software to designate the entire interface area of mobile phone software as ROI 1 to ensure that the time that the participant's eyesight entered ROI 1 and left ROI 1 was the time to complete the task.

The participants' average task completion time of the six new and old versions was in shown in Fig. 5. It is found that the task completion time of old version was longer than that of new version. The significance test results were shown in Table 3. There was significant difference in the task completion time of the old and new versions of six software, which further verified the above reasons for the non-significant difference in lostness, namely, participants spent less time completing little different clicks. It indicated that tabbed navigation has a higher page-switching efficiency than drawer navigation.

3.2.2 The Number of Fixation Points

It costs little time for participants to complete the search task and resulting in less fixation points, so that we only count the total number of fixation points when the participants doing the browsing task about old and new versions of 6 software respectively (Fig. 7).

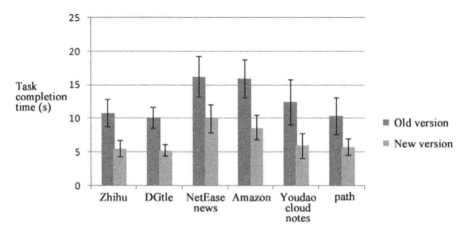

Fig. 5. The average task completion time of six software (s)

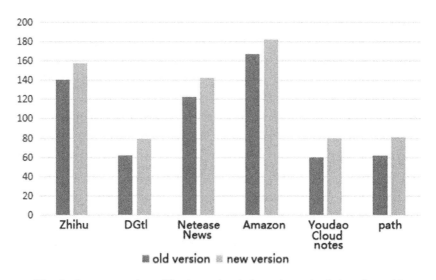

Fig. 6. Average number of fixation points in browsing task of six software(s)

Figure 6 shows that in the browsing task, the average number of points showing in the old version is less than the new version, which is valid in all the 6 software. More fixation points indicating that the interface is easier to understand, which means that participants can browse more content and process more information in the same amount of time. Older versions of the software have fewer fixation points, indicating that the interface is difficult to understand and that the participants need to spend longer time to process a message. At the same time, the study of the trajectory of the participants found that trajectory distribution of tabbed navigation is evenly and neatly while drawer is scattered and irregular (Fig. 5).

Table 3. Comparative analysis of the completion time of six software(s)

	Mean difference	Standard deviation	95% confidence interval		F	p
			Old version	New version		
Old Zhihu - New Zhihu	5.304	4.221	2.040	1.270	33.208	0.000[**]
Old DGtle - New DGtle	4.833	4.157	1.542	0.864	36.256	0.000[**]
Old NetEase news - New NetEase news	6.233	6.368	3.061	2.014	18.983	0.000[**]
Old Amazon - New Amazon	7.297	6.259	2.819	1.825	27.307	0.000[**]
Old Youdao cloud notes - New Youdao cloud notes	6.498	6.067	3.364	1.866	18.892	0.000[**]
Old path - New path	4.579	4.640	2.689	1.219	24.492	0.000[**]

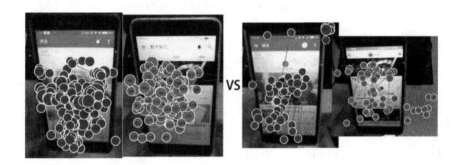

Tagged Navigation   Drawer Navigation

Fig. 7. Attention trajectory of tabbed navigation and drawer navigation

3.2.3 First Entry Time/First Trigger Time

After the experiment, the navigation area of the interface is defined as ROI 2 by the experimenter which recording when the participants enter the ROI 2 and when they click the navigation for the first time. From this, we calculated the average first entry time for the old and new version of the six software (Fig. 8). And we did an analysis of the difference significance (Table 4).

Figure 8 shows that when using the new version of the software, the first entry time to the navigation area that participants use is far less than that of the old version, and the difference is significant between the old and the new versions of the six software. As a result, the new version using tabbed navigation is more available than the older version using drawer navigation when the first entry time is rated.

The comparison of the old and new versions of one software in the first entry and trigger time shows that there are 4 kinds of behaviors of the participants: Not enter the ROI 2 (not observed navigation icon), enter but not click the ROI 2, enter but not click

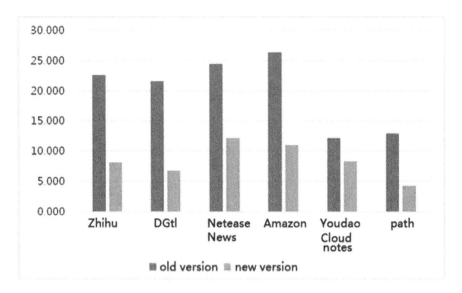

Fig. 8. Average first entry time of six software(s)

Table 4. Comparative analysis of the first entry time of six software(s)

	Mean difference	Standard deviation	95% confidence interval		F	p
			Old version	New version		
Old Zhihu - New Zhihu	14.488	16.678	11.444	2.776	8.353	0.010[**]
Old DGtle - New DGtle	14.803	10.726	6.204	1.844	18.084	0.000[**]
Old NetEase news - New NetEase news	12.230	12.978	8.272	5.007	4.917	0.041[*]
Old Amazon - New Amazon	15.329	13.573	9.490	2.856	8.004	0.012[*]
Old Youdao cloud notes - New Youdao cloud notes	3.893	7.824	4.928	2.397	8.786	0.008[**]
Old path - New path	8.666	7.230	4.131	2.582	10.941	0.004[**]

immediately, enter and click immediately. In the old versions of the 6 software, there are 3 participants not observing the drawer navigation. During the interview after the experiment, the participants said that the drawer navigation is located in the upper left corner of the interface, people usually pay little attention to this area. After analyzing the hot picture of the interface, it was found that the participants' eyes were concentrated in the middle and lower area of the screen, and the discoverability of the upper left corner area was not enough. In the task of browsing the old version of the software, there are 9 people entered but not clicked the ROI 2, 16 people entered but not clicked immediately, a total of 25 which is much high than 4 people in the new versions. After the experiment, three participants indicated that they did not understand the meaning of the drawer navigation icon, so they did not click after seeing it, which reflected that the drawer icon was not recognizable enough.

3.3 Satisfaction Index

After the eye tracking test, each group of participants was asked to complete the system usability scale (SUS). The result (Fig. 9 and Table 5) will be used as an index to evaluate the user's satisfaction. The results showed that participants were more satisfied with the new version of software than the old version of the software, and the difference was significant.

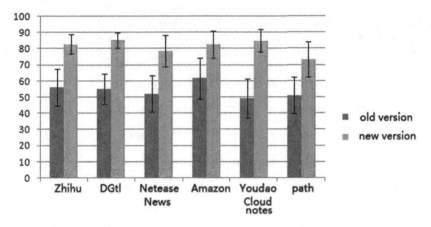

Fig. 9. The average satisfaction score of six software(s)

Table 5. Comparative analysis of the satisfication of six software(s)

	Mean difference	Standard deviation	95% confidence interval		F	p
			Old version	New version		
Old Zhihu - New Zhihu	−26.75	20.314	11.413	5.789	15.106	0.001[**]
Old DGtle - New DGtle	−30.50	19.932	9.476	4.638	28.895	0.000[**]
Old NetEase news - New NetEase news	−26.75	22.232	11.276	9.806	11.078	0.004[**]
Old Amazon - New Amazon	−21.00	20.852	12.703	8.443	6.554	0.020[*]
Old Youdao cloud notes - New Youdao cloud notes	−35.50	24.494	11.998	7.201	22.251	0.000[**]
Old path - New path	−22.00	21.626	11.286	11.002	6.737	0.018[*]

3.4   The Comprehensive Score Based on the Usability Assessment Model

In the process of establishing the evaluation model, the data collected by the eye tracker are different types of data, such as time, number, score and so on. Before calculating the comprehensive score, each data indicator needs to be converted into a unified percentile standard. There are standard scores with full marks, those with no full marks are counted as high scores, other marks are converted according to the ratio, and the standard scores after conversion are shown in Table 6.

Table 6. Standard score of the usability assessment model

	Task completion rate	Lostness	Times for help	Number of fixation points	First entry time	First trigger time	Task completion time	Satisfaction index
Old Zhihu	87.50	72.40	87.50	89.17	36.03	50.00	51.10	56.25
New Zhihu	100.00	75.60	100.00	100.00	100.00	80.00	100.00	83.00
Old DGtle	97.50	82.10	97.50	78.99	31.51	70.00	52.26	55.00
New DGtle	100.00	92.70	100.00	100.00	100.00	100.00	100.00	85.50
Old Netease	93.30	62.40	93.30	85.66	50.04	50.00	61.60	52.00
New Netease	100.00	81.40	100.00	100.00	100.00	80.00	100.00	78.75
Old Amazon	82.50	77.60	82.50	91.70	42.08	30.00	54.33	61.75
New Amazon	97.50	94.30	97.50	100.00	100.00	90.00	100.00	82.75
Old Youdao cloud notes	82.50	76.40	82.50	75.06	68.33	60.00	47.99	49.50
New Youdao cloud notes	100.00	88.20	100.00	100.00	100.00	100.00	100.00	85.00
Old path	95.00	69.30	95.00	76.86	33.32	60.00	55.92	51.25
New path	100.00	77.60	100.00	100.00	100.00	100.00	100.00	73.25

After the scores of each index are determined, according to the ratio of each index in the usability assessment model, the comprehensive score of the two navigation styles of the six software can be obtained (Fig. 10). The comprehensive usability scores of tagged navigation are far higher than the drawer navigation, and the difference is very significant (Table 7).

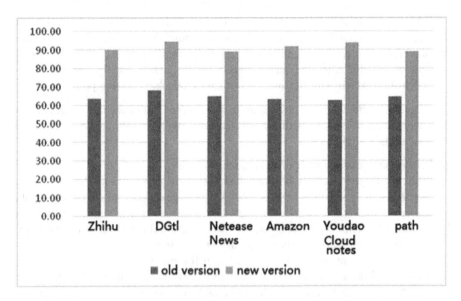

Fig. 10. Comprehensive scores of the old and new versions of six software(s)

Table 7. Comparative analysis of comprehensive availability of two navigation styles

	Mean difference	Standard deviation	95% confidence interval		F	p
			Drawer	Tagged		
Drawer-Tagged	26.97	14.23	2.48	1.98	476.81	0.000[**]

4 Comparative Analysis of Availability

The experimental results show that both group A with the same software and group B with different types of software are all better using tabbed navigation than using drawer navigation, and there is no difference between the two groups. The result shows that the influence of navigational styles on usability has nothing to do with the type of software. The conclusions drawn from this experiment are summarized as follows:

(1) Drawer navigation is lack of discoverability and recognition.
    "What you see is what you get", when users first touch a software that uses drawer navigation, it is highly likely that they only focus on the front page content because they fail to notice the navigation icon or do not understand the meaning of the icon, and this lack of detection is particularly evident in two level and below navigation.
(2) Drawer navigation has high operation costs and is inefficient.
    Even with drawer navigation and a clear software navigation architecture, using drawer navigation requires more clicks and time.
(3) Drawer navigation's classification is not clear and scattered.

Tabbed navigation usually appears at the top of the interface or the entire line below the interface, the number of tags is around 3 to 5, arranged neatly and classified clearly. While the drawer navigation information will be classified without classification, the participants need to search one by one in all the information which will increase the burden of searching for the participants.

In addition, there are some navigation icons scattered out of the drawer navigation which will result in search inefficiencies for users will be habitual to search after entering the main navigation.

(4) Drawer navigation is poor of navigation.

When the drawer navigation is switched, the navigation hide and the participants can not know where they are. As a result, the subjects continuously return to the homepage during the operation, switch their positions clearly which increases the operating burden. The label-based navigation tab, at the bottom of the page, has not been hidden, participants can always know where they are.

(5) There are different operation modes when using two navigation styles.

When using drawer navigation, participants tend to search first to find the target and then confirm to click; while using tabbed navigation, the participants are accustomed to find the target in the constant switching, thus ensuring the completion of the task to improve efficiency.

(6) In the software with many navigations and deep level, the deeper level of navigation should be shown to users.

Take Amazon as an example, in the older version, the participants need to enter three interfaces with broad categories while they are looking for books in Chinese history. In this case, participants were easily lost in any one of the navigation. In the new version of Amazon, it combines these three pages into one page, reducing the possibility of loss.

(7) Navigation style in the same level needs to be consistent.

Interface design should follow the principle of consistency [20]. There are two types of tagged navigation design style: pure icon, icon and text. But in the same software, the same level of navigation must be the same design style. There are three types of drawer navigation type: pure icon, plain text, icon plus text. And in the same software, the same level of navigation design styles are different, resulting in low completion rate of the task. We can see that consistency is very important in interface design.

(8) Drawer navigation is suitable as a sub navigation style.

Drawer navigation provides greater operating space for users taking account the invisibility of drawer navigation, though it is not suitable as the main navigation. The drawer navigation can be used as a sub navigation style, and the operation functions with low frequency of use can be placed in the drawer, which ensures that the user can efficiently switch using the tagged main navigation and the sub navigation does not occupy the user's excessive operation interface at the same time.

5   Conclusion and Forecast

Based on the above analysis, it can be concluded that the usability of using tabbed navigation software is superior to that of using drawer navigation software. The difference in availability caused by this navigation style has nothing to do with the type of software, indicating that the reason why a design approach can become a trend has its own reasons. At the same time, this study found the usability of the interface design, which provided a reference for the interface designer to choose the navigation style and design interface.

Although this paper studies the usability of drawer navigation and tagged navigation, the breadth and depth of the research are still not enough. The author believes that follow-up research can be expanded from the following aspects:

(1) This research only chooses six software for comparison, and only six software can not represent all the software. When conditions allow, we should choose more types of mobile software to research;

(2) This research proves that tabbed navigation has better usability. However, the navigation position, navigation structure and icon design in tagged navigation design are all factors that affect the usability. In the follow-up, the usability of different types of tagged navigation can be further studied.

References

1. Classic Network: Apple App Store is expected to exceed the number of applications 5000000 [DB/OL]. https://www.ishuo.cn/show/1142211.html. Accessed 15 Aug 2016
2. Qi, H., Wei, B.: Interaction Design, pp. 9–10. Zhejiang University Press, Zhejiang (2012)
3. Ku, C.J., Doong, J.L., Chen, L.C.: The effects of information architecture and atmosphere style on the usability of an ecology education website. In: Human Centered Design, First International Conference, HCD 2009, Held As. DBLP, pp. 749–757 (2009)
4. Ku, C.J., Wang, K.H., Doong, J.L., et al.: The effects of touch input modes and navigation bar styles on the usability of an ecology education system. Ac.rd.ttu.edu.tw
5. Minghui, Q., Liming, Z.: Research on the availability of information architecture in early stage of digital library development. J. Inf. Sci. 5, 18–23 (2014)
6. Chuchu, L.: Study of website navigation design usability. Jiangsu Normal University (2013)
7. Shengling, Z.: An empirical study on the influence of navigation structure on the availability of B2C E-commerce website. Huazhong University of Science and Technology (2008)
8. Xiaofang, Y.: Analysis of business webpage availability based on human-computer interaction interface. In: 2014 International Design Expo China (Wuxi) International Design Fair and Design Education Redesign Series International Conference (III) - Philosophy Concept Paper. China Industrial Design Association, Wuxi Municipal People's Government (2014). 3
9. Xiaoming, W.: Visual design of interactive interface mechanism in B2C website. Hubei University of Technology (2012)
10. Nakagawa, T., Uwano, H.: Usability evaluation for software keyboard on high-performance mobile devices. In: Stephanidis, C. (ed.) HCI 2011. CCIS, vol. 173, pp. 181–185. Springer, Heidelberg (2011). https://doi.org/10.1007/978-3-642-22098-2_37

11. Jingqian, Z., Renke, H.: Study on usability test of android mobile application interface layout. Packag. Eng. **35**(10), 61–64 (2014)
12. Hao, Y., Kai, C., Dianliang, C.: Availability of flat icons in graphical user interface. Pack. Eng. **16**, 99–102 (2016)
13. Wenming, J., Zhixin, Y., Min, J., et al.: Study on usability of icon design for smartphone application. Chin. J. Ergon. **21**(3), 21–24 (2015)
14. Yongfeng, L., Chen, J., Liping, Z.: A study on the availability of mobile phone icon size based on the preferences of the elderly. Pack. Eng. **16**, 103–106 (2016)
15. Shiwei, C.: Research on context-aware mobile device adaptive user interface design. Zhejiang University (2009)
16. Fangyuan, C.: Available evaluation of graphical user interface design for smartphone APP based on eye tracker. Packag. Eng. **8**, 55–59 (2015)
17. Yubo, Z., Peilun, R.: Study on design elements of tablet electronic reading software interface based on iOS. Chin. J. Ergon. **19**(4), 42–46 (2013)
18. CNNIC: The 38th Statistical Report on Internet Development in China [DB/OL]. http://www.askci.com/news/hlw/20160805/17065450828_4.shtml. Accessed 5 Aug 2016
19. Tullis, T., Albert, B.: User Experience Measurement - Collection, Analysis and Presentation, pp. 131–150. Publishing House of Electronics Industry, Beijing (2016)
20. Shneiderman, B., Plaisant, C.: User Interface Design - Effective Human-Computer Interaction Strategy, 5th edn, pp. 350–353. Publishing House of Electronics Industry, Beijing (2014)

Travel Navigation Design and Innovative Operation Mode

Chia-Chieh Lee[(⊠)] and Fong-Gong Wu

Department of Industrial Design,
National Cheng Kung University, Tainan, Taiwan
chiachiehba@gmail.com

Abstract. The paper aims to collect requirements and problems in travel navigation through behaviors of users, and to design and test a prototype via contextual inquiry and brainstorming. Nowadays, with the advance of traffic, tourism and the internet, access to tourist information is more convenient, like Google Maps bringing people to the world. Nevertheless, most researches put an emphasis on car and indoor navigation rather than travel navigation. Therefore, the purpose of the study is to provide direction for navigation design by the contextual inquiry, and to propose the innovative travel navigation mode.

The study acquires the needs of tourism guide by contextual inquiry. In order to fulfill the function value and operation behavior, gestures design and interface design are well combined with the design. Gestures design can decrease usage time, and with the design, a handy operation mode that can be used in intuition is invented. Then, the study combines the needs of travel navigation and the key points of operation, to plan an innovative tourism guide design by brainstorming. After designing the new mode, the study evaluates the availability, and to investigate the features of every interface and gesture. With the questionnaire based on Likert scale, the paper tests learnability, memorability, easy-to-perform and suitability of each function in the mode. The paper designs the navigation mode in accordance with tourism guide, to let users operate in intuition to get destination, and enjoy the pleasure of exploring. In the future, the new, better navigation mode will be designed for users to travel around the world.

Keywords: Travel navigation · Innovation mode · Google Map
Design method

1 Introduction

1.1 Background

Nowadays, it is easier to travel around in different countries than before. The population of Taiwan is 23.5 million people in 2017 from the statistics of Ministry of the interior. Moreover, 2.8 billion visitors visit major tourist attractions in the country in 2016. With the development of traffic, tourism, people travel for diverse reasons. Most Asian travelers prefer novel experience, indulging in luxury and participate in physical activity. On the contrary, British and American tend to absorb knowledge, and to have

A. Marcus and W. Wang (Eds.): DUXU 2018, LNCS 10919, pp. 603–613, 2018.
https://doi.org/10.1007/978-3-319-91803-7_45

excitement and outdoor activities [1, 2]. Most of the tourists expect to experience and explore different knowledge and cultures.

Moreover, new technology and the internet make us collect tourist information more easily, such as Google Maps bring people to the world. The travel navigation app helps play a role in backpacking. However, most of the studies on GPS focus on web navigation design and car navigation system. In fact, in a journey tourists usually use smart phone for information searching, favorite places saving, routes guiding and recommendation lists. Nevertheless, the reference indicates that GPS users tend to pay less attention on the routes and surrounding space globally [3], and the GPS usability requirement is different from that of travel navigation. Also, the screen of the smartphone is too small to display much information [4]. The problems of travel navigation on smart phone existed and had not been solved yet. Therefore, the foundation of the thesis is to discover main needs for travel navigation in smart phone and analyze the usability of travel navigation app prototype.

1.2   Research Purposes

In order to test the usability of mobile travel navigation, two experiments were carried out at the earlier stage. The first one was to observe the behavior of the travelers by contextual inquiry. Moreover, contextual inquiry sign can interpret and consolidate that data in a structured way as well [5]. The second was to use the results of the contextual inquiry to make Brainstorm. It is a method to stimulate creativity and strengthen thinking [6]. The study use contextual inquiry to observe and discover the larger environmental context. Therefore, contextual inquiry is based on an old community of Tainan in Taiwan, which is mainly for pedestrian. With the functions in Google Maps, including saving favorite places, routes guiding and recommendation lists, the study arranges a walking tour in Tainan to collect the needs for navigation and the problems met in journey. In accordance with the contextual inquiry, the travel navigation prototype is designed by brainstorming. In the end, the prototype is evaluated through 5 quality components to provide direction for travel navigation design.

2   Related Work

2.1   Travel

The World Tourism Organization (UNWTO)[1] announces that global outbound travel expenses maintained a 4% growth and also with 1.2 billion international tourists in 2016. The public interest in travel is still high, which is a good thing for every major destination in the world. Tourism can promote a country's economic, employment and other opportunities for development.

There are three main elements in travelers' way finding, landmarks, routes and surveys. Landmarks, which is relatively stable and conspicuous in the environment. Route knowledge infers the ability to travel from point A to point B. Survey

---

[1] World Tourism Organization (UNWTO) http://www2.unwto.org/.

Knowledge is a sense of direction that enables travelers to recognize directions or plan journeys along the routes which they have not travelled or to give relative locations of landmarks in an environment [7, 8].

In the Fig. 1, the research describes the process of individual travel. Before journey, travelers need to plan the journey and record the destinations on smart phone. At the beginning of the journey, travelers need to review the list before starting navigation. Moreover, during the journey, most of the travelers need to repeat the Routes and Survey for many times until arriving at the destination, and to refer to the Landmarks to identify the direction. In this thesis, the travel model is utilized for the contextual inquiry.

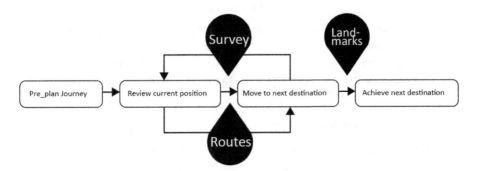

Fig. 1. Travel model

2.2 Travel Navigation

In 1957, US scientists created the first artificial satellite, which provided more accuracy at less cost to not only military but peaceful commerce [9]. Moreover, the invention of cars and air travel also led to travel trend. An increasing number of people travel to other cities and countries, and it brings about the increase on the Gross domestic product (GDP) and promotion of economic development. However, so fast the development grow that it leads to many pollution problems in the environment. Therefore, some travel modes shift back to bus and rail in 1990 [10]. Both modes reduce the GDP production for each country and provide the different travel mode. The travel modes will lead to reducing energy-cost. Nowadays, most travel modes gradually turn to walk or to take public transportation.

Most of the traveler will search for information before journey. In addition, they use smart phone to search for information and check it during the journey. However, the small screens of smart phones weaken the comprehension of users to the spatial relations of layouts. Furthermore, the fingers of the participants cover the arrow and increase the time for task completion. By contrast, with the mouse, the cursor synchronizes with the user's eyes, cursor would not cover the arrow keys [4]. The travel navigation is extremely necessary for travelers. Therefore, the principles of the travel navigation design are supposed to be emphasized on. The research complies with the principles to evaluate the travel navigation.

2.3   Location-Based Service

In 2017, Google announced that Google Maps have reached 1 billion users in Google's I/O developer conference. Hence, Google Maps could represent one of the most popular travel navigation apps. In addition to this, Google Maps is a type of the location-based service (LBS). Base on the location-based service, it includes three aspects which are navigation, information and communication. For example, the LBS has the problem like *"which objects are available in the vicinity"* [9]. Therefore, the aspects of the LBS can compare with the Google Maps features. The following features are analyzed and evaluated to collect travel problems and needs (Table 1).

Table 1. LBS with fectures

Location-based service (LBS) aspects	Google Maps features
Navigation	Routes guiding
Information	Recommend lists, Favorite places
Communication	Comment feature

2.4   Principles of Interface Design

The contents of the Location-based service include navigation, information and communication. The study focuses on different modes of operation in literature collection. Moreover, the research collects different dimensions of interface design and then apply to brainstorming. The methods of displaying information include windowshade, pop-up, hierarchical list and returned results [11]. The principles of interface design obey four rules of gesture design [12]:

- Easy to perform and remember
- Intuitive
- Metaphorically and iconically logical towards functionality
- Ergonomic; not physically stressing when used often

The prototype design refers to the principles of information design and gesture design.

3   Research Method

The literatures point out the usability problems of travel navigation. Moreover, this experiment is aim at clarify the issue and identify the aim of the innovation mode.

3.1   Environment Design

The thesis conducted the contextual inquiry to observe the users who needed the travel navigation. A navigation route in an old community of Tainan in Taiwan was planned, and the community was mainly for pedestrian. The route referred to the Tainan City Tourism Bureau, and the distance of the route was 1.2 km. It included 8 spots. The environment design was applied to LBS, which featured as routes guiding, recommend lists and favorite places. Moreover, participants walked through those spots and the researcher walked beside them. During the observation, the researcher recorded the problems that participants met with photos and print screens (Fig. 2).

Fig. 2. The navigation route in environment design.

3.2 Procedure

Contextual inquiry is the method which is developed from customer-centered approach. Through the contextual inquiry, users experience and behavior were collected by fieldwork observation, and the selected participants were the ones not familiar at Tainan City. In the observation, the process took a longtime observation and discussions of what just happened immediately [6, 13]. The aim of the contextual inquiry was to observe usability and the problems faced in the real field. In the procedure, the visual system, audio system and user behaviors were observed, and results of the experiment are shown as follows (Fig. 3).

Fig. 3. Contextual inquiry procedure.

3.3 Observation Results

In the procedure, the visual system, audio system and user behaviors were observed. The thesis summarized the observed behavior in travel navigation, and the display that needed to be improved in travel navigation app (Table 2).

Table 2. Observation result lists

Behavior	1. In navigation mode, plenty of connections to realities from point A to B were indicated. Diverse stuff, contents and exploring approaches were explored
	2. Favorites and journey routes were recorded. The participants were able to get information of spots at once but failed to record while in navigation mode
	3. The participants were supposed to close google maps for photography, which stopped navigation
	4. The participants spent excessive amount of time on screens, less on environments. It took time to check appearances of spots
Visual and Audio	1. The compatibility design of interface pointers and real directions should be improved
	2. The participants were unable to find entrances of buildings in maps
	3. Voices of navigation and outside sounds intervened mutually
	4. No precise reminder popped out for arrival. Reminders were supposed to be added in

3.4   Experiment Procedure

According to the results of contextual inquiry, the research moved on to brainstorming. To figure out the mentioned issues, seven professional designers, four graduate designers and three professor designers were invited to design within 90 min. The issues were divided into 8 dimensions, A to H. The selected participants made prototype design of operation to create innovative interfaces of travel navigation app. The results of brainstorming are shown as follows:

Journey Exploration. In navigation mode, connections to reality were provided, and diverse contents and approaches were explored. In the experiment, two new designs offered more opportunities to explore. By journey exploration 1, in order to enrich journey, multiple items on menu were supposed to be added, such as tourist attractions and restaurants, and people were allowed to select favorite items in operation mode. As for journey exploration 2, the spots which were crowded are indicated in maps, and travelers could take part in the popular activities, which enriched journeys with joy to explore (Fig. 4).

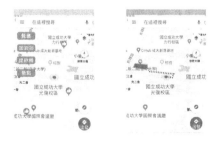

Fig. 4. Journey exploration 1(left) and journey exploration 2 (right).

Journey Record. According to the experiment, two record designs were made. Journey record 1, the function of Google search was supposed to be added in operation interface; in that case, people could search for details of spots. Journey record 2, journey routes and marked spots were recorded by GPS, and journey records were established after travels (Fig. 5).

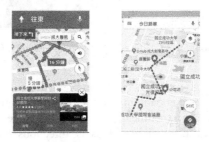

Fig. 5. Journey record 1 (left) and journey record 2 (right)

Camera Interface. The users were supposed to close google maps for photography, which stopped navigation. By the experiment, three designs of camera interface belonging to window design figured out the problem. Camera interface 1 was split screen. Camera interface and navigation were separated in the screen. Camera interface 2 was picture in picture (PIP), or the users could keep navigation interfaces small and use other apps. Camera interface 3, new camera was added into navigation interface (Fig. 6).

Fig. 6. Camera interface 1 (left), camera interface 2 (middle) and camera interface 3 (right).

Reduction in Map Looking. The participants spent amount of time on screens, less on environments. It took time to check appearances of spots. By the experiment, three solutions came out. With reduction in map looking 1, appearances of buildings were shown as POP or as PIP in navigation mode. Reduction in map looking 2 navigated with two different layers. Reduction in map looking 3, screens merely showed instant directions, which was an advanced setting (Fig. 7).

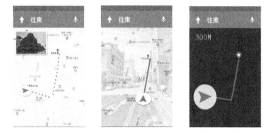

Fig. 7. Reduction in map looking 1 (left), reduction in map looking 2 (middle) and reduction in map looking 3 (right).

Compatibility Design. The compatibility design of interface arrow and real directions should be improved. In the experiment, two solutions came out. By compatibility design 1, the map layer was compatible with users' directions, like the upward arrow in GPA for cars. As for compatibility design 2, the direction on map was always northward to enhance directionality.

Entrances of Buildings. The users were unable to find entrances of buildings in maps. Three approaches came out through the experiment. Entrances of building 1, the layouts of buildings and places were loaded to show up. Entrances of building 2, the pictures of building appearances were placed in maps. Entrances of building 3, the direction of entrances was described literally (Fig. 8).

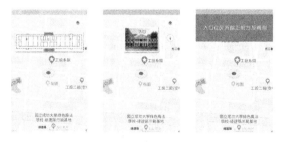

Fig. 8. Entrances of buildings 1 (left), entrances of buildings 2 (middle) and entrances of buildings 3 (right).

Interface of Arrival. No precise reminder popped out for arrival. In the experiment, two designs of interface of arrival were made. Interfaces of arrival 1, the screen zoomed in while the users were closed to destinations for clearer pictures, and the sound frequency of reminder was changed. Interfaces of arrival 2, the map was closed after arrival, and the pictures of building appearance showed up (Fig. 9).

Voice of Navigation. Voices of navigation and outside sounds intervened mutually. In the experiment, vibration was substituted for vision and audition. The vibration was directional with its frequency and direction. Nevertheless, the research was shown as

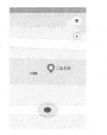

Fig. 9. Interface of arrival 1 (left) and interface of arrival 2 (right).

prototype; way of vibration was not allowed to be a part of the experiment so that it was not shown in the results.

3.5 Usability Evaluation

According to the results of dimensions above, except voice of navigation, the prototype was evaluated with Likert scale, 5 quality components, including Learnability, Efficiency, Memorability, Errors and Satisfaction. The design was made through the comparisons of above functions. The 25 participants, from 18 to 34 years old, at the average of 23, were invited to test the prototype, and all of them were digital native and frequently used navigation apps.

4 Discussion

4.1 Comprehensive Comparisons

For the seven dimension, learnability, efficiency, memorability, errors and satisfaction are calculated in t-test to make a superior navigation operation mode. Among the dimension, journey records, the compatibility of interfaces and the interface of arrival make much influences. In particular, journey records affects the most. According to the t-test, as significant level is set as 0.1, p-value equals to 0.089, reach significant level. Moreover, the mean of journey record 2 is higher than that of journey record 1, hence the participants prefer the operation mode of journey record 2.

Correspondingly, the compatibility makes a big influence. With paired sample t-test, as significant level is 0.1, p-value equals to 0.089, reach significant level. The mean of the compatibility of interfaces 2 is higher than that of the compatibility of interfaces 1, thus the participants prefer the compatibility of interfaces 2 operation mode.

The designs of arrival interfaces make a big influence. With paired sample t-test, as significant level is 0.1, p-value equals to 0.001, reach significant level. The mean of arrival interface 2 is higher than that of arrival interface 1, thus the participants prefer arrival interface 1 operation mode.

Moreover, the designs of reduction in map looking and buildings entrances have three interfaces in each. With one-way ANOVA, as significant level is set as 0.1, p-value is lower than 0.1, reach significant level. Among the designs of reduction in map looking, the total of reduction in map looking 3 is the lowest, which is not suitable for users; in terms of the design of buildings entrances, the total of building entrance 3 is the lowest, which is not suitable for users.

4.2   Usability Comparisons

According to the result of t-test, journey records 2 is the most memorable and satisfying, while compatibility of interface 2 is more learnable and memorable than compatibility of interface 1. In the designs of arrival interface, arrival interface 2 is better than arrival interface 1 in terms of 5 components, learnability, efficiency, memorability, errors and satisfaction. Among the camera interfaces, no obvious distinction is made. Nevertheless, in satisfaction scale, camera interface 1 gets lower score than the others, as camera interface 3 is the best.

4.3   Summary

In seven designs, no significant difference shows in journey exploration and camera interface. It is inferred that the participants operate; however, in satisfaction scale of camera interface, the users prefer new button linked to inner-built camera rather than split screen. To sum up, the significant distinctions are indicated as following.

- Journey record 2: Routes and marked spots are recorded by GPS automatically, and journey record list is established after journey.
- Reduction in map looking 2: other layer is added for navigation. Street view and route chart overlap to make comparison.
- Compatibility of interface 2: the direction on map is always northward so as to increase the directionality of exploring.
- Entrance of building 1, 2: In the entrances 1 the layouts of buildings and places pop out, and in the entrances 2 the pictures of buildings appearances show up.
- Arrival interface 2: The maps are closed after arrival, and the pictures of buildings appearances show up.
- Camera interface 3: the new camera button is added in the interface of navigation, which is linked to inner-built camera.

5   Conclusions

5.1   Conclusions and Future Work

With the advance of international, public traffic and independent travels, need for travel navigation increases. The study collects the problems walking travelers met in journey via the contextual inquiry, and in terms of vision and audition, the problems are divided into 8 dimensions, journey exploration, journey record, camera interface, reduction in map looking, compatibility of interface, building entrance, arrival interface and navigation reminder. The research provides direction for travel navigation design.

The study invites professional designers to make brainstorming for travel navigation prototype in accordance with the above categories. With the test and questionnaires, better design direction is provided. In the future, travel navigation design will be aimed at 8 dimensions to make further research. Moreover, the experiment is based on Google Maps, and intends to analyze different navigation systems for study. In future, travel navigation is expected to be more convenient and to enrich journeys.

5.2 Limitations of the Study

The contextual inquiry focuses on walking travel, and the primary participants are digital natives, who are familiar with smart phones, tablets and other electronic devices, hence the new functions are more learnable for them. Moreover, the prototype examines the functions separately, and does not integrate the 8 dimensions as a travel navigation app. The results suggests that integrated design is supposed to be made for further plans.

References

1. Kim, K.-Y., Jogaratnam, G.: Travel motivations. J. Travel Tour. Mark. 13(4), 61–82 (2003)
2. Jang, S., Cai, L.A.: Travel motivations and destination choice: a study of British outbound market. J. Travel Tour. Mark. 13(3), 111–133 (2002)
3. Ishikawa, T., Fujiwara, H., Imai, O., Okabe, A.: Wayfinding with a GPS-based mobile navigation system: a comparison with maps and direct experience. J. Environ. Psychol. 28 (1), 74–82 (2008)
4. Ishikawa, T., Takahashi, K.: Relationships between methods for presenting information on navigation tools and users wayfinding behavior. Cartogr. Perspect. 75(75), 17–28 (2013)
5. Beyer, H., Holtzblatt, K.: Contextual design. Interactions 6(1), 32–42 (1999)
6. Hanington, B., Martin, B.: Universal methods of design: 100 ways to research complex problems (2012)
7. Dillon, A., Richardson, J., McKnight, C.: Space-the final chapter or why physical representations are not semantic intentions. In: Hypertext: A Psychological Perspective, no. 1985, pp. 169–191 (1993)
8. Goble, C., Harper, S., Stevens, R.: The travails of visually impaired web travellers. In: Proceedings of Eleventh ACM Hypertext hypermedia, pp. 1–10 (2000)
9. B.Hofmann-Wellenhof, Legat, K., Wieser, M.: Navigation: Principles of Positioning and Guidance (2003)
10. Millard-Ball, A., Schipper, L.: Are we reaching peak travel? Trends in passenger transport in eight industrialized countries. Transp. Rev. 31(3), 357–378 (2011)
11. Hoober, S., Berkman, E.: Designing mobile interfaces. 2011 (2011)
12. Nielsen, M., Störring, M., Moeslund, Thomas B., Granum, E.: A procedure for developing intuitive and ergonomic gesture interfaces for HCI. In: Camurri, A., Volpe, G. (eds.) GW 2003. LNCS (LNAI), vol. 2915, pp. 409–420. Springer, Heidelberg (2004). https://doi.org/10.1007/978-3-540-24598-8_38
13. Holtzblatt, K., Wendell, J., Wood, S.: Rapid Contextual Design (2005)

A Comparison of QWERTY and Alphabetical Layout on Small Handheld Devices

Dagmawi Lemma Gobena[1](✉) and Addis Seifu[2]

[1] CNS, Department of Computer Science,
Addis Ababa University, Addis Ababa, Ethiopia
dagmawi.Lemma@aau.edu.et, dagmawi.Lemma@gmail.com
[2] HiLCoE School of Computer Science and Technology,
the Graduate Program, Addis Ababa, Ethiopia

Abstract. The QWERTY keyboard layout is originally designed to solve problems occurred in mechanical typewriters rather than the digital devices. The dis-ordered characters are not appearing in the order the user learns the alphabetic order. Hence, novice users need to learn the device until improving the typing performance to the acceptable level. Designing the key arrangement in a keyboard needs to consider balancing the load between the right and left hand and the fingers, distance between the keys, size of the key and frequency of character. However, some of these parameters are not applicable for designing key layout for small handheld devices. Hence, we intend to study the usability effect of QWERTY layout in comparison with alphabetically order layout. We measured the typing speed using QWERTY layout as well as alphabetical layout that we developed in the virtual keyboard for the experiment. Ten expert users have been selected for the evaluation and we run five tests with each *test-user*. We measured the typing speed in character per second then adjusted against the error. The adjusted character per second for both key layouts was 0.52 acps. This typing speed was improved in the fifth pass to be 0.78 acps and 0.68 acps for the alphabetical and QWERTY layout respectively. Regarding accuracy, during the first run 96.279% for the alphabetical and 97.674% accuracy for the QWERTY layout has been recorded. While the users were more accurate on the QWERTY than the alphabetical layout during the first run, this was changed after the fifth run having 98.837% accuracy for the alphabetical and 98.372% accuracy for the QWERTY layout.

Keywords: Keyboard layout · Usability · Character input · Handheld devices

1 Introduction

Looking to the historical background of the QWERTY layout on a standard keyboard, it is possible to note that the intention was to improve the efficient utilization of mechanical typewriters but not that of digital devices. The QWERTY layout was engineered to avoid the key-jam that occurs when a new key pressed before the previous key arm returns. Since the key-jam occurs as the result of the alphabetical key arrangement, Sholes [1] solved this problem by experimenting with the most common English two-letter sequences and assigning the most frequent couples to opposite sides

© Springer International Publishing AG, part of Springer Nature 2018
A. Marcus and W. Wang (Eds.): DUXU 2018, LNCS 10919, pp. 614–622, 2018.
https://doi.org/10.1007/978-3-319-91803-7_46

of the key layout. The Sholes design had a great initial advantage to be known by many users [1]. Further, it paved the way for the QWERTY layout to become and known as the "universal" layout in 1893. Sholes' solution was sound and greatly reduced the key-jam.

The new key arrangement (QWERTY) slower the speed of the typist (user) as well; and this means efficiency is affected. This is in contrary to the principles of usability engineering. In usability term, as the user learns the new product through time (see Fig. 1), the user's efficiency should improve and higher productivity shall follow (2).

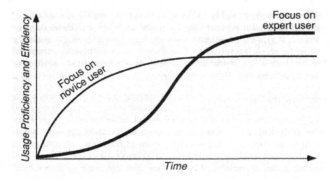

Fig. 1. Improvement on proficiency and efficiency over time [2]

In designing the key arrangement of a keyboard one needs to consider, at least.

- balancing the load between the right and left hand and the fingers,
- distance between the keys,
- size of the key and
- frequency of character (in particular language).

Some of these design goals are not applicable for designing key layout of small handheld devices. Also, the notion of the QWERTY design was to solve a problem in the context of mechanical machine (not digital). Regardless, the QWERTY layout has been adopted in digital devices; further to small handheld devices. Not only on the standard keyboard that is used with desktop personal computers but also in small handheld devices, as well as smartphones.

Hence, we intend to study the usability effect of QWERTY layout in comparison with alphabetically ordered key layout of small handheld devices. We consider comparing with alphabetically ordered layout since we hypothesize that users can perform well if the keys are arranged in the order they know. Knowing the alphabetic order would be a benefit from the cognitive perspective.

1.1 Designing Keyboard

As keyboard/keypad is widely used for inputting text in digital devices, its design might have positive or negative impact on the user interaction with the system – be it the software or the device itself. Primarily, the usability of a particular keyboard/keypad is the result of the key arrangement.

In addition to the QWERTY layout, various key layouts have been proposed. These proposals often consider the letter frequency with respect to a particular language as well as position of the control keys.

Letters Frequency in the Language. In older times, the Caligraph [3] has been designed with more keys than we know in QWERTY since there is separate key for both the uppercase and lowercase alphabet. This might improve the performance as the user doesn't require pressing additional key while shifting between the uppercase and lowercase. In the case of Dvorak keyboard, the key arrangement aims to identify most frequently used letters (A, O, E, U, I, D, H, T, N and S); and these letters are arranged in the middle row. In addition, common letter combinations are positioned in such a way that they can be typed quickly [1]. Colmak as well considers the frequency of letters in the text and puts the ten most common English letters on home row [4].

Letters Used as Control Key. While the frequency of letters in a particular language can be considered as one parameter for deciding the position of the key in the key layout, the letter function as a control key is also another dimension. For example, Colemak's design puts the ten most common English letters on home row considering their frequency in the language but keeps WAZXCV in place for the sake of shortcuts [4]. On the other hand, the Capewell design aims to reduces finger movement compared to Dvorak and designed Capewell-Dvorak. However the Capewell design, in addition to the frequency of the letters in the language, it also considers the function of the letters as a control key. As a result the modification of Dvorak moves ZXCV into QWER positions for the sake of the Undo/Cut/Copy/Paste shortcuts [1].

These kinds of design considerations are language dependent. For instance, the letters frequency varies between languages. Similarly, the use of uppercase and lowercase letters may not follow the same rule in all languages.

1.2   Performance and Accuracy of Keyboard Layouts

Norman and Rumelhart [5] present plausible explanation as performance measurement criteria and identified three factors that play a role in speed optimization:

- The loads on the right and left hands shall be balanced
- The load on the home row is maximized, hence most frequently used keys shall be placed at the home row
- The frequency of alternating hand sequences is maximized and the frequency of using the same finger for typing different characters shall be minimized.

The first factor is useful to improve the ergonomically design of the key layout. It is important to note that one of the HCI goals is making the system usable. That is, enabling the user to accomplish a task safely as well as easily, naturally, securely [6] and also with satisfaction. The other two factors are more related to efficiency and accuracy attributes of the Nelson model [2].

Efficiency is attributed to expert users and can be often valued to the experience and knowledge developed by the user while using a product. As the result, it is important to consider the user profile in the development of interaction modalities [7]. The user profile, however, not only related to the knowledge and experience but also attributes related to the psychological, social and physical state of the user.

Therefore, it is important to take into account the motor capability of the user in designing products (i.e., hardware or software). Such consideration can be useful to improve the efficiency as well as accuracy. In this regards, though it was originally meant to model movement in the physical world, Fitts's Law can be useful for designing. Fitts's Lawt provides a model of human movement, to explain and accurately predict the amount of time a human user needs to accurately select a target [8]. Fitts's Law has been formulated mathematically in a number of ways; and in designing the arrangement of keys in the keyboard it can be used to model the time that a person needs to touch a key accurately [9, 10].

This model is used to predict movement time and also to quantify the difficulty of a target selection task, which is termed as index of difficulty (ID); and it is shown in Eq. 1

$$ID = log_2 \left(\frac{D}{w} \right) \qquad (1)$$

The ID is determined using the variable D that is the distance between the current position and the target; and W, which is the size (width) of the target object. Considering this model in the design of key layout, for example, in order to type the letter 'v' and then 't', if the distance (center to center) between these keys is 4.0 cm; and if the width of the keys is 1.0 cm. Then ID will be 2.0. Similarly, if the width increases we get a smaller ID, indicating that the task is easier. If we apply a greater distance the ID will increase, meaning that the task has become more difficult. Therefore it is apparent that the performance and accuracy of the user can be equated to the way the key layout is designed. O'Riordan et al. [11] as well, indicates through their experimental research that users perform well on larger size computer keyboard than the smaller ones, but for the same key layout – QWERTY.

In summary, as keyboard is widely used being one form of text input modality, its usability apparently would have an impact on the system usability. Thus, it is worth to consider usable key layout design. Regardless, the adoption of the QWERTY layout to computers and then to small handheld might not consider the design factors above. In particular to the small handheld devices.

- Balancing the load between the two hands (eight fingers) may not be logical since users often use one or two finger/s (see Fig. 2).
- The size of the keys will be much smaller in small handheld devices and this would increase the ID.
- The frequency of the letters varies between languages but the order of the alphabetic order of the letters is similar, especially for those using Latin alphabet.

The adoption of QWERTY to the digital world is more of a coincidence but not founded on researched justification and it was without the profound consideration of the usability attributes. Or the adaptation has some logical flaw regarding the typing speed optimization.

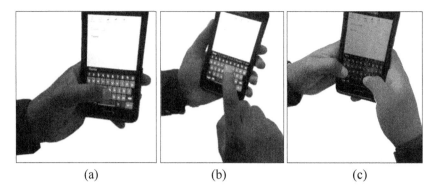

(a)   (b)   (c)

Fig. 2. Text input – common hand-orientation (a) two hands one finger (b) one hand one finger (c) two hands two fingers

Therefore, it is worth to inquire the usability of QWERTY over the alphabetically arranged key layout to propose justified design factor for deciding the key layout. In particular, we focused on small handheld devices and experimented to compare the usability impact, regarding the efficiency and error attribute, between the QWERTY layout and an alphabetical layout. Furthermore, we hypothesize that the text input performance can be improved if the letters on the key layout are ordered as per the alphabet order that the users already learnt; and the error could be reduced.

In the next sections, first the method we applied to measure the performance as well as the error is presented. Then the result obtained and discussion of the result is presented consequently.

2   Methodology

Experimental research has been followed to evaluate the performance of QWERTY against the alphabetically ordered key layout. In the experiment, we first developed android application for smartphone that measures the time elapsed for typing a text. In the application, while the built-in virtual keyboard with standard QWERTY layout is used in one hand, we also developed another virtual keyboard with alphabetical layout for comparison. In the process, we also give due consideration on selection of the *test-users* as well as the *test-input*.

2.1   Test-Users

The main usability attributes considered in the experiment were efficiency and error. Hence we were supposed to select expert users for the test. By expert, we mean users who frequently use the standard key board designed for two hands (eight fingers) use. Therefore, we use purposive sampling and considered users who give secretarial services around secretarial shops that are found around courthouse; where typing is their daily job on which they earn their income. The sample is then further filtered by considering users who are experienced with QWERTY layout. Then, we evaluated users for 35 min using Mavis Beacon. This first experiment has been conducted in four sessions.

Three of the sessions were to measure the consistency of the typing speed as well as accuracy. Measuring the consistency was important since the selected *test-input* is shorter than the preliminary evaluation used for selecting the *test-users*.

On the fourth session, users were actually tested to evaluate their experience on the QWERTY layout, where users are asked to identify for the position of a letter in blindfold. Finally for the experiment, ten of the top scorers are selected as expert users.

2.2   Test-Input

As the objective of the experiment is to compare the QWERTY layout with the alphabetically arranged one, the appropriate text that should be used for test need to contain all the English alphabet while it gives some meaning to the user. The intention of using meaningful text is not to bias the psychomotor concern related to our case which intersects the cognitive functions and physical movement. Therefore, the *test-input* is selected to be "the quick brown fox jumps over the lazy dog".

Each *test-user* entered the *test-input* using both QWERTY and alphabetic of key layout in five passes but at different time interval. At each pass, the speed and the error were directly measured in the application we developed for this purpose. After collecting the physical measurement, the learnability as well has been analyzed based on the result obtained during the five passes for each layout.

2.3   Key Layout and Design Considerations

The conventional rectangular arrangement of key layout on a standard keyboard, which is roughly with three rows and 10 columns (forming 3×10 matrix) is meant to support typing with two hands (eight fingers for the letter and two fingers for space bar). This however is not optimal for small handheld devices as users enter text mostly using one-hand-one-finger, two-hands-one-finger or two-hands-two-fingers (see Fig. 2-a to Fig. 2-c respectively). If a 3×10 key matrix is kept, the distance between the key would increase. This means, the ID that would be calculated using Fitts' Law would increase (as discussed in Sect. 1.2) and the task would be more difficult.

Therefore, while designing the new key layout, we considered a 6×4 key matrix to minimize the maximum inter-key distance (see Fig. 3).

Fig. 3. Alphabetically arranged key layout

Also, as the thumb finger can be used for entering the letters, the *space bar* and other control keys, we placed the *space bar, delete* and *enter* key to be accessible from both the right and left side of the key layout.

3   Results of the Experiment

After *test-users* entered the *test-input* that contains 43 characters, the total time used for completing the task is measured and the errors has been counted for every wrong key the *test-user* entered. The *test-users* entered the *test-input* in five passes, at five separate time interval; and the average of the result of the ten users for each pass is calculated as shown in Table 1.

Table 1. Table captions should be placed above the tables.

Pass	Alphabetic layout				QWERTY layout			
	Time (S)	CPS	ACPS	Errors (%)	Time (S)	CPS	ACPS	Errors (%)
1	79.80	0.54	0.52	3.72%	80.90	0.53	0.52	2.33%
2	67.70	0.64	0.62	1.86%	69.10	0.62	0.60	3.95%
3	67.00	0.64	0.63	1.40%	69.00	0.62	0.60	3.26%
4	58.10	0.74	0.73	1.63%	63.80	0.67	0.66	2.33%
5	54.80	0.78	0.78	1.16%	61.80	0.70	0.68	1.63%

For comparing the typing speed, characters-per-second (CPS) is used as the unit or raw speed. The raw speed is calculated by dividing the length of the *test-input*, which is 43, by the average time. In this calculation 0.54 cps for the alphabetical layout and 0.53 cps for the QWERTY was recorded during the first pass.

However raw typing speed could be misleading. Hence it is important to consider only the accurately entered characters and this gives us the adjusted CPS (ACPS). As a result, for both the alphabetic and QWERTY layout, the ACPS was equal on the first run, while on the fifth run the result was found to be 0.78 acps and 0.68 acps for the alphabetic and QWERTY layout respectively.

4   Discussion

Looking on Table 1, it seems users perform well on the QWERTY layout than the new design during the first pass. However, it has to be noted that usability is not a one dimensional attribute. Other dimensions we need to consider is the learnability aspect.

The test-users are expert to the QWERTY layout and novice to the alphabetical layout. And, it is natural if the users are not performing well at the beginning (2). Novice users do not perform efficiently and could have more error when they are introduced to new product for the first time (see Fig. 1).

Therefore, it is important to discuss the result by looking on the change in performance through time. To do this, we computed the change in performance *(P)* by equating the improvement on the adjusted speed as the difference between the ACPS (i.e. denoted as S_n) measured at the each pass and the initial ACPS (i.e. denoted as S_0) that is measured at the initial pass. Thus the performance of a user with the alphabetic layout (P_A) is given by:

$$\Delta P_A = S_{An} - S_{A0} \qquad (2)$$

And, the performance of a user with the QWERTY layout (P_Q) is given by:

$$\Delta P_Q = S_{Qn} - S_{Q0} \qquad (3)$$

The initial ACPS (S_0) in both Eqs. 2 and 3 is 0.52 acps (see Table 1) but the value used for S_{An} and S_{Qn} for each pass varies so that the value of P varies in the rest of the passes.

After computing the performance for each pass to both the alphabetic and QWERTY layout, we have noted that the performance of the users improve more on the alphabetic layout as they learn more the layout (see Fig. 4).

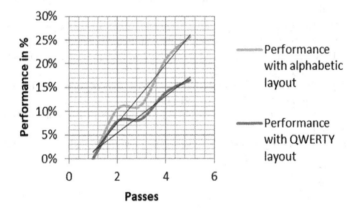

Fig. 4. Performance comparison made through time

Regarding the error, while the users were more accurate on the QWERTY than the alphabetical layout during the first pass, this was changed as they learn the alphabetic layout more; and on the fifth run, the users have performed well on the alphabetical layout having 98.837% accuracy while having 98.372% accuracy for the QWERTY layout.

5 Conclusion

Designing text input method using alphabetic order could improve the usability of the device, especially on small handheld device. Though we have used the English alphabet in our work, each language may have its own different character and order.

Hence, due consideration shall be given to the language structure while deciding the alphabetic order. Also, even if expert users (experienced with QWERTY) has well performed in our test, usually the new layout could be more appealing to novice user (new to the device or typing). Therefore, in the future designers may improve the usability of their product by introducing both type of layout and giving the option to the user on the selection of the layout.

References

1. Buzing P.: Comparing Different Keyboard Layouts: Aspects of QWERTY, DVORAK and alphabetical keyboards, Delft University of Technology Articles (2003)
2. Nielsen, J.: Usability Engineering. Morgan Kaufmann, San Diego (1993)
3. Beeching, W.: Century of the Typewriter. BAS Printers, Wallop (1974)
4. David B.: Why QWERTY - and What's Better? STAS 325 at the University of Calgary
5. Norman, D.A., Rumelhart, D.E.: Studies of typing from the LNR Research Group. In: Cooper, W.E. (ed.) Cognitive Aspects of Skilled Typewriting. Springer, New York (1983). https://doi.org/10.1007/978-1-4612-5470-6_3
6. Posland, S.: Ubiquitous Computing: Smart Device, Environment, and Interactions. Wiley, Chicester (2009)
7. Mayhew, D.: The Usability Engineering Lifecycle: a Practitioner's Handbook for User Interface Design. Morgan Kaufmann Publishers, San Francisco (1999)
8. Scott, M.: Fitts' Law as a research and design tool in human-computer interaction. Hum. Comput. Interac. 2(1), 91–139 (1992)
9. Fitts, P.: The information capacity of the human motor system in controlling the amplitude of movement. J. Exp. Psychol. 47(1), 381–391 (1954)
10. Fitts, P., Michael, I.: Human Performance. Basic Concepts in Psychology. Brooks/Cole, Belmont (1969)
11. O'Riordan, B., Curran, K., Woods, D.: Investigating text input methods for mobile phones. J. Comput. Sci. 1(2), 189–199 (2005)

SocioCon: A Social Circle for Your Interactive Devices

Ngoc Thi Nguyen$^{(\boxtimes)}$ and Hyowon Lee

Singapore University of Technology and Design, 8 Somapah Road,
Singapore 487372, Singapore
thingoc_nguyen@mymail.sutd.edu.sg, hlee@sutd.edu.sg

Abstract. Our everyday lives with technology are increasingly characterised by the use of multiple interactive devices. We are seeing more and more variety of specialised input and output devices that can connect with other devices to help the user perform a particular task in a more optimal or other beneficial way. When multiple devices are used together within a session, owing to the diversity of native interaction modalities, content representation and capabilities of each device, there are usability issues arising before, after or at the transition of inter-connectivity. In such a device-sharing situation, one device that could temporarily borrow the input or output modalities from other devices must know which devices are available or allowed to offer such connections, and how their combined use should push yet another way of end-user interactivity. In this paper, we envision a few typical usage scenarios where such multi-device interaction is expected or desirable, then from these develop an overarching concept of usability in a multi-device environment. Simple social heuristics in sharing the interactivity and resources amongst devices are employed to shape how the overall usability in these situations could be addressed and framed. We develop two multi-device interaction prototypes that correspond to some of these scenarios, conduct usability testing, report the findings and discuss further insights.

Keywords: Multi-devices · Device-to-device · Cross-devices
Transition usability · Input devices · Output devices · Context-aware
Interaction design

1 Introduction

With increasing various means of accessing information available today such as desktop PCs with monitor and keyboard/mouse, laptops with built-in camera and trackpad, tablets with multi-touch screen and Virtual Reality (VR)/Augmented Reality (AR) goggles with specialised hand-grip control devices, the communication between requests and results is vital for a useful interactive system [1]. Obviously, these interactions are currently constrained by the way input and output capabilities and one-to-one pairing are facilitated. People generally accept the interaction with a system using its pre-defined input and output components available on either separate devices (e.g. keyboard and monitor to a desktop PC) or on a same device (e.g. touch gestures and visual display on a modern tablet). This style of interaction works well in the

© Springer International Publishing AG, part of Springer Nature 2018
A. Marcus and W. Wang (Eds.): DUXU 2018, LNCS 10919, pp. 623–639, 2018.
https://doi.org/10.1007/978-3-319-91803-7_47

scenarios or environments for which the devices were designed. What if there are changes in these factors? Large displays are great for sharing information in presentation settings or public areas. However, the centralization of operations on a large display could introduce the cognitive gap between the speaker and the team members while everyone discusses about the content being displayed on the large screen. While tabletops promote collaboration by supporting multiple users working simultaneously, people sitting at one side of a tabletop are unable to read the documents displayed on the opposite side of the table. Although mobile phones have become a necessity as personal communication and management tool for our digital lives, they are not ideal for displaying large amounts of data on the screens. Smartwatches are great as a health-tracking devices as well as extensions to mobile phones, but their limited screen space can severely reduce the usability of even simple and mundane tasks such as typing or browsing information.

Usability issues arising from diverse situations in using a device as a single, self-contained unit lead us to consider the combined use of multiple devices to enhance the overall user experiences within an interactive session. Numerous techniques of coupling interactions between devices have been proposed: wall display and watch-band [2], wall screen and tabletop [3–5], presentation screen and Personal Digital Assistants (PDA) [6, 7], large public display and mobile phone [8–10], smartphone and smartwatch [11–13], or between two tablets [14, 15], etc. Cross-device interactivity often requires the explicit device connection setup at before the interaction is taken place. Making use of multiple devices at the same time may surface potentially significant usability issues which might not have been originally planned or anticipated by the developers of individual devices.

This paper addresses these usability issues, articulates and generalises the concept of coherent and consistent interaction amongst multiple devices, owned by a user or multiple users, in their own social situations. Human seeks or offers assistances among one another using languages, signals, common understanding on situations and relations. Need a helping hand? Asking a family member, a friend, a colleague or someone we know seems to come first in our mind. Not only they know us, they understand which is the best way to help us. Close family members and friends even predict when and what we need, to offer their assistances. Encapsulating these concepts with cross-device interactivity in terms of its usability, SocioCon applies such basic analogy in theoretically articulating and suggesting the mechanisms for creating and managing assistances amongst interactive devices to efficiently continue the same on-going activity or task. By augmenting our physical world with groups of pre-linked interactive devices, we are able to leverage the input and output modalities of different devices to maintain the usability in using them.

Starting with a series of typical and expected scenarios where multiple devices around us are used together to carry out one task or activity, we develop the SocioCon concept in which some of the essential usability issues in such scenarios are identified and generalised. To refine the SocioCon concept, we develop prototype systems that realise some of these scenarios to further identify the usability issues. Making various interactive devices technically connected together is one issue, but what the connected devices mean when used within an interactive session in terms of usability is an issue that deserves an in-depth study as more and more diverse interactive devices become available today and this trend will only increase in the coming years.

2 Motivation

2.1 Multiple Devices to Meet People's Needs

Having both input and output modalities on the same device allows users to perform tasks using single devices, but also bind the users with the devices' advantages as well as disadvantages. Rekimoto et al. [6] addressed the disadvantages of PDAs being isolated from the users' nearby computing devices in their proximal interaction model. Two users could connect their PDAs, acted as Internet Protocol (IP) mobile phones, to the nearby displays during a conversation to share the screens between them. Usability issues due to input/output-bound are also common on smartphones when users interact with large amount of data on the small screens. Viewing content being spread over few pages not only requires the users' short term memory to refer to the visited content, but could introduce interaction costs as well. A PC-like work environment can now be easily created by plugging the smartphone into a display dock which is connected to an external monitor/TV, a keyboard and a mouse [16]. The smartphone can still be used to make phone calls or to send messages while the output screen showing what the user is working on.

Our work seeks to leverage the advantages of each device when connected together for a more optimal overall interaction. The following scenarios illustrate how we envisage a social circle for devices would create opportunities for optimal usability. Our specific research interests are to understand the nuances of how people would transit using the input/output modalities offered from different devices during a task, whether and how it matters when those devices belong to other users or the public.

Scenario 1

Mike and his best friend Jack are watching a movie in the common room at their dormitory. Mike uses his smartwatch to remotely control the video playback on the TV. Simple operation commands such as changing the channels and increasing the volume are very easy to carry out using touch gestures performed on his smartwatch. However, when he wants to search for a TV program, typing search keywords on his smartwatch often results in typo due to the small keyboard constrained by the screen size of the watch. Before Mike starts feeling annoyed, a floating phone-icon shows up on Mike's watch surface, hinting that Jack's phone is available as an input device. Mike could choose to ignore the suggestion and carry on typing using the virtual keyboard of his watch, or he could tap on the phone-icon to start using Jack's phone keyboard for typing upon Jack's consent.

Scenario 2

Mary is showing her holidays pictures to Jane. When more friends gather around, it becomes difficult for everyone to see the pictures on her phone. Some of her friends try to crane their necks over others' shoulders to see the pictures. Mary also has to zoom in some of the pictures for her friends to see more details in the photo before moving on to the next photo. A floating tablet-icon button appears on Mary's phone screen, hinting to her that she can output the photo from her phone to her tablet for better viewing by the group. Tapping on the tablet-icon enables the photos to appear on the tablet. Mary continues showing the pictures to her group of excited friends.

Scenario 3

It takes more than 10 minutes for the bus to come. Looking around, Mark sees the public display, situated a couple of meters away, showing interesting information about a new movie. Instead of leaving his seat to approach and touch on the public display for viewing further information, Mark uses his own smartwatch to remotely interact with the public display, for example, tap on the smartwatch surface to view more information, swipe to navigate content.

One of the implications of the above scenarios is that there is no one-size-fits-all to the challenges of using a single device to meet all needs and requirements from users for any situation. In this paper, we take these as guiding scenarios in shaping the detailed concept of coherent, connected multi-device usability in Sect. 4.

2.2   Do People Want It?

The scenarios drawn above are meant to be general and perhaps soon-to-be expected situations we envisage in this study. We conducted a quick informal survey to check and confirm that they make sense and relate well to people. Ten people responded from mixed-nationality who are graduate students and researchers at a university. Almost all of them use smartphones and laptops often (Fig. 1). Each of them owns at least 3 computing devices (e.g. smartphones, tablets and laptops, etc.). We asked questions relevant to the previous three scenarios.

Figure 2 showed feedback of participants' choices. Most of respondents strongly support the idea of transit to another device to continue the current task/activity in an optimal way. Few were concerned about using other people's devices. Majority opted for using personal devices over publicly-provided devices and modalities.

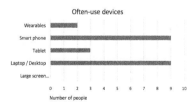

Fig. 1. Devices are often used by users

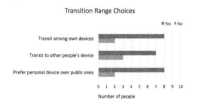

Fig. 2. Participants' choices on transitions

The three scenarios are selected amongst typical usability issues we have observed, which we believe they will become more common as we are surrounded with more devices. They demonstrate how there would be needs for a transition from one device to another for optimal interaction with a system or more efficiency in performing a task.

In the following section, we review prior work that explore multi-device interactions which our approach shares similar points of view with. In Sect. 4, we propose a novel social circle concept for connected use of interactive devices and its general guidelines, creating opportunities for interactive devices to share their advantages in input/output modalities to other devices which join the same social circle. We discuss potential applications of this model through the three scenarios, and report the studies in which two of the scenarios have been implemented and user-tested. Section 5 concludes the paper with future exploration and future work.

3   Background and Related Work

3.1   Multi-device Interaction

The concept of multi-device interaction is not new. Pick-and-Drop [17] proposed a pen-based direct manipulation technique to transfer data between displays of a PDA and a kiosk terminal, or between two PDAs. Stitching [15] applied a similar idea where a pen stroke across two tablets can be used to transfer files. InfoTable and InfoWall [18] enabled the interchanging of digital information amongst portable devices with the support of two cameras. Content sharing between a tabletop and a wall screen were possible with i-LAND [3], MultiSpace [4] and Select-and-Point [5]. Two tablets or phones could join to display a photo [14] or a canvas [19] across their device surfaces. Overall, these systems focused on distributing interactions or content resources over multiple devices for sharing resources. In contrast with these approaches, we explore the potential of utilizing input/output interaction modalities and particularly focus on the usability implications in such combined usage scenarios.

3.2   Systems with Different Input and Output Devices

Researchers have strived to enhance the system usability and improve tasks efficiency by using a device to aid the operation of another. Mobile devices such as PDA and phones have been used as customizable input devices to desktop (Shortcutter [20]), LCD displays (Ballagas et al. [8], Hyakutake et al. [10]), interactive TV (PDA-ITV [21]) and public displays (PocketPIN [22], C-blink [23]). The output of users' artefact (e.g. notes, photos) between personal devices and public displays was explored in SharedNotes [7], Hermes Photo Display [9], PresiShare [24] and Digifieds [25]. While these systems utilised handheld devices as input and/or output devices that act as controllers or companions to the larger screen displays, Duet [26] proposed join interaction in which two mobile devices can perform their input and output techniques. Interface between phone and watch was divided such as a palette was hosted on a smartwatch to work with a canvas on a smartphone. Kubo et al. [27] proposed the use of the wrist-tilt gesture on the watch combined with the push on a button on the phone at the same time to zoom out the view, which can also be achieved by using a pinch gesture on the phone. Not stopping at being used as sensing device, smartwatches were also used as sub-displays of applications running on phones [27, 28]. Our work contributes to this paradigm in terms of identifying the usability issues which may arise before, during and after the interactivity between one device to another.

3.3   Continuity in Multi-device Interaction

A number of studies have investigated the continuity of the user interfaces beyond the device physical boundary. MEDIAid [29], a set of UI sketches illustrated the shift of streamed audio-visual content from a TV to a mobile phone. FollowMe [30] provided a pluggable infrastructure for context-aware computing that enabled a user's task to be carried on when the user changed his/her environment context. Context Awareness Supported Application Mobility (CASAM) or "Application Mobility" [31] was described as the migration of an application between different devices during its execution, e.g. during a video conference, a user switched from a laptop to a tablet and continue his/her video conference from the tablet. These studies share the same focus on the transfer of the content and its state across multiple devices. Aiming to leverage the capabilities and relationships amongst devices to create a social circle of interactive symphony, we are interested in exploring the emerging "continuity" interaction concept [32] amongst connected devices. This theme refers to an interaction which starts on one artifact and ends on another to enable users to re-access the content across different devices. However, it is not clear how the same functionality, feedback and interaction technique would be achieved across multiple devices with different affordances. The seamless "continuity" in interaction while switching amongst devices is one of the usability issues when using multiple interactive devices within one session, thus warrants much more in-depth investigation. In this paper, this aspect is a part of the overall usage scenarios where various available interactive devices are to be visible, selectable and connectable for the recommendation of interaction with a target device, after which the most suitable interaction paradigm for the chosen input and output devices is to be pushed to support satisfactory user experience within that session.

3.4   Ecosystem of Connected Devices

Various studies have aimed towards creating environments for multi-device interaction. In multi-device ecosystem [29], a semi-automatic content adaptation engine would query the user in determining the most suitable way to continue streaming the media content. Turunen et al. [33] presented a multimodal media center interface based on a combination of a mobile phone and a large high-definition display. Users can interact with the system using speech, using mobile phone to physically touch on icons, and gestures. Henrik and Kjeldskov [34] explored interaction space created around multi-device music player for co-located users to listen to music together. Results of investigating the usage practices of combining multiple devices (e.g. TVs, personal computers, smartphones, tablets) in users' daily tasks and activities showed that the users continuously encountered problems in multi-device use [35]. These problems included the connection issues, incompatible content formats, unavailable applications across devices platforms and limited text-entry capability; all of which highlighted the challenges in creating ubiquitous digital ecosystems to support the collaboration and the continuity of users' activities. This work complements the concept of connected devices ecosystem by envisioning a more generic usability environment in which the factors and their relationships in pairing between interactive devices and their optimal modes of interaction paradigms are to be alerted, selected and used within a session.

4 SocioCon: A Social Circle for Interactive Devices

It is reasonable to assume that in the near future, interactive devices and their relationships will be characterised by a high level of automated connectivity and flexible ways to authorise it by the users. On-demand connections are likely to take place anytime and anywhere.

Taking privacy concerns, devices need to know which other devices have agreed to be connected and interacted to them, and what modes of interaction they are equipped with. For this purpose, sharing device input/output channels and its level (direct-share or propagation-share) needs to be defined only by devices' users. This personal definition is generally based on the trust amongst users as well as whether or not users are willing share their devices, their capabilities and data to others.

SocioCon recommendation strategy is based on a hybrid sensing of foreground and background: what application is currently in use, what activity the user is doing (e.g. standing, walking, sitting, lying, eating), what device the user is using (e.g. smartwatch, smartphone, tablet, laptop), and how the device is handled (e.g. being held by one hand or both hands, in pocket, in bag). For example, sensing its user walking while looking at the phone to suggest alternative option of output the content to a pair of AR glasses (frequent view) or a smartwatch (occasional view). In short, SocioCon examines a combination of user-device-application contexts to determine if a user requires an assistance in alternating input or output amongst currently available devices. In this paper, we focus on the usability and transition aspects of connections amongst devices as per the scenarios drawn in the previous section. With that, we construct a simple set of general guidelines as a basic mechanism for how devices in social situations should behave in terms of connectivity, then characterise SocioCon from them.

4.1 General Guidelines

- Each device shall have its own profile with information about device default status, sharing levels, sharing modalities and sharing channels.
- Each device shall have its own spectrum of roles: being a self-contained interactive device itself, or being an input and/or output sharing channel for others.
- Each device shall be able to initiate a relationship and to indicate a relationship type with other devices. Relationship type for each relation mimics the way how people feel and behave towards each other (e.g. family, friends, friends of friends or public). It shall influence how transparent multi-device handshakes would be to users and whether or not the sharing propagates.

- SocioCon shall provide adjustable sharing level between devices. Non-sharing mode shall be available for a user to stop all sharing activities of a device.
- Sharing channels shall be asymmetric. Device A could share its input and output modalities to device B, but B may choose to share either its input or output, or only accept the sharing from A.
- Based on the user's context, the device context and the application context, SocioCon would recommend the best available input/output option based on a set of available devices in the same social circle.

4.2   Conceptual Model

Device Profile
SocioCon device profile contains user's preferences on device default status (available, pending, connected, inactive), sharing levels (device-centric, user-centric, once) and sharing modalities (input, output or input + output) for sharing channels (IN-share for accepting the input and output modalities offered by other devices, and OUT-Share for offering its own modalities to others).

Establish Relationship with Other Devices
When a device is within proximity of another device, any of the device owners can initiate a SocioCon relationship if there is none existed. The user can indicate the relationship type between devices (SocioCon-Buddies, SocioCon-Family, SocioCon-Friends, SocioCon-Friends of Friends and SocioCon-Public) (Fig. 3) and can further customise the device sharing parameters. Device role is dynamic, each device could take a role as an input device in one scenario and an output device in another, or both. The transparency of multi-device handshake - the basic rules for the way input and output modalities are shared between them, is highest with the SocioCon-Buddies type and decreases with others.

The proposed social connections amongst devices use analogy of human relationships in defining relationships between devices, but not necessarily the same (e.g. devices belonging to family members could belong a SocioCon group other than SocioCon-Family, likewise devices belonging to two close friends could participate in a SocioCon-Buddies group). The main objective is to establish basic guidelines for a device to understand which devices are available as alternative input and output options, and how much willingly they want to share.

Transition Composition
One of the important design consideration in such a multi-device environment is when the user *switches* between the input/output device within an interactive session, i.e. a transition of device and its modalities. The transition to alternative input/output modalities comprises of 3 components:

1. A *set of available devices* that offers sharing their input/output modalities. The devices social circle provides the knowledge of available devices.
2. A *set of trigger factors* that invokes the recommendation for alternative input/output from other devices.

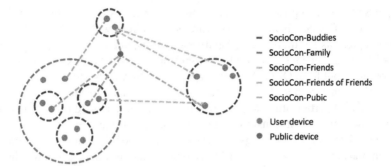

Fig. 3. Relationships amongst devices as social circles

3. A *transition model* that depicts how multiple input/output devices support one another.

Trigger Factors
The recommendation for input/output options can be triggered by the contexts of user, device, application, or a combination of any of them. These trigger factors can be implicit (SocioCon recommends the transition) or explicit (user indicates the transition).

Transition Models
Transitions of input/output can be categorised into 4 models: Input Shift, Input Shift-Relay, Output Shift and Output Shift-Relay, illustrated in Fig. 4. ('I' denotes input, 'O' denotes output).

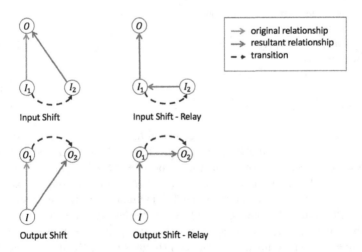

Fig. 4. Transitions of input/output devices

Input Shift model represents a situation when there is a switch of input device from I_1 to I_2, both of which belong to the same social circle with O. Input Shift-Relay similarly represents the transition of input from I_1 to I_2, but with I_2 not participating in any social circle that involves O. Output Shift and Output Shift-Relay represent the transition of output from O_1 to O_2, each differentiated by whether O_2 is within the same social circle with I or not. This particular categorisation is based on the social relationship amongst participating devices, which may impact on the future user interaction guidelines of input/output transition, and is transparent to the users.

The social relationship amongst devices influences how instant the input transition or output transition happens. SocioCon-Buddies relationship type allows the input transition and output transition to occur upon the user's positive response to SocioCon recommendation amongst its participating devices (usually belonging to the same user). For other SocioCon relationship types, depending on their settings such as sharing levels, channels and modalities, a minimum level of consent by the user is required before the input/output channel transits from one device to another. SocioCon status for each participating device is automatically updated accordingly (e.g. stopping a device from participating to a particular relationship or all relationships by simply changing its status to Inactive for that relationship (local) or in device profile (global)).

Table 1 enlists some examples of using user's physical activity, device-in-use and current task as trigger factors to suitable transition models.

Table 1. Examples of trigger factors and transition models

Trigger factors	Trigger contexts	Transition models
Frequency of typos when typing on a small screen device (scenario 1)	Device + App	Input Shift-Relay
Crowd-sensing while sharing resources on personal devices (scenario 2)	User + Device + App	Output Shift
Interaction with a large display at close-up vs far distance (scenario 3)	User + Device	Input Shift
Output music from smartphone to hall speakers	User + App	Output Shift-Relay

To aid understanding of the trigger factors and the transition models, we use our 3 scenarios (see Sect. 2.1) to illustrate. In scenario 1, as Mike's watch and Jack's phone join the SocioCon-Friends group, when the typo rate exceeds a threshold, SocioCon suggests to use Jack's phone as an alternative device for typing the search text. If Jack's phone participates in the social circle of the TV, the input transition is classified under the Input Shift model, else the Input Shift-Relay model. Jack's consent is a decision factor to make the input transition happens. SocioCon updates the transition status from the time Mike taps on the floating phone-icon (Input-Receive Request) to the moment when Jack taps on the floating watch-icon (Input-Offer Accept). This is illustrated in Fig. 5a. An adaptation to Input-Offer interface may take place on Jack's phone. Either

Mike or Jack can interrupt the request or the offer an input modality by choosing the Disconnect option in the context menu of the respective floating icons.

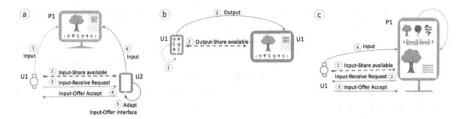

Fig. 5. Transition models: Input Shift/Input Shift-Relay between devices of 2 users (a), Output Shift between devices of the same user (b), Input Shift between personal and public devices (c)

In scenario 2, both the phone and the tablet are owned by Mary, thus belong to the SocioCon-Buddies group. Crowd-sensing and the browse of pictures on Mary's phone triggers the Output Shift. When she taps on the floating tablet-icon showing on her phone, the pictures are instantly output to her tablet. This is because Mary's tapping action gives her consent to the output transition. This is illustrated in Fig. 5b.

The transition in scenario 3 (Fig. 5c) happens in a similar way to that of scenario 1, but only for the first time when Mark's watch joins the SocioCon-Public group. Public displays are situated with a general purpose of sharing information to everyone, hence the viewing and browsing their information are strongly encouraged. For this reason, a social profile for a public display would have a default settings of SocioCon-Buddies type for its IN-Share channel, which accepts the input commands for the navigation and selection of objects from other devices. Mark, who wishes to use his smartwatch as an input device to a public display could establish a social relation between his watch and the display using the SocioCon-Public type. Input Shift model enables Mark to interact with the display using his watch by simply tapping on the public display icon showing on the watch social circle list.

Instant input/output transition possibilities would likely encourage more opportunistic switching between devices when situations arise in ways that will benefit the tasks the users are engaged in. We developed prototypes for some of these situations and conducted usability testing to understand the usability aspects of the device transition and the implications for the interaction modalities, described in the next section.

Transition Usability

Similar to the way human interact with one another using their best suited languages and protocols, we expect optimal interaction interfaces and methods would be required for our devices to participate effectively in their own relationships on SocioCon. Basic interface adaptation on connected devices during input/output transitions may be required to accommodate the differences in interaction techniques between devices. User interface of substitute device may take a different form to adapt with the interaction technique and to differentiate the substitute mode from its host mode.

The nature of interacting with public display involves consideration on easy and quick information retrieval. The scenario 3 involves the interaction between a smart-watch and a large public display, both of them tend to have better supports for tasks and activities that do not require objects manipulation in details. We envisage that this particular arrangement of multi-device interaction will become a common and typical situation in our public, urban setting, thus we investigated further as one of our pro-totypes[1]. To overcome the challenges of huge differences in screen sizes of a large display and a smartwatch, we applied the 'hop-to-select' traverse style which enables the jumping from the current-selected object to the nearest selectable object in our prototype applications (Fig. 6). This traversal style combines the navigation and the selection of an object, thus the name 'hop-to-select'.

Basic object manipulations, such as viewing the context information of a selected object, are possible with simple common touch gestures performed relatively on the smartwatch. This is achieved by mapping a subset of common gestures (Tap, Long Tap, Swipe, 2-Finger tap and Shake) sent by the watch to the common input commands (select an object, show/hide context information, show all interactable objects, traverse previous/next/up/down, exit current screen or undo) on the large display. As the touch gestures performed on the watch screen do not require an exact spatial coordination between the watch face and the wall display, users remain visually focused on the screen while continuing to interact with the system (Fig. 7).

Fig. 6. Hop-to-select traverse

Fig. 7. Eyes-off interaction with large display using smartwatch

We developed three applications with this interaction strategy (Photo Browser, Slides Presentation and Planets Explorer) to demonstrate a seamless multi-device user interactivity using a smartwatch (input) and a large display (output) in conducting a task (information sharing) in a particular setting (on university campus). Ten partici-pants were recruited one by one to engage in the interactivity during which all inter-action, comments and other particulars were video-recorded and analysed afterwards. Each participant tried all three applications one by one in a free, explorative manner. Most participants enjoyed the interaction, effortlessly tapping and swiping for browsing the contents of each application. Although all participants had experience of interacting

---

[1] The interactive prototype for this scenario was demonstrated to elicit further feedback [36].

with large displays, only two were familiar with using the smartwatches. Notably, those who have not used the smartwatch navigated skillfully after few minutes of using the system. Participant 5 and 9, who had been already experienced with smartwatches, praised the intuitiveness and responsiveness of this interaction technique. At least eight out of ten agreed on the ease of learning, ease of use and the usefulness of this eyes-off interaction, particularly in making presentation or collaborative learning using large displays. Figure 8 shows overall users experience rating from this usability testing.

The connected use between smartwatch (as input) and public display (as output) implies a particular usage setting where the user has his/her own multi-touch device that can serve as input but wants to share the output on a separate, large screen. As the user looks around the environment to identify any such large screen, the Output Shift model (lower left in Fig. 4) is determined based on the device sociality as mentioned in the previous section, the pre-defined hop-to-select interaction strategy is then pushed to this combined interaction system.

Another potential situation that could employ this interaction style is when a user, who has been browsing the content directly by touching on a large interactive display, decides to step back in order to be able to take in a full view of the large display content. The change of the user's spatial context triggers the recommendation of the user's personal devices (e.g. smartwatch) that participate in the same social circle with

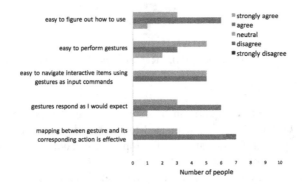

Fig. 8. User experience rating of multi-device interaction: smartwatch as input and large display as output

the large display. Suppose the user agrees to use his/her own smartwatch as input device to the large display as suggested by SocioCon, the Input Shift model (upper left in Fig. 4) will apply the hop-to-select interaction strategy to this connected interaction. In summary, depending on what each of the connected devices is and the details of their interaction modalities, the optimal interaction strategy will need to be identified and replace the ones each device had been using at that moment.

We also expand our input modalities to tangible input devices in our experiment with the Visual Field Visualizer (VFV) system, based on a real needs of eye-specialists identified by collaborating with a local hospital [37]. The VFV system comprises of a smartphone, a VR headset and tangible input devices (Fig. 9). It measures one's visual field by presenting stimuli (light) at different location in the tested visual field region, records the user's response of seeing the presented stimuli to construct the user's visual region. During our on-site observation of how visual field tests are conducted at a local hospital, we observed some patients having difficulty in pressing the response button connected to the machine. To eliminate the external factors which impact users' timely responses, multiple choices of input options were considered before being narrowed down to 3 Bluetooth devices: a round-shape button, a joystick and a mouse (Fig. 9c). This setting loosely implements the scenario 1 in which a user may want to switch to another input device due to the usability issue of current input modality. Usability testing with the system involved 39 participants, each wearing the VR headset and responding to the visual stimuli with an externally connected input device. Situations for switching the input device happened, for example after a participant expressed her difficulty in pressing the small Bluetooth round-shaped button, we quickly passed her a Bluetooth mouse to resume her visual field test. The idea of providing multiple choices of input was welcomed by the participants as some felt easier to click on a mouse button than a round-shaped button while others prefer the button or the joystick for their compact sizes. We received positive responses from participants on the system usability.

Fig. 9. VFV components: Android phone (a), VR case (b) and Bluetooth button/joystick/mouse (c)

A VR headset typically requires an on-device input button or separate hand-held input device(s), both of which are dedicated to the brand or model of VR headsets. The VFV prototype is a manifestation of the Input Shift model (upper left in Fig. 4). Considering a user might want to switch the system-provided input modality for a particular sub-task where the switched-to input device is more optimised for it. Other trigger factors include the usability issues of an input device or user's personal preferences. The transition to alternative input devices would be possible if their social relationship exists.

The Bluetooth button/joystick used in the VFV system could flexibly take a role as an input device as well as an output device (see general guidelines in Sect. 4.1) to the VR headset. An example for this case is when a separate haptic feedback is output to the connected input device (e.g. in the form of an armband or textile wearable) due to the discomfort of vibration on the VR headset itself. The Output Shift model determines the details of the output transition. Auditory feedback can be output to the user's earphone by the Output Shift-Relay model (lower right in Fig. 4). Using different forms of feedback to acknowledge the user's positive response in seeing a stimulus would be seen as a contribution to the overall usability improvement to the VFV system in particular and to the visual field test practices in general.

5   Conclusion

As more and more interactive platforms emerge offering different interaction modalities and their associated benefits, more burden is eventually imposed on the end-users to make the right choices in the devices, their combined uses in ways not necessarily anticipated or expected by the developers of the individual devices. We expect that such situations will only increase in the coming years.

While a sizable number of studies are available and conducted today to experiment the technical possibility and feasibility in such multi-device connectivity and cross use, the usability side of the picture (i.e. how the user is aware of such possibility in a given situation and how to switch between them, what is the best interaction modalities and style, and how to ensure to minimise a negative experience in the transit as well as during the consequent interaction) needs to be studied in itself.

In this paper we outlined a possible way to frame this transition usability issue by suggesting three expected usage scenarios. We contribute with the general guidelines and the SocioCon conceptual model that will support how multi-device transition and their usability implications should be addressed and studied. We are interested in the design issues that arise when considering multiple computing devices, each of which is more capable of input and output modalities than others, which might be combined in many different ways. Transition usability emerges when a user switches between the input/output modalities on the same device, or between input/output modalities provided by difference devices in a session. With the growing interest in Internet of Things (IoT) devices and AR/VR applications in which the interaction modalities and styles may not be natively fixed or pre-designed but most likely require some level of cross-input/output device connections, we believe that our study in transition usability is timely and important.

References

1. Jacob, R.J.K., Leggett, J.J., Myer, B.A., Pausch, R.: Interaction styles and input/output devices. Behav. Inf. Technol. **12**(2), 69–79 (1993)
2. Bolt, R.A.: "Put-that-there": voice and gesture at the graphics interface. ACM SIGGRAPH Comput. Graph. **14**(3), 262–270 (1980)
3. Streitz, N.A., Geißler, J., Holmer, T., Konomi, S.I., Müller-Tomfelde, C., Reischl, W., Rexroth, P., Seitz, P., Steinmetz, R.: i-LAND: an interactive landscape for creativity and innovation. In: Proceedings of the SIGCHI Conference on Human Factors in Computing Systems, pp. 120–127. ACM, Pittsburgh (1999)
4. Everitt, K., Shen, C., Ryall, K., Forlines, C.: MultiSpace: enabling electronic document micro-mobility in table-centric, multi-device environments. In: First IEEE International Workshop on Horizontal Interactive Human-Computer Systems, TableTop 2006. IEEE (2006)
5. Lee, H., Jeong, H., Lee, J.H., Yeom, K.-W., Shin, H.-J., Park, J.-H.: Select-and-point: a novel interface for multi-device connection and control based on simple hand gestures. In: CHI 2008 Extended Abstracts on Human Factors in Computing Systems, pp. 3357–3362. ACM, Florence (2008)

6. Rekimoto, J., Ayatsuka, Y., Kohno, M., Oba, H.: Proximal interactions: a direct manipulation technique for wireless networking. In: Interact 2003 (2003)
7. Greenberg, S., Boyle, M., LaBerge, J.: PDAs and shared public displays: making personal information public, and public information personal. Pers. Technol. **3**(1), 54–64 (1999)
8. Ballagas, R., Rohs, M., Sheridan, J.G.: Sweep and point and shoot: phonecam-based interactions for large public displays. In: CHI 2005 Extended Abstracts on Human Factors in Computing Systems. ACM (2005)
9. Cheverst, K., Dix, A., Fitton, D., Kray, C., Rouncefield, M., Sas, C., Saslis-Lagoudakis, G., Sheridan, J.G.: Exploring bluetooth based mobile phone interaction with the hermes photo display. In: Proceedings of the 7th International Conference on Human Computer Interaction with Mobile Devices & Services. ACM (2005)
10. Hyakutake, A., Ozaki, K., Kitani, K.M., Koike, H.: 3-D interaction with a large wall display using transparent markers. In: Proceedings of the International Conference on Advanced Visual Interfaces. ACM (2010)
11. Rekimoto, J.: Gesturewrist and gesturepad: unobtrusive wearable interaction devices. In: Proceedings of Fifth International Symposium on Wearable Computers. IEEE (2001)
12. Morganti, E., Angelini, L., Adami, A., Lalanne, D., Lorenzelli, L., Mugellini, E.: A smart watch with embedded sensors to recognize objects, grasps and forearm gestures. Proc. Eng. **41**, 1169–1175 (2012)
13. Xu, C., Pathak, P.H., Mohapatra, P.: Finger-writing with Smartwatch, pp. 9–14 (2015)
14. Hinckley, K.: Synchronous gestures for multiple persons and computers. In: Proceedings of the 16th Annual ACM Symposium on User Interface Software and Technology. ACM (2003)
15. Hinckley, K., Ramos, G., Guimbretiere, F., Baudisch, P., Smith, M.: Stitching: pen gestures that span multiple displays. In: Proceedings of the Working Conference on Advanced Visual Interfaces. ACM (2004)
16. Microsoft Display Dock Overview - Microsoft - Global (2018). https://www.microsoft.com/en-ww/mobile/accessory/hd-500
17. Rekimoto, J.: Pick-and-drop: a direct manipulation technique for multiple computer environments. In: Proceedings of the 10th Annual ACM Symposium on User Interface Software and Technology, pp. 31–39. ACM, Banff (1997)
18. Rekimoto, J., Saitoh, M.: Augmented surfaces: a spatially continuous work space for hybrid computing environments. In: Proceedings of the SIGCHI Conference on Human Factors in Computing Systems. ACM (1999)
19. Lucero, A., Keränen, J., Korhonen, H.: Collaborative use of mobile phones for brainstorming. In: Proceedings of the 12th International Conference on Human Computer Interaction with Mobile Devices and Services, pp. 337–340. ACM, Lisbon (2010)
20. Brad, A., Myers, B.A.: Using handhelds and PCs together. Commun. ACM **44**(11), 34–41 (2001)
21. Robertson, S., Wharton, C., Ashworth, C., Franzke, M.: Dual device user interface design: PDAs and interactive television. In: Proceedings of the SIGCHI Conference on Human Factors in Computing Systems. ACM (1996)
22. De Luca, A., Frauendienst, B.: A privacy-respectful input method for public terminals. In: Proceedings of the 5th Nordic Conference on Human-Computer Interaction: Building Bridges, pp. 455–458. ACM, Lund (2008)
23. Miyaoku, K., Higashino, S., Tonomura, Y.: C-blink: a hue-difference-based light signal marker for large screen interaction via any mobile terminal. In: Proceedings of the 17th Annual ACM Symposium on User Interface Software and Technology, pp. 147–156. ACM, Santa Fe (2004)

24. Geel, M., Huguenin, D., Norrie, M.C.: PresiShare: opportunistic sharing and presentation of content using public displays and QR codes. In: Proceedings of the 2nd ACM International Symposium on Pervasive Displays. ACM (2013)

25. Alt, F., Shirazi, A.S., Kubitza, T., Schmidt, A.: Interaction techniques for creating and exchanging content with public displays. In: Proceedings of the SIGCHI Conference on Human Factors in Computing Systems. ACM (2013)

26. Chen, X.A., Grossman, T., Wigdor, D.J., Fitzmaurice, G.: Duet: exploring joint interactions on a smart phone and a smart watch. In: Proceedings of the SIGCHI Conference on Human Factors in Computing Systems, pp. 159–168. ACM, Toronto (2014)

27. Kubo, Y., Takada, R., Shizuki, B., Takahashi, S.: Exploring context-aware user interfaces for smartphone-smartwatch cross-device interaction. Proc. ACM Interact. Mob. Wearable Ubiquit. Technol. 1(3), 1–21 (2017)

28. Noh, W., Lee, M., Cheon, H., Kim, J., Lee, K., Cho, J.: TakeOut: drawing application using distributed user interface for being close to real experience. In: Proceedings of the 2016 ACM International Joint Conference on Pervasive and Ubiquitous Computing: Adjunct, pp. 173–176. ACM, Heidelberg (2016)

29. Trimeche, M., Suomela, R., Aaltonen, A., Lorho, G., Dossaji, T., Aarnio, T., Tuoriniemi, S.: Enhancing end-user experience in a multi-device ecosystem. In: Proceedings of the 4th International Conference on Mobile and Ubiquitous Multimedia, pp. 19–25. ACM, Christchurch (2005)

30. Li, J., Bu, Y., Chen, S., Tao, X., Lu, J.: FollowMe: on research of pluggable infrastructure for context-awareness. In: 20th International Conference on Advanced Information Networking and Applications, AINA 2006. IEEE (2006)

31. Johansson, D., Wiberg, M.: Conceptually advancing "Application Mobility" towards design: applying a concept-driven approach to the design of mobile IT for home care service groups. Int. J. Ambient Comput. Intell. (IJACI) 4(3), 20–32 (2012)

32. Sørensen, H., Raptis, D., Kjeldskov, J., Skov, M.B.: The 4C framework: principles of interaction in digital ecosystems. In: Proceedings of the 2014 ACM International Joint Conference on Pervasive and Ubiquitous Computing, pp. 87–97. ACM, Seattle (2014)

33. Turunen, M., Kallinen, A., Sànchez, I., Riekki, J., Hella, J., Olsson, T., Melto, A., Rajaniemi, J.P., Hakulinen, J., Mäkinen, E., Valkama, P.: Multimodal interaction with speech and physical touch interface in a media center application. In: Proceedings of the International Conference on Advances in Computer Entertainment Technology, pp. 19–26. ACM, Athens (2009)

34. Sørense, H., Kjeldskov, J.: The interaction space of a multi-device, multi-user music experience. In: Proceedings of the 7th Nordic Conference on Human-Computer Interaction: Making Sense Through Design, pp. 504–513. ACM, Copenhagen (2012)

35. Jokela, T., Ojala, J., Olsson, T.: A diary study on combining multiple information devices in everyday activities and tasks. In: Proceedings of the 33rd Annual ACM Conference on Human Factors in Computing Systems, pp. 3903–3912. ACM, Seoul (2015)

36. Nguyen, N.T., Lee, H.: 'Hop-to-select' traverse with gestural input in an eye-off interaction. In: Proceedings of the 29th Australian Conference on Computer-Human Interaction, pp. 597–601. ACM, Brisbane (2017)

37. Nguyen, N.T., Nanayakkara, S., Lee, H.: Visual field visualizer: easier & scalable way to be aware of the visual field. In: Proceedings of the 9th Augmented Human International Conference, pp. 1–3. ACM, Seoul (2018)

The INmobility Project: Modes of Textualities and Unpredictable Visualities of Everyday Life

Luisa Paraguai[✉]

Pontifical Catholic University of Campinas, Campinas, Brazil
luisa.donati@puc-campinas.edu.br

Abstract. The text is concerned with the contemporary condition of everyday life transformed by mobile technologies and digital networks. The article discusses new possibilities for behaving and for occupying urban space since mobile phones connected to the Web enable real time informational exchanges – data access, and interpersonal communication processes. In big cities such as São Paulo, pedestrians, drivers, and motorcyclists have diverse modes of choosing their routes and moving because they use mobile technologies, which superimpose the urban landscape with layers of data. By understanding other possible perceptions of urban space, the INmobility project – a digital artwork – makes visible personal experiences, using topological structures of users' visual perception by the recombination of images of the city. As a result, visual narratives emerge, structured through computational algorithms, and create different perspectives and visual patterns of people's everyday routine.

Keywords: Art and design · Art and technology
Everyday experiences and perceptions · Computational codes and visualities

1 Introduction: Mobilities in Physical and Wireless Networks: Urban Transport, Hybrid Space, and Mobile Communication

The INMobility project draws on the concept of "automobility" as an urban condition that helps understand ways of travelling in a big city. Following Urry (2004: 26) it "captures a double sense, both of the humanist self as in the notion of autobiography, and of objects or machines that possess a capacity for movement, as in automatic and automaton" [1]. The use of the car has proposed particular relationships between human and technological objects, and in some way, organized possible complex models of social and cultural organizational structures to approach the urban landscape. People use cars to move between work and home, leisure and work, home and leisure, and face lenghty commuting times in this process. As a "machine space" (Horvath 1974: 167–168) [2], people are able to change physical mobilities and social contexts across particular distances; this technological embodiment has spatially stretched and time-compressed ways of perceiving and constructing everyday life, by encapsulating people in a personal, cocooned, and moving capsule. For this art project it needs to figure out transformations of temporal relationships and visual perceptions, when, for example, people look at cityscape while driving in congested traffic; there are

© Springer International Publishing AG, part of Springer Nature 2018
A. Marcus and W. Wang (Eds.): DUXU 2018, LNCS 10919, pp. 640–652, 2018.
https://doi.org/10.1007/978-3-319-91803-7_48

resynchronizations of current time-space patterns, with perceptive implications about signifying distances and occupying temporal intervals.

Second, it is necessary to comprehend mobility as users' behavior between distinctive spaces – physical and digital – that have as many dimensions as interconnections. Mediated communication devices have configured a mode of existence, juxtaposing actions in physical domains and connections in the digital contexts simultaneously. The concept of "hybrid space" (De Souza e Silva 2004) [3] is quite important to comprehend the symbolic and aesthetic perspectives of everyday life. The term hybrid implies the combination of elements from distinct natures and the proposal of unexpected results when the author investigated cultural changes from the use of mobile devices. According to Santaella (2007: 224) [4], "interstitial space" is another theoretical term to understand users' actions combining urban spaces and digital contexts through mobile technologies. The term interstitial points out the possibility of forming or occupying interstices – spaces in between, and defines the dynamic condition of behaving while dealing with distinct natures – digital and physical universes – during any mobile call. Lemos (2010: 4) [5] affirms that "place is now the result of a set of physical, cultural and economic characteristics: physical dimensions and a database". These actual configurations have enabled a dynamic perspective on everyday interactions, combining face-to-face and mediated relationships through synchronous and asynchronous exchanges. People renegotiate space-time organizations as they circulate in the world. As a result, they deal with different modes of interaction simultaneously 'to be on the move' – to operate and produce within in-between physical and digital spaces and times. So, the mediated body combines "bodily zones" (Hall 1990a) [6] with possible presences established by online interactions - virtual borders of control and privacy. It can no longer only be sustained by an identity, or a physicality; it expands according to its ability to make connections, to access and to be accessed. The constant possibilities of interfacing with other networks have established a constant renegotiation of the body space's boundaries.

Third, mobile devices and wireless communication can create some flexibility for people's movements modelled by circumstances, producing multiple activities such as writing a text or sending a tip to the radio station about the traffic while driving, spatially desynchronized from each other, but integrated by the temporal dimension. This means that users can compose complex structures, contingent patterns of social life – self-created narratives – juggling fragments of time and actions. Thinking about networks and flows of information and bodies means to consider other perceptions and configurations of movements to perform daily life, and so, to perceive and comprehend the world. "Movement often involves an embodied experience of the material and social modes of dwelling-in-motion, places of and for activities in their own right" (Urry 2007: 11) [7], and people have articulated those organizations and systems upon physical and informational – data networks. Therefore, the world can be understood as a negotiation process among different actual events, according to different protocols of communication and networks such as telecommunication systems and wireless networks. Reality is understood as a dynamic process of flows.

The INmobility project is concerned with visualities of temporary physical and digital networks, juxtaposed by synchronous live messages and images shared. The proposal of narratives to be produced is to visualize daily actions as ways to perform everyday activities in big cities, and so, modes of perception and reading the surrounding space. Nowadays, mobile technologies have evoked from drivers other distinct behaviors, creating the condition of driving a car with a participative way of creating their routes in urban areas.

2 Everyday Life: Modes of Spatial Occupation

Motion and emotion – the car is a place to exercise subjectivity in urban spaces, a private cocoon in which feelings and experiences are released in behaviors and gestures; those movements are modes of perception, affecting ways of sociability - formal and informal attitudes. According to Featherstone,

> The automobile is one everyday object where human beings regularly encounter new technologies in their everyday lives and learn to 'inhabit technology'. More and more aspects of everyday driving becomes [sic] a mediated process in which technology ceases to be a visible tool or technique, but becomes a world in which the boundaries and interfaces between humans and technological systems become blurred, refigured and difficult to disentangle (Featherstone 2005: 10) [8].

As such, driving a car is a technologically ritual process, in which people nowadays perform their everyday life remotely while organizing unexpected physical displacements like being stuck in traffic jams. The vehicle is a ubiquitous object embedded with new features, for example self-parking, adaptive cruise control, and multi-zone climate control, which augment people's actions, since being in the automobile is not only driving. In the context of drivers and mobile gadgets, symbiotic relationships between the object and the user improve those possibilities when accessing information remotely on the Web. They articulate different protocols of communication and modes of uncoordinated distribution of information, and they question other space and time relationships through the process of virtualization. So, it is related to potentialize modes of driving, transforming routines and activities of everyday life, and this is related to the INmobility project.

Information is flowing, dependent on cultural, economic, and political relationships, and it is globally structured; nevertheless, information is also structured as negotiation processes of local experiences. It means that "depending on the relevance of each segment for the dominant logic of each network' there are 'different geometries and geographies" (Castells 2009: 26) [9]. Social inclusions and exclusions are still present, reaffirming and creating individualized experiences in physical spaces – "differential mobility", and developing other informational filters attached to them – "differential spaces" (De Souza e Silva and Frith 2012: 155–156) [10]. During periods of traffic jams in the city of São Paulo, it is quite common to share streets and avenues with people selling snacks, drinks and mobile chargers. Usually, areas occupied by cars in traffic jams or waiting for the traffic lights, such as main roads, are populated by both vehicles and an informal transient market of ambulant vendors – a situated space by an activity, nowadays even more common.

The densest parts of the city of São Paulo are the repositories of recent immigrants (Burdett and Sudjic 2011) [11], explaining the increase in informal jobs around those areas such as street vendors. "In Brazil and Mexico it is estimated that about one million people are directly involved in street foods and in India over three million" (Fellows and Hilmi 2011) [12]. Those activities qualify the modes of spatial occupation as fluid, with no defined period of time, and moveable, since street vendors change location easily. They can be on foot, on bicycle, or using a push cart. Finding an opportunity to sell emerges from the unpredictable condition of the congested avenue. Signing or creating displays, hawkers improve the way in which street and snack foods are displayed and sold, while walking between cars. Because they must share the streets, drivers find the streets congested with not only vehicles and motorcycles, but bikes and people walking in between. Those moments can be dissolved and created in another location of people's routes, as temporary conditions of behavior. Assuming those spatial conditions and agents – drivers, riders and pedestrians – as a complex system, patterns arise out of a multiplicity of relatively simple interactions among them.

Comparing the concepts of borders and boundaries in the natural world (Sennet 2011: 324) [13], dialogues among hawkers and drivers can be assumed as momentary borders, zones of interaction not fixed and determined dynamically. Those attitudes create spatial relationships – specific localities for occupation, able to exchange and influence both perspectives. While drivers are immobile physically and situated dynamically on digital networks – through email, Facebook, Skype, and SMS – local pedestrians emerge from nowhere developing strategies of living and being noticed – spaces of life. They configure other attributes to usual artefacts by remixing formal elements and material characteristics to design other functionalities. The practice of driving and looking outside through mirrors, determines another perception of the world. These other modes of seeing evoke a 'fluid choreography' (Featherstone 2005: 8) [8], but still suggest an effective private space. The mirrors enable drivers to experience other ways of perceiving the world. Blind spots such as the A-pillar (also called the windshield pillar), side-view mirror, and interior rear-view mirror can influence the visibility and the identification of the objects and people around the vehicle. So, when people and cars move, those visual readings are constantly changing and embodying different elements of the scene. Drivers and pedestrians engage in constant negotiation on those avenues.

Therefore, the everyday practice is the "investigation of ways in which users operate' or 'ways of operating, or doing things" (Certeau 1984: 474) [14] – an operational logic in which pedestrians and drivers can go through and organize places creating their own routes – spatial narratives. "It is impossible to discuss experiential space without introducing the objects and places that define space" (Tuan 2011: 136) [15]. According to Santos (1999: 181) [16], scientific-technical-informational objects have been created to work systemically, revealing inner discourse as modes of use, seduction and actions: "space is a system of objects and a system of actions". From those perspectives, the space occupied by people, constituted by technical objects and actions, has transformed cultural entities and even created new ones. It is not possible to comprehend the full meaning of an object, without taking into account the intentionality of the human action that has produced the object and placed it in a location in space.

This process of movement and practice between ideas, intentions and actions, actualized by mobile technologies, has the possibility of expanding, and, even improving, the understanding of a certain urban order. The occurrence of those movements needs a previous order, determined by the functional cartography of the city – urban mapping, which nowadays has been superposed by singular experiences through distributed networks. As Simondon observed,

> *the individualised technical object corresponds most directly to the human dimension. The human individual is not dominated by it as he is in the mining or any other network. Nor does he dominate it, making it an extension of his hands or prosthetic device, as happens in component technology. He neither dominates nor is dominated but enters into a kind of dialectic (Simondon 1980: 9) [17].*

Taking into account Simondon's perspective, technological objects should be embedded into everyday life as a negotiation process, changing behaviors, rethinking values, and choosing other ways of life. Mobile devices create other possibilities for people being temporarily 'on the move', and in a way, create new possibilities for using these devices, demanding from users the comprehension to accommodate real-time choices and feedbacks in time and space. For Tuan,

> *Spatial ability is essential to livelihood, but spatial knowledge at the level of symbolic artic-ulation in words and images is not. (…) Spatial ability precedes spatial knowledge. Mental worlds are refined out of sensory and kinaesthetic experiences. Spatial knowledge enhances spatial ability (Tuan 2011: 74) [15].*

The author recognized spatial experience as a process of negotiating life and producing knowledge. Different from the knowledge elaborated on an iconic or a metaphorical mode, the enacting paradigm of cognition is centred on sensory motor dynamics –corporeal activities– and presents physical mediations between individuals and their contexts as fundamental and decisive for the production of meaning. According to Stewart (2007: 90) [18] "without action there is no world nor perception". For the author, the action is a pre-requirement for the perception; the understanding of the surroundings can make sense as actions take place. So, knowledge can be under-stood as patterns of embodied experiences, which necessarily have to be culturally and socially shared.

Mobile technological context, based on distributed networks, generates a spatial structure with specificities dynamically adapted to the communicational demands and necessities from own nodes. As a result, for each new connection the network topology can be modified based on the existence of nodes/users' mobile phones and their abilities for communication. Networks import not only the organizational structure with potential rhizomatic characteristics, but it needs to understand the production of information in dialogues, exchanges. The attempt to comprehend and incorporate the operational network structure is to formalize a social shared space as zones of fluxes, and not determined spaces of information distribution. As Gordon and De Souza e Silva (2001: 97) [19] affirm "information is not just something to consume. One's awareness of nearby information (and people) can also be a context for performance".

Space as material support for social practices has incorporated historical and technological characteristics, which constantly transform it through the simultaneity of uses and meanings. This dynamic and complex condition – the juxtaposition of distinct information and diverse temporalities of urban life, defines the contemporary urban space can no longer be exactly discerned because many activities can be carried on at the same time, thus configuring an overlapping construction of reality.

3 The INmobility Project: Textualities, Visualities and Narratives

The INmobility project is concerned with the organization and processes of visible structures and their meanings defined by computing languages and/or script that accesses data and creates media objects and physical environments – digital and material artefacts.

As Tuan (2011: 164–165) [15] wrote, "the art project seeks visibility, as an attempt to give sensible form to the moods, feelings, and rhythms of functional life". Working with computational algorithms, the INmobility project creates visual interfaces to mediate modes of perception and everyday activities. The algorithm runs as mediator of distinct procedures and domains of information – computational objects, syntactic elements, and symbolic meanings – to configure the art context. The visual results of this project formalize human and machine relationships and models to present the sensible. So, understanding the ways that code is used in the processes of creation and production requires a general knowledge of how form is manipulated by the computer. For Manovich, working with software now is:

> a layer that permeates all areas of contemporary societies. Therefore, if we want to understand contemporary techniques of control, communication, representation, simulation, analysis, decision-making, memory, vision, writing, and interaction, our analysis can't be complete until we consider this software layer (Manovich 2011: 8) [20].

Manovich recognized computational language and its elements in contemporary methodologies of producing content and knowledge. It is not about symbolic meanings or metaphors translated to the digital domain; for the author, modes of behaving and thinking are interconnected and modelled by the numeric layer. Hayles (2002: 24) [21] had a similar theoretical approach when writing about machines and their textualities; according to the author the computational code can be counted as "an inscription technology because it is possible to produce material changes, read as marks". Those models of formal creation and production evoke other attitudes, practices and methodologies in creative processes. One important difference, however, is that there is no systematic way to predict the behavior of a software application by inspecting it; actually, the only way to assess it is to run it. Its non-deterministic characteristic can produce non-controlled results, and thus, poetics validate the uncertainty as an experiential process.

Working with encoding and decoding processes, I use syntactic and semantic behaviors to actualize everyday routine by computing laws and their unpredictable visualities. Assuming those models of creation and production, some intrinsic conceptual elements of computing languages, such as repetition and parameterisation, elaborate other perceptions of the INmobility project visually as presented in the images bellow (Figs. 1 and 2). "Within the visual realm, repetition encourages our eyes to dance. Controlling repetition is a way to choreograph human eye movement" (Reas, McWilliams and Barendse 2010: 49) [22]. Repetition is deeply embedded into the language of computing as other visual art languages; therefore it modulates and creates sensations of depth and motion, as for example optical's art proposals. Repetition can also be an important element within time-based work such as video, animation, and live software. In this domain, repetition becomes a form of rhythm and can be used to produce complex forms.

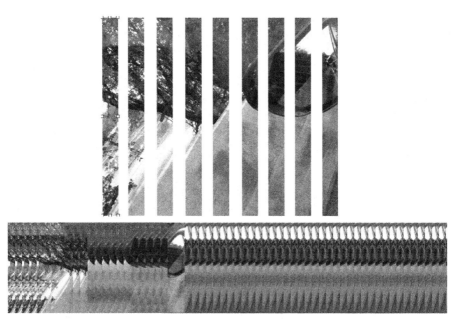

Fig. 1. High speed and more repetition of thinner slices, 2012, Luisa Paraguai, photographic media. (Used with permission.)

By modulating the slices and their repetitive composition in the INmobility project, the visual results recreate sensations of time spent and therefore the reading and perception of the outside context. The focus is on the instant, precisely used because it is recurrent. The MobMesh algorithm processes embedded iterations and repetitions as a contemporary aesthetic proposal to produce visualities. It emphasizes the way in which the interface presents the content – a metalanguage process. "It is the 'infinity' of the process that gives a new sense to the device of variation" (Eco 2005) [23].

The construction of slices determined by parameters is also important. "Defined broadly, a parameter is a value that has an effect on the output of a process; parameters can describe, encode and quantify the options and constraints at play in a system" (Reas, McWilliams and Barendse 2010: 95) [22]. For the authors, while transformation describes a parameter's effect on form, repetition offers a way to explore a field of possible designs for favored variations. Both visualization and simulation require the use of parameters to define the system, and they describe how data or other inputs will influence the behaviors of that system. In contrast to using random numbers to explore a field of possible designs, parametric systems are under control to determine the final result.

In the INmobility project, each image, grabbed and uploaded is decoded and divided into vertical slices according to local values: distance travelled and time spent.

Fig. 2. Low speed and less repetition of bigger slices, 2012, Luisa Paraguai, photographic media. (Used with permission)

Therefore, parametric control can make the management of complex and unpredictable forms possible, by connecting multiple elements. Modularity involves the arrangement of one or more elements to produce a multitude of forms; elements are not transformed, but simply repositioned. The new visual composition arranges each element in such a way that it occupies a unique part of the image space. In this way, parameters and possible values in conjunction with repetition are used to generate multiple versions – singular pieces into the complex system.

With this in mind, the INmobility project articulates mathematical relationships to determine the number and the width of the slices as well as their repetitions. The use of those elements as patterns to be repeated, according to the driver's speed, considers the transformation from the semantic content – meanings of those captured images, to the syntactic dimension – to data visualization. The aesthetic exploration of variable elements and the range of possible values create relationships between repetition and transformation of those images, and consequently, the narratives.

In the field of art and design, the use of computing algorithms based on statistical methods translates mathematical abstraction into visible material results, and according to Martin-Barbero (apud Santaella 2007) [4], they "hybridise the symbolic density of the numerical abstraction with the perceptive sensoriality". The Paulo Costa and Luisa Paraguai's proposal is to think about the relationship between materialities and textualities in the digital context – mathematical models with possibilities of developing artefacts, not as a mimesis pattern but as a simulation model of behaving. According to Hayles (2002: 22) [21] "material metaphor" can explain the relationship between codes and visualities, defining a "term that foregrounds the traffic between words and physical artefacts". The visual results are not totally predictable, but the poetic concerns with the cultural and social dimension of people behaving in big cities. In other words,

> *our contemporary society can be characterised as a software society and our culture can be justifiably called a software culture – because today software plays a central role in shaping both the material elements and many of the immaterial structures which together make up 'culture' (Manovich 2011: 8) [20].*

The INmobility project explores images and narratives (Fig. 3), trying to track ad-hoc networks and to map those activities. The visual results create landscapes that expand or contract the passing concerns of people, aesthetically exploring their perception. The understanding of location can take place through the visual exercise of different scales. From those visual narratives, parallel dimensions are exercised in order to question the feeling of belonging to those metropolitan areas. The materialization and extension of a driver's time spent can be clearly understood during traffic jams, admitting interventions as inscriptions from other dimensions of the information through remote data. In this context, the temporal dimension is considered a management element of dealing with the city. According to Urry (2004: 28) [1] "automobility develops 'instantaneous' time to be managed in complex, heterogeneous and uncertain ways".

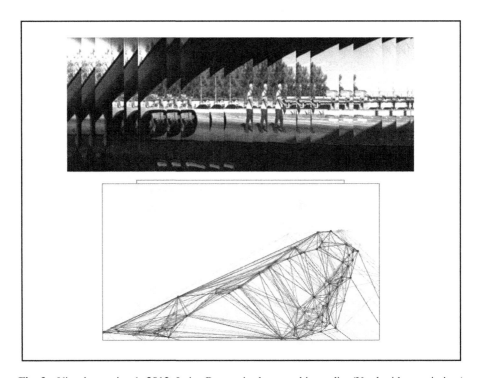

Fig. 3. Visual narrative 1, 2012, Luisa Paraguai, photographic media. (Used with permission.)

The project intends to represent the tension between distinct materialities of space-time relationships simultaneously operated by people with mobile devices. The operational model transforms informational patterns – computational and bodily, electromagnetic and spatial – into shapes and visual spaces. The aesthetic choice for a recursive technique generates forms with multiple effects and patterns; the software processes embedded iterations and sequences as a part of its functions.

By understanding the visual narrative as a computational system, unpredictable operations turn to a method of writing. But, more important than creating representations through different visual characteristics, the intention of mapping the attributes of data is the topology of subjectivities. The poetic procedure based on mathematical operations can recreate, in some way, and question the relationships between public and private spaces, body and space contours, to express dynamic organizational practices of the city.

The visual discourse can be understood as negotiations about spatial orientations. In other words, the construction of situations, momentary ambiances, defines perpetual interactions between people's behaviors and spaces, which gives rise to and transforms them, behaviors and actions in time contained in transitory visual arrangements. The narrative as a poetic object, according to Lefebvre (1960) [24], plays with moments to be repeated. The repetition is a law, modelled by possibilities of extending and condensing the perception of the time according to the traffic. It is important to affirm that the idea of movement, visually defined by the rhythm of the slices (Figs. 1 and 2), is related to different moments of tension and ease – day-to-day personal experiences while driving in the city of São Paulo. Considering the visual results of the INmobility project, when there is no traffic, people do not notice the outside and the contours of the cityscape become a blurred image with no definition. On the other side, the heavy traffic expands and potentializes other attitudes since drivers combine physical (brushing hair, doing make-up, writing any note) and digital (reading and sending emails, checking facebook feeds, taking pictures) domains. Behaviors are context dependent. The environment serves as an ever-changing mode of perceptions and actions. The artist's intention is to evoke other cartographies for perceptions by the pleasure experience of recombination and reinvention.

The blur limits of compounding physical spaces and informational contexts evoke other dimensions for people's daily lives; the narratives proposed here have pointed out mediated practices to create particular visual objects and subjects in specific localities. The concept of location, broadly dependent on organization of information, considers both geographical aspects (space and place) and social constructions (networked interactions). So "new interfaces such as mobile, location-aware technologies and mapping software make it clear that both places and locations are still important to the construction of people's identities and to the development of sociability" (De Souza e Silva and Frith, 2012: 169) [10]. The authors connected locality and networks to identities and being social, but these connections need to change habits of seeing to criticize boundaries, to experiment with undisciplined attitudes, to try different negotiations between self and circumstance. The mobile condition of behaving can make the city more open and flexible, and stimulate a social difference.

The human sense of space is quite dynamic because it is related to "action – which can be done in a given space, rather than what is seen by passive viewing" (Hall 1990) [6].

Perception and action relationships present themselves as phenomenological experiences in which the individual and the ambient are included by mobile media. The understanding of mobile devices does not reside in the technology itself but it is determined by its ability to extend and model human activities and relationships over time and space. Locality and recognition define possibilities of inclusion in distinct social networks, and mobile gadgets augment opportunities of working, studying and living.

So, mobile users, technologically mediated, operate simultaneously in different, unrelated contexts and dimensions, like several folds of existence. Therefore, those artefacts do shape and "alter the way in which we engage with the places we move through" (De Sousa e Silva and Frith 2012: 45) [10], proposing other cultural constructions in which people interact with and perceive the world.

4 Final Considerations

More recently, people have incorporated mobile devices to perform formal and informal everyday activities, and now it is possible to observe the frequent repetition of behaviors everywhere, establishing other social bonds and borders – cultural spaces and zones of dialogues. By establishing those contours, people have expanded physical limits and reconfigured body spaces, mediated by mobile artefacts, determining other distinct comfortable distances already established (Hall 1990) [25], combining physical distances and informational connections.

The occupation of space is also important, specifically as modes of behaving aesthetically – the sensible (Ferrara 2007) [26], and their possibilities of redefining cultural attitudes. The experience of objects, surroundings, and/or people evokes an "aesthetic perception" (Seel 2005) [27] when a particular ordinary or extraordinary situation is created, a potential condition of transformation. For Ferrara (2007) [26], spatiality, visuality/visibility and communicability are categories of space, and phenomenological processes to enact (Noe 2008) [28] in the world; so they have been manifested differently, combining different structures and media. The actual spatiality, dependent on the hybridization of everyday practices, technologies and subjectivities, is a dynamic construction of a certain order – a manner of experiencing.

Mobile technology is a potential framework and people's attitudes are combining the actual scenario with information during every day practices. Physical and cartographic maps usually offer defined routes, such as street and road networks, but the localities determined by mobile technologies have established other sources of information about the city; they function as a drivers' live map about directions and particular ways between places, for example, where vehicles reduce their speeds because of flood area. The use of mobile devices creates cultural filters about how to walk and to drive in the city of São Paulo, attributing new significances to everyday routine. The intention of the INmobility project is to give visibility to personal experiences, including those of place. Thinking about relationships between visibility and spatial perception, the enactive approach is considered since looks are not mental entities, but environmental properties – contextual negotiations; they are relational, to be sure – relationships between objects and the location of users – an encounter between appearances and existences (Noe 2008) [28]. So, the visual proposal is to evoke other perception of topologies by the recombination and reinvention of images. It means that from visual narratives created by computational algorithms, patterns not usually perceived are evoked (Paraguai 2017) [29]. The binary logic can add information and abstract content in complex processes, and the project aesthetically evokes these symbolic messages working with numbers, such as the speed of cars. This aesthetic articulation between distinct texts - codes and images – can materialize and present some structure, not perceived before (Manovich 2010) [30].

According to Santos (1999) [16] the logic of the device proposes other spatial and temporal perceptions, and so affects human behavior and relationships. The INmobility project makes other connections possible, questioning location and awareness of codes and decoding processes, as modes of behaving and perceiving others and the world. Assuming the dialogue to comprehend machine and human relationships, the materiality of codes drives aesthetical choices as parameters to generate visual results.

The final consideration is about different processes of visualisation between humans and machines, and how an artist-engineer can appropriate that content as poetic proposal. The act of reading and understanding the world depends on the ability of recognizing its patterns, and human and machine approaches constantly reveal the differences in what is visible for each system. Working with computing means developing mental abilities of comprehending mathematical sentences in order to be figured in numerical representations. So, the narrative forms produced on the INmobility project can be defined as a process of "direct visualization" (Manovich 2010: 24–25) [30], understanding that the produced images spatially recompose their values, linking the captured image and its transformed versions to modes of living and behaving situated spaces.

In conclusion, the act of reading and understanding the world depends on the ability to recognize and signify patterns. Patterns reside in the domain of modules and interconnections to prompt rethinking attitudes, practices and methodologies in the process of creation. The INmobility project uses non-deterministic characteristic of software and their unpredictable results to validate uncertainty as a process to be experienced. The project embodies the poetic aspects of writing and creating visualities.

References

1. Urry, J.: The system of automobility. Theory Cult. Soc. **21**(4/5), 25–39 (2004)
2. Horvath, R.: Machine space. Geogr. Rev. **64**, 167–188 (1974)
3. De Sousa e Silva, A.: From multiuser environments as (virtual) spaces to (hybrid) spaces as multiuser environments: Nomadic technology devices and hybrid communication places. Tese de Doutorado. UFRJ/CFCH/ECO, Rio de Janeiro (2004)
4. Santaella, L.: Linguagens líquidas na era da mobilidade. Paulus, São Paulo (2007)
5. Lemos, A.: Locative media and surveillance at the boundaries of informational territories. In: Firmino, R.J., Duarte, F., Ultramari, C. (eds.) ICTs for Mobile and Ubiquitous Urban Infrastructures: Surveillance, Locative Media and Global Networks. IGI Global, Hershey (2010)
6. Hall, E.T.: The Hidden Dimension. Anchor Books Editions, Garden City (1990)

7. Urry, J.: Mobilities. Polity, Cambridge (2007)
8. Featherstone, M.: Automobilities, an introduction. In: Featherstone, M., Thrift, N., Urry, J. (eds.) Automobilities, pp. 1–24. SAGE Publications Ltd., London, Thousand Oaks, New Delhi (2005)
9. Castells, M.: Communication Power. Oxford University, New York (2009)
10. De Sousa e Silva, A., Frith, J.: Mobile Interfaces in Public Spaces: Locational Privacy, Control, and Urban Sociability. Routledge, New York and London (2012)
11. Burdett, R., Sudjic, D.: Living in the endless city. The Urban Age Project by the London School of Economics and Deutsche Bank's Alfred Herrhausen Society. Phaindon Press Ltd., New York (2011)
12. Fellows, P., Hilmi, M.: Selling Street and Snack foods. FAO, Rome (2011)
13. Sennet, R.: Boundaries and borders. In: Burdett, R., Sudjic, D. (eds.) Living in the Endless City. The Urban Age Project by the London School of Economics and Deutsche Bank's Alfred Herrhausen Society. Phaindon Press Ltd., New York (2011)
14. De Certeau, M.: The Practice of Everyday Life. University of California Press, Berkeley (1984)
15. Tuan, Y.F.: Space an Place. The perspective of Experience. University of Minnesota Press, Minneapolis (2011)
16. Santos, M.: A Natureza do espaço: Técnica e Tempo. Razão e Emoção. Editora Hucitec, São Paulo (1999)
17. Simondon, G.: On the Mode of Existence of Technical Objects. University of Western Ontario, London, Canada (1980)
18. Stewart, J.: Enactive cognitive sciences_1. In: Luciani, A., Cadoz, C. (eds.) Enaction and Enactive Interfaces: A Handbook of Terms, pp. 89–91. Enactive Systems Books, Grenoble (2007)
19. Gordon, E., De Sousa e Silva, A.: Net locality: Why Location Matters in a Networked World. Wiley-Blackwell, Oxford (2011)
20. Manovich, L.: Software takes command (2011). http://manovich.net/content/04-projects/070-cultural-software/67-article-2011.pdf. Accessed 09 Feb 2018
21. Hayles, N.K.: Writing Machines. The MIT Press, London, UK (2002)
22. Reas, C., McWilliams, C., Barendse, J.: Form+Code in Design, Art, and Architecture. Princeton Architectural Press, New York (2010)
23. Eco, U.: Innovation & repetition: between modern & postmodern aesthetics. Daedalus, J. Am. Acad. Arts Sci. **134**(4), 191–207 (2005)
24. Lefebvre, H.: The theory of moments and the construction of situations Internationale Situationniste #4 (1960). http://www.cddc.vt.edu/sionline/si/moments.html. Accessed 09 Feb 2018
25. Hall, E.T.: The Silent Language. Anchor Books Editions, Garden City, New York (1993)
26. Ferrara, L.D. (ed.): Espaços comunicantes. Annablume, Grupo ESPACC, São Paulo (2007)
27. Seel, M.: Aesthetics of Appearing. Stanford University Press, California (2005)
28. Noe, A.: Action in Perception. The MIT Press, Cambridge (2008)
29. Paraguai, L.: Image, flux, temporalité: narrations fluctuantes. In: D'Angelo, B., Soulages, F., Venturelli, S. (eds.) De la photographie au post-digital. Du contemporain au post-contemporain, 1st edn., pp. 100–110. L'Harmattan, Paris (2017)
30. Manovich, L.: What is visualisation? (2010). http://manovich.net/content/04-projects/064-what-is-visualization/61_article_2010.pdf. Accessed 09 Feb 2018

Bridging the Digital Divide: One Smartphone at a Time

Kathryn Summers[1(✉)], Noel Alton[2], Anna Haraseyko[1],
and Rachel Sherard[1]

[1] University of Baltimore, Baltimore, USA
ksummers@ubalt.edu
[2] Western Governors University, Salt Lake City, USA
noel.alton@wgu.edu

Abstract. Growing use of smartphones among low-literacy/low-income urban populations is increasing access to the internet for this group, a group that has been historically disadvantaged in terms of internet access. This digital divide has had enormous historical importance and many negative practical effects on health, income, civic participation, and education [1–4]. While providing internet access through libraries made the internet available to many people, library-based access to the internet did not guarantee its use (i.e., penetration). Now that the rise of smart phones [5] is finally narrowing the access gap, we need to understand how adults with low literacy/low income are using smart phones. What are their assumptions about the internet? What do they value? What barriers to successful use persist?

This is a small-scale exploratory and descriptive study of smartphone use by low literacy/low income urban residents who are smartphone dependent or smartphone dominant. Understanding the information behaviors, attitudes, and goals of this demographic, as well as the barriers and opportunities provided by smartphone-based internet access, is an essential step in making online information and services more broadly available.

Keywords: Smartphones · Low literacy · Digital divide · Information behavior
Ethnography

1 Introduction

Benefits of access to the internet include access to information; increased connection to other people; mapping and locational services; financial tools for banking, paying bills, and shopping; and even opportunities for making money. Internet access correlates with both economic status and literacy level, and poorer, less literate adult Americans are less likely to have internet access at home. However, a growing number of U.S. adults obtain access to the internet through smartphones. As of 2018, 77% of American adults own smartphones (up from 35% in 2011) [6]. The Pew Research Center defines smartphone dependence as "[having] a smartphone but [lacking] other broadband internet service at home, and/or [having] limited options for going online other than their cell phone [5]. Many of the benefits of internet access can be obtained by those who are smartphone

© Springer International Publishing AG, part of Springer Nature 2018
A. Marcus and W. Wang (Eds.): DUXU 2018, LNCS 10919, pp. 653–672, 2018.
https://doi.org/10.1007/978-3-319-91803-7_49

dependent, but we need a deeper understanding of how low-literacy/low-income populations, who are the most likely to be smartphone dependent, navigate the challenges of internet access.

1.1 Internet Access

According to recent Pew Research Center reports [5–8], there has been a rapid increase in internet use in American adults across all socio-economic statuses; in 2000 roughly half of all American adults used the internet, today that total is nine in ten adults [9]. Despite this near ubiquitous use of the internet, there are still marked differences in adoption based on race, age, geography, and economic status. There is a nearly 20% difference in adoption from low-income adults (less than $30,000) to high-income adults ($75,000 plus). Across different community types, only 78% of adults living in rural communities have adopted use of the internet [9]. Nor does internet use correlate directly to broadband access in the home, as adults who make less than $30,000 per year have a home broadband rate of only 53%, and only 63% of those in rural communities have home broadband [9].

Most research on the digital divide has focused on economic factors [4, 10, 11], age [12], country [13], or race [7]. Many researchers have focused on internet access in less developed countries (e.g., [14]), but research in the U.S. demonstrates that low-income residents' in the US experience similar "disruptions" to their internet access as those described for low-income residents in other countries [11]. One-fifth of adults in the low-income bracket of less than $30,000 per year consider themselves "smartphone-only" users for internet access, compared to only 5% of adults who make $75,000 or more [8, 9]. Nor does smartphone ownership guarantee consistent internet access, as those in the lower income brackets who are smartphone dependent often find their services cut off due to non-payment or broken technology [7, 11, 15].

1.2 Literacy Considerations

Literacy is defined as the ability to use "printed and written information to function in society, to achieve one's goals, and to develop one's knowledge and potential" [16]. In the 2003 National Assessment of Adult Literacy (NAAL), it was reported that 42% of adult Americans were considered low-literate, defined as scoring at Below Basic or Basic in prose literacy [17]. A rating of "Basic" indicates that an individual can "[read and understand] information in short, commonplace prose texts" while individuals with a "below basic" rating can range from "non-literate" to being able to "[locate] easily identifiable information in short, commonplace prose texts" [17].

Low literate populations are often forgotten when websites are being designed. As recently as 2005, text on federal and state government sites was measured as well above an 8th grade reading level, and often at an 11th grade level or above [18]. Some research has been done on how to design websites for low-literate users [19–22]. However, we do not yet have sufficient information about how smartphones are used by low literate users, or about the additional barriers these internet users may encounter when they are smartphone dependent.[1]

This ethnographic study examined the everyday use of smartphones by low literate users. It also sought preliminary understanding of low literate users' behaviors, attitudes, and goals when using their smartphones to access the internet.

1.3   Smartphone Usage

Smartphone owners in general use their phones in the following ways:

- 62% of smartphone owners have used their phone in the last year to look up information about a health condition.
- 57% have used their phone to do online banking.
- 44% have used their phone to look up real estate listings or other information about a place to live.
- 43% to look up information about a job.[2]
- 40% to look up government services or information.
- 30% to take a class or get educational content.
- 18% to submit a job application. [5]

In addition, 68% of smartphone owners use their phones to read breaking news reports at least "occasionally" while 33% say they do this "frequently" [5]. However, these statistics, and most studies of how smartphone owners interact with and feel about their devices, fail to address the specific experiences of those who are smartphone dependent.

2   Methods

This study has two parts: qualitative analysis of 12 in-depth interviews in order to understand the smartphone usage of adults with low literacy skills, and quantitative analysis of phone activity logs for ten participants.[3] The goal of the interviews was to engage participants in discussion and storytelling about their experiences with their phones—what they believe, how they feel, what they do, and why—in order to better understand the complex nature of their experience. Interviews took place at the University of Baltimore during January and February, 2018.

---

[1] Some research has been done to investigate the use of smartphones in low literate users [23], but this research was conducted in India and focused on better understanding information security among literate users, and helping to protect their privacy.

   Research on smartphone-dependent access to the internet from outside the US has generally focused on using graphics and voice overs to help low literate users [24–26].

[2] Note, however, that 58% of households making less than $30,000 use their phones for job seeking, while only 32% of households making $75,000 or more use their phones for this activity.

[3] Two participants did not return for the phone log analysis. Multi-visit protocols can be challenging with this research population.

The qualitative data was supplemented by analyzing two six-day periods of data from the "MyActivity" logs as collected by Android phones. Ten participants participated in the activity log analysis.

The semi-structured interviews examined the following issues:

- The participant's history of smartphone ownership, including their type of contract, their provider, and their history of upgrades and replacements.
- The range of activities participants perform with their phones, including social connectivity, access to information, entertainment, mapping, and economic activities such as shopping or paying bills.
- Participants' feelings about smartphone ownership and usage, as indicated by the adjectives chosen, spontaneous statements about emotional state or emotional impact, and presented affect during the interview.

2.1   Participants

Participants were recruited for the study from a database of participants maintained by the University of Baltimore, through street recruiting, and using snowball sampling, a non-probability sampling technique used in sociology and statistics research in order to research a population which may be difficult for researchers to access.[4]

All participants but one were African Americans living in or close by Baltimore, Maryland. One participant was Caucasian, working in Baltimore but living in Baltimore County. All participants were Android phone users. Participants ranged in age from 29 to 59, with an average age of 49.4 years. In order to participate in the study, the participants were required to qualify as low literate, i.e., reading at the eighth grade level or below as measured by the Rapid Estimate of Adult Literacy in Medicine (REALM) [27].[5] Participants' REALM scores ranged from 36 to 58, with an average score of 48.1 (Table 1).

---

[4] Snowball sampling is the most commonly used sampling technique for studying hard-to-recruit populations. Its potential disadvantages are minimized by using a diverse seed (a diverse group of initial contacts, found in a variety of ways), which was done, and multiple recruitment waves (asking at least three rounds of participants to recommend additional participants), which was done [27].

[5] The REALM is one of several possible instruments for estimating adult literacy levels. It is comprised of a list of 66 words that a participant reads aloud as a facilitator keeps score of words pronounced correctly; the score is the number of correct words a participant pronounces. Although originally designed to measure health literacy, REALM has several advantages for field work— primarily in that it takes 2–5 min, requires minimal training to administer, and does not feel like a literacy test to participants. The REALM has been shown to reliably distinguish between adults at lower literacy levels [29], although it does not distinguish between adults at a 9th grade reading level or above. The REALM is also highly correlated with the Wide Range Achievement Test-Revised ($r = 0.88$), the revised Slosson Oral Reading Tests ($r = 0.96$), the revised Peabody Individual Achievement Test ($r = 0.97$, and the TOFHLA ($r = 0.84$) [30, 31]. The REALM also has a high test-retest reliability ($r = 0.97$) [28].

Table 1. Demographic characteristics of study participants.

Gender	
Male	5
Female	7
Reading level (REALM) of participants	
3rd grade or less (0–18)	0
4–6th grade (19–44)	4
7–8th grade (45–60)	8
Average REALM	48.1
Average age	49.4

2.2 Analysis

Audio recordings of the interviews were transcribed and converted to a spreadsheet format for qualitative analysis. The primary researcher conducted open coding to identify patterns and themes related to the research questions. Axial coding was then conducted to identify relationships among the open codes, and a set of standardized thematic categories was developed for systematic analysis [32–35].

Each transcript was then reviewed for matches to the thematic categories by the primary researcher and a second researcher. Differences in coding decisions between the two researchers were discussed and settled by consensus agreement.

The phone logs were recorded without condensing items into categories. The researchers developed categories in a coding process similar to that used with the transcripts. The final set of categories was agreed upon by the primary and secondary researchers. Both researchers sorted the logs into the final categories; differences were discussed and settled by consensus agreement.

3 Findings

In our analysis of the interview transcripts, we focused on participants' feelings about their smartphones, the types of usage they engaged in, the types of usage they valued most highly, and the relationship between their smartphone-based access to the internet and other ways they might use to access the internet.

This qualitative information about phone usage was then supplemented by activity log analysis for two six-day periods.

3.1 Qualitative Findings — 12 Participants

Smartphone Ownership History. Most (70%) of our participants had owned smartphones for more than four years, but only 33% of our participants had purchased their own phones. Most participants had received their phone as a gift from a spouse or a grownup child, but most smartphone owners learned to value their phones fairly quickly, and then moved on to encourage adoption by peers or purchase phones for others. One participant bought her own first phone, along with phones for her grandchildren, because her grandchildren begged for them.

P8   My husband bought us new phones, and that was the one he chose. I have no idea why.

P5   …I have three grandchildren. At first I was gonna get them one of them [phones], but Boost and Cricket and Metro came up with the four [phones] for something something price. So it was like getting close to Christmas and they wanted a phone…. Then Metro came up with the four for four plan, and that's how they got it.

Five participants had phones that were less than two years old (58%), and six (50%) participants had phones that were less than a year old. However, "new" phones did not usually correspond with high-end phones. One participant had a Samsung Galaxy S8 that was just a few days old (a gift from a grown daughter), but another participant had a Samsung Galaxy S4 that she had owned for just over a year.

Participants' ownership history was sometimes dominated by breakage and theft (one participant had owned ten phones in ten years, and another had owned seven phones in ten years). Other ownership decisions were driven by economic ups and

Table 2. History of smartphone ownership (12 participants).

Number of years as smartphone owner		
0–3 years	3	25%
4–7 years	5	42%
7+ years	4	33%
Length of ownership of current phone		
0–1 years	7	58%
2–3 years	5	42%
4+ years	0	
Source of phone		
Purchased by self	4	33%
Received as gift	8	67%
Other internet access		
Wi-fi at home but no desktop or laptop	3	25%
Use wi-fi at public locations	2	17%
Own laptop or desktop and wi fi at home	4	33%
Own laptop or desktop but no wi fi at home	2	17%
Disruptions in service within the last year (6 out of 8 reported)		
Disruptions to home wi-fi	4	50%
Disruptions to smartphone service	2	25%
Employment (9 out of 12 reported)		
Working full-time or part-time	4	44%
Not working or on disability	5	56%

downs—one participant had twice been forced to purchase new phones in order to change carriers, but the changes in carriers were triggered by difficulties in paying the phone bills. Some decisions were a response to pressure from others to upgrade. One participant upgraded because her daughter insisted; two upgraded because their service providers sent texts saying it was time to upgrade. These participants thought they "needed" to upgrade (Table 2).

Benefits of Use. Participants reported the same range of benefits from smartphone ownership as the larger population of smartphone owners: increased connections with other people, ability to find resources and locations, access to information, financial management or financial opportunities, and entertainment. However, some participants only used a few of these opportunities.

Nearly every participant mentioned the benefits of access to information about doctors or other professionals, and of being able to find locations. Several mentioned looking up the meanings of words. One participant works as a certified medical technician, so she regularly looks up the meanings of words for her job.

Similarly, all twelve participants used their phones for communication. But only seven out of twelve participants used email. Eight out of ten used social media.

Two types of benefits merit more detailed discussion because of their close connection with financial well-being: explicitly financial activities supported by phones, and activities related to making purchases.

Financial Benefits. Several participants did receive tangible financial benefits through their phone. One participant had been required to buy a smartphone for her job at Amazon, and she received notices about opportunities for overtime or for taking time off through text messages. Another participant used his phone to create music videos and monitor traffic on his YouTube channel. One participant used his phone to participate in paid online surveys, and one participant used his phone to document the before/after state of his construction and demolition jobs. Two participants had applied for jobs and two for social services on their phones. Two participants checked their benefit card balances on their phone.

Only four participants had used their phones to monitor their bank account or their benefit card balance, or to pay bills. One participant uses her smartphone to call an automated phone line to check her bank balance. But most participants did know it was possible to do banking online:

P8 I will just dial the number and go on and check my balance...But I don't go and like pull it up.

P3 Nope, but .... my niece said something to me last week about it – she say, "You know, you can put that on your phone. You ain't got to go to the bank," and pay your bills off your phone and all that. I said, "yeah." So I don't know how to do it yet, but she's supposed to be showing me, take me through the steps.

One participant had previously paid her AT&T bill with her phone, but had been unsuccessful in setting it up on her new phone, even after six months, so she was calling AT&T to pay her bill.

Shopping. Although only two participants had made purchases on their phones, five participants (42%) had used their phones to find information to support their purchasing decisions—either by looking up current sale offers, comparing prices, or receiving coupons. Two participants had store apps on their phones to provide deals and notices (McDonalds and Safeway). Three participants had looked up or browsed items for sale between 33 and 86 times during a 12-day period, although all three participants would then go in person to make purchases.

P10 I usually go to a physical store or I'll pull up online what I want. I'll go to Google and find out who has a particular item there and they give me a map right to the store. There's usually a map that goes along with it, as well as the stores address and all that..

 P9 I Google like stores I go to, like JCPenney. And I Google Walmart for my mother.

Feelings about Smartphones. Overall, participants had strong positive feelings about their phones, with the exception of one participant with lukewarm feelings who was required to carry a smartphone for her job. The strongest feelings expressed were a sense of empowerment created by access to information and resources, and a growing sense of ownership. These positive elements were counter-balanced by some feelings of vulnerability, inadequacy, and risk.

Security and Empowerment. Participants felt that their phones made them more knowledgeable and more qualified. In particular, participants mentioned the value of being connected to local and world events. All but two participants reported looking at news items on their phones (Facebook was sometimes mentioned as a source of news), and seven out of ten participants had evidence of regular news activity in their phone logs.

P3 I read it all, world news, I go all the way down, and I might be sitting there now for two hours – I read all this, I read all that, I read all this, and I just scroll on down.

P2 I can get gobbled up in reading all kinds of what's happening, in all the clickbait...

The emotional satisfaction related to having easy access to information was a strong theme:

P6 I use [it] for if I want to find a definition of a word. If I want to find a place, a location of the place. I use it for everything....for the information.... It's like a library all at once to me.

P5 I use [the phone] because it [is] more convenient for me at my age.... I can go in on Google and get [the] majority of what I need or want and it shows you a lot. And then with the smartphones I like program it, like I tell with my voice. I can say dial such and such number.... I say Google where is 1420 North Charles Street. Bam. [Snaps fingers.]

P8   You know, I think it's cool for me at age 59. It's teaching me…. It keeps you excited. It keeps you focused….and you learn something new every day. You live your life.

Smartphones also enabled a sense of playfulness around information, including the fun of pursuing random interests:

P7   Okay, so me and my friends were just researching the Goatman on Google satellite… So we looked up Bowie State, we looked up St. Mark's School, Governor Bridge, Moll Dyer, like, we was sooo gone….these are just things that I look up, places, stuff like that. Most times we use Google Maps to try to see if A) we're going to an event or B) we're just being idiots try to see if we find anything on there just so we can screenshot it and put it up on people's Facebooks.

P1   Taraji P. Henson, I looked her up last night…I looked her up because she in the movie I want to go see come out Friday….[S]he was on a talk show last night.

Similarly, participants talked about how their smartphone enabled them to do new things—find new recipes, or fix a car door.

P8   What about my Christmas cake? [Speaks into phone] "Jello Christmas cake." I made that over the holidays…In fact, I'm making my brother one today, when I go home. He loved it so much.

Sense of Ownership. The apps and capabilities that participants felt confident about tended to be described with possessives—my messages, my contacts, my pictures. It was notable that most participants also talked about the resources provided by Google, such as the Play Store or the Google page, as if they were personal belongings. For most participants, the Google page was their home base for all information activities, and the suggested content items below the search box received a lot of attention.

P4   [O]nce I'm finished I watch that completely and then I go back to my page. I go back to that and then I slide down and see what else.

P5   You can go into your Play store and get your games.

Safe Storage. Most participants had come to see their phones as an important and reliable place of storage. Important memories and other media have a place in the phone; they are preserved as photos and videos and made available for sharing— whether through social media or by showing someone on screen.

P6   When I go to church, I take pictures. I record it … so I can look back on it. And then I get home with my husband, he'll put it on the tv, got all hooked up to the tv. …like I sing in the choir in church and I get home, and …I say, "Look, babe, I'm on the screen. I'm on the TV." And he'll put me there.

P5   That the girl, the boxer [pet dog]. She is terrible…. Now, see, that's her again. She stay in my phone.

P8   If something funny is going on, if someone's dressed for a really nice event, I [take] video of my grandkids a lot…someone I haven't seen in a while, and I want to take a picture of us together…But mainly my grandchildren. That's what I take pictures of.

However, only two participants showed any awareness of the cloud, or of the potential need to back up data. Of these two, one was a musician with his own YouTube channel, and the other was a more advanced phone user—the only participant to show usage activity in every category used in this study.

Memory Aid. Many smartphone owners use their phones to support prospective memory tasks such as future appointments or grocery lists. Most of our participants did the same, but not necessarily with the tools designed for such purposes. Only one participant used her calendar to record appointments, although several said they might open their calendar to look up a particular date. Instead, one participant would use his voicemails from doctors or other providers as his record of appointments, and he would sometimes transfer his voicemail reminders onto a paper calendar at home. Another participant would take screenshots of event information that would go into her photo gallery. Participants would take pictures in their kitchen of items they wanted to remember to purchase, or screenshots online of clothing or other items that they hoped to purchase. Another participant regularly used her camera to record video reminders to herself.

P3   [L]et me show you…right where I've got my appointments set up…whenever I need or have an appointment I'll call my voicemail, and my voicemail play back all the appointments that whoever left me, and I'll hear them.

Insecurity and Self-doubt. Despite their positive feelings about their phone usage, nearly half of the participants had a lingering sense of inadequacy with regards to their phone. But most had found strategies for dealing with questions that felt safe—strategies that often involved children or grandchildren. They felt both successful and uncertain with regards to their phones.

P6   [M]atter of fact I'm still figuring it out, but at least I'm further than I was at first.
P5   When I first got it I was getting frustrated and mad…And then I start to wander through it…I found out this smartphone can do a lot…I think people should get the smartphones.
P8   My family is beginning to make me use more of the phone…. Because my grandkids, I think, are tired of me calling them to do things…. One time they would just do it. Now they'll say,…"Grandma, this is what you do, you do this, blah blah blah."…. So I'm learning more…. When I want to ask a question, if I think no one's around that would know it, I Google it. So I'm Googling a lot. So it is becoming to be…a smart phone. (laughs)

Sense of Risk/Lack of Control. Participants also saw the phone as a potential site of vulnerability. The phone could be used to "steal" their financial information, and thus their fiscal resources. The phone itself is vulnerable to breakage and theft. Even the information provided by the phone was occasionally seen as problematic.

P9   I be so scared. Because people get your information, and they will use it. So I'm skeptical of even paying my phone bill on the phone, but I have done it. 'Cause I'm thinking that people can get my account numbers from my phone, and try to go and do what they do.

P1   If someone uses your phone and [a site has saved your credit card information], and it come up and it say "Slide to pay", they just take whatever card, the last card you had and transfer the money.

P10 [We] don't do any banking from the phone because we had a bad experience. Someone got hacked, or someone close to me, it must have downloaded from my phone because they got my banking information.

In practice, the security of the phone itself is an area of significant vulnerability. More than half of the participants had lost a phone to theft. Yet four out of the twelve participants had no security code blocking access to their phones. One of those participants had used fingerprint security on her previous phone, but has not figured out how to set up fingerprint security on the Galaxy S8 (because there is no home button), and she doesn't dare use a password because she might forget it.[6] For now, her solution is to keep "personal" or financial information off her phone.

Only three participants had any kind of antivirus software on their phones. Two participants—without antivirus protection—had clear evidence of virus activity on their phones.

Most participants had a lot of applications on their phone that they had not chosen and did not use; often they did not know the purpose of the applications. The applications that were pre-installed, or were unexpectedly installed with updates, worked against the fledgling sense of ownership and empowerment that participants were developing.

Participants also perceived risks posed by the information coming through the phone. Two participants rejected Facebook in particular as a negative influence:

P5   I don't mind everybody else have Facebook, but I just don't like it. 'Cause like, you know, Facebook is nationwide and all them people comment,…but certain things I don't believe I can deal with [others' comments].

P3   I just don't like it because most of the things that come up on there, people put on there now. And most of the time my nieces and nephews have my phone, and a lot of things I don't want them to read, hear, or see on my phone. So I don't put [Facebook] on there.

Another participant was worried that the wealth of information available to her grandchildren through Google was a form of "cheating," and she would sometimes take the children's phones away during homework—not because they were a distraction, but because they were a source of information:

P9   I takes they phone because they're, "Google give me something something something."….[T]hey'll tell you that they have to. And I ask the teachers, teachers say, "Yeah, they have to use the phone."….[But] still.

---

[6] Passwords in general pose challenges to internet users with low literacy skills [36]. This participant normally plays Word Feud every day, but she was getting ready to delete the game from her new phone. Accessing the game from her new phone required a password that she could no longer remember.

Participants also experienced pressure from others about their phone decisions:

P3   They kept sending me text messages saying I need to upgrade…. So I went on and upgraded.

P9   [M]y other one, it wasn't right, and my daughter was like I need to upgrade my phone. So, she told me about the Samsung, so I got that one.

P8   I was going to change my greeting. I change it at least once a year. Because one time I had one on there for like four years, and somebody said, "Oh my God, you need to change that, that's been there forever!"

Smartphones as Shared Resources/Use by Others. Participants reported a lot of phone usage by relatives—mostly children and grandchildren, but sometimes by a parent, spouse, or a sibling. This sharing seemed to elicit some mixed emotions. Grandparents felt good that they were making their grandchildren happy, but were sometimes annoyed by the constant struggle to keep track of the device. Borrowed devices were often returned with no charge, less available storage, and even unexpected and undesired new applications.

P8   I noticed [my 17 year old granddaughter—who has her own phone] will say, "Grandma, can I hold your phone?" and keep it until I say, "I need my phone."

P5   [A]s soon as you put your phone there they just picks it right up…

The most common problems with this secondary usage were children using up storage space on the phone, with photos, videos, or music, or installing games and other unauthorized applications.

P3   [M]y nephew and my great-nephew and my great-nieces [say] 'Oh, let me borrow your phone' [to play games].

P8   She [grand-daughter] took the phone and made a whole video, like "You guys, we're moving in a new house. This is going to be my room, this is going to be my Mom and Pop's room, this is the kitchen," oh, she was just on…. [A]fter a while the phone is going to be telling me, "Look you're going to run out of space." And what made me realize that, I was going to record something and I couldn't. And I just had my grandson to remove a whole bunch of stuff.

In two cases, secondary users had inadvertently infected the phone with a virus. Neither of the participants whose phones were infected knew why their phones had begun to behave strangely.

3.2   Phone Log Activity—Ten Participants

Android phones connected to Google accounts preserve an activity log of all phone usage, although different devices capture data at different levels of granularity. As a supplement to the story-based, qualitative data provided by our interviews, we gathered phone log data from two six-day usage periods for our participants. Two of the participants who began the study, and completed their interviews, did not return to the lab for their final log analysis. Thus, this quantitative discussion only includes data from ten participants.

The data logs were captured, then coded based on the following categories:

Communication

- Phone calls
- Texts
- Email
- Contacts
- Voicemail
- Video calls

Photos and document storage

- Camera usage
- Gallery
- Cloud storage

Tools

- Calendar
- Calculator
- Scanner (photo or document)
- To do list
- Text magnifier

Maps

Information resources

- Search
- Google Assistant (search)
- Weather
- News
- Webpages
- Books and podcasts

Social media

- Facebook
- Instagram
- Snapchat
- Other social (Google+, Birthdays)

Entertainment

- Games
- Video (non-YouTube)
- YouTube
- TV
- Music
- Bible
- Fitness
- Other (gambling, horoscopes, dating, pornography)

Shopping

- Purchases
- Shopping information (deals, ads)

Money

- Banking, paying bills, transferring money
- Earning money (managing online assets, participating in paid surveys

Antivirus

These categories were based on joint analysis of the logs by the primary and secondary researcher.

The range of activities performed by each participant varied. One participant's log only showed activities in two of these categories, and one participant had activities in all ten categories, with a median of eight categories of activities documented for most participants (see Fig. 1).

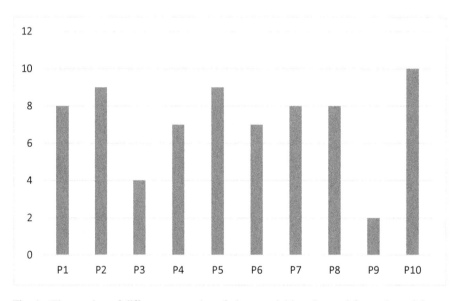

Fig. 1. The number of different categories of phone activities observed for each participant.

The number of participants who had performed activities from each category is shown in Fig. 2. The most widely used categories were communication, information, maps, and entertainment, with photos and social media in the next tier.

All but one participant used their phone for communication activities of some sort—usually phone calls and texts. The single participant who did not use phone calls, texts, email, contacts or voicemail during the logged period was instead a heavy user of searches, news, and YouTube, and a moderate user of games.

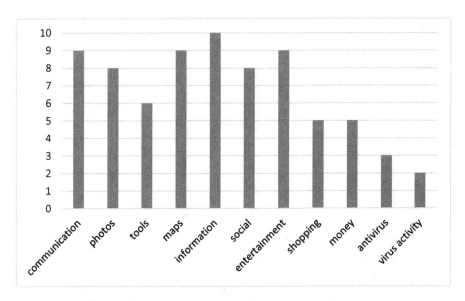

Fig. 2. Number of participants with activity in each category

Every participant did some searching for information. All but one participant used Google search, between 34 and 235 times, with an average number of 106 searches over twelve days. Only five participants (50%) visited webpages on their phone, but the average number of pages visited among those five participants was 61, with a range of 5 to 134. All participants checked the weather on their phones. Five participants (50%) had enabled Google Assistant.

Eight (80%) participants had used their cameras or accessed their gallery. Four participants (40%) had used a form of cloud storage. Based on their interviews, none of the other six participants had thought about backups, except insofar as they knew that pictures could be copied from one phone to another during a replacement or upgrade.

The largest usage of participants' smartphones was to access information and for entertainment, with communication activities such as phone calls and texts in third place (See Fig. 3). The activity logs showed very minimal use of productivity tools, antivirus protection, and very limited financial activities such as banking or paying bills. Slightly more use of maps, photos, shopping resources, and social media was observed. In a future study, we hope to compare this usage to similar activity log analysis for high-literacy/high-income urban residents; however, two notable differences stand out when our participants' usage is compared to usage reports from a broader sample [5]. Our participants made very little use of phone tools such as calendars, to do lists, scanners, etc. Moreover, despite being smartphone dependent, they made comparatively little use of their phones for banking or shopping activities.

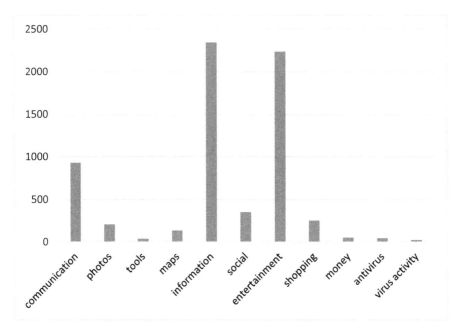

Fig. 3. Total activity for all participants summarized by category

4   Implications

4.1   Barriers

Barriers to internet access by these low-literate/low-income smartphone users definitely persist. Some barriers to internet usage by this group are intrinsic to being smartphone dependent, such as the barriers to accessing information and services that are caused by small screens, tiny keyboards, data limits, poorly designed or unresponsive websites, etc. Other barriers faced by this group pre-existed smartphone-dependent internet access, but are highlighted by the increased internet access made possible by smartphone ownership: such as, barriers to use caused by low civic literacy, low levels of social knowledge, webpage text that requires high literacy to read, or complex site structures that are hard to navigate. Nor have economic barriers disappeared—participants reported disruptions based on broken or stolen phones, and interruptions in service as their ability to pay their phone bills fluctuated. Participants primarily learned about the capabilities of their phones, or the resources that were available online, through word of mouth. While learning from peers was manifestly helpful, reliance on this left them with significant knowledge gaps. Participants' imperfect understanding of security practices and threats left them unnecessarily wary in some areas and vulnerable in others. Participants had fairly low information literacy, with poor skills in finding information or evaluating information quality. Many of the participants relied on sensationalized or entertainment-focused sources of news, for example. Moreover, the complex reading-based activities required to navigate the internet safely can lead to some anxiety or lack of confidence for this group.

Overall, however, it was encouraging to see participants' positive experiences with information access. Smartphone usage among this demographic continues to grow, making it likely that their propensity to find information online and their success in doing so will increase with their growing levels of experience.

4.2 Facilitators

The study also provided insight into a number of facilitators that increase access for this group, as well as facilitators that help individuals with low literacy feel confident about their ability to access the internet, and feel motivated to pursue information online. The growth of higher-quality phones and coverage available on a pre-paid basis, with small, local phone stores (particularly MetroPCS), played a role in most of these participants' path to smartphone use. Economic incentives from other carriers were also mentioned, such as falling monthly fees as a reward for consistent, on-time payment (Boost), or deals that provided multiple phones at a time. Google's progress in supporting natural-language, spoken search has clearly empowered (and delighted) this group. The benefits of social cognition provided by widespread adoption were also evident. Participants saw peers enjoying their phones and benefiting from their use, and the many opportunities for observational learning this entailed, led to both increased desire and self-efficacy. We also saw some positive inter-generational dynamics at work—grandparents in particular had strong positive relationships with their grandchildren, and so grandchildren enjoyed being experts and teaching their grandparents. At the same time, grandparents generally felt safe and valued by their grandchildren, so they felt comfortable asking for help and being taught.

5 Limitations of This Study

This small-scale study was conducted in a single large urban center. The average age of our participants was 49 years. It is likely that the experience of smartphone ownership and usage patterns would be different for participants with low literacy who are teenagers or young adults, or who live in rural areas, or perhaps for smartphone owners from other ethnic groups, such as Hispanics or Latinos. Other cultural or geographical differences may also be relevant.

Participation in the study was also limited to Android phone owners, because iPhones do not currently provide access to phone activity logs. A diary study could be performed with iPhone users; however, this approach was judged impractical for this initial study for a number of reasons.[7]

---

[7] IPhone owners are less common in this group, making it difficult to recruit a comparable sample size. Since phone activity logs would not be available, researchers would have to rely on a diary study, placing a higher burden on participants to collect and report their own usage. The exigencies of life at a lower income level can make it harder to sustain regular participation in a research study over time. The combination of these factors would have led to a high administrative burden for researchers, and much less complete data. We plan to pursue this approach in a later study.

Moreover, restricting the study to Android phone users did not guarantee access to equal records of phone activity for all participants. The variation in phone quality among participants affected the granularity of the data available. Some phones would capture actual search queries; other phones did not. Therefore, for this study, data was captured at the level of granularity that was consistently available across all devices.

We were unable to differentiate in the logs between activity that used data plans versus activity that relied on wi-fi, although some information could be inferred from the interviews. Thus, we cannot draw conclusions about how access to wi-fi affected phone usage patterns.

A further study focusing on exploring specific information behaviors, search queries, and use of search results is planned.

References

1. Lorence, D.P., Park, H., Fox, S.: Racial disparities in health information access: resilience of the digital divide. J. Med. Syst. **4**, 241–249 (2006)
2. Fallis, D.: Social epistemology and the digital divide. In: Weckert, J., Al-Saggaf, Y. (eds.) Proceedings Selected Papers from the Computers and Philosophy Conference (CAP2003), Canberra, Australia. CRPIT, vol. 37, pp. 79–84. ACS (2004)
3. Jennings, M.K., Zeitner, V.: Internet use and civic engagement: a longitudinal analysis. Public Opin. Q. **3**, 311–334 (2003)
4. Wong, Y.C., Ho, K.M., Chen, H., Gu, D., Zeng, Q.: Digital divide challenges in low-income families: the case of Shanghai. J. Technol. Hum. Serv. **33**, 53–71 (2015)
5. Pew Research Center: The smartphone difference 18 February 2018. http://www.pewinternet.org/2015/04/01/us-smartphone-use-in-2015
6. Pew Research Center: Mobile fact sheet, 18 February 2018. http://www.pewinternet.org/fact-sheet/mobile/
7. Pew Research Center: Smartphones help blacks, Hispanics bridge some—but not all—digital gaps with whites, 19 February 2018. http://www.pewresearch.org/fact-tank/2017/08/31/smartphones-help-blacks-hispanics-bridge-some-but-not-all-digital-gaps-with-whites/
8. Pew Research Center: Digital divide persists even as lower-income Americans make gains in tech adoption, 19 February 2018. http://www.pewresearch.org/fact-tank/2017/03/22/digital-divide-persists-even-as-lower-income-americans-make-gains-in-tech-adoption/
9. Pew Research Center: Internet/broadband fact sheet. 19 February 2018. http://www.pewinternet.org/fact-sheet/internet-broadband/
10. Harris, C., Straker, L., Pollock, C.: A socioeconomic related 'digital divide' exists in how, not if, young people use computers. PLoS ONE **12**(3), 1–13 (2017)
11. Gonzales, A.: Technology maintenance: a new frame for studying poverty and marginalization. In: Proceedings of the 2017 CHI Conference on Human Factors in Computing Systems, pp. 289–294 (2017)
12. Delello, J.A., McWhorter, R.R.: Reducing the digital divide: connecting older adults to iPad technology. J. Appl. Gerontol. **1**, 3–28 (2017)
13. Hillbert, M.: The bad news is that the digital access divide is here to stay: domestically installed bandwidths among 172 countries for 1986–2014. Telecommun. Policy **40**, 567–581 (2016)

14. Mimbi, L., Bankole, F.O., Kyobe, M.: Mobile phones and digital divide in East African countries. In: Proceedings of the South African Institute of Computer Scientists and Information Technologists Conference on Knowledge, Innovation and Leadership in a Diverse, Multidisciplinary Environment, pp. 318–321 (2011)
15. Gonzales, A.: Health benefits and barriers to cell phone use in low-income US neighborhoods: indications of technology maintenance. Mob. Media Commun. **2**, 233–248 (2014)
16. Kirsch, I.S.: Adult literacy in America: a first look at the results of the National Adult Literacy Survey. U.S. Government Printing Office, Washington, DC 20402 (1993)
17. Kutner, M., Greenberg, E., Jin, Y., Boyle, B., Hsu, Y., Dunleavy, E.: Literacy in everyday life: results from the 2003 National Assessment of Adult Literacy. NCES 2007-490. National Center for Education Statistics, Washington, DC (2007)
18. West, D.M.: State and federal e-government in the United States, 2005. Taubman Center for Public Policy, Brown University (2005). http://insidepolitics.org/egovt05us.pdf
19. Summers, K., Wu, J., Abela, C., Souza, R., Langford, J.: Designing web-based forms for users with lower literacy skills. In: Proceedings of the American Society for Information Science and Technology, pp. 1–12 (2007). https://doi.org/10.1002/meet.14504301174
20. Kodagoda, N., Wong, W., Kahan, N.: Behaviour characteristics: low and high literacy users information seeking on social service websites. In: CHINZ 2009, pp. 13–16 (2009)
21. Chaurdy, B.M., Connelly, K.H., Siek, K.A., Welch, J.L.: Mobile interface design for low-literacy populations. In: IHI1 2012, pp. 91–100 (2012)
22. Alton, N.T., Rinn, C., Summers, K., Straub, K.: Using eye-tracking and form completion data to optimize form instruction. In: Proceedings From the International Professional Communication Conference, pp. 1–8 (2014)
23. Doke, P., Joshi, A.: Mobile phone usage by low literate users. In: IndiaHCI 2015, pp. 1–9 (2015)
24. Taoufik, I., Kabaili, H., Kettani, D.: Designing an e-government portal accessible to illiterate citizens. In: ICEGOV 2007, pp. 327–335 (2007)
25. Lalji, Z., Good, J.: Designing new technologies for illiterate populations: a study in mobile phone interface design. Interact. Comput. **20**, 574–586 (2011)
26. Medhi, I., Patnaik, S., Brunskill, E., Gautama, S.N.N., Thies, W., Toyama, K.: Designing mobile interfaces for novice and low-literacy users. ACM Trans. Comput.-Hum. Interact. 1 (2011)
27. Heckathorn, D.D.: Snowballs versus respondent-driven sampling. Soc. Meth. **41**, 355–366 (2011). https://doi.org/10.1111/j.1467-9531.2011.01244.x
28. Davis, T.C., Crouch, M.A., Long, S.W., Jackson, R.H., Bates, P., George, R.B., Bairnsfather, L.E.: Rapid assessment of literacy levels of adult primary care patients. Fam. Med. **23**, 433–435 (1991)
29. Alqudah, M., Johnson, M., Cowin, L., George, A.: Measuring health literacy in emergency departments. J. Nurs. Educ. Prac. **4**, 1–10 (2014)
30. Davis, T.C., Kennen, E.M., Gazmararian, J.A., Williams, M.V.: Literacy testing in health care research. In: Schwartzberg, J.G., VanGeest, J.B., Wang, C.C. (eds.) Understanding Health Literacy: Implications for Medicine and Public Health, pp. 157–179. American Medical Association, Chicago (2005)
31. Parker, R.M., Baker, D.W., Williams, M.V., Nurss, J.R.: The test of functional health literacy in adults: a new instrument for measuring patients' literacy skills. J. Gen. Intern. Med. **10**, 537–541 (1995)
32. Charmaz, K.: Constructing Grounded Theory: A Practical Guide Through Qualitative Analysis. Sage, London (2006)

33. Glaser, B.G., Strauss, A.L.: The Discovery of Grounded Theory: Strategies for Qualitative Design. Transaction, Rutgers (1967)
34. Strauss, A.L., Corbin, J.: Basics of qualitative research: techniques and procedures for developing grounded theory, 2nd edn. Sage, Thousand Oaks (1998)
35. Saldana, J.: The Coding Manual for Qualitative Researchers, 3rd edn. Sage, London (2015)
36. Rinn, C., Summers, K., Rhodes, E., Virothaisakun, J., Chisnell, D.: Password creation strategies across high- and low-literacy web users. In: Proceedings of the Association for Information Science and Technology, pp. 1–9 (2015). https://doi.org/10.1002/pra2.2015.145052010052

An Interactive Recommender System
for Group Holiday Decision-Making

Lanyun Zhang and Xu Sun[(✉)]

University of Nottingham, Ningbo, China
{Lanyun.Zhang,Xu.Sun}@nottingham.edu.cn

Abstract. Various types of applications are available on mobile devices that support the holiday decision-making of individual tourists. However, people often travel in groups and existing applications lack the services to support the decision-making of tourists who travel in a group. In group holiday decision-making, intra-group interaction plays a major role. In this work, we design an system that provides recommendations for tourist groups based on their travel preferecnes. Meanwhile, the system allows each group member to participate in the process of such recommendation through the design of interactive features. The recommendation mechanism is based on an ontology that describes the tourism-related information of a destination. This paper presents the design idea, the development of the system (including the ontology, the aggregation strategy, the recommendation mechanism, and the interactive features), and the preliminary findings of evaluating the user experience. The results show that the system facilitates the group holiday decision-making and provides users with an engaging experience.

Keywords: User interface · Holiday decision-making · Tourist group
Recommender system · Ontology · Mobile devices · EEG

1 Introduction

Holidays have played major roles in people's lives, providing opportunities for them to experience something that are different from their everyday routines [1]. The process of holiday decision-making is considered an important part of the whole travel experience. In many cases, people tend to travel with a group of people, so that they may socialise, enjoy the company of each other, and better fit into their communities [2]. Therefore, the process of group holiday decision-making has drawn attention by many researchers and the characteristics of intra-group interactions among group members are examined, such as group cohesiveness and congruence [2]. With the development of Web 1.0, Web 2.0 and social media, tourists, especially those who travel in groups, now rely more on the Internet to obtain tourism information and share information among themselves, and to make decisions. Online tourism domains are examined and categories are put forward, such as review websites, virtual communities, blogs, etc. [4]. Existing travel planning applications and designs have explored some functions for tourist groups, where group members can work on their itineraries together and acquire personalised services, such as Tripomatic (tripomatic.com). However, the designs of

© Springer International Publishing AG, part of Springer Nature 2018
A. Marcus and W. Wang (Eds.): DUXU 2018, LNCS 10919, pp. 673–683, 2018.
https://doi.org/10.1007/978-3-319-91803-7_50

interactivities to support understandings among group members in the decision-making process have not been examined adequately, especially in personalisation applications. This paper aims to explore how group recommendation with interactive features can facilitate the group holiday decision-making experience.

We focus on the two main characteristics that are essential in this design: making recommendations for tourist groups and allowing group members to participate in the recommendation process. Firstly, existing studies have proposed different types of mobile-based recommender systems in the field of tourism [3, 5]. Among those recommendation mechanisms, ontology-based mechanism is the most efficient and accurate, that it represents the domain knowledge and later is to be used in recommendation processes [6]. In the recommendation for a group of users, studies have explored ontology-based mechanisms in various fields, such as tourism and movie [7]. The underlying mechanism of this system is adapted from Garcia et al.'s work [8]. They propose a recommender system for tourist groups based on an ontology of tourism information of a certain destination. Secondly, understanding each other's opinions among group members is essential in group work [9]. Interactive features are found to have positive effects on user experience in the studies of human-computer interaction for entertainment, such as interactive music sharing [10]. However, very few have the interactive features that involve the users in the recommendation process. This system aims to make use of the recommendation mechanism, allow group members to participate in the recommendation process, and further support a better understanding of each other's travel preferences and opinions.

We further develop a prototype of the interactive group recommender system that provides tourist groups with tourism recommendations based on users' preferences and their interactions with this system. To evaluate the system, both subjective approach (questionnaire surveys and interviews) and objective approach (electroencephalography) are employed to examine the usability of the system, the degree of engagement when interacting with the system, and the performance of the interactive features.

2 Literature Review

2.1 Ontology-Based Recommendation Mechanism

Ontology-based recommender systems are examples of how semantic technologies may be integrated with Web services to leverage each other's strengths. Existing studies have explored how ontology-based recommender mechanisms can facilitate the holiday decision-making process. For example, Wang et al. [11] propose an ontology-structured tourism recommender that allows the automatic and dynamic integration of heterogeneous online travel information. To realise personalisation for tourists, individual's travel preferences are also involved and considered in the ontology-based recommendation mechanism [7].

With regards to a group of users, existing studies have explored how to make recommendations for groups based on individual's travel preferences. One more step is added before the recommendation mechanism - aggregation of individual preferences to obtain a group preference. *e*-Tourism is designed by Garcia et al. [7, 8], that it aims at recommending a list of tourist activities for a group of tourists based on an ontology of the city of Valencia (Spain). Firstly, *e*-Tourism requires the tourists to build their user profile, enter their travel preferences and general likes. Secondly, group preference is generated through aggregating the individual preferences. Lastly, group recommendation is calculated based on the group preference. The mechanism of the system in this paper is built on Garcia et al.'s work with a newly designed aggregation strategy that allows users to participate in the group recommendation process and interact with the system.

2.2   Interactive Features in Recommendation

Developing novel interactive features is an important research area in the studies of human-computer interaction, such as supporting for learning [14], enhancing newspaper reading experience [15], etc. In the context of group work, interactivity is a particular medium, which has the ability to facilitate two-way communication among the group members [16]. Such communication can be supported via direct dialogues, such as face-to-face, phone calls, and instant messaging applications (WhatsApp). It also can be supported indirectly through certain interactive features provided by technologies. For example, animated representatives of each group member is generated to enhance visualisation, mimic intra-group dialogues, and facilitate the communication experience [17].

With regards to the interactive features in personalised recommendation, a collaborative group recommendation has been developed that enables four users to simultaneously engage in parallel recommendations, in which personal and group profiles are exploited through the interactivities with the device [18]. In this paper, interactive features are designed for the purposes of: (1) making group members aware of each other's travel preferences, and (2) allowing group members to participate in the group recommendation process.

2.3   Evaluation Method

Evaluation of user experience is practised in various fields (e.g., gaming, website [19, 20]) using different methods. Subjective methods (e.g., questionnaire surveys [20]) are convenient, but they are inherently biased by the participants' personal feelings and opinions. Therefore, physiological metrics have also been employed, as objective methods, to simultaneously acquire physiological data, e.g., electroencephalography (EEG), skin conductance, etc. Existing studies have used physiological metrics to identify human emotions [20], psychological stress [22], and working memory load [21]. In this paper, both subjective methods (questionnaire surveys and interviews) and objective method (EEG) are used to investigate the usability of the system, the degree of engagement when interacting with the system, and the performance of the interactivities.

3   System Design and Development

3.1   Design Principles

The goal of this system design is to facilitate the holiday decision-making of tourist groups. Our system needs to meet two main design principles. First, it should be able to provide recommendations for a group of tourists based on their individual travel preferences. Second, it should allow users to participate in the recommendation process through the design of interactive features. An ontology-based recommendation mechanism was developed and the following sections introduce the ontology, the aggregation strategy, the recommendation mechanism, the interactive features, and the development of the system.

3.2   Ontology

This system aims to provide personalised tourism recommendations for tourist groups about Nanjing, China. The ontology of this system describes the tourism information of Nanjing, which is built based on the knowledge of ten senior travellers from Nanjing. The structure of the ontology is adapted from Garcia et al.'s [7, 8] work, while the building of the ontology is based on the guidance by Noy [22].

Firstly, nine *classes* are identified based on a tourism ontology developed in SigTur [23]. They distinguish the sightseeing attractions in Nanjing. Ten sightseeing attractions are chosen as *instances* (items) in the ontology. Secondly, *relationship* between classes and instances are built. It is a link to connect the classes to each instance and each instance can link to more than one class. The value of each relationship (d_{ij}) shows how much an instance represents a class (in a range from 0 to 100). Lastly, a *score* is assigned to describe the popularity of each instance (S_i). See Fig. 1 for parts of the ontology.

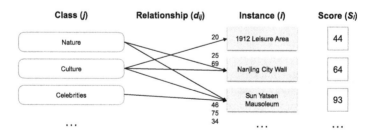

Fig. 1.   Parts of the ontology used in this system.

3.3   Aggregating Group Profile

This system records a profile for each user that contains individual users' general tastes in terms of travel preferences. The individual profile of a user (IP^u) is represented by a list of tuples in the form $IP^u = \{(u, j, p^{uj})\}$, where $j \in Class$, and $p^{uj} \in [0, 100]$ is the degree of preferences given by the user u to a certain class j. In case of a group of users, all the individuals must be previously registered and have submitted their individual user profiles. This system will consider all the individual profiles in a group as whole to make group recommendations. And there is one step before making recommendations: obtaining group user profile.

To obtain group user profile of a tourist group, firstly, travel preferences of each group member is obtained explicitly from the users through a questionnaire; secondly, aggregation of the individual preferences is conducted to derive a group preference. This aggregating machenism is fed with individual profiles (IP^u) of all group members, and returns one aggregated group profile, $GP^G = (G, j, p^{Gj})$, where $j \in Class$, and $p^{Gj} \in [0, 100]$ is the degree of preference of group of user G to a certain class j.

While there are different types of aggregation strategy [13], one strategy was chosen in this system to support one of the interactive features. This aggregation strategy begins with a standard average calculation over the travel preferences of all the group members towards one class, in which each member has the equal influence on the group preference. Then the interactive features allow users to manually change the influences of any group member by modifying the weight, $W_u \in [0.5, 1.5]$, of any group member u in a tourist group. The range of the weights was from 50% to 150%, which means that the minimum influence of a group member can be set to 50% of its normal influence, and the maximum influence is 150%. Every time when the aggregation strategy is manually adjusted, the system will provide new recommendations for the tourist group.

GP^G is the result of aggregating all individual profiles in a tourist group. This system calculates the average values of the preference-degrees of n users in G for the class j, with a weight on each user u that is adjustable by any user. An example is shown in Table 1. More formally:

$$GP^G_j = \frac{\sum_{u=1}^{n} W_u p_{uj}}{n}, u = 1 \sim n, j = class\,1, class\,2, \ldots, class\,m \qquad (1)$$

Table 1. Example of aggregating mechanism

	Class 1	Class 2	Class 3	Weight
Profile - user 1	10	94	55	100%
Profile - user 2	30	65	38	60%
Profile - user 3	40	45	91	140%
Group profile	(10 × 100% + 30 × 60% + 40 × 140%)/ 3 = 28	(94 × 100% + 65 ×60% + 45 × 140%)/ 3 = 65	(55 × 100% + 38 × 60% + 91 × 140%)/ 3 = 68	N/A

3.4   Recommendation Mechanism

The model of calculating of recommendations is in charge of selecting the items (*instances* in ontology) that satisfy the group's preferences, based on group profile GP^G and the ontology introduced previously. This recommendation mechanism produces a list of recommended items, RI^G. It is a set of tuples of the form $RI^G = \{(i, D^{Gi})\}$, where i is the recommended item, and D^{Gi} is the estimated degree of interest of a group G in the item i. The degree of interest (D^{Gi}) of the group G in an item i is calculated as follows:

$$\begin{cases} D^{Gi} = per(S_i) \times \sum_{\forall (j, p_{Gj}) \in GP^G} \left(d_{ij} \times per(p_{Gj}) \right), \\ per(p_{Gj}) = \frac{p_{Gj}}{max(GP^G)}, \\ per(S_i) = \frac{S_i}{max(S)}, \\ i = item\ 1, 2, \ldots, k;\ j = class\ 1, 2, \ldots m \end{cases} \tag{2}$$

The recommendation mechanism then rearranges the order of the items (*instances*) in descending order based on the degree of interest assigned to each item (D^{Gi}). The final recommendation will display the top 7 items for the tourist group G. In their work, degree of interest, D^{Gi}, calculates the sum of the three entries, $per(S_i)$, d_{ij}, and $per(p_{Gj})$. We calculate D^{Gi} using the multiplication to better describe the degree of interest towards each instance (first equation in Eq. 2).

3.5   Interactive Features

Two interactive features are designed in this system. First, as introduced in the aggregation strategy, users can participate in the recommendation process by manually adjusting the influence of each group member. So users can repeatedly check the recommendation results with different inputs (group member's influence – Fig. 2 left).

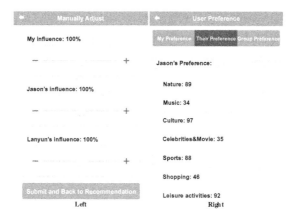

Fig. 2. Screenshots of the interactive features.

Second, this system allows users to check the travel preferences of all the individual group members and the travel preferences of their group as a whole (Fig. 2 right). This feature enables the users to be aware of each other's travel preferences, so that a holiday decision is made to have the maximum satisfaction.

3.6 Development of This System

The development environment used to build this system is appery.io, which is a rapid development, integration and deployment platform for delivering cross-device applications. It provides browser-based development environment; integrates the interface and backend services; enables rapid creation of a mobile application for immediate evaluation.

This system requires the establishment of communication between the mobile interface (graphic user interface), a web server, and a database. To understand the entire architecture, Fig. 3 shows the components and their functions in the building of this system.

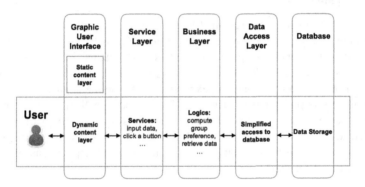

Fig. 3. Architecture diagram of this system.

4   User Study

4.1   Aim and Experiment Design

The aims of this user study were to evaluate the usability of the system, the degree of engagement when interacting with the system, and the performance of the interactive features. A between-subject, scenario-based experiment was designed to compare the group trip planning experience with the assistant of two types of tools: this system vs. commonly used mobile applications for trip planning. These commonly used mobile applications were selected freely by participants, which include mafengwo, qiongyou, tripadvisor, C-trip, and baidu travel.

Firstly, usability was measured by Nielsen's 10 usability heuristics [23], in which 4 question items were omitted as they were not applicable to this system evaluation. The measured 6 question items are listed in the result (Table 2). Secondly, the level of engagement when interacting with a piece of technology (this system and the commonly used mobile applications) was measured via a commercial EEG device - NeuroSky Mindwave headset. This device has been used in the evaluation of user experience [12]. Lastly, the performance of the interactive features was evaluated through face-to-face interviews of participants.

Table 2. Median values of usability heuristics.

Usability heuristics	Other apps	This system
1. Simple and natural dialogue	6.5	6
2. Speak user's language	6	6.5
3. Minimise user's memory load	6	6
4. Consistency	6.5	6
5. Clearly marked exits	6	6
6. Shortcuts	6	5.5

4.2   Participants

18 groups of participants were recruited from the University of Nottingham, Ningbo, China. Within each group, there were three members (apart from one group that was a couple), and in total there were 53 participants (31 females, 22 males). All of the participants were Chinese. The requirements of recruiting the participants were: (1) they had prior group trip planning experience with mobile applications, and (2) at least one of the group member in each group had not been to Nanjing. To compare the user experience with and without the assistant of this system, 9 groups of participants were asked to make a group trip plan to Nanjing using this system, while another 9 groups to make such trip plan using their commonly used applications. Participants were compensated for their time.

4.3   Procedure and Task

After the participants had signed off the consent forms, they were given an instruction of the task and the scenario: "*The three of you are planning a two-day trip to Nanjing as a group. You can use this system (for 9 groups)/any mobile applications that you are familiar with (for another 9 groups) to help you. The task is for you to think about what you want to do in Nanjing. The only requirement is that the three of you cannot have verbal communication in this part. You will need to produce a trip plan by the end of this task.*" During the period of performing the task, two participants in each group were required to wear EEG headsets (due to the limitation of the devices). After the tasks were completed, participants in the groups using this system needed to fill out a questionnaire survey regarding usability (7-point Likert questions). Lastly, follow-up interviews were given to obtain participants' opinions towards the performance of the interactive features.

4.4   Data Analysis

The questionnaire in this study aimed to measure the usability of using this system. Frequency and descriptive statistics were employed to gain an overall understanding of the opinions of the participants. Data collected from EEG devices was ranged from 0 to 100, which represented the attention level of interacing with the system. Independent t-test was used to compare the attention level between two groups of participant (i.e., one group using this system vs. one group using other commonly used mobile applications). The performance of the interactive feature was evaluated through face-to-face interviews. Interview data was qualitative in nature. The Emergent Themes Analysis [26] was conducted to understand the data.

4.5   Results

Usability. The 53 datasets of the usability questions (7-point Likert questions) were not normal distributed, so median values were analysed and Mann-Whitney tests were used for statistical analysis. The outcomes show that the median values of the 6 usability items were no smaller than 5.5 (Table 2), which indicate that the participants had positive views regarding the usability of this system. Across the 6 items, Mann-Whitney tests show that there are no significant differences between the usability of other commonly used mobile applications and this system ($p > 0.05$). This finding indicates that this system performed quite well in terms of usability, which is found to be as well as the commonly used mobile applications for travel and holiday planning.

Degree of Engagement. The brainwave data derived from the NeuroSky headset included an attention indicator to indicate the mental focus and the degree of engagement of participants. The values of the attention indicator ranged from 0 to 100. Over the 18 groups of participants, independent t-test shows significant difference in participants' attention level ($p < 0.001$) that participants using this system (M = 57.58, SD = 17.19) were more focused and engaged in the group trip planning task compared with participants using their commonly used mobile applications (M = 56.31, SD = 16.13).

Interactivity Performance. First, this system allows users to participate in the recommendation process by manually adjusting the influence of each group member. This interactive feature has been used in different ways and received positive feedbacks from the participants. For example, one participant said: "*Since I had been to Nanjing before, and the other two had not. So I wanted to know what they might like to do. Then I just reduced my influence in the group to the minimum, and maximised their influences. I quickly got the recommendations for them and then made decisions. It helped a lot.*" Second, this system allows users to check the travel preferences of all the group members. This interactive feature has also obtained positive comments, "*I had a look at the preferences of the other two people and quickly knew what they generally liked in travelling, so I immediately had an idea of where we might go in Nanjing. It is really helpful.*"

5   Discussion and Conclusion

How to better facilitate the experience of group holiday decision-making through technology? Based on the findings from existing studies, it is essential for a group of tourists to reach a congruence through intra-group interactions [2]. From this perspective, we design and evaluate an system that provides recommendations for tourist groups and supports group members to participate in the process of the group recommendation. The empirical results demonstrate that, first, the functions and interactivities in this system are able to support usability.

Second, the 'attention level' derived from EEG headsets shows significant increase when using this system to make a group trip plan. This finding might be confusing if relating 'attention level' to 'cognitive load'. Attention is the behavioural and cognitive process of selectively concentrating on a discrete aspect of information, and ignoring other perceivable information [24]. 'Cognitive load' refers to the total amount of mental effort being used in the working memory [25]. In other words, a high level of cognitive load can be caused by multiple tasks processed in a person's brain, while a high level of attention represents that the person can focus on one thing and ignore the distractions. This finding indicates that this system can increase the user's degree of engagement during the holiday decision-making.

At last, the interactive features of this system have received positive feedbacks from participants, that they are able to support the understandings among group members and positively assist the group trip planning experience.

We plan to further explore this issue through extending this system from two aspects. On the one hand, different aggregation strategies [13] in the group recommendation mechanism are worth exploring for different types of tourist groups. On the other hand, novel interactive features should be designed to facilitate the intra-group interactions during the group trip planning process.

Acknowledgement. The authors would like to thank participants for the empirical study, the paper reviewers, and the support of International Doctoral Innovation Centre at the University of Nottingham, Ningbo, China. We also acknowledge the financial support from National Natural Science Foundation of China for a Grant awarded to the authors (Grant No. 71401085).

References

1. Decrop, A., Snelders, D.: Planning the summer vacation: an adaptable process. Ann. Tour. Res. **31**(4), 1008–1030 (2004)
2. Decrop, A.: Group processes in vacation decision-making. J. Travel Tour. Market. **18**(3), 23–36 (2005)
3. Braunhofer, M., Elahi, M., Ricci, F., Schievenin, T.: Context-aware points of interest suggestion with dynamic weather data management. In: Xiang, Z., Tussyadiah, I. (eds.) Information and Communication Technologies in Tourism 2014, pp. 87–100. Springer, Cham (2013). https://doi.org/10.1007/978-3-319-03973-2_7
4. Xiang, Z., Gretzel, U.: Role of social media in online travel information search. Tour. Manag. **31**(2), 179–188 (2010)

5. Borràs, J., Valls, A., Moreno, A., Isern, D.: Ontology-based management of uncertain preferences in user profiles. In: Greco, S., Bouchon-Meunier, B., Coletti, G., Fedrizzi, M., Matarazzo, B., Yager, Ronald R. (eds.) IPMU 2012. CCIS, vol. 298, pp. 127–136. Springer, Heidelberg (2012). https://doi.org/10.1007/978-3-642-31715-6_15

6. Borràs, J., Moreno, A., Valls, A.: Intelligent tourism recommender systems: a survey. Expert Syst. Appl. **41**(16), 7370–7389 (2014)

7. Garcia, I., Sebastia, L., Onaindia, E.: On the design of individual and group recommender systems for tourism. Expert Syst. Appl. **38**(6), 7683–7692 (2011)

8. Garcia, I., Pajares, S., Sebastia, L., Onaindia, E.: Preference elicitation techniques for group recommender systems. Inf. Sci. **189**, 155–175 (2002)

9. Forsyth, D.R.: Group Dynamics. Cengage Learning, Boston (2009)

10. Wu, M.: Interactive music playlist sharing system and methods. U.S. Patent Application 11/321, 571 (2005)

11. Wang, W., Zeng, G., Tang, D.: Bayesian intelligent semantic mashup for tourism. Concurr. Comput. Pract. Exp. **23**, 850–862 (2011)

12. Sourina, O., Liu, Y.: A fractal-based algorithm of emotion recognition from EEG using Arousal-Valence model. In: Biosignals, pp. 209–214 (2011)

13. Masthoff, J.: Group modeling: selecting a sequence of television items to suit a group of viewers. User Model User Adap Inter. **14**(37), 37–85 (2004)

14. Kennewell, S., Beauchamp, G.: The features of interactive whiteboards and their influence on learning. Learn. Media Technol. **32**(3), 227–241 (2007)

15. Chung, D.S., Yoo, C.Y.: Audience motivations for using interactive features: distinguishing use of different types of interactivity on an online newspaper. Mass Commun. Soc. **11**(4), 375–397 (2008)

16. Torres, F.A.: Towards a Universal Theory of Media Interactivity: Developing Proper Context. California State University, Fullerton (1996)

17. Jameson, A.: More than the sum of its members: challenges for group recommender systems. In: Proceedings of the Working Conference on Advanced Visual Interfaces, pp. 48–54. ACM (2004)

18. McCarthy, K., Salamó, M., Coyle, L., McGinty, L., Smyth, B., Nixon, P.: Cats: a synchronous approach to collaborative group recommendation. In: Florida Artificial Intelligence Research Society Conference (FLAIRS), pp. 86–91 (2006)

19. Takatalo, J., Hakkinen, J., Kaistinen, J., Nyman, G.: Measuring user experience in digital gaming: theoretical and methodological issues. In: Proceedings of SPIE (2007)

20. Siegfried, B.: Enhanced student technology support with cross-platform mobile apps. In: SIGUCCS: User Services Conference (2011)

21. Grimes, D., Tan, D.S., Hudson, S.E., Shenoy, P., Rao, R.: Feasibility and pragmatics of classifying working memory load with an electroencephalograph. In: Proceeding of CHI 2008, pp. 835–844. ACM Press (2008)

22. Noy, N.F., McGuinness, D.L.: Ontology development 101: a guide to creating your first ontology (2001)

23. Nielsen, J.: Usability inspection methods. In: Conference Companion on Human Factors in Computing Systems, pp. 413–414. ACM (1994)

24. Anderson, J.R.: Cognitive Psychology and Its Implications. Macmillan, New York (2005)

25. Sweller, J.: Cognitive load during problem solving: Effects on learning. Cogn. Sci. **12**(2), 257–285 (1988)

26. Wong, B.W., Blandford, A.E.: Analysing ambulance dispatcher decision making: trialing emergent themes analysis. In: Proceedings of the Human Factors Conference: Design for the Whole Person: Integrating Physical, Cognitive and Social Aspects. Ergonomics Society of Australia (2002)

Author Index

Printed in the United States
By Bookmasters